# THE ARSONIST PROFILES

# THE ARSONIST PROFILES

## Analyzing Arson Motives and Behavior

Ed Nordskog

ISBN-13: 9781530983070
ISBN-10: 153098307X
Library of Congress Control Number: 2016906296
CreateSpace Independent Publishing Platform
North Charleston, South Carolina

# Prologue: The Arson Problem

Arson is easily the most misunderstood crime in all of criminal justice. The public, and consequently the jury pool, has almost no concept of the crime of arson other than what is portrayed on television, in movies, and in popular culture. Those portrayals have almost always been wrong or grossly exaggerated and continue to be so. Worse than the public having a poor understanding of the crime of arson, most prosecutors, defense attorneys, and judges, along with police and fire department administrators, have just as poor of an understanding of this complex crime.

If that's not bad enough, the overwhelming majority of the psychiatric community is mired in a mind-set of the portrait of an arsonist that was formed over fifty years ago in the wake of meager and poorly understood psychiatric "research." Most modern criminal profilers agree that the past studies and clinical history of understanding arson behavior have been sparse, erroneous, and over reliant on self-reporting. They have also been based on sketchy and largely flawed "evidence" gathered by untrained corrections staff.

However, this flawed information is the very basis of the training and education of our mental-health experts specializing in this field. These mental-health "experts," with their flawed training, are the same people the public and the courts turn to for advice when deciding how to treat or rehabilitate a fire offender. Finally, the very group of people that is tasked with understanding, tracking, and apprehending this criminal—the arson investigators, as a community—has historically had no better of an understanding of the arsonist than the aforementioned groups.

The intent of this book is to help the arson investigator and the courts to understand the complex nature of the crime of arson and the individuals who commit this crime. The book is based on the author's work on nearly two thousand arson cases and his review and analysis of several thousand more. The author is also friends with or associated professionally with some of the more enlightened minds in the arson-investigation world. The author is not an academic conducting sterile research; he is also not a clinician attempting to assign a diagnosis to an odd behavior. The author is a working detective in the arson/explosives world and is attempting to use the analysis of arson crimes in hopes of translating that into a better understanding of people who use fire as a weapon. The end goal is catching them, prosecuting them, and shipping them off to prison where they belong.

This book will feature selected true case histories that illustrate the profile of each subtype of arsonist. There are tens of thousands of more cases out there that will do the same, but I have selected cases with which I am very familiar.

# Acknowledgments

As usual, this book is a compilation of the efforts of dozens of detectives, investigators, prosecutors, profilers, crime-scene technicians (CSI), special agents, and other professionals whom I know and have worked hundreds of cases with. The following have been my partners, coworkers, or professional associates, and they have allowed me to tell their case histories (in a somewhat abbreviated fashion). I thank them for their years of service to their communities.

Arson Detectives Rob Harris, Cindy Valencia, Dana Duncan, Rick Velazquez, Mike Digby, Kim Ponce, Alex Miller, Irma Gonzales, Greg Everett, Mike Cofield, Arnold Van Lingen, Barry Miller, and Ray Falcon; Arson Sergeants Joe Acevedo, John Hanson, Craig Anderson, Derek Yoshino, Mike Costleigh, Dan Tobin, Wendy Zolkowski, Ron Ablott, Greg Collins, Walt Scheuerell, Guy Peach, and Mike Rompal; Arson Investigators David Liske, Dan Gaytan, Tim Crass, Mike Camello, Patrick Leonard, Jose Sanchez, John Kabala, Alan Campbell, Christine Saqui, Pat Wills, Andy Anderson, David LaClair, Tim Chavez, Andrea Buchanan, Jim Iammatteo, Steve Flaherty, David Westfield, Chuck Doremus, Greg Smith, Jim Allen, and Rob Rappaport; Homicide Detectives Todd Anderson, Gary Sica, John Corina, Mark Lillienfield, John O'Brien, Steve Fisk, and Pat Tapia; Det. George Elwell, Sgt. Rob Hernandez, Det. Ken Schiffner, Det. Felix Osorio, Det. Eric Tscharanyan, and

Det. Claudia Delgado; Special Agents Suriya Khemradhipati, Chad Campanell, Keith McAuliffe, Paul Steensland, and Pat Kelly,; Sr.Criminalists Phil Teramoto, Steve Phillips, Dr. Joseph (J. J.) Cavaleri, and Deputy Larry Mitchell; Crime Analysts Theresa Olaes and Priscilla Billet,; Forensic Artist Sandra Enslow and Dr. John DeHaan; Deputy District Attorneys Sean Carney, Renee Rose, Angela Brunson, Susan Schwartz, Marion Thompson, Richard Simon, Andrew Katz, and Shawnalyse Ochoa; Assistant US Attorney Andrew Dunne; insurance investigators Shannon Hubbard and Catherine Nash; and civil attorney David Werner.

The professionals who have contributed to the development of criminal and arson/explosives profiling work before me and whose notes, papers, journals, publications, and books I have studied include Professor Hans Gustav Gross; Dr. James Brussel; Capt. Pierce Brooks; Dr. Robert Keppel; Special Agents Robert Ressler, John Douglas, Tim Huff, Gordon Gary, and Kevin Kelm; Dr. Allen Sapp; Dr. David Icove; Dr. Gerard Labuschagne; Dr. Dian Williams; and Investigator Brett Martinez.

As usual, a special nod to my mentors in the arson business. Thanks to Rich Edwards, John Ament, Joe Konefal, and Ron Michel.

# Contents

# Introduction

## THE TIGER HUNTER

The courts, prisons, and parole and probation departments have long sought out expert advice on how to deal with special criminals that they just don't seem to understand. These types of special criminals commit crimes that even the average criminal doesn't understand. This class of special criminals includes child molesters, stalkers, rapists, serial murders, sexual deviants, bombers, and arsonists, among others. These groups are the weirdos in society, even in the jails or prisons, where they are usually segregated and treated differently than other typical violent offenders.

During the course of the lives of many of these offenders, various judges, counselors, and parole officers are forced to make critical decisions on treatment, incarceration, or release from custody. There are countless case histories of someone urging release of one of these subtypes only to have the criminal reoffend within days or even hours. These guys just aren't wired like the rest of society. Because of that, and because of the ramifications of these decisions, the courts and counselors often consult the only person who *might have an idea* on how to deal with this sort of odd criminal. The persons usually consulting on this are psychiatrists or psychologists, with varying degrees of education, clinical work, and expertise. Many of these "experts" have gained their knowledge about these offenders by studying them and interviewing them in a custody setting. This behavior is noted and analyzed, and an attempt is made to classify this offender.

All of this activity starts out often in the youth phase of the offender after some sort of "incident" has occurred. The analysis continues as the offender ages and goes through various foster homes, schools, juvenile hall, county jail, and eventually prison. Over their entire lives, these offenders are subjected to dozens of interviews and questionnaires by court appointed "experts."

Most, if not all, of these psychiatric experts have gained their only real-world experiences by studying these offenders in a custody setting. This, in my estimation, is the crux of the problem. In my thirty years in law enforcement, with twenty-six of them as a detective involved in criminal investigations, I am well aware of the difference between interviewing an offender who has never been to jail and the offender who has a lot of experience in custody.

The experienced offender is a natural survivor. He can be a very savvy and cagey individual who has learned through trial and error how best to get what he wants by manipulating "the system." The experienced offender quickly learns the "correct" answers to give to counselors and mental-health evaluators that will get him special privileges or even early release. Even offenders with the most fragile grasp on mental health can understand the concept of "reward-based incarceration." This concept means if you go along with the program and tell "the man" what he wants to hear, good things will come your way. Besides all of this, the inmate/prisoner has been bombarded with advice by jailhouse lawyers and cons, who have been working the system for decades. It is well known in detective work that jailhouse lawyers have much more influence over an inmate than their own legitimate legal advisors.

The entire system is subject to manipulation. This concept of manipulation is exactly the way the custody/criminal justice field has worked for the past two hundred years and continues to work until today.

The entire purpose of the above observation is to show that any analysis of an incarcerated offender is skewed by the norms and mores of the prison system, the manipulative skill level of the subject, and the gullibility index of the interviewer. Whatever information you get from that subject should be treated with great suspicion. The more sophisticated and savvy the offender, the more he will tell you exactly what you want to hear.

Arsonists are generally a very clever group, even more so than many other offenders. They learn quickly in prison to lay low, get along, and be model prisoners, which most of them are. They are outcasts in the criminal world and soon gravitate toward their jailers and counselors for better treatment and rewards. They seldom engage in gang activity, violence, or any of the normal prison activities. They have listened and learned from any number of psychiatrists their entire lives and often regurgitate psychiatric babble when you speak to them. Many can be true chameleons, and all have found a way to minimize or escape blame for their past activities. They are indeed a manipulative group of survivors.

I was asked once by a prosecutor about my qualifications to render an opinion on the danger level of a very serious arsonist so that a judge could make an informed decision about incarceration or release. I recalled something an experienced street gang investigator once told me. He called himself the "tiger hunter." He explained his *nom de guerre*, which he had adopted while offering opinions on street gang behavior in criminal court. He had been investigating gang members for twenty years. He knew their living conditions, their brothers and sisters, their parents, their grandparents, their homes, what their bedrooms looked like, what drugs they took, what girls they slept with, the guns they preferred, the manner of their assaults, their favorite beverages, the movies they watched, the clothes they wore, the cars they drove, the heroes they admired, and even where they ate. He told me once, "If you want to catch a tiger, you have to be a tiger hunter."

I heard him explain in court that a zoologist might study tigers in captivity for thirty years and still never know how to catch one in the wild as the actions of a tiger in a zoo are decidedly different than the actions of the tiger in the jungles of Bengal. He said a tiger hunter in the bush knows where a tiger sleeps, when it hunts, how often it drinks, what's in its fecal matter, how long its stride is, and all the other factors that make him capable of hunting, tracking down, and killing the beast. This investigator had very little formal education beyond high school but claimed to have the equivalent of a doctorate in street gangs. I knew him, all the gangsters in the area knew and feared him, and the judge agreed with his assessment of his abilities. He was allowed numerous times in his career to give opinions on cases as an equal peer to medical doctors and psychiatrists.

This analogy applies directly to the arson-investigation field. After having done nearly two thousand arson investigations, having tracked down, arrested, and interviewed over three hundred fire starters, and having been involved in the prosecution and court testimony of nearly a hundred arsonists, I have been privy to a ton of documents and reports related to the behavior of these offenders. I have reviewed over nine hundred case histories, court records, psychiatric reports, criminal profiles, and probation and parole files on these offenders, and I am quite sure of one particular fact. The folks that know the absolute least about fire offenders appear to be the very mental-health professionals and counselors who are charged with treating and releasing them.

Other groups, in my estimation, that have little to no credible information about arsonists include judges, prosecutors, defense attorneys, the media, fire and police administrators, and, sadly, many members of the arson-investigation profession. These are the very groups charged with catching, understanding, defending, and judging these complex offenders, and yet they appear to know almost nothing about them!

The small number of prosecutors, mental-health professionals, and arson investigators that do understand this group of offenders are truly "tiger hunters." They are interested in tracking down, catching, understanding, and incarcerating this group for as long as possible. They know that many of these offenders are beyond treatment or rehabilitation. They know you cannot alter or change the "hard wiring" or DNA of some of these weirdos. They know the only place for some of these arsonists is in prison. I am in this group. I only care about understanding them to the point that it helps me catch them. I am the tiger hunter!

After I explained this theory to the prosecutor, he rolled his eyes, looked at me with some trepidation, but then decided that I knew more than the three experts who had appeared in court already. He then had me generate a written opinion or profile of this particular arson offender, where I assessed the sophistication of his attacks, the intended targets of the assaults, and the future danger level of the arsonist. My profile was accepted in court by the judge, who read it into the official record and then assigned a penalty more consistent with the danger level of the offender. This was very heartening to me as both the prosecutor and the judge had the ability to realize that they knew very little about this type of offender and were looking for someone, anyone, who might have a more learned opinion on the subject. That case was one of the first of my formal profiles that I have provided to prosecutors and courts on this complex subject matter.

# 1

# Criminal and Arson Profiling

## CRIMINAL PROFILING AND INVESTIGATIVE ANALYSIS

Modern fire investigation is steeped in science, technology, engineering, and theory. The understandings of these subjects, along with their implementation during investigations, have caused massive improvements in the investigation of fire scenes that have long been plagued by myths and legends. Much more work in these areas is needed. However, while the science of fire investigation has notably improved in the past twenty years, the observation of the "human side" of fire and arson investigation still lurks in the Dark Ages with a myriad of myths and misconceptions. None of the major books or manuals on fire investigation delves very deeply into all the "human factors" related to both accidental and incendiary fires. Since this is a mostly unscientific aspect of the profession, it is given very little attention by the bulk of the writers, instructors, and self-appointed "leaders" in the fire-investigation profession.

The purpose of this book is as a natural follow-up to my previous two books on the analysis of serial fire setters and obsessive, stalking fire setters. This book is being offered as a study and explanation of the fire-setting behavior of a wide range of arson subtypes.

The term ***profiling*** is the layman's name for the analysis of crime scenes, criminals, and criminal behavior. As times change and analysis evolves, along with the heavy influence of political correctness, the media, and the entertainment industry, various terms have come into vogue to describe basic criminology techniques. These techniques have been called "offender profiling," "criminal profiling," "psychological profiling," "behavioral analysis," "crime-scene analysis," "event analysis," and the Federal Bureau of Investigation's (FBI) current title, "criminal-investigative analysis." The differences in the names might mean something to attorneys, agency heads, and psychiatric professionals, but to the real practitioner in the form of the working detective, agent, or investigator, the names are all synonymous with a single practice: the analysis and interpretation of crime scenes and the behavior of the offender in an attempt to classify and identify a perpetrator. To avoid all of these messy names, this book will call that practice either "profiling" or "criminal profiling."

On a personal note, I have been a criminal investigator in Los Angeles (LA) for over twenty-five years, beginning in 1990, and have led or participated in nearly eight thousand criminal investigations of every type. I have worked as a plainclothes detective, undercover operator and detective, narcotics detective, and finally as an arson investigator / bomb technician on over twenty-five hundred cases. I am an ardent believer and practitioner in crime-scene analysis and profiling. I live it and use it every single day, and I routinely preach it and teach it in many classes, lectures, and schools. I also have had the occasion to employ these techniques, explain them, and defend their usage in several major criminal-court cases that resulted in the imposition of sentences ranging from many years in prison to **life in prison**, and even the **death penalty**.

## Standard Criminal Investigation Techniques

There are two main sub classifications within criminal profiling. The most well-known classification is called ***behavior profiling***. Its slightly lesser known partner is called ***geographic profiling***. Geographic profiling will be discussed at a later juncture.

While I am a major proponent of **criminal profiling as an investigative tool** or technique**,** I am just as strongly opposed to those who use it as **the sole basis for an arrest**. Any investigator who relies on a single strategy or technique to "solve" his case is both lazy and a fool and possibly criminally negligent. The arson-investigation profession has been particularly hard hit in recent years by the lack of employment of standard criminal-investigation techniques and the overreliance on gadgets, gimmicks, and toys. Many arson investigators (the lazy ones) have gotten into serious trouble for their overreliance on the "odor of a flammable liquid," the appearance of "flammable-liquid pour patterns," or the blind acceptance of a positive K-9 "hit" or similar "hit" by a mechanical-accelerant detector despite the crime lab not being able to independently verify these claims with hard evidence.

Additional issues that plague the profession are the blind acceptance of possible false confessions by juvenile suspects or those who have serious mental-health issues, along with the overdependence on polygraphs. These are all nice investigative tools, but all should be verified, corroborated, and employed in conjunction with multiple other investigative techniques. The proper use of profiling is nothing more than just another great tool in an investigator's toolbox. I don't believe that a criminal profiler can "catch the bad guy" or even accurately identify an offender as has been poorly characterized in many television and movie depictions. I especially do not believe that a profiler can predict such things as when the suspect will attack next and who or what will be the next target. That is pure Hollywood fantasy.

Used properly, a profile fits nicely into other standard investigation techniques such as scene photography and diagrams, detailed canvassing of the area, witness interviews, surveillance, pattern analysis, and the collection of physical evidence. Certain types of profiling, such as geographic and temporal profiling, may assist in narrowing down a suspect list or even eliminating entire groups of suspects. An experienced profiler can assist investigators in more oblique means. He can offer guidance on how to use or deal with the media, how to possibly "stimulate" the suspect, what to look for during a search warrant, and how to prepare for an interview with a suspect.

## REVIEW AND HISTORY OF CRIMINAL PROFILING

No other subject in law enforcement has caused more confusion and controversy in recent years than the word "profiling." In many agencies and courtrooms today, it is considered a taboo subject as it is thought to mean an officer was engaged in "racial profiling." Many agency heads, afraid of media backlash, have foolishly made public proclamations that their agency doesn't profile. What nonsense! Every intelligent or experienced police officer and detective in the world uses, on a daily basis, a form of profiling or behavior analysis, whether consciously or subconsciously.

The person who is considered to be the founder of the study of criminality and criminal profiling was an Austrian jurist and professor named **Hans Gustav Gross**, who, in 1891, wrote a *Handbook for Understanding Criminality* for magistrates, police officers, and lawyers. Gross's writings brought together several different topics that he believed should be part of routine criminal investigations. These topics included the study of motives, the study of modus operandi (MO), the use of crime-scene photography, the idea of maintaining objectivity during an investigation, the study and analysis of physical evidence, and the close study of offender behavior, or as we now refer to it, behavior analysis. After reviewing Professor Gross's work over his lifetime, I can affirm that he was a hundred years ahead of his time. His principles are still to this day valid and important principles in criminal investigation.

Criminal profiling came into popular culture during a nationally famous **serial bombing** case in the mid-1950s. The notorious Mad Bomber, a.k.a. George Metesky, had conducted a seventeen-year bombing campaign, where he placed forty-seven bombs in locations throughout New York City. During that campaign Metesky had sent several written manifestos to local police and the media. Eventually the police contacted a forensic psychiatrist named **Dr. James Brussel**, who analyzed crime-scene photos and the oddly phrased manifestos. As part of an investigative strategy, Dr. Brussel urged the police to publish the manifestos in the media. He said that this bomber would be identified quickly by his unique writings. He also gave police investigators an idea of what the offender's social history would look like and his probable life circumstances. Dr. Brussel's now-famous profile even went so far as to describe the unique clothing the bomber would be wearing when arrested.

In the end, Dr. Brussel accurately predicted several characteristics of the bomber including what state he lived in, in what part of the world he was born, how he dressed, his religion, his mental-health state of paranoia, and the fact that he would be in his fifties, unmarried, and living with a female relative. He also told investigators that the bomber would be a disgruntled former employee of the Con-Edison power company. When he was caught, George Metesky immediately confessed to all of the bombings and claimed that he was upset over his treatment by the power company nearly twenty years earlier. His very first targets in the campaign had been Con-Edison offices.

Dr. Brussel was the first person to formally describe what we now know as "profiling." To him it was merely looking at the actions of an unknown offender and then comparing them to the actions of known offenders through extensive studies of the latter groups. Basically, a profiler has to have a large amount of experience and education examining the case histories of offenders.

The Mad Bomber case was a resounding success for the study of criminal profiling as a legitimate investigative technique. It would take the arrest of the first known **serial killer** in the United States to bring it to the forefront. A legendary homicide detective with the Los Angeles Police Department (LAPD), **Capt. Pierce Brooks** is credited with being the first person of investigative stature to recognize the existence of serial killers in the late 1950s. He learned through his arrest and interrogation of Harvey Glatman that serial killers often have consistent behaviors from one crime to the next. Capt. Brooks conducted painstaking research on serial murderers by going through newspapers at local libraries, and he spent twenty years trying to convince LAPD brass to invest in computers and crime-tracking systems. Brooks eventually linked up with the FBI and was instrumental later in life with establishing the National Center for the Analysis of Violent Crimes (NCAVC).

The FBI was highly interested in profiling as it pertained to serial criminals, particularly serial murderers. By 1972, the FBI formally established the **Behavior Science Unit**, or BSU, at its headquarters in Quantico, Virginia. From there this new field of study expanded exponentially by the 1980s. The BSU (later changed to the BAU—Behavior Analysis Unit) became engrossed in studying sexual homicides in the form of serial murderers. Emerging stars in the profiling field included **Robert**

**Ressler** and **John Douglas** of the FBI, and **Robert Keppel**, a Seattle-area homicide investigator. These men and several of their colleagues interviewed dozens of incarcerated serial murderers, rapists, and child predators, and amassed a large amount of data about these special criminals. The data has been studied over the years and used as a base for analyzing the behavior of unknown suspects.

Criminal profiling has gone through many phases, not the least of which is the "Hollywood Effect." The exposure of this field of study in such movies as *Silence of the Lambs* and various television shows has elevated it to an almost mythical level of reliability and "science." It clearly isn't science, and the many mistakes in the field have demonstrated this very well. The most famous and commercially successful profiler of them all, John Douglas, a.k.a. "the Mind Hunter," made several very important erroneous findings in his analysis of "the Green River Killer." To this day, Douglas is scoffed at by the homicide and arson investigators in the Seattle area.

Other famous profiles that were dead wrong included the Olympic Park Bomber case and the Beltway Sniper investigation. The data has been morphed and modified over the years after several embarrassing errors made by profilers. Since these highly publicized goofs, the FBI has taken great pains to announce regularly that they have a Behavioral Analysis Unit, but that they do not employ persons whose job title is that of "profiler." They now conservatively consider it an investigative tool that many, if not all, of their agents use. They also maintain that profiling is not designed to solve crimes and catch suspects but is an investigative tool, which is offered via consultations to investigating officers.

## ARSON SCENE PROFILING

Many persons before me have made attempts at "profiling" the behavior of arsonists. Some of these people have done admirable work, some have been led astray by their own poor analysis of the actual events, and some in this profession should be embarrassed by their ridiculous use of "profiling an arsonist." Unfortunately, there are still many expert witnesses who make their living giving opinions in court about arsonists, who have very little understanding of the crime or the criminal, and who continue to rely on outdated studies from a half century ago. By their hefty resumes alone, these folks get away with making outrageous claims about a subject matter when they have no real proof or documented case histories.

I have met several of the early criminal profilers for the FBI and read practically all of their published works. I have also spoken to or corresponded with many of the persons first interested in profiling arsonists. They all freely admit that the bulk of the early profiling interviews were designed to inquire about sexual homicides and serial murders. All of these people admit that arson and fire-setting behavior was attached to this, but the analysts were much more interested in the murder aspect of the cases. The arson aspect of these serial killers was almost an afterthought. As such, specific, important details of the fire-setting behavior were omitted or not researched in depth. To this day, there is very little in-depth study of fire-setting behavior by analysts or investigators.

Much of the early arson-profiling work was haphazard at best and was overly reliant on the study of only incarcerated arsonists. From these studies, the profilers attempted to come up with profiles that fit every type of arsonist, which we will soon find are many.

My biggest criticism of the earlier attempts at gathering data from arsonists is that the researchers used a fairly limited pool of arsonists and seldom differentiated between serial arsonists and one-time arson offenders. There are massive differences between the groups, just as there are massive differences between serial killers and a person who murders his or her spouse.

The other major criticism to the early arson profilers is that almost none of them were fire-scene investigators. Because of this, very critical crime-scene behaviors were missed or omitted. The exact methods and manner in which an arsonist sets a fire is extremely critical information when attempting to profile the event. In a related field, one cannot study a serial bomber without first studying the design and implementation of his devices.

A final criticism I have of some arson profilers is their fixation on being able to predict where the arsonist will next strike. This has been attempted numerous times in several countries as researchers attempt to make sense out of patterns in an arson spree. After having met a few dozen serial arsonists, I find it almost laughable that researchers would attempt to predict what the arsonist himself has no idea he is going to do. The overwhelming numbers of serial arsonists select targets of opportunity and put very little planning into their event.

*The size of the fire event has very little to do with the intent of the arsonist.*

### Two Main Types of Arson

When all is said and done, the crime of arson can be broken into two main categories or types: ***goal-directed arson*** and ***emotionally based arson***. Readers should be cautioned that arson attacks can have a blend of motives and a mixture of both goal-directed and emotionally based behavior. Nothing is black and white in this business, and nothing is simple.

### Goal-Directed Arson Behavior

Goal-directed arson basically describes all arson motives where **the arsonist has a specific goal and target in mind prior to his attack**. Goal-directed arson accounts for the overwhelming majority of arson attacks, possibly up to 90 percent. Examples of goal-directed motives include **revenge/spite**, **financial gain**, **crime concealment**, **extremism**, **vandalism**, **suicide by fire**, and **organized crime / gang related**. In each of these motives, the arson attack fulfills the need of the motive. These goals and motives are easily understood and simple to investigate. (I didn't say they were easy to solve, they are just easy to understand and investigate.) There is frequently some sort of connection between the arsonist and the target of the attack.

### Emotionally Based Arson Behavior

Emotionally based arson describes **fires set with no known connection between the arsonist and the target and for no known motive or reason.** Emotionally based arson behavior is fairly rare and is the least understood, even by investigators. However, it is the type of arson that gets the most attention and is often used by defense attorneys to obfuscate or hide the true (goal-directed) motive behind the arson. It is the most studied type of arson by mental-health professionals even though less than 10 percent of arson attacks are related to emotionally based fire setting. Examples of emotionally based arson attacks include **vanity** or **hero fire setting**, **juvenile fire setting**, **curiosity fire setting**, **attention-seeking arson**, **excitement-based arson**, **female arson (mommy fires)**, and **serial arsonists**.

These fires often make no sense to investigators, may appear as "nuisance fires" or even accidental fires (mommy fires), and involve mostly random targets. It is much more difficult to begin one of these investigations as there appears to be no apparent motive and no connection between the arsonist and the target.

### Profiling Steps

The profiling steps in the next section, if followed properly, will assist the investigator in defining the target, identifying potential suspects, and determining type and motive of the arson attack.

## TARGET ANALYSIS

Target analysis is a poorly understood aspect of arson investigation. That's too bad because **target analysis is the most critical clue** in an arson attack as to who the offender might be.

The early study of serial murderers was illuminating in that it clearly showed that serial murderers were most likely to target five specific groups of victims. These groups are babies and infants, the elderly, gay men involved in high-risk sex, teen runaways, and the most targeted group, people involved in prostitution. These groups are most victimized in that they are either unable to defend themselves, are in the care of others, or have placed themselves in a secluded environment or a high-risk situation. These are targets that are fairly defenseless and with no support group nearby to protect them.

This type of analysis has some correlation to the serial arson world in that the most common targets of serial arson attacks are also easily identifiable groups. The most common targets of serial arsonists include vegetation in remote areas, trash containers in hidden areas, abandoned vehicles, outbuildings, and abandoned structures. Like the human targets described above, these nonhuman targets are usually not occupied, are hidden from public view, and have no one who is actively watching over them. Like their human counterparts, they are the targets that are easy to access with the lowest risk to the offender.

Sometimes in large fire events it is difficult to determine the exact target of the attack. Often, if a fire grows into a large event, the actual target of the arson attack may be hidden or missed in all of the damage. An example of this is taken from the bomb-investigation field. The Oklahoma City Bombing in 1994 was one of the most heinous crimes in American history and certainly the most significant criminal bombing on our soil. From the moment the event occurred, the media and their paid "talking-head" criminal profilers began to guess as to whom might have committed this major attack. The guessing immediately focused on Middle Eastern terrorist groups as this level of attack on American soil was something that those groups had long dreamed of committing.

However, any reasonably experienced expert on bombings or terrorists would have quickly excluded this attack as having been committed by an international terrorist group by merely looking at the general target of the attack. The general target, a US government office building in the American heartland, is hardly on the radar of any international terrorist group. I would wager that if these groups kept detailed target lists in order of importance, the Murrah building would not have made it into the top two hundred desired targets. International terror groups are intent on hitting targets of major emotional, financial, or even symbolic importance. While it did represent the government somewhat, the Murrah building paled as a symbol in comparison to the White House, US Capitol, CIA Headquarters, or any other major facility. No offense intended, but it is doubtful that Middle Eastern terrorists in 1994 had ever heard of the state of Oklahoma, let alone a federal building in one of its cities.

Any experienced profiler or investigator would have first thought of a homegrown, right-wing antigovernment extremist group as the *most likely* offender in this attack. The 1980s and 1990s were rife with antigovernment groups in the heartland of the Midwest. The Militia Movement, Christian Identity movements, White Separatist Movement, and the antiabortion, antigay, and similar groups absolutely hated "big government" and everything it stood for. There was any number of likely specific targets within the Murrah building that day that had long been the focus of many of these groups. These targets included the Internal Revenue Service (IRS), the FBI, and the Bureau of Alcohol, Tobacco, Firearms and Explosives (ATF). Of all of these targets, the one that had drawn the most sustained hatred by these right-wing groups was easily the ATF.

The ATF's role of enforcing gun laws has historically been unpopular in a country that practically worships firearms. Further, the ATF had been involved in several high-profile botched investigations that had extremely tragic results. These right-wing extremist groups had serious issues with the manner in which the ATF had operated in the Ruby Ridge standoff; the raid on the Covenant, Sword, and Arm of the Lord compound in Arkansas; and most notoriously, the horribly botched raid on the Branch Davidian Compound in Waco, Texas, exactly one year prior to the Oklahoma City bombing. Only after detailed analysis and investigation did the FBI conclude that Tim McVeigh, the Oklahoma City bomber, specifically targeted the ATF office within the Murrah building. To him, everything else was collateral damage in his war against the government.

Several years ago we had a serial arsonist in Los Angeles who lit over two hundred fires in his *second arson spree*, after being released from prison for a previous spree of seven fires. His name was Christopher Dominguez, and I described his activities in detail in my first book on serial arsonists, *Torchered Minds*. When we originally arrested him for the first seven arson attacks, he was charged with setting several Mexican-owned bars on fire. He refused to speak to us in that case, and only talked to us nearly a decade later when he was arrested for the next two hundred fires.

We were confused as to why he set buildings on fire in his first arson spree and then seemed to reverse his intensity during his second arson spree by attacking mainly trash, vegetation, and minor items he found in alleys and behind structures. He explained that he had always lit the same things on fire. He had an odd fixation on messy things (untrimmed vegetation/trees, overflowing trash barrels/Dumpsters, and furniture in yards and alleys) and believed it was his duty as a good citizen to clean up the area around his town by burning away all the messy or unsightly items. He further explained that he was setting overflowing trash Dumpsters on fire during his first spree, and that they just happened to be placed up against bars. In his mind, he did not burn the bars at all; he merely burned the trash Dumpsters. It didn't matter to him that the fire from the Dumpsters spread to the bars and caused major damage because that was not his intention. His target was the Dumpster.

This type of target analysis can be extremely important when attempting to classify a fire and narrow down a list of offenders. As an example, a major strip mall burns from an arson attack at two in the morning. A natural first instinct for an arson investigator may be to suspect that this attack could be associated with the owner of the strip mall or one of the tenants attempting to commit insurance fraud. A close examination of the fire scene reveals that the fire originated outside of the structure in a pile of cardboard boxes stacked up for normal recycling the next day. Further analysis and maybe a video shows that the fire was set in the cardboard by a transient who is also suspected in other small fires in the area. By this sort of detailed fire-scene examination and analysis, the investigator can quickly eliminate some motives and suspects.

*The time when an arsonist sets a fire is at his convenience.*

## TEMPORAL ANALYSIS

Many past studies have been conducted with the intent of being able to predict the behavior of an arsonist. Several of these studies focused on the time of day that the fires were set. It is an excellent idea to track the times of all arson attacks, especially those set in a series. The analysis of this data will later help you to include or exclude certain people from your pool of suspects. The term used to analyze the dates, days, and times of criminal events is known as ***temporal analysis***. In the arson world, temporal analysis applies to both serial arson cases and to cases involving one-time arson offenders.

Some of the early studies of this have been downright ridiculous. Several pioneers in the world of profiling conducted studies to see if arson activity coincided with the phases of the moon, tides, or on specific days of the month or year. Psychologists have long associated arson with abnormal behavior and have long sought out exotic reasons for this to occur. I really don't believe any of these bizarre theories.

A recent analyst from Scripps News Service has relied heavily on mathematics and statistical data. He has found that there are serious upticks in reported arson activity on specific dates in the year. Halloween, New Year's Eve, and the Fourth of July have been identified as days with significant arson activity surrounding them. The surge in reported arsons on those days appears commonsensical as they all involve holidays associated with a liberal amount of drinking, fireworks, and chicanery. Most of the "arsons" on those dates are probably related to vandalism-type fires.

However, one theory that I am sure about, after interviewing several hundred arsonists of every subtype, is that arsonists usually **set their fires at a time that is convenient for them** and for really no other reason. An arson investigator may note that there is a pattern but will not understand why until the arsonist is arrested. There is usually a very practical reason for when an arsonist sets his fires, but only he knows why. As an example, studying a serial arsonist may reveal a pattern of fires set only on Tuesdays between four and six o'clock in the late afternoon. After the arsonist is identified and arrested, it is learned that he is a fourteen-year-old boy whose mother normally is home at four o'clock when he gets back from school. On Tuesdays, she has a staff meeting at work and is unable to get home until after six. That is the time and day of the week that the at-risk youth is unsupervised, and therefore it is the only time he has the opportunity to conduct his fire-setting activity.

It is true that the overwhelming number of arson attacks occur in the time of darkness as it is easy to remain hidden, and there are few witnesses around. It is a matter of pure practicality to set fires during the darkness. One notable exception to the rule of darkness is the **wild-land arsonist**. Because the wild land offers its own hidden areas, and there are very few people about, there is no need to operate in darkness. Also, wild-land fires are most devastating when set in the afternoon hours because of higher temperatures and wind activity. It is more common for a wild-land-arson incident to occur during daytime hours than nighttime hours.

Juvenile-set fires are more often set during daylight hours but at a time when they are unsupervised. This could be during after school hours or at a time when the childcare provider is asleep or not paying attention. "Housewife" or "mommy fires" are also set during daylight hours because that is usually the time when their husbands are at work.

Each subtype and case is unique and needs to be evaluated individually. If an arson fire occurs at an odd time, there is usually a practical reason for this. If the investigator can identify that anomaly, then he can usually identify the suspect.

## GEOSPATIAL-PATTERN ANALYSIS / GEOGRAPHIC PROFILING

A heavily studied field in criminology is criminal-pattern analysis. There have been dozens of studies from all over the globe that have focused on possibly predicting criminal behavior by studying geographic patterns in the locations of the attacks.

This field of analysis is called either ***geospatial analysis*** or ***geographic profiling***. In the arson world, geospatial analysis usually only applies to serial arson cases.

Most modern police agencies have learned the value of mapping crimes and crime trends as a way of noticing problem areas. They have hired or trained people in the role of **crime analyst**, and they use that person to plot crimes in their jurisdictions. Police administrators then use this information to allocate additional resources to trending areas. All arson investigators should form a close relationship with a police crime analyst in their area. This is an invaluable resource during a serial arson event.

Serial crimes of any type are extremely common in police work, and an astute crime analyst is worth his or her weight in gold. Experienced crime analysts can, within a day or two, pick out trends in burglaries, car-theft locations, dumping grounds for stolen cars, robberies, and sexual assaults.

Many researchers have discovered that several types of criminals have developed patterns within their behaviors that give clues as to who they are and where they reside. These patterns may be developed through subconscious thought, social norms, or by barriers that impede their expanding out of a certain area. The first step in the process is to plot every single crime in your series on a map, including the day, date, and time of the event. After enough attacks in your area, patterns may emerge. This sort of pattern analysis has proven reliable during many serial murder, serial rape, and serial arson cases.

However, a word of caution should be given here. The pattern analysis of predatory crime, such as stranger rape, child abductions, flashers, and serial murder, does not always compare equally with nonpredatory crime such as arson and burglary. In the case of predatory crime, the target of the attacker must be taken into consideration when looking at pattern analysis. As an example, if a serial rapist has targeted teenage girls, his geospatial pattern of attacks will center around areas where there is a likelihood of teenage girls, such as near a mall, a high school, or any other similar venue. A serial killer whose targets are streetwalker prostitutes will have a geospatial-pattern analysis focused in an area's "red-light district." These are called "**hunting areas**" for these types of predatory criminals.

Burglars, on the other hand, will target areas where they expect to find the items they are interested in stealing. If they are high-end commercial burglars, they will target areas with electronics businesses and the like. The patterns established by a serial arsonist are often a good indicator of where the arsonist lives and what mode of transportation he is using to access his targets.

### Serial Arson Geospatial Analysis

As stated earlier in this book, the crime of serial arson is not the same as other crimes. There are two main subtypes of serial arson: ***urban serial arson*** and ***wild-land serial arson.*** Both types of offenders operate within a "**comfort zone**." The comfort zone of an offender is usually an area he is familiar with, lives in, or works in. The area traveled between home and work or school may also be part of the comfort zone. The wild-land offender's comfort zone is usually much larger than his urban counterpart's zone.

Urban serial arsonists do tend to have some pattern behavior in their actions. For the most part, urban serial arsonists do not drive and are usually limited in their operating area by their lack of transportation. Most urban serial arsonists access their targets via foot travel or bicycle. A few will use public transport, such as busses or trains, and a rare few might have an automobile at their disposal. The first goal in a serial arson investigation is to see if you can eliminate any of these modes of transportation from the scenario. By plotting all the fire scenes and the times of the fires, you might be able to definitively state that the arsonist is walking to his scenes or, by the great distances involved, that he must be driving to his scenes.

Many urban serial arsonists will tend to set fires in the areas around their home or work. Most studies suggest that 70 percent of urban serial arsonists will set their fires within two miles of their homes, using their residence as a base of operations. Crime analysts have called this type of behavior as being a "**hunter**."

Next, after you have plotted a number of fires in a series, you may tend to see **clusters** or groups of fires in a small area. These clusters are usually very important and are known as **anchoring points** for the arsonist. Many past case histories have shown that urban serial arsonists often light fires in clusters near where they live, work, go to school, or have some other personal connection. It may take until the end of the case to determine what connection the arsonist has to a particular cluster, but it is something that is usually practical and makes sense. For instance, several serial arsonists have set fires in and around their own homes and then set additional fires at or near their job sites or their mothers' homes or at schools they are connected with. A cross analysis of clusters and temporal patterns may tell the investigator which anchoring point represents the home of the offender and which anchoring point represents the school or work site of the offender.

Another pattern that may evolve in an arson case is a "**travel pattern**." This is a pattern of fires that are between anchoring points for the arsonist. In this type of pattern, the arsonist may set fires while traveling between his home and work, or home and school. In a case highlighted in my second book, *Fireraisers, Freaks, and Fiends*, serial arsonist Tevin Gibson worked at a supermarket where he was closely monitored. He lived a mile away with his parents, who also closely monitored him. He routinely walked home each night after work through a greenbelt in a suburban neighborhood. While walking home, Tevin set a total of twenty-three small fires in the only travel path between his work and his home. There were several keys to the case that pointed at him, including the fact that he reported at least two of the fires

A theory that I have developed somewhat in my own lectures and training is called "**the first fire in a series theory**." This theory has been developed during my own casework on over three dozen serial arson cases and my studies of hundreds more. The theory is that if we, as investigators, can identify the very first fire in a series, then the arsonist will likely have a personal connection to that fire scene or target. If we begin a detailed canvassing of all the neighbors near that first fire scene, it is a decent bet that they will know the arsonist or at least someone acting peculiar. This theory has worked for me on at least a dozen cases, including the massive Hollywood Arsonist case, where a suspect lit fifty-two fires in three days. We went to the very first fire that he lit in our area and found out that he had a personal connection to the people who lived there. In fact, in that case the suspect had a personal connection to at least four of the first eight structures he burned that night.

Wild-land serial arsonists have a completely different type of pattern (if any) in their behavior. Most wild-land serial arsonists drive to their fire scenes, and therefore most of their fires are not near their homes. Crime analysts have called this type of behavior as being a "**poacher**." Most of their fires will be on a linear path of sorts, but that isn't a subconscious pattern. The fact that there are very few roads through the wild land is the main reason that serial arsonists tend to set fires in a linear fashion. Any other method is inaccessible to them. Wild-land serial arsonists tend to set their fires at roughly the same time of day (midmorning to late afternoon), so interpreting temporal-analysis information is more difficult. Close attention should be paid to the day of the week during serial wild-land cases.

Serial wild-land arsonists can also have travel patterns similar to urban serial arsonists. They may live in a town but have to drive through the wild-land areas to get to work or school. It is during this time that they may have the opportunity to set their fires. Crime analysts have labeled this type of offending as being a "**troller**."

The key to all geospatial and temporal analysis is to gather as much information about each event as possible, attempt to decipher all of this information, and see if there are any patterns that emerge. Once patterns are identified, then the investigator can focus resources in a more useful manner. Once a suspect is identified, you can then compare the information you have gathered to his life, his work, his home, his school, and his travel patterns and see if he fits into those patterns. Pattern analysis alone will not prove that a suspect is an arsonist, but it will aid in identifying or eliminating potential suspects.

A few rare serial criminals, including rapists, murderers, and arsonists, may actually monitor the media during a crime series. This is an extremely rare phenomenon, but if the arsonist is doing this, he may intentionally set a fire outside of his normal patterns in an effort to throw off the investigation. This rare event is called a "**displacement crime**" and is only done by the most savvy and narcissistic of criminals. Famous examples of very cagey arsonists who set "displacement fires" in an effort to throw off investigators include DC Arsonist Thomas Sweatt and the most famous arsonist ever, John Orr. It is truly a rare and unique phenomenon. A way to minimize this from occurring is to carefully guard all investigative information during a crime series and to release only information that has been carefully vetted. Many a serial arson investigation has been compromised by investigators or fire chiefs releasing way too much case sensitive information to the media.

*Efficient fire setting is learned behavior.*

## IGNITION SCENARIO

The ignition scenario is just a fancy way of asking, "Exactly how did the arsonist start the fire?" The ignition scenario is just that: the exact methods, style, materials, and manner in which the arsonist got the fire to ignite and spread. The ignition scenario differs from the next section on method of operation (MO), in that MO covers every aspect of the event while the ignition scenario only covers the fire-starting aspect.

This is the time in the investigation where the fire-scene investigator (a.k.a. the origin and cause investigator) earns his money. By examining the fire-movement patterns at the scene, he hopes to locate a room or area of origin. If he finds the room or area of origin, he narrows his search further and hopes to find a point of origin. If he is clever enough to find the point of origin, then he must find two items: the ignition source and the first fuel that was ignited by that ignition source. He then develops a finding of the ignition scenario: What element or actions caused the ignition source to come into contact with the first fuel ignited? This determination is the most important aspect of arson scene investigation, and it can and often will indicate a probable offender type or at least a profile of an offender. The proper analysis of the ignition scenario can also eliminate specific persons and possibly entire groups from the suspect pool.

An example of a detailed ignition-scenario statement is as follows. An investigation into an elementary-school classroom fire, which occurred after school hours, revealed that some paper matches were left on the teacher's desk among a pile of crumpled, burned papers, resulting in a fairly small fire. The detailed ignition scenario for that arson attack would read something like this: "The fire was ignited by an unknown suspect crumpling papers found on the desk and arranging them into a pile. The suspect then applied an open flame from three paper matches to the pile of crumpled papers, causing the ignition of them."

In this manner, the investigator specifically identified the fact that an unknown offender used **available combustible materials** (papers found on the teacher's desk), arranged them into a pile for ease of burning (crumpled them and stacked them), and used at least three paper matches to light the pile of papers. A profile or analysis of this ignition scenario would indicate that the likely pool of suspects would be juvenile offenders who lived nearby and were probably students of the school. Further assessment of the scene would divulge if the offender brought matches with him or used matches found at the scene. It would also show how the offender entered the school either via an unlocked door or window or by force.

Additionally, school fire attacks are usually in conjunction with theft, graffiti, and other forms of vandalism. An assessment of this activity is needed to clarify the MO of the entire event. All of these assessments would go further to identifying the type of offender. In this case, the first place to start an investigation of this sort would be to consult the principal of the school or even the victim teacher, who would have the best information on troubled or at-risk students at the school.

In the above scenario, the suspects did not bring flammable materials with them, and the arson fire was likely not a preplanned event. The scene was extremely crude and haphazard, and the suspect left evidence behind (matches), which is a classic aspect of juvenile fires. The fact that the suspect crumpled the paper before igniting it reveals that the suspect has lit fires in the past and has shown that this method of "**arranging fuels**" causes the paper to burn more efficiently. In this scenario the suspect has probably lit other small fires before this event and is perfecting his fire-setting behavior. The arranging of fuels before a fire suggests a higher level of sophistication than the pure novice or first-time offender.

If no other classrooms or teachers were targeted in this attack, then the offender is likely a current or past student of the teacher, or at least has some sort of connection. That type of analysis greatly reduces the list of potential suspects for this attack.

## METHOD OF OPERATION OF EVENT

After processing an arson scene and determining the ignition scenario, the next most important analysis to undertake is to determine the **method of operation (MO)** of the offender. This will give a major clue to the arsonist's skill level and sophistication. It may give a clue if his behavior had been taught to him in some manner.

*MO is everything an offender does to successfully complete his crime.*

MO can include the time of day of the arson, the type of target selected, the method of accessing the target (e.g., by vehicle, bicycle, bus, on foot), the clothing worn by the arsonist (for protection or camouflage), the use of a scanner to detect police, the use of tools to access a building, the use of lights or night-vision devices, the scouting of the target, the disabling of the sprinkler or alarm systems, the use of the Internet to research information on the target, and the return to the target after the attack to assess damage. The ignition scenario is also included within the overall MO.

MOs tend to develop, evolve, refine, and become more efficient as the offender matures. A very seasoned offender (without serious mental-health issues) will tend to have a very efficient MO. For example, a seasoned burglar will have learned through bad luck or trial and error to avoid homes with dogs or alarm systems. He will tend to select homes without these safeguards, in areas that are hidden from street view, and enter them in daylight hours when the occupants are presumably at work. A highly skilled burglar was Richard Ramirez, the notorious "Nightstalker" serial murderer in Los Angeles. Ramirez was a drug addict who needed to feed his addictions. He committed several burglaries on a daily basis. He most often entered homes through unlocked windows. He chose his targets for burglary by looking at the home and seeing if the windows had vegetation near them to obscure his entry.

Only late in his burglary career did he step into the world of being a serial killer. By this time he had perfected the art of clandestine entry into homes. His MO for victims was that he chose targets in an Asian area of Los Angeles as he believed that Asian victims were smaller, more compliant, and less likely to attack him during his assaults. The Nightstalker had perfected his MO as a burglar way before he began killing people.

Suspects who have refined or perfected their MOs include older or experience offenders; offenders who have spent time in gangs or prison as it is common behavior for gang members and prisoners to discuss tactics and police-detection techniques; and finally offenders who have been mentored by an older, more experienced crime partner.

MOs for arson attacks will vary based on the skill level of the arsonist and the type of target he is trying to burn. Fire starting is a learned behavior, and an arsonist will soon learn that certain materials are very difficult to ignite. He may refine his MO by bringing kindling wood or flammable materials to a scene with him. An example of a famous arsonist whose MO evolved greatly was Bruce George Peter Lee, the deadliest serial arsonist ever identified.

In my first book, *Torchered Minds*, Lee is the keynote case study. He started his serious arson activities at age twelve. He broke into occupied homes at night and poured petrol (gasoline) onto victims as they slept. This high-risk behavior was dangerous to Lee in many ways. He was at risk of getting caught, at risk of getting beaten by one of his victims, at risk of being seen carrying a can of petrol down the street, and at risk of being burned by the highly volatile petrol. He, in fact, did burn himself on multiple occasions and was detained by suspicious police at numerous scenes.

By the time he was eighteen, Lee had dramatically refined his methods and carried a squirt bottle hidden in his clothes. The bottle contained paraffin, a much less volatile liquid than petrol. He stopped breaking into homes and instead squirted the paraffin into open mail slots of homes where his victims slept. He then gave himself a safe ignition distance by placing a burning paper through the mail slot. Lee killed twenty-three people with fire before he was caught. Even though his first attacks were deadly and highly successful, his MO continued to evolve as he matured and sought a more discreet and safer method of committing arson/murder.

### The Myth of Experimentation and Small Fires

Once a suspect refines his MO to an efficient method, he tends to stay with that MO until it fails or he hurts himself. He may then switch MOs again until he finds another that works well for him. This information is in contrast to a theory posed by many veteran arson investigators (with very little documentation to back it up). Many past "experts" in the serial arson world have told the courts that all serial arsonists experiment with their devices by lighting small fires, and they always evolve to better devices and bigger fires. This has happened occasionally, but for the majority of the time, once a tactic or device is found to work, the arsonist will tend to stay with it until it fails him. I have documented many serial arsonists who have used the same crude tactics or devices for their entire lives, spanning sixty years and hundreds of fires. It is a pure myth that all serial arsonists evolve and experiment with their methods or devices.

MOs can be quite unique or ingenious but will not rise to the level of a "signature," which will be discussed in the next section. Serial arsonists all tend to develop an efficient MO. Paul Keller, the "Seattle Arsonist," used an open flame via a cigarette lighter to ignite all of his eighty-plus fires, which is not unique at all. Keller had an interesting MO in that his fires were set on items or materials that hung off homes or structures such as tarps, awnings, and wood piles. He also set his fires at waist level or higher and almost never lower than that. There may be many practical reasons for that, including the fact that he capered in Seattle, a very humid environment where it is difficult to ignite things, the fact that he often wore a suit or dress clothes when he lit his fires, or the fact that he was too drunk or lazy to bend down. Thomas Sweatt's ("DC Arsonist") MO included a consistent targeting method, a consistent simple incendiary device, and a method of carrying the device in a very innocuous manner directly up to the target. His tactics made him appear as just a middle-aged man carrying a jug of milk home in a bag.

Understanding an arsonist's MO will give investigators clues as to what to look for when searching the arsonist's home, phone, and computer and when attempting to link him to various fire scenes.

## SIGNATURE

One of the most misused terms in criminal investigation is ***signature***. It has frequently been misused by investigators when they are actually describing the MO of the attack or arson. When a rapist-murderer targets street prostitutes, wears a ski mask, uses a belt to strangle them, and discards them in a river, he does not have a signature. Those are his targets, tactics, and method of operation necessary to find an easy victim, not be recognized, silently kill, and discard in a manner that will take care of all forensics. It is a reliable and efficient way for him to kill over and over again. It is not his "signature." If, before he dumped the body into the river, he put makeup and panty hose on the victims, then he would have included his signature.

The term *signature* became very popular when describing certain serial killers, and by the late 1980s, the arson world erroneously adopted the term when referring to incendiary devices used by serial arsonists. The term was somewhat invented during the early profiling years, and its correct use is generally seen only among sexual murderers.

In profiling, the term *signature* refers to an act done at a crime scene that is completely unnecessary to complete the crime but is done to satisfy some sort of psychological need of the suspect. It is an act that is usually very unique and deeply personal to the suspect, and usually only he knows why he does that signature act. Signatures are most often done after the criminal act (rape, murder, arson) has been completed. Typical examples of signatures at sexual-murder scenes include the suspect urinating or defecating in the scene, the suspect posing the body or body parts in a manner to shock the person finding the body, the suspect mutilating the body after the rape or murder, the suspect dressing the victims in particular clothes, wigs, or makeup that he has brought to the scene, and the suspect leaving messages at the scene.

Robert Keppel, one of the original criminal profilers who worked on the Ted Bundy and Green River Killer cases, writes in his book *Signature Killers* that a signature is the suspect's "calling card" that he leaves at every scene. He and other profiling experts say that the signature, if it exists, runs through every crime scene of the offender and seldom changes. Keppel devoted an entire chapter of his book to explain the stark differences between MO and signature.

There have been many signatures used in the sexual-murder world but almost no documented cases of true signatures in the arson world. Many arson investigators believe that John Orr used a "signature device," when in fact he used multiple styles and types of incendiary devices, and he lit fires in multiple types of targets. Orr did favor a specific device design (cigarette, rubber band, three paper matches), but that was more for utility than for a psychological need. I have seen only one serial arsonist who appeared to leave a signature at the fire scenes. This arsonist lit approximately thirty structure fires in Los Angeles in 2001 in a similar manner. He broke into a home, urinated on a bed, stole a small child's toy, and then lit a fire in the bedroom. It appeared to us that his urination and theft of the toy at every scene were his signatures. The suspect never spoke to us and was never convicted of his arsons. He fled to Mexico shortly after making bail on his case and hasn't been seen in almost fifteen years.

An example of a person who had a signature was serial bomber/murderer Ted Kaczynski (the "Unabomber"), who actually had two different signatures. He wrote the letters "FC" at some point on every explosive device and in his letters mailed to authorities, which nobody had any idea what that meant until after his arrest. Kaczynski admitted that it stood for the name of his own social movement (of which he was the only member) called "Freedom Club." His second unique signature was that on all of his mailed bombs, he placed an unnecessary stamp with the image of playwright Eugene O'Neill. Again, the item was completely unnecessary to complete the bombings but was more symbolic in nature, as O'Neill was sort of a counterculture-themed playwright.

Ted Bundy's signature was the fact that he left postmortem bite marks on many of his victims. It should be noted that Bundy was also quite famous for choosing targets that looked remarkably similar as most had straight, long hair parted down the middle. There is some debate whether this was a signature or just his target of desirability.

To reiterate, the use of a signature in the arson world is practically unheard of. Consistent targets or devices are usually related to MO.

## STAGING

The act of "**staging**" at any crime scene indicates that the suspect was attempting to hide the true intention or motive of his actions and arranged the scene to make investigators believe something else occurred or some other person committed the crime. This type of action indicates an offender with a fairly high degree of preplanning and sophistication. A classical criminal act involving crime-scene staging is a man who wants to kill his wife but knows that he will likely be considered one of the prime suspects in the investigation. He may murder his wife and then "break in" to his home and possibly leave items to indicate she was killed by a random burglar. A suspect like that may leave gloves, a pry bar, or other item near a forced or jimmied door.

In the arson world, the most common form of staging a scene is when a businessman wants to burn his business for profit but stages the entire event as a burglary to throw off arson and insurance investigators. Another classic act of staging concerning arson is when a vehicle owner stages the "theft" of his vehicle, which is then found burning in a remote area. It should be remembered by arson investigators that, typically, burglars and car thieves commit crimes for profit and seldom, if ever, find profit in burning the place they burgled or the car they stole. There is very little documented case history to show that thieves and burglars burn their scenes. The most likely person to burn property is the property owner.

More unique types of staging include when a church official, engaged in theft or embezzlement, stages the burning of his church as a "hate crime" in order to hide evidence of his misdeeds. A prudent arson investigator will probably find that this fire originated in the church offices, which is a major red flag toward a possible theft or embezzlement. Most "hate" arsons toward churches occur from outside the church or, if they are inside, usually within the sanctuary or worship area and not the business offices.

## SOPHISTICATION OF EVENT

The ultimate goal of fire-scene investigation and analysis, after finding the ignition source and first fuel ignited, is to determine the sophistication level of this event and, therefore, of the suspect. This aspect is the most important step in determining a potential pool of suspects and the elimination (or at least the marginalization) of a large number of suspects.

In reality, very few people know how to efficiently build a fire. A skilled fire setter can build a massive fire with a single match, while an unskilled fire setter can bring a case of highway flares and fifty gallons of gas to a scene, and the fire can fizzle out. Every experienced arson investigator has seen dozens of examples of too much fuel or ignition material at a scene that only smoked and smoldered. All of this plays into the skill level and sophistication of the fire setter.

Most people that set criminal fires understand only two of the three sides of the fabled fire triangle: fuel plus ignition/heat plus oxygen equals fire. Most arsonists forget the importance of oxygen and fail to start a fire in a well-ventilated area. Others forget that fuel must be arranged in a continuous fashion or the fire will die due to lack of fuel.

A huge mistake that I have seen many arson investigators make is that they equate how a typical arsonist starts a fire to how they (the arson investigator) would start a fire. That is a very bad investigate strategy, as we in the firefighting/investigation business have unique knowledge on how an efficient fire should be built. Remember, the overwhelming number of people who set criminal fires are novices and not at all skilled at this act. When we identify someone who has unique fire-setting skills, it is truly a rare subject, and one who likely has some sort of related training or experience.

Sophisticated actions at a fire scene, ranging from fairly unsophisticated to hyper sophisticated, include the following: bringing a continuous flame source such as a candle or flare, bringing any form of accelerants, using ignitable trailer material designed to spread the fire from one area to another, arranging fuels in the area of origin, using more efficient ignition devices such as small hand torches, establishing multiple areas of origin, creating the **laddering of fuels** (a very sophisticated technique where fuels are arranged from lighter combustibles to more substantial fuels, arranged at ever-increasing levels, which will cause the fire to race up the ramp of fuels), demonstrating an **awareness of ventilation** to enhance fire spread, and reconfiguring the structure (holes in walls, doors removed) to enhance fire spread.

Staging the arson scene as something else is also a form of higher sophistication. A highly sophisticated arsonist may disable sprinkler or alarm systems, block the scene so as to impede fire department response, create another diversionary fire in another part of the town, and employ the use of a sophisticated time-delay incendiary device.

Arsonists who engage in some of the more unique actions of sophistication are giving investigators a huge clue as to who they might be. Very few people in the world actually understand fire behavior, and any exotic methods would indicate that the arsonist is highly experienced or has unique training in starting fires. Remember, the more exotic an action at the scene, the more rare and unique your arsonist.

In direct contrast to the previous ignition scenario at the school, I offer a true-case scenario from the other end of the spectrum. In a chapter from my previous book, *Fireraisers, Freaks, and Fiends,* I outlined the case history of Tim Komonyi. Komonyi set a long-delay ignition device into the floors and walls of his home and built a backup device into the furnace of his home. He arranged for containers of flammable liquid and a large amount of polyfoam material to be placed into the floors and ducting as fuel for his long-delay ignition devices. The ignition sources themselves were heating elements taken from coffeepots and wired into the main electrical wiring of the home. Komonyi then sealed these hidden materials into the flooring, walls, and ducts of the home. Komonyi was being evicted and had built his entire home into one large incendiary device. This device was discovered by contractors before it could function.

An analysis of the device by me and my partners found this to be the most unique item we had ever heard of. We believe that it was set on a multiweek delay and was intended to kill his neighbors and the future tenants in the home. We knew that only a few highly sophisticated people in the world could have constructed this sort of device. We also learned that Tim Komonyi had worked as an engineer and had a college degree in microelectronic circuitry. The highly technical nature of the device excluded about 99 percent of the people in California from being suspects. Komonyi was convicted and got an eighteen-year sentence in prison for this sophisticated ignition scenario.

## RED FLAGS OF ARSON

A peculiar phrase used in most arson schools, books, and training is ***red flags***. Red flags are those observances at a fire scene, or affiliated with the fire or insurance claim, which tends to make an investigator's "spidey sense" tingle and is a red flag begging the investigator to look further. While not always rising to the level of suspicion, a red flag is an observance that makes the investigator's eyebrows rise slightly. A single red flag is fairly normal at any type of fire and should not be used as the sole basis for a conclusion. However, multiple red flags at any scene should cause the arson investigator to hyper focus on the event as possibly an act of arson.

Each sub motive of arson will have its own set of red flags, but a short list of the typical red flags found in arson events include fire during times of darkness, vacant properties, unnaturally burning fires, run-down properties, properties for sale, rental properties recently vacated, owner behind on payments, property in foreclosure, bankruptcy, dissolution of a partnership/marriage, loss of employment by owner, signs of a break-in, gang graffiti, items stolen from the fire scene, the removal of (non valuable) personal items such as pictures, papers, and toys prior to a fire, the absence or removal of pets prior to a fire, indicators of accelerants at the scene, ignition devices left at the scene, and odd alibis or "out of character" activity by the property owner before, during, and after the event.

Some business-arson red flags not already mentioned are dissolution of a partnership, rival business recently opened in area, arson fire in an office/accounting area, or the business carries products that are seasonal or fashionable (e.g., home furnishings, clothing) and may be out of style or date.

Vehicle arsons have their own set of red flags: "staged" theft, lack of removal of valuable parts, history of mechanical problems, expired registration tags, end of a lease, high mileage, excessive wear on tires, traffic-collision damage, prefire vandalism, and the vehicle torched in a remote location.

Boat arson events have their own unique red flags. Besides the ones previously listed for the other property categories, boat/vessel fires while underway on the water can show red flags if there is insufficient fuel onboard for the planned trip, lack of fishing/recreation gear, removal of valuable navigation and other electronics before the fire, expiration of lease on slip rental, and lack of maintenance, care, and use of the boat for weeks or months prior to the "accidental fire."

Red flags associated with the insurance claims stemming from a suspicious fire include recent policies, recent changes to a policy, a lengthy history of odd property claims, multiple fire claims within the same family, and "padded" or excessive claims for loss.

Each chapter of this book will start with a reminder of potential red flags for the subtype of arson. Each case history will have numerous red flags present.

## VICTIMOLOGY

In profiling and criminology, the study of the victim of the attack is an important aspect in locating a potential offender. There are seldom arbitrary victims of arson attacks. In my long study of the crime of arson, I have found that in over 80 percent of arson attacks, the victim knows the suspect. Using rough figures, about 40 percent of arson attacks are motivated by **revenge/spite**, usually involving a very personal dispute. Another 40 percent of arson attacks involve **financial gain** via fraud. In this case, the victim is the suspect. **Vandalism arsons**, **extremist**, **organized crime**, and **crime-concealment arson** also involve many cases where the victim knows the suspect. With this in mind, the most important person to interview after an arson fire is the victim or property owner. They are very likely to know exactly who did this to them.

Many persons who are victims of murders or arson have put themselves in that position based on their **lifestyle** and family relations. People who are vulnerable, or who live with a violent or mentally unstable person, have placed themselves in a dangerous position. Persons involved in crime to include drug sales, gang activity, or prostitution are in a very high-risk environment for assault. This holds true for arson as well.

## SERIAL ARSON

Serial arson is a theme woven throughout all of my books. In this book it is covered again several times in both the urban and wild-land setting. There are several different subtypes of serial arsonists, each with his own unique characteristics. I will not attempt to rewrite everything on serial arson in this book but will remind readers of the common traits and characteristics of serial arsonists.

In general, urban serial arsonists are fairly common in every large town or city and may be active for weeks at a time and then go dormant for weeks or even years. Urban serial arsonists tend to walk or ride bicycles, set fires at night, and set fires in a fairly random fashion, with very little preplanning. There are very few cases of an urban serial arsonist using a device of any type. Many have moderate to severe mental-health issues, and many have a history of institutionalization, health issues, and possibly visible abnormalities. Many have a criminal history that includes theft, vandalism, prowling, peeping, and burglary. Serial arsonists are of both genders, transgender, any age, and generally reflect the racial makeup of the target area.

## COPYCAT ARSONS

Every time a serial arson case is played out in the media, the phrase "copycat" arises from investigators, the fire chief, or the media. In reality there are very few documented "copycat" offenders. There have been a few persons who took advantage of the hysteria of an ongoing arson spree and set their own property on fire in an attempt at fraud. In this manner, they were hoping to use the arson spree to cover their own fraudulent actions.

The easiest way to prevent copycat arsons is to not release case-specific information to the media. US Forest Service (USFS) Special Agent (SA) Paul Steensland related a story addressing this. Over twenty years ago an arsonist was setting dozens of wild-land fires in Northern California with a particular type of delay device. The media, hot on the story, got a state arson investigator to not only describe the device in detail but to actually construct one in front of a news camera. This act of idiocy would surely destroy an ongoing investigation as a suspect arrested with something like this could say that he had seen it on TV. This buffoonery has been replicated by dozens of other arson investigators and fire officials since then. John Orr, when acting in his capacity as an arson investigator, was notorious for showboating and showing the media arson devices and case-sensitive information.

# 2

# Incendiary Devices

## A BIT OF HISTORY

In the ten years after the American Civil War, a group of former Confederate guerilla fighters formed a gang of outlaws in Missouri known as the James-Younger gang. This gang was headed by legendary outlaws Cole Younger and his brothers, along with Frank and Jesse James. This gang of skilled cavalry veterans ran amok to avenge their civil-war defeat and robbed dozens of banks, stagecoaches, and trains. By the mid-1870s, the railroads brought in the famed Allen Pinkerton Detective Agency to deal with this menace. The Pinkertons believed that the only way to get into the tight enclaves that protected this group was to have undercover operatives pose as outlaws in an attempt to infiltrate the gang.

By 1874 the Pinkertons had infiltrated a detective into Clay County, Missouri, the home of the James clan. A day after his arrival, the undercover operative's body was found shot and fed to the hogs on a rural farm. In retaliation, Mr. Pinkerton sent a group of his detectives to engage the gang in a shootout in another part of Missouri. This shootout was a disaster and resulted in the deaths of three more Pinkerton men. An enraged Allen Pinkerton then sent a large posse of men and detectives directly to the James family farm, with orders to burn them out. The night of this event was January 25, 1875. At the time of this incident, the Pinkertons had information that Frank and Jesse James were holed up in the home, along with several family members. The family members included the James boys' mother and a cousin with an intellectual disability.

The plan for this raid was for the detectives to sneak up on the property and simultaneously break out all of the windows while other members tossed in a couple "fireball" incendiary devices. In this instance, the Pinkertons had designed incendiary devices using metal balls filled with a flammable liquid similar to lamp oil. The device was lit with a burning fuse and was designed to start a flash fire that would burn the rural home down and drive the occupants out into the hands of the waiting posse.

The plan went immediately awry when members of the James family saw the items enter the home and, by using fireplace implements, pushed one of the burning balls into the rock fireplace. Instead of bursting and burning as designed, one of the fireballs detonated when it came into contact with the roaring fire. Instantaneously an explosion rocked the farmhouse, and the mother and cousin of Jesse James were severely injured by both blast and fragmentation. The mother, Zerelda Samuels, had to have her arm amputated later that night while the cousin died of his injuries. Naturally, the James bothers had left the farmhouse a couple of hours prior to the raid and were not present for this legally sanctioned firebombing.

This revenge-inspired firebomb attack had the opposite of its intended effect, and angry citizens soon called out to have the Pinkerton detectives arrested for murder. No charges were ever filed, but the reputation of the famous agency suffered mightily from this botched event.

*Proper analysis of an incendiary device, its materials, and its construction will give the investigator an excellent starting point as to who the suspect may be.*

### Incendiaries

A general description for an incendiary device is **any arrangement of items or materials** used by the arsonist to accelerate the growth of, delay the start of, or assist in the spread of a criminal fire through a structure in an unnatural manner. Incendiary devices can be made of commercial items, military items, safety items, improvised items, or any combination of all of these. There is no limit of imagination when it comes to the construction of an incendiary device.

**Author's note:** Many states and the federal government may have actual statute descriptions that define "incendiary devices" and "Molotov cocktails." The descriptions given here are only for analysis purposes and may conflict with your local laws.

Incendiary devices, like any improvised weapon or bomb, have failure rates. Many fail due to poor design or construction. Some fail due to poor weather conditions. Others fail during their deployment. The failure rate of a device is a direct reflection of the skill level of the suspect who built and deployed the item.

In September of 2015 I was speaking to an ATF engineer/fire scientist about a style of incendiary device used by a cell from the Earth Liberation Front. He mentioned that this type of device functioned nearly 100 percent of the time when he and his colleagues at the Fire Research Lab tested them. I countered with my review of case history on the items and found that they had a failure rate of up to 20 percent. He initially disagreed, but then I was able to change his mind with an explanation. If an engineer-trained fire scientist assembles a device in the lab, it should work nearly 100 percent of the time. However, in the real world the devices are made in cars, hotel rooms, and under great stress by sometimes stoned or drunk college kids, without engineering degrees, who are about to commit a major felony. The device failure rates can almost always be attributed to stress, inexperience, and possibly drugs and alcohol use. The "real world" explanation made sense to the fire scientist.

Incendiary devices continue to be fairly rare items during arson attacks. With that in mind, they should be treated like gold when they are found. Every effort should be made to collect and analyze the device at criminal laboratories with the intent of linking it to an offender.

## MOLOTOV COCKTAILS, FIREBOMBS, AND PETROL BOMBS

Like many aspects of arson investigation, firebombs in the form of Molotov cocktails are a poorly understood weapon, even by experienced arson investigators. For the sake of clarity, in this book the terms *firebomb*, *Molotov cocktail*, and *petrol bomb* are interchangeable and will be used to describe a glass bottle containing a flammable liquid and possessing some form of "wick." The item is generally ignited at the wick by the suspect and then thrown at a selected target. Once the glass container breaks, the aerated flammable liquid (normally gasoline/petrol) is ignited by the burning wick, and then a flash fire occurs.

The term Molotov cocktail has a historical reference. In 1939 the massive Soviet Union attacked its smaller neighbor Finland. The Russian foreign minister at the time was a man named Slava Molotov. At the time of the invasion, the Finnish Army was not yet modern and still used ski troops and horse cavalry to fight Russian tanks and armored vehicles. As they had no tanks of their own, and no anti-armor weapons to speak of, the Finns improved on an item that had been used in several earlier wars, known as the "petrol bomb." They took glass wine bottles and filled them with just about any flammable liquid they could get from petrol to kerosene and even grain alcohol.

Because these fuels were very volatile and burned away quickly when they hit the tanks, the Finns added thickening materials in the form of soap, rubber, and baking soda. This caused the burning fuel to be more persistent and remain on the armored vehicles longer, causing larger fires to disable the vehicles. The weapons were used in clusters with several thrown at a single tank. Despite their crudeness, the firebombs were fairly effective and have been used by armies and terrorist groups ever since. To spite the Russians, the Finns called their special antitank weapons "Molotov cocktails." The name has stuck ever since, even though the materials have varied through the years.

Molotov cocktails in various forms are the most common incendiary device used in the world. In my neck of the woods, Los Angeles, Molotov cocktails are used on a weekly basis, mostly by urban youth or street gangs. My unit has handled hundreds, if not thousands, of these items over the years, and we find them to be an extraordinarily ineffective weapon. Our own statistics show that the Molotovs used in our area fail at a rate of over 90 percent of the time.

Many factors play into this high-failure rate. The main factor is poor target selection. The device was invented to be used against tanks and vehicles covered in steel plate. In modern times, most of these devices are lit and thrown at homes or automobiles. Since most homes in Los Angeles are made of wood and stucco, these glass bottles seldom break against the home. If they are thrown through a glass window, they often end up landing on a wood or carpeted floor, and again don't function as designed. Molotovs thrown at vehicles have an even higher failure rate as most will not break against the soft metals or glass on vehicles. Many just bounce off the vehicle and end up breaking on the pavement, causing almost no damage. The vast majority of our Molotov cocktail attacks end up with us recovering an intact or mostly intact device, with very little fire damage at all.

Molotov cocktails are an extremely crude and ineffective incendiary device when used against targets. They reflect the builder of these devices as most are crude and unskilled teens and gang members. Despite their many failures, they are an incredibly intimidating device, and the victim is usually quite alarmed even after failed attacks.

## INCENDIARY-DEVICE ANALYSIS

The remainder of incendiary devices, other than Molotovs, is up to the imagination of the arsonist. They differ in design and sophistication level in a direct correlation with the skill and sophistication level of the arsonist. The US military has developed an explosive-device program in Iraq/Afghanistan based on groups of specialists known as CEXC teams. The term *CEXC* stands for Combined Explosives Exploitation Cells, and in short these teams go into the field to recover as much from an improvised explosive device (IED) as they possibly can. Their goal is to analyze every possible aspect of the device, with the end result of identifying all persons responsible for the purchase, assembly, transportation, and planting of that IED.

The exact same principles are applicable to our analysis of every single incendiary device we come across. The investigative steps are listed below:

1. Recover device and components at the scene.
2. Conduct a detailed lab analysis of every component.
3. Give a detailed description of the device and design.
4. Describe all materials used in constructing the device.
5. Find the source of each component of the device: Where was it acquired or purchased?
6. How was the device delivered to the target (e.g., hand placed, thrown, mailed, launched)?
7. Diagram exactly how the device functioned.

8. Did the device function as designed? Partially? Complete Failure?
9. Reconstruct and test the device for court.
10. What was the exact target of the incendiary attack?
11. How did the arsonist access the scene (e.g., vehicle, roof job, entered structure)?
12. What is the sophistication level of the device and the attack?
13. What suspect or group would have sophistication and desire to do this attack?
14. What is the suspected motive for the attack?
15. Conduct a search of the suspect's home, work, vehicle, and computer for components and information about the device.
16. What is the technical skill or work history of the suspect? Is that commensurate with the sophistication of the device?

Incendiary-device analysis is extremely critical on any arson attack where a device occurs. It is the most critical aspect used to profile the offender. Currently, incendiary-device analysis is often done poorly, haphazardly, or not at all, and valuable information is lost forever.

The design of **a suspect's incendiary device tends to remain constant** once satisfactory results are obtained. Past profilers have speculated that arsonists always experiment with devices for larger and larger fires. In truth, the device has almost nothing to do with the size of the fire. The fire size is more related to fuel load, ventilation/wind, and fuel arrangement. Devices evolve and change as the arsonist runs out of materials or begins experiencing failures in his fire setting. Normally, once a device becomes successful for an arsonist, it will tend to remain constant and only evolve out of necessity.

# 3

# Case Histories and Analysis

## ARSON SCENE PROFILING: REINSCHEID—A CASE HISTORY ORANGE COUNTY, CA, 2012

*This case is a formal profile I conducted at the request of the Orange County District Attorney's Office and a superior court judge regarding a unique serial arsonist. It is included as an example of how I conduct analysis and profiling of arson events.*

### The Triggering Event

Claas Stubbe was the fourteen-year-old son of Rainer Reinscheid. Claas was a student at University High School in Irvine, California. His father, German-born Rainer Reinscheid, was an associate professor of pharmaceutical sciences at the University of California, Irvine. Rainer was considered a very rigid man, who was exceedingly smart and disciplined. He was very controlling with his family members and demanded high performance from his children.

Claas Stubbe got into minor trouble at University High School on March 13, 2012, when he was caught stealing a small item from the campus store. The event was not a major incident, and the police were not called. Instead, Assistant Principal Michael Georgino opted to handle the incident "in house" and imposed minor discipline on the young boy. His "sentence" for the theft was to pick up trash at the school property in off-hours. The young boy beseeched the principal to not inform his father (Reinscheid), as he knew that his dad would be extremely upset by this. The principal told the young boy that he was compelled to report all discipline and that this was a fairly minor event, and his father would understand. The very next day, the fourteen-year-old boy was found hanging in a park near the school. The boy had chosen suicide over telling his father that he had gotten into trouble at school. Toxicology tests would conclude that he did not have any drugs or alcohol in his system.

The suicide was a very traumatic event for the Reinscheid family, the school, and the school staff. The school staff soon became aware that Rainer Reinscheid was extremely unhappy with them, the way they handled the discipline of his child, and the way they handled the aftermath of the death. This sort of reaction is normal and to be expected when such a horrific tragedy occurs. Reinscheid advised the school that he blamed them for bullying his child and causing this suicide. After several confrontations with school district administrators, he seemed to go away and was not heard from. The school staff hoped he had gone off to grieve his son's loss in private.

### The Computer

Shortly following this tragic event, Rainer Reinscheid began doing secret Internet searches. The subject matter of these searches was discovered by police several months later after Reinscheid became a suspect in a series of arson fires. Following Reinscheid's arrest for the arsons, a forensic search of his personal laptop was conducted and revealed the following alarming searches. Reinscheid was found to be actively searching for the home address and personal family information of Assistant Principal Georgino on sixty-four occasions over a two-month period. During that same time and continuing until his arrest in July, Reinscheid conducted forty computer searches for gun purchases, gun laws, explosives, explosions, vehicle explosions, and specific information about explosive combinations and formulas.

## A Good Plan

The computer search showed that on April 26 and 28, 2012, Reinscheid drafted two emails to his wife. These emails were never received by the wife, but they gave great insight into Reinscheid's mind-set. An excerpt from the email on April 26 reads as follows:

> *"I will find this vice-principal and find out where he lives, then I will wait for him and kill him. I will force him to tie a rope around his neck, and if he is too coward, I will do it for him, in front of his wife and children. I will make him cry and beg, but I will not give him a chance, just like he did to Claas. I will make him die, slowly, surely…Next I will set fire to Uni High and try to burn down as much as I can."*

The computer search showed that two days later, Reinscheid drafted an email to himself, where he very graphically described his intentions for the school, the staff, and other students, along with his own fate. The email was entitled "a good plan," and in part reads as follows:

> *"I have dreams about going to Uni High and setting the place on fire, burning down every single building, and then killing myself in the same place where Claas died. I am thinking about getting a dozen machine guns, then going to the school and shooting down that asshole*

*vice-principal, then the principal and the stupid counselor lady, but I will stick the gun inside her pussy before I pull the trigger; she deserves it. Then I will shoot at least two hundred students before killing myself..."*

### The Fires

On July 4, 2012, an arson fire was set on the front patio of Assistant Principal Georgino's home. The fire was set in the middle of the night when the family was asleep. The fire was started by a suspect igniting available combustible materials found at the scene to include shoes and plastic patio chairs. The fire did minimal damage.

On the very same night, an arson brush fire was set at the park where young Claas Stubbe had committed suicide. Normally, brush and vegetation fires at the height of summer in Southern California are cataclysmic events. However, due to the fairly cool and humid conditions that night, the fire did not spread quickly and was brought under control within an hour. The fire burned about a quarter acre of vegetation.

Just over a week later, on July 10, 2012, an arson fire was set on a window sill of a classroom at University High School. This time the attack was conducted with much more purpose, and the arsonist brought two fire logs (Duraflame type) and placed them in the window of the large building. Because the structure was made of modern materials, which were mostly masonry, the fire did not progress as desired and only caused minor damage to the window area.

### Computer

After the first three fires in this series, Reinscheid's computer revealed that on July 11, 2012, he conducted an additional fifty-two searches for explosives, bomb-making tutorials, car bombs, and the phrase "Michael Georgino Death."

### New Fire

The day after the additional computer searches on Reinscheid's computer, a second arson fire was set at the home of Assistant Principal Georgino while he and his family were sleeping. This time the scene was prepared and arranged a bit, with the arsonist taking a stack of newspapers and placing them along with other combustible materials up against the wood siding of the victim's home. The items were then set on fire. This fire was adjacent to the bedroom window of the victim. The smoky fire alerted neighbors and awakened the victim, and he extinguished it with a garden hose before authorities could arrive. He immediately told the police the story of Rainer Reinscheid, and how he suspected him in these arson attacks.

### Computer

On July 17, five days following the latest attack on Assistant Principal Georgino, Reinscheid drafted another email to be sent to eight recipients. This email advised friends that he was planning suicide and admitted to his past failures at starting the arson fires. He urged his friends to follow his lead and murder named school officials and then to take their own lives. In part this email read as follows:

> *"Make sure you kill Michael Georgino (and the female counselor)...before you take your own life. They both need to suffer before they die; make sure it will be painful before they die, please. I have tried to burn down Georgino's house and the fucking school, but I was not strong enough; I tried multiple times, but I failed."*

### Final Fires

Two days after this final message, a third arson attack occurred at Georgino's home, when an unknown attacker placed a large book against the wood side of the home and ignited it. The family was not home during this event. The fire caused minor damage.

That very same night a second brush fire/arson occurred back at the park where young Claas had hung himself. This fire was quickly extinguished with minimal damage. Three nights later a third fire occurred in the same park, again causing minor damage.

That same night as the park fire, a larger fire occurred on the campus of University High School. This time an arsonist used two fire logs (identical to prior attack) as an ignition device and placed them against two different wooden doors to the gymnasium. Both caused moderate damage to the doors but did not impact the rest of the fire-resistant structure.

After this serious attempt to burn the school, police and fire investigators in Irvine and for the Orange County Fire Authority joined forces and began to link all of these fairly moderate arson events. Their investigation pointed directly at Rainer Reinscheid as he had personal, emotional connections to every fire scene. He had also been very vocal in past months about his hatred for the school and the assistant principal. A full-time surveillance operation of Rainer Reinscheid was commenced.

Inv. Barry Miller and Inv. Ray Falcon were in charge of the investigation. They put a surveillance team on Reinscheid and on the night of July 24, 2012, followed him to the same park where his son had committed suicide. On that night surveillance officers watched as Reinscheid attempted to ignite the fourth brush fire within that park. Police officers emerged from the darkness and attempted to take him into custody. Reinscheid briefly resisted arrest and then was captured. The detectives searched him and found a can of lighter fluid on him. An additional search of the area located newspapers that had been soaked in lighter fluid. Reinscheid had been caught red handed, as it were, in the act of committing an arson attack. He spent the next year in jail while he awaited trial.

### The Court Case

The prosecution in this case eventually charged Rainer Reinscheid with eight felony counts of arson and one felony count of attempted arson. Reinscheid had no prior criminal history but was looking at potentially twenty years in state prison. Nearly one year after his arrest, he took an offered plea deal and pled guilty to several counts of arson. As part of the deal, he was pleading to an open sentence that could range from three years to eighteen years in prison.

In August of 2013, the presiding judge held a hearing to learn about aggravating and mitigating factors in order to determine the actual amount of prison time to be served. Prior to this hearing, Reinscheid had gone through court ordered mental-health analysis by qualified psychiatrists. The length of his sentence was going to depend greatly on the opinions of various experts as to the true intent of Reinscheid's fire setting and the future danger level he posed to the intended victims.

Speaking for the defense was the defense-retained arson investigator in this case, Nina Scotti. This private fire investigator had reviewed the evidence from the police investigation and had written her opinion about Reinscheid and his fires. In part it stated that the fires were all carefully planned and calculated events by the arsonist as a means to be noticed and not to cause major damage or harm. Ms. Scotti also determined that "I do not consider Mr. Reinscheid as a serial arsonist." She went on to add about Reinscheid, "If his intentions were to cause great property damage or injury, his (choice) of materials and the arrangement of the materials would have been different."

In rebuttal, the prosecuting attorney, Andrew Katz, was able to get Ms. Scotti to admit on the stand that she had never before investigated a serial arsonist and thereby was not qualified to render an opinion on this matter. Deputy District Attorney (DDA) Katz gave a further scathing review of her opinion that Reinscheid was not a serial arsonist, when literally every major arson manual and study classifies a serial arsonist as someone who is involved in three or more arson events with a cooling-off period in between. In this case Reinscheid was charged with and convicted of nine different arson events. By anybody's definition, he was clearly a serial arsonist.

Another defense expert, clinical psychologist Dr. Veronica Thomas, conducted an analysis of Reinscheid and gave this written opinion of his fire-setting activities. "Given Dr. Reinscheid's intellect and capability to carry out any actions he would choose, the crimes he committed were about letting others know how hurt and angry he was. He certainly had the means and ability to inflict great harm on others." In her statement, the defense expert was saying that Reinscheid, by virtue of his very high intellect, had the ability to cause great damage with his fires, but he chose not to. Instead his fires were more of a warning and a way of letting people know he was angry.

Dr. Thomas described Reinscheid's arson attacks as "his expression of his out-of-control emotions and were aimed at regulating his mood." She went on to describe his arson wave as "a pressure-reducing strategy, albeit irrational." Most importantly, the defense witness said, "His risk for recidivism is low." The defense cited a myriad of mitigating circumstances and asked for the bare minimum sentence of three years in prison.

To rebut this defense-hired psychiatrist, the prosecutor pointed out that she, too, did not have any experience or expertise when dealing with a repeat arsonist. In her opinions, the psychiatrist had only cited general information on every type of arsonist and not specific information on serial arson offenders. DDA Katz gave a blistering rebuttal stating that it was an "illogical idea" to suggest that any arsonist intended to cause only minimal damage. The astute prosecutor correctly pointed out that an arsonist has no control whatsoever of the fire event once it is set in motion.

The prosecutor was also able to introduce evidence that Reinscheid had not voluntarily stopped his attacks but had been caught in the act of committing one. He had shown no indications of slowing down or stopping. The prosecutor also introduced written evidence and computer records showing that besides arson, Reinscheid had a very dark and disturbing personal side not associated with his son's suicide. Reinscheid's computer and written notes showed ongoing extramarital affairs with multiple women, very dark and disturbing sexual-rape fantasies, and strong indications of anti-Semitism and homophobic sentiments.

The judge in this case was in a real quandary. He acknowledged that Reinscheid didn't appear to be a "typical arsonist." Reinscheid held multiple advanced degrees as a professor, was well regarded in the academic community, had a minimal criminal history, and was the head of a family. Added to that, the court recognized that the fires had caused no injuries and fairly minor property damage. The judge had to weigh the safety of the victims in mind with the mitigating circumstances surrounding the defendant. He had the power to sentence Reinscheid to three years if he viewed him as a minimal risk to the public or up to eighteen years if he was considered the highest risk.

One of the biggest questions the court had was how a man of such high intelligence and intellect, like Reinscheid, could have botched so many arson attacks. The defense theory was that Reinscheid was only trying to scare the school and get noticed. The prosecution theory was that despite his high intellect, he was a terrible fire setter. The judge questioned both prosecution and defense experts and learned that neither side had an expert who had much experience dealing with serial arsonists. The judge asked the prosecutor if there was anyone who actually may have some sort of experience in dealing with this unique type of offender. One of the lead investigators, Ray Falcon, had read my first book, *Torchered Minds*, and had attended a lecture I delivered on the many subtypes of serial fire setters. He offered my name to the court and the prosecutor, and the judge agreed to allow my input.

The prosecutor sent me all of the files on the case to include both the prosecution and defense investigations. I was leaving the next day for a conference in China and could not be present for the final hearing in the case. The prosecutor agreed to deliver a written opinion or "profile" I developed after studying the entire case. Attached to this profile were my curriculum vitae and a brief synopsis of my expertise dealing specifically with serial arson cases. At that point in my career, I had investigated thirty-four serial arsonists and had studied case histories of over seven hundred other serial fire setters. I had lectured at a dozen conferences and at several universities, to include speaking engagements with both the ATF and FBI on the subtypes of serial fire setters.

Below is an excerpt from the profile I submitted on the case of Rainer Reinscheid:

## *Opinion on the Rainer Reinscheid Arson Series*

*The case against the defendant is fairly unique but not unheard of. I have personally worked at least four similar cases to his. I have researched and written about dozens more. He belongs to a small and unique category of serial arsonists classified as "revenged based/obsessive." He is on the very high end of the danger scale and will most likely continue his behavior after release from incarceration. He is what I have classified as a "man on a mission." I have written a second book to be published in October about obsessive arsonists, and there is an entire chapter of case histories nearly identical to the defendant.*

***Danger Level***

*In short, the defendant is a serial arsonist, as nearly every single book, study, or research on arson investigation classifies a serial offender as a person with three or more arson events (with a cooling-off period in between), which absolutely includes failed attacks or attempted arsons. There should be no debate; he is a serial offender.*

*The true analysis of assessing an arsonist's danger level* ***does not include*** *the amount of damage or size of the fire. These facts are usually irrelevant as the size of a fire event is often out of the control of the novice fire setter. Fuel arrangement, weather conditions, and wind are the primary factors that control the size of a fire and how much damage is done. The true assessment of the danger level of an arsonist is his intent, targeting methods, sophistication of attack, and ignition scenario (exactly what methods he used to start the fire).*

***Sophistication of Attacks***

*The defendant in this case, while highly educated in one field, is clearly a* ***novice fire setter****, who is using methods he has copied or learned recently. He would have gotten more successful and had more dramatic results with more practice, similar to a marksman with a firearm. High intelligence and education does not always translate to a successful fire setter. I have personally arrested/*

*convicted a successful doctor, who finished second in his medical school, for setting a string of arson fires, all of which were failed events. Likewise, I have prosecuted three different engineers, all who set a series of revenge-related arson fires.*

*Despite their high level of education and intelligence, most of their attacks were low-performing or failed events. Lastly, many firefighter serial arsonists, who understand ignition dynamics and fire behavior better than most people, and who have lit dozens, hundreds, or even over a thousand arson fires, have many failed fire events in their respective series. The most famous firefighter serial arsonist ever, John Orr, was convicted because of the evidence left behind on his botched arson attempts, despite having set an estimated 2,500 fires over his lifetime.*

*My review shows that the tactics and methods used by the defendant were crude and ineffective, with low-performing fires as a result. However, his intent in all his fires was for maximum damage. He was just not skilled at carrying out his attacks. Fires in a brush land in summer, in Southern California, are always potentially catastrophic events. Had he chosen a better time of day for his attacks (afternoon), the defendant's outdoor fires would have become major events. Nighttime cool temperatures, high humidity, and low winds are the only reasons the fires were ineffective. He is clearly not an expert on fire behavior.*

***Evolving Method of Operation***

*Fire setting is learned behavior. Successful arsonists use a consistent method or device until it becomes unsuccessful or they injure themselves. Unsuccessful arsonists will research or experiment with various ignition materials and methods. The defendant was an unsuccessful arsonist who was using a variety of methods to achieve maximum destruction of a target. For instance, at the school he was well aware that he could not burn the masonry block of the walls, so he placed his devices at windows and at doors, which he thought would be easier to breach. He wasn't aware of the fire-resistant properties of most modern-construction materials. Eventually he would have actually broken into the structure and placed his incendiary materials inside, which would have been much more effective.*

*The fires at the school were set with the intent to burn the structures to the ground. The use of a fire log is somewhat rare in the United States by arsonists but is a common tactic in Europe (Germany in particular). I was recently the lead detective on the massive Hollywood Arsonist event, where a German national (Harry Burkhart) lit fifty-two major fires in four days with an identical device (fire log placed under a car). Reinscheid used an adequate device to burn the buildings down, but his placement of the device was poor. This was not a call for attention as has been speculated, or he would have set the fire logs by the masonry instead of the doors if he just wanted to be noticed. These were clear attempts at causing maximum damage.*

*The fires at the home were easily the most dangerous. Attacking an occupied home at a time of day where persons are expected to be asleep is clearly* ***attempted murder****. The defendant brought incendiary materials to the scene in two cases and set the fires against the home. A pile of newspapers provides as much heat energy and temperatures as a gallon of gasoline. He was unskilled at* *the ignition of these items and did not arrange the fuels in the correct fashion to achieve better results. The exterior of the home was combustible, and a more skilled arsonist would have done more significant damage with the same materials. With practice, he would have achieved his goals with the newspapers.*

### *Motive*

*His motive is the* ***most dangerous of all arson motives: revenge****. The few experts in the field believe that the revenge-based arsonist will refine and continue his attacks until his goal is achieved. Incarceration of any sort will only be an interruption in his revenge-seeking mission. He will be just as dangerous the day he is released as the day he was arrested.*

### *Defendant Behavior*

*The defendant is not the classic arsonist with a lifetime of fire-setting activity (that I am aware of). His fire-setting series was triggered by a traumatic event that overwhelmed his ability to cope. Most serial arson behavior is based on anger, revenge, and an inability to cope with stress. The defendant is at that juncture.*

*His pattern of behavior before his arrest is extremely alarming. He was researching weapons and explosives and at some point settled on* **fire as a weapon***. He is likely unfamiliar with other weapons and decided to use a weapon (fire) that was easy to get, affordable, and seemingly easy to use. The defendant's computer searches for the school official are the clearest indicators of his actual intent. He is absolutely* **stalking and hunting** *for this person with the intent of destroying him, his family, and his home. He is bent on revenge and will remain an extreme* *danger to the victim for a long period of time as he is convinced the victim caused this trauma. At this time fire is his weapon of choice, but he may resort to an alternative weapon in the future.*

### *Targeting*

*The defendant is showing* ***obsession*** *with a specific target: the institution and official he believes caused his loss. They are all the same target—the park (next to the school), the school itself, and the official from the school. This is not the wandering target selection of a "firebug" type arsonist, but these targets are clearly defined and consistent.*

*The outcome of this obsession will likely result in the death of the defendant. He is on a mission to exact revenge, and he has little expectation to survive his successful attack. This type of attacker often commits suicide or "suicide by cop." The suspect will not get over the death of his son anytime soon, if ever, and he will have little to live for. This series is a classic "end of life" scenario employed by mass murderers and terrorists who strive to end their life with a horrific, dramatic event. There are historically dozens of cases like this.*

*The defendant's written threats of torture, rape, and mass murder are not whimsical musings but are indications of his true intents and desires. Most arsonists are true cowards. They have a need to get even but lack the courage to face a victim in person like other violent criminals. Instead, they plan and conduct surreptitious nighttime attacks. All of the defendant's targets, threats, and future planned attacks revolve around the same institution or persons at that institution. He is completely obsessed with revenge and likely will not stop until he has achieved that revenge.*

### *Tempo of Attacks*

*After his first four failed attacks, the defendant wrote of his frustration and failures and implored others to carry on with the attacks after his planned death. Immediately after writing this, the defendant's actions increased in tempo and sophistication. This* ***frenetic activity*** *is a very common occurrence as serial offenders get paranoid, become frustrated, and begin to lose all control. His actions were deliberate, planned out ahead of time, and carried out in darkness. He brought incendiary materials with him for maximum results, only to fail over and over again. At the time of his arrest, he was lighting fires at a faster pace.*

### *Overall Opinion*

*In a final analysis, I would rate his* ***level of danger at extremely high****, with the same victim as the likely target for future attacks. He will never forgive this victim (or himself) for the loss of his son. Suicide or attempted suicide is a very likely scenario for him. He may not use fire in the future but may use an alternate weapon to complete his revenge mission if given the chance. I would rate his chances to reoffend as extremely high. He is a clear danger and will remain so for many years. He will need lengthy incarceration and intense and ongoing therapy to cope with all of these events.*

*My curriculum vitae has been submitted to the prosecutor.*

### *Reviewed Documents*

*Reinscheid Sentencing Brief (Katz 3-21-13)*
*Reinscheid Supplemental Sentencing Brief (Katz 8-01-13)*
*Nina Scotti CV*

*Nina Scotti Report (7-18-13)*
*Reinscheid Sentencing Memorandum (Glotzer 8-01-13)*
*Veronica Thomas PhD Report (7-29-13)*

***Detective Ed Nordskog***
***Los Angeles County Sheriff's Department***
***Arson-Explosives Detail***

### Reinscheid Sentencing

The prosecutor received my profile and made copies for the court and defense, and the item was presented in open court. The defense had no significant rebuttal to the document, and the judge accepted me as an expert in serial arsonists. The prosecutor advised me that my analysis appeared to answer the remaining questions for the judge. Orange County superior court judge Gregg Prickett then read the entire document into the official record of the court. Based partly on my analysis in the document and the facts of the case, Judge Prickett deemed that Rainer Reinscheid was indeed a clear and continuing danger to the victims in this case. He sentenced Reinscheid to the high end of the sentencing scale. Rainer Reinscheid was given in excess of fourteen years in state prison for this series of arson attacks.

### Afterword

Judge Prickett in this matter showed incredible enlightenment on seeking guidance and help in the difficult sentencing phase of this case. In my first pages in this book, I lament that most lawyers, judges, and court-appointed psychiatrists have very little credible information on arsonists and serial arsonists. Yet these are the very people relied upon to assess the danger level of these unique criminals. Rarely does a court consult with someone like me to give them an analysis of the entire arson event. This case shows a judge who realized that he did not have an actual serial arson expert to advise him, and he had the vision to seek out someone who may be able to add credible analysis to the event. I applaud Judge Gregg Prickett's wisdom.

If you read my analysis/profile, you will note that I needed to review every aspect of the case to include photos, notes, history of the suspect, fire-setting scenario, targets, and the triggering event for the case. The local detectives must gather as much information as possible through crime-scene work, interviews, surveillance, search warrants, and computer analysis in order to give a profiler a complete and clear picture of the event. In this case the detectives and prosecutor in Orange County did an outstanding job.

*The Rainer Reinscheid case was investigated by several members of the Orange County Fire Authority and the Costa Mesa police and fire departments. The lead investigators were Barry Miller and Ray Falcon, along with Inv. T. Blincoe. The prosecutor was Orange County DDA Andrew Katz. I (Nordskog) conducted the criminal profile on this event.*

## HOLLYWOOD FIRE DEVIL: THE MOST INTENSE ARSON INVESTIGATION...EVER! HOLLYWOOD, CA, NEW YEAR'S 2012

**Colead Investigator Dan Gaytan—LAFD**
**Colead Investigator Ed Nordskog—LASD**
**Det. Ray Morales—LAPD**
**SA Suriya Khemradhipati—ATF**
**DDA Sean Carney—District Attorney's Office**

*"They are working hundreds of clues, interviewing dozens of witnesses, picking up countless pieces of evidence"* (LAPD commander Andrew Smith

commenting on the Hollywood Arsonist Task Force, January 1, 2012).

*This case is from the author's personal case file and is told from his perspective and recollections of this massive investigation. Included in this case history are a sampling (in italics) of the endless sound bites released to the media by the involved agencies, shameless politicians, and talking-head experts.*

For four nights straddling New Year's 2012, the Hollywood area of Los Angeles was rocked by the most intensive arson spree by a single individual ever in American history. The case would tax the resources of four of the largest public agencies in the United States and would nearly bring the many professional fire departments in the Los Angeles basin to their collective knees.

It all started with a very confusing side note. At 1:20 a.m., on Thursday, December 29, 2011, a party was taking place in an apartment in Hollywood. It was just off the Sunset Strip. A young man named Samuel Arrington was "over served," and grew drunk and belligerent to his hosts. The twenty-two-year-old was eventually tossed out of the party because of his rowdy and obnoxious behavior. He promptly went downstairs to the open carport directly under the apartment and, with a cigarette lighter, set fire to the bumper of a car parked there. Arrington then drunkenly wandered down the street, setting fire to a trash Dumpster and a trash can. Eventually, he focused his bleary eyes on a gas tank affixed to a work truck.

He walked over to the truck and attempted to light the gas tank on fire. The driver grabbed Arrington, pummeled him a bit, and threw him onto the ground. He then held him there while he summoned an LAPD patrol car. Even while he was being arrested, the carport fire he had set grew quite large and caused significant damage to the apartment complex.

Because news was slow that night, a film crew from Channel 4 was nearby and arrived in time to see a very drunk and foul-mouthed Arrington shouting threats from the back seat of the patrol car. This image would be plastered over the news for the next week, causing two things. One, it caused any number of armchair detectives to believe that Arrington was the leader of an antigovernment group of arsonists who were hell bent on setting the city on fire; and two, it caused a few arson investigators, who were normally very clear thinking, to doubt their instincts and go along with their chiefs in a mad attempt to confirm this amateurish theory.

Arrington had unknowingly caused a huge amount of confusion that would not manifest itself for another forty-eight hours. Sam Arrington did have one bit of luck. He was in jail at the time of the greatest arson spree in California history and, therefore, was positively eliminated as a suspect in the onslaught of fire attacks that occurred just one day after his arrest.

In a separate side note, an LAPD patrol car, at almost the same time of Arrington's arrest, observed a down-and-out street transient named Alejandro Pineda set fire to two trash cans along Sunset. He was quickly snatched up and brought to jail at the same time as Arrington. It was just another typical night in Hollywood. Both of these men were charged with separate arsons and stayed in jail for the next several days.

### The Frankfurt Fire Devil and Federal Court

Hours after the arson arrests of Arrington and Pineda, a seemingly unrelated event was taking place at the federal courthouse in Los Angeles. A federal judge was holding a hearing for a German woman named Dorothee Burkhart. Dorothee was facing extradition to Germany on an international arrest warrant. In a bizarre life story, Dorothee had been born in the Soviet republic of Chechnya. In 1994, during the Chechen war, she had fled with her son and daughter to Germany and had received asylum. The three became German citizens and lived there for the next several years.

Dorothee made her living in a shady manner as a scam artist and "grifter." She was thought to have been engaged in numerous fraud schemes possibly associated with Russian Mafia activity. She was fluent in Russian, German, and English, and soon she began posing as a property manager. She would dress nicely and approach tenants and accept their monthly rent payments in cash. The only problem was that she never was associated with the landlord. Dorothee was always one step away from being arrested and knew that her time in Germany was short.

In 2004 she went to a plastic surgeon for breast-enhancement surgery. She paid for the large implants with a fraudulent check. When German authorities arrested her in 2007 for the fraud, she feigned a heart attack and was rushed to a hospital. While there, she escaped out a bathroom window and fled via train, calling her family to bring passports and cash to help her leave the country. Her son, Harry, assisted her in leaving Germany via Amsterdam, and the two ended up in Vancouver, Canada. During their two-year stay in Vancouver, Dorothee and Harry shuttled several vehicles over the Canadian border and down into Hollywood. These vehicles would later be linked to Russian mob types in Los Angeles.

In one of their stays in Hollywood, law enforcement responded to their apartment, where Harry had attacked his mother with scissors. The charges were never filed in that case. Later, in 2010, after all of their immigration and asylum appeals were refused in Canada, the two made their way to West Hollywood and Hollywood, where for a couple years Dorothee continued her landlord scam. She collected thousands of dollars in cash with this scheme and was always being chased out of one apartment complex or the next. Finally, Dorothee put her fraudulently obtained breasts to good work. She set up a massage parlor on Sunset Boulevard, in Hollywood and began placing online ads for erotic prostate massage services, which featured very enticing photos of her enhanced cleavage. Her son, Harry, shuttled occasionally between Germany and Hollywood.

Normally Dorothee Burkhart would be considered nothing more than an amusing scoundrel and prostitute. However, she did one thing that investigators would find to be deplorable. Her adult son, Harry, had several "special needs" and moderate mental-health issues. He was on the autism spectrum, and although he drove a car and had held jobs in the past, he was dealing with bipolar disorder and obsessive/compulsive issues. He was also severely paranoid. His medical history showed that he had been institutionalized more than once in Germany for erratic behavior.

In order to cover up her schemes and hide her prostitution activities from her son, Dorothee had played on his mental disabilities and had long ago concocted stories about why they had to always avoid the police and move around a lot. She had convinced the very gullible Harry that "Nazis" had been chasing them for years. She further convinced him that the Nazis often wore police uniforms in an attempt to fool them. She had drilled into him the evil of the Nazis and the necessity to avoid police.

Eventually the German government began actively seeking Dorothee Burkhart. She had accumulated over nineteen counts of fraud that was related to "gang activity." They went looking for her first in Frankfurt, Germany, and found her autistic son, Harry, instead. He had obvious mental-health issues, so the authorities left him alone. Harry, despite his mental-health issues, maintained a job with an airline company. On October 14, 2011, shortly after Harry had been visited by German authorities looking for his mother, a fire broke out in a duplex owned by the pair. The large fire destroyed the apartment, and authorities soon began examining it as a probable arson and insurance-fraud scheme.

Shortly thereafter, Harry Burkhart dropped out of sight in Germany. About the same time that Harry disappeared, the town of Frankfurt was rocked by a string of car fires. German newspapers showed photos of over twenty burned cars in parking lots with the headline proclaiming that a "fire devil" was on the loose in Frankfurt. By the time the newspapers were printed, Harry Burkhart was on his way back to the United States.

German prosecutors issued an international arrest warrant for Dorothee Burkhart and eventually learned that she was running the massage parlor in Hollywood. They forwarded their arrest warrant through Interpol and asked the US Marshals Service to serve it on Dorothee. The case was assigned to Deputy US Marshal Louis Flores in Los Angeles. The Marshals Service is a very small and obscure federal agency, and Deputy Marshal Flores needed a partner. He enlisted the help of another agent from an even smaller and more obscure federal agency, the Diplomatic Security Service, which worked for the State Department. Together, Flores and his fellow agent Jonathan Lamb began to look for Dorothee Burkhart in Hollywood. They soon found her apartment/massage parlor on Sunset Boulevard.

The two federal agents had done a work-up on Dorothee and her son, Harry, and the two quickly identified Harry as he came and went from the apartment. They noted that Harry, who appeared painfully thin in a prior booking photo, was actually quite robust. In truth, he had gained about eighty pounds in the previous year or so. By monitoring Harry for a few days (in hopes of seeing Dorothee), the two agents quickly realized why he had gained so much weight. Harry Burkhart spent the bulk of his days sitting in a pastry shop eating endless amounts of the sweet baked goodies. The agents were able to quickly spot Harry on each of their surveillance missions as he had an odd look that stood out, even in the colorful crowds of Hollywood. He had a ghostly white complexion and wore nothing but dark black clothing. He had long, dirty-blond hair and very feminine features.

After a few days of monitoring the strange looking young man, the two agents eventually saw him with his mother, Dorothee. She was driving a blue Dodge van with British Columbia license plates. They stopped her on the street and found Harry sleeping in the back. The agents took Dorothee into custody on December 28 and turned the van over to her agitated son. The agents had no idea at this point that he was autistic or had any other issues.

The next day, on December 29, in a federal courtroom in Los Angeles, Dorothee Burkhart appeared in front of a federal judge. As he was going through the legalese of her case, the judge was irritated to hear two outbursts, which are not common at all in federal courtrooms. First, Dorothee, with a heavy European accent, began arguing, interrupting, and cutting off the judge. She refused his orders to be quiet. When the judge finally ruled that she would be held in custody until she was extradited to Germany on her warrant, a second outburst occurred. This time, a very agitated Harry Burkhart, who had been sitting in the audience, jumped up and began screaming at the judge, the courtroom, and the United States in general. He shouted, "Fuck all Americans" and "Death to America."

The normally hallowed halls of the American federal court system seldom heard such blasphemy, and the judge lost his temper. He immediately ordered Harry Burkhart to be held in contempt of court and to be arrested by the marshals. However, upon hearing this, Dorothee immediately became docile and pleaded with the judge that her son was crazy, had autism, and couldn't control himself. She agreed to behave and cooperate if the judge would not arrest her son. Realizing that Harry likely had some sort of mental-health issues, the judge rescinded his order and asked the marshals to identify the young man and just escort him out of the courthouse. Witnessing this entire event were the two arresting officers, agents Flores and Lamb. At three o'clock on December 29, 2011, an extremely agitated Harry Burkhart was physically escorted out of the federal courthouse and released into the Los Angeles afternoon.

## Firestorm

Nine hours later, at twenty-two minutes after midnight, on December 30, 2011, a fire was observed burning under a white BMW parked in a carport at 7763 Romaine Street, West Hollywood. LACoFD Engine No. 8, commanded by Captain Brandelli, responded and found the car burning from the engine area. Captain Brandelli and his crew quickly extinguished the fire before it could do significant damage to the other cars in the carport and to the building under which the carport was located. Still, damage exceeded $200,000 for this incident.

In Hollywood and other areas surrounding Los Angeles, high-density housing consists of small apartment complexes of about eight to twelve units, usually no more than two stories in height, and all with an open, unsecured carport area either next to them or quite often built under the housing units. The buildings are all designed for earthquake mitigation and are built of stucco exterior over a wood frame. There are very few single-family homes in Hollywood and in neighboring West Hollywood, and over 80 percent of the population resided in these types of small apartment complexes.

Captain Brandelli and his crew didn't realize it as they were responding to the Romaine Street fire, but they and their comrades would not have a minute's rest for the next ninety-six hours. Brandelli was the first fire captain to realize that "something was up," for the moment he arrived at Romaine Street, he could see another larger fire in a carport just fifty yards away. Before Brandelli and crew could hook up to a hydrant and unroll a hose, they received calls of two more fires in carports within about six blocks.

Brandelli immediately called for a major response from additional units of the gigantic Los Angeles County Fire Department (LACoFD). As part of this response, he asked for "mutual aid" support from neighboring Los Angeles City Fire Department (LAFD), whose jurisdiction was in Hollywood just four blocks to the east. Brandelli was stunned to hear that LAFD was too busy to respond as their engines were receiving calls to multiple carport fires in the Hollywood area as well. Before Brandelli had extinguished the Romaine Street fire, he learned that there were at least six other identical fires in carports within a half mile of his scene.

The fire department dispatch-radio bands were jammed with everyone calling for mutual aid and everyone getting confused as to who was responding to what scene. Despite being the two largest and most modern fire departments west of the Mississippi River, with years of mutual-aid training and responses to the massive wild-land fires that plague Southern California, these two august agencies were soon embroiled in chaos and confusion. A later review showed that both agencies responded to the same fire scenes as there were multiple fires on the same street, but the street crossed over both jurisdictions. Some fires were missed for several minutes in the confusion as the dispatchers and battalion chiefs got confused as to which fire was of a higher priority or which fire had already been attended to.

Adding to the confusion, the calls kept coming in for the next few hours and did not get fully sorted out until well after dawn. There was so much confusion by the fire-suppression agencies that by ten o'clock the next morning, nobody could positively tell the investigators exactly how many fires had occurred. The totals ranged from fifteen to twenty-seven. It would take all the next day to sort it out. The one thing everybody realized was that something truly extraordinary had occurred within a four-hour span.

I should rephrase that last statement. At least one person who was involved early on didn't have a clue as to what an extraordinary event this was developing into. My unit, the Los Angeles County Sheriff's Department (LASD) Arson-Explosives Detail, was the arson-investigative unit for Los Angeles County. As such, we have a team of twenty-two full-time arson-explosives investigators, with at least two on duty every minute of the day. Because Los Angeles County is so large and has nearly eight million citizens, there are several fires to investigate each night.

Our policy is to triage the fires and respond immediately only to those that we consider high priority. Included in high-priority fires would be any fatal fires, any fires with major injuries, any fires where there is a suspect being detained, any fires where there is critical evidence to be seized, and any fires of major dollar loss exceeding a half-million dollars. The rest of the fires that come in during the night are of a lower priority and are handled by a crew the next day. It is up to the on-duty night team to determine if a fire is high priority or not. A caveat to this informal rule is that it is up to the discretion of the night crew to immediately respond to any fire or fires they believe may be of an extraordinary nature or involve a possible major interest by the media.

With all of the above in mind, the on-duty detective that night started receiving calls from West Hollywood patrol deputies by one in the morning, advising him that there were four similar fires burning simultaneously in their small area. Not impressed by a carport fire with no injuries, the arson detective advised the patrol deputies that he would not be responding to their scenes, and they would be handled the next day as routine events. Ten minutes later, a more seasoned patrol deputy called back and advised the arson detective that this was not a normal event, and he even added that the city's LAFD, just four blocks away, was experiencing an identical issue and that at least six fires were burning there along with the four in the sheriff's area.

The arson detective, a legendary jerk throughout his career, reprimanded the patrol deputy and advised him that we "don't care what's going on in the 'city.'" He told the patrol officers to stop calling him. Before he went home for the night, that same arson detective took twenty-two minutes of his precious time to draft a scathing email chastising the patrol deputy's efforts to get him to respond to the scene. He then blissfully drove home while an entire section of Los Angeles erupted in flames. I spent the next four days apologizing to patrol deputies for the lazy and unprofessional performance by a member of my unit. It wouldn't be the last time we apologized for him for this sort of behavior.

### The First Night

By one fifteen in the morning, while Captain Brandelli had his hands full with two fires fifty yards apart, I was sleeping at home, twenty-five miles away. Since I was due to get up to cover the night duty starting at two in the morning, my cell phone was laying on a nightstand a foot away from my head. It began to ring, and I picked it up, not knowing that I would not visit my own bed again for nearly seventy-five hours. The caller was my partner, Det. Cindy Valencia, a detective I had spent the past eight months training to be an arson investigator. These next two nights would be our last ones working together as she would be released from training status and begin her career as a full-fledged investigator.

Working with Cindy was interesting because she had been on the department for over a dozen years and had spent the past several years as a street gang detective in the worst area of Los Angeles. Cindy was well known and well liked by a lot of the patrol deputies and investigators on the department and had hundreds of personal friends and contacts. In this case, she knew a patrol deputy at West Hollywood Sheriff's Station, and he, having grown frustrated and pissed at the arson detective he spoke to a few minutes before, called Cindy on her personal cell phone. This determined and intelligent patrolman knew that something big was happening, and he wasn't going to let the other lazy detective kiss this thing off. He explained the developing event to Cindy, and she recognized this as a major event in the making. She told her friend that she and I would be heading his way in a few minutes. She then called me and filled me in.

By two o'clock in the morning, Cindy and I, both still trying to wake up, were standing in front of a heavily burned apartment complex on Harper Avenue in West Hollywood. In a really odd coincidence, I recognized that I had been to this very same complex three years earlier to a fire in the underground carport. That case had finally made it to a civil courthouse, and I had testified on that case just two days prior to this fire. It was a really bizarre coincidence that in the end had nothing to do with these latest fires.

A sheriff's deputy contacted us as we started to approach the heavily damaged apartment building. He pointed to a nearly identical building next door and advised us that when he arrived at the large fire, he noticed that there was smoke coming out from under a car parked at the unburned building next door. We saw that the car was a burgundy Mercury Grand Marquis sedan, which looked very much like a plainclothes detective's car. I could see a small amount of burn damage under the car and a pile of burned plastic. I got the key to the car from the owner and moved the vehicle back ten feet so we could look under it.

I saw that the black plastic molding from under the front bumper had caught on fire, melted, and dropped down into a mass that had eventually re-solidified. The mass had a unique-looking rectangular bump in it about the size of a brick. I used my knife and dug into the plastic, flipping it over. I saw that the plastic, when it was molten, had covered a brown, fibrous block of material. I examined the material and quickly smelled a chemical odor consistent with kerosene. I picked at the material and was shocked to soon realize that it was a small fire-starter log, similar in texture to a Duraflame log.

This greatly surprised me as I had conducted over seven-hundred vehicle fire investigations by this point in my career, and this was the first such incendiary device I had ever found at a scene like this. I had seen a couple dozen firebombs in the form of Molotov cocktails at car arsons, but almost all of them had failed in some manner. This was the first device I had ever seen placed under a car. This device had been placed in front of the driver's side front tire, under the bumper. It had been ignited and had caused the plastic on the bumper to melt down on top of it. At one point a large glob of plastic had dropped down onto the log and had extinguished the item. The plastic cooled and solidified in place. We got an extreme amount of luck to find a fully intact incendiary device.

By this time, the patrol deputies had informed Cindy and me that there were six total fires in West Hollywood and another dozen or so in neighboring Hollywood. Something truly extraordinary was occurring, and now I had found an incendiary device in our very first scene. I quickly realized that this sort of information was highly valuable and needed to be kept secret. I called my partner over to bring her camera and held the device so that she could take a photo. We then quickly stuffed the entire item into an evidence bag and stashed it into the trunk of my car. We were very aware that something unique like this incendiary device was critical, case-sensitive information and needed to be secured quickly before any other persons, including patrol officers and firefighters, could get their eyes on it.

Neither one of us realized that at the time I was holding the small fire-starter log in my hand, an eager patrol deputy had taken a photo of it over my shoulder with his cell phone. Before it had been secured in the trunk of my car, he had already forwarded it to the entire night patrol shift at West Hollywood Sheriff's Station. A few of them, in turn, forwarded it to some contacts in LAPD, the LAFD, and throughout the sheriff's department. We didn't realize this for two hours, but miraculously the media never got that photo and never showed it to the public.

As soon as we had bagged the first incendiary device and taken our photos, we hustled next door to look at the much larger fire scene. This large twelve-unit structure had a row of open carports beneath it at below-ground level. Two cars were fully destroyed by flame, which then extended through the carport, into the building, eventually doing over a half million dollars in damage to at least four apartments. Because I had already found an intact device, I took a chance and looked under the front bumper of the most seriously damaged car—a Volkswagen.

I found a similar fire log device in the exact same spot. This device had undergone a tremendous amount of fire and had lost its original shape. However, once the fire department had poured thousands of gallons of water into the scene, the item had resolidified. It was still the size of a brick but had degraded into a pile of material that looked very much like vomit. I smelled it and recognized the kerosene odor. This confirmed that both fires in adjoining carports were set with the same type of device placed in an identical manner. We grabbed this item and left the scene for the next fire.

West Hollywood patrol deputies took Cindy and me to four more identical scenes that night, all within eight blocks of each other. In each scene, a near-identical event had occurred. A suspect had placed a small fire-starter log under the front engine area of a car that had been parked in a carport under an occupied apartment building. The results varied a bit, with some of the fires doing moderate damage to the car, and other fires destroying one car and extending to several other cars and into the apartment structure itself. We knew one thing for sure. We had a very energetic individual setting these fires. We also knew that we had a serial arsonist the likes the city of Los Angeles had never seen before. As it turned out, nobody in US history had seen someone like this before this event.

*"We had a very busy night with several car fires… and extension into several apartments. It was a long, tough night"* (LACoFD battalion chief Tom Sullivan).

### The Right Person at the Right Time and Place

In an incredible twist of fate or luck or karma, I had been placed at the head of one of the most intense arson investigations in the history of the United States. Eventually, there would be two lead detectives in this case, but it was fortuitous that I was one of them. I later realized that I was the exact right guy in the right place at the right time. This egotistical-sounding claim has some merit as I will explain.

Five years before this week, I had been embroiled in a major trial against a very wealthy suspect. This suspect was a serial arsonist who had attempted to murder seven people with his fires. During that case the suspect hired a well-known celebrity attorney to defend him at the cost of nearly $2 million. Wanting to fight fire with fire, so to speak, and out duel a celebrity attorney with another high-profile witness, I convinced the DDA in this case that it would be a great idea to bring in an "arson profiler" from a national agency. This sexy-sounding witness would surely be able to counter any dirty tricks or legal sleight of hand this celebrity attorney was known to use in the past.

I contacted a nationally known profiler and told him what kind of case I had, what I wanted him to do for us, and who we were facing in trial. He agreed that the suspect was truly a vicious serial arsonist, but he expressed great trepidation about facing a well-known "Hollywood attorney" in a major case. He confided to me that he really was only an analyst, had never been an investigator, and had really only reviewed a couple of cases. In the end, he refused to come to court and eventually forwarded me a bunch of his profiling or analyst material for me to study. He told me, "You guys out there are way more experienced at this than me."

Disgusted by this act of professional cowardice, I resolved to learn everything I could about serial arsonists, including their motives and the analysis of their crime sprees. When I received the material from this national-level profiler, I realized that a good deal of it was vague, generic profiling material published by the FBI for many types of offenders. In short, it gave a very rough "profile" of a serial arsonist, stating that he was most likely the standard "lone white male, aged eighteen to twenty-four, who was a lower achiever in school and at work, worked below his skill level, had extremely poor relationship skills, didn't like authority, argued with his boss, couldn't keep a wife or girlfriend, had a fascination for the military and police, made poor choices, drank too much, had sexual performance issues, was unhappy with his life, his wife, and his job, and was obsessed with pornography and masturbated excessively."

After reading this assessment and giving it much thought and reflection, I realized that this profile covered about 80 percent of my fellow investigators, most of the men in the fire and police service, all of the guys in the military, pretty much everyone in jail or prison, and about three quarters of the US population of adult males. It was and still is an inane, practically useless "profile" that was just vague enough in every category to be always right, sort of like a horoscope. It didn't help me one bit.

That case and several other serial cases I worked over the years caused me to intensely study serial arsonists and their case histories. I soon was able to amass entire cases or portions of over seven hundred case histories of serial arsonists. I studied the cases, the trial transcripts, the probation reports, and the reports from private and prison psychiatrists. I compared the findings with serial murder profiles and the profiles of serial poisoners, snipers, criminal bombers, and persons who tamper with products. By 2010, I had personally worked on thirty-four serial arson cases, had personally interviewed a couple dozen serial arsonists, and had read and studied the cases of another seven hundred more. From that expertise, I felt I had amassed enough information to come up with nearly a dozen subtypes of serial arsonists. I eventually took my findings and, through over sixty case histories, described the various serial arsonist subtypes in my first published book, *Torchered Minds: Case Histories of Notorious Serial Arsonists.*

That book was published in November of 2011. In late November, I convened a meeting at the local ATF Headquarters in Glendale, California, with over fifty arson investigators from the Los Angeles region to talk about my work in the analysis of serial arsonists. Specifically, we discussed the issues of how to run and manage a serial arson task force in the Los Angeles area if ever we should get a large case. My case studies had pointed to other major serial arson task forces and the numerous problems they had.

Previous serial arson task forces had been organized in Washington, DC, Seattle, East Texas, Alabama, and in Los

Angeles twenty years prior. While all of these groups eventually solved their series of fires, all had been cursed with mismanagement by fire officials, incompetence by some investigators, poor working relationships between agencies, and, the most common curse to every modern crime task force, information leaks. We vowed to learn from the mistakes made by these previous multiagency task forces. Within one month of that meeting and before a single book of mine had been sold, I was to be one of a small group of guys running the largest serial arson task force ever assembled. I couldn't have been more prepared, and yet still every one of the previously cited mistakes was made.

*"The mechanism used to set off the fires seemed to be timed and chemical. [It's not Sterno because] Sternos have a metal can, and we haven't seen any metal cans at the scenes"* (LACoFD captain Rick Brandelli discussing possible incendiary devices to the media).

### The Device

By four in the morning on that first night, Cindy Valencia and I had finished six arson scenes, albeit in a very hasty manner. We knew absolutely that we had a serial arsonist and that he used a nearly identical device, method of attack, and targeting tactic in all six fires. We also knew that we had a unique device, one of which I knew had seldom been used as an incendiary device in the United States. This knowledge stemmed from my studies on serial arsonists.

I knew that there were two main subgroups of serial arsonists: those who operate in a town or urban area, and those who operate in the wild lands or forest. Case analysis had told me that wild-land serial arsonists were more likely to use a delay device than any other type of serial arson subtype. The reasons for that are many, but the main reason is that many wild-land serial arsonists are, in fact, related to the fire service in some manner and, as such, have had past training in the construction of incendiary-delay devices.

My studies had also proven to me that it is extremely rare for an urban serial arsonist to use an incendiary device. Most fires set by urban serial arsonists are set with the use of an open flame. Nowadays that almost always mean the use of a small disposable cigarette lighter purchased practically anywhere.

In this case in Hollywood, we clearly had an urban serial arsonist, but he was defying the odds by using an incendiary device. We knew immediately that we had to alert other investigators about our findings, and we also had to maintain the secrecy of this device. We took great pains to hide it from our own patrol deputies, or so we thought. We knew that if the presence of a device was kept secret from the public, then there couldn't be the possibility of a copycat arsonist as occasionally occurs during big cases. Also, we knew that the device was the secret to identifying the suspect, and we didn't want him to discard additional devices, switch tactics, or rid himself of other incriminating items. We left this scene thinking we had a really cool secret.

We heard on the radio about an active fire two blocks away from our final fire scene that was over the border into Hollywood. Cindy and I drove over there and saw a large complex on fire, with fire originating in the carport. I contacted an LAPD patrol officer, and he directed me to a detective. I approached the older detective, identified myself, and asked if any of the arson investigators from LAFD were on hand. He sent a patrol officer to fetch them from nearby. He then pulled out his smart phone and said, "Hey, check this out. The arsonist is using a fire-starter log." He then opened his phone to a picture of a semi burned fire-starter log.

I stood, completely stunned as I realized that the log in the picture was being held in my gloved hand, with my watch included! I could only stammer, "That's my hand and device. Where the fuck did you get that?" He said it was forwarded to him by a patrolman. It was at that point, less than two hours since I had first picked up that sensitive and critical piece of information, that I realized our device, and possibly the case, was compromised.

*"There are so many fires; it will take a while to sort that out"* (LAPD spokesperson Officer Wendy Reyes).

### The Task Force

By four thirty in the morning I had linked up with my counterparts at the LAFD and had shared all of my information with them. They were a very good arson-investigation unit. The same could not be said for the bulk of the other units in Southern California and, for that matter, most of the United States. Most were staffed by either new, untrained arson investigators or old salts who had been doing it wrong for twenty years and weren't about to change. Such is the state of the arson-investigation world going back a hundred years in this country. The main reason for this is the extraordinarily poor leadership provided by fire chiefs throughout the United States regarding their arson units.

The vast majority of fire chiefs know nothing about criminal investigations, the court process, and the massive amount of training it takes to keep an arson investigator up to date. Fire chiefs have traditionally neglected training and budgeting for arson units and would much rather buy a new truck (whether they need one or not) than spend a few thousand dollars training an investigator. Most agencies consider their arson units to be tremendous risk-management issues for their departments and secretly wish they could give the job to the cops. In my career, numerous fire officers at chief level have told me that they really don't care for their own arson investigators as what they did was not traditional fire-service work. Many viewed their own investigators as outcasts, oddballs, and wannabe cops. They treat them accordingly in many cases.

The sheriff's department (my agency, the LASD) had learned the hard way over the previous eighty years that fire chiefs were probably the worst persons to lead a criminal investigation as they had no training in that field. Worse, a fire chief could not keep an investigative secret to save his life. As such, the LASD had almost never joined a local arson task force, except in the rarest of occasions. The last time they did, they secretly joined the very clandestine John Orr arson task force, which was in effect from about 1988 to 1995.

A unique feature of the sheriff's department, which very few law enforcement agencies possess anymore, is that it still allows its investigators to actually run an investigation. Most agencies have long since ended that practice, with many large investigations run by captains, chiefs, or some other form of middle management. The sheriff's department is an extremely aggressive agency and has long held the opinion that it train and pay us (the investigators) to be the experts. It normally just turns us loose to conduct an investigation as we see fit, within reason of course. This case would be no different.

At four thirty in the morning on a dark street in Hollywood, I shook hands with Investigators David Liske and Dan Gaytan of LAFD, and we agreed on the spot to a gentlemen's agreement to operate as a task force. We planned our first "investigators only" meeting at eight in the morning at the old LAPD Hollywood Station, which had recently been deactivated. Cindy and I got some quick breakfast, called our boss, Lt. Larry Lincoln, and told him to meet us at the Hollywood Station for the "investigators only" meeting.

*"We are not going to rest. We are going to work tirelessly"* (LAFD assistant chief Pat Butler).

## The First Investigators Meeting

By around nine in the morning, we arrived to the "investigators only" meeting. To say we were shocked would be an understatement. To say I was mad, irate, flabbergasted, or even livid wouldn't half begin to describe my emotions. We walked into the meeting room with just two investigators and a lieutenant from the sheriff's department. We knew from dozens of past major events that only the obnoxious bureaucrats at the FBI bring dozens of agents to meetings, mostly as a show of force and intimidation to smaller agencies. We left most of our investigators back in the office or in the field and only brought the decision makers. Such could not be said for the other agencies that showed up.

By the time the meeting started, it was clear to me that this was going to be a circus of epic proportions. The LAFD had indeed brought its arson investigators, about ten of them. Besides them, the LAPD arrived as expected, with about forty persons, only about five of which were investigators, the rest being patrol leaders from the Hollywood Station area. Also in attendance were several investigators from the LACoFD, an agency with no jurisdiction in the criminal investigation of any of these fires. All of these folks were a bit much, but I could deal with them. However, I could not deal with the other fifty or so folks from fire-suppression units, public-information units, homeland-security details, and staffers from local politicians' offices. There were way too many politicians and midlevel fire chiefs in the room, and too few investigators.

What made this meeting start to go south fast was when a midlevel chief from the LAFD announced that he would be running this "event," and since he was soon retiring after a long thirty-five-plus-year career as a fire chief, this event would be the crowning achievement of his career. He seemed positively giddy about this. He then took control of the meeting and asked the local city councilman to stand up and give the task force a pep talk. The local political hack obliged and added that he too was going to be monitoring this investigation and wanted frequent briefings and updates. This political blowhard then asked each person in the room to stand up, introduce himself or herself, and give a status report as to what had occurred and what they were going to do to fix things.

About this time, my counterparts at LAFD could feel my glare of hatred staring at them from across the room. They knew what I was thinking: How the hell is this an "investigators only" meeting? We motioned each other to the side, and we spoke quietly. They explained that their arson chief was outranked by the midlevel chief in the room who had "assumed command" of this event. As such, we would have tremendous issues for the next two days, as a fire-suppression chief (not an investigator) would be telling his arson investigators how to go about conducting a major investigation.

This sort of thinking drove me crazy. Fire agencies have established, through dealing with countless major emergencies and catastrophes, a response system called the Incident Command System, or ICS. This system works extremely well in coordinating resources and multiagency responses to major events such as wildfires, floods, earthquakes, and the like. In the ICS, the chief that heads it is practically a military general, and he issues orders and directives to lesser commanders in charge of operations, administration, logistics, communication, and several other disciplines. This type of system is effective in dealing with a highly chaotic, emerging, and developing crisis such as a major fire event. A fire boss can quickly assess the problem, allocate resources, and even change control and command to another commanding officer in the blink of an eye. It is so effective that it is taught as a near religion in every fire-management school for supervisors.

The problem with this mind-set is that the system has proven that it is not effective at all in dealing with a criminal investigation. A major disaster and a major investigation are two completely different problems and cannot be attacked in the same manner. On the street we say, "Firemen do, and cops think." You just cannot brutishly throw resources at a problem (serial arsonist) that you haven't yet identified and analyzed. Police work always has been, and always will be, the polar opposite of fire-suppression work. For this reason, I have long advocated in my books and writings that the two should always remain separated and that a fire-suppression officer has no business running a criminal investigation, any more than a homicide detective should be putting out a structure fire.

So, to start out the largest arson case in Los Angeles history, we had an older, near-retirement-age fire-suppression chief attempting to run the event as a nice "feather in the cap" of his career. I was pissed. I went back and sat down as the people around the room made it clear to each other that there was going to be a lot of political ass kissing and not much investigating going around. I heard the usual platitudes and buzz phrases about "forming partnerships" and "working as a team."

By the time it got around to us, my boss, Larry Lincoln, who was well aware of my temper and uncensored speech, gave me a verbal warning to "Relax, Hoss, and let's just get through with this meeting." I stood up, introduced myself, and stated that the sheriff's department had six carport fires in the West Hollywood area, had found significant physical evidence at every scene, and would be pursuing the investigation with me as the team leader. The local politician asked that we share what we knew of the evidence, and I boiled over a bit. I announced that I would not be involved in any other meetings, except with fellow investigators, and would not be discussing evidence, motives, or suspect information with anyone but another investigator or the prosecutor. A chilly silence prevailed for a few seconds until the ranking fire chief stated, "Well, we are all on the same team, so let's hope we work well together."

I left the meeting seething but was immediately stopped by someone with a clearer head. I met LAPD detective Ray Morales, of the Criminal Conspiracy Section, and he quietly agreed with my opinion. Ray was a calm, cool customer who had a taste for nice suits. He was very experienced with major cases and ended up being the voice of reason many times over the next few days. He became the case manager for the entire case, and we soon convened an investigators' mini meeting. We were joined by the LAFD folks who sheepishly apologized for their suppression chief. It was quickly established that Inv. Dan Gaytan would be the lead investigator for the LAFD, I would be the lead investigator for the LASD, and Det. Ray Morales would be the case manager for LAPD. Also joining us in the "lead group" would be a local ATF agent named Suriya Khemradhipati. Filling out this command group would be the lead arson prosecutor in Los Angeles, DDA Sean Carney. We didn't know it then, but none of us would sleep for the next four days.

*"These are very serious fires with huge loss-of-life potential because they are set in structures with people sleeping inside"* (LAFD captain Jamie Moore).

We sat in a quiet room and discussed what we had and where to start the investigation. By this time we had sorted out all the fires from the previous twelve hours and realized that in one six-hour flurry, an arsonist had set seventeen similar, if not identical, fires in the Hollywood/West Hollywood area of Los Angeles. All seventeen had been set under parked cars with the use of an identical incendiary device placed in the exact same spot under the vehicles. It was crystal clear to me that it was a lone offender, based on the devices, the targeting, and the closeness of the attacks to one another. These seventeen fires were so close to each other that an energetic person could have set all of these fires while on foot or bicycle. This was the hallmark of an urban serial arsonist.

We agreed at that point to consolidate the case and make it a single investigation, with two joint-lead investigators, Dan Gaytan and me. As such, we worked out several administrative details that would bore the average person but were highly critical when conducting a long, multiagency investigation.

I agreed, for the first time in my career, to turn over all of my evidence to the LAPD so that it could be booked and processed in a uniform manner. We agreed on a simple method of identifying the fire scenes since, at this point, four agencies had been involved in the seventeen fires, and each agency had assigned its own numbers to the fires. We knew that would not work in court, so we simply classified the fires by time of reporting (alarm time) and address. This gave us a clear map, or time and location, of each fire for future geospatial and temporal analysis. I also agreed that since two-thirds of the fires were in the city of Los Angeles that the command post would remain with LAPD, and if any suspects were detained or arrested, they would be processed at the LAPD command post and with LAPD evidence technicians.

After this short meeting established who was who among the investigators, we all resolved to work our own clues and scenes in our own areas. We would then bring the results to the task-force manager, Det. Ray Morales, for him to arrange in a logical investigation. We truly felt that a single arsonist would be so emotionally exhausted after such a wild night that we would have a few days or even a couple of weeks to get organized before he struck again.

It was at this point that I got my first kick in the nuts on this case. An investigator from LAFD had quietly told me that one of their chiefs had determined that this was not the work of a single arsonist and was most likely the work of a dedicated terrorist group or at least some local extremists. In the few months prior to this, Los Angeles and several other American cities had been beset by a civil disobedience group called the Occupy movement. This group was a loose affiliation of several professional protest groups who usually protest big government and big business. They had taken their tactics to new, unheard of levels by staging weeks-long "camp ins" in many cities, creating chaos and filthy living conditions in several massive tent cities.

The Occupy LA group had held the city of Los Angeles hostage for weeks by crowding thousands of protesters into squalid conditions in downtown. This fire chief had determined that this arson spree must be related to the Occupy LA movement. The fire chief, who had proclaimed himself in charge of this investigation, was now directing his investigators as to whom he wanted them to look at. He even suggested that this was a terrorist attack and should be handed to the FBI.

What this hapless chief did not know was that no credible investigator, upon reviewing the facts and evidence, would believe that it was an organized group who conducted these attacks. There was already a clearly defined MO of the arsonist, and it is impossible for a group to maintain a consistent detailed MO Secondly, the foolish chief assumed that the FBI knew a damned thing about arson, which they don't at all. They are seldom, if ever, involved in arson cases as that crime is usually not under their jurisdiction and clearly not their field of expertise. Nonetheless, the chief had ordered his investigators to start looking at the Occupy movement for possible suspects. He also wanted them to look at friends of Sam Arrington, the drunken college student, as possible suspects.

After the meeting, I arranged to turn all of my evidence (six fire-starter logs) over to two LAPD major crimes detectives. So far, LAPD had dedicated two very good detective units—Criminal Conspiracy and Major Crimes—to this investigation. This would be very helpful as I knew that these units were excellent at putting together a large criminal investigation, something that fire departments are woefully unprepared to handle.

As it stood, the LAFD arson unit would respond to and process its fire scenes and then bring all of its evidence and intelligence back to the LAPD case managers. The LASD would handle all of its scenes, evidence, and intelligence and bring a completed report back to the LAPD detectives managing the case. The DA would be sitting in the command post monitoring the progress of the case. The LAPD had also shuffled resources and dedicated a patrol platoon of about forty officers to respond to the Hollywood area for saturation patrol duties. They were instructed to conduct patrol stops on any type of suspicious person, whether they were on foot, bicycle, or in a vehicle. By early Friday evening, there were at least one hundred police officers and arson investigators assigned to this ad hoc task force.

### Incident at the Consulate

While the investigators were starting to put together the semblance of a task force and criminal investigation, a strange incident occurred at the German consulate across town on Wilshire Boulevard. At around ten thirty in the morning, a young white male wearing dark clothing and having his hair pulled back in a dirty-blond ponytail approached the security kiosk in a hallway of the consulate. The young man looked a bit odd and slightly disheveled, so the consulate security officers kept video tabs on him. Security guards monitoring the man saw him remove some items from his pocket, place them on the floor in an empty hallway, and then proceed through the security checkpoint. He went to an operations desk and appeared agitated and upset. He was a German national and identified himself to the consulate as Harry Burkhart. He was highly upset that his mother, Dorothee Burkhart, had been taken into custody by the American government.

While Harry Burkhart was ranting and railing at the desk officer, a curious security guard walked over to examine the items Burkhart had placed on the floor. He didn't recognize them but snapped a picture of them with his cell phone. Several minutes later, after Burkhart had finished his rant and left the building, the guard walked over to find that the two items were gone. Burkhart had taken them with him. Nearly ten days later, the guard would finally realize what those items were and would forward the photos to the arson task force. Harry Burkhart had placed a small Duraflame Firestarter log on the floor along with a small square package containing a chemical booster block. The arson investigators recognized these two items as the components of the incendiary devices that had been found at nearly every fire in this spree. It would take several days after his eventual arrest, but there were at least a few eyewitnesses that could testify to Burkhart having incendiary devices in his hands.

The rest of the day I spent writing all of the crime-scene reports for the cases in the sheriff's department's area. I knew that cases like this were highly unpredictable, and we could go weeks without making an arrest, or we could arrest a suspect the next day. I wanted my cases ready to be filed the moment we made an arrest. I advised my LAFD counterparts to do the same as the sheer volume of fires would make this case a bit overwhelming.

I also requested that the sheriff's department match LAPD's investment of personnel. That would prove to be a rare problem for my agency. The LASD is massive, with around nine thousand uniformed deputies, which is just a few hundred less than LAPD.

On a given day, if the circumstances warrant it, I can summon several hundred patrol officers and several dozen detectives to assist in a high-profile case. I could do that any week of the year except, as it turned out, this week.

One of the long-standing traditions of the LASD has been to provide patrol support to the megaevent that occurs every year—the Rose Parade—and the following Rose Bowl football game. The City of Pasadena contracts with the LASD to provide a couple thousand patrol deputies and hundreds of other support personnel to assist in policing these two high-profile events. This typically takes away over one-third of the sheriff's department's resources. The remaining members of the agency must continue to staff the sprawling jail system and the twenty-seven patrol stations, along with all the normal murders, shootings, and other mayhem that occurs in Los Angeles County on a given night.

I called my boss and advised him of my needs. I wanted to set up a team of major crimes investigators out of my office, along with at least fifty patrol officers to conduct saturation patrols out of the West Hollywood Station. He denied the major crimes teams as they were all dedicated to collecting intelligence about possible attacks at the Rose Parade. He promised that he would set up a formal investigative team in two days, when the Rose Bowl commitment was complete. In the meantime he was able to send a platoon of forty patrol deputies to the West Hollywood area. They would come on duty at about nine in the evening.

I finished my reports and began setting up a "clues management" system within my office. We knew that major events spawn a number of phone calls, tips, and clues being sent in to the investigative agency. These clues would hopefully be directed to the Arson-Explosives Detail. As such, I created a clues sheet for this event and gave blank copies to the night-duty team from my office. Unfortunately, the night-duty team included that same lazy detective who had attempted to kiss off all of these fires the night before. That guy would continue to be a pain in the ass throughout this case.

By six in the evening I was bone tired and wanted to go home. Cindy and I had been up since one in the morning and we needed to be back on duty early the next morning. I sent her home, but I needed to stay on until about eight thirty that night so I could go to West Hollywood Station and brief the oncoming platoon of forty deputies specially assigned to provide saturation patrol.

I finished my reports and began looking at phone tips that were coming in already. By seven thirty I got into my car to make the drive over to West Hollywood. My phone began ringing before I was halfway there. It was LAFD investigator Dan Gaytan, the other lead detective on the task force. "It's starting again, Ed," he said in a voice hoarse from talking all day. "We have a car fire burning in a commercial underground structure in Hollywood." This was a slight deviation in the pattern, as all seventeen of the first night's fires were either to cars in carports or to cars parked on the street. We hadn't had one in a commercial lot before this, so there was a bit of doubt if this one was connected.

Gaytan and his crew sped to that lot and began processing the scene to see if he could find a device. I secretly couldn't believe the suspect would try something this crazy two nights in a row, but I kept my mind open to the possibility. The only nice thing about a fire in a commercial structure was that there was a decent chance that the event may be captured on security cameras.

By the time I pulled into the lot at West Hollywood Sheriff's Station, Dan Gaytan had called me back and confirmed that he had found an identical device under the car in the structure. He was in the process of looking for video evidence. Incredibly, our arsonist was back to work at nightfall.

I walked into the sheriff's station and saw a large briefing room full of eager, aggressive, and a bit agitated sheriff's department's deputies. I was exhausted but gave them as detailed a brief as I could up to this point. By this time I was aware that at least twenty-five arson investigators were running around the streets of Hollywood, attempting to catch the arsonist in the act. By the time I started talking at West Hollywood Station, rumors were already coming over the radio that the arson investigators were looking for someone on a Vespa-type motorcycle. A second report said that the arsonist was possibly driving a beige-colored Lexus. I knew from hundreds of prior investigations that citizens were reporting any suspicious person or vehicle anywhere near one of the fires. I also knew that none of this information had been vetted or corroborated and that I was unwilling to forward it as a legitimate clue or tip.

The patrol deputies were not dumb. They knew that we had found incendiary devices the previous night as some of them had seen the photo. They demanded to see it so they knew what to look for. I refused to show them the devices and told them to look for anything suspicious. I assured them that if they found a suspect with the device, they would recognize it immediately for what it was. I admonished them not to discuss the device or forward any photos at all as that was case-sensitive information. They had all heard LAPD talking on the radio about the Vespa and Lexus and asked me if that information was good. I told them it was not. They seemed quite pissed with me, and I totally understood their feelings. I was holding some information back from them, and they knew it. However, I had long lectured to other investigators the importance of protecting some information, and I had to stick with my instincts.

I gave the patrol deputies very vague orders to patrol around and stop anybody they thought was suspicious. I wanted the person positively identified, and I wanted the deputies to summon me or another arson investigator if they thought their "contact" was a legitimate suspect. With that, I sped home to try to get some sleep. It was just before midnight on December 30.

*"We are pulling out all the stops...the person responsible will be brought to swift and complete justice"* (LAFD spokesman Brian Humphrey).

### The Second Night

On my way home I was called four times before I even got out of Hollywood. Patrol deputies let me know that a man on a Vespa was stopped near a hotel, and they wanted me to respond to the scene. Minutes later a second man was stopped on another small motorcycle in West Hollywood. Neither of these guys was carrying incendiary devices, and they were released. Somehow, LAFD and LAPD had told the sheriff's deputies that the arsonist was on a motorcycle. I then was called to meet the ATF and LAFD investigators at another spot in Hollywood, where a suspect in a beige-colored Lexus was stopped. Again this didn't pan out. When I got there I was surprised to see at least half the arson squad from the LAFD at the scene. They had all responded to the fire in the commercial parking structure and then just stayed on the streets "looking for the arsonist." I was surprised to see that they had been joined by some investigators from the LACoFD, who really didn't have a role in this case at all.

I met quietly with my counterparts and told them that having investigators running around the streets of a large city in the hopes of catching an arsonist in the act was ridiculous and a complete waste of time and manpower. This is an ongoing problem in the arson-investigation world, where for some reason investigators believe that the only way to catch a suspect or prove a case is to drive around aimlessly hoping to see an arson attack in progress. I reminded them of my age-old quip that I give in my training classes: there has never been a homicide detective that actually caught a suspect in the act of committing murder, yet they constantly put people in prison for it. Every homicide investigation is solved by crime-scene work, interviews, canvassing of the area, and detailed follow-up investigation.

I told these guys that they needed to get home and get some sleep so that we can began a detailed investigation in the morning. I also reminded them that our role was to solve the case and link a suspect to the attacks. If we do this correctly, then usually a uniformed patrol officer or tactical team member would make the actual arrest of the suspect. I could see that my little scolding was falling on deaf ears as this was such a unique event that these guys were caught up in the excitement of it all.

I also learned at this little meeting that the information about the arsonist driving a small motorcycle or Lexus was from the most recent fire, and that witnesses had seen both of these types of vehicles speeding around at the time of the fire. This was hardly solid information, and I asked the investigators to stop leaking fragmented information to the patrol cops. This case was quickly starting to lose its luster with me, as even veteran investigators were getting caught up in the hype. I drove home and made it by one in the morning. I took a long-needed shower and prepared to jump into bed when my phone went off.

At just before two in the morning, on December 31, Inv. Dan Gaytan, my colead partner, called me and said, "The guy is active, Ed. He's burning up North Hollywood." LAFD was responding to multiple fires in North Hollywood, which is about an eight-minute drive from Hollywood. I got dressed and drove to Hollywood. By the time I arrived, it was about three thirty, and Gaytan had called back to say that he had at least a dozen active fires burning in the San Fernando Valley.

My own phone started blowing up shortly after I started back in to work. A staffer at LASD Headquarters (HQ), who normally managed media inquiries, was demanding that I call him and provide him with all of the information that I had accumulated. He wanted to "get ahead of the media storm" and release a detailed report by the sheriff's department. I told him that I wouldn't be releasing any information other than that we were working in a joint task force with the city fire department and LAPD. The HQ staffer was not at all happy with me and immediately called my boss. My boss stood tall and told the staffer to stay off my back.

I got to Hollywood Station and began looking for the task-force crew, but they were already in the field chasing fires. I drove over to West Hollywood and met with the station commander, who was also completely jacked up by events. She said that there weren't any fires as of yet in West Hollywood, but she had over fifty sheriff's deputies standing by. I sat drinking bad coffee and kept getting updates from the LAFD about the fires burning in the nearby San Fernando Valley. There were ten fires in North Hollywood, a couple further out in Burbank, one way the hell on the other side of the valley in Sunland, and then a break for about a half hour. Then a couple more broke out in North Hollywood, followed by two more in Hollywood.

The suspect clearly was mobile in a car and had taken a fairly straight path north from Hollywood, into the valley, and had then returned to Hollywood on roughly the same path. By four thirty, he had fully returned to West Hollywood and lit his last two fires of the night. In total, a suspect lit seventeen fires in about a five-hour period—a fire frenzy that matched his previous night's total. Even the most veteran of us couldn't even begin to fathom this volume of activity. Now, even I started to doubt my "lone offender" theory. However, within just a few hours, the LAFD investigation teams would report that they had found fire-starter logs at all but two of their scenes.

Not wanting to get bogged down processing fire scenes, I sent my two night-duty detectives to handle the pair of fires in the sheriff's department's area of West Hollywood. One investigator immediately found a fire-starter log under a car at a very large fire scene in a carport. This massive blaze destroyed the entire structure and half a dozen cars.

My co lead investigator, Dan Gaytan, did not have as easy a night as me. He directed the investigation of fourteen arson scenes, spreading from Hollywood and out into the Valley. The single Burbank fire necessitated the addition to our task force of an investigator from the Burbank Police Department. By the time I met Gaytan the next morning at the second task force meeting, he was exhausted. He also had some interesting news about the evidence he had seen.

### Evolving MO

Serial criminals tend to develop methods of operation, or MOs. Successful MOs tend to remain constant with little deviation or evolution. In this case, the Hollywood Arsonist, as we were calling him, had mixed results, with most of his fires being fairly successful, large events, and only a few failures. By the second night, however, his device began to evolve, as did his target selection. On the first night he targeted about fourteen vehicles within carports and three parked in driveways or on the street. By the second night, he continued to target vehicles in an identical fashion, but more of them were in private driveways or on the street. Less than half of the second night's attacks were to vehicles in carports.

His device, however, remained fairly consistent, with a couple of notable deviations. In at least three of his fires, he added small, camp-stove-sized propane cylinders to the top of the fire-starter log. This crude attempt to "blow up" these items failed in every case, as it is close to impossible for that to occur in these items. However, this activity confirmed to us that we were not dealing with a super sophisticated individual, just someone who was intent on maximum damage. On a couple of other devices, he added entire boxes of wooden matches to the top of his log.

These items all survived the fires, and again, he had mixed results with his success at starting large fires. It would be a few days before we could figure out why he had altered his devices.

*"We've reassigned dozens of detectives. Those detectives are now working together around the clock"* (LAPD commander Andrew Smith).

### Second Task-Force Meeting

At eight in the morning, on December 31, after the second crazy night, an exhausted group of fire administrators and investigators reconvened at the old Hollywood Police Station. The energy and euphoria of the first night was long gone, and now I saw the same senior fire-suppression chiefs looking downright distraught and worried. A fire chief who had seemed so confident the day before was now literally crying in a hallway. He was being consoled by another older chief. The first chief told him, "I feel so helpless and embarrassed. Why can't we stop this guy?" This chief, so giddy the previous day, was personalizing this event as his own failure. He clearly needed to leave and go home as he was too emotionally involved.

The second day's meeting was shorter and much terser. There were way fewer people at this meeting and almost nobody wanting to be in charge, as some viewed this event as a potential career killer. A few small, worried speeches were again made by some senior suppression chiefs from a couple of agencies. One chief was certain that this was an organized attack by terrorists and demanded the FBI be called in. A second chief made possibly the dumbest statement I have heard in my thirty-year career. He seemed completely frustrated by the scope of these fires—now over thirty-four in two nights—and he did the only thing his years as a fire manager had trained him to do: he called for more assets.

He stated, in frustration, "I want to declare martial law in Hollywood." He followed that up by announcing a firefighting method more aptly applied in a major wild-land fire. "I'm declaring this region a disaster area, and through mutual aid, I want to bring in twenty-five strike teams to patrol the streets and drive this guy out of here." The investigators all stood with their mouths agape. This chief was stating that he was going to declare martial law and bring in twenty-five teams of firefighters, each team consisting of four engines and a battalion chief. That was roughly the equivalent of three hundred and twenty-five firefighters. The chief did not want them to fight fires but to use their engines and uniforms as a visual deterrent to patrol the streets and drive the arsonist out of Hollywood. We were incredulous!

At that announcement, the four sheriff's department's detectives in the room, me included, started to fold up our notebooks and decided to quit the task force. This suggestion was ridiculous. We knew that two things had to happen for this case to move forward. First, we needed to immediately separate the fire-suppression chiefs from the investigative teams. These well-meaning veterans knew nothing about conducting a criminal investigation and were trying to apply firefighting techniques to the problem. Second, we needed a senior police official in charge of the investigation as there was really no one of high enough rank to deal with all of these inept fire chiefs.

As we walked out the door, I was stopped by the head of the LAFD arson section. I told him that this method was idiotic and that unless things changed, the sheriff's department would just go back to our side of town and work our own investigation of our fires. I told him that he needed some serious brass from the LAPD to come in here and help out his guys as this was really turning into a massive, complicated case. The chief was one step ahead of me. He told me that a major LAPD official was coming to the station in a few minutes. My boss and my team left to conduct further investigation, but I stuck around to see if this was going to get better. I would not be disappointed.

About a half hour later, Deputy Chief Michel Moore, the number four guy in charge of the LAPD, walked through the door with several commanders and captains. Moore met with all the fire brass and then finally came over to me. He and I were friends and had known each other socially for over twenty years. I pulled no punches and told him my thoughts on the case and the horrible job the fire chiefs had done so far. Chief Moore asked me what I thought was needed. I told him that we needed more cops here, and not knuckle-dragging patrol officers but some high-octane detectives. We had lots of clues and leads and plenty of crime scenes to work on.

Moore agreed and got on his cell phone. Incredibly, within two hours, dozens of LAPD detectives descended on Hollywood Police Station. They were led by Commander Mike Moriarity, who was leading a detail from Robbery-Homicide, the cream of the LAPD. Now I was impressed! By noon we had about two hundred total LAPD detectives and officers dedicated to this case. They were the best LAPD had to offer, and they came from three elite units: Robbery-Homicide, Major Crimes, and Criminal Conspiracy. Det. Ray Morales remained in charge of case management, but now he had several experienced helpers and some leaders with some clout.

Chief Moore then made his most significant contribution to the case, which ended up being the critical factor. He stood up and in a no-bullshit tone demanded that this case be worked twenty-four hours a day, with as many assets as needed, and with no stone left unturned. He also lit a fire under the middle-management guys and said he wanted this suspect in custody in seventy-two hours. I was impressed with the tone and the speech, but I was well aware that major arson cases often took weeks or months to bring to justice. Still, this was the best news I had heard in two days. Reenergized, I went back to the field with a new partner, Det. Dana Duncan.

*"We're not resting, and we're not stopping. We'll continue all through the night. We've got many, many clues and many, many leads to follow up on and a lot of other work to be done"* (LAPD commander Andrew Smith).

### Amateurs

By this second day the media had started to whip this event into a massive news story. As such, all sorts of fire agencies wanted to be involved in this task force. Like I stated before, the sheriff's department seldom worked with other agencies in the arson world due to issues with information security and the lack of skill or expertise by their investigators. In this case, I was asked several times by another agency to include their investigators into my portion of the case as they wanted to be "in the game" despite having no jurisdiction and a history of rather poor fire investigations. The other task-force leaders asked me to give a couple of investigators something to do, so I finally relented and met two arson investigators from the other agency. I told them that I need someone to canvass the first four fire scenes for witnesses or evidence. It was also part of a theory, which I discuss in the following paragraph.

These two investigators seemed disappointed at this somewhat inglorious assignment. I told them that real detective work was fairly mundane and not at all exciting, but it was what is required in order to solve cases. These two guys went to work, and I never heard from them the rest of the day. By normal investigation rules, they were to go to the scenes, conduct a detailed "canvass," record the results, and report back to me so that I could eliminate those tasks and assign new ones. Dozens of other investigators were doing exactly the same thing.

I didn't hear from these two all day and just assumed they went home as I knew they really didn't know how to be good investigators. That night I came upon them driving around the streets of Hollywood in an undercover role, looking for the arsonist. I asked them about their assignment, and they told me they had finished it in an hour and had no results. They didn't write a report, didn't record any names, and didn't complete a proper canvass at all. I told them that they didn't complete their tasks, and they replied that they didn't want to do boring work but only wanted to cruise around hoping to catch the arsonist in the act. Like I knew they were before that day, these two proved that they were true amateurs. Unfortunately there are a lot of arson investigators across the country similar to them.

### First Fire in a Series Theory

During my studies of serial arsonists, I had developed a theory about the fires these people set. I knew that the most common motive for serial arson was revenge so that meant that serial arsonists would have a direct connection to their fires, or at least the first few fires in their series. They often went out to settle old scores, and then after they had burned a few items owned by their enemies, they gravitated toward the excitement of the fire setting and just began selecting random targets, or so I believed. I explained this to Dana Duncan. He had replaced Cindy Valencia in the past two days; with the start of a new year (that night), our team schedules changed in our office. Dana was one of the sharpest detectives I knew, and he bought into my theory. He and I drove back to West Hollywood and began knocking on apartment doors in the buildings that were torched in the first wave of attacks two nights before.

I didn't have much luck, but Dana found a tenant at the very first fire scene who described what a female witness had told him. The tenant said that a local drug-user girl told him that she had seen a "crazy Russian" right before the very first fire, and that she recognized him as a guy who used to live at the complex. The tenant described the girl, gave us her first name, but warned us that she was a methamphetamine addict, a.k.a. a "tweeker," and was a bit erratic. Dana noted this information. We spent the rest of the day working on these leads. That afternoon I went back to the office to help set up a "clues and leads" program with the desk crew. The same lazy detective was on duty (the guy who kissed off the original fires) and mentioned casually that a female drug addict had called claiming that she knew who the arsonist was. She gave the usual complicated, drug-addict-style story, and our lazy detective didn't have the patience to listen to her. He just told her to call back later when I was on duty.

By now I was near comatose from lack of sleep. I stumbled to a bunk room behind our office and tried to get a couple of hours of sleep before the maniac started lighting fires again. The stress was starting to get to me, and due to a lack of sleep and too much coffee, my heart was racing. I couldn't fall asleep. My phone kept ringing at least every hour, with a patrol officer reporting that he had stopped some guy on a bike or in a car or something. I had left a message for them to call me only when they found someone very suspicious, but apparently they believed they were supposed to call me with every person they stopped. I was starting to lose my mind. By evening I just couldn't fall asleep, so I ate and went back to my desk. The leads had started to pile up, and I now saw dozens of tips.

### The Freelancers

By the late afternoon and early evening of December 31, I had caught up on the reports of all eight fires in the sheriff's department's area. I truly believed the guy would get caught fairly quickly (within a couple of weeks) and that we needed to be ready to present the case in court immediately. The average citizen is unaware that from the moment you put handcuffs on a criminal suspect, you had about three days to get him formally charged in front of a judge, or you were forced to let him go. The more complicated the case, the more difficult it was to get all the victims, witnesses, and evidence lined up. For each fire so far, we had a minimum of about four victims, usually meaning the building owner and the owners of each damaged vehicle, along with all of the witnesses, which included any citizen eyewitnesses, firefighters, and police officers who had attended each fire. Besides that, we needed to track down any 911 callers and get statements from them.

It was New Year's Eve, and many of the victims were out of town and unavailable. This was a huge logistical problem as we needed as many cases as possible ready to go so that we could raise any potential bail to a large enough level that a suspect could not be bailed out. I kept up to date on my reports, but I knew that any cop could write about eight times faster than any fireman, and surely my counterparts were not going to have their casework up to date. As it turned out, I was correct.

Complicating my life were the dozens of tips that were pouring in via the media, phone calls, and car stops made by uniformed police officers. I looked at the "clues/tip" sheet and saw at least a half dozen really interesting-looking tips. One came from a police chief in North Dakota, describing a kid from his area who had just relocated to Hollywood and was bragging to his buddies about lighting the fires. Another was a great tip from an arson unit in a major eastern city, who knew one of their suspected serial arsonists had just moved to West Hollywood. A third came out of San Diego County Sheriff's Department, also describing one of their registered arsonists having recently moved to Hollywood. Another was from a retired detective from my own unit who gave me the name of a serial arsonist in West Hollywood who had lit thirty cars on fire in the early 1980s. Coincidentally, many of that suspect's fires were on the exact same streets as this current arsonist.

All of these tips looked good, and we actually chased down all of these potential suspects. Indeed, at least three looked like they were probably serial arsonists that had just moved into the area. None of these tips panned out.

*"We got some valuable tips from social media. I personally passed on to investigators at least three pieces of information from Twitter that were useful"* (LASD captain Mike Parker).

Additional problems arose, which did not allow me to get to sleep. The most persistent was the staffer from LASD HQ who wanted to be actively involved in every aspect of the case. This staffer called me every few hours demanding the latest information on the case. When I refused to release more than vague information, someone at HQ concocted his own fake press statement that they believed I would have made. This was an embarrassment and was a distraction for me for a week. Other staffers were attempting to use social media to solve this case. In the end, social media was merely a nuisance to investigators. Neither social media nor the tip line provided a single clue related to this case. The bulk of the tips on social media involved commentary, jokes, and the usual conspiracy theories. It may have a role in future investigations, but it was not a factor at all in this case.

A second "armchair detective" arose to give me a large headache. The sheriff's department is a massive agency with dozens of small commands within it. One such command is our Transportation Division, which polices the rail lines, bus lines, and related facilities. This is a large and high-profile unit within the sheriff's department, and it has a huge budget. As such, it has its own bomb-sniffing dogs, tactical teams, and intelligence squads, all in place to immediately react to anything involving the trains or busses.

The Hollywood Arsonist case so far had nothing to do with this unit; however, that did not deter one of their "intelligence squad" sergeants from coming up with his own investigative theories. He had decided that the Hollywood Arsonist was riding the trains as most of the fires were within walking distance of a train station. While it was true that all of the first night's fires were within walking distance of a metro rail station, the second night's fires were nowhere near any train stations.

I contacted this sergeant, explained what I knew, and told him I had found no evidence of his theory, but he should just advise the deputies on the trains to look for any suspicious individual and check them out. I told him we believed the suspect was most likely in a car. Not satisfied with my answer, he demanded that I send him a photo of what devices we were looking for, as he too had heard that we had found devices. I gave him the same story as the other patrol units, and he lost his mind and began yelling about me holding back information and risking the lives of deputies, believing that this fire series was related to international terrorism.

I hung up on him in the middle of his rant. I found out the next day that this same idiot had written a memo to all transit deputies before he had talked to me. The memo stated that he was working with me on the task force, and we had concluded the suspect was traveling by rail. He gave out several pieces of wrong information, including his theory on international terrorism and the use of explosives and incendiary devices. This guy clearly wanted only to glorify himself in front of his bosses.

With all of this swirling around, I got some very disturbing news from some patrol deputies. They were aggressively stopping and checking out dozens of suspicious persons in the Hollywood area. One such car stop revealed a white male in his thirties, wearing a wig and a fake mustache and carrying a loaded gun under the seat. When detained, he flashed a firefighter identification card and said he was working on the arson task force. The shrewd deputies probed further and discovered that this guy was a firefighter from over one hundred miles away and had nothing to do with the task force. He was not an arson investigator and had "self-deployed" to the area to help arrest the Hollywood Arsonist.

"Self-deployment" has become a serious phenomenon ever since the Oklahoma City bombing, where virtually everyone in the emergency-services business within a three-state area sped to the scene to help, without any official role. While 95 percent of these folks are well meaning, caring people, a few are fake rescue workers, who show up for their own glory and self-serving reasons. They have been a huge problem in every major event since the Oklahoma City bombing, including the 9/11 attacks, Hurricane Katrina, and other catastrophes. Some have been involved in theft and more serious crimes, and others have actually made claims and received federal compensation for "on-the-job injuries" when they were never actually rescue workers.

In this case, the deputies identified this clown, copied down his gun number, and let him go. They forwarded me his information, and I had him checked out within the arson business. I also told the patrol officers that if they saw him again, I wanted him detained, and I would come and interview him.

I forgot about this guy and went back to my other clues. Twenty hours later, another deputy stopped the same guy in West Hollywood. This time I had the firefighter detained and driven to a sheriff's station where I met them. We thoroughly searched his car and found no evidence that he was the arsonist. He no longer had the gun. He told me that he was helping with the task force but had no idea that I was one of two guys running the task force. This guy was a true clown, and the absurd disguises he carried were right out of the John Orr book of "wannabe" police detectives.

I called his fire chief and asked him about the guy. The chief said the firefighter was a regular fireman but was trying to get assigned to his arson unit. I told the chief that I could arrest his guy for carrying a loaded firearm and interfering with a police investigation. He admitted that his guy was a bit too "gung ho" and immature and begged for me to not ruin his fire department career with an arrest. I agreed to let the guy go but told the chief that this guy was too much of a loose cannon and glory seeker to be an arson investigator, and he should probably be dropped from that program.

We kicked the freelancer loose with a stern warning that this was his last chance. He was told to get out of Los Angeles County and to return immediately to his home city. To my knowledge, he has never been selected as an arson investigator with his agency. Before this investigation was over, two more firefighters and a police reserve officer, who were all "freelancing," would be detained by patrol officers. All four of these knuckleheads had sped to Hollywood, hoping to make an arrest of what was emerging as the most intense arson investigation ever. It just gave me a worse headache than I already had.

*"We are tracking down every possible lead or rumor to catch these guys"* (LASD captain Kelley Fraser).

### A Suspect Emerges

By the evening of December 31, Inv. Dan Gaytan, my co lead investigator from LAFD, called me and filled me in on what was going on with his part of the task force. He and I had held to our handshake agreement and remained in constant contact with each other. Gaytan told me of two significant developments. First, he said that a segment of his group had been pursuing the idea that these attacks were part of the Occupy LA protest movement, and they had a belief that all of these fires may have been set by friends of the drunken kid, Sam Arrington, who had been arrested on December 29, for lighting three fires. It was found that Arrington had some sort of loose connection to anarchists or a similar group. This theory had been further bolstered by the fact that the fires on the second night of this spree had led all the way out to a small community called Sunland, very close to where Arrington and his friends lived. Right now a segment of the task force had developed enough information to get a search warrant on the home of Sam Arrington's friends.

I was not pleased with this information as I was 100 percent sure this was a lone attacker and not an organized group. Gaytan somewhat agreed but confided that his chiefs were behind the organized-group theory. They wanted this aspect of the case to go forward. I considered this aspect to be a total waste of time.

The second news that Gaytan had for me was a bit better. He had finally gotten some security-camera video footage from the very first fire scene on the second night—the fire in the commercial structure. He described a lone white male with a dark or dirty-blond ponytail. He was wearing black clothing and walking to and from the burned vehicle. The suspect had a "European look" and was suspected of being Russian. He also had a ghostly white pallor. This description caused me to get excited as this was an identical description to the one forwarded to us by the "tweeker" girl in West Hollywood. I let Gaytan know that we were going to pursue that angle the next day. Gaytan told me that he had several video techs checking out other scenes for video footage.

LAPD detective Ray Morales told us even more. LAPD detectives received a tip from a citizen on the "tip line. A witness on the second night of the fires described a male who looked "European" near one of the fire scenes. The male was described as white, in his twenties, and wearing black clothing. He had his hair in a tight ponytail and had a receding hairline. He was seen walking oddly and then leaving the area in a dark Dodge van. The van had British Columbia plates and its hazard lights operating.

Dana and I then drove over to West Hollywood Station and again briefed the night-shift patrol teams. I urged them to stop more vehicles and to identify anyone they believed was suspicious. Again they pressed me for insider information, which I was reluctant to give out. At the conclusion of this briefing, we were approached by a West Hollywood patrol sergeant named Brian Lutz. He gave us the full name and address of the same "tweeker" girl who had been calling our office about the suspect. She had called the West Hollywood Sheriff's Station at least five times, trying to get her information out to an investigator. Because she was somewhat of an annoying, half-coherent drug user, her information was only partially taken or she was hung up on. Sgt. Lutz had taken the time to investigate this information and to find the name of the tweeker girl's boyfriend.

Armed with her full name and address, Dana and I went looking for her for the next few hours, until about midnight. We couldn't find her, as she was already out and about.

Unbelievably, on New Year's Eve, the Hollywood Arsonist was quiet and lit no fires. I drove back to my office and attempted to get some sleep in the bunkroom. Again, I got less than two hours of sketchy sleep. I was called almost every thirty minutes throughout the night, and agencies as far away as San Diego were reporting fires in their cities.

## The Media Circus

The media in Los Angeles is one of the most aggressive and voracious in the world, rivaled only by New York and London. During this four-day event, it was one of the quietest media times in LA, with really nothing going on. The Hollywood Arsonist soon became the only story in town, and by New Year's Eve it was being covered by all of the Los Angeles media, the national media, and even the international media. It quickly spiraled out of control on New Year's Day.

The second night of fires included one attack where a car was torched as it sat next to a home in the hills of Laurel Canyon. The fire spread to the old wooden home and caused severe damage to the structure. The media leaped at this one fire because the home had been a past residence of the deceased front man for the group the Doors, Jim Morrison. Of course, the next day's headlines couldn't wait to invoke the hit song of the Doors, "Light My Fire." And so the insanity continued.

Another continuing theme the media harped on for at least a week was the fires set by Sam Arrington (drunk kid) and Alejandro Pineda (transient) on December 28, which they included as part of this series. They concluded, erroneously, that all of these events were linked and that the suspects must be linked. Many pseudo "experts" weighed in on news shows with their own theories about how all of these things were connected. None of them were right.

By New Year's Day the fire agencies were holding multiple press conferences every few hours. Several outlying fire agencies had fires overnight and had determined (incorrectly) that the Hollywood Arsonist was now capering in their cities. This hysteria was spread by the media as it quickly descended on every single fire in Southern California. Soon, "arson experts" were appearing on all of the local and national news shows, talking about the "profile of a serial arsonist" and exactly what motivates this particular arsonist, even though none of them knew the details of the investigation.

To counter some of these stories, LASD HQ called me and told me they wanted me to sit in for a television interview by several local and national media broadcasts. They told me it would be okay for me to feature my new book on these broadcasts. As much as I wanted to promote my new book on serial arsonists, I knew from my studies and my own lectures that it was a really bad idea for any of the main investigators to appear before the media until the case was over. It was not very professional, and it would possibly jeopardize my ability to be a witness in a future criminal proceeding. Defense attorneys would have a field day analyzing my comments and comparing them to the actual results in the case, which invariably would be different. I declined to appear and was happy that all of the lead investigators in the task force would do the same. None of us ever appeared on any press release or in front of any news conference.

What local fire chiefs seemed to have forgotten was that there are over twenty-five million people in Southern California, and it was common to have several fires every single night in many of the cities. Despite this, the media believed that the arsonist was striking everywhere. We, on the task force, knew better.

Another amusing thing that occurred during the media frenzy was the amount of tips and suggestions by security experts on how to prevent the serial arsonist from selecting you as a target. Several news stories cited security experts on this subject, despite none of them ever having dealt with a serial arsonist in the past. Lastly, and perhaps most amusingly, the east-coast-based neighborhood watch/vigilante group "Guardian Angels" came to town and announced that they too would be patrolling the streets of Hollywood. Finally, as can only happen in America, a small company began printing T-shirts immortalizing "Hollywood Arson." I am not ashamed to admit that I wanted one as a souvenir but somehow missed the opportunity.

By the end of the second day, the *Los Angeles Times* ran a short story citing "law enforcement sources." The story stated that investigators within the task force believed that there were multiple arsonists and even copycat arsonists lighting all of these fires, as "a single arsonist would have to be superman to have set all the blazes" that occurred the previous two nights. We, in the task force, knew there was only one arsonist, and because we had released no information, we knew there couldn't be any copycat arsonists. This information leak was an expected problem, and we narrowed the suspect list of "leakers" to a fire chief, an LAPD homicide detective, or an LASD HQ staffer. We began to isolate them from future information.

We couldn't stop all the leaks. A city councilman named Tom LaBonge, who had gained access to the fire chiefs early on and told them to keep him informed, was spilling information left and right. He gave multiple statements to the media, one of which gave the entire MO of the arsonist: "The arsonist is mostly targeting underground parking in midcentury-type apartments that have no security gates and putting some kind of incendiary device under cars." Thankfully no one leaked the pictures of the device to the councilman, or he would have described that to the media as well.

I had one personal sidelight. The media had finally gotten wind that we had found devices at several of the scenes and that the devices were in the form of fire-starter logs. We started receiving dozens of calls and inquiries about these logs, along with some crazy speculation. We knew that the media would pursue this angle and attempt to get our photographs, which had miraculously not been leaked. To try to cool off the media, my boss authorized me to confirm that we had found devices in the form of a fire-starter log. That seemed to do the trick, and the press never pursued it any further. We kept out the specific details of the device, hoping the arsonist wouldn't change his MO.

### New Year's Day (Day Three)

I pulled myself out of the bunkroom about dawn on New Year's Day 2012. I called Inv. Dan Gaytan, who like me still had not gotten any sleep, and we confirmed that there were no fires to report last night. He told me that search warrants were going to be served in a few hours on Occupy LA types, and I told him that Dana Duncan and I would be trying to run down the "tweeker girl" who witnessed the suspect on the first night.

After breakfast, Dana and I sped to Hollywood and finally located our "tweeker" girl. She sat and talked to Dana for an hour and gave a pretty good description of exactly the same guy that was seen on surveillance video at another fire. She told us that she was driving up Harper Avenue on the first night and saw a male she recognized coming out of the parking structure at 1226 Harper. She said that he was walking quickly, and she knew that he wasn't supposed to be at the address. She turned her car around to follow him and finally caught up to him a block away. He walked directly across a street in front of her and passed in front of her headlights.

She said the male was a "Russian" guy. He used to live at the Harper address or had bought drugs there in the past; she wasn't sure. She said her ex-boyfriend knew the guy well and could give investigators his name. She said that she was fighting with her ex-boyfriend who lived at the Harper address. Like a true "tweeker," she concocted a scheme on how we could get her boyfriend to cooperate and name the arsonist. She said her ex-boyfriend was a drug dealer and had drugs in his apartment right now. If we raided his apartment and arrested him for drugs, then we could force him to tell us the name of the suspected arsonist.

This crazy scheme was our only way to put a name on the face of the guy we were starting to think was the arsonist. We began looking at the tweeker girl's ex and found out he truly was a drug dealer, and the local narcs had been trying to put a case on him for a couple months. However, we just didn't have enough probable cause to kick in his door. So, we went with a second plan, which was to just go to his place and to appeal to his sense of citizenship and get him to cooperate with us. This may have worked, but we found out the drug dealer wasn't home. The "tweeker girl" tapped into her network of other tweekers, and she found out where this guy was staying in another city. We set up a plan to go meet this guy the next morning. By now it was late afternoon on New Year's Day.

Dana and I drove over to the task force headquarters and checked in. A lot had happened. First, the team that served the search warrant on the Occupy LA movement guys had failed miserably. They devoted a lot of time, resources, and energy into raiding a place that was no more than a hangout for pot-smoking kids. There was no evidence whatsoever that the group had anything to do with the ongoing arson attacks.

By this time, LAPD deputy chief Moore had convened a strategy meeting with the various leaders of the task force.

He introduced us all to Special Agent Brian Hoback, the commander of the ATF's National Response Team. Hoback's team was just arriving in Los Angeles.

Amazingly, in the wake of poor results, the large number of fire chiefs at the task-force meeting faded and went home. Only one or two remained in the room when I walked in. The bulk of the group comprised just a couple of sheriff's department's detectives, a couple of LAFD arson investigators, an ATF agent, and a dozen investigators, captains, and commanders from LAPD. Chief Moore pointed out immediately that he was not amused at having chased an empty lead for the past two days with a large amount of assets. He wanted to know what other credible clues or leads we had and wanted to get moving on them immediately. He also reminded everyone that he wouldn't tolerate chasing crazy theories. He wanted to get back to doing what cops do best: following legitimate evidence and leads. He was clearly voicing his disapproval of the Occupy LA theory.

One thing that jumped up in the meeting was that the follow-up investigators, video techs, and canvassing operations were getting results. During this meeting, we determined that we had at least four decent videos of a white male with a dirty-blond ponytail and wearing black clothes at four different arson scenes. Additionally, LAPD detectives had found an eyewitness and video of that male exiting a blue van at one of the scenes. On the second night of fires, a neighbor of one of the victims on Stagg Street, in North Hollywood, had a security camera running. The footage showed a stocky male fitting our guy's description exit a blue Dodge van, leave the flasher lights on, run across the street, and light a fire.

We decided that although we had numerous other potential suspects still to vet, this guy was the one who began appearing at several scenes. He was also the same guy that our "tweeker girl" witness had described. We now had two live witnesses and at least four video witnesses of the same individual, along with a blue Dodge van. Finally, the task force was focused on a single individual, and we had information that he may be Russian and may have lived at one of our victim locations. He was the best suspect to emerge. At this point we were pleased with how much information we had found in just the past twenty-four hours. We now believed that we were less than a day behind this guy, despite not knowing his name or where he lived.

Task-force leaders then decided to implement a tactical investigative strategy. We now had some very good video footage of our potential suspect. We sat in a room and made the decision to release a clip of the video to the general public in hopes that someone would recognize this guy. We decided to have a small press conference and let managers from LASD, LAPD, and LAFD release the clearest piece of video that we had. The rest of us waited in our offices by the phones.

*"People were so scared; they were setting up patrols in their neighborhoods"* (LA City councilman Eric Garcetti).

### The Arrest

On January 1, at 5:30 p.m., a prepared media release was initiated by the task force, with an LASD captain delivering the video and still photos of the suspect to a bank of local and national news cameras. The news conference would repeat throughout the evening. Sitting at home watching the ten o'clock edition of the local news, a federal agent assigned to the US Marshals Service looked up to see a male he recognized on the surveillance video. Deputy US Marshal Luis Flores first contacted his partner to confirm the identification. He then attempted to call the fire department, the LAPD, and finally the duty desk at the ATF. He finally got someone with a brain, and that person eventually put him into contact with the Hollywood Arsonist Task Force.

It would take some time, but by eleven thirty that night, he met with two of the task-force leaders and told them, "That guy looks like Harry Burkhart." He supplied the task force with Burkhart's identification, address, and a list of vehicles. Flores and SA Jonathon Lamb, from the Diplomatic Security Service, had been on a three-week-long surveillance attempting to locate Dorothee Burkhart to arrest her on her German warrant. During that time, the two agents identified Harry Burkhart as her very odd-looking adult son. They had watched Harry several times and saw that he obsessively ate sweets all day, hung out at a bakery and barbershop, and occasionally drove around in one of several vehicles with a British Columbia license plate. He appeared to actually live and sleep within the same apartment where his mother was operating a "hand-job joint."

When they eventually spotted Dorothee, she was driving a van with Harry sleeping in the back. The two agents arrested Dorothee, and then released the car to her son. The next time they saw him, he was throwing his tantrum in federal court, the afternoon before the arson spree.

As soon as the task force got the information on Burkhart and matched his photo to the surveillance footage and the few descriptions provided by the witnesses, we knew we had finally put a real name to the face of the arsonist. A specialized surveillance and arrest team from LAPD, the legendary Special Investigation Section (SIS), deployed to set up on his apartment. Their initial goal was to identify him, follow him, and watch him approach a target with the incendiary material in hand. At that point they would conduct an arrest and hopefully seize evidence to link him to the other fires.

A few administrative technicalities slowed down the deployment of the surveillance team. Before they could even set up around his apartment, they knew they were too late. Burkhart and his blue van were gone. Reports started coming in by one fifteen in the morning of January 2 that cars and carports were bursting into flames in neighboring North Hollywood. Harry Burkhart was on the loose!

The task-force leaders, once they had Burkhart's home identified, began to write a search warrant for the property. Part of that warrant was to find out which cars in his possession were home and which one was unaccounted for. By two in the morning, with several fires already reported, surveillance teams finally confirmed that the vehicle missing appeared to be the blue 2004 Dodge Caravan, with British Columbia plates. This was the same vehicle that had been described at two of the fire scenes. The surveillance team also looked through the trash behind Burkhart's apartment and located two empty cases of fire-starter logs. This was solid evidence linking him to the fires!

The one-day reprieve from fires that Burkhart took only seemed to reenergize him. This final night his frenzy started anew. From 1:15 a.m. until 2:50 a.m., Burkhart cruised the darkened side streets of North Hollywood, placing his incendiary devices under cars at nine locations. He then hopped over the Hollywood Hills on Laurel Canyon Boulevard and dropped back into West Hollywood, where his spree had begun four nights earlier. Burkhart lit a large fire in a carport on Alfred Street, and then two minutes later he lit his fifty-second and final fire in an underground parking structure on La Cienega Boulevard.

At this final fire scene, Burkhart parked his blue Dodge van in a 7-Eleven store parking lot and walked next door to the parking structure to light the fire under a white BMW. He was then seen on the video at the business as he entered, ordered a coffee and donut, and ate his donut while staring out the door toward the fire. The store video captured him taking his coffee cup, entering his blue van, and driving out of the parking lot toward Sunset Boulevard.

*"I hate America"* (Harry Burkhart, upon his arrest).

At ten o'clock, on the night of January 1, Shervin Lalezary, LASD deputy, began his shift in a single-man patrol car out of the West Hollywood Sheriff's Station. Like all sheriff deputies that week, he was out on routine patrol, but he was primarily focused on the hunt for the serial arsonist. Lalezary and his brother, Shawn Lalezary, were very similar to the other 150 deputies assigned to the West Hollywood Sheriff's Station in all respects except for one. They were part of a cadre of Sheriff's Reserves, and only worked in a patrol car one night a month. Their salary for a year totaled one dollar, less taxes.

The two Persian brothers were not that concerned about their meager reserve-deputy salary as both men held day jobs as civil attorneys. They were part of a proud cadre of 844 citizens who had taken great pains to become reserve sheriff's deputies and volunteered their time on a regular basis to the department. Shervin Lalezary was relatively new to the reserves and was in his first deployment in his own one-man car. This would prove to be the most eventful night of his career.

When the night-shift patrol cars for both LASD and LAPD went on duty in West Hollywood and Hollywood, they had received the latest briefings about the arsonist and the latest intelligence, which wasn't that much. Lead investigators, heavily concerned about information leaks, had kept a good deal of information back from the patrol officers. This infuriated the patrol officers, but investigators had told them to continue making stops of any suspicious persons, whether on foot, bike, or in a vehicle. The patrol officers felt left out and were sure the detectives knew more than what they were releasing, which was completely true.

On that particular night, all of the patrol officers had been provided a still photo of Burkhart taken off the security footage. Policemen, left to their own devices, can be a very clever bunch, and within a short time period, word had leaked from the task force that the suspect had been identified and that he lived somewhere on Sunset in Hollywood. Immediately the patrol cars began to heavily cruise Sunset. For the next several hours, LASD and LAPD patrol cars kept bumping into one another and exchanging all manner of gossip and intelligence about the arsonist.

When the fires started in North Hollywood, about eight miles away, several of these gung ho patrol officers began drifting out of their own patrol zones and onto the few roads in the hills that the suspect may return to Hollywood on. Everyone knew somehow that the guy had to be based in Hollywood as all of his fire sprees started and ended there. By about 2:30 a.m., they could hear radio calls of the fires. Based on their location, everyone realized that the arsonist was heading back toward Hollywood, setting fires along the way.

By 2:45 a.m., Deputy Shervin Lalezary, who was cruising the Sunset Strip, still did not have a name or vehicle description for the arsonist. At about the same time, an LAPD car had stopped a strange-looking man in a suspicious car a few blocks away. The man turned out to be an undercover detective from the LAPD's SIS unit, sitting on the Burkhart apartment, waiting for him to return. The SIS guy told the LAPD patrol car the suspect's name and vehicle description. Five minutes later, the LAPD car drove up to a sheriff's car and passed on the information. The deputy in that car then put it out to all West Hollywood Sheriff's Station units, and it arrived on Lalezary's computer terminal at about 2:50 a.m., exactly the same time that Harry Burkhart was sipping coffee and watching for smoke from his final fire.

At about 2:55 a.m., on January 2, Deputy Shervin Lalezary copied the arsonist's vehicle information into his notebook, looked up, and was shocked to see a blue Dodge Caravan passing him. It was going eastbound on Sunset. Lalezary pulled in behind the van and confirmed that it had British Columbia license plates. Still not quite sure, the deputy pulled alongside the van at a stoplight and saw a profile view of a chubby-faced male wearing dark clothes and his hair pulled tightly into a ponytail. The male's face was so white that he looked like a vampire. The male did not acknowledge the police car, but only stared straight ahead. That view was an exact clone of the photo of the arsonist that Lalezary had seen on television and during briefing.

Because he was very new and still not quite sure of himself, Deputy Lalezary did not summon backup but initiated a traffic stop of the van. A passing LAPD car saw the lone deputy making a traffic stop and circled in behind to back him up. The LAPD officer approached the van on the passenger side while Lalezary walked cautiously up on the driver's side. They made contact, and the two officers could see a dark bag in the car next to the driver. The LAPD officer shined his light into the bag and saw several fire-starter logs. It was him! They had caught the Hollywood Arsonist!

Lalezary removed a compliant Harry Burkhart from the van, handcuffed him, and placed him into the back of his patrol car. He immediately summoned his field sergeant, who sped to the scene like a madman. A sidelight of the arrest was that as Burkhart was moved from his van to the patrol car, he yelled out, "I hate America!" And with that spontaneous outburst, the question of motive was settled. A citizen watching the arrest reported the words to the media and within minutes the "I hate America" utterance made international headlines.

A brief tug-of-war match ensued in the middle of Hollywood as the news that the Hollywood Arsonist had been arrested raced through three large agencies. Soon, brass from LAPD and LAFD raced to the scene. Meanwhile, the on-duty sheriff's sergeant made several frantic phone calls to reach me as I was the lead investigator for the LASD. I had left instructions with my desk that if the arsonist was arrested, nothing was to happen until I had been notified. The poor sergeant was soon besieged by high-ranking detectives and brass from LAPD Homicide and Major Crimes Units, and of course several high-ranking fire chiefs. All wanted to see the arsonist and have him sent to LAPD HQ.

Adding to his misery, the poor patrol sergeant was getting screamed at by his own shift commander, a female sheriff's lieutenant not known for her daintiness. She yelled, "I don't care what Nordskog said; bring that body (arsonist) to West Hollywood Station." Meanwhile, Deputy Chief Mike Moore, fourth in command of the LAPD, arrived at the scene and spent several minutes trying to convince the sheriff's sergeant that we had an agreement and that he wanted to take custody of the arsonist. The poor sergeant was greatly intimidated by seeing so many stars on a collar, but again refused to yield. He kept trying to call me or anyone in my office who would answer. Everyone was sensing that this arrest was going to be one of the biggest in recent history in Los Angeles. I was nowhere to be found. For the first time in four nights I had turned off my cell phone. This was the first sleep I had gotten in days.

LAPD deputy chief Moore called his home, spoke to his wife, and she gave him my private home number. He then dialed it, and when I answered in a fog, he calmly said, "Ed, one of your deputies arrested the arsonist, and you agreed that we would book and process him at LAPD, remember?" Nobody in my agency knew that Mike Moore and I had been friends for over twenty years as our wives had been friends since their teens, which was the reason why his wife had my personal number. Chief Moore explained the situation in the street, and I told him to hold on; I would be there in thirty minutes. He then put me on the phone with a very relieved-sounding sergeant. I instructed him to leave the suspect in the sheriff's car until I arrived, and I would make my decision. I made it to the scene in twenty minutes, driving at over one hundred miles per hour.

While on my way I called my unit commander, Lt. Larry Lincoln, and my partner, Dana Duncan. We all arrived simultaneously to see a carnival in the making. The media had swarmed on this scene, and we passed dozens of television trucks. I explained to my boss that when we joined the task force three days prior, we had agreed that the booking of a prisoner would take place at LAPD. I was going to honor my word. My boss advised me that several high-ranking LASD brass were now demanding that the arsonist remain in LASD custody, but that he would back my decision. We approached Chief Moore and told him that LAPD could have the prisoner as agreed, but that he would ride to the jail in a sheriff's car. Everyone was happy.

When I arrived at the scene at about three thirty in the morning, I took a quick look into the bag between the seats of the van and saw that it was filled with fire-starting materials. A day later, when Burkhart's Dodge Caravan was processed by LAPD evidence technicians, they found a veritable treasure trove of evidence, leaving zero doubt that Harry Burkhart was indeed the lone wolf Hollywood Arsonist. The evidence ledger would record that his "arson kit" between the front seats consisted of a black messenger-type bag, seven fire-starter blocks, nine quick-start fire sticks, seven packages of the Zip brand fire booster, a full box of three hundred wooden stick matches, thirteen packs of Ignite-O fire-starter boosters, four packs of a different brand fire starter, a spray can of mace in a holster, a hammer, a flashlight, a cigarette lighter, a small torch lighter, and a reusable grocery bag from Ralph's grocery chain. He had with him upon his arrest enough material to make twenty more devices. There was no sign that his spree was going to end anytime soon.

Before we left the scene, we took Burkhart out of the sheriff's car and examined him. He was sober but disoriented. He made spontaneous statements that he had rented this van in Las Vegas just a few days ago and that the fire logs had been in it at the time. We saw that his hands were covered with the dark, sticky residue from handling the logs, and he had bits and pieces of the material on his clothes and shoes. He was photographed in detail at the scene, and a scientist took swabs of his hands. When he got to LAPD HQ, he was processed in a sterile room. He was photographed in his original clothes from all angles, for later comparison to surveillance videos. He was then stripped of all clothes and put in a sterile suit. Many photos and swabs were taken from him.

We had three major tasks ahead of us. First, we needed to search his apartment for other evidence. Second, we needed to interview Burkhart. Finally, we needed to prepare our reports and file this megacase within the next forty-eight hours or a judge would release him back to the streets. This is normally quite difficult, but the two lead investigators, Gaytan and I, had hardly slept in four days, and we were nearly catatonic. We pulled it together with lots of coffee and some bad food. DDA Sean Carney stayed with us throughout, and he was also instrumental in this phase.

From the moment Burkhart was positively identified, through his arrest a few hours later, and in the hours before his interview, we all began an intense study of the actions of Harry Burkhart. For the first time in my long law enforcement career, I was given access to all the information sources I could ever want, with no delay. In the two hours before I sat down with Burkhart, I reviewed reports from immigration, customs, and border patrol units from Canada and the United States; the German national police agency known as BDK; the US State Department; Interpol; the Canadian Mounties; Vancouver (Canada) fire and police agencies; Las Vegas Metro Police; and a German psychiatrist.

Burkhart's most recent activities showed that he had been in Frankfurt, Germany, in September 2011, when over twenty vehicle fires were set in a chaotic spree known as the "Frankfurt Fire Devil." No suspects were ever identified. He was still there when the arson fire to his home had occurred. Six days later he got on a plane to Las Vegas, Nevada, where he rented a car. His other history showed him in Vancouver around the time of a dozen arson fires that were still unsolved. Border records showed him over the past several years shuttling vehicles over the Canadian border into the United States. We were able to get a description of every vehicle linked to him. One of which was a blue Dodge van with British Columbia plates.

We began to prepare to interview Burkhart. Before we did this, we consulted with the prosecutor, several senior homicide investigators, and even made some phone calls back to Germany officials to get their advice on how to approach him. We prepped for about two hours, and then when we believed we were ready, we walked into the interview room. It was the shortest interview of my career, as Burkhart, who had been sitting quietly since his arrest, leaped to his feet and began screaming, "Nazis, Nazis!" He refused to calm down and then immediately invoked his rights and screamed for a lawyer, his mother, and the German consulate, in that order.

Despite the hours of prep, we weren't even able to get our names and introductions out before he legally invoked his rights. I consulted with the DA, and even though Burkhart had invoked, we sat down and spoke with him for about ninety minutes, trying to get a gauge on his mental health and possible motive. After several minutes of him being quite animated, he eventually calmed down enough to speak to us for a while. All of this was unusable in court. A few weeks later, when we received information from various psychiatrists who had examined him, we learned that no amount of prep on Burkhart would have worked. His extensive mental-health issues, along with the incredible amount of paranoia about police instilled in him by his mother over his life, overrode any reasonable attempt to communicate with him.

While we were prepping and attempting our ill-fated interview of Burkhart, LAPD detective Ray Morales ran the search warrant operation of Burkhart's apartment. The LAPD Criminal Conspiracy detectives found a pile of fantastic evidence to further solidify Burkhart as the sole suspect in the arson attacks. In his home they found Internet printouts from German newspapers, all talking about the "Frankfurt Fire Devil." The pictures and descriptions of the events depict nearly identical fire scenes occurring in Burkhart's hometown of Frankfurt, just two months prior to this spree. In all, there were over twenty fires set under cars using a fire-starter log in the town of Frankfurt.

Additionally, there were Internet printouts and photos of Burkhart's own home in Germany fully engulfed in flames. He clearly kept souvenirs and was showing an interest in the fires he had set the week he left Germany. He also had several local papers from Los Angeles depicting the previous three days of the attacks of the Hollywood Arsonist. There were numerous pieces of identification and other items linking Burkhart to the blue van used in many of the arson attacks, and then a final gift for the investigators was located. On a key ring in the apartment was a Ralph's club card. This matched the one on his key ring to his van and to the Ralph's shopping bag found in the van.

The shrewd LAPD detectives noted there was a Ralph's grocery store directly across the street from Burkhart's apartment. They entered the store and found a shelf containing a large supply of fire-starter logs and chemical boosters. They got a court order to search store records for purchases made by Burkhart. Using his club cards, the store management found that Burkhart had made nearly seventy purchases of fire-starter logs, matches, and boosters since the December 28, literally the day his mother was arrested. This was still more tangible evidence linking Burkhart to the fires.

By the end of that day we all went home. Dan Gaytan and I, the two lead investigators, along with DDA Sean Carney, LAPD detective Ray Morales, and ATF agent Suriya Khemradhipati, finally got back to our own beds for some sleep. I slept straight for fourteen hours and woke up with a massive hangover despite not having had the pleasure of a drink. The next day I brought my entire case down to Sean Carney's office for filing. I had eleven fires in the LASD area, constituting thirty-seven counts of arson. Those counts alone had Burkhart facing over three hundred years in prison. I was not surprised to find out that the LAFD did not have a single count ready to go. It would take weeks before they brought the remaining counts in for filing. It always takes firemen much longer to write reports than cops.

*"I feel very good that we've got the right guy"* (LAPD chief Charlie Beck).

### The Perkins Operation

After I filed my case with the DA, Dana Duncan and I went over to the task force headquarters at LAPD to follow up. We were there to ensure that although a suspect was in custody, the dozens of other good leads were followed up on as well. At that time we were approached by a couple of highly experienced homicide detectives from the LAPD. They wanted to know if we were interested in setting up a "Perkins Op" with Burkhart.

A ***Perkins Op*** is a unique and highly sophisticated undercover operation. It entails finding the appropriate undercover officer and placing him into a custody setting near the inmate. The inmate is then stimulated in some manner in hopes that he begins talking to the undercover officer. All of this must occur before a suspect is arraigned on charges. All of this must take place in the county jail or on the busses used to move inmates about. This is a very delicate operation in that most inmates are very aware of the normal activities within a jail and would easily notice an undercover operation. Only the most skilled of operators can pull off a caper like this.

We agreed to try this operation and enlisted the help of veteran LASD homicide detective Mark Lillienfeld and a specially selected undercover detective (UC) from the LASD Major Crimes Bureau. Incredibly, the LASD had an undercover detective who looked like a maniac and spoke both German and Russian fluently. The undercover detective, whose name I won't mention due to keeping his identification secret, underwent a several hour briefing by Dana and me regarding this case and what we knew about Harry Burkhart. He was then outfitted with a special jail uniform indicating he was a "ding" (psychiatric inmate) as Burkhart was being held in the mental-health section of the county jail.

Burkhart and the UC came into contact in a jail hallway, and Burkhart soon engaged the UC in conversation. Over the next several hours, the two were shuttled back and forth to the courthouse, where Burkhart was to make an appearance, and then back to the psych ward of the jail. Throughout this ordeal, the UC and Burkhart had several lengthy conversations, all of which were recorded by multiple listening devices placed on the UC and in the jail cell. Burkhart switched in conversation several times from English to German and then to Russian. He eventually admitted that he had lit many fires over the last week. He told the UC that he was mad at the United States and wanted to recreate the LA riots of 1992. He said that if he could get some fires going, then he hoped it would spur on others to do the same. He believed that he could get the blacks and Hispanics involved in this activity as they were always being picked on by the police. Burkhart told the UC that during a major riot he would be able to help his mother escape from jail. He also told the UC that he had targeted several undercover LASD cars in his attacks as he believed they were following him. Lastly, he described his device, how he placed it under the car, and how he had taken precautions not to get caught.

In short, Burkhart gave a fairly detailed admission of the fire spree set by the Hollywood Arsonist. He also gave us proof that while he did, indeed, suffer from some moderate mental-health impairments, he clearly was aware of what he was doing and that what he did was wrong or illegal. By this admission, he would undermine any sort of mental-health defense. The Perkins Op was a quiet success, and the exhausted undercover detective was soon sent back to his normal undercover duties.

Two days later, Harry Burkhart was formally charged and arraigned on all of the fires in the LASD's area. The media, stealing a line from the German papers, labeled him "the Hollywood Fire Devil." In my filing affidavit I cited Burkhart's hatred for Americans as a motive for his fire-setting spree. A very liberal judge attempted to set his bail extremely low, citing the fact that these were all merely "car fires." DDA Sean Carney countered the judge and gave an impassioned argument about the incredible danger that Burkhart posed and that his "car fires" actually were set under the occupied homes of dozens of families. The judge finally set bail at $2.3 million.

During the hearing, which was attended by dozens of media members, Burkhart began yelling and screaming and stood in the "crucifixion pose." He then collapsed into the waiting arms of several bailiffs. That was the first and last court appearance that Harry Burkhart made for a long time.

The ATF's National Response Team had barely landed at LAX when Burkhart was arrested. As such, they had nothing to do with the actual investigation leading up to Burkhart's arrest. However, these thirty-five professionals were instrumental for the next few weeks as they revisited each fire scene and conducted a second, incredibly detailed investigation, to include computer-generated diagrams and studio-quality photos. They also helped LAPD detective Ray Morales organize the hundreds of pieces of evidence and combine the entire massive case into fifty-two identical case files. The ATF did an incredible piece of work organizing the case and managing the paperwork. When they left Los Angeles three weeks later, there was no doubt we could prove all fifty-two fires against Harry Burkhart.

*"Our long, four-day nightmare is over"* (LA County supervisor Zev Yaroslavsky).

### Awards Season

Hollywood is well known for its awards season, which occurs in a two-month span after New Year's. In 2012, the Emmys, Oscars, Golden Globes, Director's Guild, People's Choice, and other annual awards galas were joined by a unique phenomenon: the Hollywood Fire Devil Awards. This lengthy awards spree started the day of Burkhart's arrest, when city-council members and the mayor of Los Angeles began issuing citations, proclamations, and all sorts of commendations to everyone and anyone vaguely associated with this massive case.

While the two lead investigators, Dan Gaytan and I, were still filing papers against Burkhart with the DA, the two federal agents who recognized him from our press release received major commendations from the City of Los Angeles. City leaders nearly broke their arms patting the two on the back for cracking the Hollywood Fire Devil case. The two would receive similar awards from their respective agencies and special awards from the US Justice Department. Both of their agencies would claim in the media that their men solved the case, despite merely being good witnesses.

At a similar news conference later the same day, the sheriff of Los Angeles County, Lee Baca, would nearly fall over himself gushing and bloviating about reserve sheriff's deputy Shervin Lalezary and his role as the man who solved the Hollywood Fire Devil case via an astute traffic stop. The shameless sheriff, who until the day he left office never knew that one of his headquarters detectives was actually a lead investigator on the case, believed the entire thing was just a fortuitous traffic stop. He later paraded Deputy Lalezary in front of several TV shows to include *Good Morning America* and *Ellen*. Lalezary received Deputy of the Year, Reserve Police Officer of the Year, and about a half dozen other awards. Ellen DeGeneres awarded him with a free trip to Australia.

The humble young man showed extreme embarrassment when he kept receiving awards for the next several weeks. He told me in a quiet moment that he had only about ten minutes of work into this case but was receiving all of the adulation. We told him to just enjoy the spotlight; it would be gone the moment he had a minor mishap on the job. The investigators all thanked Lalezary and admired the way he handled the spotlight that followed him for several days.

*"I can tell you this is a lot more exciting than my day job"* (reserve sheriff's deputy Shervin Lalezary).

The awards season continued a week later when the City of West Hollywood honored over fifty deputies from that station for their role in the case and then gave yet another special award to Shervin Lalezary. I was asked to attend as the lead investigator, but no mention was made of me or my unit's role in this case. To add insult to neglect, the LACoFD sent two investigators to the awards ceremony to receive acknowledgement for their role in the arrest. To be clear, the LACoFD investigators were not involved in running the task force, and the two guys they sent to get awards had almost nothing to do with the case.

LASD staffers also received recognition and gave interviews for their claims that they "aided in solving the case" by creating new media and other innovations. In reality the case was solved by the work of several detectives, and all the administrators and staffers contributed absolutely zero to the investigation.

All told, dozens of LAPD and LASD officers, along with numerous fire commanders, received commendations and awards for their roles in the Hollywood Fire Devil case. To this day, none of the cadre of lead detectives have received so much as a verbal acknowledgement or even a commendation for their role in actually identifying and tracking down the most significant arsonist in Los Angeles's history. We are probably just a little bitter about that. Over a year after the arrest, the Los Angeles County Police Officer's Association gave a group award to over one hundred persons whose names appear on the roster of the Hollywood Arsonist Task Force.

### Legal Matters

Within weeks of Burkhart's arrest, his main defense attorney contacted the prosecutor and advised him that Harry Burkhart had developed a massive cancerous tumor in his chest, between his lungs. The tumor was so large it was impinging on both lungs. The attorney stated that Burkhart was not fit to appear in court and needed to undergo treatment for his cancer in the county jail. Not known for great medicine, the county jail began treating Burkhart. We all considered this basically a death sentence. The case sat dormant until late 2014. The defense re-contacted the prosecutor and advised that Burkhart was recovering (incredible!), and that they were seeking a compassionate plea deal. They believed that although technically recovering, Burkhart was expected to live no longer than five more years. They wanted a fifteen-year plea deal so that Burkhart could be sent back to Germany to serve his time near his mother and sister. The investigators had no problems with the deal, but senior prosecutors did not want to set precedence for other inmates. They urged that the case go forward.

On Wednesday, March 4, 2015, the Hollywood Fire Devil case finally made it to a courtroom. On the thirteenth floor of the Criminal Courts Building in downtown Los Angeles, DDA Sean Carney brought the massive case in front of the county grand jury. These twenty-seven citizens sat through five days of rapid-fire testimony by about a dozen arson investigators from the LASD, the LAPD, and the LAFD. A week later they handed down the indictment on Harry Burkhart. He was indicted on fifty felony counts of arson, exposing him to several hundred years of jail time. For our roles as the co lead investigators, Inv. Dan Gaytan and I each testified for several periods in front of the grand jury.

Immediately after the indictments were unsealed and made available to the media, we learned that again, Harry Burkhart's cancer was back. His time on earth seems limited.

*"Most dangerous arsonist in the county of Los Angeles I can recall. This is one of the most significant arrests anyone can make...in the history of law enforcement"* (Los Angeles sheriff Lee Baca).

### Scope of the Event

The Hollywood Fire Devil, in a short two-month span, placed himself among the top five arsonists in history. He joins the lofty company of John Orr—the "Fire Lover," David Berkowitz—the "Son of Sam," Paul Keller—the "Seattle Arsonist," and Thomas

Sweatt—the "DC Arsonist," for the pure intensity of his arson spree. While the other four "heavyweights" lit many more fires than Burkhart, they spread their arson sprees over several months or even several years. Burkhart lit more fires in a shorter period of time, fifty-two in seventy-five hours, than any arsonist in recorded history.

His frenetic fire setting has never been matched and likely will never be by a sole offender. Added to his total was a similar, intense few days in Frankfurt, Germany, just two months prior, where he set over twenty fires, including the arson fire of his own home. At the same time in Berlin, there were an additional thirty car fires all set in the same manner. Canadian investigators noted a spike in car fires in Vancouver in the short time Burkhart was there and believe he may have set up to a dozen cars on fire in their area. These acts constitute over 110 fires in roughly a two-month span.

Burkhart's actions in Hollywood were incredible! He unknowingly crossed into three jurisdictions and, as such, involved four massive public agencies: the LAFD, the LACoFD, the LAPD, and the LASD. In addition, the City of Burbank and the ATF pumped resources into this event. By the third day of this investigation, over four hundred detectives, officers, and technicians were working on the task force. That doesn't even take into account the firefighters who actually fought the flames. Each night of the event, firefighters were simultaneously fighting about seventeen fires in a very small area.

Despite being bipolar, autistic, obsessive-compulsive, paranoid, schizophrenic, addicted to sugar, and having Asperger's syndrome, asthma, and hepatitis B, Harry Burkhart took on the four largest public agencies west of the Mississippi River, and quite literally brought them to their knees. Despite the claims of the "police source" who leaked the information that multiple suspects or international terrorists were involved in this case, "superman" is apparently an autistic, bipolar Chechen man who likes sweets and merely misses his mother.

*"Everything is lie. I and my son* [sic] *were persecuted from fascist Nazi organization…if you send us to Germany, we will be killed! He can exist only with me. He is twenty-five [years old], and he is mental ill, and he's like a small child. One little mental child cannot cause big fires. My son is not biggest arsoner; he is biggest sufferer"* (Dorothee Burkhart describing her life and son to a federal judge).

Dorothee Burkhart made several appearances in federal court to fight her extradition, citing her son's mental handicaps as reasons for her to remain in the country. Sympathetic federal judges, aware of both cases, allowed her to remain and perhaps rightly so. Harry Burkhart did have incredible mental-health issues, and possibly deadly physical-health issues. Even the most hardened investigators and prosecutors felt a bit sorry for Harry as more information about his mother surfaced.

A year after his arrest, his mother went on an extended tirade in federal court, yelling and screaming over the judge and proclaiming all sorts of Nazi persecution and conspiracy theories. It was clear that his wasn't an act. This lady, who had been inseparable from her son his entire life, was truly a nut job. Harry's defense attorneys seemed pleased as Dorothee's outbursts were reported in the media. They hoped this would help his defense case.

*"This is the first time that the district attorney has gotten the benefit of seeing the type of person that raised Harry Burkhart, who is*

*developmentally, psychologically, and mentally disabled"* (public defender Gustavo Sztraicher, defense attorney for Harry Burkhart).

## Aftermath

While Harry Burkhart stayed in jail and got treatment for his cancer, his crazy, manipulating mother, Dorothee, was given a reprieve on humanitarian grounds. She remained in US custody for over a year so that she could be near her son. During her appearances in court, she constantly argued with judges and made up elaborate stories about being tortured by all her jailers. Eventually, her crazy antics in the courtrooms and her failure to listen to a judge finally got her extradited back to Germany. She was barred from returning to the United States.

If truth be known, the investigators felt somewhat sorry for Harry Burkhart. He had emotional and mental-health issues, which his mother exploited for her own personal gains. She had him completely brainwashed, and once she was in jail, he had no support group whatsoever to lean on. She had told him after arrests and hearings in Germany and Canada that she was tortured routinely by the cops and that she was subjected to sexual assaults, electric shock, and all manner of horrors. No wonder he attacked police vehicles and acted in the manner he did! He reacted in a bizarre and dangerous manner, which easily could have cost the lives of a large number of people. Despite our sympathy toward him, we realize he is one of the most dangerous serial arsonists ever identified, as most of his fires impacted occupied homes. He needs to be locked up in a mental-health facility for the rest of his life.

Reserve sheriff's deputy Shervin Lalezary still diligently patrols the streets of West Hollywood with his brother, Shawn, one to two nights a month. They each earn one dollar per year, minus the taxes.

### The Task-Force Leaders

LAPD deputy chief Michel Moore, the energy and muscle behind the task force, retired from the LAPD in 2014. He was hired back immediately as an adviser to other administrators within the department. LAPD commander Mike Moriarity retired within a month of Harry Burkhart's arrest. He had spent over three decades running major homicide cases for the LAPD. SSA Brian Hoback, the commander of the ATF's National Response Team, retired from the agency about eighteen months after Burkhart's arrest. He is now a private consultant on major arson and explosion investigations.

Los Angeles sheriff Lee Baca was eventually forced to retire in 2014 due to ongoing scandals within my once-proud department. Baca spent fifteen years as the befuddled head of one of the top-rated law-enforcement agencies in the world. From the day he took office until the day he quit, he didn't have a clue what his detectives and patrol officers did; nor did he really seem to care. He had no idea of the involvement of several of his senior detectives in this case. His leaving should help the department significantly.

Most of the main investigators are still active in the business. Inv. Dan Gaytan continues to work major arson cases for the LAFD. SA Suriya Khemradhipati is still assigned to ATF and works arson cases with the LAFD. Det. Ray Morales continues to run major investigations for the Criminal Conspiracy Section of LAPD. His boss, Lt. John Carle, another major player in this task force, continues to run the Criminal Conspiracy Section. LAPD Det. Dan Jenks from Robbery-Homicide continues to stalk murderers in Los Angeles. DDA Sean Carney is the senior arson DA in Los Angeles and has prosecuted over a dozen serial arson cases. Det. Cindy Valencia now has a bomb detection K-9 partner and still works at the Arson-Explosives Detail for LASD.

My boss at the time, Lt. Larry Lincoln, retired as the commander of the LASD Arson-Explosives Detail in the summer of 2014. Det. Dana Duncan retired in January of 2014 from the Arson-Explosives Detail. His retirement party was attended by a veritable "who's who" of major prosecutors and detectives from Los Angeles, who lauded Dana for his thirty-plus years of major crimes detective work. I continue to work major arson cases for the LASD, and have now written my third book on serial arsonists. To date I have been involved in forty-five serial arson investigations and have consulted other agencies on two dozen more. All of the rest of those cases combined do not match the scope and intensity of the Hollywood Fire Devil case.

### Investigator's Analysis

*"Me and my mother…the most vulnerable in society. I'm several* [sic] *disabled, we are alone, I have no father, no family members, or friends"* (Harry Burkhart in a written letter to a Canadian court, in 2010).

The profile for Harry Burkhart is classic for a serial arsonist. He is besieged with numerous mental-health and physical problems. The list begins with autism and Asperger's syndrome and goes on to schizophrenia, paranoia, obsessive-compulsive disorder, addiction to sweets, anxiety, posttraumatic stress disorder, depression, and sleep and learning disorders, and it concludes with a few physical ailments to include asthma and hepatitis B. Added to this is that Burkhart is a very effeminate-appearing male and had a dominating, manipulative, almost matronly mother running his life. He had an extremely traumatic childhood, growing up in a war-torn country and having to flee and seek asylum in another country, where he was likely treated as an outsider.

He was not physically fit, had been institutionalized in Germany for psychiatric issues, and was unable to control his own activities. He had documented learning disorders and sleep disorders going back to his childhood. The triggering event for this latest spree was obviously when his mother was arrested. His profile pretty much fits most of the common traits of serial arsonists. He is classified as a **goal-directed arsonist**.

Burkhart set his fires for maximum destruction of occupied dwellings, at a time of day where victims would be sleeping. He traveled by vehicle and on foot, which made him a bit more difficult to pin down. He was arrested before we could do a complete pattern analysis, but he seemed to set fires in a **travel-pattern** fashion, which originated from his home, spread outward as he drove, and then returned back to his home. He was involved in **trolling** after his first night and appeared to just pick targets of opportunity as he traveled or trolled.

He moved quickly and efficiently when setting his fires, never staying at a scene longer than a minute. He used an accelerant and booster device to enhance his fires and set them under cars to provide an easily combustible and massive fuel package. He had mixed results with his devices and adjusted them as his results dictated. He admitted to having a motive, preplanned targets, and utilizing tactics to avoid detection. Harry Burkhart is off the charts dangerous and should never be let out of jail or a mental-health facility.

### The Experts Weigh In

During this case, the sound-bite hungry media looked for any expert or pseudo expert who could give them an opinion on the suspect. Luckily, for the most part, the investigators on the case—many of them highly qualified experts—stayed out of the media spotlight. Below are some quotes from the "experts":

*"Arsonists can be motivated by a range of things—the desire for recognition or revenge among them. Often mental illness is a factor. Sometimes the numbers grow because there's a thrill involved. It becomes a kind of game to see how many more they can light before they are caught. Whoever he is, he is very dangerous. He definitely means business...It could be anybody. Attention seeking pops out in my mind...someone is trying to make a statement"* (Rob Rowe, retired arson investigator).

*"Sometimes there are various patterns to these fires that arsonists are establishing unwittingly. It's going to be tough until they get some witness information or something is left behind"* (Brad Hamil, retired arson investigator).

*"Usually, someone setting these types of fires will have some kind of history behind them"* (Brett Martinez, Suffolk County, NY arson investigator/author).

*"True serial arsonists are relatively rare. Another motivation is sex. Others get sexually aroused from watching the fire trucks"* (SA Jim Parker, ATF).

*"Sometimes it's pathological in nature. I think motives are going to be hard to come by. We may never know"* (Chief James Lopez, LASD).

*"This frequency is unusual, as well as the pattern. There are so many of them in a short period of time. This is one of the largest sprees of arson fires I have witnessed"* (Captain Erik Scott, LAFD spokesman).

> *"This is a form of communication. Something causes him to be enraged, and he doesn't know what to do with it. There's enough people in LA; you're not going to find the person from a profile"* (Dr. Jeffrey Geller, expert on pathological fires setting, UMass Medical School).

> *"It can be about revenge, power, vandalism, or for profit. It can be about someone trying to conceal a crime. It can be politically motivated. Some people do it because they get excitement out of it"* (Dr. Steven Pitt, forensic psychiatrist).

> *"Often over the course of their life, they've fused an association between angry feelings and fire. I would expect that they will have this solved within the week"* (Dr. Robert Stadolnik, psychologist/owner of a fire-setter treatment program).

Some of these experts were too vague, some were spot-on accurate, and some were just plain idiots.

This case was the most intense case I have investigated in my thirty-year career. It began and ended so fast that it has been almost completely forgotten in Los Angeles.

Normally, within my world, there is a natural rivalry between the fire departments and the police. The firemen are always the good guys, and the cops are always the bad guys in the eyes of the media. If I were to be truthful, I would have to say I thoroughly enjoy the rare moment when the media picks on a fire department or chief for some sort of mistake they made. It just doesn't happen very often, especially in Los Angeles.

Within a week of Harry Burkhart's arrest, a local newspaper reporter wrote a story about how the LAFD screwed up the Hollywood Fire Devil case, and it was just another example of the incompetence of the city's fire department. The reporter remarked that it was a lucky car stop by a sheriff's department's deputy that saved the fire department's ass. The reporter clearly had an axe to grind and was looking for anything to blame on the fire department. I always have had my differences with the fire department's chiefs when it comes to them handling crime scenes. In this case I was downright pissed at them for their inability to function for the first couple of days. However, I wondered why this reporter was coming down so hard on the firemen, considering that Burkhart was arrested fairly quickly.

I took the very rare step of contacting the reporter and giving her the hard facts that she obviously didn't know. I told her that this was the most intense fire spree in the history of the United States, that the arsonist had attacked over forty occupied structures in the dead of night, that there had been no deaths and no serious injuries, and that a task force totaling up to four hundred investigators had been assembled in a matter of three days. I further stated that those four hundred investigators had looked at fifty-two fire scenes, interviewed over a thousand persons, sifted through hundreds of hours of video footage, and had identified, located, and arrested a suspect within four days from the first fire! That "lucky patrol stop" was, in fact, the result of that deputy being fed detailed information that was gleaned through seventy-five hours of nonstop sleuthing.

Seldom in the annals of crime, and certainly not within the field of arson investigation, had a case of this magnitude been solved in such an efficient manner. In all other major arson cases, it took months for the task forces to run down a suspect. This was possibly one of the best, well-coordinated investigations I had ever heard of. The ATF agreed, as their supervisor on scene reported back to Washington that this was the best run task force they had ever been involved with, and this was the two hundredth time they had been involved in arson task forces! The reporter was polite and eventually agreed with me after hearing the facts. I noted that she never did print a retraction or clarification to her story.

I teach courses nationwide on the investigation of serial arsonists, along with profiling and pattern analysis. This case was a fantastic case with which to employ some of my investigative strategies and theories and to test other recommended investigation techniques. Many of the things we did worked very well for us. My **first fire in a series** theory was spot on, as we later learned that Harry Burkhart had personal connections to at least four of the locations he burned on his first night. We were correct in believing that he was settling old scores. Because the case moved so quickly, we were unable to amass data to conduct a detailed **temporal analysis** of the fires. The only time frame we could come up with was that he lit his fires in the darkness and probably kept going until he was out of incendiary devices.

Our **spatial analysis** was crude, but it only told us that he was based somewhere in Hollywood and was moving outward from there and then returning at the end of his night. By the second and third nights we knew he was operating in a vehicle as his targets were so far apart. We conducted **target analysis** and soon found that Burkhart had two distinct patterns of targets. He targeted German cars in over half of his fifty-two fires. We were never able to come up with a reason for that. In another dozen or so attacks, he targeted vehicles that appeared similar to detective sedans. Through his admissions to the UC, we learned that he believed those cars to be sheriff's department's cars. We also noted that he more frequently targeted vehicles that were in the left-hand corners of carports. Again, we never came up with a reason for that and assumed that it was because the corners of the carports were darker and more hidden.

Our final bit of analysis was to his devices. We made one very large, glaring error here. We didn't understand the use of the fire-starter logs. We had hardly ever seen these items used anywhere in the United States as incendiary devices and never in the attack on vehicles. One call to the German authorities made us feel like idiots. We told them about Burkhart's devices and how unique they were. The German cops laughed and said that all young people in Europe use these things to burn cars. They gave us the reason that the items were cheap, plentiful, and safer to use than gasoline. It was easier to carry these down a street without someone being suspicious.

In the end, the **device analysis** should have pointed to someone from Europe, as indeed these were very commonly used items there for incendiary events. Our analysis of why his device evolved was simple economics. Burkhart was setting so many fires and using so much material that the stores near him were running out of fire-starter logs and boosters. He began breaking the logs in half to double his number and had to improvise his boosters by using matches and propane cylinders. There is a reason for everything!

What made us the happiest in this case was that Harry Burkhart was tracked down, identified, and arrested through the use of basic police-investigation techniques. Sending experienced detectives to the fire scenes to conduct interviews and canvass the neighbors was what made the case. Using special video techs to locate and download security footage gave us our first glimpse of the arsonist. Using forensics at every scene helped us locate Burkhart's fingerprints and DNA on some of the devices that failed. Even without the identification by the two federal agents, we strongly felt that we were just a few hours away from catching Burkhart on our own.

The amount of evidence we found against Burkhart was staggering. He resembled the arsonist on at least five videos. At least two different eyewitnesses identified him and his van at two fire scenes. His DNA and fingerprints were both found on devices at fire scenes. Eyewitnesses at the German consulate show him in possession of an incendiary device hours after the first night of fires. His van held over twenty of the incendiary devices when he was stopped. A Garmin navigation device in his van would link him to several of the fire scenes. He had lived previously at four of the fire scenes. His Ralph's club card showed him buying over seventy-five incendiary items during this event. He maintained a record of the media coverage of these fires and the fires in Germany. Finally, he gave a recorded admission to an undercover sheriff's detective of how and why he set many of the fires.

My anger and frustration early on in this case was aimed at misguided fire chiefs and a couple of my own peers, who got caught up in the excitement of this dynamic event and wanted to stray from basic investigation principles. Many of the cowboys, amateurs, and lazy investigators in the region just wanted to drive around all night in a pseudo undercover capacity, hoping to bag the serial arsonist in the commission of the crime. Truly, even in well-trained agencies, that immature and unprofessional attitude continues to exist. This mind-set is what keeps many arson cases unsolved or prosecuted at a much lower level than they should be.

Detective work is not the glamorous lifestyle as depicted in the movies with stakeouts, surveillances, car chases, gun battles, and the lead detective catching the suspect in the act. It is hard work that is often monotonous and boring. It is work best suited for thinkers and analysts, and less suited for armchair detectives and adrenaline junkies. In great investigations, the detective seldom makes the arrest. He compiles information, clues, and data, and exploits forensics and explores leads. He identifies a suspect and then builds a solid case around that suspect with physical evidence and witness statements. Then, he tasks a professional surveillance team or even a uniformed patrol officer to go out and arrest the suspect. It is that simple.

Again, to reiterate, all of this evidence against Harry Burkhart was recovered through utilizing the basics of criminal investigation: crime-scene work, forensics, interviews and canvassing, and exploitation of video technology. Any reasonably trained detective could have solved this case eventually, but the employment of a couple hundred highly trained police detectives, as only a major city like Los Angeles or New York can amass, caused this "whodunit" case to be solved in seventy-five hours. It truly is one of the best major criminal investigations I have ever seen or heard of in my entire career.

It was a personal honor for me to work alongside Inv. Dan Gaytan as the two lead investigators for this massive task force. I would also like to thank the other members of the leadership group of this unit.

*"This has been a very unusual level of cooperation between different agencies and levels of government, and to have pulled it off over a holiday weekend makes it all the more remarkable"* (Mary Powers, president of National Coalition on Police Accountability).

# 4

# Motives of Arson

Understanding the motives for any crime is the basis of all criminal investigation. If you can study the target/victim, you will learn the motive. If you understand the motive, then you can realize the potential suspect pool. If you study and analyze the sophistication of the act, then you can further reduce the size of a suspect pool to just a few people or even a single suspect. It is that simple. Yet, motive analysis seems to be one of the least studied topics in arson investigation.

There are several generally accepted main motives for arson, followed by several subtypes within the motive. Once the motive is realized, then identifying the suspect becomes rather easy. Based on practically all arson-investigation books, the following motives are considered the most common in the field of arson. They are listed in declining order of most common to least common.

- Revenge/spite
- Arson for profit
- Vandalism
- Crime concealment
- Excitement-based fire setting
- Extremism

The motives shown above are general motives, and each case needs specific study and analysis to locate a possible subtype of motive. Additionally, many cases encompass multiple motives or a blend of motives. Arsonists are very complex people and cannot easily be defined or described in a single category.

Besides the main groups of motives and their subtypes, arson is further classified in other "types." Female arsonists are semi-common and add their own unique styles and targeting methods. Juvenile arsonists light nearly half of all incendiary fires, and their crimes can be broken down into still further subgroups of offenders. Wild-land and serial arsonists are completely different breeds of offenders than all the rest. Each chapter of this book will offer a profile, key traits, and red flags associated with each subtype of motive or offender

*The three main visceral motivations for the crime of arson are* ***anger****,* ***power****, and* ***frustration****. All of these motivations are manifested in the following motive subtypes.*

## REVENGE/SPITE

### The Profile

Revenge and spite (used interchangeably for this book) are the most common motives of all violent crime, particularly arson. Roughly, by my own lengthy studies and estimates, revenge or spite account for 40 percent of all arson attacks. Revenge-based arsons are those where the arsonist is usually known to the victim and most often stems from a failed personal or business relationship. It can be an extremely personal crime done with much anger and passion. As such, the revenge-based arson is filled with so much emotion and anger that often the arsonist cares very little (during the event) about getting away with the crime.

This type of arson involves suspects that are so enraged that they often don't plan the crime well and, therefore, do a very poor job of hiding their actions and evidence. They also don't foresee the possible consequences or additional victims of their attacks and, therefore, place many innocent persons in jeopardy. Revenge/spite-based arsons are the easiest arsons to solve in that evidence is often recovered, the act is often done in full view of the victim or other witnesses, and the act occurs after many other smaller attacks leading up to it. In more modern times, with the heavy use of social media, the attacker often leaves messages bragging about the attack—Internet posts and taunts and even video recordings of himself committing the crime.

Typical events that lead up to revenge/spite arsons include arguments, failed relationships or partnerships, physical altercations, vandalism attacks in the form of graffiti, "keying" of cars, flattening of tires, window breaking, minor theft, annoying/harassing phone calls, texts, online posts, and stalking or surveillance behavior at home, school, or the workplace. A natural event during all of this behavior is that the victim seeks a court order or restraining order to force the offender to stay away or cease this activity. I have noted in countless cases that as soon as the offender is served the court order, he flies into a rage, and an arson attack on the victim soon follows.

The revenge/spite arson is one that is committed by female offenders quite often, although still not as often as males. Revenge/spite arsons are very personal in nature, and the target may be something highly coveted by the victim, such as a car, special clothing, photos, or even a home.

The good news is that revenge/spite arsonists most often tend to be "one-time offenders," wherein fire just happened to be their weapon that they used that day. Most revenge/spite arsonists are not habitual users of fire.

Lastly, and most importantly, revenge/spite arson attacks historically are the **most dangerous**, causing more injuries, damage, and death than any other arson motives. Quite often in revenge/spite fires, **unintended victims** are injured or killed as they are in the wrong place at the wrong time when two parties settle their dispute by arson. Such is the following dramatic case.

## HAPPY LAND SOCIAL CLUB ARSON/MASS MURDER NEW YORK CITY, NY, 1990

Easily the most notorious act of arson and mass murder in American history started out as a typical boyfriend-girlfriend dispute. It is included in this book as it is a classic example of this very common form of arson attack.

Julio Gonzalez is a Cuban immigrant to the United States, arriving on our shores during the notorious Mariel Boatlift of 1980. As a reminder, Cuban leader Fidel Castro ordered thousands of mental patients and career criminals freed from custody in Cuban prisons and asylums and cast them adrift on leaky boats in the Caribbean. These "at risk" prisoners soon mingled with tens of thousands of other Cuban refugees and landed on the shores of the United States. Many of these folks were highly dangerous criminals and were held in federal detention centers for months. This is the group that committed murders and staged huge riots in the detention centers while demanding their release into American society. Some of these refugees entered society and lived crime-free lives, but a good number of them were such hardened criminals that they started huge waves of crime wherever they ended up.

The 1983 movie *Scarface* depicted the life of a "Marielito" named Tony Montana (actor Al Pacino), who through sheer brutal violence rose to the top of the Miami drug-trafficking world.

Law enforcement investigators who have dealt with vicious "Marielitos" believe the depiction in that movie was not that farfetched.

In the case of Julio Gonzalez, there is no obvious evidence he took the path of Tony Montana; however, he did arrive on these shores as a former prisoner from Cuba's notorious prison system. He claimed to have been imprisoned for being an army deserter in Cuba. Gonzalez ended up in the Cuban enclaves in New York City and spent seven years working as a laborer in a lamp factory in Queens. At some point he met a Cuban woman named Lydia Feliciano, and the two engaged in a long relationship.

By 1990, Julio Gonzalez's life started to spiral downward. He lost his job at the lamp factory, and eventually Lydia left him. In that era, New York City was in the throes of its worst economic times and was still in a state of decay. The city had numerous social and economic issues that the public agencies could barely cope with. Among these issues was the proliferation of illegal, underground social clubs and bars in poor and ethnic neighborhoods. Most of these clubs were hidden in older, dilapidated buildings and were not suitable for permits or licenses. The clubs were notorious for having unsafe and unsanitary conditions, along with countless violations of the fire codes. Lydia Feliciano worked at one of these underground clubs. It was called the Happy Land Social Club.

After the breakup between Julio Gonzalez and Lydia Feliciano, Julio made several desperate attempts to reconcile and win his girlfriend back. He was rebuffed at every turn and soon grew agitated and angry. At three thirty in the morning, on March 25, 1990, Julio went to the club to speak to Lydia. She rebuffed him again, and he exploded in rage. The club's bouncers intervened and had to physically throw Julio out into the street, warning him not to return. Before he left, witnesses heard

Julio say to Lydia, "You won't be here tomorrow." He was then heard to say he was going to "shut this place down."

Gonzalez stomped off into the night. He didn't go very far. He walked directly to a nearby gas station and bought one dollar's worth of gasoline, pumping it into a plastic container. This act was witnessed by an attendant at the gas station. Gonzalez returned to the Happy Land club and approached the staircase leading down to the only door of the business. Gonzalez was observed pouring less than a gallon of gasoline down the stairway and into the only door of the crowded club. He lit the gasoline with two matches and stood there to watch the fire for a few moments. He then walked back to his nearby apartment.

At the time of this incident, there were ninety-two people inside the Happy Land club, including Gonzalez's ex-girlfriend, Lydia. Only five would emerge from the ensuing holocaust. Amazingly, the target of the attack, Lydia Feliciano, would be one of the lucky five escapees.

The fire that resulted from this attack was not that large and did not do that much structural damage, in the grand scheme of things. However, the actual design of the structure and the lack of fire-protection systems and escape routes sealed the fates for the eighty-seven people that died within minutes. The entrance to the club was below street level, so the stairs leading to the door went downward from the street. There were no other escape portals, and there was a medium-sized fire at the only exit, which was at the base of the stairs. The fire in the entryway created enough smoke to fill the small, packed club, which caused an immediate panic and rush to the only door. All of the victims died of smoke inhalation, but many of them also had severe crush injuries due to their escape attempt at the only door. Some of the smoke-inhalation deaths occurred so fast that victims were found with drinks still in their hands.

The Happy Land fire was the deadliest arson attack in American history. Its fallout rocked New York City and caused immediate enforcement and crackdown operations on similar clubs.

The arsonist/mass murderer, Julio Gonzalez, was arrested nearby that same day with his clothes still smelling of gasoline. He immediately confessed to the attack, telling investigators "I got angry; the devil got to me, and I set the fire."

Julio Gonzalez was convicted of multiple counts of second-degree murder and arson in August of 1991 and was sentenced to 174 separate twenty-five-year terms in prison. The total prison sentence of four thousand three hundred and fifty years is the longest in the history of New York.

## LEFT EYE
## ATLANTA, GA, 1994

Lisa Lopes was an international singing star before she became a convicted arsonist. Lisa Lopes was born in 1971 in Philadelphia. She later talked about her childhood, and while it was not a horrific upbringing, she did endure parents who she described as alcoholic and somewhat abusive. Lopes herself admitted later in life to constantly struggling with ongoing issues concerning alcohol. Beautiful and with a talent for singing, rapping, and dancing, Lisa Lopes joined the girl group TLC when she was just seventeen years old. She moved to Atlanta to pursue her career, which would quickly lead the trio to superstardom.

By her early twenties, Lopes, now using the stage name "Left Eye," was a multimillionaire, and in early 1993 started dating pro football star Andre Rison, from the local Atlanta Falcons team. She eventually moved in with him at his mansion outside of Atlanta. Left Eye later described her life with Rison as tumultuous, confining, and abusive. She began drinking more and was known for bouts of violent behavior. She told investigators later that Rison had been both mentally and physically abusing her. In September of 1993, the two were seen physically fighting in a grocery-store parking lot. When people tried to intervene, Rison pulled out a handgun and fired it into the air. No charges were ever filed, and the two resumed their relationship.

On June 9, 1994, Andre Rison returned home from a night of clubbing and got into a physical confrontation with Left Eye. He said she was drunk and assaulted him. She later claimed that he beat her, with him saying the combat was mutual. After the altercation, Rison left the mansion to cool off. When he left, Left Eye found some cardboard and shoes belonging to Rison and placed them into the upstairs whirlpool tub that did not have water in it. She said she then lit the items on fire as a way to get revenge on Rison for his abuse.

Rison's brother witnessed her standing over the burning tub and muttering, "I don't care anymore." The fire soon spread to the fiberglass and plastic of the tub, which spread to the walls, ceilings, and floors and eventually burned the sprawling mansion to the ground. The near-million-dollar property was a total loss! While the fire was still burning, Left Eye, not completely spent of her revenge, went outside and attacked three cars owned by Rison with a pipe from a vacuum cleaner, causing major damage to all of them.

Left Eye went to her high-priced attorney, and he had her turn herself in the next day. He also enrolled her in a substance-abuse program as soon as she made her $75,000 bail.

Lisa "Left Eye" Lopes eventually pled guilty to arson and was given five years of felony probation with the condition that she spend just six months in a halfway house and maintain her alcohol counseling and treatment.

The rest of her life she struggled with alcohol issues and admitted that she was the "crazy one," who was well known for eccentricities and unpredictability. She was quoted once as saying, "There's a thin line between genius and insanity." Left Eye stayed out of legal troubles the rest of her life but tragically died in a car accident in 2002 at the young age of thirty.

### Investigator's Profile

Both the Happy Land fire and the large mansion set on fire by "Left Eye" Lopes are included in this same profile as they are basically the same event. The consequences for each event were dramatically different, as were the punishments. Despite the size of the fires, the loss of life, and the sentences, the motive for both fires is nearly identical. One romantic partner is extremely upset with his or her mate and believes the only way to solve this issue of "love" is by starting a fire. This is an incredibly common act done almost as often by females as males, but usually not with these horrific results.

This is the most common arson to investigate, and the offender is often witnessed doing the act, as in both of these cases, and makes little effort to flee or hide evidence. Both of these arson offenders quickly confessed which is fairly common with this motive of arson. These attacks were both preceded by heavy drinking, a failing relationship, and the unwillingness of one partner to listen to or obey the other partner. Therein lays the **frustration,** which is followed shortly by intense **anger**—two of the main motivations for fire setting.

Regarding the ignition scenarios of each fire, the fire set by the male was enhanced with the use of gasoline—an accelerant the suspect acquired and then brought back to the scene. Flammable liquid, most often in the form of gasoline, is the most common flammable material brought to a scene. In many cases of revenge/spite arson, the flammable materials are acquired or gathered from fairly close to the arson scene. That is what occurred in this case. These case comparisons highlight some differences between male and female fire setting. Males are more likely to bring an accelerant to the scene, while females are more likely to use available combustible material at the scene. The female ignition scenario was consistent with the bulk of female fire setters. The female used only the available combustible material found at the scene to start her fire.

In a cold and sober assessment, I doubt very much that either of these arsonists had any intent to do the scope of damage and destruction that they eventually caused. However, their acts were so outrageously dangerous that they endangered the lives of all persons near their fire scenes.

## DENMARK PLACE ARSON/MASS MURDER CENTRAL LONDON, UK, 1980

Ten years prior to the Happy Land arson/mass murder event, a nearly identical attack occurred in Central London. The Denmark Place was a location that had a pair of rundown clubs habituated by prostitutes, rent boys, pimps, the barely employed, and other seedy and down-on-their-luck Londoners. The clubs were very popular as illegal, after-hours joints that catered to many foreigners who worked low-paying jobs in the restaurant industry. The three-story building had two clubs, with the upper club nicknamed the "Spanish Club" as it was a haven to many people from Colombia who liked to go there and dance to salsa music.

The London cops had heard of the illegal clubs and were aware that they likely were in violation of any number of codes, specifically the fire code, as often over one hundred people were jammed into the small rooms of the two clubs. The ground-floor door to the building was kept locked, and patrons had to yell upstairs to be allowed in. This was a disaster waiting to occur. This site was on a long list of clubs that the police eventually wanted to close down.

On the night of August 16, 1980, the building was packed with well over 150 people. A regular at the Spanish Club, who went by the name "the Gypsy," became involved in an argument and then a fight with a barman over the price of a drink. Eventually the Gypsy was physically tossed out of the club. The Gypsy, whose real name was John Thompson, was a Scottish small-time hoodlum, who did not handle insults very well. He got a ride to a nearby petrol station and purchased a small amount of the volatile fuel. He returned to the club building and poured the petrol through the locked front door, via the mail slot, and onto the stairs leading up to the crowded bars. He lit the stairs on fire and then disappeared into the night.

Within just a few minutes, fire had raced up the stairs, and the smoke and heat killed thirty-seven people. Many of the survivors made it only by clawing their way through the walls into an adjoining structure. Over the price of a drink, John Thompson became one of the most notorious mass killers in Britain's history. It was the largest single-fire death incident in England since the end of World War II.

If one were able to interview responding firefighters from both the Happy Land fire in 1990 and the Denmark Place arson in 1980, they would describe eerily similar circumstances. Both fires moved so fast and consumed so much oxygen that patrons in both locations were found dead with drinks still in their hands and with no indication that they knew anything was wrong. Many were slumped in their original positions and had made no attempt to escape. It is likely that many in both scenes had no idea that a fire was even occurring. The invisible, undetectable poisonous gasses lurking below the smoke layer of a fire literally dropped many victims in their tracks.

John Thompson was eventually identified and arrested nine days later while drinking in a club on the same block. He was tried for a single count of arson and murder and was convicted.

He received a life sentence for the fire. Thompson died in a prison hospital twenty-eight years later.

## CLUB MECCA FIREBOMBING LOS ANGELES, CA, 1957

The Club Mecca was a small neighborhood bar in South Central Los Angeles. It sat near the corner of Fifty-Eighth Street and Normandie Avenue. On April 5, 1957, the club had twenty-one patrons who were all drinking and dancing. Sometime in the evening, a group of four men entered the club and began drinking hard. Two were described as white, and two were described in the vernacular of the day as "swarthy," which is vintage police talk for a darker ethnic color than white. In this case the two "swarthy" men were actually Mexican. The group of four men was described by all as fairly drunk.

Apparently the club had very loose social rules because soon two of the waitresses accepted invitations to dance with two of the men. This quickly went sideways as both men became aggressive and abusive toward the waitresses, and the bartender was forced to evict them. He and others apparently did so with some gusto, and a witness described the four men as "getting worked over." After a bit of a skirmish, all four of the men eventually left the bar. They walked just a block and purchased a two-gallon pail full of gasoline from a Union Oil gas station. The four drunks then quickly returned to the bar and yanked open the front door. One man, thirty-six-year-old Clyde Bates, hurled the bucketful of gas into the crowded club. A second man, twenty-five-year-old Manuel Chavez, made three attempts to light a book of matches. When he finally got it lit, he tossed the book of paper matches onto the floor, and immediately a fuel vapor explosion occurred, turning the entire room into an inferno.

While not technically a true "firebomb," the aerated gasoline probably ignited rapidly in the form of a low-order explosion. The *Los Angeles Times* printed a story about the event using the vivid descriptions of the day. The paper's writers described the fire as turning the small bar into a "charnel house of molten metal and charcoal," and a "seething mass of flame." The entire revenge attack was labeled an "orgy of violence." If you were one of the unfortunate patrons trapped inside, these garish descriptions probably seemed quite apt. Six of the bar's customers never escaped the flames, with one victim being found still seated at the bar with a drink in front of him. His body was almost unrecognizable from the flame damage.

The LAPD soon rounded up all four suspects, who were laborers in the area. One agreed to turn state's evidence and testify against the others. Both Bates and Chavez were tried and found guilty of mass murder and arson, and both were sentenced to death in the gas chamber. A third man named Hernandez was sentenced to life in prison. Years later Bates and Chavez had their sentences reduced and eventually both were released from prison by the late 1970s.

At the time of this fire, the Club Mecca arson was the worst mass murder in the history of Los Angeles. This would not be the last horrendous act in this area. In 1992 the Los Angeles riots and ensuing firestorm of hundreds of arson attacks would begin on a street corner just a few more blocks south on Normandie Avenue, in South Central Los Angeles.

### Investigator's Profile

This small case is included as it is a virtual clone of the larger incidents in London and New York, which would follow years later. There have been hundreds of revenge/spite arson attacks similar to these, and they are usually quite simple to solve. The perpetrators often commit these crimes in great passion, with very little preparation, and often in full view of several witnesses. They are so inflamed by rage that they have not thought at all about the dangerousness of the act or their means of getting away with it. These are all classic revenge/spite arson attacks.

## THE EXPLOSION ALHAMBRA, CA, 1998

On Sunday, November 16, 1998, just before sunset, a major explosion decimated an occupied apartment building in the 1300 block of Fremont Avenue, in Alhambra, California. The building had four units, three of which were occupied at the time of the event. LASD's legendary rescue helicopter, Air-5, happened to be flying close by as it had just dropped off a patient at a nearby hospital. The massive heavy lift copter was staffed by two pilots and three airborne paramedic/SWAT deputies. The crew chief of this rescue copter was Sgt. Mike Connelly.

Connelly spotted the fireball and explosion that burst through the roof of the apartment building and made a critical decision. Since three members of the crew of Air-5 were trauma-trained paramedics, and it was obvious that this large explosion happened in a neighborhood with dozens of residents, Sgt. Connelly determined that there was a high likelihood of deaths or severe casualties. He ordered the massive machine to land in the middle of the intersection of Fremont Avenue and Valley Boulevard (both are major thoroughfares) and to begin immediate rescue operations. He also radioed for assistance from nearby sheriff's stations, the LACoFD, and the Alhambra police and fire departments. The giant helicopter shook the residential neighborhood as it shuddered to a landing in very tight quarters.

As soon as the big bird could safely land, Sgt. Connelly saw that they had a major incident on their hands. The exploded structure was now on fire. The building was a four-unit, two-story residential structure that was made out of wood frame and had a stucco exterior. The entire roof of the building had been blown upward and had come to rest on the building next door. The side of the building that faced the street had literally come apart and had exploded out to a distance of one hundred feet. The area around the building was buried in shattered wood, masonry, roofing materials, and the contents of three of the apartments. The other homes and apartment buildings on all sides of the burning structure suffered blast damage and were covered in debris from the exploded building. Sgt. Connelly reported that he believed that a large bomb had exploded.

After the SWAT/paramedics made a crisis entry, they found several stunned occupants inside the building. One had been in a bathtub at the time of the explosion and had been thrown out of his apartment. He suffered blast and burn injuries. An upstairs apartment was the only one on fire. Two residents were rescued with moderate to severe burn injuries, and an additional five victims had minor to moderate blast injuries. A car passing by on the street at the time of the explosion was heavily damaged by blast and debris. The mother and child inside the car had minor injuries. SWAT paramedic Sgt. Connelly could not believe that there were no fatalities.

The apartment that was on fire was quickly suppressed by the Alhambra Fire Department. All of the casualties were treated and then transported to the area hospitals. Almost immediately residents told the Alhambra police that a former tenant had recently threatened to blow up the building. The tenant had been seen entering his former apartment just a half hour prior to the explosion. Recognizing that the size and scope of this massive event was beyond their abilities, the Alhambra Police Department called the LASD Arson-Explosives Detail to manage this potential major crime scene. The LASD Arson-Explosives Detail sent a half-dozen arson-explosives investigators to the scene. They would later be joined by arson investigator John

Kabala of the Alhambra Fire Department and a couple of agents from the local ATF offices. LASD detective Rich Edwards and Sgt. Greg Collins would be the lead investigators on this complex case.

The investigation team stayed on-site and processed this explosion/fire scene over the next three days. It was fairly simple to spot the seat of the explosion for this event. An apartment on the upper floor had been blown to bits, with just a few interior walls remaining. That same apartment was where the fire had originated and had done the most damage. All other apartments had suffered lesser degrees of damage from the explosion and fire. The investigators learned from tenants that this apartment was vacant and had been the source of a dispute between the prior tenant and the landlord. The landlord had evicted the tenant just a few days prior to this explosion. Neighbors were saying that the tenant had threatened to blow up the building after his eviction. After an initial assessment of the entire building, the investigation team focused on the vacant apartment.

The investigation team cleared a path to the worst damaged apartment and then reconstructed the room. They found that the fire and explosion originated in the same location. They saw that a gas stove was in place in the kitchen and that the fire and explosion had originated behind this appliance. The investigators noted that the stove had been moved away from its original position before the fire. They saw that the burners and stove top had both been removed from the appliance before this event. The investigators closely examined the gas-pressure regulator on the stove and noted that it had fresh tool marks on it. They also saw that the gas-delivery shutoff valve had been removed from the appliance.

The investigator now knew that this appliance had been deliberately tampered with. The blast damage to this structure was mostly at the ceiling and roof levels and appeared consistent with the detonation of natural gas. Natural gas is lighter than air, and any explosions due to the leaking of natural gas tend to damage structures in high areas. They also tend to take the roof off buildings, as occurred in this case. The LASD Arson-Explosives Detail had dealt with a dozen or more natural gas explosions in the past, and the damage to this building was consistent with that type of explosion. However, in almost every past case, the cause of the natural-gas leak had been accidental in nature. In this case, it was evident that someone had manipulated the gas appliance, which in turn caused the gas to leak. The gas leak appeared deliberate. At this point, the investigators were still trying to figure out the source of ignition. They searched the crime scene carefully.

One result of the crime-scene search was a bit surprising. The investigators opened the stove/range and found that the interior had been stuffed with pages from a newspaper. The dates on the paper suggested that this had occurred within recent days. Det. Mike Digby, one of the sheriff's department's investigators on scene, scoured the kitchen area for any source of ignition. Since it was a vacant apartment, there was not the normal household supplies and clutter to deal with. One of the upper cabinets was ajar, and Digby located a decorative candle, which appeared to have been lit at the time of the fire/explosion. This candle had been placed in an area in the upper part of the kitchen, and suggested that whoever had placed this item there had some knowledge of volatile gasses and that natural gas would rise when released.

After they completed their scene investigation, the investigators formed the opinion that the incident was intentional and that someone had deliberately arranged this gas appliance to explode and catch fire. They believed that an unknown suspect had opened pages to a newspaper and stuffed them in the oven. That same suspect had then attempted to remove the pressure-regulator valve on the stove/range, and when that failed, finally removed the inline gas shutoff valve, which led to the apartment slowly filling with natural gas. The investigators theorized that either the intentionally placed candle, or some other flame or spark, ignited the natural gas and caused the explosion and fire. The act was deemed an arson attack, with the use of a very unique incendiary device.

Meanwhile, the Alhambra police detectives were doing their own good work. Within an hour of the explosion, a neighbor approached the police and pointed to a young man who was watching the scene. The neighbor said that the man was the same tenant who had recently been evicted from the vacant apartment. The neighbor had seen that same man enter the apartment building an hour prior to the explosion. This was the same person whom other neighbors had described as being irate and had earlier threatened to "blow up" the building. The Alhambra cops contacted the man, whose name was Kermit Kyle. He was later interviewed and eventually arrested for this event.

Kermit Kyle and his girlfriend, Darlene Nevarez, had lived in the vacant apartment up until they were evicted just a few days prior to this explosion. Kyle had been upset with the manager and had gotten into a dispute with him. Kyle was soon evicted but prior to leaving swore in front of more than one witness that he would blow up the building. More than one witness saw Kyle and his girlfriend enter the building in the days after they had been evicted. At least one witness confirmed that Kyle had entered the burned building just an hour prior to the explosion. He had either stayed at the scene to watch the explosion or had returned shortly after it occurred.

Shortly after he was arrested, sheriff's department's detectives joined Alhambra police officers as they drove to a nearby home where Kyle was staying with relatives. They had a warrant to search the home, looking for any evidence linking Kyle and Darlene Nevarez to the crime scene. They were a bit surprised to find a large amount of firefighting uniforms and equipment at the home. They learned that Kyle was a seasonal firefighter who worked part time for the California Department of Forestry fighting wild-land fires. This may have explained his knowledge of volatile gasses.

Eventually both Kyle and his girlfriend, Darlene, were charged with attempted murder, arson, and the use of an incendiary device. The lawyers got involved, and everyone settled in for what would probably be a long, drawn-out court battle over the source of ignition.

After filing the case, lead detective Rich Edwards met with the prosecuting attorney Marion Thompson. DDA Thompson was an aggressive prosecutor who had made a name for herself prosecuting Colombian drug lords and Mexican Cartel members on major narcotics violations. She consulted with the experts in the field and took the suggestion of Edwards to hire an outside fire and explosion expert to test the theory of the investigators. The District Attorney's Office brought in Dr. John DeHaan, an internationally recognized fire scientist, to review the detective's work on the case.

Dr. DeHaan reviewed the case file and then conducted his own calculations and analysis regarding natural-gas explosions. DeHaan noted that the natural-gas supply had been tampered with and determined that, in the given circumstances, it would have taken approximately forty-five minutes for the apartment to fill with natural gas and reach an explosive level. This coincided with the time frame that witnesses had established by placing Kyle at the scene.

DeHaan concluded that the explosive levels of gas and air were ignited by some unknown, outside flame source. He theorized that it was possible that the gasses had migrated into another room and may have been ignited by a furnace. Either way, whether ignited by the candle or some other flame source, the gasses were purposely introduced into the structure by the illegal act of Kermit Kyle tampering with the gas system.

DDA Thompson filed several major charges against Kyle and his girlfriend. Eventually, Darlene Nevarez pled guilty and admitted her role in preparing the home for a large fire. She was sentenced to three years of felony probation. Shortly after her conviction, Kyle saw the writing on the wall and also pled guilty to arson of an occupied structure and several other charges. He admitted that he had been upset with being forcibly evicted from the building. In May of 2000, Kermit Kyle was sentenced to twelve years in state prison for blowing up and burning the apartment building.

**Author's note:** Photos and a very brief synopsis of this crime scene appear in *Kirk's Fire Investigation*, Seventh Edition (2012), by John DeHaan (pp. 491–493).

### Investigator's Profile

This case was a very short and straightforward investigation. It was easy to find the suspect since he had remained at the scene of the event. He was linked to the scene by eyewitnesses and the fact that he had been the tenant of the unit just prior to this event. Lastly, he had voiced his intent to several witnesses to "blow up" the building. It is doubtful that even he expected the dramatic results that occurred. Kyle was extremely lucky that no one died in this explosion and fire.

The fire scene was the tricky part of this investigation. In truth, most explosions like this are accidental events. A cursory investigation or one done by inexperienced detectives may not have found the evidence that proved the event was intentional. In this case the handling agency, Alhambra Police Department, knew that this was a complex case, and they wisely brought in a much larger agency that had highly experienced arson-explosives investigators. This was the crux of the case.

Kermit Kyle was a very unhappy tenant and acted out in an open and dangerous manner. The fact that he was a firefighter, even part time, showed that he had a depth of knowledge of fires and explosions that greatly exceeded the common citizen. Since his fire was a clear act of revenge and spite, he is classified as a **goal-directed arsonist**.

*The following professionals worked on this case: Det. Rich Edwards, Sgt. Greg Collins, Det. Mike Digby, Inv. John Kabala, and DDA Marion Thompson. Dr. John DeHaan was retained as an expert witness for the prosecution.*

## MARIJUANA ARSON SERIES WEST HOLLYWOOD AND BEVERLY HILLS, CA, 2009–2012

*This case comes from the author's own case files.*

### The Sunset Super Shop

In December of 2004, Andrew Kramer pulled a permit through the City of West Hollywood to open a medical-marijuana dispensary. In order to open this business, he needed to give the city the address of a legitimate commercial site. This was not an easy task as the city only wanted to have a total of three or maybe four marijuana dispensaries. Because the city had several concerns about drug trafficking, violence, and the like, any marijuana dispensary had to be at least so many feet from a school, day care, park, et cetera. A good deal of thought and planning went into the selection of the proper site. Kramer researched the area and found a likely storefront at 8921 Sunset Boulevard, in the same block as the famous Whiskey a Go-Go club. Next to the shop was an Asian nail salon called Melody Nails, and next to that was a gypsy psychic shop. Highlighting this historic area was the world-famous Hustler store directly across the street.

The building selected by Kramer was owned by a man named George Lanning. Lanning, along with his wife, Nansee, were longtime real-estate speculators and investors, who had made loads of money from past property deals. They struck up a rental agreement with Andrew Kramer, and the two sides started on a mutually profitable business deal. Kramer called his store the Sunset Super Shop. He immediately began to advertise it in the underground newspapers and on business cards and flyers throughout the area

Kramer was no dummy and was not a novice in the marijuana game. His sister had been involved in marijuana dispensaries in the past, and Andrew himself had been dealing for years in the less legal side of the pot business. By this stage of the game, Andrew Kramer had tons and tons of connections between growers, brokers, and distributors in the marijuana trade. With this license from the City of West Hollywood, he became legitimate overnight and was able to sell marijuana fully legally.

The City of West Hollywood had no problems whatsoever with issuing Kramer a business license. He was a well-known person in the marijuana industry, and his name had been bandied about for years as an expert in medical marijuana. He had, in fact, done significant research over the years on how to open up and run a medical-marijuana dispensary (clinic) in a legitimate fashion. Kramer had been involved, either on paper or behind the scenes, in the opening of a dozen dispensaries in Los Angeles, the San Fernando Valley, Marina Del Rey, the San Gabriel Valley, Long Beach, and now into West Hollywood.

Kramer had a smooth presentation for skeptical city council members who met and voted on these dispensaries, and he had a fairly clean and neat business appearance. He was no dummy. He grew up in nearby Beverly Hills, had a spotless criminal record, and had been a school teacher in the distant past. His family appeared to have significant finances, and his mother owned some very expensive properties.

Andrew Kramer also had a very successful strategy when dealing with city council members of the various cities he had met with. He knew that he needed a majority of any council to carry a vote, and most city councils had five voting members. As such, Kramer used a time-tested tactic on three of the members. He bribed them. In most cases, he, through some sort of intermediary, usually an attorney, gave a $5,000 bribe to at least three of the council members, thereby carrying the vote. We didn't know this in 2005, but by 2012 we had gotten information from several of his partners that Kramer routinely used bribes for all sorts of favors. Kramer himself confirmed the city council bribes to us in front of his criminal-defense attorneys and the district attorney.

While he never admitted to bribing the West Hollywood City Council members back in 2005, Kramer made it well known that he was close friends with several of the council members, their legal counsel, and even the LASD's commander in the area. Besides those powerful contacts, Kramer seemed to have very close ties to the local newspaper in West Hollywood, the *Patch*.

### The DEA

Even though marijuana dispensaries had become legal in California, and clinics or shops began to appear in many cities, the federal government still considered marijuana an illegal drug. Politics aside, the confusing state of marijuana left cops, particularly narcotics detectives, confused, and it kept the marijuana attorneys ecstatic because of all the litigation that was occurring. Cities had no idea what was legal or how to issue licenses and to regulate this burgeoning industry. Pot shops were springing up everywhere, and many of them were not licensed. To complicate matters more, the marijuana shops gave themselves any number of names to appear legitimate, including dispensary, collective, pharmacy, care center, caregiver, and clinic.

To the feds, however, it was quite simple. Growing and selling marijuana was illegal. Medical marijuana was not recognized as a legal remedy by the US government, and the dispensaries were clearly illegal criminal enterprises. Thus, the local Drug Enforcement Administration (DEA) had a unit called Group Two, which had the primary responsibility of enforcing marijuana-trafficking laws. Even the hard asses within the DEA didn't want to waste their time dealing with small dispensaries, which appeared to be operating within California law. The feds had received tons of tips and other intelligence to convince them that several dispensary owners in California were actually engaged in all-out drug trafficking and moving hundreds of pounds of the high-quality weed under the guise of "medical marijuana."

One guy who came to their attention almost immediately was Andrew Kramer. By 2005, the DEA in Los Angeles was convinced that Andrew Kramer was running one of the largest distribution networks of high-quality marijuana that they had ever identified. They began to look very carefully at him.

### The Falling-Out

The building owner, George Lanning, and his adult son, Justin, had a friendly and lucrative relationship with Andrew Kramer. He had a thriving business, appeared to make a lot of money, and always paid the Lannings in a timely manner. From 2005 to 2007, the Lannings and Kramer got along quite well. George Lanning began watching how Kramer did business. George soon believed that he, too, could make a pile of money in the "legitimate" marijuana business. He began to study and take notes of how things were done.

The one thing that George Lanning did notice was that any number of marijuana growers showed up unannounced to the Sunset Super Shop to sell their high-grade product to Kramer. Kramer bought everything that was brought in. The Lannings noticed that Kramer bought many pounds at a time, and they couldn't believe that he could legally sell that much pot, one-eighth of an ounce at a time, out the front door. They were wondering if Kramer was actually involved in legitimate transactions.

In 2007, Kramer and the Lannings received a rude surprise. The DEA had gotten good information that Andrew Kramer was indeed buying and selling excessive amounts of marijuana through the Sunset Super Shop. One day they arrived *en masse* and served a search warrant on the business. During that raid, the DEA seized Kramer's computers, phones, records, and a few hundred thousand dollars in cash. They also seized over thirty pounds of high-grade weed worth easily over $150,000. He was in violation of federal laws and very probably in violation of the state's extremely liberal marijuana laws.

The DEA had a clever little tactic they used on guys like Kramer, whom they had dubbed as "potrepreneurs." They had identified several guys in the dispensary business who were making millions of dollars in profits from running businesses they called "nonprofits." The DEA was well aware that even federal juries might sympathize with "marijuana caregivers" and would excuse them for making a bit of profit off the deal. As such, even the DEA was reluctant to arrest these folks for their obvious drug-dealing activities. But, like in the Al Capone case eighty years before, the DEA knew they could impact these guys with federal financial statutes.

At the start of the dispensary craze, the feds just patiently waited until the potrepreneurs deposited their vast profits in a bank. They then swooped in and seized the cash, and then charged the pot dealers with any number of money-laundering, banking, or tax-code violations. In response to this aggressive tactic, the pot dealers now had to find ways to hide all of these monies from the feds. This made them very vulnerable to robbery and theft as they usually were forced to keep large sums of cash around. Andrew Kramer was no different. Anyone who knew him or did business with him was well aware that he always had upward of $200,000 in cash on him or in the safe upstairs in his office. He needed it to buy whatever weed walked in the back door from the growers who flocked to him. He also had no legal way to put it into a bank.

After the first raid, and then a few subsequent raids, the feds were able to seize more than $2 million in cash from Andrew Kramer. His response was to just shrug. He never even asked for it back through his various high-powered attorneys. Everyone was beginning to wonder just how much money this guy had. We later learned the extent of Kramer's brilliance. His own employees told how he had devised a way to "launder" his cash. He bought several portable ATM machines and placed them in the lobbies of any dispensary he was associated with, thereby laundering the money and receiving the transaction fees from the ATM withdrawals. This money he could later bank in a legitimate fashion.

While the 2007 raid and seizure didn't seem to even remotely affect Kramer, it had a profound effect on the Lannings. George, the owner of the building, was contacted by DEA investigators and advised that Kramer was clearly running a criminal enterprise, and if George allowed him to do that, he risked having his entire building (worth several million dollars) seized under federal-asset forfeiture rules. So, while Andrew Kramer merely called his lawyers and accepted the losses of cash and drugs to the feds as a cost of doing business, George Lanning freaked out at the prospect of losing his building.

Shortly after the federal narcs left the scene, George and Justin Lanning had a meeting with Andrew Kramer and asked him to close the shop. They were scared! A calm Kramer came up with an alternative idea. He offered to buy the building from the Lannings. They tentatively agreed to a sale, and Andrew Kramer soon came up with $1 million in cash to place into escrow as a partial payment. Several months later George Lanning began to get worried about the legality of it all and backed out of the sale. Kramer demanded his escrow money back immediately, but George Lanning was unable to pay it. Kramer came up with an alternative plan. He said he would sell the shop and its license to the Lannings, and they could run it as they see fit. He would allow them to pay back his monies piecemeal and even offered to stay on as a hired consultant to ensure that the shop continued to make money. For a fee of $40,000 a month, Kramer was to be a consultant to the Lannings and show them how to make much more money than that. They all agreed to this deal.

Several months into this deal, the Lannings felt that they had learned the tricks of the marijuana trade and decided that Kramer's fees were too much of an expense. They had paid Kramer back most of his money and wanted to terminate his services. When they told Kramer their plan, he refused, saying that he would stay on. George and Justin Lanning responded by stopping all payments to Kramer. Kramer responded in an unexpected and intimidating manner. In July of 2008, he showed up at the shop with several of his "security guards." By security guards, I mean that Kramer had hired an entourage of several large black ex-convicts and street gang members as his personal security force.

The crew, while unarmed as they were ex-cons, was extremely intimidating to anyone in the business. The Lannings were not impressed by the pale, skinny, nonthreatening Andrew Kramer, but the hardened, muscular, and mean-looking ex-cons certainly got their attention. Kramer forced them out of their own business. Later, sheriff's deputies from the West Hollywood Station were called to keep the peace and couldn't figure out what two soft-looking white businessmen were doing among a group of muscle-bound black ex-convicts.

Kramer and George Lanning then did what all businessmen do with a dispute. They took it to civil court. The Lannings opened up a civil suit against Andrew Kramer in late 2008. The court ruled in their favor in the spring of 2009 and ordered Kramer out of the Sunset Super Shop and to pay monies back to the Lannings. Kramer responded in a very sneaky manner. Kramer was forced out of the Sunset Super Shop, so being an expert in the dispensary business, he knew that the only thing of value was the license for the shop, not the shop itself. He went to the City of West Hollywood (who knew nothing of the dispute and civil court case) and told them he was closing the Sunset Super Shop and transferring the license to his new dispensary on Santa Monica Boulevard, known as Zen Healing. Because Kramer was a legitimate licensee, the city had no problems with the transfer. It would take George Lanning months before he realized that he was operating a dispensary (Sunset Super Shop) without a license.

Kramer refused to pay the Lannings their money, and they went back to court and got an order on August 4, 2009, for Kramer to pay. On August 5, Justin Lanning's car was firebombed outside of the family home in nearby Beverly Hills. Justin told the Beverly Hills Police Department (BHPD) that he suspected Kramer for this attack due to the business dispute. The police could never find a suspect. Three years later this firebombing would be linked to another two dozen attacks connected to Andrew Kramer. We would eventually discover that this connection between civil court hearings for the Lannings and Kramer and fire bombings and other attacks would follow a very peculiar pattern.

Andrew Kramer had yet another sneaky trick up his sleeve. Through his close friends on the West Hollywood (known locally as WeHo) City Council, he informed them that George and Justin Lanning were running an unlicensed marijuana dispensary as the license had been transferred to Kramer's new shop. The City of WeHo immediately served notice to George Lanning that he was to cease his dispensary operations. It was only then that Lanning realized he had been snookered by Kramer. In his own litigious fashion, Lanning went back to civil court but continued to operate his business. Meanwhile, WeHo officials informed the WeHo Sheriff's Station that the Sunset Super Shop was operating illegally. Soon, George Lanning was considered a bit of an outlaw by both the city and its LASD substation.

Like many citizens, George Lanning also had his own family issues. He and his wife were semi separated. Nansee lived in the family home with Justin in Beverly Hills, just blocks away, while George lived with his adult daughter in an apartment above the Sunset Super Shop. The daughter had a series of mental-health and drug-related issues and was a constant source of attention by the local law enforcement. Her erratic behavior caused the sheriff's deputies to respond several times to the Sunset Super Shop for any number of wild and crazy accusations. She had accused family members of theft, sexual abuse, and physical abuse. All of these accusations were soon recanted by the troubled young woman, and no charges were ever filed or even considered.

Deputies soon tired of responding to disturbances at the Sunset Super Shop. City council members, probably at the latent prodding of Andrew Kramer, began to suspect George Lanning of all sorts of crime. He and the city soon engaged in a very bitter and protracted legal fight over the shop, which the city now considered a nuisance. Even the local newspaper, with very suspicious ties to Andrew Kramer, began hinting that the

Sunset Super Shop was a rogue operation not in keeping with the other legitimate dispensaries in the city. Lanning began to hunker down behind his attorneys as he was soon attacked from all corners.

### Marijuana Mayhem

While this seemingly petty squabble between Kramer and the Lannings was going on, something much larger and more sinister had been playing out for a couple of years in Southern California. Law enforcement and the local media began noticing an increasing volume of violence surrounding the marijuana dispensaries in the Los Angeles basin. Nobody really knew how many shops actually existed, but at one point it was believed that an estimated four to five hundred dispensaries were doing business in Los Angeles. Records would show that only about a third of those were actually licensed to operate, with the remainder being rogue operations.

The over strapped cops from several cities were unable to keep up with the laws, the licenses, and the rules regarding these dispensaries and soon basically gave up trying to regulate them. They quickly lost count of all the robberies, burglaries, and assaults that were occurring in and around these shops. Small cities like West Hollywood were aggressively monitoring their dispensaries and seemed to have much less violence, at least at first. However, the list of mayhem was growing.

On January 30, 2008, two black gang members armed with a pistol and a shotgun did a "takeover robbery" of a pot clinic in Studio City, just five miles from Hollywood. The robbers stole cash and high-grade weed. This robbery was indicative of dozens of similar robberies and some late-night burglaries of medical-marijuana clinics spread throughout the city of Los Angeles. Shops in the San Fernando Valley, Hollywood, the Marina area, Mid-City, and West Los Angeles were all targeted for the large amounts of cash they kept on hand and the very valuable weed that was stockpiled in the back rooms. The robbers fit virtually every description from black and Hispanic street gang members to Armenian, Russian, and even Asian thugs.

Within just a year, most pot shops had learned to build a sally-port system that could lock in any would-be robbers if they failed to pass the hidden metal detectors. All shops had numerous large security guards, high-quality camera systems and alarm and panic buttons. Still, the robberies and burglaries continued throughout Southern California.

On October 26, 2010, gunshots rang out inside an apartment on King's Road, in West Hollywood. Responding sheriff's deputies found three dead men in the apartment along with a quantity of high-grade marijuana and packaging materials. Sheriff's detectives, utilizing state-of-the-art license-plate-reader technology, identified a vehicle that had been parked near the murder scene. Two days later they located the vehicle twenty miles away near the Los Angeles Harbor, by tracking it through digital license-plate readers. Inside the car they found a thirty-one-year-old Korean American man named Harold Young Park, who fit the description of the shooter.

Park was arrested and found to be in possession of three pounds of stolen weed. He admitted that he had gone to the apartment to buy five pounds of the weed and got into an argument with the three sellers. At that point Park admitted that he decided to rip them off, and he then gunned the trio down. Park knew the three and had conducted past marijuana business with the men, who were buying large quantities of pot from West Hollywood's dispensaries and reselling them on the street at a substantial mark up.

Park was subsequently charged with robbery and murder in a case of a drug deal gone sideways. Two years after this triple murder, I learned from one of the informants in this case that

Harold Park had originally been introduced to the three bulk-marijuana dealers by none other than Andrew Kramer. While Kramer had nothing to do with the deal gone bad, he had at some point connected the two parties together. On September 29, 2014, Park was convicted of burglary, robbery, and three counts of murder. Two months later a judge sentenced Harold Park to three life sentences in prison.

In response to this triple murder, just a few days after Park's arrest, Los Angeles sheriff Lee Baca, a very liberal law-enforcement officer who had been extremely tolerant of the use of "medical marijuana," finally conceded in public that "criminal enterprises are buying and reselling pot purchased at local dispensaries." Despite the sheriff's admission, the code-compliance manager of West Hollywood, Jeffrey Aubel, firmly stated to the media, "We are happy with the way the four clinics are legally operating in the city [West Hollywood]." Aubel was not referring to the fifth, unauthorized clinic—George Lanning's Sunset Super Shop.

The WeHo code-compliance manager may have been happy, but by 2010 the gang, narcotics, and major crimes teams from the LASD and LAPD were becoming very concerned that these crimes associated with the dispensaries were growing more organized and sophisticated. Several seminars, meetings, and conferences were set up among the local law-enforcement agencies to try to get a handle on the emerging problem of violence associated with the dispensaries.

A dramatic incident occurred in November of 2011, when three young black gang members brandishing handguns burst into a dispensary in West Hollywood called the Farmacy. The males tied up the owners, ransacked the location, and left with tens of thousands of dollars in cash and several pounds of high-grade pot. The suspects also took the owners' cell phones with them. During the ordeal, one of the owners noticed that one of the robbers was on a cell phone at the time and appeared to be taking orders from someone on the other end of the call. The person on the cell phone seemed to be directing the young trio on where to look for cash and hidden pot. The robbers, who were very young gang members, seemed almost like first-time offenders as they stumbled through the robbery.

Their escape was short lived as sheriff's detectives soon began "pinging" the stolen cell phones, and within the hour had the robbers tracked down to the desert region, fifty miles north of Los Angeles. Within three hours the robbers were located, arrested, and booked into jail. Shortly thereafter, the three were sent off to state prison for several years each. We would later come to realize that the Farmacy was located directly across the street from Andrew Kramer's dispensary known as Zen Healing. We came to believe that Kramer had possibly arranged for this robbery of his neighbors.

Another interesting attack occurred in early 2009. A marijuana shop on Pico Boulevard, known as Shiva's Garden, was attacked by two Armenian gunmen in an attempted robbery. The owner, a young guy named Bryan Lalezari from Beverly Hills, armed himself and chased the two robbers out the door and down the street, firing rounds at them. LAPD would later count Lalezari as a victim and declined to file charges against him. It was learned several months later that Lalezari was a close friend and confidante of Andrew Kramer. Kramer had help set him up in the marijuana-dispensary business. By this time Andrew Kramer's name had come up numerous times in some really shady events.

By early 2010, the local arson units would join the fray as a disconcerting number of suspicious fires were now routinely springing up in marijuana shops. Between 2010 and 2012, pot shops in Marina Del Rey, Long Beach, Orange County, the San Fernando Valley, San Diego, the Riverside area, and Hollywood had all been attacked by arsonists. Examination of security footage from over twenty marijuana-shop fires showed that almost all of the suspects appeared to be black street gang members.

Soon pot-shop arson attacks by black gang members spread to Northern California and Denver, Colorado. These attacks were markedly different from the robberies and burglaries. In those earlier crimes, cash and valuable dope was taken from the dispensaries. In almost all of these arson attacks, there was no clear attempt to steal cash or pot. The places were simply torched in a very public manner. Insurance-fraud schemes were quickly ruled out. Veteran arson detectives could only assume one of two possibilities with these torch jobs. They believed that it was possible that an organized black gang was conducting extortion of the pot-shop owners, or a second scenario was that a pot-shop owner was attempting to rid himself of the competition. Either way, the arsons, robberies, and burglaries continued to occur on a weekly basis. This was getting out of hand.

One such place that was torched was a brand new dispensary in the city of Rosemead, fifteen miles east of downtown Los Angeles. On February 27, 2010, the entire front of the store burst into flames in the middle of the night. Responding sheriff's deputies found a melted gasoline can on fire in a planter outside of the front door. Detectives from the sheriff's department's Arson-Explosives Detail (my unit) responded and were able to recover security-camera video of the event. The footage showed two males wearing dark hooded jackets and skeleton masks pouring gasoline into the mail slot of the business. A few minutes later, one of the men ignited the gas, which caused a violent vapor explosion. The fireball briefly engulfed the arsonist, but he was seen brushing off fire and running from the scene.

Like all of the other arson attacks, the suspects in this case made no attempt at all to enter the building and steal money or the valuable marijuana. Two years after this incident in

Rosemead, Beverly Hills detective George Elwell and I would speak to a person who was Andrew Kramer's director of security. That man would confirm that Andrew Kramer had ordered the torching of that pot shop in Rosemead that night.

Other confidantes of Kramer confirmed that he had tried to act as an "advisor/consultant" to the shop's owner, and when his services were turned down, he ordered the arson attack. The owner of the shop had no idea at all that Kramer had been behind the torch job. Another place that suffered a suspicious fire was familiar to investigators: Farmacy, the shop across the street from Kramer's business, which had been robbed by three gunmen and had a suspicious fire just three months after the robbery. This shop was Andrew Kramer's closest competition.

### The Conspiracy—Yaron Bassa and Russian Mike

By early 2010, the feud between the Lannings and Kramer had been going on for nearly a year. During that time George Lanning continued to do business in the Sunset Super Shop, and Andrew Kramer continued to run Zen Healing just ten blocks away. Kramer also kept his hands involved in several other shops as a consultant. Meanwhile, their civil case was progressing in a nearby Beverly Hills courthouse. In April of 2010, a trial conference was scheduled between the parties. In the two weeks prior to that hearing, a meeting took place in Andrew Kramer's office above his Zen Healing shop. The meeting was attended by a close friend of Kramer's known as Yaron Bassa and a street thug known as "Russian Mike."

Bassa knew Kramer from Beverly Hills and had grown up in a wealthy Israeli family. He had become addicted to drugs and had dropped out of school and gotten into a lot of trouble. He was involved in crime and drug sales on the street and soon was convicted of several felonies, sending him to prison. In 2010 he was out of prison for a few months and reconnected with Kramer. Kramer was extremely wealthy and successful in the pot business, and he was also known as very generous to his friends. He helped Bassa out and got him involved in brokering some deals with marijuana growers.

At one point Kramer approached Bassa and told him about his dispute with the Lanning family, whom Bassa also knew from Beverly Hills High School. Kramer offered Bassa money to put the Sunset Super Shop out of business by vandalism or fire or something similar. He offered Bassa $5,000 to smash the windows out of the dispensary. Bassa declined the offer but introduced Kramer to a real sketchy guy who was known for extreme violence on the street. He was a white Russian kid, who was a member of a black Crip street gang. His name was Russian Mike. Russian Mike met with Kramer and Bassa and accepted $5,000 to vandalize the Sunset Super Shop. Kramer also asked Russian Mike if he could beat up George Lanning or make him disappear. Kramer also mentioned that there would be extra money if the shop was somehow firebombed.

On April 18, 2010, a few days after the civil court hearing, the front windows of the Sunset Super Shop were smashed by a rock. Two males were seen on surveillance video attacking the business. Russian Mike later claimed to have committed this attack in fulfillment of his agreement with Andrew Kramer. A few days later, George Lanning was sleeping in his room above the Sunset Super Shop when a neighbor alerted him to a small fire on his roof. He ran outside and saw a very small fire, which he extinguished from the ground with a hose. He assumed it was from an ember from someone's fireplace. He didn't report this incident for nearly three years, at which time Det. George Elwell and I climbed the roof and found physical evidence to prove that the fire was, in fact, a Molotov cocktail firebomb. This device was later attributed to the paid attack by Russian Mike.

Russian Mike was truly one of the most opportunistic and treacherous characters in this long saga. He was the most experienced criminal in the bunch and as such knew how to profit from both sides of a dispute. He eventually got a large amount of money from Andrew Kramer despite his attacks being fairly poor in quality. Kramer wasn't even sure that Russian Mike had committed the attacks because there was very little evidence. Still, Kramer was intimidated by Russian Mike and paid him his money. He also asked Russian Mike if he could kidnap George Lanning and take him up the mountains and either make him disappear or scare the hell out of him. Russian Mike agreed to study the problem.

Nobody really knows what Russian Mike did or did not do, and if he actually attempted to firebomb the shop or not. Russian Mike and his weasel of an attorney would later claim that Russian Mike was a good guy trying to stop Kramer and save the life of the Lannings. We never believed Russian Mike a bit when we finally spoke to him some time later. However, what most parties agree on is that Russian Mike was a true opportunist and saw profit in this Lanning-Kramer feud.

Sometime in the spring of 2010, Russian Mike walked into the Sunset Super Shop and spoke to George Lanning. During that visit, Russian Mike informed George and Justin (whom Mike knew from high school) that Kramer wanted the shop torched and wanted the Lannings either killed or kidnapped. Russian Mike then asked George for some money and marijuana, and he assured them that he wouldn't do these things requested by Kramer. Eventually the Lannings supplied Russian Mike with cash and an amount of high-grade pot. Russian Mike, truly a professional criminal, was soon arrested for some other more serious crimes and was out of the picture, probably much to the relief of both the Lannings and Kramer.

Most cops I know would consider the acts of Russian Mike to be extortion, at the very least (he got money and drugs in exchange for not attacking the Lannings), and probably conspiracy in his role of attacking the shop in the first place.

In July of 2010 the civil case between the Lannings and Kramer continued with still more hearings and still more legal setbacks for Andrew Kramer. Mirroring these hearings were a continuing and escalating series of attacks. On July 28, two black men were seen on video throwing bricks through the windows of the Sunset Super Shop. A week later a similar attack broke the windows of the next-door nail salon.

### Kim Maybee, Bolo, and California

Every major case has a watershed event. That point where through luck, a mistake, or incredible police work the bad guys screw up or the case starts to come together. We got ours through a combination of all of these factors. On August 9, 2010, two black men were seen breaking windows and throwing Molotov cocktails into the Sunset Super Shop and the adjacent nail salon. This was a clear and deliberate attempt to destroy the building owned by George Lanning. I would become involved in this case a few days later.

At thirty minutes after midnight on August 9, George Lanning called the WeHo Sheriff's Station to report the firebombing. That night a detective named Greg Everett from the sheriff's department's Arson-Explosives Detail also responded to investigate the fire scene. He found two partially broken Snapple iced-tea bottles filled with gasoline at the scene. Each had a cloth wick made of a towel. One bottle had been placed on the sill of the broken window of the nail salon, and the second was found on the ground at the base of the door to the Sunset Super Shop. A small fire had occurred and was quickly extinguished by a nearby worker.

George Lanning showed Det. Everett a video of the event taken from security cameras. The video showed two older (forties) black men dressed in dark clothing. The pair walked past the location a couple times and then one of them broke the windows of the shop. Of note, one of the men walked with an odd, arm-swinging gait and appeared to have something physically wrong with his back or legs. That same suspect wore a dark hoodie with white lettering on the front.

A few minutes after breaking the windows, they returned and one of the pair, a bald man, placed the firebombs into the broken windows and ignited them. The devices flashed and got fire on the arsonist. The arsonist quickly ran from the scene, patting out the fire. Additional security footage from nearby stores showed the two suspects had emerged from a dark SUV that had been parked around the corner on a side street. The SUV was a blue Ford Explorer. An eyewitness said the same vehicle had driven by to examine the fire, and the witness supplied detectives with a partial license plate.

Det. Everett and the patrol deputies then did some good detective work. They walked the route of the suspects and examined the area where they had parked their car about fifty yards away. Next to where their vehicle had been parked, the cops found a black "do-rag" head cover. This item may have been dropped by one of the suspects. Everett collected that to be analyzed for DNA. He then gave the partial license plate to a West Hollywood traffic deputy who had access to a new system called ALPRS—the Automated License Plate Reader System.

This system was a great tool for investigators. Certain law enforcement agencies had patrol cars mounted with the ALPRS system, which automatically focused on and recorded license plates from vehicles as the patrol car drove down the street. It could capture tens of thousands of plates every week from moving or parked cars. The system would scan the plates and run them for "wants or warrants." The computer would automatically tell the patrol officer that a plate he had just scanned was a stolen vehicle or had a felony warrant or want associated with it.

For investigators this was pure magic. Witnesses often supplied partial or erroneous information when copying license plates. This system could take partial information and match it to a vehicle description and give investigators a list of vehicles that matched that description. A day or so later, the traffic deputy sifted through the ALPRS information and found that the partial plate matched a blue Ford Explorer that had frequently been stopped in the Hollywood/West Hollywood area. The vehicle was driven by a female name Kim Maybee.

## Kim Maybee

Most cops in the Hollywood area knew Kim Maybee. She tended to stand out a bit by her looks and her actions. Kim Maybee ended up being the key to this entire case. Her personal history was extremely colorful. Kim Maybee had grown up in Los Angeles and had been a superstar athlete in her youth. She had the build for it. Maybee was over six feet tall and weighed just under two hundred pounds. She had rippling muscles and not a whole lot of body fat. She had been one of the very first professional female boxers and had several fights under her belt.

All of that incredible size, strength, and athleticism was long gone, fading over twenty years ago when Maybee tried crack cocaine. She had been an addict ever since and had spent most of the last two decades in an out of jail and prison for an unbelievable amount of criminal arrests. During that same time, the very bright woman also had clerked for a lawyer, and through various stints in prison had become extremely well versed in criminal law.

Kim Maybee was a one-woman crime wave. By 2010 she had twenty-eight felony arrests with thirteen felony convictions, and multiple state prison sentences. A true scam artist as well, she had been booked under three different races and under twenty-eight different aliases. Despite being clearly black, she had conned jailers into booking her as Hispanic, black, and Filipino. Her criminal specialties included fraud, forgery, burglary, and narcotics sales, and in recent years she had graduated to the violent world of strong-arm robbery.

By the time her car had been located in the ALPRS system as being associated with this firebombing attack, Kim Maybee was already on her third level of felony probation and had an active warrant out for grand theft from a person by the LAPD. An LAPD detective later told us that she was suspected as a "knock-out" artist on the streets in dozens of physical robberies of tourists in the Hollywood area. Kim Maybee, completely strung out on crack cocaine, would run up to unsuspecting tourists and rip their purses off their arms. If any of them resisted at all, she would punch them in the head, invariably knocking them down or out. Even at forty years of age, and worn down by a life of prison and drugs, she still possessed some impressive punching skills.

One more thing that the WeHo deputies knew was that Kim Maybee, who always cut her hair very short to her scalp and wore dark, baggy clothing, looked very much like a man. She had been described as a man in several of her prior crimes.

On August 12, 2010, at about two in the morning, three nights after the firebombing attack on the Sunset Super Shop, sheriff's deputies saw a dark SUV speeding down a major street in West Hollywood. The deputies pulled it over and immediately recognized two hard-core looking convicts in the car. The driver was Kim Maybee, and her passenger was a heavily tattooed convict who also was a former boxer. Kim Maybee was high as a kite on cocaine, and the car was filled with burglary tools and what appeared to be items stolen during vehicle burglaries. Both persons were found to be on active probation and were arrested for possessing burglary tools and the probation violations.

Maybee was booked into the WeHo Sheriff's Station, and an astute training officer noticed that her car resembled the fire-bombing vehicle from three nights earlier. He rechecked the ALPRS system and found the partial plate number. He realized he had the right car. He had also seen video of the attack and noted that the "male" suspect, who had been walking oddly and wearing a dark hoodie with white lettering on it, was an exact match for Kim Maybee. The deputy had seen her walk after her arrest and had noted that due to back, neck, and leg injuries suffered during sports competition, she walked just like the suspect from the firebombing. Even better, when she was arrested this night, she was wearing the exact dark hoodie with the white lettering on it that had been seen in the firebombing video.

It was crystal clear that Kim Maybee was the "male" suspect seen in the firebombing video. The training officer called the Arson-Explosives Detail attempting to get a hold of Det. Everett, who was out of town. I was working the on-call duty and picked up the phone. Within a half hour I was heading to WeHo to fill in for Everett.

At this point I knew that something had been going on with the marijuana dispensaries around Hollywood. We knew of some ongoing attacks and were told they were being worked by a couple of detectives from the Major Crimes Bureau. Up until this arson attack, these events hadn't concerned my unit, the Arson-Explosives Detail. However, most of the guys in my unit were ex-narcs and knew very well the incredible amounts of cash involved in the marijuana business. When I interviewed Kim Maybee that night, I only knew of a few isolated fire bombings to dispensaries in other parts of the county and the most recent attack to the Sunset Super Shop. I assumed that all of these attacks had been committed by black gangs attempting to get a hold of the huge amounts of cash.

Before talking to Kim Maybee, I spoke to the passenger in her car that night. He admitted that he and Maybee were in Hollywood to "do a job." He didn't know what the job was, but because he was a good fighter Kim had asked him to come along as "muscle." While driving she told him about a wild scheme she was involved with. She said a man named "Bolo" was doing favors for a white guy. The white guy wanted the owner of a marijuana shop beat up and the shop burned down. Maybee had told her partner that she had helped burn the shop a few nights earlier, but that it had failed. She told him a rich white guy wanted the shop burned and would pay up to $25,000 after the job was completed. The passenger admitted that he was willing to beat up someone for money but was not at all interested in torching a building. He said they were stopped by the cops before they could do anything.

At four in the morning I walked into a cramped and smelly interview room in the rear of the WeHo jail. A jailer led a shuffling and half-awake Kim Maybee into the room and closed the door. I looked at her, having seen about fifty thousand other crackheads like her. She was dirty and disheveled, with bleary red eyes, and you could smell her rotting teeth from ten feet away. She had every appearance of the longtime crack addict that she was. I had no trouble making this assessment as I had worked the streets of Compton, Watts, and South Central Los Angeles for seven years during the height of the rock cocaine or crack epidemic. Kim Maybee was a crackhead. She was also big, muscular, and very tough looking. She easily could pass for a guy, even in the daylight. She had an odd, rolling gait with swinging arms that she told me was a result of several injuries. Later, everyone who saw the video of the firebombing would clearly be able to pick out Kim Maybee's unique gait.

Like all crack addicts, Maybee, while half-asleep, was in the mood to talk. She rambled incessantly and then drifted off to sleep. The audio recording of that interview has me waking up Maybee several times by rapping on the table. In between her crack-ramblings and snoring, Maybee actually was lucid for several minutes and gave some surprising revelations about the firebombing. After some initial denials, she admitted to her car being at the firebombing because she gave a ride to a guy named "California" to the scene. Maybee explained that she often works for a street thug named "Bolo." She described Bolo as a very large ex-convict and former "Rollin 60s Crip" gang member who was a major drug dealer on the street.

She said that she often did favors for Bolo in exchange for money or crack. In this case she said that Bolo had asked her to meet a man named "California" on a street corner and take him to the marijuana shop on Sunset. In exchange she was given gas money and several rocks of crack cocaine. Maybee did as she was told and met the man named California. She said she knew him from the street, and he was a drug addict and burglar. She said that California was also an ex-convict and was about fifty years old. When she picked up California, he asked her to take him to a gas station nearby where he went inside and bought two Snapples. She said he poured out the tea and then filled the bottles with gasoline. He then had her drive him to the Sunset Super Shop.

At this point Maybee's story became very self-serving. She described that California burned the shop but conveniently left her own role out of the story. She said she saw him come running around the corner while the burglar alarm was sounding. She said he had been wearing a black head scarf "do-rag," and that he dropped it somewhere. She said they both got into the SUV and drove past the front of the shop. At that point she said she saw the windows burning. Despite leaving her own role out, the story was an exact match to the video.

Maybee went on to tell me a fantastic story. A few weeks ago she was approached by Bolo to go with him to speak to some Armenians. She was to be the interpreter. They drove to a shop on Pico Boulevard. Kim Maybee went inside and spoke to the owner, a young guy she described as Armenian but was in fact Bryan Lalezari of Persian/Iranian descent. Kim and Bolo eventually were told by Lalezari that he wanted the Sunset Super Shop torched and the owners beaten up, or worse. He promised $25,000 for this job and said it was in retaliation for a shooting that happened at this shop previously (Lalezari had been involved in the running gunfight with two would-be robbers several months prior).

Bolo promised Lalezari that he would make this happen and then directed Kim Maybee to get the job done. On the night she and California drove to the shop for the firebombing, she was aware that Bolo was following them to monitor their activities.

This very confusing story didn't make a lot of sense to me since I didn't know the entire background of the Lanning-Kramer dispute or the fact that Lalezari was Kramer's closest confidante. I told Maybee that all of the dispensary attacks were done by black street gang members. Even in her drug-addled brain, the streetwise Maybee said, "Wake up, Detective; there's two rich white boys doing this." She explained in street terms that all of the attacks on marijuana dispensaries were being ordered by a rich white guy from Beverly Hills who was mad at another rich white guy. She said that blacks were being hired to do this to give it the appearance of random black-gang violence.

Kim Maybee was facing over twenty years in prison for all of her criminal charges, along with her horrible criminal record before this firebombing. She decided to fight these charges not in front of a jury but in front of a single judge in Beverly Hills Court. During Maybee's brief trial, DDA Angela Brunson had me testify and then play Kim Maybee's own admission. The video of the attack was shown, and the judge was easily convinced that the person onscreen with the funny walk was Kim Maybee. She was convicted after just a few short minutes' consideration by the judge.

Somehow, though, Kim Maybee had a bit of luck. For a peculiar and suspicious reason unknown to anyone but himself, a superior court judge set aside several of Kim Maybee's previous convictions just a few weeks prior to this trial. The DAs researched this odd ruling and found that the downtown court clerks had merely made an unfortunate paperwork error, but Maybee bragged to friends that she had dirt on the judge in that case. Either way, the Beverly Hills judge had to give Kim Maybee a much less severe sentence than what she deserved. He ended up giving her the maximum that he could give, which was fifteen years in state prison. Because of her previous serious criminal record, she had to do a minimum of 85 percent of her time, or over twelve years in prison, before she could be considered for parole.

### Enter Det. George Elwell, BHPD, a.k.a. Big George

I thought after Kim Maybee's conviction that my role in this case was ending, but it was just beginning. Immediately after Maybee's arrest, the Sunset Super Shop was vandalized again. Two weeks later, another property in WeHo owned by George Lanning was broken into and vandalized. Lanning owned a vacant home a few short blocks from the WeHo Sheriff's Station. The home was empty but going through rehabilitation to be a high-dollar rental property. A week after this attack, the Sunset Super Shop was again vandalized by a black male throwing rocks through the windows.

Just two weeks later, on September 24, 2010, two males were seen throwing firebombs onto the roof of the Sunset Super Shop. This last attack did very little damage, and an intact firebomb (Molotov cocktail) was recovered. During all of these attacks, George Lanning and his daughter were sleeping in the upstairs apartment. The firebombing assaults were clear attempts to murder.

The carnage continued into October. George Lanning's vacant house in WeHo was again vandalized and burglarized. Two nights later, the family home in Beverly Hills was attacked by fire. Unknown persons had poured gasoline along the edge of the home and set it on fire. The fire self-extinguished, and a gardener the next day noticed the smell of gasoline and the burned plant material. The Lannings did not report this until a later, more significant event.

In December of 2010, unknown suspects threw a rock through the front windows of the Lanning home in Beverly Hills. In January of 2011, the Sunset Super Shop was again vandalized with its signage being broken and splashed with paint. A week later, yet another significant attack by fire occurred. The vacant home George Lanning owned in WeHo was attacked by fire, with it being completely destroyed by gasoline-enhanced flames. This was the first major loss in this series, and caused the Lannings tremendous financial issues as the home had very little insurance coverage.

After this arson attack to the vacant home, we sent Sgt. Derek Yoshino of the Arson-Explosives Detail to the scene. He gathered his evidence and spoke to George Lanning. Lanning told him about all of the other incidents and how they were now occurring about once a week. Derek and I were old partners, and when he returned to our office, he was greatly bothered by the increasingly dangerous tempo of this case. The overall case had been assigned to another investigative unit, and they had made no progress. I told Derek about all the information I had learned six months earlier with the arrest of Maybee. We began to quietly put together all of the incidents.

On February 4–5, 2011, back-to-back incidents brought the case back to life. On the fourth, a black male was seen on video pouring gasoline into the mail slot at the Sunset Super Shop while George Lanning slept in the apartment above. The fire was very small and quickly burned out. The very next night, the Lanning home in Beverly Hills was attacked by fire, with the same male seen in security footage. This time the attack was much more serious in that the male and two others threw a rock through the front window of the home, followed by a one-gallon paint can filled with gasoline and a burning rag.

The fire did major damage to a custom music room within the very pricey home. During this attack, Justin Lanning and his mother, Nansee, were asleep in the house. These two most recent events were clear attempts to murder the Lanning family. This time I got called to the Lanning family home at the request of the BHPD. At that point, we learned of all the attacks in Beverly Hills and agreed to assist the BHPD on all of its fire scenes since it did not have an experienced arson-investigation unit.

We all agreed to a meeting at the WeHo Sheriff's Station in the spring of 2011. Before we could even meet, there was yet another arson attack on the Sunset Super Shop, where a male was seen on video pouring gasoline through the front door slot. Again, this occurred when people were sleeping above the shop, and again there was very little damage. We convened the meeting of the investigators, and the arson unit eventually took the case back from another LASD detective unit that hadn't done much on it. We immediately formed a pact with BHPD and started working the case hard. The rest of the case was a joint venture between the LASD's arson unit and the BHPD. The investigation was kept extremely covert.

BHPD Sgt. Rob Hernandez was a technical wiz and soon began building a computer program to chart all the cell phone calls in this case. Rob would be moved to a technical unit within a month, and the BHPD side of the case would be carried forward by Det. George Elwell. He would prove to be one of the hardest working detectives I had ever met. For our part, we (LASD Arson-Explosives Detail investigators) began a semi covert relationship with the BHPD. We were aware that the WeHo City Council was chummy with Andrew Kramer, so we wanted to hide all our activities from them. We began filtering all of our clues, leads, and cell phone information to Det. Elwell at BHPD. He began exploiting the cell phones and comparing them to the incidents. Soon I began a detailed time line of all the events surrounding the Sunset Super Shop and its owners, the Lanning family. Eventually we all would combine to unravel an incredibly intricate and sophisticated criminal conspiracy.

Meanwhile the attacks continued. In June of 2011, the Lanning family's cars were vandalized in front of their home. In July, a black male drove a stolen car into the front of the Sunset Super Shop and then fled on foot. Three nights later a black male drove a stolen car into the front of the Sunset Super Shop and fled on foot in an identical "car accident." Sadly, the same deputy took both reports and chalked them up to drunk drivers. One year later, a third stolen car was driven into the front of the shop with two black males fleeing on foot. It took over a year for these incidents to be discovered by investigators.

Worse things were happening than these "car accidents." Things were pretty quiet from June to October of 2011. On October 26, three black males came to the front of the Lanning home in Beverly Hills and sprayed the door with lighter fluid. They then placed a delay incendiary device at the base of the door, and several minutes later it functioned, causing a large fire and major damage to the front of the home, where three family members were sleeping.

By far the most sinister event to occur in all of this series happened on the night of January 30, 2012, at the Lanning family home in Beverly Hills. Nansee Lanning awakened in the middle of the night to a noise in her home. She got up to find five large black males wearing masks, standing in her home. One of them smashed her over her head with a steel pipe. Her son, Justin, came out to investigate the noise and saw his bloodied mother on the floor. The men grabbed him and prepared to tape him up and carry him away in a probable kidnapping or murder scheme. One of the men did not wear a mask, as he didn't seem to be worried about being identified. This caused the petrified Justin to believe that this man was here to kill him. Just as Justin was being dragged out the door, a houseguest came home and scared the intruders, causing them to drop Justin and flee. Justin Lanning barely escaped a horrible fate that night.

This failed event was certainly the scariest in the series, but it wasn't the last. Three months later two men were seen on video breaking into the rear of the Sunset Super Shop with a pair of bolt cutters and a gas can. They were scared away by George Lanning's guard dog before they could torch the place. Two nights after that, an alert BHPD patrol officer, sensitive to the many attacks on the Lanning residence in his city, found a lone black male parked on the street near the Lanning home. The male's name was Rene Johnson, and he had an empty plastic bottle that smelled like gasoline sitting on the floor of his car. He was identified and released. We later connected Rene Johnson to other attacks.

From 2009 to 2012, black street thugs committed a total of twenty-six attacks against the Lanning family at the Sunset Super Shop, their empty rental property in WeHo, or their family home in Beverly Hills. In almost every one of these attacks, video footage showed various black males, all of whom had the appearance of street people or gang members. These attacks included five different attempts to murder by fire, one attempt to kidnap, eleven arsons or attempts to commit arson, and a dozen felony vandalisms. The Lanning family was in dire danger.

### Untangling the Web of Conspiracy

By early 2010, some of the above events had yet to occur, but we were starting to figure out this conspiracy. The ineptitude of the previous investigators on the case put our investigation six to eight months behind schedule.

First things first, BHPD detective George Elwell, a.k.a. "Big George," and I decided to track down "Bolo" and "California," who had been involved in the Kim Maybee firebombing incident. We knew that to get to the top of any conspiracy, you had to start with the easiest street-level guys and work your way up. We decided to do it through a combination of cell phone records and interviews. The BHPD guys had started doing wonders with the cell records taken from Kim Maybee. This process quickly identified Bolo and California from the night of the fire. Within just a couple days we located both of them. We found Bolo, a.k.a. Grace Cox, in just a few hours via phone records. California, a.k.a. Jimmie Jones, took a couple days longer, but we soon located him.

After the arson attack, Bolo had been arrested on another charge and was sent to Wasco State Prison on a parole violation. California had also been arrested on another charge and had sat in the county jail for three months. By the time we began looking for him, he too had been transferred up to Wasco State Prison on a parole violation. Incredibly, both men were housed in the same dorm in state prison.

### "California," a.k.a. Jimmie Jones

California was a longtime drug addict, burglar, forger, and street criminal. He was nearing fifty years old at the time he was involved with Kim Maybee. He was a lifetime felon and had been sent to prison multiple times. Det. Elwell interviewed him in prison. We had also identified him via the security video at the Sunset Super Shop. He was clearly the bald-headed suspect along with Maybee. Several months later the crime lab through a DNA match would positively identify Jimmie "California" Jones as having worn that "do-rag" found at the crime scene. We owned him, and he knew it. When Det. Elwell spoke to him, Jones acknowledged his role but would not name Bolo as the guy who paid him to do the crimes. He knew Bolo for a long time and was petrified of him. California was facing up to twenty years in prison for the firebomb attack.

### "Bolo," a.k.a. Grace Cox

Bolo is one big and scary dude; just ask anyone who knows him. He had a long and active street gang history connecting him to murders, drug dealing, vehicle theft, and assault. He was in his forties and retired from street gangs, but he was still a very active criminal and hardened by several years on the street and several more spent in jails and prisons. Det. Elwell visited him too at Wasco State Prison, and off the record Bolo admitted that we had him in a corner. He wasn't worried about Maybee or Jimmie Jones snitching on him, but he knew his cell phone showed that he was near the Sunset Super Shop at the time of the firebombing.

Just as Kim Maybee had described, Bolo had followed her and California to the shop to insure the job was done. While Bolo never gave a full admission, he told us that he was open to make a deal someday if we ever filed charges. We let him stew in prison for several more months, and he was eventually released on parole. By late summer of 2012 we had built up a decent case against Grace "Bolo" Cox. We also learned that he was in violation of his probation, and we went out to pay him a visit to see if we could persuade him to cooperate.

On August 7, 2012, Big George and his BHPD team hit Bolo's mom's house on a probation search. Upon his release from jail, Bolo was required to give the probation officials his new address so that they could check up on him. The problem was that Bolo lied to the probation department and had never stayed at the home since his release from jail. Mom was livid after the SWAT team came through the door. She demanded that the probation department "violate him" and give him six months back in the joint just for the violation. Not only did she disown her son but she gave investigators phone numbers and clues to where he was likely staying and what kind of car he was driving.

It wouldn't take long to track him down. We picked him up a couple of days later, and he sat in county jail looking at a possible life sentence in prison for the firebombing attacks. Still, like the hardened convict he was, he refused to implicate anyone above him.

### "RJ," a.k.a. Rene Johnson

When we really started working hard on this case in the spring of 2011, we began developing information about a black guy known as "RJ." RJ's name popped up over and over during the case. He was a close confidante of some of the top guys in this group, and his phone number was closely associated with at least three arson events. He was also the guy who had been stopped outside the Lanning home with the gasoline container in his car. RJ claimed to have run out of gas. Prudently, the alert patrolman, after carefully checking the man out, filled out a field interview card. The suspicious man's name was Rene Johnson.

The reason we wanted RJ was that he was supposedly the man who had hired Bolo to burn the Sunset Super Shop. Phone records showed Bolo talking to a man named RJ around the time of the fire and later showed RJ speaking to one of Kramer's closest friends, Bryan Lalezari. RJ appeared to be the link between

Kramer and the black street thugs. We wanted to talk to him very badly.

RJ had an active warrant out for his arrest. It seems that two sheriff's deputies had noticed some suspicious activity in a park a few months back and had detained people in two different cars. RJ was one of them, and he was in the possession of a stack of phony marijuana prescriptions. He said that he had worked for Kramer and was carrying the cards as a normal part of his business. Other informants told us that RJ stole the cards to resell on the street. He was yet another lifelong criminal associated with Andrew Kramer.

In the other car was a real prize. The white male in that vehicle was a defense lawyer. His name was Kenneth Markman. Sheriff's department's officials already knew who Markman was. We will revisit Markman a bit later.

Det. Elwell began knocking on doors and looking for RJ. After showing up at a few places where RJ had lived, Elwell got a call from RJ demanding to know what we wanted. Det. Elwell explained a bit and then asked RJ to come meet with us at a neutral location. We wanted to talk about Andrew Kramer. RJ agreed to meet us several times, and each time he failed to show. On the phone RJ was adamant that he wasn't involved in any of these events, and he would never admit to them. He refused to talk about his relationship with Kramer and vowed that he would never go to jail for the firebombing.

RJ had an extensive criminal history with several arrests for narcotics and fraud. He was suspected in numerous thefts, burglaries, and fraudulent activity. Amazingly, he had never been to state prison. We hoped to change that.

### Kenneth Markman

Ken Markman is a forty-seven-year-old attorney with a lot of history. Markman's famous father is noted courtroom forensic psychiatrist and author Dr. Ronald Markman, who diagnosed many notorious criminals including Charles Manson and the Hillside Stranglers. This strong reputation did not get passed down to his son. Ken is a longtime documented substance abuser who had been kicked out of drug rehab at least once for cocaine use. His work record is equally shoddy. A mere search of attorney websites will find more than one serious complaint about his lack of ethics, alleged theft of monies, and the dispensing of poor legal advice. His law license had been suspended multiple times.

Besides these personal and professional issues, Ken Markman had some other serious problems. In late October of 2011, while working as a criminal defense attorney, he walked into the Criminal Courts Building in downtown Los Angeles to visit an incarcerated gang member client. Like all criminal defense attorneys, he was allowed access into the jail portions of the courthouse to interview his client, who was in an attorney room. However, there was no inmate in the room that day. Jail investigators had been tipped that Markman was an addict and was supplementing his income by smuggling narcotics into the jail.

Jail investigators searched him and found twenty-six balloons filled with heroin and methamphetamines, several needles, and several small bags of marijuana. He was arrested for transporting narcotics into the jail system. He was released on bail pending trial. One month later the troubled attorney was arrested again by a sheriff's officer at another courthouse when crack cocaine was discovered in his wallet.

We don't know for sure, but we suspect that Markman's detention with RJ was an attempt at some sort of drug deal in exchange for the stolen prescriptions. In March of 2013, Ken Markman was convicted and sentenced to a year in jail for smuggling drugs. His law license was suspended. A year later, in August of 2014, the California State Bar finally disbarred the fifty-year-old Markman. It seems that everyone associated with Kramer and the marijuana business was dirty.

### The DEA

The Los Angeles office of the DEA kept looking into the activities of Andrew Kramer. Their lead investigator was Special Agent Pat Kelly out of Group Two, the marijuana enforcement unit. SA Kelly advised us that Group Two was working on several tips that Kramer was now moving hundreds of pounds of high-grade marijuana across the country to New York, where it was sold at three to five times the amount of its California prices. Kramer was thought to have made millions of dollars in the past few years on illegal marijuana sales and trafficking.

The DEA was still actively chasing the heavyweights in the marijuana business, even with the reality that the drug was practically legal in this country. During their original raid on Kramer in 2007, they had seized large amounts of pot and cash. They did another raid a couple years later and seized even more dope and cash, along with his computer and cell phones. In early 2011 they had gotten wind that we (BHPD and LASD Arson-Explosives Detail) were attempting to link Andrew Kramer to several arson attacks. They met with us and agreed to work a joint investigation into Kramer and all his activities. To support our investigation, the DEA staged yet another raid on Andrew Kramer in March of 2011, this time hitting his shops and his home. They seized a bunch more marijuana and cash and several phones and some computers.

By this time we had heard a rumor that Kramer had hired an Israeli military guy to assist him in keeping his phones and computer secure. Whether this was true or not, we knew that Kramer compartmentalized his operations and routinely dumped his phones and got new ones on a regular basis. He assumed that the DEA was tracking his cell phones, so he constantly switched them. He also brought in an expert to "clean" the memory out of his computer hard drives on a weekly basis. The DEA told us that Andrew Kramer was one of the cleverest drug dealers they had ever seen.

The DEA in the past had attempted to access Kramer's computers and phones to see what information existed about illegal activities. The cleaning process Kramer used erased all incriminating information and frustrated the feds. This time, though, we caught a break. A young analyst from the DEA tried a new technique when accessing Kramer's computers after they were seized. He was aware that many people actually charge their cell phones on their computers. What most people did not know was that if you do that, the computer automatically "vampires" the information out of the cell phone, to include any call records or, even better, any text messages. This information is dumped into a hidden file on the computer hard drive and is seldom noticed. The DEA analyst soon confirmed that Andrew Kramer had finally made a huge mistake. He had indeed been charging his phones on his computer, and the hard drives now held hundreds of call records and thousands of text messages.

All of this information was soon forwarded to the BHPD to add into their ever-growing computer program of phone information. This information is what would bring Andrew Kramer's marijuana empire crashing to the ground.

### Anderson Byrd

Anderson Byrd was one of Andrew Kramer's inner circle, if there was such a thing. Byrd was a mid-forties, thickly built, muscular, clean-shaven, former black-street-gang member and ex-con who had somewhat gotten his life back on the right track. That is until early on the morning on June 26, 2012, when detectives from BHPD raided his home and found the ex-con sleeping with a loaded pistol just inches from his head.

The reason the detectives were there is because there had been a successful arson attack on the Lannings' vacant home at 370 San Vicente Boulevard, West Hollywood, in February of 2011. After the DEA seized Kramer's computer and were able to find his cell phone records of that night, they found that Kramer and Byrd had been communicating in a suspicious manner at exactly the same time as the attack on the vacant home. Kramer received several highly suspicious texts from Anderson Byrd's phone both before and minutes after that arson attack. The texts were somewhat coded with song names referring to "firemen" or "burning." We knew early in the case that Anderson Byrd was head of security at Kramer's Santa Monica Boulevard pot dispensary.

Like most drug dealers, Andrew Kramer was a racist. He did what many other white criminals do. He knew that white people were generally afraid of bulky, intimidating-looking black guys, so that's exactly who he hired as his personal security in his shop. To emphasize the point, he even made sure that all his security guards were ex-cons to get an even more intimidating presence. The funny part of this was that the black guys themselves were totally aware that they were being stereotyped solely on their appearance and didn't seem to mind as long as the money was good.

So, for the past several years, Anderson Byrd and his team of black, ex-con, thug-looking security guards had been hovering around Kramer's shop, intimidating potential rip-off artists and business rivals. They had also helped Kramer intimidate George Lanning out of his own shop.

The morning when Det. George Elwell spoke to Byrd at his home with his wife, kids, and grandchildren, and pointed out the possibility of a lengthy return to state prison on the gun charge alone, let alone the arson events we were aware he was involved in, the astute and experienced Byrd, like most veteran criminals, realized that it was time to make a deal with the devil. He agreed to come to the station later in the day and talk openly about Andrew Kramer, the pot biz, and all things arson. True to his word, Byrd showed up at BHPD at precisely the appointed time. Big George and I sat down and spoke to him candidly for about two hours.

Byrd was strong, in control, matter-of-fact, and poised. He spoke in the vernacular and cadence of most ex-cons who were trained in their actions and words by the animalistic world of the penitentiary. He spouted prison-like phrases such as "I do my own program" and "I keep to my own business," when we were well aware that he was an experienced and shrewd operator who likely missed nothing during the day-to-day activities of the dispensary. He was confident and appeared open and honest. But like most crooks, we knew he would only admit about 75 percent of what he was involved in.

Byrd told us that he had been employed originally by Andrew Kramer's sister. When Andrew took over the business several years ago, he retained Byrd and the other ex-cons as his security force. Byrd, who called Kramer "AK," was present nearly every day the shop was open and saw everything that went on.

He related that Andrew Kramer was a punk and had bad karma following him as he routinely treated people badly. He believed Kramer had some anger or psychiatric issues and that he was probably a drug user, other than marijuana. He said Kramer had a public face that showed him as a "medical provider," but in truth he hung out with a multitude of bad guys, convicts, and serious drug dealers.

Specifically, Byrd was well aware that Kramer had an ongoing dispute with the Lanning family over a failed deal with the marijuana shop on Sunset. At one point, Byrd was asked by Kramer to take the other security guards (all black ex-cons) and stand outside of Lanning's business and not let anyone in. Byrd told us that Kramer wanted him to intimidate the Lannings.

In 2011 Kramer was at the shop again and fuming openly about George Lanning. He abruptly approached Byrd and asked him if he could take care of a problem for him. He wanted Byrd to burn down Lanning's vacant home in West Hollywood. Both Kramer and Byrd passed by the home on a near daily basis on their way to work. The home was vacant and under construction. Kramer indicated that he wanted the place torched in an effort to intimidate or frighten Lanning into getting out of this business and leaving the Hollywood area.

Byrd told Kramer that he didn't do that sort of stuff and told him not to ask him anymore. At that point, Kramer recalled that there was another black guy who routinely came around the business to detail the cars. His name was Jonathon. Kramer asked Byrd if Jonathon would do this job, and Byrd told him to go ask himself. Byrd saw Kramer walk outside to speak with Jonathon.

Later that night, at about one thirty in the morning, Jonathon called Byrd and told him that the job was done—the house was burned. He asked Byrd to text Kramer with the information. Byrd immediately sent a text message to Kramer, in a crude code, indicating the fire had taken place.

The next day, there were follow-up text messages between Kramer and Byrd regarding the fire. Finally, later the following day, Kramer came up to Byrd with a white business envelope with a number written on it. He asked Byrd to hand deliver it to Jonathon, who was detailing a car behind Kramer's pot shop. Byrd recalled the number on the envelope was either $2,500 or $3,500. The envelope held what felt like a stack of money.

Jonathon took the money from Byrd without comment. A later evaluation of Byrd's, Kramer's, and Jonathon's cell phone records for that night would verify this story. Jonathon's phone showed him near the property at the time of the fire and talking to Byrd. Kramer's text messages made several references to fire and the results of the incident. He was very pleased with the results. In Byrd, we finally had a witness who could directly connect Andrew Kramer to one of the attacks. Because Byrd was a lifetime criminal, his testimony would be tainted by his record. We needed more corroboration.

After some computer work, we finally identified "Jonathon" as Jonathon Livingston. We didn't have to look too hard to find him. Within just a few minutes we found him cooling his heels in the county jail. Not surprisingly he was in there for possessing marijuana for the purpose of sales.

Big George and I then convinced Anderson Byrd to work for us as an informant. He agreed to wear a recording device in his future dealings with Andrew Kramer. For the next year he helped build a case against Andrew Kramer.

Anderson Byrd filled us in on a lot we didn't know. Byrd said that Kramer routinely kept large amounts of cash on him and in his safe for the purchase of bulk amounts of marijuana. Byrd said that Kramer compartmentalized his operations and worked with several different groups of people. He said that he never told one group what the other group was doing. Byrd described that growers of high-quality pot showed up nearly every day to the shop and sold Andrew Kramer between five and fifty pounds of marijuana. That dope was then given to a different group of males, usually black gangsters or sometimes Jamaicans, and then shipped out of the state to the East Coast. Byrd said that Kramer had some sort of magic touch and had worked deals with Russians, Armenians, Jamaicans, Crips, Bloods, and was even talking to Mexican Cartel members. No one in the history of illegal drugs in California had been able to do business with all these violent criminal groups. They usually ended up dead.

Byrd also confirmed rumors that Kramer had millions of dollars stashed somewhere at his mother's home in the San Fernando Valley. He said that Kramer made so much money that he had to bury large amounts of it on his mother's property. Byrd had also been told that Kramer had over $10 million in some offshore accounts.

### Jonathon Livingston

Anderson Byrd had provided us the name of Livingston as the arsonist in the vacant house fire. Big George and I interviewed him one day at the sheriff's jail facility. Jonathon Livingston was as hard core an ex-convict as we had ever seen. He had already been arrested for murder, spent a couple of years in jail fighting the case, and had been released. He had spent several years in the penitentiary for assaults, drug sales, and other serious crimes. He had spent over a decade of his life in jail or prison and was hard as stone. He was currently fighting a case for selling marijuana. When we interviewed him, we got absolutely nowhere. He refused even to listen to his rights being read. He was adhering to the old convict rule of never speaking to the cops. He never did.

Talking to Livingston was not a complete waste of time. Big George and I had been knocking on doors and talking to crooks for months on this case. We knew that the word had gotten around on the street that people were looking into the marijuana shop attacks. We knew that we were getting close when after George introduced himself to Jonathon Livingston, Livingston stated, "So, you're the famous detective Elwell." Even in jail Livingston had heard that we were talking to people. The thugs had learned who Det. Elwell was, and Big George has worn that title ever since that moment.

### Bryan Lalezari

Big George and I had studied this group for a long time. The text messages we recovered from the phones showed a connection between a twenty-eight-year-old Persian kid named Bryan

Lalezari, Rene Johnson (RJ), and Andrew Kramer. The texts were pretty damning and concerned some attacks of the Sunset Super Shop early in the case. We'd heard through various people that Lalezari was a confidante of Kramer, and we felt that he might be the best person to exploit in this case.

Lalezari was a middleman, somewhere near the top. He was the go-between for Kramer to the thugs. By all accounts, he was a complete dope fiend and addicted to any number of hard drugs, including crack cocaine and heroin. He also owned a pot shop on Pico called Shiva's Garden. Shiva's had been robbed one day by a couple of Armenian thugs, and Lalezari had engaged them in a running handgun fight. He was never prosecuted for that shooting.

On a later date, just a few months back, Lalezari had been nabbed on Skid Row in downtown Los Angeles, just after he purchased a vial of crack and heroin from a street dealer. He was fighting that case in court. His lawyer in that case was the notorious Ken Markman, who was currently fighting his own charges for smuggling drugs into county jail.

Det. Elwell and I knew that Lalezari would be the guy to exploit because he was near to Kramer and had no serious criminal convictions. The rest of the thugs in this case were truly hard-core gangsters, kidnappers, robbers, and murderers, and a jury would look at their testimony with a jaundiced eye. Lalezari came from a wealthy Persian family and was a former student of Beverly Hills High.

In early July 2012, Big George decided to hit Lalezari with a search warrant for evidence in this case. Lalezari had "failed to appear" in court one day, and the judge issued a warrant for his arrest on his recent dope-possession case. We learned that he had possibly fled to Mexico. We knew we were likely to find dope and guns in his home as well. BHPD hit Lalezari's mother's pad and learned that he had fled the country just two days prior.

He was believed to be headed to the Caribbean for yet another drug rehab stint. Det. Elwell did find a couple of pounds of pot, a ton of syringes and balloons for heroin and crack, and some cash. He also found a very interesting piece of paper stating that Bryan Lalezari has just this past week sold his Shiva's Garden dispensary to Andrew Kramer for $50,000 in cash.

A phone call to the feds showed Lalezari's passport heading from Mexico to Panama. Panamanian authorities were notified and opted to use a handshake agreement they had with the US Marshals Service, where they agreed to return any wanted felons to the United States, provided that two officials escorted the felon back, for free, and got a two-day stay in the States for free. Naturally the lure of a trip to Hollywood and Disneyland was all that was needed for an older male official and his young, curvy, and beautiful "assistant" to bring a bewildered and doped-up Bryan Lalezari back to LAX. He was met by Big George from BHPD, and they cleared customs about two hours later.

George and I interviewed Lalezari at BHPD that same night. He was a bit stoned on methadone but was quite eager to talk to us—that is, until he saw a picture of the menacing Bolo and turned almost to stone. Lalezari said he wanted to talk to us, and two weeks later, on July 30, we sat down in BHPD with Lalezari, his criminal lawyer, and Renee Rose, the special DA assigned to the case. This session was called a "proffer," where Lalezari got to tell us everything he knew, and the DA would weigh its value and determine what kind of deal she would give him in exchange for testifying.

Bryan Lalezari came as clean as we had hoped. He said he went to Beverly Hills High along with several other guys involved in this case, including Justin Lanning, Russian Mike, and Yaron Bassa. Lalezari told us that all of them were connected in some way to Andrew Kramer and his marijuana empire. In Lalezari's words, Kramer truly had an empire. Lalezari stated that he had been working for and with Kramer on and off for years and that Kramer had made millions of dollars off of illegal marijuana sales. He said that Kramer had his hands in a dozen or more dispensaries and charged them huge fees to act as a "consultant." He said that if a dispensary did not hire Andrew Kramer, Kramer would just walk quietly away and not make a fuss. A few weeks later Kramer would casually remark to any of his crew, "Oh, did you hear that dispensary had a fire?" The implication was that Andrew Kramer paid some unknown thugs to have the dispensary burned.

Lalezari said that Andrew Kramer was a true mystery. On one hand, he often gave money or jobs to out-of-work street people and former cons, just to help them. He was friendly and cordial and truly believed in the healing powers of marijuana. On the other hand, if someone crossed him or got the better of him on a deal, Kramer sent some real scary black thugs to scare him, beat him, or worse. He said Kramer never had guns around but always stayed close to a contingent of muscular ex-convicts.

According to Lalezari, Kramer did not seem to be concerned about local law enforcement as he seemed to be very friendly with the local sheriff's commander, and was well known and respected by the entire West Hollywood City Council. He was supposed to be especially close to the attorney for the city council. However, Kramer was extremely paranoid of the DEA. He hired security and computer experts to help him thwart DEA surveillances and wiretaps. He always changed his phones on a near monthly basis and used a series of females to buy new phones under fake names.

Lalezari said that despite Kramer's great care with his information security, he routinely carried large amounts of cash and conducted large purchases of marijuana out in the open. Lalezari confirmed that any grower of high-quality marijuana could come to the back of Kramer's business with a duffel bag full of pot, and Kramer would buy it. A day or so later, Kramer would hand this pot off to any one of several gangs or groups who worked for him to move the dope out of state. Lalezari said that Kramer made so much money, he had a hard time hiding it and had buried a large amount on his mother's property.

After a significant debrief from Lalezari about Kramer's activities, he finally got down to the Lanning-Kramer feud. He filled in the details about Kramer, who was a millionaire many times over, getting upset about George Lanning beating him on a business deal and in court. He said Kramer asked any number of people to burn down the Sunset Super Shop or assault the Lannings. Lalezari admitted that he had helped Kramer broker the deal that led to California and Maybee firebombing the Sunset Super Shop in August of 2010. He said that he and Kramer had contracted with RJ, who in turn subcontracted with Bolo, who in turn farmed the job out to California and Maybee. Lalezari said Kramer liked these types of jobs because the suspects who actually committed the crime never knew who Kramer was.

Lalezari also admitted that he had been the middleman between Kramer and RJ when Kramer wanted the Lanning family home burned in October of 2010. Big George Elwell and I studied the text and cell phone records for these men and found corroborating evidence to back up Lalezari's admission. We now had Kramer linked by evidence and admissions to have paid for at least three of the arson/attempted murder attacks. Bryan Lalezari would stay in jail for the next two years cooperating with the investigation.

Lalezari also explained to us the reason he had fled the country. Big George had sent Bolo a letter when Bolo was still in prison. The letter spelled out our case against him and what we wanted from him. After Bolo got out of prison, Bolo came to see Lalezari in his shop and showed him the letter that Big George had sent him. He then asked Lalezari if he was "snitching" or cooperating. Lalezari denied this, but Bolo asked him to leave the shop and meet him at a nearby Taco Bell. Lalezari believed that Bolo would likely kill him if he showed up at the Taco Bell so that Lalezari couldn't tell on or testify against Bolo. Bryan Lalezari felt it prudent at this time to get out of the marijuana business and flee the country to avoid characters like Bolo. It was probably a very wise decision.

### Yaron Bassa

A week or two after "flipping" Bryan Lalezari, Big George sent me and a partner to interview Yaron Bassa, another close friend of Andrew Kramer. Bassa had been in prison for several months on a parole violation. On September 20, 2012, Det. Dana Duncan and I drove to Wasco State Prison, in the Central Valley of California, to interview Yaron Bassa. Yaron was another of those rich-kids-gone-bad, whose parents were wealthy Israelis living in Beverly Hills. He attended Beverly Hills High School along with Justin Lanning, Bryan Lalezari, and Russian Mike. Like Russian Mike, Yaron didn't graduate and instead drifted quickly toward a life of crime, despite the affluence of his parents.

We met Yaron in a small interview room within the guards' office at the prison. We didn't play around much. Dana and I told Yaron we were there to talk about Andrew Kramer and his marijuana dealings. Bassa immediately told us that if Kramer knew he was talking, then Kramer would pay to have him killed. He also was concerned that Kramer might have his parents killed. I asked him if Kramer had the sort of inclinations and connections to make something like that happen. Without hesitation Yaron stated flatly that Andrew Kramer had millions of dollars at his disposal and could easily get anything he wanted done.

Yaron Bassa then told us about his life around Andrew Kramer. He said that Kramer was a friend of his, treated him well, and had always been generous with him. He said that Kramer had been involved in the marijuana business for over a decade and had even helped Bassa get started in the business. He said he frequently sold between one and three pounds of high-grade pot at a time for Kramer, for around $4,000 a pound. He said Kramer moved massive amounts of pot in deals like this. Bassa reiterated much of the same history of Kramer that we had heard from both Byrd and Lalezari. He said Kramer could be generous, helpful, and friendly, and in the same day order a vicious attack on someone if they did him wrong. He said Kramer had a massive ego and didn't like to come out second best on any sort of business deal.

Getting to specifics, Bassa told us that he had helped connect Andrew Kramer with some street thugs, who agreed to vandalize and attack the Sunset Super Shop. Text messages between the two in 2010 confirm this. He then connected Kramer to Russian Mike and was present when Kramer asked Russian Mike to burn the Sunset Super Shop for $5,000. He then amended his order to have it burned at night when George Lanning was sleeping upstairs.

Bassa, like several other of Kramer's acquaintances, could not understand why Kramer wanted to risk jail for a couple hundred thousand dollars that George Lanning owed him. Bassa said he had seen up to a half-million dollars in Kramer's safe once and knew him to always keep a couple hundred thousand around. He said he once looked at Kramer's computer and saw accounts in Switzerland and another place totaling $50 million. Bassa said that Kramer was obsessed with the Lannings as they had taken his shop from him. He said that several of the thugs around Kramer had tried to talk him out of attacking the Lannings.

Yaron Bassa, because he was facing serious charges for a lengthy stay in prison, agreed to cooperate and testify against Andrew Kramer. By now we had three good witnesses—Bassa,

Byrd, and Lalezari—who all had confessed and agreed to testify against Kramer for paying to have the shop burned down several times. In each case there was digital forensic evidence in the form of cell phone records to back up each person's story. We were slowly tearing Kramer's world down.

### Russian Mike

Russian Mike (a pseudonym) was a longtime criminal who was currently in county jail for a drug-sales arrest. He was considered by the other informants to be one of the most dangerous people in this conspiracy. Everyone was afraid of him, and there were stories that he had been involved in any number of assaults, robberies, kidnappings, and major narcotics deals. We had tried to engage him in conversation about Kramer, and he had deferred to his attorney. The attorney and the DA agreed to let us talk to Russian Mike.

Within a very short time we could judge that Russian Mike was a true criminal and opportunist. He admitted in a roundabout way that he had been paid by Kramer to torch the Sunset Super Shop and beat up or kidnap George Lanning. When he got there, he instead took the opportunity to make even more money. We believe he committed extortion by demanding money and drugs not to beat up Lanning. Russian Mike was a real bad guy, and Big George and I didn't want to use him as he was clearly not reliable. The DA agreed, and we put Russian Mike on the back burner and chose not to use his testimony. He eventually was sent back to prison for ten years on his latest narcotics conviction.

### Byron Ellison

On September 18, 2012, Big George's hard work had paid off yet again. In April of 2012, two males were seen on video with a gas can, trying to break into the back of the Sunset Super Shop.

We saw on the video where one of them had touched a block wall with his hand. Big George brought an evidence tech to the scene and recovered DNA from that spot. A few days earlier, the lab techs told George that they had a positive DNA sample. Now, it was a matter of entering it into a database called CODIS, where it would be compared against millions of other samples in the rare hope of a "hit." Big George's luck held true, and it "hit" with authority. The DNA came back to a forty-something ex-convict black guy named Byron Ellison. George cross-referenced Ellison's name with the ever-expanding phone number database to the case and found that Bolo had called Ellison's number several times in the past. This was clearly another of Bolo's paid thugs sent to the shop to torch it.

Big George located Byron Ellison. Ellison was purported to be hiding out in a place in the south bay city of Lawndale. Once located and positively identified by undercover detectives, Big George got a Ramey Warrant for the arrest of Ellison in the amount of $1 million. On September 20, 2012, LASD detectives set up a surveillance on the location where Ellison was holed up. After a slight glitch in the case, (the Major Crimes Bureau team shot another suspect at the location), Byron Ellison was arrested and brought to jail.

He was very irate about being arrested, and when we spoke to him, he denied knowing anything about this attempted arson at the dispensary. He very much surprised us by spontaneously saying, "I didn't burn anything, but I did drive a stolen car into the front of the dispensary." With that, we had yet another crime in the series solved. Like all of the other people associated with Bolo, Ellison was a lifelong criminal and drug addict. He was an ex-con and a subject in a murder investigation in another state. Yeah, he "fit the profile" of one of Bolo's friends and one of Kramer's employees. He sat in jail for months waiting for a trial.

## The Attempted Kidnapping—Ronald Samuel and Howard Offley

On January 30, 2012, easily the most terrifying act of this entire crime spree occurred at the Lanning home in Beverly Hills. It would take weeks for us to unravel it all. At 7:22 p.m., Nansee Lanning received a cell phone call from a strange number. When she answered, the caller hung up. Due to the elaborate techniques he used to hide his phone information, it would take us months to discover that the call was from a phone registered to "Chris Cruel." According to Anderson Byrd, Kramer's head of security, who was now secretly working of us, Chris Cruel was identified as one of Andrew Kramer's fake names under which he registered phones. In short, Andrew Kramer called one of his enemies, Nansee Lanning.

Less than an hour later, Nansee received another call and hang up from a phone registered to a man named Ronald Samuel. Twelve seconds later Ronald Samuel's phone called a man named Howard Offley. Nansee Lanning didn't know either one of these young black men, and she really didn't want to know them. Both were longtime criminals actively involved in drug dealing and drug-house rip-offs. Samuel was on federal probation for trafficking internationally in ecstasy. Surprisingly, the young black gang member was as highly connected in the drug world as Andrew Kramer. Samuel was well known in Amsterdam and was the sole black partner in a major drug-trafficking ring. He was so high up in the ring that he was actually able to take possession of tens of thousands of dollars' worth of ecstasy on credit, which is pretty much unheard of in the dope world. He was also the leader of a specialized crew who would pose as drug buyers on the street, and when they found a drug dealer, they would kidnap, beat, torture, and rob the dealer.

Howard Offley was one of the "heavies" in Samuel's crew. They had been sought for violent drug-house takeovers in the desert areas east of Los Angeles. They were extremely violent guys who were thought to be involved in several unsolved murders of drug dealers. The mystery of why the phones of those two black street maniacs would be linked to a middle-aged white woman was solved a few hours later.

An hour or so later, a man in Beverly Hills heard a disturbance outside of his apartment. He looked out and saw BHPD cars responding with lights and sirens to some sort of emergency call a block or two away (not related to this assault). As the citizen watched the police cars speed by, he saw a car in an alley near his window with four tough-looking black males standing near it. When the cops passed by, the four males appeared to duck and hide behind the car. The citizen called BHPD to report the suspicious activity, assuming the cops were looking for these men for some reason. He gave a vehicle description and a partial plate. Cops responded, but the males and the car were gone. This was just a few blocks from the Lanning home.

Shortly after receiving the strange phone calls, Nansee Lanning went to bed in her room while her son, Justin, was hanging out in the garage. In the late evening, five black men, two of whom were later identified as Samuel and Offley, surreptitiously entered the Lanning home and walked into Nansee's bedroom. One of the men bashed her in the head with a steel pipe and then dragged her unconscious body into a hallway. Hearing odd noises, Nansee's son, Justin, entered the kitchen to find five black males, with four of them wearing masks. He saw his bloodied mother being dragged through a hallway as the remainder of the males grabbed him.

Offley then demanded, "You know what we want, Justin. You owe money." The men then began beating him, and he believed that they were ready to drag him out of the home. At this time a houseguest appeared and scared off the would-be kidnappers. Justin Lanning felt absolutely sure that he was going to be kidnapped, beaten, and probably killed that night. After we identified the suspects and looked at their track record of violence, we were positive Justin Lanning was to be murdered. Justin later identified the male without the mask as Ronald Samuel.

Again the ALPRS license plate system served as an excellent investigative tool. A check of the system identified a suspicious car in the area. Det. George Elwell cross-referenced the plate with police records and found the earlier call in another part of his city of the four suspicious black males. They had obviously parked and were planning their home-invasion mission at that scene. The vehicle was a rental car, which had been rented by a black female in the desert region northeast of Los Angeles. That female was the girlfriend of Howard Offley, one of the numbers that had come up the night of the attack. The Lannings had security video in their home, and Howard Offley was identified on it prior to putting his mask over his head. Howard Offley's associates were checked in the computer, and his crime partner was Ronald Samuel, a federal probationer.

The Lannings were shown photo lineups of the crew and immediately picked out Ronald Samuel as the male who was not wearing a mask during the attempted kidnapping. Through federal-probation records, Ronald Samuel listed his sister as a family contact. All of these numbers were fed into our ever-expanding cell phone database and cross-referenced. The database churned out some incredible connections. Andrew Kramer's phone, under the name of Chris Cruel, had contacted Ronald Samuel's sister over 564 times. She, in turn, had contacted Howard Offley's phone over 112 times. This staggering number of contacts showed that Kramer had an active business relationship with Samuel, who was a convicted marijuana smuggler and known home-invasion specialist.

On the very night of the attack at the Lannings, the phones show Kramer and the kidnapping crew contacting each other no less than seventy-one times by voice, voicemail, or text. The phone analysis also identified the girl who rented the car the night of the kidnapping and the girl who acted as the "phone center" for Samuel's criminal gang. It was well known to all law enforcement, prison, and parole staff that street gangs almost always use a female relative as a "phone center" to connect members who may be in other states or prison. These phone centers coordinate hundreds of dealings and activities of street gangs.

Finally, we had incredible digital evidence directly linking Andrew Kramer to a very violent street gang and a vicious act. Big George set out a hunt for Samuel and Offley. Samuel was grabbed in Las Vegas and interviewed by Big George. Once shown the evidence against him, Ronald Samuel, a hard -ore felon, agreed to cooperate with the investigation at a later date. Howard Offley was arrested shortly afterward and refused to cooperate. The rest of Samuel's kidnapping crew was never identified.

### The Humanitarian Andrew Kramer

In late 2012, Big George Elwell and I met with the DA, the assistant US attorney, and a representative of the DEA. We now believed we had several strong cases against a diverse group of offenders, all appearing to take orders and money from Andrew Kramer. We felt very confident that we could present a strong case against Andrew Kramer for conspiracy. We knew by now that he had nearly unlimited funds and would have the assistance of the best legal team money could buy.

Our evidence included witness statements, physical evidence from the fire scenes, video evidence of all the attacks, and the admissions of several coconspirators. While all of the coconspirators were lifetime thugs and criminals and their testimonies would be somewhat tainted, we had developed great physical evidence to corroborate their statements. That evidence was in the form of the cell phone matrix developed by BHPD. By 2013 we had accumulated over forty thousand cell phone records from tower dumps, we had identified sixty different cell phones used by the coconspirators, we had written court orders for over thirteen thousand subscriber records, and the data bank now held over two million cell phone calls and text records. Despite their attempts at using three-way call centers, changing cell phones on a regular basis, using fake names to purchase cell service, and speaking and texting in codes, we were able to positively link Andrew Kramer to eight of these criminal events.

We planned to arrest all of the coconspirators not yet in custody on the same day in a blitz attack. This would be coordinated with the DEA, who would be doing more search warrants against Kramer and his family. This planning took a couple of months to put together and coordinate.

Andrew Kramer had by now become aware that the BHPD and the LASD Arson-Explosives Detail had been speaking to his coconspirators. Fearing an imminent arrest, Kramer hired a public-relations firm to go on the offensive. The local newspapers, the *Patch* and the *WeHo News*, had long been running negative stories about the Lanning family and their rogue pot dispensary. They had made several references that, of all the pot shops in the city, the Sunset Super Shop under the Lannings was the only one violating the law.

In other articles over the years, the newspapers lauded Andrew Kramer as one of the true medical-marijuana advocates in the city, who had been running dispensaries the "right way," as the law had intended. Additionally, the WeHo City Council and its legal advisor, John Duran, seemed extremely close to Kramer and decidedly against the Lannings. Big George and I had always wondered about how much influence Kramer's money had bought him. We had found no substantial evidence to show corruption, but it was clear that Kramer held a very favored position with the City of WeHo.

Through Anderson Byrd, Kramer's head of security, we learned that Kramer had donated lots of money to the local newspapers and possibly the local politicians. Byrd told us that Kramer was aware that we were possibly going to arrest him and that he had taken countermeasures by hiring a public-relations firm. Indeed, in December of 2012, a company called PRWeb, a public-relations firm, issued a glowing and syrupy press release on Andrew Kramer and his efforts to help veterans and the homeless. It stressed how Kramer was a pioneer in the medical-marijuana field and was a "humanitarian" and "well-respected" advocate for free medicine for veterans and the homeless.

### The Arrests

By the spring of 2013 we had built as strong a case as possible. We had fantastic charges against most of the major players in this ongoing conspiracy to murder the Lannings. We were well aware that we had not identified at least twenty additional coconspirators, based on the images we had seen on surveillance videos. It didn't matter to us because the focus of this case was the leader of the group, Andrew Kramer.

On April 16, 2013, we threw eleven simultaneous police raids throughout the Hollywood area, targeting Kramer, Bolo, and RJ, along with Kramer's shops, again. All of the suspects were brought to BHPD for interviews. We made attempts to speak to Bolo and RJ and got the usual "get fucked" from both of these professional criminals. Andrew Kramer, when brought in, was clearly shocked and disoriented. He was a wealthy guy not used to being pulled out of bed by the police but instead used to a high-powered attorney handling his legal issues. Our raids clearly rattled him. He clearly did not expect to be swept up like this as in the past he had been politely contacted by authorities through his various attorneys. The shock value of this raid was overwhelming to Andrew Kramer. He could barely speak. Eventually he asked for his attorney, and the meeting was over.

We had a couple of extra tricks up our sleeves and got Kramer's bail set extremely high at $3 million. We knew he could pay the bail, and we were prepared to seize any bail money he put up that was not from a legitimate source. Since we knew he hadn't made an honest dollar in ten years, we knew he couldn't post bail without risk of it being seized. Because of this strategy, the multimillionaire Kramer sat in jail with the rest of the common criminals.

The next day we deliberately released a public statement about the case to the media, describing Kramer as an arsonist, kidnapper, assaulter of women, and a true drug lord. The shock effect was palatable within the marijuana advocacy groups. After seeing most of the violent charges spelled out in newspapers, almost immediately any allies in the marijuana legalization movement turned their backs on Andrew Kramer. To say that his powerful friends and connections were shocked would be an understatement.

The *Los Angeles Times* had published an article on March 15, 2011, after the DEA and other law enforcement agencies raided two marijuana dispensaries in West Hollywood, including Andrew Kramer's Zen Healing shop. The article was very critical of the federal government's perceived rough tactics (raids) against shops that appeared to be operating legitimately. The article stated that "West Hollywood had prided itself on diligent oversight of the dispensaries" in its area.

Immediately after the arrests of Kramer and several of his henchmen for the arsons and attempted murders, the legal counsel for the City of West Hollywood, John Duran, expressed outrage in the media for the intrusion of BHPD into his city. He sent a scathing letter to the Beverly Hills City Council and police, expressing this outrage for their police having invaded his city. He was shocked and even more upset to find out that the LASD had been involved in the investigation from the start. He made several angry phone calls to the local sheriff's commanders, who passed on his outrage to me.

Throughout this investigation, even we became amazed at the reach and scope of Andrew Kramer. His associates believed that he had orchestrated dozens more attacks and other arsons than what we knew about. He openly acknowledged in an interview his role in bribing city officials and of being involved in a few dozen dispensaries that had been attacked in some way. We were also aware that Andrew Kramer was secretly paying for the attorney bills of some of his coconspirators. We realized in the end that his stated goal to some of his cronies was to control the entire marijuana business in Southern California. We certainly came to believe that he had his hand in dozens of violent incidents.

Lastly, we learned that hardened felons of several ethnic groups feared Kramer as they knew (or believed) that he could and would pay to have anyone killed. He had successfully led people to believe that he was affiliated with such violent groups as the Crips, Bloods, Russian Mob, and Mexican Cartel. He also led people to believe that he "owned" the media, local politicians, and possibly police commanders. True or not, street people believed this, and that gave Andrew Kramer incredible stature and power in the criminal world.

### The Convictions

On May 21, 2013, Bryan Lalezari pled guilty to arson, and in return for his agreement to testify against Kramer, he received a sentence of five years in prison.

On June 12, 2013, Jimmie "California" Jones pled guilty to multiple felony counts in a plea deal with prosecutors. This plea was based on his decision to come clean to investigators and admit his role in the firebombing of the Sunset Super Shop. California admitted that he had been recruited and paid by Bolo to torch the Sunset Super Shop. He fully admitted that he and Kim Maybee purchased some gasoline and placed it into iced-tea bottles. He and Maybee drove to the shop in her car, where she broke the windows of the nail salon. California then threw both bottles into the broken windows of the nail salon. California reluctantly agreed to cooperate with prosecutors in the case against Andrew Kramer.

On July 3, 2013, Anderson Byrd also pled guilty and admitted his role in helping Kramer arrange for the firebombing of the vacant home owned by the Lannings. He agreed to cooperate with prosecutors against Kramer.

On July 25, 2013, Ronald Samuel struck a deal with the prosecutor and pled guilty to robbery and assault with a deadly weapon for orchestrating the kidnapping plan. He agreed to take an easy three years in prison for his cooperation, which would cause him to violate federal parole and expose him to several more years of federal incarceration. He too was set to testify against Andrew Kramer. We opted not to use Russian Mike as a witness. He was eventually sentenced to ten years in prison for his role in an unrelated narcotics deal.

By the time he was ready for court, Andrew Kramer had learned that Jimmy "California" Jones, Ronald Samuel, Anderson Byrd, and Bryan Lalezari had agreed to testify against him in court, if needed. They would be able to describe to a jury Kramer's operation, sophistication, and massive amounts of money he had made by illegal drug transactions. They would also be able to describe the intense obsession and hatred Andrew Kramer had with the Lanning family. Kim Maybee's rambling, taped admission to me would also be played, explaining the dynamics of at least one major event.

We would never get to hear all of these juicy details in a courtroom. When court started, Andrew Kramer was facing eighty-eight years in prison. We knew he would take a deal to minimize that. He sat through four hours of testimony by me to see what we were willing to present, and then he and his high-priced legal team took the deal. The case finally came to a close on March 27, 2014, in Department Fifty-One of the Criminal Courts Building in downtown Los Angeles. The Honorable Judge Michael Pastor sat for nearly three hours taking guilty pleas from a variety of defendants. Once Andrew Kramer pled guilty, the rest fell into place in what seemed like just a few minutes.

Grace "Bolo" Cox, easily the scariest guy in the room, pled guilty to arson and conspiracy and got nine years in state prison. Jimmy "California" Jones received an eight-year sentence for arson and conspiracy. Kim Maybee was already serving her fifteen-year sentence for arson, use of a destructive device (Molotov cocktail), and conspiracy. Yaron Bassa, still in jail for his previous conviction, was convicted of conspiracy and would serve a total of eight years. Jonathon Livingston, the hard-core lifelong convict who refused to talk, finally pled guilty to arson and conspiracy and was given six years back in the penitentiary where he truly belonged. Byron Ellison, the man whose DNA appeared on a block wall near the attempt at a burglary and arson of the Sunset Super Shop, was convicted of burglary and received five additional years in state prison, on top of the sentence he was serving when we finally found him.

If the truth be told, there were two people who we really, really wanted to send to prison more than the others. The first was, naturally, Andrew Kramer. The second was Rene "RJ" Johnson. Nobody had been in more denial of his actions than RJ, even when confronted with a mountain of evidence. He was obnoxious, threatening, and refused even the normal cordialities. He vowed that he would not admit to anything ever; nor would he spend one day in prison. We offered him a very hefty incentive package when we first dealt with him, and his massive ego refused to accept it. In the end, we wanted him to go away just as bad as Kramer. RJ was finally forced in open court to admit to conspiracy to commit arson along with the arson of a structure. He was sentenced to seven years in state prison.

Howard Offley, one of the would-be kidnappers, got sentenced to eleven years in prison. Anderson Byrd, who had pled guilty to conspiracy and assisted us in an undercover capacity for several months, was eventually given immunity. With the long tentacles of Kramer's money, he will have to look over his shoulder for the rest of his life.

Andrew Kramer, with all his money and resources, expected to get less than five years in prison for his role in orchestrating over two dozen serious attacks against the Lanning family. He was visibly upset when he learned that the very minimum time he could do was twenty-five years in prison. If he took that deal with the state, the federal government agreed to sentence him to a similar sentence for drug trafficking and to let him serve both sentences at the same time. This deal included Kramer making cash restitution to the victims and authorities, totaling something near $1 million. When told of this hefty sum, Kramer merely said, "No problem."

In the end, nobody ever gets what they were supposed to get. Samuels, whose attorney cleverly confused the situation with the federal government got his federal violation somehow dropped and was released from jail shortly after his sentencing. We felt cheated out of about five years on him.

Kramer stayed in county jail for almost two years, working the system and stalling prior to being sent to state prison. He also vigorously fought giving the Lannings so much as a dime in restitution as he had agreed to do. In the end, his hatred of being bested by George Lanning in a business deal for something around $100,000 caused his spectacular downfall. Even the hard-core convicts that surrounded him had attempted on several occasions to talk Kramer out of his insane attacks on the Lannings. His vanity prevailed and would cost him his freedom for the next two decades. In what had to be a major blow to his vanity and status in the underground culture, the newspapers the day after Kramer's sentencing told the world what he truly was: a big-league narcotics trafficker and conspirator in the attempted murder of his rivals. Andrew Kramer became the biggest drug lord in Los Angeles.

However, true to form, Kramer still did not own up to his much of his crime wave. On November 2, 2015, he pled guilty in federal court to a single count of the interstate trafficking of marijuana in excess of one thousand pounds. He received a sixteen-year sentence in federal prison, plus forfeited over $2 million the feds had already seized from him. In his plea to the federal judge, he also admitted to owning eight marijuana dispensaries in the Los Angeles area. Coincidentally, at least five of those shops were the victim of a fire at one time or another. He further admitted to earning between $200,000 and $400,000 from his shops each and every month from the years 2006 to 2013. Despite this enormous pile of cash, Kramer in the same month had told the Los Angeles courts that he was unable to make the restitution of $2 million to the Lannings as he had agreed.

The judge who had dealt with Kramer finally was sick of him and threw out his plea agreement in late 2015. We took the entire Kramer case to the Los Angeles Grand Jury in early 2016, and Kramer was indicted on all counts. Now he is facing a trial and over eighty years in prison. We expect to go to trial in late 2016.

On a really rude note, I was called on March 12, 2015, by a counselor at Chowchilla women's prison. The counselor stated that Kim Maybee was being considered for a possible release under a new program to get rid of "non-serious and nonviolent" inmates. I nearly had a seizure while speaking to the man. Kim Maybee was the definition of a serious and violent offender as she had made a living for years out of strong-armed street robberies, paid beatings, intimidation, burglary, and arson for hire. She was truly a professional criminal with over a dozen convictions behind her.

She had spent weeks convincing beleaguered prison officials that her arson attack was against a "noncombustible" building, and as such it shouldn't be considered a serious offense. They were at the brink of releasing her from her fifteen-year sentence after just six years served. This travesty was on top of the fact that a judge had mysteriously set aside her other convictions at time of sentencing, or she would have been a "third striker" life-in-prison candidate. Despite her one-woman crime wave over the past twenty years, Kim Maybee was released after serving just over a third of her time. This "justice" system really sucks.

*The following detectives and investigators played major roles in this four-year-long complex investigation: lead investigators George Elwell, BHPD, and Ed Nordskog, LASD Arson-Explosives; Sgt. Rob Hernandez, BHPD; Det. Mike Cofield, LASD Arson-Explosives; Det. Greg Everett, LASD Arson-Explosives; Det. Cindy Valencia, LASD Arson-Explosives; Det. Dana Duncan, LASD Arson-Explosives; Sgt. Derek Yoshino, LASD Arson-Explosives; Sgt. Wendy Zolkowski, LASD Arson-Explosives; Sgt. John Hanson, LASD Major Crimes; Inv. Tim Crass, LAFD; DDA Renee Rose, District Attorney's Office; and SA Pat Kelly, DEA.*

### Investigator's Profile

This case describes one of the most unique and best-organized arson conspiracies I have ever heard of. Andrew Kramer had made untold millions in the pot business and had used his brains and energy to manipulate an entire industry into believing that he was operating legally. His ego couldn't stand losing a small amount of money, and he then risked everything he had to fulfill his need for revenge in a petty squabble against the Lannings. Kramer cleverly used black street gang members to conduct the attacks in an attempt to mask them as generic street gang violence. In truth, he fooled us for a few months and clearly befuddled two major crimes detectives the entire time.

However, simple profiling techniques would clearly show that these attacks were not for profit and didn't attempt to take money or valuable drugs. Instead they were attacks against the owners, which was a personal crime. This sort of analysis quickly changed the scope of the investigation and refocused us on the aspect of revenge. Revenge-based fires are the easiest ones to solve, and in this case, knowing it was Kramer was the easy part. Proving it was Andrew Kramer took a couple of years of hard work, some luck, and some very ingenious detective work.

The arson scenes themselves were quite telling. They were crude, low-tech, and with very little chance of success. It was clear that the arsonists had very little knowledge on how to light a fire and kept failing at trying to burn the shop down. The use of Molotov devices is also a hallmark of gang members. These crude devices fail over 90 percent of the time. This would definitely point to a gang member as they are notoriously uneducated and poor fire starters. The only fires with any success were late in the series and involved the suspects actually having to enter the structure to get better results.

We conducted an analysis of the victimology of this crime series. The Lanning family was clearly the victim and intended target of the multiple attacks. Normally the victims of arson have a failed personal relationship with someone, or they have an "at risk" lifestyle, which brings them into contact with the arsonist. In these attacks, the Lanning family had both. A failed business relationship with Kramer and the fact that they were involved in a business considered to be extremely high risk—the selling of marijuana. Any suspects acting on behalf of Kramer were **goal-directed arsonists**.

By the time we figured this out and formed our own three-agency task force, Kramer had attempted to kill the Lannings several times. However, the key to unraveling a conspiracy is deliberate and detailed detective work. Once I linked up with "Big George" Elwell and his BHPD mates, I knew I was working with true professionals. We kept our minds open and used creative investigative strategies such as cell phone programs, visiting inmates in state prison, undercover operations, and modern license-plate reader systems. We also selected specific low-level conspirators to isolate and exploit the entire time while building a comprehensive case against the target at the top of the conspiracy.

I have worked several large arson cases in my career, with a couple having been recognized at the national level for their size and scope. I have seen no better detective work than that done by my partner on this case, Det. George Elwell of BHPD, a.k.a. "Big George," a.k.a. "the Famous Detective Elwell." He was relentless and tireless and did a remarkable job. My compliments, Big George.

### An Observation from a Weary Detective

The victim in this case, George Lanning, barely muttered a thanks to us at the conclusion of this case despite us (mostly Det. Elwell) being responsible for stopping the attacks on his life and getting him hundreds of thousands of dollars in restitution. He and his greedy legal team just kept demanding more money.

I have had an over twenty-five-year association with the marijuana industry, first as an undercover narc specializing in marijuana growers, and now as an arson-explosives investigator.

Back in the day we only had to worry about violence from the Mexican Cartel growers and distributors. With the passage of several initiatives in California and other states to make the drug legal, or at least partially legal, the violence has skyrocketed. Now, the old hippy growers with their natural-growing methods are long gone. They've given way to the gang-financed, industrial indoor growers, whose constant crossbreeding and use of performance-enhancing chemicals has created a semi addictive form of superpot.

Despite pot being mostly legal in California, the price still remains astronomically high, causing thefts, burglaries, rip-offs, robberies, beatings, kidnappings, arsons, tortures, and murders. Added to this mayhem is a new chemical process for purifying the "shake," or residue of the marijuana plant, called the Butane Honey Oil Process. This technique basically injects an explosive material (butane) into marijuana and alters its chemical makeup. The highly volatile process has brought THC levels in marijuana from the near-addictive 25 percent levels to dangerous 90 percent levels. The problem with this process is that it has resulted in hundreds of explosions and fires, with buildings destroyed and dozens of people badly burned or even killed.

Where do growers learn this stuff? They go to pot conventions hosted around the country, pay a pile of money, and are taught this by the darkest denizens in the pot world—the activists and lawyers (sometimes one and the same), who have always profited off the plant.

No matter how much marijuana has changed over the years and the various crime groups that have come and gone to profit from it, only one group remains constant and reaps a healthy profit year in and year out—the pot activists/attorneys. One semi famous pot attorney once shook my hand after court and thanked me for my work at busting pot growers. He told me that was what put his daughter through an expensive college. He was known for being a very public advocate of marijuana but in person confided that he never wanted to see it fully legalized. He explained that all the lawyers in the business wanted it kept illegal or semi legal so that it remained in a foggy, legal haze that would leave the cops confused. He told me that was where the profit was—in the litigation. If it was legal, he'd have to find something else to do.

So, in the end, I guess I couldn't dislike George Lanning any more than any other seller of pot in the business. I'm glad he didn't get killed or seriously hurt, but he was just like all the other profiteers in the business. They are all a pretty despicable bunch if you ask me.

## FINANCIAL GAIN—ARSON FOR PROFIT

*"Fraud is learned behavior"* (Ed Nordskog).

### The Profile

**Financial-gain arsons** are almost as common as revenge/spite-based arsons. My studies and assessments show that financial-gain arsons occur in nearly 40 percent of all arson attacks. I will point out here that the national arson databases do not agree with my statistics. I will explain why.

Financial-gain arsons are often the most difficult arsons to identify and therefore solve. As such, a significant number of financial-gain arsons are missed by the responding fire-suppression crews or misdiagnosed by inexperienced arson and insurance investigators. Another aspect that adds to my argument is that many civil fire investigators are so focused on finding an accidental cause for a fire, in the interest of subrogation and cost recovery for their client (insurance company), that they miss (either purposely or inadvertently) numerous red flags indicating the fire event was a cleverly staged fraud scheme.

A last argument as to why financial-gain arsons are underreported is that very few agencies investigate vehicle fires. In my area, greater Los Angeles County, we, the LASD, are one of the last agencies that investigate vehicle fires, as most fire chiefs refuse to waste resources on them. We investigate hundreds of vehicle fires each year and have concluded that over 90 percent of our vehicle arsons are "owner set," or insurance-fraud schemes. If a large number of fire agencies across the country don't even investigate these vehicle fires, then the entire arson statistical system is in shambles, which it is.

The analysis of financial-gain fires shows that more than any other arson motive, these events tend to be extremely well planned and thought out. A businessman planning the arson of his failing business may think about and plan this event for months or years. This includes preparing the scene, establishing ironclad alibis, and hiring subcontractors to "torch" the property at the perfect time. Financial-gain arsonists are more likely to use an incendiary device than any other arsonist except for a wild-land arsonist or extremist arsonist. Financial gain arsonist will most often use an accelerant and devise flammable trailers so as to maximize the damage at a scene.

Other unique aspects of financial-gain fires related to insurance fraud include the fact that most often the fire is set from **within the interior of the structure** to be burned. It is a rare arsonist, indeed, who is brazen enough to enter a property in the dead of night to start a fire, unless of course he is the property owner or a hired agent for the owner.

Another unique aspect of financial-gain / insurance-fraud arsons is the presence of a phenomenon known as "**staging**" the scene. Staging is when a criminal does specific acts at a scene to make investigators believe something else occurred. Typical staging techniques during an insurance-fraud scheme will be to force entry into the location and leave some sort of pry tool to make it appear as if this fire was due to a burglary. The staging will go so far as to upend furniture, remove drawers, and make the business appear to have been ransacked. In truth, real burglars seldom resort to arson as there is no money in it for them, and all the ransacking nonsense is just too much work. True burglars seldom engage in these sorts of activities.

Staging during car arsons for insurance fraud is extremely common with the owner staging the theft of his car, only to have it found burning in a remote area. In truth, car theft by professional thieves does exist but mainly in high-end vehicles. Those professional car thieves would not waste the effort or expense on torching a vehicle. Their goal is merely to remove expensive parts or to completely renumber the car and ship it overseas. The idea that car thieves always burn cars is yet another myth in the arson business.

Other unique types of staging that occur include staging an incident as a hate crime or gang attack by leaving graffiti at the scene. Close analysis of the graffiti by a gang expert should reveal this as staged or planted evidence.

Arson investigators should remember that there are numerous ways to profit financially from arson. Insurance fraud is the most straightforward method, but there are other methods as well. Burning a competing business is another aspect of a financial-gain arson. Burning out-of-style inventory or stock is another way to profit from a fire.

Wild-land fires bring another aspect to financial-gain fires as many firefighters work on a "call" status, where they are paid only when they fight a fire. Other entities make large amounts of money off wild-land fires. These companies may supply equipment and supplies to Western wild-fire crews worth millions of dollars each year. There have been several cases of people from these companies starting fires so that they can cash in with the rental of their equipment.

## VALERIO
## VALENCIA, CA, 2009

*This case is from the files of LASD arson-explosives detective Mike Digby.*

The city of Valencia is a high-end neighborhood in the Santa Clarita Valley, thirty miles north of downtown Los Angeles. The area is directly next to the famed Magic Mountain Amusement Park. Across the Interstate 5 Freeway from Magic Mountain is a large industrial park filled with dozens of modern tilt-up buildings that house small factories, manufacturing plants, movie studios, and warehouses. At the very north end of this large industrial park sits a small group of identical buildings, all being used to house small businesses. One of these businesses was called Globo-Tech.

At around eleven thirty at night on Saturday, October 24, 2009, an explosion rocked the small group of businesses surrounding Globo-Tech. A local security officer heard and felt the rumbling explosion and assumed that it had been a minor earthquake in the area. He drove around looking for indications that something was wrong but could find nothing. At 11:36 p.m., the automatic fire-sprinkler system within Globo-Tech activated and began dumping water throughout the interior of the business. As per the local fire code, the sprinkler was also alarmed to the LACoFD, who immediately responded to the scene with an engine and crew to determine why the alarm had activated.

Captain Ken Sotro, of LACoFD Engine No. 156, responded to the scene and immediately saw debris strewn from the front glass doors of the business, well out into the parking lot. The debris was in a large, pie-shaped wedge, fanning out from the broken door and windows. Capt. Sotro recognized the signs of an explosion. He also saw light white smoke and water pouring from the broken windows of the business. He summoned LASD deputies to the scene. As soon as the captain approached the building, he could smell the strong odor of gasoline everywhere. He asked the first sheriff on scene to summon his arson investigators. Eventually, several arson investigators from the LASD would arrive, with Det. Mike Digby taking overall charge of the investigation.

Globo-Tech was the source of the explosion, and the building was fairly small in size, occupying two units of the large, tilt-up structure. One unit held the Globo-Tech office, and the second was a garage/warehouse that held an amount of inventory on the shelves, plus two boats on trailers. The walls and floor were made of concrete, with the roof covered in thin, one-inch-thick plywood and a rolled-composite-shingle roof. The fire damage was confined mainly to the office of the business, with just minor burning and scorching to the items within the garage area.

Almost immediately firefighters located highly suspicious items that they later pointed out to the arriving arson investigators. The first was a five-gallon gasoline container lying on its side in the office. It was somewhat burned and scorched and still contained a small amount of gasoline. The second was a large pool of gasoline that had been poured through the office and into the rear of the business. All of this fuel appeared to have come from the gas container. The firefighters accessed the roof of the building to insure that no fire or damage had occurred there. They immediately noted that there were several burned highway flares lying on the roof in large pools of a dark fluid that resembled motor oil. It appeared that someone had attempted to set the roof on fire, but that no fire had developed. The scene was secured for the arson investigators.

Det. Rick Velazquez was one of the first investigators on scene, and he quickly sized up the event as a mostly botched attempt at starting an arson fire to destroy the business. He immediately recognized this as a scheme likely concocted by the business owner. Rick had been to over 1,300 arson scenes in his career and could easily recognize the red flags and indicators of a fraudulent arson. He knew it was imperative to locate an owner as soon as possible to establish his whereabouts during the fire.

Rick found information in the office listing the owner of Globo-Tech as Mr. John Valerio. Messages were left on Valerio's phone, but he did not respond that night. The detectives left the scene that night, and a patrolman stayed to guard it. The detectives planned to come back with additional assets in the morning to conduct a proper post blast/arson investigation of the scene.

Shortly after the detectives left the scene, the patrolman who remained behind was approached by an older male who showed him a fire department badge. The male stated that he was there to examine the fire damage. Since most patrol officers are not at all experienced in handling fire scenes, the young patrolman just waved the man with the fire department badge through the barrier tape and allowed him access into the building. He assumed he was with the arson investigators. The mysterious man was named Amparran. He walked through the scene for several minutes and then made a phone call from the interior of the building on his cell phone.

Weeks later, Det. Digby would find out that the man was a relative of the business owner, Valerio. One of the burned boats in the business was registered to him. It would take some additional weeks to realize what he was doing there. In the end, the man was a long-retired firefighter and certainly not an arson investigator. His "scouting mission" actually had a purpose.

Months later, investigators would conclude that Amparran was also an investor in this business. It was believed that he had invested over $500,000 in the failing business before the fire. Digby pieced together the event and later determined that Amparran was there to tell Valerio how much damage had occurred as Valerio had two distinctly different claim forms filled out. If there was a lot of damage, then Valerio could claim that a large number of items were in the building and all had been consumed. However, the fire was not actually that damaging, so when the former fireman told Valerio that everything was damaged but recognizable, then Valerio could only make a smaller claim. This was a typical mistake made by law enforcement in a case like this, in which an unauthorized person is granted access to an arson scene.

A day later the sheriff's department's arson investigators returned with a full complement of seasoned professionals. Mike Digby had now taken over the case, and the scene processing was commenced. Detectives fanned out and quickly found numerous indications that their original suspicions were starting to look true. The business had been locked and secured at the time of the fire, and the alarm had been set. There were no signs of forcible entry. However, the fire/explosion originated in the office area, on the floor near the pool of gasoline, indicating that the arsonists somehow accessed the interior of the location. This was a classic red flag in a business fire as most insurance-fraud arsons are ignited from the interior of the structure.

Other red flags began to appear. The detectives found two expensive bass boats, motors, and trailers in the garage area of the business. These items belonged to the owner, John Valerio, and it would later be revealed that they were only recently placed into the business, shortly before the fire. A quick look at the inventory for the business revealed that there were very few items on the shelves. Digby and his partners recognized both of these factors as consistent with a fraud-related fire.

Often people engaged in fraud "pad the claim" by placing unwanted items within the scene to be burned. In this case the two boats, motors, and trailers were worth tens of thousands of dollars and were added to the scene in the weeks prior to the fire. This was a huge red flag. Additionally, the lack of inventory at a business, or the stocking of shelves with cheap items, is another indicator that means the owner had some sort of involvement in staging this scene prior to the event.

The arson aspects of the case really jumped out. It was determined that a vapor explosion had occurred as the front doors were blown out, a roll-up garage door in the garage was blown out, and a plastic skylight over the boats was blown out. The explosion was consistent with the rapid ignition of the gasoline vapors.

The scene yielded several other pieces of significant evidence. Besides the gasoline on the floor and the gas can found in the office, investigators located a yellow plastic butane cigarette lighter out in the parking lot among the blast debris. The early speculation was that this was the item that ignited the fire, and it was probably blown out into the lot during the vapor explosion, which followed the ignition of the gasoline vapors. Digby and partners believed that it was likely that the arsonist for this fire may have injured himself during the act and may have visible burns or blast injuries. We had seen this before on several other occasions.

A close examination of the burned items in the garage revealed the presence of gasoline and a thick, dark oily substance around the boats and around the shelves that held the inventory. There was a blue plastic fifty-five-gallon drum sitting in the middle of the garage area, with no apparent purpose for this business. The drum contained an ignitable liquid. On the floor all around was a thick liquid similar to waste oil. Digby processed this scene and found that the building had three different points of ignition for the fire. One was in the area between the boats and the inventory, the second was in the bathroom of the office, and the final ignition point, which was the largest, was on the floor of the office near the front door. Gasoline was detected in all of these areas.

The final determination was that it was probable that an arsonist had attempted to start a fire on the roof of the business but had failed. A second attempt occurred by pouring gasoline in the garage and office area. Based on the blast damage, it was believed that the arsonist may have been standing outside of the front door and had probably lit the fire by reaching through the mail slot. He was lucky to be alive!

By the end of this day, Digby was certain that this was an insurance-fraud scheme as the items targeted (boats and inventory) were things that only an owner would want to burn. Buttressing his suspicion was his examination of the office. The office had desks, chairs, cabinets, and storage. All furniture items were practically empty of personal items, work materials, or the normal paperwork and supplies needed to run a business. Digby's team became convinced that this was a "bust out" operation.

Digby and team ascended the interior roof ladder and examined the items the firemen had found on the roof of this unit. They were utterly shocked by the evidence. They found that there was no exterior access to the roof, and whoever had been here had either brought a long ladder with them or more likely had accessed the roof from the interior ladder in the garage. About twenty gallons of a thick, dark liquid were spread across the roof. The liquid appeared consistent with a mixture of waste motor oil and possibly diesel fuel. Three expended highway flares were lying in the liquid, although the liquid had not ignited. Most astounding of all was that the detectives found that someone had drilled nearly fifty holes in the roof, all about one inch in diameter. After examining this, the investigators concluded that this was an incredibly serious attempt to burn the entire building to the ground!

The arsonist(s) had taken a great deal of time to enter the business and drag a drill and a large amount of fluid to the roof. They then drilled the holes in the roof and poured the fluid over the roof so that it would seep in through the holes. The roof holes were directly over the inventory and the boats below. This was the source of the oily fluid on the inventory and on the floor near the boats. The arsonist(s) then (presumably for safety reasons) went outside and threw the lit highway flares onto the roof, assuming they would ignite the liquid.

This "roof job" apparently did not work, and the arsonist(s) was forced at some point to come back to the scene, reenter the business, and then do things the old-fashioned way—by pouring a lot of gasoline. Based on what Mike Digby and his team were seeing, this arson attempt had turned the entire business into a massive incendiary device. For weeks after this, we speculated that the fire was possibly lit over a two-night time frame as the main fire started on Saturday, but we believed all of this work may have taken place over two different nights. We would never get the true answer on that, but it really didn't matter.

A roof job is one of the most dangerous and technical arson attacks that anyone would have the guts to attempt. We had seen these rare attacks before, and all of them had been insurance-fraud schemes orchestrated by the building owner. This was the investigative tack that Mike Digby started on.

Digby and his partner, Sgt. Mike Costleigh, made contact with business owner John Valerio just a couple of days later. They took a statement from him, and at the end of it, both Digby and Costleigh smiled to themselves. When asked where he was at the time of the fire, John Valerio had told the investigators that he was with his family at Disneyland. Unofficially, this was practically an admission of guilt. Every arson or fraud investigator in the Los Angeles area knows one thing for sure. If you are out of town in Las Vegas or at Disneyland and something like a fire, break-in, robbery, or major vandalism occurs to your car, boat, home, or business, then you did it!

It is almost comical how many fraudsters use those two locations as their alibi when they orchestrate the fraud. I am told by old-time arson investigators that these two alibis have been in use for decades. The rationale for their use is simple. In modern times, there are video cameras and cell phone tracking systems everywhere. However, in days gone by, sometime just a decade or more ago, the only places that had detailed surveillance systems were the casinos of Vegas and Disneyland.

Most fraudsters seldom do the deed themselves as they know only too well that we will suspect them and ask for an alibi. So, they establish an alibi that can be verified, like being seen on the security cameras at the casinos or amusement park, and then they contract out the dirty work to an associate or relative. We have seen this hundreds of times, and incredibly the same alibis are used continuously. Of course, knowing that Valerio staged this event and proving it would be two completely different things.

Digby and Costleigh listened to the rest of Valerio's story. He seemed well rehearsed and filled with details and not at all upset by this fire and explosion to his business. Valerio advised that he was in a niche business that was a wholesaler in electronic components. Valerio had a sole local employee. The only other employees of the business were in foreign countries. Valerio said that his business was doing fine and that he had insured it through Farmers Insurance. He did mention that he suspected this arson attack may have been done by "Nigerians," as both he and his former business partner had a falling out with a group of them recently. Valerio confirmed that he personally closed the business on Friday the twenty-third, the evening before the fire. He said he set the alarm code as was his normal custom.

After the interview, Dets. Digby and Costleigh both believed that Valerio was a well-rehearsed schemer as he was able to provide exact details and even receipts for all of his activities on the day of the fire. That is not something that is normally found in legitimate victims of major events. Digby knew then that Valerio had planned this for months and likely had done something like this before.

Digby began a records check through law enforcement sources on the history of John Valerio. Simultaneously, he contacted two insurance experts to assist him on what would be a several year investigation. First, he contacted the best National Insurance Crime Bureau (NICB) agent in the United States, Ron Michel. Ron had worked with our unit numerous times and was a multi-time winner of NICB Agent of the Year. Digby also contacted a hard-charging investigator from the California Department of Insurance, Detective Catherine Nash. All three of them began detailed inquiries into the life of John Valerio.

Within hours, Digby's suspicions were confirmed. John Valerio had a lengthy criminal history and a lengthy personal history of suspicious or fraudulent insurance claims. He, as suspected, was a seasoned pro at the fraud game. In 1985, as a juvenile, he had been arrested for burglary. In 1989 Valerio had been convicted of petty theft. In 1996 Valerio was convicted of burglary and sentenced to felony probation. In 2000 Valerio was convicted of fraud as he had stolen over $56,000 from a bank where he was a manager. He got a two-year prison sentence for that theft. He already had two felony convictions on his record.

Digby learned that Valerio was no stranger to suspicious fires. In 2005 Valerio reported that someone had torched his personal vehicle with gasoline and road flares. Digby noted that the same incendiary materials were in use at this latest fire. Valerio received $24,000 from that vehicle fire claim. That case was still an open/unsolved arson investigation. Over the Fourth of July weekend in 2007, Valerio reported a "spontaneous combustion" fire at his home. The fire was classified by arson investigators as "suspicious in nature." An insurance company paid Valerio over $180,000 for that loss.

Valerio had another suspicious claim in his insurance file when in 2005 he made a large claim to Lloyd's of London for a major burglary/theft to a storage locker. The carrier ended up paying Valerio $1.9 million for the loss. It was not hard to see that Valerio was a man who had grown accustomed to collecting insurance-claim money. We, having seen all of this before, recognized these prior events as all being probably staged by Valerio. We were up against a true seasoned pro when it came to fraud. Valerio had also declared bankruptcy in 2001.

Digby verified that Valerio was going through some serious financial difficulties in the months leading up to the fire/explosion at his business. Valerio was in a bitter dispute with his former business partner over finances. He was also going through a very contentious divorce and was in danger of losing his home and half his assets. Lastly, just ten months prior to this fire, the IRS had placed a half-million-dollar lien against Valerio for failing to pay taxes.

The NICB found out that although Globo-Tech had been at that site in Valencia since 2007, the business was not insured until just a couple of months prior to the fire. The insurance experts began delving into Valerio's claim. It was a major red flag waving in the air. The circumstances of the purchase of insurance were quite strange. Valerio had personally walked into a local Farmers office exactly two months prior to his fire. He asked for $4 million in coverage for his business. To get this large amount of insurance, Valerio put $5,500 in a down payment and the first two months of $2,700 each, all in a cashier's check. The nearly $11,000 in a single payment raised the eyebrows of his broker and the administrators at Farmers. They were so suspicious of this large purchase that they ordered the broker to physically go to Globo-Tech and inspect the premises, something that is rarely done.

Digby and his partners began pounding the pavement. They spoke to the owner of the building leased by Valerio. The owner said that all was not well with Globo-Tech as past rent checks had been returned with nonsufficient funds, and that during the past four months in particular the rent had been substantially late. The owner of the building believed that Globo-Tech was soon to be out of business.

Digby found Valerio's former partner. That man confirmed that Globo-Tech was losing money badly. He said that in just four months, early in 2009, Globo-Tech had lost over $800,000. He said they owed a large amount of money to several investors. He said he parted ways with Valerio as he viewed Valerio as spending extravagantly on motorcycles, boats, and lavish gifts for a girlfriend even as the business was failing. The former partner's name was not at all associated with the insurance claim on the business. The partner also confirmed that Valerio had taken investors' monies and sent tens of thousands of it to Nigeria in support of one of those "get rich" schemes that had been making the Internet circuit. Like everything else associated with the Nigerian schemes, the money disappeared, and the investors were hounding Valerio for their cash.

The investigators also contacted a former employee, who had stopped working several months prior to the fire. That employee told them that the business was failing miserably and that Valerio seldom ever showed up for work. He said that he quit after Valerio had cheated him out of $18,000 in sales commissions. He also mentioned that he suspected that Valerio had been involved in several shady, if not illegal, deals buying old computer equipment and passing if off as new.

Lastly, this employee gave Digby a true gem of information. He said that Valerio had hired him several years ago to do staining in his home. When he had finished the staining operation, he put the staining materials outside as he knew that they could possibly cause a fire. The next day he heard that the materials indeed started a fire but inside the garage, which was not where the employee had left them. The employee told Digby that Valerio was not at all upset and told him not to worry as the insurance company would pay for everything. Ever since that event, the employee was sure that Valerio had deliberately started that fire.

Digby and his mates had noticed during their fire investigation some things within the office. Of note was a distinct lack of personal items on the wall or on desks. Additionally, Digby had astutely noted that the business received a regular water delivery from the local Arrowhead company. Digby met with them and confirmed that John Valerio had a water contract with them starting in 2008. The company kept up a steady service until just one month before the fire when it was terminated for lack of payments.

Within ten days after the arson fire, John Valerio walked into the local sheriff's station and reported that someone had entered his damaged business and had stolen some computers that he had there worth over $10,000. This act was either a staged event to further "pad the claim" or was a crime-concealment move. We later learned that the insurance company had asked to review Valerio's business records as part of the claim process. They wanted to confirm that he had conducted as much business as he was claiming. The "theft" of the computers made doing that verification impossible. Yet another bright red flag had popped up as Valerio was clearly trying to hide evidence.

After just a couple of weeks of investigative work and interviews, Mike Digby and his team had a fleet of red flags waving at them about this event. Valerio had just split with his business partner, and he was going through a nasty divorce. His business was hemorrhaging money at the rate of $200,000 a month, yet he was buying luxury items like boats, motorcycles, and gifts for a girlfriend. Valerio was behind on his rents and on his water service. Several personal items were missing from the fire scene, and a large amount of odd items appeared to have been placed in the scene prior to the fire. Valerio had an established history of criminal behavior to include theft, fraud, and possible arsons. If anyone was a ripe candidate to have an arson fire, it was John Valerio. His past and most recent history almost predicted that he would be the "victim of arson." Digby and team now had all the circumstantial evidence they could possibly use. They now needed to positively connect Valerio to the arson event.

Digby contacted the alarm company that was hired by Valerio. The alarm contract was issued in July, just two months before the fire. There were only two codes used by the business: Valerio's and that of his sole employee. On the night of the fire, the alarm code used solely by Valerio accessed the business at 10:36 p.m., or about one hour prior to the fire. This was in direct contrast to Valerio stating that he had been at Disneyland. Later confirmation would show that Valerio was indeed at Disneyland; therefore, the investigators concluded that he gave his alarm code to another person, the arsonist.

Likewise, the locksmith who had made the only two keys for the doors of Globo-Tech was interviewed. He advised that only Valerio and one employee had laser-cut keys. The doors were all locked during the incident, so only a properly cut key could have opened the door. The employee was checked out, and it was verified that he didn't open the door. That left only Valerio's key unaccounted for. Again, it was believed that he likely loaned that key and alarm code to the arsonist.

Digby began a detailed cell phone search and analysis of all the numbers that Valerio had been in contact with in a several day period, both before and after the arson attack. Since we believed that Valerio had hired someone to burn this building, surely he would be in contact with that person both before and after the event.

Digby interviewed Valerio's insurance broker. That man told him that he had been very nervous and wary of this deal since the moment Valerio had walked into his office. He said after he sold Valerio the $4 million policy, he took the extraordinary step to visit Glob-Tech no less than four times over a six-week period. He noted that there was very little business activity and not a large amount of inventory for such a large policy. He did notice that Valerio kept many personal items, such as photos and trophies, in the office area. Valerio had assured the insurance man that his inventory was small but expensive and that sales were actually quite strong. He said he bought the large policy as he was about to greatly expand the inventory.

On the very last visit to the business, about one month prior to the fire, the insurance man was shocked and a bit alarmed to see that Valerio's personal property—the photos and trophies—was missing from the office.

The laborious investigation continued for weeks. Digby was able to get search warrants for Valerio's bank accounts and found something interesting. He found a check for $195,000 deposited into Valerio's account just three weeks before the fire. The check had the endorsement of Valerio's former partner. The bank confirmed that the check was forged and fraudulently endorsed. Valerio's partner had never given Valerio the check. It was clear upon seeing this fraudulent document that Valerio had attempted to take $195,000 from his bank by using his former partner as a scapegoat, but the bank refused to cash the check.

On the exact same day, another nearly identical fraudulent check for $225,000 was deposited into Valerio's other bank account. This check too was recognized as fake, and the bank did not cash it. It is notable that the same illegal activities totaling over $420,000 occurred on the same day to both of Valerio's accounts. It is important to remember here that John Valerio formerly worked as a bank manager and was familiar with the workings of banks.

The results of Digby's cell phone inquiries were mixed. The cell phone data established that Valerio was physically at Disneyland the night of the fire. However, the cell data results also showed that he was in contact with another male who was in the immediate area of Globo-Tech an hour before and an hour after the fire. That male was identified, and Digby found that the male had met on more than one occasion with Valerio in the weeks prior to the fire.

Digby met with an insurance adjuster named Rob Kassi. Kassi had been hired to complete a detailed inventory and adjust the loss of the building. Kassi told Digby that the items of inventory were actually cheap, outdated, and worth very little money. He said that when he first spoke to Valerio, that Valerio had given him a very detailed list of items that was incredibly inflated in quality and price. Mr. Kassi, an insurance expert, believed that the items in the business were worth less than $60,000, when Valerio put in a claim stating they were worth over $700,000.

Kassi had something else to add. He told Digby that he recognized Valerio from a previous fire scene. Kassi had been called to another city several months prior to adjust a loss at an electronics business. At that scene, Kassi had noted that a large amount of electronics had smoke and ash damage, which makes those items useless. Kassi told Digby that he recalled that Valerio had been present, attempting to buy the damaged electronic components. He now believed that the items within Globo-Tech were now the same items damaged in that previous claim.

Between Digby's investigation and the insurance company's own inquiries, Farmers began to seriously doubt Valerio's side of the story. They stalled on settling the claim, and in fact demanded that he come in for an examination under oath in early 2010. Shortly after this examination, Farmers Insurance, citing numerous misrepresentations by Valerio, officially denied the claim. This didn't seem to slow down Valerio's greed one bit, as less than a month later he submitted an amended claim for a total of $4.7 million. There was no end to his gall!

Nine months after the fire, on July 24, 2010, in the city of Palmdale, Valerio entered a Costco store and took detailed digital photos of SKU labels on low-priced computer boxes. He then went home, reproduced the labels, and put them on sticky tape. He took the labels back to Costco and affixed them to the most expensive computers in the store. He then pushed a cartful of these fraudulently labeled computers up to the checkout registers. Store video shows him selecting the busiest register and never removing the boxes from his cart. He then pushed the six computers out of the store.

Within a day or so, Costco realized that they had been scammed out of several thousand dollars and reviewed their security tapes. Palmdale sheriff's detectives determined the suspect was John Valerio and arrested him four days later for the commercial burglary. They raided his home but were unable to locate the stolen merchandise. It is important to note here that Valerio in the past had been a manager of a Costco and would have known how to beat the system. That theft case stalled as the stolen evidence could not be located.

Several months later, Digby got information that Valerio had been involved in the Costco scam and a couple of other similar scams since the arson fire. He dug deep and found that Valerio was renting a storage locker in a desert town under another person's name. On January 12, 2011, Digby and crew served a search warrant on Valerio's storage locker. In that locker Digby found the new computers and equipment that Valerio had taken via fraud from Costco in July of 2010. The Costco case would later be added on to a growing list of felonies filed against John Valerio.

It had taken a long time of unraveling all of Valerio's schemes and scams, but in early January of 2011, Det. Digby filed multiple felony charges against him with the district attorney. On January 13, several arson investigators from LASD arrested John Valerio at his Palmdale home. He refused to speak to the detectives and shortly was able to post his $100,000 bond.

Valerio did what all others of his ilk are prone to do. Instead of owning up to getting caught fair and square, he ran sniveling behind a battery of high-paid attorneys. It only cost him more money as he eventually lost the preliminary hearing and was soon headed for jury trial. Despite the doom on the horizon, Valerio still thought he could make a few bucks off this deal. While criminally he was looking at several years in prison, he nonetheless hired a civil attorney, who continued to pursue his large claim against Farmers Insurance.

Even while out on bail on this arson case, Valerio went to Utah and pulled a similar scam to the Costco scam. He again stole thousands of dollars of merchandise from a large retail store by switching labels. He was quickly arrested and just as quickly made bail. Over the next several months, Valerio kept fighting one case in Los Angeles, another in Palmdale, and began accumulating more fraud-related arrests for scams he pulled in Utah, in Florida, and in Costa Mesa, California. One of his scams involved purchasing cheap, almost useless computer parts, repackaging them, and selling them as high-quality items with a massive markup. At the same time Valerio had become involved in some sort of major car chase due to a fraudulent act. Digby couldn't keep up with all of Valerio's scams

Finally, because Digby was persistent, he was able to get John Valerio in front of a judge and a jury in November of 2014.

The five-week trial was filled with endless testimony about the high degree of sophistication exhibited by Valerio during his many scams. Eventually it all came to a merciful end when, in December of 2014, John Valerio was convicted of arson, use of an incendiary device, and multiple insurance-fraud charges. He remained in the local jail while he fought some of his other fraud cases. He also continued his ridiculous civil suit against Farmers Insurance.

Despite the mountain of criminal evidence against him that was presented at his conviction, Valerio still thought he deserved a payout from the insurance company.

Valerio resorted to his fraudulent habits, and in 2015 he somehow enticed a jailhouse "informant" to write a letter and claim that he was the one who had lit the fire at the behest of Valerio's old business partner. Oddly, this inmate's admission was not mailed to the LASD, the district attorney, or even to Valerio's criminal attorney, but somehow the informant had sent it to Valerio's civil attorney. This was clearly a ploy. A close examination of jail records would show that the "informant" inmate and Valerio had shared a cell block for several weeks prior to the letter being sent. It was yet another desperate scheme by Valerio to get out of his crime and to try to make money off of a scheme. I think he would have had better luck trying the Nigerian scheme again.

John Valerio is a **goal-directed arsonist**. He was sentenced to eleven years in prison for this highly sophisticated insurance-fraud/arson scheme. He has also been convicted for some of the other scams as well. He has continued his civil suit even as he wastes his life away in jail.

*The following detectives and criminalists worked on this lengthy criminal investigation: Det. Mike Digby; Sgt. Mike Costleigh; Det. Rick Velazquez; Det. Jim Gonzales; Det. Gary Spencer; Criminalist Joseph (J. J.) Cavaleri; Investigator*

*Catherine Nash, DOI; SA Ron Michel, NICB; Investigator Nancy Keech-Brown, Farmers Insurance.*

## PROFESSOR GREEN EYES
## LANCASTER, CA, OCTOBER 24, 2004
### LACoFD Investigation

At 8:27 p.m., Lancaster Sheriff's Station deputies responded to a structure fire at 1310 Marion Avenue, Lancaster. When they arrived, they saw that LACoFD Engine No. 135 was extinguishing the blaze. The deputies could see that the roof area near a chimney was on fire. After the fire captain declared a "knock-down" several minutes later, he entered the near-vacant home and began a cursory investigation.

In much of the United States, fire captains are routinely assigned the duty of conducting a preliminary investigation of all fires. If they are confident in their own opinion, they do not call their own department's trained arson investigators. Sadly, engine captains are given exactly one day of arson training when they are promoted. In reality, arson investigation is one of the most scientific and technical of all criminal investigations and takes hundreds of hours of formal instruction and hundreds of fire scenes to master.

In this case, like in so many across the United States and the rest of the world, the captain was dead wrong. In the real world, engine captains are wrong on their determination approximately 50 percent of the time. It is little more than a guess for them. This erroneous decision by the captain caused a domino effect to take place and caused an insurance carrier to give away a couple hundred thousand dollars to a greedy, scheming arsonist and fraud artist. (On a side note, I don't blame the fire captains of this country for this ongoing mess; I blame their bosses, the fire chiefs of the United States, for continuing to allow this disaster to unfold, even though they have been aware of this problem for over forty years.)

The fire captain in this case believed the fire was related to an electrical malfunction in a swamp cooler, or older style air conditioner, in the upstairs bedroom of the home. He ruled the fire as "accidental/electrical" and declined to call his own arson investigators for assistance. The fire captain estimated that the fire caused over $150,000 in damage to the structure. The captain would later fill in a "check off" list in the department's computer and would classify the event as an accident, with the cause of the fire listed as "failure of equipment" in the master bedroom. As the home was sparsely furnished, he listed the contents loss at $25,000.

While sheriff's deputies were still at the scene, a thirty-four-year-old black female, along with her nineteen-year-old nephew, arrived at the home and stated that she was the landlord of this property. She said that the home had been vacant for the past two weeks as she had been attempting to find new renters. In essence, the home was a vacant rental property, which would normally cause eyebrows to rise on any sort of suspicious fire. The owner was a striking black woman, very well built, with brilliant green eyes. She identified herself as Tiffany White, a professor at a local school district.

### LASD Investigation

That night the on-scene sheriff's deputies, in accordance with departmental protocol, placed a call to their own arson detail and advised them of the fire. They then left the scene to the firefighters. By eleven that same night, the fire department had completed its duties at the scene and had driven away, leaving the home unattended and unsecured. At this point nobody really cared about security as the fire was called an "accident" by the fire captain. At eleven thirty, LASD arson investigator Rich Edwards arrived at the scene to find the home empty. Edwards was a thirty-five-year veteran of the LASD and a twenty-five-year veteran arson/explosives investigator. He had investigated over four thousand fires up until this point of his career. He was probably the most senior and best-trained arson investigator in the state of California that particular night.

Det. Edwards's notes and reports classified the building as a normal two-story tract home, of wood and stucco construction, with an attached garage. He entered the home and found it to be sparsely furnished. The garage, which received no fire damage, had been filled with furniture, clothing, and personal items. Several of these stored items were marked with cheap prices, as if they were set to be sold at a garage sale.

Det. Edwards determined that the fire originated in the upstairs master bedroom and had caused extensive damage to the upper story, with the bottom floor sustaining minor damage. Because he was working alone at night in an unstable property, Det. Edwards left the scene at about one o'clock. He would return to resume his investigation at just after seven the next morning. Prior to leaving, he walked completely around the home and took photographs of the scene.

Several hours later Edwards returned and finished his scene investigation. He found fire patterns and evidence indicating that the fire had originated near a mattress on the floor of the master bedroom, which had almost no other furniture in it. The patterns were indicative of an accelerated fire, and Det. Edwards took eight different evidence samples of fire debris to analyze for ignitable liquids.

Det. Edwards asked for a technician from the electric company to respond to examine the electrical service. The technician confirmed that the electrical service had been terminated by a prior tenant sixteen days before this fire. Det. Edwards, with this information, ruled out an electrical problem as a cause for this fire.

Before he left the scene, Det. Edwards encountered the property owner, Tiffany White. He interviewed her at length.

She advised that she owned the property for the past thirteen years and that it had been a rental for her for the past few years. She currently lived nearby with her sister. She said that her last renters had vacated the property a couple of weeks before and that she was going to move into the property in just two days. She said the contents of the garage were her personal property. The prior renters had also been relatives of Ms. White, and she asked them to leave after they were unable to pay the rent.

Det. Edwards advised Ms. White that the fire was an act of arson. She said she had no idea who would start this fire as she had no problems with anybody. The two walked around the home and property. Det. Edwards was very suspicious of the lack of furniture in the home. He and Ms. White conducted a detailed assessment and only found a mattress, table, couch, and an old television. In the kitchen, there was no refrigerator and no dishes, pots, or pans. He pointedly asked Ms. White if she had set this fire or had anything to do with this arson attack. She denied any involvement in the fire.

The following day, on October 26, Det. Edwards returned to the scene with another LASD arson investigator and an accelerant-detection K-9. The dog alerted in the same areas where Edwards believed an accelerant had been poured. The LASD crime lab would analyze the samples at a later date and positively confirm that the samples contained a liquid accelerant.

Det. Edwards left the scene for the final time that day, classifying the event as an arson attack. He wrote the details of his scene investigation onto a police report. What he left out of this original report was his belief that this scene had all the hallmarks of a staged arson for the purpose of insurance fraud. Normally, Det. Edwards would have conducted a detailed, several week follow-up investigation. In this case, due to a family medical emergency, he was forced to end his investigation two months later with not much follow-up investigation. He classified the event as "arson," but was unable to investigate further due to personal reasons. The case was inactivated on December 30, 2004. Det. Edwards, after one of the most respected and lengthy careers in the LASD Arson-Explosives Detail, would retire shortly thereafter.

### Private Fire Investigation

On October 28, two days after Det. Edwards left the scene, the insurance carrier California Casualty hired a private fire-investigation firm to conduct a scene investigation at the home. The investigator who responded had learned that the fire department originally believed the fire was related to a failed swamp cooler above the master bedroom. The private investigator, a former fire marshal and arson investigator for a small city, had been a fire investigator since 1980. At the time of this case, he was working for a private company in fire investigations.

He would later acknowledge that he had no idea that a seasoned LASD investigator had classified the event as arson. He also would admit that he was unaware that there was no electrical service to the home at the time of the fire. For some reason, it didn't dawn on the private investigator at the time of his scene investigation that it seemed very odd that someone would even have a swamp cooler plugged in during the fall, winter, and spring months in that area. Lancaster sits in the middle of the high desert in northern Los Angeles County and is extremely cold during those times of year. It would be very rare for anyone to be operating a swamp cooler in those conditions.

When the investigator arrived at the home, he was met and escorted around the property by Bruce Copeland, a public insurance adjuster retained by Ms. White. The private investigator examined the scene and concluded that the swamp cooler was likely at fault. He didn't collect the entire bulky unit to be examined but instead recovered the remnants of the swamp cooler's power cord and the power outlet to which that cord had been plugged into. His company later brought those two electrical items to an electrical engineer who specialized in fire-damage analysis.

Shortly thereafter, the private investigator's firm informed the insurance carrier (California Casualty) that they believed the fire to be electrical in nature due to a failure in the power cord of the swamp cooler. From that point, California Casualty, completely unaware that the LASD's investigation had concluded that the event was a staged arson for insurance fraud, took the steps necessary to settle this claim.

At some point after that, the private fire-investigation firm sent the power cord to an electrical-engineering firm that would conduct a detailed forensic examination of the burned cord and outlet. The examination was inconclusive. The engineering firm reported the items had suffered electrical failures, but that the failures could have either caused the fire or been caused by the fire. They recommended in their engineering report that the private fire investigator conduct further investigation of the burned property or interview the victim to try to make a better conclusion. Whether anyone ever read this engineering report or not, the private fire investigator never went back to the property. He was never able to tell the engineering firm that there was no electrical power at the scene prior to the fire.

It took six months before the insurance carrier learned from the electrical engineer that the private fire investigator hired by them had not taken enough evidence at the scene and that the results of their analysis were inconclusive.

### Insurance Claim by Tiffany White

Immediately after the fire, Tiffany White contacted her insurance company, California Casualty, and informed them of the fire loss. Despite being told the event was a criminal arson by

Detective Edwards, she informed California Casualty that the fire was electrical in nature, caused by a failure in the swamp cooler. A review of Tiffany's insurance policy showed that she was covered for $136,000 in replacement costs for the home itself, and $102,000 in personal property (contents).

Tiffany listed her employment as a "professor" at a local college and that her income the previous year was about $35,000. Employment records show that she worked in a local school district as a temporary employee for about five months, with a pay scale of under $5,000 per month, which is hardly "professorial pay." The prior year she had worked as a part-time employee, less than twenty hours per week as an English instructor at a local junior college. For the remainder of the case, Tiffany demanded that several attorneys and investigators she came in contact with refer to her by her title, "Professor Tiffany White," despite the fact that she appeared to be little more than a tutor or substitute teacher.

Tiffany White was born Tiffany Peppers, the daughter of a bus driver. She was raised in South Central Los Angeles and later graduated from California State University, LA. She was employed as a teacher and tutor on and off since 1991. In 1997, she received a master's degree from Chapman College. At some point she was married to a man named White. They divorced in 1991. In 2002 she divorced husband Kevin Harris. In July of 2004, just months prior to the fire, she filed for personal bankruptcy.

On November 10, seventeen days after the fire, Tiffany met her insurance-claims adjuster in person and gave a formal recorded statement about the fire loss, the condition of her home prior to the fire, and the contents of her home at the time of the fire. She was accompanied by her retained public insurance adjuster, Bruce Copeland. In that statement, Tiffany told her claims adjuster that prior to the fire, she had instructed her tenants to remove her stored "custom furniture" from the garage and place it into the vacant home. She indicated that it was all in place throughout the home at the time of the fire.

Another bit of information Ms. White gave the claims adjuster was that she was present at the burning home at almost the exact time the fire department arrived. She watched them break down the door, and she saw "fire going up the stairs."

During that interview she said that the fire department told her that the air conditioner may have started the fire. She was asked if she had spoken to anyone from the LASD, and she replied, "No." At a second deposition in 2006, she again reiterated that she had never been told the incident was classified as arson, and she had never spoken to an arson investigator.

**Author's note:** An astute reader will note that both of these claims are in direct contrast to an accidental fire occurring near the swamp cooler. According to both the fire department and the private investigator's theory, the fire started and remained upstairs near the swamp cooler. Det. Edwards, from LASD, believed that the fire started in the upstairs and possibly on the stairway leading up the stairs. This would indicate a liquid accelerant or "trailer" poured in those areas. The lab confirmed this and, in fact, matches exactly what Tiffany White claims she witnessed. In her statement, she inexplicably told the insurance company the truth that the fire was arson. Additionally, she was absolutely lying about any custom furniture being spread through the home. Her tour with Edwards, along with his scene photos, show only three pieces of old furniture in the entire home.

On December 2, 2004, a restoration specialist hired by the insurance company gained access to the locked garage of the burned home. It still contained all the household items from before the fire. The specialist examined the items to see which could be cleaned and salvaged. He noted in his report that many items had hand-drawn price tags on them, for very little money, as if they were to be sold at a garage sale. These price tags had soot on them, and it was clear they had been in place prior to the fire.

**Author's note:** The reader will recognize that this "custom furniture" was, in fact, little more than yard sale junk that Tiffany White attempted to sell prior to the fire. At some point she apparently made the decision to "sell" it to her insurance carrier via a staged fire.

On May 13, 2004, the claims adjuster sent a letter to Bruce Copeland informing him that there were "several inaccurate statements" in a demand letter he had previously sent them. On that same letter, the adjuster advised Copeland that they could only agree on a few of the items listed as lost in the fire. They forwarded a settlement check for those items to Tiffany White in the amount of $11,122.

On February 24, 2006, an insurance attorney retained by California Casualty took a deposition of Tiffany White. This was in response to her claim of losing a large amount of property in the fire. She was accompanied by her public adjuster, Bruce Copeland. Prior to the deposition, the attorney had asked Tiffany to produce any and all receipts for the lost property that she had claimed. In the first minutes of the deposition, she told the attorney that because of the fire "everything was lost" and "I have nothing." She gave the same answer when asked about any video or photographic evidence of the property, which may have been taken prior to the fire occurring. When asked to produce utility bills and other household documents, she again maintained that all were destroyed in the fire. Tiffany also testified that she had always maintained the home as her residence, despite previously telling the fire department and LASD investigator that she was renting the property out to others.

During this deposition, Tiffany provided a handwritten list of items that she purchased to replace those "lost in the fire." That list included a $3,800 refrigerator, dishwasher, washer, dryer, stainless steel freezer, food processor, blender, a $2,500 vintage curio cabinet, a $400 coffee table, a three-hundred-piece set of antique china, a $2,000 to 3,000 set of gold flatware, $7,000 worth of crystal glasses, and office furniture. Additionally, she claimed that she lost $32,000 worth of books, $2,200 worth of towels, $8,000 worth of bedding, and $4,200 worth of makeup and applicators. This medium-sized tract home in a low-income neighborhood in the desert was also stocked with $60,000 worth of additional furniture in the downstairs alone and tens of thousands more in artwork.

Tiffany gave a second deposition on October 10, 2006. This time she continued to describe even more damages and lost items. She told the attorney for the insurance company that she had over three hundred pairs of shoes and a large amount of clothing in the master bedroom of the burned home. She said it was all burned up in the fire. When she was grilled by the attorney about this astonishing number, she was forced to admit that just after the fire, she only listed eighteen pairs of shoes burned and not three hundred. She blamed the huge difference on a mere clerical error. One year later, the lawyers for the insurance carrier would be stunned to receive a fifteen-page itemized addendum of loss for the home, detailing 236 additional lost items worth tens of thousands of dollars.

Tiffany surprised the attorneys when she told them that some of the expensive items were purchased with cash given to her by one of her boyfriends over the past few years. One boyfriend lived out of state, and he gave her several thousand dollars each time he saw her. A second boyfriend gave her over $10,000. She also claimed to get regular cash gifts of up to $15,000 from her father.

In August of 2002 and again in 2004, Tiffany White had submitted insurance claims for floods within her home to California Casualty.

### Bruce Copeland

Bruce Copeland was a husky black man in his early forties. He drove a variety of large, showy vehicles including a Hummer and another massive, custom SUV. Bruce Copeland was a licensed public insurance adjuster in the state of California in the early 2000s.

On August 18, 2006, Larissa Kosits, a staff counsel with the California Department of Insurance's (DOI) legal division, issued a formal accusation against Bruce Dwain Copeland and the many companies he was associated with. The accusation was a legal action that outlined numerous citizen complaints to the DOI, and it was a legal instrument designed to suspend or cancel Copeland's public adjuster's license. This particular document was the end result of a many-year investigation by DOI investigator Verdis Felton into the actions of Bruce Copeland. The document alleged numerous counts of fraud, embezzlement, theft, and incompetence by Bruce Copeland acting as a public adjuster in fire losses. It also linked Copeland to a man named Ignacio Navarro, who was a convicted felon and mastermind of the largest arson-for-profit ring ever prosecuted in California.

I was the lead investigator into the Navarro case and linked eighty-eight staged arson-for-profit cases to the ring run by Navarro from 1998 to 2002. I became aware that Navarro and Copeland were suspected of working together from about 1999 until 2003 and were suspected of dozens more fraud schemes linked to structure fires and staged arsons and floods.

This massive investigation, which resulted in numerous convictions, showed that Navarro, acting mainly in the Mexican American community, would solicit or instruct homeowners to commit an arson on their property, with the promise to rebuild the home better, add rooms, and hand the owners $5,000 in cash. In reality, Navarro's crew burned the homes, pocketed hundreds of thousands of dollars in insurance money, did token rebuilds, which seldom passed inspection, and then fled the scene, leaving the property owner with a home that was in very poor condition.

It was learned by the NICB, the DOI, the ATF, and the LASD that Navarro, while out on bond fighting his huge fraud/arson case in the Mexican American community, had created a business relationship with Bruce Copeland to continue this fraudulent activity in the African American community in South Central Los Angeles. By 2004, these above agencies were getting numerous complaints that Navarro and Copeland were ripping off dozens of victims in the black neighborhoods of Los Angeles. When each was confronted, they quickly blamed the other for the fraud.

One of the many facets of the ongoing fraud schemes by both Navarro and Copeland was that there were many admissions by coconspirators that the two often "coached" homeowners in how to stage a fraudulent fire and then how to greatly inflate the claim after the fire. The Tiffany White case seemed to be a classic Navarro-Copeland fraud/arson scheme.

By 2006, Bruce Copeland, hounded by the DOI, the NICB, and the LASD had decided to relocate out of California. Dozens of sources would later confirm that Copeland fled to New Orleans and was back in business there immediately following Hurricane Katrina.

### Insurance Attorney David Werner

As Tiffany White, through Bruce Copeland's company, began submitting more and larger claims for property lost in the fire, California Casualty began to realize that they were being victimized by a crude but brazen fraud scheme. They finally turned to a highly skilled attorney named David Werner.

In October of 2006, almost two years after the fire, David Werner undertook an examination under oath of Tiffany White. This time, Tiffany was not accompanied by Bruce Copeland. The more than 250 pages of transcripts of this examination are pure comedy gold as Mr. Werner struggled mightily to make sense of Tiffany White's ever-evolving claims and fantastic explanations for the endless discrepancies in her statements. In a never-ending game of cat and mouse, Mr. Werner kept trying to pin Tiffany down on specifics, such as the number of shoes and clothes in her home. In one brief exchange, she maintained that she kept three hundred pairs of shoes in individual custom boxes in a walk-in closet, while a few minutes later she claimed to only have one bra in her wardrobe. When Attorney Werner vigorously confronted her on the unlikelihood of fitting even half that number of shoes in the closet, she upped her estimate to say that she possibly had four hundred pairs in the closet!

Despite fantastic exaggeration, Tiffany White didn't hesitate to offer outright lies in the face of obvious evidence to the contrary. Among her many claims was that she had very expensive stainless-steel kitchen appliances at the time of the fire that were destroyed in the blaze. She was shown Det. Edwards's photos taken within ninety minutes of the fire being extinguished. These were taken in her presence the night of the fire. The photos depicted that the kitchen had no refrigerator, no microwave, and no other appliances or pots, pans, or dishes. The only appliance present was a several-year-old stove that came with the tract home. Despite this obvious evidence to the contrary, Tiffany steadfastly maintained that she had top-of-the-line, very expensive items throughout her kitchen. When pressed even further, she insinuated that someone must have removed her expensive appliances (for which she had no receipts) and replaced them with cheap tract-home appliances, all in a ninety-minute span in the middle of the night after the fire!

Mr. Werner became further exasperated when he read Tiffany's claim that she had lost all her kitchenware, silverware, and small appliances in the fire. He showed her Det. Edwards's photos again and pointed out that there was no fire damage in the kitchen as the fire had been upstairs. The photos clearly showed open cabinets that were empty. Again, Tiffany maintained that someone must have removed the items or they were burned up.

### Rental Property, Bankruptcy, Divorce, Perjury, and Fraud

California Casualty noticed from the start of this incident that Tiffany White had told various persons, including the sheriff's department and fire department, that her burned home was being used as a rental property at the time of the fire. As soon as they heard that information, the insurance company sought to confirm that, as that was in violation of the conditions of her policy. Tiffany White knew that her insurance only covered her if she was the actual person living in the home. From the start of their inquiries, California Casualty sought to negate much of the policy coverage by confirming that Tiffany had been renting out the property.

The cagey Tiffany, however, realized this, and from the first statements she made until two years later after several examinations under oath, she maintained that she always had lived there but that she often spent the night in other places. She gave vague answers over and over about who actually lived there, who paid the utilities, and where she actually was staying. It was finally determined that up to six people lived at the home in the months preceding the fire. The insurance attorneys had requested over and over for Tiffany to produce her tax records, divorce records, and any receipts she had. She had stalled for nearly two years, claiming alternately that these things had been burned, lost, missing, or destroyed.

On November 10, 2006, the final examination under oath took place in this case. Prior to starting this exam, Werner gave Tiffany a lengthy admonition about the crime of perjury and lying under oath. By this time, cornered by numerous inconsistencies and outright lies, Tiffany finally produced some of her tax and legal records to David Werner. The astute attorney immediately pointed out that many of the documents she had sent to him had areas that were "whited out." Tiffany claimed that the "whited out" areas must have occurred during copying. Attorney Werner also pointed out that in her 1999 federal tax records, she claimed her home as a rental property, in order to receive depreciation benefits. She denied that it had been a rental, basically admitting that she either had lied to the federal government in 1999 or was lying now.

She was forced to admit that she claimed it as a rental property every year from 1999 until the fire in 2004. This was in direct contrast to the earlier statements she had given to insurance reps and attorneys. Mr. Werner also got her to admit that the electricity had been turned off some weeks prior to the fire and that she had no recollection of ever turning it back on again.

Mr. Werner then pulled out the papers from Tiffany White's bankruptcy. This was started just three months prior to the fire. He pointed out that on her bankruptcy papers, she listed a total of "wearing apparel" of only $150 worth. Months later she would claim tens of thousands of dollars of clothing lost in the fire. In the same document she told the bankruptcy court she had "none" under the category of household goods, furnishings, and computer equipment. Her insurance claim a few months later would be for well over $200,000 worth of these things.

David Werner started to get downright ugly with Tiffany as he confronted her on her bills versus how much property she claimed to have. She was forced to admit under questioning that she owned a Mercedes-Benz and a Ford Expedition and hadn't made car payments on either vehicle for nearly a year prior to the fire. She owed over $58,000 on the vehicles. She had taken out a student loan in 1987 and had never made a single payment since then, owing over $75,000 to the federal government. She had numerous unpaid credit cards and owed several lawyers for various civil-court hearings.

Werner pulled out Tiffany's court papers for child support during a divorce hearing. She was forced to admit that she told the judge over her divorce/child-support case that she made only $533 per month, when she had claimed making over $35,000 per year several times already to the insurance carrier. Werner deftly pointed out that in court papers over a four-month period, all under penalty of perjury, Tiffany had told a bankruptcy judge she made $5,000 per month and a divorce judge that she made $533 per month. She later told the insurance company a completely different figure. More importantly, in her bankruptcy papers of August 2004, she told the judge, "I can no longer afford to live in my home in Lancaster." This statement was made just ten weeks before the fire.

Mr. Werner then focused on the child-support payments Tiffany was required to make. He showed court records that she had never made any child-support payments despite several court decisions ordering her to do so. In the face of clear court records, Tiffany denied that any of that was true. She, in fact, maintained that she was the one who was owed child-support money. She refused to acknowledge official court records in several civil proceedings.

Lastly, Werner pointed out that Tiffany had refinanced her home two years after the fire, pulling an additional $250,000 in cash out of it.

### Guy Friends

David Werner began pressing Tiffany White hard on some of her early statements. Tiffany, in answers as to how she had acquired so many things on her modest income, had made several statements that she was often given cash and gifts by several "guy friends." One in particular named "Al" gave her up to $50,000 in cash and gifts. She claimed he lived in Atlanta, Georgia, and would shower her with gifts and cash each time they met, which was several times each year for the past several years. When Mr. Werner began pressing her about the details of other "guy friends," she became very defensive and didn't want to reveal their names or the nature of their relationships with her. Eventually, after more questions, she gave the names of a few more, including the owner of the Los Angeles Lakers, Dr. Jerry Buss. Another name she gave was Kevin Cohee, a wealthy banker who controlled a bank catering to African Americans.

**Author's note:** By 2010, Kevin Cohee would find himself embroiled in scandal as he was accused of being involved in a congressional ethics scandal, drug use, and a past arrest for sexual assault. He was also accused of living an outrageously opulent lifestyle while claiming to cater to the underprivileged in the nation. His bank was named by federal regulators as one of the worst-performing banks in the nation.

Finally, Mr. Werner got to the point of this line of questioning. He had found a phone number linked to her, where she had a message on her phone inviting men to take her on dates for compensation. In truth, he was accusing her of acting as an escort, call girl, or prostitute. An outraged Tiffany denied that was her on the phone. Mr. Werner's investigation also turned up an escort ad that coincided with Tiffany's phone number. The ad was for the companionship to wealthy gentlemen of an African American woman in her thirties named "Professor Green Eyes," which seemed a clear indication of Tiffany White as she gave herself the title "professor" and had vivid green eyes (real or contacts).

### The Water Loss

During further questioning under oath, Attorney David Werner focused on a large-loss water-damage claim by Tiffany White at the same home in 2002. In that claim she alleged that a toilet had overflowed and destroyed thousands of dollars' worth of clothing and shoes and tens of thousands of dollars' worth of furniture. Mr. Werner adroitly pointed out that at the time of this "flood," all of the property in the home was in litigation in front of a civil judge, who was presiding over Tiffany's divorce from her last husband. The judge hadn't decided how to split the furniture and other household items. The "flood" made the point moot, as Tiffany received a large insurance settlement from California Casualty for this water-damage loss. This "flood" also conveniently deprived her ex-husband of any of the contested items in the home.

**Author's note:** A modern phrase in the arson-investigation world calls a staged "water loss" in a property a "wet arson," as the two events are quite often used by the same insurance-fraud scammers. This appears to be the case here as well.

### Civil Court Trial

On June 13, 2008, a very unique civil proceeding commenced. California Casualty, via its retained attorney David Werner, sued Tiffany White for the crimes of arson, insurance fraud, and perjury. It is a rare but not unheard of tactic for a civil attorney to actually sue a defendant for a criminal act that has never appeared in criminal court. Trial was conducted before a civil judge in Department Seventy-Four of the downtown Los Angeles Civil

Court. Tiffany White opted for a "court trial," meaning that there would be no jury in this case.

I was called as a witness on June 18. The reason I got involved is twofold. Det. Rich Edwards had retired before this and was unavailable. More importantly, I had been involved in a five-year investigation into a major arson-for-profit ring throughout the Los Angeles basin. This ring involved corrupt public insurance adjusters and phony contractors who were staging home fires for the purpose of profit. The ring had strong links with Bruce Copeland. The insurance-fraud schemers in this ring, all of whom were sentenced to prison, advised me that Bruce Copeland was conducting this same sort of fraudulent activity on a near-weekly basis within the black community. By this time I had examined several dozen complaints by persons who had been defrauded by Bruce Copeland. My role at this trial was to describe to the court how this scam by Tiffany White had been a classic Bruce Copeland-inspired caper, as by this time I had become quite an expert at identifying his scams. Basically I was called in as an expert on this type of fraud.

I had never met Tiffany White until that day. I was wearing a business suit and sitting in the hallway outside of court when she approached me. Tiffany was over forty and an extremely attractive black woman. She had bright green eyes. To me, the eyes appeared so bright they were almost bizarre, and I strongly suspected she wore contacts. Her dress was skin tight, with a deeply plunging neckline. She was overly made up and reeked of perfume. It was hardly courtroom attire, but she seemed to be like a lot of pseudo celebrities in Los Angeles who just didn't believe in social norms. She definitely wanted all eyes focused on her.

She sat down next to me and, possibly assuming I was an attorney, began chatting almost immediately. She seemed to have few secrets and told me all about the fact that she was here for some silly misunderstanding, and the judge would soon see things her way and award her about a half-million dollars. It appeared to me that this woman had no clue she was due in court on several felony charges.

Tiffany was soon joined by the private fire investigator who originally examined the fire after the event. This man was the private investigator hired by the insurance company, who made the determination that this fire was electrical in nature and, therefore, an accident. The investigator, who also didn't recognize me, assumed I was an attorney and immediately began talking about the case to a couple of people in the hallway. He was highly agitated and appeared very nervous. He told an attorney that "those damn sheriffs'" were completely wrong in their assessment of the fire and that it was clearly an electrical incident with arcing on the wiring to prove it. He went on with the usual fireman's complaint that cops didn't know anything about fire and shouldn't be in this business.

Silently, I raged. This private investigator was claiming that Rich Edwards had screwed up the fire-scene investigation. I knew, as most fire investigators in Southern California knew, that Rich Edwards was among the top three fire investigators around. He had been doing this work for twenty-five years and had looked at thousands of fire scenes. He had prosecuted some of the largest arson cases in California history, including the infamous John Orr case and the Universal Studios arsons. He was among the best of the best. I also felt a little bad for the private investigator as I knew what he didn't know. The private investigator didn't know that Edwards and the insurance company had found proof that there was no electrical power at all in the home at the time of the fire and that the crime lab had found accelerants around the origin of the fire. The case had been conclusively ruled an arson.

The private investigator's day was going to get worse as the insurance carrier, California Casualty, had also determined that he had made several mistakes. California Casualty, which had originally hired the private fire-investigation firm, had determined that the firm's own investigator was completely wrong in his findings, which eventually cost them over $200,000. In a very rare move, California Casualty, as part of this case, was going to go after its own fire-investigation firm for damages. By the time the private investigator arrived at the court, it was a mostly done deal. A lawyer representing the fire-investigation firm was present to propose some sort of settlement with California Casualty, as they too had recognized major errors in the private fire investigation.

I was present in the hallway when this attorney advised the private investigator of these facts. If he was agitated before this, the private investigator was downright distraught about learning all the true facts of the case. His errors would cost his company a pile of money. The lawyer for the insurance carrier (a different attorney than David Werner) later advised that the private fire-investigation firm had settled with them, but in true attorney fashion, he withheld the details.

My testimony about this case was pure profiling at its best. I explained that I was somewhat of an expert in staged arson-for-profit schemes and had won national recognition in this field. Specifically, I had looked at dozens of cases involving Bruce Copeland, and I testified that this was very typical of a Copeland-inspired fraud scheme. I also was able to testify for retired LASD detective Rich Edwards and about the veracity of his investigation. I gave my expert opinion on the heavy staging of the crime scene, which is a hallmark of insurance-fraud arsons. The fire was set near an electrical appliance (swamp cooler) in an attempt to pass this entire event off as an accident.

This sort of simple scheme has been fooling naïve fire investigators in both the public and private sectors for a hundred years, and it looks like it will continue for the next century. In this case, this very crude and simple scheme fooled the fire captain that fought the blaze, a private fire investigator with over twenty-five years of experience, and any number of insurance adjusters. The only persons not fooled were the highly experienced LASD investigator Rich Edwards and the equally astute civil attorney David Werner.

After I was done explaining my profile of this event and of the design and scheme of a typical Bruce Copeland-influenced incident, I sat back and awaited a stiff cross-examination by the defense. In this bizarre case, it came from none other than Professor Green Eyes herself. Tiffany White, acting a bit as her own attorney, made several weak attempts at cross-examination. She appeared to have no concept of the law and none whatsoever of courtroom tactics and strategy. She exasperated the judge by asking me such nonlegal questions like "What do you have against me?" and "Why are you saying negative things about me?" To me, she was no more a lawyer than she was a professor.

After her inept questioning, the judge mulled the case over for just a few minutes and found that she was civilly guilty of arson and many counts of insurance fraud and perjury. He found completely in favor of the insurance carrier and advised a tearful Tiffany White that it was likely the LASD would be arresting her in the near future. He awarded California Casualty a very hefty settlement in this case.

In a rare move for me, I had to tip my hat to a civil attorney. David Werner, counsel for California Casualty, had painstakingly unraveled one of the better fraud schemes I had ever seen. Well done! Years later he would tell me that while he had obtained his arson conviction and the judge had awarded financial damages to the insurance carrier, the company never received a dime from Tiffany White. Like she had so many times in her life, she avoided any responsibility for her actions.

After she emerged from court a convicted arsonist, a completely mystified Tiffany White still could not understand why no one believed her. She had told so many lies in her life that at this point, even she was starting to believe them. This "professor" with the green eyes was finally officially exposed for what she had always been: a fraud, a liar, and an arsonist.

*This case was the result of the work of Det. Rich Edwards, LASD Arson-Explosives Detail, and Mr. David Werner, a private civil attorney. Det. Ed Nordskog was a profiler and expert witness for the courtroom portion only.*

### Investigator's Profile

Way before I got involved in this event, Det. Rich Edwards had made an accurate, on-the-spot profile the night of the fire that this had all the appearances of an owner-involved arson-for-profit scheme. This is a huge problem in the arson-investigation field. What was very apparent to Rich Edwards just minutes into his investigation was missed by several important people: the responding fire captain, the insurance-claims adjuster, the insurance company's privately retained fire investigator, and the insurance executives who originally had settled this claim. The real crime here is that this same thing occurs several times each day in this country (and the world), and the same types of people are fooled over and over again.

Tiffany White is a **goal-directed arsonist**. This scene is the easiest scene in the world to profile. Any fire in a vacant home is suspicious on its face. The fact that the owner showed up to the fire scene almost immediately is also highly suspicious. When the fire occurs at night with the use of accelerants, along with the fact that the property was recently vacated, well then, it practically screams "arson." All of these red flags should have called for an immediate arson investigation from the insurance carrier.

The investigator that was sent out was clearly focused on finding an accidental cause for the carrier to subrogate its losses and missed the extremely obvious signs of an incendiary fire. This is an ongoing bias with private arson investigators who may look to "please" the insurance carrier by finding a way for them to save money on this loss, as opposed to actually investigating a crime. While it involves a different subject for another time, this sort of fanaticism for pursuing loss subrogation has greatly degraded the quality of civil fire investigations.

Tiffany White, being a woman, probably did not start her own arson fire. This sort of act during an arson-for-profit scheme is seldom carried out by a woman but instead is often done by a male acquaintance or relative. We will never know the answer to who actually lit the fire, but we know assuredly who profits from the fire. Tiffany White clearly had some skill and experience in committing fraud. Her entire life had been spent lying in courts and to attorneys. She had numerous previous court cases involving bankruptcy, insurance claims, divorce, and child custody in which to practice her craft. Despite all of this experience, she inexplicably stuck to incredibly inflated insurance claims and outrageous statements that were easily proved false.

Tiffany also represents a type of con artist who, through her good looks, manipulative ways, and sheer audacity and boldness, had fleeced any number of men and entities out of hundreds of thousands of dollars. Hers is a textbook case of a fairly simple and crude fraud scheme that would have been very successful for her had she not gotten so greedy after her initial claim.

The investigation done by Attorney David Werner also points out the excellent investigative axiom of looking backward for the truth. He recognized in Tiffany White a skilled liar and con artist, and went backward in official records to use her own lies and past crimes against her. I have done this same technique on dozens of fraud-related arson cases, and almost every one of them shows the fraud arsonist having committed several other lesser frauds before he graduated to arson. Fraud is indeed a learned behavior.

## SODA MACHINE ARSONIST LANCASTER, CA, 2008

In the fall of 2008, an arsonist began attacking specific targets in the town of Lancaster, which sits in the desert region north of Los Angeles. Like all arson series, the first few attacks went virtually unnoticed by the local cops. They responded but really didn't put too much info on paper as they considered it a pretty small event.

On September 29, a small fire was reported in a mobile-home park on the east side of the city. Responding deputies found two vending machines on fire. The vending machines were in the common area of the park and were both owned by the Pepsi company. One machine dispensed Pepsi sodas, and the second one dispensed bottled water called Aquafina. The fires were both set on the right side of the face of the machines near the money slots. A responding arson investigator from the LASD Arson-Explosives Detail examined both machines and determined that they had been set on fire by some sort of flammable liquid poured into the coin slot and ignited. The fires had been extinguished by park personnel and had not completely destroyed the machines. It should be noted that both machines were metal framed, but the faces were plastic. No suspects were seen, and no leads were available to follow. The investigator chalked up this one event as a probable prank or act of vandalism. Despite the limited damage, each machine cost $2,000 to replace.

Two months later in a public park in the same city, a Pepsi machine was set on fire. This fire seemed unrelated to the previous two fires as the scene was at least five miles away. Like the previous attacks, the fire was concentrated on the right side of the face of the machine in the vicinity of the money slots.

Things were quiet until about two months later in January of 2009, when four identical arson attacks occurred to Pepsi machines in four city parks on the east side of the city, close to the original attack. All of the attacks occurred at night. February brought even more fires as Pepsi machines were set on fire in city parks on the first and the eighth of the month. This time the attacker switched back to the west side of the city.

On February 12, the attacker went into high gear and hit four vending machines in three different parts of the city. This time it was evident that he was clearly mobile in a vehicle as the scenes alternated between the east and west sides of the city, an area about five miles apart. Like all of the previous attacks, the fire was set on the face of the machine at or near the coin box.

The local fire department began talking about a serial arsonist who was attacking vending machines in the public areas of Lancaster. Fire department investigators wanted to go out on stakeouts of all vending machines to see if they could catch the arsonist in the act. They had no idea that there were hundreds of machines spread across the city. The LASD arson investigator assigned to this case had over twenty years of experience as a detective and quickly profiled this event for what it was. He recognized that while the targets of the attacks were all very similar, their locations were spread around quite a bit, which is not normal for a "typical" serial arsonist, who may be setting fires for excitement purposes. That type of arsonist normally sets fires in a very finite geographic area or sets clusters of fires related to something in his daily life like where he works, goes to school, or visits a relative.

In this case, the fires were spread a long way apart and too far for a typical serial arsonist, who usually does not have access to a vehicle. Besides the distances, the LASD arson investigator recognized that the intent of the arsonist did not seem to be in lighting a large fire or burning the machines to the ground. All of the fires had caused only localized damage and had all originated inside the cash area of the machine. Very quickly the detective recognized this activity as probably a fire set for financial gain. In this case the fire was actually a burglary designed to burn the area of the machine near the cashbox so that it could be compromised and accessed by the person who set the fire. We were looking for a burglar, not an arsonist. In this case fire was just a tool used by a burglar to commit theft.

The LASD started looking for burglars in the area. We also knew that if our suspect was a burglar, he was likely a drug addict and probably addicted to the drug of choice in the desert—methamphetamines. Unfortunately, the desert area is swarming with meth addicts, burglars, parolees, and probationers. Finding this guy would take a string of luck. By late February the luck would come.

Luck was on the side of the LASD as a witness had seen a fire start in some vending machines on a train platform. The train platform had many security cameras, and soon an excellent picture of the burglar/arsonist emerged. The suspect was a shaved-headed white male about twenty-five to thirty years old. Responding LASD deputies later viewed the video provided by the rail authorities and then released it to the local media. Phone calls came in rather quickly as the suspect was soon recognized as a local burglar named Walter Reeves.

Detectives quickly tracked him down and arrested him. A couple of the local deputies recognized Reeves because he was currently on felony probation for sales of narcotics. As part of his probation, and to avoid actual jail time, he was ordered to work in a "work-release" assignment, in essence to pay back his debt to society by working. His work place was the local Lancaster Sheriff's Station, where he swept, raked, and pumped gas for all the patrol cars.

The arson investigators looked at the criminal record of Walter Reeves. As predicted, he had a slew of crimes associated with drug use, theft, fraud, forgery, and burglary. As important, he had none of the crimes typically associated with a firebug. This guy was clearly using fire as a means to commit burglary and therefore feed his drug habit.

Reeves was eventually interviewed and found to be in possession of a significant amount of quarters and other coins, consistent with having broken into vending machines. He gave a partial admission and had his probation revoked. He was sent back to jail to await a new trial on the arson charges. In August of 2009, Walter Reeves took a plea deal on two counts of arson and was sentenced to state prison for three years and eight months. He got out after a little more than two years and within just a year committed another felony and was sent back to prison. He has been released twice since then and subsequently violated his parole on both occasions, landing him back in prison.

### Investigator's Profile

The profile on this case was very simple and fairly basic for an experienced arson investigator. The target selection by the offender was very consistent: plastic-faced machines that held money. The method of access was by flame, but in fact Reeves was found to have used a small amount of accelerant poured into the coin slots and then ignited, which was a fairly unique ignition scenario. These identical ignition scenarios and the consistent selection of targets were the factors that enabled investigators to link numerous fire scenes that were some distance apart. The fires were very small and caused localized damage, as opposed to someone wanting to burn the machine to the ground.

The one factor that threw investigators off a bit was the geospatial pattern of the fires. The offender's first fires were set very close to his home. He then hopscotched back and forth from the east to the west side of the city, sometimes in the same night. This obviously meant that the offender was mobile with a vehicle as the scenes were over five miles apart. It also meant that he had to drive some distance to find machines that were hidden in a dark area of a city park. While this guy has the word *arsonist* associated with him for the rest of his life, his motivation is not fire setting, but is in fact profit, with fire having been used as merely a tool for him to earn his profit. He's simply an ingenious burglar. He is considered a **goal-directed arsonist.**

This was not the first or last time my unit dealt with an offender using this technique. The very first time we heard of this was nearly a decade earlier at a time when vending companies were just switching to plastic-faced machines. In 2002 I attended an arson seminar for investigators from the Los Angeles area. About sixty arson investigators were in attendance discussing major cases and trends. A team of two investigators from a beach city stood up and gave a thirty-minute talk on a serial arsonist in their area. They had worked on this case for months and proudly proclaimed that they had detected a "sexually motivated" offender who was targeting Coca Cola machines. They had consulted with FBI profilers and had even contacted Coca Cola corporate headquarters in Atlanta.

After careful consideration, they came to the conclusion that the mysterious arsonist had burned over twenty-five Coca-Cola machines because he was sexually excited by the image of the Coke bottle on the front of the machine. The intrepid investigators believed that the classic curvature of the Coke bottle resembled a curvaceous woman and thereby enticed the arsonist to satisfy his sexual urges through fire.

For several minutes most of us were dumbstruck as we thought this was just an elaborate joke. Several of us in the room had already found vending-machine fires in our areas where the cashbox was literally burned out of the front of the machine. When we realized that these two investigators were completely sincere, we all burst out laughing and ridiculed them off the dais. They had clearly and foolishly bought into the old arson myth about serial arson being a sexually motivated offense. The two red-faced fire investigators quickly got a lesson in the operations of tweekers and burglars. Eventually, the vending companies placed metal plates in their machines surrounding the cashboxes and the arson fires to these machines quickly abated.

## PEERNOCK
## LOS ANGELES, CA, 1987

*This case is from the files of the Los Angeles police and fire departments. Some information was taken from the book* A Checklist for Murder *by Anthony Flacco, while additional portions were told to me by retired LAFD investigator Mike Camello.*

Robert J. Peernock was a fifty-year-old pyrotechnical engineer who lived in the northern Los Angeles County suburb of Saugus. He had learned this trade so that he could work in the motion picture and television industry in the San Fernando Valley. Some pyrotechnicians learn their craft via on-the-job training, while others have a higher level of education derived from a degree in engineering. Robert Peernock had learned his trade via the engineering route. He had worked in this very technical field for a short time but eventually lost his job. Although he had training as a pyrotechnic engineer, Peernock worked professionally in a state government job for the Department of Water Resources.

He was retired on a stress disability from that career in 1987 at the time this case came to light.

Peernock married his wife, Claire, in 1967. The two separated around 1982. The couple had an eighteen-year-old daughter named Natasha, along with an eleven-year-old daughter named Tanya. Claire and Robert Peernock had serious marriage difficulties, and Robert had moved out of their Saugus home in the early 1980s. For several years he lived with a girlfriend in the San Fernando Valley. However, he occasionally visited his wife and two daughters in Saugus up until the date of this incident.

### The Incident

On the evening of July 21, 1987, Robert Peernock was visiting the family home in Saugus when he became enraged at eighteen-year-old Natasha for wasting electricity. He grabbed her violently by the throat and choked her until she fell onto the ground. Natasha later testified to these events in court and remarked that she was not overly alarmed at this assault by her father as she had grown accustomed to his violent outbursts over the years. This sort of activity seemed fairly normal to the girl. She told the court, "He flipped out like this all the time." She remarked that after the assault, her father had apologized to her. He then left the home.

Several minutes later, Robert Peernock returned to the home, and things started to get evil. He approached Natasha again and immediately grabbed her and placed handcuffs on her. He then forced a macabre-looking cloth hood over her head. The hood had been premade and had no eyeholes, only a hole for her nose and mouth. He then led the girl into a bedroom where, through an odd pumping device that he affixed to the hood, he forced a large amount of whiskey and a white pill down her throat. He then pulled out a revolver and began spinning the cylinder and cocking the gun next to the girl's head. He told the girl that he was going to "blow her brains out" with the gun unless she and her mother signed some papers. He then bound her legs and hog-tied them to her handcuffs. She was forced to lie in a bedroom and was again fed more whiskey.

This went on for a couple of hours until the young girl was quite drunk. Natasha asked her father if he was going to kill her. He simply answered, "Yes." Natasha, who was by now semi-conscious from the booze and pill, lay in the bedroom after Peernock left. She heard her mother come home and then a loud disturbance coming from the kitchen area of the home, where she believed her mother was.

Several hours later, the drunk/drugged girl recalled being placed into the back seat of her father's Cadillac, along with her mother. She said that her mother was breathing but unresponsive to her questions and nudges. Natasha said that her father then entered the car, and they drove somewhere. She awoke to hear him exit the car and go to the rear of the vehicle. She heard him tinkering with something mechanical at the rear of the car. She then felt him place both her and her mother into the front seat of the Cadillac. She could tell by the sounds outside that they were near both a freeway and a railroad line.

While seated in the front of the car with a hood over her head and her hands and feet still bound, Natasha felt the first of several violent blows to her head from a tire iron. Mercifully she passed out after the first vicious blow. She wasn't awake to feel the several additional blows, which fractured her skull. Nor was she aware that her mother was beaten to death in the same manner while sitting next to her.

### The "Accident"

At about four in the morning on July 22, 1987, a passing motorist came upon a car accident on a quiet side road in Sun Valley. This road was in a dark industrial area between the 5 Freeway and the Union Pacific rail line. This area is about twenty miles from the Peernock home in Saugus. Arriving LAFD firefighters and LAPD officers found that a black Cadillac sedan had veered off the road and sheared off a wooden utility pole. Firefighter paramedic Clyde Piephoff entered the damaged car and found two women in the front seat. FF Piephoff found that the older woman was dead due to severe head trauma, but the younger woman, although badly injured, was still alive. Both victims reeked of whiskey, and there was a whiskey bottle on the floorboards. There was blood splattered across the inside of the windshield. The entire inside of the car had been soaked with gasoline, but luckily there had been no fire within the car.

Piephoff and other firefighters noted that while the two women in the car were badly injured, the interior of the car suffered almost no damage at all. The damage to the car did not match the women's injuries. The scene did not make any sense at all.

The firefighters noted that there was an odd rope or fuse extending from the rear of the car that had been burned, and there was a small fire in the trunk area above the gas tank. This situation was extremely suspicious to the police and fire crews. The barely alive girl was transported to the hospital, but the older female (deceased) remained at the scene.

Arson and police investigators descended upon the death scene. LAFD arson investigators Michael Camello and Rick Chew arrived first. Camello would eventually be the lead arson investigator for this case. Inv. Camello spent over thirty-three years as an arson investigator and attended nearly four thousand arson scenes. He would recall this case as the most devious and bizarre one he had ever been involved with. Camello first took note of the victim. He noted that she had blisters on her skin that appeared as if it had been burned. Closer inspection would prove that the blisters were from a caustic chemical in the form of gasoline that had been splashed onto the skin. Camello saw that the older female was on the floor of the driver's side and that her right foot was jammed down on the accelerator pedal. There was a whiskey bottle on the floor of the car. He found the remnants of a rope tied around the gearshift lever.

Inv. Camello found this scene to be increasingly bizarre. His suspicions were so high that he called an LAPD homicide investigator over to the scene. Det. Steve Fisk arrived, and both he and Camello carefully examined the car. The veteran investigators were completely stunned by what they found. First, they found that the gasoline from the interior of the car had not come from a leak in the gas tank. Someone had poured gasoline over the bodies of the interior passengers. They found the source of that gasoline in the trunk of the vehicle, where a gasoline container was located. The trunk also held a stick, some wood, and other combustible materials. These articles appeared to have been burned by fire. Secondly, the fire underneath the rear of the car was not caused as a result of the "accident."

The arson expert determined that a rope extending from the rear bumper had been soaked in gasoline and set on fire before the car crash. Inv. Camello followed the burned rope into the trunk area where it connected to the gasoline container. The fire on the rope appeared to have self-extinguished at some point while in the trunk and, thankfully, had not ignited the gasoline poured through the interior.

Lastly, Inv. Camello found a very bizarre item affixed to the rear axle area of the car. He found an L-shaped piece of heavy metal, ground down to a very sharp point affixed near the axle, with the pointed end next to the gas tank. While the entire underside of the car was dirty with road debris and dirt, this piece of metal was cleaner and newer in appearance. It appeared that this item had been recently added to the car as a device designed to penetrate the gas tank when the car impacted something hard.

At the end of his investigation, Inv. Camello would later describe the car as having an incendiary device rigged in "the most elaborate way I've ever seen." He later described in jury trial that the car was one large incendiary device with the interior filled with gasoline, and the metal piece designed to puncture the gas tank to add several more gallons of fuel to the fire. The investigation revealed that the car's gas tank had been completely filled with gasoline shortly before the crash. Inv. Camello said that the fire from the burning rope was supposed to act as an ignition fuse and eventually ignite the gas container in the trunk and then the spilled gasoline from the punctured gas tank of the car. It was obvious from the large amount of fuel at the scene that the bodies of the two women were intended to be cremated in the large fire that was to have ignited.

The investigators at the scene took note of the terrain and saw that the car had been intended to be driven from the top of a hill, down toward a solid block wall at the bottom of the hill. Inv. Camello concluded that this event was staged to appear as a traffic accident, where the car would explode into flames when it crashed into the wall. Camello and Fisk developed the theory that someone had placed the women's bodies in the car, had started the vehicle in "neutral," and had jammed the older woman's foot down on the accelerator pedal. The suspect had ignited the gasoline-soaked rope at the rear of the car and then used another rope around the gearshift lever to remotely pull the transmission shifter into "drive." The revving car then sped down the hill toward the wall but veered off before impact.

This exotic movie-like plan was thwarted as experts determined that the older car was out of alignment and had veered off the roadway sooner than the suspect had planned and before it could gain enough speed to activate the penetrator device near the gas tank as it struck the solid wall. Like many exotic incendiary or explosive devices, this one failed and left investigators a ton of incriminating evidence. Needless to say, no one had ever heard of such a farfetched plan, and the homicide brass initially did not believe this was possible. They eventually came around to believe the two investigators.

### The Investigation

Homicide investigators ran the car on police computers and found that it belonged to Robert Peernock. They soon identified the live passenger as his eighteen-year-old daughter, Natasha, and the deceased woman as Peernock's wife, Claire. Both women had severe head wounds, but the investigators determined that the wounds did not match the damage to the car from the accident. The wounds were more consistent with an instrument such as a metal pipe or bar. They soon recognized this as a bizarrely staged event by someone who wanted to murder the women and make it appear as an accident. Eventually the detectives were able to interview Natasha, and she told them the bizarre story about her father.

The detectives immediately went out to locate and interview Peernock. Inv. Camello called Peernock on the phone to inform him of the incident and the fact that the investigators needed to speak to him. Peernock told them he was on his way to the scene. He never showed up, and when investigators went looking for him, they found that Robert Peernock had vanished!

The coroner examined Claire Peernock and confirmed that she had been beaten to death before the accident and that her injuries did not match the car crash scene. LAPD detectives learned that Robert Peernock and his wife had amassed a large amount of money during their marriage through real-estate investments. There was also life insurance on the wife, Claire. If both Claire and their adult daughter had died, then Robert Peernock would control all of the money in the estate, which amounted to over $1.5 million. The investigators also found out that Claire was just weeks away from beginning divorce proceedings against Robert.

During their investigation, the detectives learned about Peernock's highly technical background, his hair-trigger temper, and his obsessive and paranoid personality. They found out that on the day after the car crash, instead of visiting his daughter in the hospital, Robert Peernock had visited a local bank, where he attempted to withdraw over $50,000 jointly owned by he and his (now deceased) wife, Claire. A few days later a friend of Claire's contacted the police and told them that she had heard of the "accident" but was sure that Claire had been murdered. When questioned, the woman said that several months earlier Claire had predicted her own death. She had told this friend that Robert would try to kill her before settling on a divorce, and he had the abilities to make it look like an accident. She worried openly to her friend that her oldest daughter would be a target as well. Claire Peernock eerily and accurately predicted this event months before it occurred!

Several days later Claire's divorce attorney called the investigators after she had heard of the death. She said that Claire had instituted divorce proceedings several months earlier, but Robert had convinced her to hold off until early August. This "agreement" was to expire in just a week. At that point Claire would continue with the divorce and divide up the civil assets. With her now dead, Robert Peernock owned 100 percent of their assets. This was the motive the detectives were seeking. Robert Peernock was soon determined to be the only possible suspect in this exotic murder scheme.

The arson and homicide investigators located the residence where Robert Peernock had been staying before the incident. They served a search warrant and found that he had fled that scene as well. They also found a treasure trove of evidence. In the garage they found pieces of cut metal that matched the device found affixed near the gas tank of the car. They also found metal shavings on the floor and on tools indicating that the pointed item had been manufactured in the garage. A large vise at the residence would be forensically matched to the imprints it had left on the metal device from the car. Additionally, they found the remaining portion of rope in the garage that matched the pieces from around the gearshift lever and the gas tank "fuse." The physical evidence was pointing directly at Robert Peernock.

A week or so after the car crash, Peernock's personal car, a small Datsun, was found near the Los Angeles airport. The detectives searched that car and found two handguns and a tow-bar connection at the front of the bumper. This filled in the mystery of how Peernock had fled the scene. He had driven the Cadillac with the two unconscious women in the back seat from the Saugus home to the crash site. The Cadillac had a tow hitch on the back, and Peernock had apparently pulled his own small Datsun behind the Caddy via the tow bar and tow hitch. He then uncoupled the cars, staged the crash, and fled the scene in the Datsun.

Several weeks later investigators learned that Peernock was in contact with a girlfriend and that she appeared to be helping him get money. Investigators arrested the woman and stuck her in a jail cell as an accomplice to the murder. After spending a few hours in a cell with prostitutes, the woman decided that prison life was not for her. She began cooperating with the cops and told them that Peernock was out of state but would be returning to Los Angeles to pick up money on a given date. Six weeks after the staged car crash, on September 4, 1987, Robert Peernock was located and arrested for murder. He had been found in a motel room in the San Fernando Valley, registered under a fake name. He was driving a Nevada-registered car, and was believed to have recently returned from Las Vegas, where he had undergone plastic surgery on his face in an effort to alter his appearance. He had also changed his name. It was clear that Peernock had fled after he learned that his daughter had survived to tell her story.

Upon his arrest, Peernock threatened suicide to "save the taxpayers a lot of money." At the time of his arrest, Peernock had $28,000 in cash on him. He later accused arresting officers of taking some of the cash and placing it into their own pockets. This would be the first of hundreds of accusations he made against the cops, the coroner, doctors, lawyers and all of the judges of Los Angeles County.

### The Criminal Case

Robert Peernock was eventually charged with murder for financial gain, attempted murder, kidnapping, and arson. Like many suspects with obsessive and paranoid histories, Peernock would not accept his fate quietly. His case was delayed for nearly three years as experts evaluated him and debated his sanity. Eventually he was deemed fit for trial and began the long court process. During this same time he began a vicious legal battle with his daughter, Natasha, and her attorney over the family estate. He fought from his jail cell with his own attorneys and then employed a more sinister tactic.

Peernock had a lot of money at his disposal and was rumored to have hidden large amounts of cash. Peernock began a wave of threats and intimidation toward anyone who opposed or spoke ill of him. He targeted all the investigators and prosecutors with complaints, threats, lawsuits, and intimidation tactics. Peernock hired private investigators to collect information on the cops and prosecutors targeting him. During the trial, the head prosecutor, Craig Richman, had a family vehicle torched in his driveway. While the cops could never link Peernock to that arson attack, they later found the home address of the prosecutor in Peernock's cell, and there were several jailhouse rumors that Peernock had paid someone to torch the car. Peernock was later charged with soliciting other jail inmates to murder his daughter and her attorney. An inmate eventually testified that Peernock offered him $20,000 to murder his daughter, who was the only witness against him.

The Peernock legal saga was a complete and utter circus! Every new court hearing brought a new antic or outrageous claim from Peernock. He frequently fired attorneys and demanded to represent himself. Each time he angered judges and often yelled over them. Several times he was led out of the courtroom due to his outbursts. Once a judge ordered him restrained and gagged in court because he refused to listen to the judge and stop yelling. Peernock openly railed that the judges and his own attorneys were conspiring to convict him to "keep me quiet" about government corruption. He petitioned judges in other counties to take over his case so he could get a fair trial and expose all the corruption in the courts of Los Angeles. Despite his increasingly bizarre behavior, Peernock's case was eventually heard by a jury.

On October 23, 1991, Robert Peernock was convicted of murdering his wife and attempting to murder his daughter, along with kidnapping and arson. That same jury also convicted him of the additional charges he received during his jail stay. The additional convictions were for soliciting other inmates to kill his daughter and her attorney. Peernock was sentenced to life in prison without the possibility of parole.

During sentencing Peernock again disrupted the proceedings and had to be gagged. At this hearing the presiding judge called Robert Peernock "one of the most dangerous men I have ever dealt with in my career." It was learned at sentencing that Peernock had discovered the identities of the jurors who had convicted him and made attempts to contact some of them. The investigators got a search warrant and searched Peernock's jail cell. They were surprised to find the names of the jurors and the home addresses of all the investigators, judges, and prosecutors on the case.

From that point on Peernock was housed in a high-security jail wing. After the case was concluded, DDA Craig Richman apologized publicly for not seeking the death penalty against Robert Peernock. He too believed him to be one of the most evil and dangerous suspects he had encountered in his career.

### Conspiracy Theories

Shortly after beginning their investigation against Robert Peernock, the LAPD's investigators would recognize that they were dealing with a very dangerous man who was highly intelligent but extremely paranoid. He was also delusional in that he had a deep-seated belief that his entire life was being controlled, set up, and staged by dark forces within government.

Peernock's work history showed that he had worked as an engineer at both the Jet Propulsion Lab and at TRW. He left those jobs and worked for the State of California in the water department, dealing with contracts. It was during that time that he became disgruntled with government and became a "whistle-blower." He then engaged in a several year battle with the state through the civil courts. A relentless complainer and highly litigious, Peernock launched an avalanche of lawsuits against anyone who opposed him. He eventually won several of his lawsuits and received a large amount of income from the settlements, along with a fully compensated retirement. Peernock took all of these legal winnings and successfully invested in several small real-estate deals. At the time of the murder/car crash, Peernock was living off his pension and investment income.

It would take years to hear all of Robert Peernock's wild conspiracy theories as they slowly emerged through dozens of court hearings and legal briefs. In a nutshell, Peernock adamantly believed the following theories. He had become a self-described "whistleblower" at his job with the water department after exposing waste, theft, lies, and laziness among his fellow employees. He believed that every government contract was fraudulent. After he reported this ongoing "criminal activity," he asserted that the judges, police, and attorneys of Los Angeles formed an intricate conspiracy to discredit him, take his wife and children from him, and take all of his substantial investments from him. His ongoing theory was that the LAPD, real-estate agents, and lawyers helped get his wife, Claire, and daughter, Natasha, addicted to drugs so they could steal their Saugus home from them.

As part of this elaborate plot, he believed that LAPD officers had helped to stage the car crash involving the two women. When the car crash was discovered, the LAPD officers noted that the women were still alive, so they had known felons beat the women with metal pipes, trying to kill them. When this did not kill Natasha, the LAPD conspired with hospital doctors to treat the girl for her head injuries and to manipulate that part of her brain that controls memory. Peernock maintained that the doctors, along with LAPD detectives, then subjected the girl in the operating room to intense brainwashing so she would "remember" the incident the way that the government wanted her to. Peernock then stated that the defense bar, the coroner's office, the prosecutors, and the judges all conspired to steal what remained of his fortune. They plotted and schemed to get Peernock convicted and sent away to prison so that they could divide up his monies.

In his many courtroom appearances and legal briefs, Peernock railed against the judges, the civil courts, LAPD, and others. He named names and conducted his own inquiries via private investigators from behind bars. He named LAPD detectives by name as murderers, drunks, felons, et cetera.

Another target in Peernock's elaborate conspiracy theory was the Los Angeles County Department of Children and Family Services (DCFS). After his arrest, his eleven-year-old daughter, Tanya, was taken for foster placement by the DCFS. Her case moved into the juvenile courts system, and at one point she was placed in a home to be raised by a foster family. Since Peernock still had a large amount of money within the disputed estate, the foster system tapped that account for $165,000 to facilitate the raising and education of the young girl. Peernock went on another rant against "the system," adding the juvenile judge, the DCFS, the court-appointed child psychologist, and the foster family to his growing list of coconspirators against him and his money. He wrote a 170-page legal brief (more of a rant or manifesto) detailing this ongoing government conspiracy.

Among the many people Peernock believed were in a massive conspiracy against him was a state judge who oversaw the distribution of the assets of his wife after her death. Peernock, from prison, filed a suit in federal court citing that the state judge was involved in an ongoing criminal conspiracy against him, along with his own attorneys, the LAPD, his surviving daughters, and the entire District Attorney's Office and judges within Los Angeles County. Peernock asked for federal Racketeering Influenced Corrupt Organization (RICO) charges against the state judge and others, and he asked for $50 million in fines and triple that amount in damages against the judge. In 1992, the Ninth Circuit US Court of Appeals denied this wacky petition after just two days of studying it.

After Peernock was convicted and sentenced to prison, he had one more court battle to deal with. Like all his other courtroom fights, he lost this one too. A civil jury ordered the convicted murderer, Robert Peernock, to pay his own daughters $11 million in damages and suffering. Of course he will never pay it.

Robert Peernock is out of appeals and remains in prison until this day. Somehow he (or an ally) is able to maintain a website where he rants about his case and any number of ongoing government conspiracies against him.

**Author's note:** During a 2015 interview I conducted with retired LAFD investigator Mike Camello, he told me that he had heard that Robert Peernock died in prison due to an illness. I have been unable to confirm that information.

*The following professionals worked on this case: LAFD arson investigators Mike Camello and Rick Chew, LAPD homicide detective Steve Fisk, and DDA Craig Richman.*

### Investigator's Profile

The incredibly elaborate incendiary device that Peernock attempted to use in this case is a perfect example of a very unique subtype of arsonist. This type of arsonist is one I have personally encountered on at least four prior occasions, with each one being a near clone of the others. This type of arsonist is something called the ***engineer/scientist arsonist***. While that title is something I just made up, it is the only way I can describe this unique subtype.

In general, this type of arsonist or criminal is best described as someone with incredible intellectual skills but horrible social skills. Many engineers and scientists fit into this category. However, only the most extreme examples become criminals and arsonists. This type of personality becomes obsessed with facts, figures, and analysis and can be completely out of touch with normal human interaction and emotions. These are the people who live in a fact-based world and cannot tolerate mistakes, errors, or human emotions. The extreme versions of these folks are intolerant of others and completely obsessed with exactness, neatness, and perfection. These people have an inordinate distrust or paranoia toward the government, despite the odd fact that many of them are employed by that same government in some capacity.

These are the people who see conspiracies everywhere and view mistakes as intentional acts. There is no compromise in their thoughts, actions, or views. Everything in their life is black and white, with no shades of gray.

In my previous books I talk about two other arsonists who are examples of this subtype of offender. Tim Komonyi and Gary Glazier were both arsonists who used incredibly exotic incendiary devices in an attempt to murder their neighbors, who did nothing more than annoy them. Their devices were straight out of a Hollywood screenwriter's nightmare, and both failed to an extent. Both of these previous examples were clones of Peernock in that they had engineering backgrounds, were overly litigious in nature, believed that everything in life was part of a dark government conspiracy, and refused to accept their fates in court despite an incredible amount of evidence against them.

Most of these types of offenders take the smallest slights in life and magnify them into murderous revenge plots. They hold grudges forever and are just as dangerous the day they are let out of prison as the day they were sent in. Like Peernock, many of the others in this small subtype are highly litigious and engage in endless and petty lawsuits throughout their lives, even after incarceration.

These people use incredibly intricate crime scenarios and attempt to set fires and/or kill others through very complex methods not seen in any other type of offender. The nice thing about these cases is that their methods and devices are so complex and intricate that only a small fraction of people in the world could create them, which gives the investigator a very small pool of suspects to look at. Their very actions eventually point directly at them as the only person who could possibly commit this sort of crime.

Like many arson-for-profit schemes, there was an extreme amount of **staging of the scene** to make the fire appear accidental in nature. It was meticulously planned and prepared, and it was clear that Peernock schemed this out over weeks and months. Despite all his intelligence, preparation, and planning, it failed, as many exotic scenarios tend to. Robert Peernock was a **goal-directed arsonist**, whose goal was strictly financial gain.

## CRIME CONCEALMENT/ANTI-FORENSICS

### The Profile

Crime concealment and anti-forensic fires are goal-directed arsons. They are growing increasingly common in murder cases where a fire is set after the murder. In those cases, normally the dead body itself is the target of the attack. As career criminals are becoming warier of leaving DNA evidence at scenes, we are seeing an increase in these types of anti-forensic fires.

Other classic crime-concealment fires include fires set in offices, desks, file cabinets, and other places where records are kept. These fires are bright red flags indicating that someone is likely involved in internal theft, embezzlement, or fraud, and needs the records destroyed to avoid discovery. In the real world, burglars and car thieves seldom set crime-concealment fires.

## CELEBRITY FIRE CHIEF COMPTON, CA, 2011

*This case comes from the files of the Los Angeles County Sheriff's Department, the Compton Fire Department, the Area E Arson Task Force, and the Los Angeles County District Attorney's Office.*

### The Rock Star

Marcel Melanson was a rock star! He lived it and believed it, as did many people around him. I met him about four years prior to these events, and he made an immediate impression. One day I was called by an arson investigator from Compton to assist them with a home-explosion investigation. While at the scene with the investigator and about a dozen Compton firefighters, a very young man showed up in civilian attire that included shorts and a tank top. He was a tall, lean, light-skinned black man, with green eyes and a large grin. He had the exotic looks of a male model. I saw that his bare arms were covered with colorful "fully sleeved" tattoos. I heard him before I saw him as he approached several firefighters and vigorously shook their hands and started a nonstop banter with them. He appeared to know all of the firefighters, and I judged him to be about twenty years old. I figured he was a college student who was maybe the son or relative of one of the firefighters.

A few seconds after he arrived, he abruptly walked over into the explosion scene and began addressing the Compton arson investigator. He was standing in the middle of the area where we were seeking evidence. At that time I saw that this "civilian" was muddling up the evidence, and I said something along the lines of "Hey, partner, you're in the middle of a crime scene. Go stand outside the tape." My tone, while civil, told him that I wasn't asking; I was telling. Almost immediately everyone from Compton looked shocked and stared at me. The young man looked at me and just grinned. "No problem, dude," was all he said. He complied and walked back out to joke with the firefighters.

The Compton arson investigator slid up to me and whispered that the "civilian" was, in fact, his battalion chief, and was soon slated to be one of the top three guys in the Compton Fire Department. Despite looking like a teenager, he was in fact nearly thirty years old. Chief Melanson took it well that day and shook my hand and talked to me after we were done. He was friendly and energetic. I ran into him a couple more times over the next few years. Each time he was always friendly and bursting with energy. Each time I saw him, he seemed to have a couple more tattoos. I must confess that I wasn't a huge fan of the tattoos as they were quite garish and actually spread up his neck and were clearly visible even with his uniform shirt on. They didn't look professional, especially for someone destined to be the future chief of the fire department. He was hard to take serious due to the visible ink, his very youthful appearance, and extremely outgoing personality.

In the fall of 2009, the Black Entertainment Television (BET) channel started filming a reality TV show about the Compton Fire Department called *First In*. While doing so, the production company was introduced to one of the top commanders of the department, Deputy Chief Marcel Melanson. By the second episode, the good looks, flamboyant tattoos, and over-the-top personality of Melanson were features on the show. He soon became perhaps the main focus of the show. In October of 2009 he was featured in a *Los Angeles Times* article talking about the show and the resurgence of the city of Compton. The article pointed out that Melanson was the star and was Compton's new hope to show the world that it was emerging from its gang-ridden, violent past. The channel and the city loved him.

A year later, the show *First In* had closed production, but Marcel Melanson's fame was just beginning. In late 2010, Marcel and his tattoos were featured in the tattoo magazine *Inked*. He had emblazoned his entire back with a vivid tattoo of the firefighter from the movie *Backdraft*. In firefighter tradition, he of course added flames, skulls, and the ubiquitous dragon. This ink covered his back, neck, and arms from his wrists to his ears. His face, tattoos, and story were online and in more than one magazine. He hosted ride alongs for reporters and writers and was the subject of several articles. A firefighter's blog called *The Fire*

*Critic* lauded him in early 2011 as one of the youngest deputy chiefs (of an urban fire agency) in the entire United States. He was a star on his way up. He even had his own Twitter following under the account @cptkid.

Professionally, Melanson was on his way to the top. He was loved by all the other firefighters and was the most "gung ho" of them all. He was a macho swashbuckler who loved the excitement and danger of firefighting. He was known as a very aggressive and fearless firefighter who craved the action and didn't hesitate for a second to jump into harm's way. There was a story (or perhaps a myth) of him responding to a fire while in the middle of a workout and attacking the flames while still wearing workout gear and shower shoes.

City officials loved him and openly called him a "media darling." He was giving Compton a very positive public image. He was also very smart and ingenious. He was a whiz with electronics and had helped build up Compton's communications abilities within a very tight budget. Through his work as a communications specialist, he had formed close ties with large companies who were suppliers of first-responder communications equipment. He received national recognition in 2010 by Fast Company, an entity who named him one of the "top one hundred creative people in business."

The Compton fire chief loved him and was grooming him to be possibly the youngest chief of a full-time fire department in the nation. Melanson did have a bit of baggage with him that the chief tried to overlook. In one particular case he was disciplined for being out of his area while on duty. Another senior chief had discovered that Melanson, while allegedly on duty in Compton, was in fact over thirty miles away on a college campus. This was learned by an audit of the GPS tracker on his vehicle. Shortly after this audit, it was learned that someone with high technical skill (like Melanson) had purposely disabled the tracker on

Melanson's car. After this incident, Melanson was busted back down in rank to battalion chief.

### Corrupt Compton Police et al.

Compton has always been a screwed-up city. Back in 1991 I was a detective in the City of Lynwood, which borders on the north side of Compton. At the time Compton was hands down the most violent, gang-infested, drug-ridden city in the United States. It was the birthplace and breeding ground for both the Crips and Bloods street gangs and had the most inept and corrupt police department in the western United States. This went on for years until 2000, when the police department was formally disbanded due to corruption and incompetence. From that point until now, Compton has been patrolled by the LASD under a contract with the Compton City Council.

The Compton police were not alone in their alleged corruption. I personally became involved in investigations involving several city officials, the school district, the trash companies, the water board, and virtually every other public entity in Compton around 1992. From the outside it appeared that the entire city was corrupt. I didn't know much about the Compton Fire Department until we (LASD) took it over. When the LASD patrol an area, it also supplies all detective resources for that area. When Compton came under LASD jurisdiction in 2000, it became the number-one response area for most of the sheriff's detective units including Homicide, Gangs, Narcotics, and the Arson-Explosives Detail.

We got buried by arson calls to Compton in the first few months of us taking over. However, in under just a couple of years, the Compton fire chief, who we did not work for, convinced the Compton City Council that it would be better if the Compton Fire Department retained its arson-investigation duties. This caused some rancor as we believed in our unit that the Compton Fire Department was vastly underreporting its arson statistics to appease the city council. This is a very common tactic done by many fire chiefs throughout the United States, and Compton was no exception. So, from about 2002, the LASD patrolled and policed every crime in Compton with the exception of arson. It was a really weird arrangement.

### Police Radios

The corruption and shenanigans within Compton politics did not end with the LASD's takeover. By 2004, federal, District Attorney's Office, and LASD investigators had opened up several corruption and fraud probes against various officials within Compton. One of the targets of the probes was the mayor of Compton, Omar Bradley. This guy was the self-proclaimed "Gangster Mayor" and even wrote a book entitled *King of Compton*. Bradley had always been suspected of any number of fraud schemes. Bradley was eventually unseated as mayor and later convicted of fraud. He was replaced by a mayor who had been a former Compton police officer.

The new mayor despised the LASD and vowed early on to restart the Compton Police Department. By 2010 he was tired of the LASD's oversight and had publicly threatened to reinstate a Compton Police Department. Nobody was impressed by these threats or boasts because everyone knew that with insurance, union rules, hiring issues, and a floundering economy, it was virtually impossible for a small town of one hundred thousand people to start its own police or fire department from scratch. The LASD was a large, professional agency that could do the job at half the cost.

Everyone understood that financial logic—that is, except for the people running Compton. In a bizarre and foolish move, as if to intimidate the LASD into believing their threat, they took the first step toward restarting their own police department.

Before they had hired one person, before they had dealt with the insurance carriers or the unions, the defiant city went out and purchased two hundred of the highest-quality handheld police radios on the market, at a price of $5,000 apiece. The city didn't have a person to assign them to, but they had a million dollars' worth of radios! Everybody knew this was a foolish act even if Compton could muster a police department. It would take at least three to five years to create a department, and everyone in the technology world knew these radios would be obsolete before the first patrolman ever saw them. Battalion Chief Marcel Melanson sat on the acquisition committee for this large purchase.

The city had no place to store these radios in the meantime, so they turned them over to the fire chief. The fire chief in turn gave them to the guy who handled all the equipment orders for the fire department, Deputy Chief Marcel Melanson. The chief had Melanson store them in an old racquetball court in the main fire station in downtown Compton. The room was dry, secure, and locked by a key that only Melanson and the chief possessed. The radios were still new in the box and were sealed in original packaging. They sat in storage for the next several months while Compton attempted to form a police department.

By 2011, Compton was almost bankrupt, and any plans at reestablishing a police department were out the window. Compton officials decided to sell the nearly new radios. Very few agencies used these modern radios, and almost none could buy the entire lot of two hundred from Compton. Ironically, the only agency large enough to purchase that number of radios was Compton's rival, the LASD. In the first few months of 2011, the sheriff's department's officials agreed to examine the radios and make an offer to purchase them from Compton. The bad blood continued still as the sheriff's department knew that Compton was in a bind, and the sheriff's department would not be willing to pay full price. Still, sometime in the spring or summer of 2011, the Compton fire chief told Marcel Melanson to inventory the radios and get them ready for inspection by LASD.

Over the next few months, Melanson assured the chief that everything was in order. He then told the chief he intended to move the items out of the locked racquetball court in the main fire station and into a storage facility for easier access. Noting the high incidence of crime in Compton, the chief told Melanson to leave the radios where they were. Melanson persisted and urged this move more than once. The chief ordered that the radios remain where they were in the racquetball court. In early December of 2011, the chief advised Deputy Chief Melanson to have the radios ready to be inspected by the week of December 13, as the LASD was coming over to audit them at that time.

### The Fire

On the evening of December 11, 2011, Compton firefighters from their main station were ordered to conduct a drill in another part of the city. It was later determined that Deputy Chief Melanson had set up this training for that crew. Melanson was not on duty that night but appeared at the main station before the firefighters left for their training. He told them he was going to strip and stain an old wooden ladder used for adorning an antique firetruck for parades. Several firefighters saw him carry the ladder into the racquetball court and set up some saw horses. As they left for training, the firefighters saw the deputy chief with an electric sander and staining materials.

This sanding/staining operation was being done within several feet of the large stack of radios within their cardboard boxes. More than one firefighter thought this was extremely odd as there were no parades on the horizon, and the ladder Melanson was going to strip and stain was in pristine antique condition. It was not the type of ladder that should have been altered in any way. Further, everyone thought it odd that a deputy chief would be doing this sort of menial labor when he had an entire shift of firefighters to do it for him. The deputy chief was left alone at the station while everyone else went off to train.

Shortly after leaving the main station, two ambulance drivers for the department realized they had left their jackets back at the station. They returned to the main station less than fifteen minutes after leaving. When they arrived, they found smoke seeping out of the locked racquetball-court area. They investigated and saw a small fire burning near the ladder, and a larger fire burning on the stack of boxes that held the radios.

They immediately ran to a wall-mounted hose, charged it, and prepared to fight the fire. As they were about to start, Deputy Chief Melanson arrived from some other area of the station and ordered them to stop. He said that they were not qualified to fight the fire. Both young men were astonished. They had both completed a fire academy and had been hired temporarily as ambulance drivers/medics while they waited to be hired as full-time firefighters. They were certainly qualified to fight this small fire within this room.

Nonetheless they obeyed the chief and stood alongside him while all three just watched the fire grow as the on-duty crew responded. One of the rookies was astute enough to pull out a cell phone and record the small fire and the response by the deputy chief. All who viewed it later were stunned and shocked to see the most aggressive firefighter on the department stand by and watch a fire grow in his own fire headquarters station. The engine company soon returned and was able to knock down the fire before it could cause structure damage to the building.

The arriving fire captain was immediately suspicious and called the Compton Fire Department's arson investigator Vince Capelli. Capelli was out of town and could not respond. When told of the circumstances he was uneasy and suggested they call the local arson task force to assist them. That night two outside investigators from the local task force arrived and conducted an interview and investigation. They were Captains Pat Wills, of Long Beach Fire Department, and Kurt Johnson, of Montebello Fire Department.

Melanson told the investigators that he had set up the staining operation in the racquetball court. He had sanded a portion of the ladder and had then applied some stain. He then took a break to get some fresh air. Within minutes he was alerted to the fire by the returning rookies. He maintained that it was unsafe for the young ambulance drivers to attempt to fight the fire, so he admonished them to wait for the engine company.

At the time of this fire, the two arson investigators knew nothing of the history of the radios or the upcoming audit/inspection. They only knew what the small fire scene told him. They saw that there was very little fire near the wooden ladder, but there was a significant amount of damage to the stack of boxes containing the radios. This scene appeared to be fairly suspicious, but at the time they did not know why. It was a highly suspicious event, and the statements and inaction by Deputy Chief Melanson made no sense at all.

I later spoke to Inv. Capelli, and he told me that he recommended to his chief that this case be investigated by an outside agency like the LASD. His chief had no big love for the sheriff's department, so he continued the use of the two investigators from the Area E Arson Task Force.

### The Investigations

This case had some bizarre complications right from the start. The city of Compton is policed by the LASD but maintains its own small fire department. This case in any other part of the county would have been investigated by the largest arson unit around—the LASD Arson-Explosives Detail (my unit). However, shortly after the sheriff's department took over the policing of the Compton area, the City of Compton specifically demanded that they conduct their own arson investigations with their own fire department, and as such the LASD Arson-Explosives Detail was not welcome there, with the exception of rare instances.

From the moment this event occurred, the local sheriff's captain had been told that one of the Compton fire chiefs was the likely suspect. That sheriff's captain called me and demanded we (LASD Arson-Explosives Detail) investigate. However, there was bad blood between the agencies, and besides that, the LASD were an interested party in the loss of the radios. We were probably not the best choice to lead this investigation as the City of Compton or the suspect could claim some sort of bias. Several days later, the sheriff's department dispatched veteran arson investigators Derek Yoshino and Marcus Friedemann to the scene, but they were asked to remain uninvolved and left after just a preliminary investigation.

Inv. Vince Capelli from Compton did not want to be the lead investigator on this case within his own department. He had been a battalion chief at one point and was subordinate to Deputy Chief Marcel Melanson. When Melanson was demoted, that caused a ripple effect below him, and Capelli was demoted back to captain. He had an ongoing civil action against the City of Compton for this demotion. Capelli believe it would be a conflict if he investigated his own department at the same time he was suing them.

The choice of Kurt Johnson as one of the investigators was also complicated. Johnson was the arson investigator for a small city called Montebello. Unfortunately, he was the former arson investigator for Compton and had been a subordinate to Deputy Chief Marcel Melanson. The two had an uneasy history as Melanson had been selected for promotion over Johnson in the past. After being passed over for promotion at Compton,

Johnson left the department and became the arson investigator at Montebello. Johnson, while a capable investigator, was not the best choice to lead this investigation as he had a relationship with Melanson and a possible grudge against the City of Compton. Either side could claim that he, too, was biased.

Capt. Pat Wills, a longtime investigator from the Long Beach Fire Department and a member of the local Area E Arson Task Force, eventually was selected as the lead investigator. It was a good choice as Inv. Wills was one of the few impartial investigators on this case. He had no ties to or grievances against Compton or any of its employees. Kurt Johnson was then added on to assist Wills. Capelli also acted as an assistant.

Wills, Johnson, and Capelli spent many hours laboring over the fairly small fire scene. They originally were a bit stumped as there had been an electrical power surge in the area at the time of this event, and they had some issues with ruling out an electrical issue as a cause. Originally they were unable to determine the cause of the fire. This all changed a few weeks later when Inv. Capelli did a detailed analysis of the burned radios. He soon discovered that a large number of them were missing before the fire. As soon as this was confirmed, the City of Compton asked the LASD for help. This was an internal matter and required internal experts.

After some consultation with the ATF and the LASD, and a fresh look at all the evidence, the fire-scene investigators eventually ruled out all accidental events. This scene was dubbed an "incendiary" fire. Further, the investigators believed the scene had been "staged" to appear as either an electrical fire or possibly a "spontaneous combustion fire" from the staining operation. This was a huge clue toward a probable suspect.

The arson side of the investigation was supplemented by fraud and internal-affairs experts from the sheriff's department. The lead LASD investigators on the case ended up being Sgt.

Dan Tobin and Sgt. Amy Hanson. They pursued the fraud and theft aspect of this case. Sgts. Hanson and Tobin learned about the history of the radios and the impending sale to the LASD. Not knowing much about these radios, Sgts. Hanson and Tobin approached two civilian radio experts assigned to the sheriff's department to give them some advice.

The sergeants were very fortunate in that these radio experts had actually purchased two of these radios from Melanson on eBay. The radio techs explained that off duty they were radio geeks and liked listening to police calls. Knowing it was illegal to use sheriff's department's equipment off duty, they went online looking for the same type of radios used by the LASD. They found that a Compton firefighter was selling some, and they purchased one. The radios were delivered in person by Deputy Chief Marcel Melanson, who was in a department car and wearing a uniform at the time. This was several months prior to the arson fire. The LASD radio experts directed Sgts. Hanson and Tobin online, and they conducted a historical search for other sales by Melanson. They found plenty!

Sgts. Hanson and Tobin eventually determined that Melanson had stolen nearly one hundred of the radios and sold them all over the country and the world for approximately $2,000 apiece. The investigators eventually located fifty radios that Melanson had sold via eBay. None of the buyers had any idea that the items were stolen. They all believed they were buying surplus equipment from a municipality, which is quite common. Hanson and Tobin found that besides the radios, Melanson had been selling surplus firefighting equipment embezzled from the Compton Fire Department for a few years. Included in this list were handheld radios, vehicle radios, and a thermal-imaging system.

It appeared that Melanson, while assigned as a battalion chief and in charge of supply and equipment, had "padded" several orders for communication items and other gear. Once the order came in, Melanson had taken the excess items and had sold them under his own name on the Internet. The loose accountability standards within the fire department had allowed this to go unchecked for a long period of time. The two sheriff's department's sergeants located similar sales by Melanson going back five years. Marcel Melanson had embezzled over $300,000 worth of equipment from this scam. Sgt. Hanson and Tobin spent months tracking down radios and equipment that Melanson had embezzled and sold to unwitting buyers. Sadly, many of these buyers were small volunteer fire departments that had very little money to spend on equipment.

The investigators took a thorough look at Melanson's lifestyle. Melanson's personal history showed ominous warnings. In 2005 the State of California placed a $29,000 tax lien against him. A couple of years later, the feds hit him with an $80,000 lien. He was living a rock star life on a fireman's wages. He also had a recent divorce and the demotion, both of which affected him financially.

*"I'm just waiting for the sheriff's [department] to arrest me for that fire at the fire station"* (text taken from Marcel Melanson's phone).

The investigators eventually drafted several search warrants for Melanson's computer and personal records. They produced proof of his Internet transactions and accounts. The investigation was closing in around him. They drafted a search warrant for his home and then seized his cell phone and got a warrant to search that device. The investigators were surprised to see that Melanson had been conducting Internet searches from the days shortly after the fire. He had researched online to find out if any fire agencies would hire convicted firefighters, and if there was any work for a guy like him with a criminal conviction. They also found searches inquiring about prison inmate firefighting jobs.

Lastly, they found a text to a friend that Melanson had made. In the text he said, "I'm just waiting for the sheriff's [department] to arrest me for that fire at the fire station." He knew they were coming for him. Another aspect that the investigators learned was that prior to the fire, Melanson had apparently been attempting to stage a burglary. His reason for wanting to move the radios to the storage facility was that he could stage a theft more easily than he could stage a fire. When the chief refused to have them moved, it left Melanson with only one option.

Shortly after the fire, the Compton fire chief relieved Melanson of duty based on "negligence." They cited the fact that he had allowed a fire to start within his own fire house as the "negligence." By February of 2013, the Compton fire chief became aware that Melanson was the only suspect in the theft of the radios and the subsequent arson fire. Melanson's role as the "hope of the fire department" was coming to an end. The City of Compton fired him. On May 15, 2013, LASD detectives arrested Melanson for a bevy of fraud and arson-related charges. The case was assigned to special arson prosecutor DDA Renee Rose. She filed significant charges against Melanson that exposed him to over ten years in prison. Because Marcel was a bit of a local celebrity, his shocking arrest was covered in the national media. The rock star had finally come back down to earth.

*"I always thought he was the smartest guy up there. I thought he should've been chief"* (Compton City official discussing the arrest of Marcel Melanson).

In April of 2014, Melanson pled "no contest" to the arson and fraud charges. He was sentenced to three years and four months in prison for the arson attack on his own fire station. He was also ordered to pay a restitution of over $500,000. Marcel made good on some of this restitution by pulling all of the money out of his retirement accounts. He was able to repay about $100,000.

In a feel-good note, the City of Compton legally owned all the embezzled radios that Melanson had sold. Many were recovered, and the city got a large insurance payout for the burned ones. In the end they didn't lose that much money. One small volunteer fire department in New York, the Amityville Volunteer Fire Department, had purchased over a dozen radios from Melanson, and the legal seizure of these embezzled items would have been disastrous to the small department. In a show of good will, and at the urging of the investigators and prosecutor, the Compton City attorney drafted a document proclaiming that while the radios were the legal property of Compton, they would be on permanent loan to the Village of Amityville, NY. Something good did come out of this embarrassing mess.

Inv. Pat Wills retired shortly after this case after a thirty-plus year career with Long Beach Fire Department. Inv. Vince Capelli remained with Compton Fire Department and has since been promoted back to Battalion Chief. Sgt. Dan Tobin finished this case and was subsequently assigned to the LASD Arson-Explosives Detail. As I write this in January 2016, Marcel Melanson has been released from prison and is on active parole. The word on the street is that he is still an adrenaline junkie, now working as a "stringer," or one of those guys who chase fires, accidents, and violent crime via police radios so they can film it and sell it to the media. That seems like it's right up Melanson's alley.

The City of Compton and its fire department continue to be in disarray. If the embarrassment and shock of their number-three man being convicted of arson and fraud wasn't enough, in July of 2015 the *Los Angeles Times* reported that county regulators had just finished an investigation into the fire department and recommended a "sweeping overhaul." Many of the ninety-man department's paramedics had lost their certifications, and heart defibrillators had all been removed from their vehicles. The regulators said that training and record keeping within the department was in shambles. I'm not at all surprised. It's Compton. Things have been in shambles there for decades.

*The professionals who worked on this high-profile investigation include Lead Investigator Pat Wills, Inv. Kurt Johnson, Inv. Vince Capelli, Sgt. Derek Yoshino, Sgt. Dan Tobin, Sgt. Amy Hanson, Det. Marcus Friedemann, and DDA Renee Rose.*

### Investigator's Profile

Marcel Melanson is an arsonist who used fire as a tool in which to **conceal his crime** of embezzlement. He is a **goal-directed arsonist**. He should not be lumped into the general category of "firefighter arsonist" as the majority of them are actually **emotionally based arsonists**. There is no evidence whatsoever that Melanson set any other fires.

A brief investigation into this event points directly at Melanson as the only possible arsonist. He had been embezzling and selling the radios for up to five years and only recently learned that an inspection would occur within a few days. He had to cover up this crime in a very short time period. The chief had refused to let him move the radios to a storage locker, where he could have easily staged a burglary. He was forced to set the fire.

The type of fire that was set speaks directly toward someone with a good knowledge of fire, like a fireman. This event was **staged** to appear as a **spontaneous-combustion fire**, which does occur in certain circumstances. Only persons with a detailed knowledge of fire would know how to stage such an event, such as a firefighter. The fact that it occurred within a fire station could only mean that it was a fire department employee. Lastly, the fact that it occurred when only Melanson was present makes him the only possible person capable of staging such an event. He had the clear motive, means, and opportunity.

All that being said, Melanson was not a skilled or clever criminal or fire setter. The barest of arson investigations would have easily concluded that this was a staged event and that the radios were the intended target of the attack. The out-of-character actions and inactions by Melanson (known as crime-scene anomalies) make him the very first suspect to examine. A few questions by even the dumbest investigator should have focused on "Who stood to gain by the loss of the radios?" Again, all leads would have pointed back toward Melanson.

There is another case in this book under the chapter on excitement-based arsonists. In that case a fire chief in Minnesota named Ryan Scharber was a serial arsonist. He was a white male in a small, semirural town in Minnesota, but he and Melanson shared several similarities. They were both probably too young and too immature to be in the "chief" roles that they held. They were both whiz kids in that they were each the smartest, most motivated guys within their respective departments. Both were talented and gifted at getting loads of equipment for their respective units through clever use of the grant system. As such, both were allowed great freedom and very little supervision in their duties.

Scharber became a serial arsonist, and Melanson became a serial thief. Each thought they were too clever to get caught, and they got away with their crimes for years. In the end each brought great embarrassment and discredit to their agencies and professions. Both are a product of failures within city government and the fire department to monitor, audit, and discipline them.

This situation should never have occurred. The Compton Fire Department brass should have been ashamed of themselves as they let this situation develop. They let a bright and energetic young man go uncontrolled and unmonitored for years. He had obvious immaturity issues, and his ego started to get the better of his judgment. He saw himself more as a celebrity than as a public servant. He turned to theft to live a rock star's life. His supervisors should have monitored him closer, and the City of Compton should have been doing regular audits. This sort of poor oversight and lack of supervision is exactly the reason that problems occur in the firehouse, the police department, and any other job where there is no discipline or supervision.

## HOLLYWOOD VAMPIRE
## WEST HOLLYWOOD, CA, 2014

On January 2, 2014, I was working with a new partner named Alex Miller, a.k.a. "Angry Alex." Miller was new to the Arson-Explosives Detail in Los Angeles, but he had already earned a reputation as a skilled detective working out of the Compton area and for the Technical Crimes Unit. Angry Alex had a gift for working with computers, tracking systems, cell phones, and all the new toys that solve modern crimes. He was a perfect fit for me as I had a lot of experience as a detective but had serious problems just dialing my cell phone. I had yet to embrace the digital age.

At around eight in the evening, we got called to a small fire at an upscale apartment building in West Hollywood. The call stated that the fire started in an outdoor stairwell for the building. The deputies on scene reported that there was a clear video of the incident showing a suspect starting the fire. We didn't normally get that kind of good luck, so we sped to the scene.

While driving there I regaled Angry Alex with my seemingly infinite knowledge about arson, particularly those arson fires that are set in West Hollywood. I had investigated dozens of cases there and had reviewed dozens more as I wrote my first two books on serial arson investigation. West Hollywood is a wealthy small city that has a very liberal outlook on life. As such, they have a large and aggressive population of homeless transients. Almost all of these transients have significant issues with alcoholism, drug addiction, and mental illness. As a result of that, West Hollywood has always had a large number of small fires set outside of buildings near trash areas. We, in the arson unit, have linked many of these fires to several serial arsonists, a.k.a. "crazy transients," that roam the area.

I told all of this to Angry Alex as we drove, and said that based on the location of the fire (outside of a secure building) and time of day (early evening), my preliminary guess was that this fire was possibly set by a transient. Of course I ended up being wrong.

The building was a three-story apartment building with twenty-four units. All units were full and housed a clientele of upscale citizens. Because of this, the building had a very good security system in place with locking gates and access doors and security cameras spaced liberally throughout.

The location of the fire was in an outside stairwell at the rear of the building. The stairwell was not locked as it sat outside of the locked doors. The stairwell was enclosed by stucco over wood frame. The exterior of the building was undergoing painting, and an empty area under the stairs on the ground floor was used as temporary storage by the painters. In that area they had placed about twenty one- to five-gallon paint cans and some other materials including a gallon can of paint thinner. All of these items had been covered by a large canvass tarp. The painters left these materials at the scene when they stopped work at about five o'clock.

We saw that a small but intense fire had occurred within this stored painting material. Most of the paint containers had vented (exploded from the heat) and spilled paint into the area.

The fire consumed paint, clothing, buckets, and rollers that were stored under the tarp. We could not find an ignition source but could smell a strong odor of chemicals all through the area. We also found a heavily burned gallon can that had held paint thinner.

The manager of the apartments took us to the video room, and we viewed the incident on a very clear camera. The camera was less than ten feet from the scene and looked directly downward at it. At seven thirty in the evening, a stocky male entered the stairwell area with a small flashlight clenched in his teeth. The male walked around for a few seconds and then lifted the tarp off of the materials. He then used his small flashlight and, for the next minute or so, seemed to be searching for something among the materials. He couldn't find it and was visibly agitated. The male walked away for a minute and then came back and again looked under the tarp. He again appeared agitated. This time he picked up the square can containing paint thinner and began pouring it all over the tarp and stored paint supplies. He threw the empty can on top of the materials and bent down with something in his right hand that appeared to be a lighter. A second later the entire scene exploded in a brilliant fireball of light.

The small vapor explosion knocked several of the paint cans backward and started most of them on fire. The male was seen stumbling backward and then falling down for a second. He then was seen lurching and running from the scene. The fire burned for several minutes until residents helped extinguish it.

We studied the suspect in the images and realized that he was not a street transient and appeared to be a male around thirty years old, whose race was either Hispanic, Armenian, or possibly Russian. The Hollywood area has a large population of all three of these groups of people. The suspect had a unique hairline with a pronounced widow's peak, and cul-de-sac-style fading. He had very low-set ears and an odd shape to the back of his hair. He also had a very odd gait as he walked, as if he had an old injury. The suspect had on a short-sleeve shirt and several tattoos were clearly visible. He had multicolored rings around his left wrist and a line of writing down the back of his left arm. He had a large colorful star on his right elbow. The unique identifiers were a tattoo of Vlad the Impaler, or the original Count Dracula, on his left arm, and the word "Omerta" on his neck. These were somewhat rare markings for criminals, and we knew that they could be the key to this case.

The apartment manager told us that he had noticed a similar appearing guy on the video system a couple nights prior. The manager did not have the necessary security codes to access the system for a historical search, but Angry Alex the computer whiz stepped in and quickly bypassed the security codes so that we could view past events at the apartment complex. We saw that on the previous night that same suspect who had lit the fire entered the complex via the parking garage. There was video of the male along with a female reaching through a security fence and somehow activating the door opener. The two then entered the complex.

The manager confirmed that they were not residents of the location. We viewed further back and found on that same night that the same male had broken into a car in the parking lot and had removed a gift box from the seat. The male was seen carrying the gift box and other items and then placing them under the painters' tarp under the stairwell. By viewing the security footage back a few more days, we were able to find the same male using a lockpick and flashlight to access a security door in the lobby three days prior.

Based on our viewing of the security video, we confirmed that the same male suspect who had set the fire had illegally entered the building at least twice prior to this and had broken into a car in the lot. He was a burglar, not an arsonist.

Within a day of this event, we confirmed through interviews at the complex that residents had lost several small items in the past few days to include expensive sunglasses, credit cards, and cash. The burglar had not taken any large items. We also found through interviews that the burglar appeared to have stashed a box of stolen items and sunglasses under the painters' tarp one evening. He had come back for them the next evening, and they were gone, which is why he appeared agitated and started the fire. We determined that one of the painters had found the valuable items and had kept them himself.

### Tattoos and Crime Analysis

Both Angry Alex and I had been burglary detectives in our distant past, and we quickly recognized that this arson suspect was a professional burglar. He took only selected items out of apartments and was likely involved in identity theft. He used a penlight and lockpicks, which are items that are extremely rare and not seen among typical burglars. This guy was special. We also knew he would probably have a criminal record, and since we were in the Hollywood area, he would also likely be a heroin addict. In our experience, nearly every burglar in that area was a heroin or methamphetamines addict, and they need to steal to finance their habit.

Alex Miller took the video, enhanced it, and removed still photos of the suspect and his unique tattoos. I researched online and found "Omerta" to be a word associated with the Mafia. It was meant to symbolize that Mafia members never talk. In Hollywood there is a known group of Russian Mafia, so we thought our guy could be Russian. We also learned that certain Gypsy bands used the word as well. There was a small population of Gypsies in Hollywood, with a few of them actively involved in crime. We also studied the tattoo of Vlad the Impaler and found that it was also associated with Roma groups or Gypsies. Since our guy had darker skin and jet-black hair, we determined that he might, in fact, be Gypsy or Roma.

Taking our profile to the local West Hollywood Sheriff's Station, we went directly to the crime analyst named Theresa Olaes. A crime analyst is usually a civilian who catalogues crime trends and statistics via computers. Good crime analysts can make sense out of emerging crime sprees and can help allocate resources or focus detective operations toward these issues. Every detective unit in the LASD has a dedicated crime analyst. Theresa Olaes had a great reputation as one of the brightest and more innovative crime analysts in the entire department.

We told her about our crook and showed her still photos of the video images. When she suggested we query groups of arsonists, we stopped her and said that we believed this arson was in anger or frustration or even for crime concealment. We didn't believe that this guy would have a history of arson. We wanted to look for burglars, not arsonists. We said our suspect was likely a Gypsy, Armenian, or Russian, and was probably a burglar and heroin addict, and likely lived near Hollywood.

Theresa took our suspect info and the sketchy info we had on the tattoos and started building a computer-search model. We left her to her work, and before we could even get back to our offices, she had found a "hit." She forwarded us information for a male named Tristan Duvall, a thirty-two-year-old man with recent addresses to motels in Hollywood. He had a lengthy criminal history and was currently on probation for burglary, and he had several past arrests for theft, heroin, and methamphetamines. According to jail records and old booking photos, he also had a tattoo of the word "Omerta" on his neck, an image of Vlad the Impaler on his arm, and the word "Dracus" next to it. He had a large star on his elbow. He was a perfect physical match to our arsonist.

Crime analyst Olaes didn't stop there. She began a detailed computer query of all acquaintances associated with Tristan

Duvall and eventually identified a female Hispanic who had been arrested with him several times. This girl was a close match to the female we had spotted on surveillance video. She was now working in Hollywood as an "out call" prostitute, specializing in bondage. The computer work by this expert was spectacular, and we knew we had our guy.

### Forensic Artistry

The LASD employs thousands of people associated with our work. One such person assigned to the headquarters of the department is a highly skilled forensic artist named Sandra Enslow. She has made a long career assisting homicide and robbery investigators by identifying suspects and victims through just partial photos and descriptions. She has also developed techniques where she can view just small portions of video of a suspect who may be hidden from view due to clothing, disguise, hats, or a bad camera angle, and she can fill in the hidden features through forensic reconstruction.

In our case we had good, clear photos, but the suspect's face was mostly hidden through camera angles. We took our photos to forensic artist Sandra Enslow and had her recreate the tattoos and fill in the facial features we couldn't see. She then asked us to photograph the suspect from specific angles once we arrested him.

That was the sticking point in this case. We couldn't find the suspect. Angry Alex and Theresa Olaes began an exhaustive search looking for recent addresses of Tristan Duvall. This guy was a true professional! Most of his listed addresses were fake or were motel rooms long vacated or were to friends or family who were not cooperating with us. Over the next several weeks, Alex and I checked out numerous leads and empty buildings where Duvall had previously stayed. We learned that he was probably heavily engaged in credit-card theft and identity theft, and he was very careful about covering his tracks.

Still, Alex persisted, and a couple of months later he found that Duvall had a court appearance in a downtown courtroom from a recent narcotics arrest. Alex went to a Los Angeles courthouse and sat in the audience as Duvall appeared for a hearing. He immediately confirmed through his looks and odd walking gait that Tristan Duvall was the same guy who had set the stairwell on fire. Angry Alex had Duvall arrested on the charge of arson.

That evening Alex and I went to the main jail to interview Duvall. Just like his tattoo "Omerta" suggested, he was not at all talkative. He did tell us that his family was from Romania, and he was Roma (Gypsy) by birth. He denied ever being at the apartment building where the burglaries and fire had occurred. We recognized him as a longtime professional criminal, who was well aware of the pitfalls of talking to police. However, we were able to pose Duvall in several ways so that we could take photos of him consistent with the camera angles from the fire scene. We closely photographed and documented every tattoo on his body. We noted that he had lost a lot of weight and had shaved most of his hair since the arson attack.

We then took the new photos of Duvall back to forensic artist Sandra Enslow, and she did an official comparison of his many unique features through the eyes of a forensic artist. In the end, besides the tattoos, Enslow found several unique body and head features that matched Duvall to the person on the video. This was the final evidence we would need in this case.

Arson and burglary charges were filed against Duvall, and he eventually appeared in a Los Angeles courtroom. The first witness we brought in was the apartment manager (who had never personally seen Duvall). He was to testify that the images he retrieved from the video cameras were accurate. He surprised everyone in the courtroom when he pointed at Duvall, who was sitting at the defense table, and spontaneously stated, "That is the person seen on the video lighting the fire and the same person who broke into the car and picked the lock on the lobby door." This ended all discussion on the identification of Tristan Duvall. He was held over for trial on all charges. Because of his lengthy criminal record, he was facing a very long sentence in state prison.

Special arson prosecutor DDA Sean Carney was assigned to this case. After many courtroom delays, finally on May 7, 2015, Tristan Duvall took a plea deal and, in lieu of the arson charge, pled "no contest" to residential burglary in the first degree, a serious strike felony. That plea is the same as "guilty" in California. Tristan Duvall, the Hollywood Vampire, was sentenced to four years in state prison.

*The following professionals from the LASD investigated this case: Det. Alex Miller, Det. Ed Nordskog, crime analyst Theresa Olaes, forensic artist Sandra Enslow, and DDA Sean Carney of the DA's Arson-Bomb Prosecution Unit.*

### Investigator's Profile

Det. Alex Miller and I approached this case looking for an arsonist. In Hollywood, the area is filled with transients and homeless persons who set a large amount of small fires. Since this fire occurred outside of the building and was fairly crude in design, it had the initial appearance of a fire set by a homeless person or transient. However, a very good security-camera system pointed out that the arsonist was a younger, fairly healthy person who did not resemble a street transient or homeless person. He, in fact, was carrying a small penlight in a fashion where he appeared to be a burglar or thief. His use of lockpicks in another video confirmed this to us. We quickly stopped looking for an "arsonist," and began looking for a professional burglar or thief who was also a drug addict.

The Hollywood area is filled with drug addicts, transients, and people of all types just passing through. It is normally very difficult to identify someone just from video images. However, in this case we were greatly assisted by the fact that the security cameras were of a high quality, and that the suspect had fairly unique and highly identifiable tattoos. We consulted a skilled crime analyst (Theresa Olaes), and it took her less than one hour to identify the suspect by combining his tattoos with our profile of a burglar and heroin addict. That's pretty damn good in an area of nine million people! Because Duvall was a professional burglar/thief, it took a lot of work by Det. Alex Miller to run down this guy.

True to his "Mafia" heritage, Tristan Duvall refused to cooperate with us or admit anything. He was a professional criminal, and his body tattoos proclaimed that as well. This was the first fire on his record, but he had a long history of theft, burglary, and narcotics use and possession. In his case, arson was not the main crime but was used to cover up any possible evidence of a crime. We believe he lit his fire out of frustration after he found out that his stolen items had been taken by someone else. It was also possibly a method of antiforensics behavior. We label him a **goal-directed arsonist**.

## CITY CLERK
## MILL CITY, OR, 2010

*This case comes from the files of the Oregon State Police, the Oregon State Fire Marshal, the ATF, and the Linn County Sheriff's Office.*

On September 13, 2010, at eight in the evening, a citizen of Mill City, Oregon, stopped by the city hall to drop off a payment to the city. The citizen was surprised to see the city's financial clerk near the building as she dropped off her payment. The two said a quick "hello" to each other, and the citizen drove home.

Thirty minutes later an explosion and fire ripped through the city hall. The fire continued to burn until the building was mostly destroyed.

Someone hearing the explosion and seeing the building engulfed in flames called 911, and a nearby citizen who was monitoring a scanner sped to the scene. The citizen rescuer, Ann Holaday, arrived to see a white van parked across the street from the burning city hall. Ms. Holaday could see a lone female sitting in the van, and she appeared to be in great distress. Holaday rushed to the van to find a woman named Joy Cronin in great pain and suffering from burns to her body. Holaday said that the injured woman "reeked of gasoline." She recognized Joy Cronin as the finance clerk for Mill City.

When Emergency Medical Service officials arrived, they immediately began treating the badly injured Cronin. She was taken to a nearby hospital and then later transported to a burn unit for specialized care. Her injuries, while quite serious, were not life threatening. The city councilor for Mill City, Lynda Harrington, announced the next day that Joy Cronin had been an unfortunate victim of this fire. She explained that Joy Cronin told rescuers that she happened to be driving by her offices at night and had spotted a bright glow within the building. She opened the door with her key to investigate, and the building literally blew up in her face, causing her injuries. City clerk Cronin was held at a local hospital for several days to the severity of her burns and cuts.

Within one day of the fire, local arson and sheriff's office investigators classified the fire as "incendiary." They had detected gasoline evidence within the burned building. Immediately, the Mill City mayor provided to the media a possible motive for the attack. Mayor Roel Lundquist said that it was no secret that a couple of citizens had been highly upset with the city over a local water-rights issue. The pair had been disruptive and threatening to the city council and had forced the city to have a sheriff's deputy attend all meetings for the past six months as security. Still, another clue came in. A local student reported that he had seen a man standing outside of the city hall, and the man had thrown something inside the building. Moments later the building blew up.

Mill City is a town of just under two thousand people and is situated in northern Oregon, south of Portland, and just thirty miles east of Salem. The small city used the Linn County Sheriff's Office as its law enforcement branch. Mill City had a small building it used as its city hall. Due to the small size of the town, every single record for the city was housed within this small building. The fire that destroyed many of these records was truly a disaster.

The investigation eventually involved assets from Linn County Sheriff's Office, the Oregon State Fire Marshal, and the ATF. Arson investigators began a detailed dig out of the burned building. In the area where the fire had been originated, investigators located the heavily burned remains of two six-gallon red plastic gasoline containers. They later served a search warrant on the van owned by Cronin and found two green inserts, which corresponded to the plastic nozzles of two gasoline containers. Cronin's statement of how she happened to be driving by the scene was in stark contrast to the citizen who put Cronin at the scene thirty minutes before any fire was noticed. Additionally, rescuers recounted that there was a very strong odor of gasoline on Cronin when they found her.

The investigators focused on the probable motive for this arson fire. After numerous interviews and a detailed analysis of the affairs of the city, investigators concluded that Joy Cronin was under scrutiny prior to the fire for some financial irregularities. In her role as city finance clerk, Cronin presided over a system that had very few checks and balances within it, and she had unsecured access to substantial amounts of cash. Worse, she was aware that there was only one computer that monitored all of these financial transactions and that there was no off-site backup system for the computer. Any destruction of the computer or files would cause a permanent loss of all city financial records.

This loose accounting system was ripe for a theft. City officials had suspected possible theft as a significant amount of cash was unaccounted for. A preliminary audit took place earlier in 2010, and it showed that Cronin did not have adequate receipts to account for missing cash. She was advised to find the receipts, and the official audit would resume in three weeks. The arson fire occurred shortly after Joy Cronin had been advised of this. The investigators were able to prove that at the same time as this cash was missing, Joy Cronin opened up a personal bank account separate from her normal bank account in another city. This second account had cash deposits of over $25,000 in the early months of 2010. Investigators also determined that Cronin had spent thousands of dollars in cash clearing up debts for her unemployed husband and giving money to her son. Investigators proved that she had paid for a car and a trip to Mexico in cash.

A grand jury was seated and eventually indicted Joy Cronin on several charges of theft, embezzlement, and finally the arson of the city hall. On August 19, 2011, over eleven months after the fire, Linn County Sheriff's Office investigators arrested Joy Cronin for the arson attack. On the day of her arrest, her booking photo of a sobbing Joy Cronin made national headlines.

*"The destruction of city hall was the act of Joy Cronin's attempts to cover up her theft. This is a case where she's the only person who could have done it"* (Deputy District Attorney Ani Yardumian).

Cronin obtained a defense attorney, and the case eventually went to a jury trial in February of 2013. As part of the ridiculous side story to this case, Cronin had received over $12,000 in workers' compensation for her injuries from the fire. Additionally, she was accompanied in court by a "service dog," which her attorney claimed was necessary for her recovery as she suffered from posttraumatic stress disorder from the fire. Both of these benefits were obtained for a fire, which she was now accused of setting. The trial lasted for five days, the jury deliberations not quite as long. After just ninety minutes of deliberations, the jury found Joy Cronin guilty of all three felony counts associated with this arson attack. On March 30, 2013, Joy Cronin was sentenced to three years in prison for arson. She was also ordered to pay over $370,000 in restitution.

### Investigator's Profile

In the arson biz there is an older phrase that comes to mind when looking at this case. We would call this one a "Ray Charles Fire." Obviously the dated reference to the blind music legend is crude cop/fireman humor indicating that a blind person could solve this case from the onset.

There is little doubt that the very first investigators involved in this incident quickly focused on Cronin as the probable suspect in this case. They then had to set about building a case and physically proving that theory. Knowing who the probable suspect is is the easy part in most arson cases. Proving it is what separates the armchair detectives from the true professionals. In this case, the investigators were practically handed a solved case from the onset. If this fire had occurred and the suspect had not been injured, then this would have been a much more difficult case to prove. It would still be provable but would take much more work. Targets like a city hall or courthouse could have any number of potential suspects who would want to burn it, from antigovernment groups, tax protesters, or any angry citizen. The suspect list might be quite lengthy.

The key in a case with numerous potential suspects is to look at the exact target of the arson attack. In this case the investigators worked very hard and found that the target was the computer and financial records of the city. The question would be "Who benefits from this fire?" After an investigation, it was proven that only one person could benefit from a fire that would destroy these items. In this case the presence of an overly large amount of fuel (twelve gallons of gas) indicates that the suspect wanted maximum destruction. With that determination, as the DA would later quote, Cronin was "the only person who could have done it." It is that simple.

In this case the suspect list was narrowed immediately by the presence of the city clerk at the scene of the event at an odd time. The fact that she suffered severe flash burn and explosion injuries indicates that she was there when the fire was ignited, making it very difficult to come up with a legitimate reason for that. After that, the investigators only had to ask a few questions to figure out a probable motive. In this case the motive is clearly **crime concealment**, with the suspect utilizing fire as a tool to **cover up embezzlement and theft**. Joy Cronin is a **goal-directed arsonist.**

The rest is simple criminal investigation. You can't steal and hide large amounts of money without some sort of trail. All of this occurred within a small town, and it is very difficult to keep secrets in such an environment. Since the overwhelming majority of arson attacks by female offenders occur within their homes or at work, the detectives had a likely candidate from the start. The method of arson was crude, overkill, and bespoke of an unseasoned and inexperienced arson offender. It also indicated that the arsonist lit a fire from within the structure, which greatly narrows down the list of offenders. Most other offenders (e.g., vandals, antigovernment types) would probably have targeted this structure from the outside. Everything about this event pointed at just one potential suspect. It was inevitable that Joy Cronin would have been caught.

## EXTREMISM

### The Profile

Extremist-related arson attacks are some of the easiest to identify and some of the most difficult to solve. The extremist arsonist is a dedicated zealot to his or her cause and has often undergone some sort of training in relation to the attack. The extremist is usually part of an organized or semi organized group and has pledged his or her loyalty to the group and to the cause. Many extremist arson attacks employ the use of some sort of premade incendiary device. The design and employment of the device is directly related to the type of extremist group involved, the amount of training the attacker had received, and the skill level of the actual device builder and attacker. The investigator should keep in mind that sometimes the actual attacker did not construct the device but was merely supplied with the incendiary device just before the event.

Incendiary devices used by extremist groups have a fairly high failure rate (often exceeding 30 percent of the time), and as such, investigators frequently find substantial physical evidence left at the scene of extremist-related arson attacks. It is imperative that all components of any burned or unburned incendiary devices get to a crime lab for detailed forensic analysis!

The key to recognizing an extremist-based arson attack is to study the target or victim of the attack. Certain extremist groups have specific targets in mind and consistently attack those targets in various ways. In the 1980s in the United States, there was a wave of right-wing extremist groups and militias active throughout the country. The most common right-wing extremist target was an abortion clinic. There have been hundreds of fire bombings and arson attacks against any sort of institution that conducts or supports abortion activities. Other targets of right-wing extremist groups in that era included gay/lesbian clubs and bars, IRS offices, and any targets that represented America's involvement in international groups. An example of that would be the attacks associated with the Atlanta Olympics. Other related activities by these same right-wing groups were protests of the same facilities, sniper attacks, bombings, vandalism attacks, and stink-bomb attacks. These types of attacks have waned dramatically since the 1980s and have become rare in this country.

Since the 1970s, leading all the way up to current times, left-wing extremist groups have also been active in bombings, fire bombings, and arson attacks. The target lists for left-wing attacks include government facilities, prison/probation facilities, courthouses, and major corporations. The most active left-wing groups involved in arson attacks are the Earth Liberation Front (ELF) and the Animal Liberation Front (ALF) and all of their associated groups. The ELF/ALF groups are the most prolific groups of arsonists in history and have been responsible for thousands of attacks worldwide. Almost all of their attacks entail the use of some form of incendiary device. Another hallmark of these types of groups is their penchant for taking claim for their attacks either through graffiti left at the scene or online posts. ELF/ALF attacks are easily identifiable.

The targets of ELF/ALF attacks can be quite varied, and luckily the groups often claim their attacks. This helps investigators in the end. The targets include any facilities related to animal research, animal exploitation, urban sprawl, destruction of wild lands, corporate offices, or officers of companies involved, even tangentially in any type of animal research, hunting/fishing companies, and any large construction project bordering on wild lands.

Fire/arson investigators must treat these events as highly sophisticated terrorist attacks and glean every single piece of forensic evidence possible from the scenes. This work will identify the group and perhaps the attackers themselves. The follow-up investigation should be forwarded to the FBI as they are the agency responsible for maintaining an intelligence file on these types of extremist groups.

## POISON OAK CAPER
## ELF ATTACKS
## AUBURN, CA, 2004–2005

*From the files of the California State Fire Marshal's Office.*

North central California has always been a fairly liberal area. While not as wildly liberal as the nearby San Francisco Bay area, the rural areas to the east of the Bay are known for an odd mixture of farming, ranching, wine making, and pot growing. This rural-but-liberal lifestyle clashes with the rest of the country, where rural areas are notoriously conservative. Besides the cities in the Bay area and Sacramento, the region is policed by very small police and sheriff's departments and the State of California's investigative agencies. Any arson or bomb investigation in this semirural area normally falls under the bailiwick of either the California Department of Forestry and Fire Protection (Cal Fire) or the California State Fire Marshal's Office, or both. Sometimes, as in this case, even the feds become involved.

On February 7, 2005, Joe Konefal, a supervising arson/bomb investigator for the State Fire Marshal (SFM), was called to an arson event in the town of Sutter Creek. Sutter Creek is in "Gold Country," which is in the western Sierra foothills forty miles southeast of Sacramento. Although the fire was not that large, the on-scene fire commander, Brian Kirk, recognized a potential major event. As soon as Inv. Konefal arrived, he too recognized this as an extremist-related arson attack and summoned investigators from the ATF and FBI. The clue that Konefal and the fire chief immediately spotted was a large storage container at the fire scene that had been spray-painted in garish red letters: "WE WILL WIN ELF."

The structure that was attacked was a classic ELF target. It was a new apartment housing development encroaching into the wild Sierra foothills. The development was still under construction and about halfway finished. No tenants had moved in as of yet. There were fires in several areas of the complex. Luckily, only one of these blazes was significant, and it was quickly brought under control by Cal Fire firefighters.

While ALF, a close cousin and sympathizer with ELF, would normally attack targets that were involved in animal issues, ELF targeted locations that they believed were assaulting the environment or mother earth. Inv. Konefal had been in the arson/bomb business for well over two decades, and while all early indications showed this was an ELF event, he took great care to keep an open mind to the other possibilities. In this case, this event may possibly be a very cleverly staged insurance-fraud scheme by the contractors or building owners. The possibility of a labor/union-related arson was also on Konefal's mind. With the assistance of the FBI's Evidence Recovery Team (ERT), Konefal began to process the fire scene.

Of great interest to Konefal was that there were clearly seven different areas of origin for the fires in this apartment complex. Each origin was in an area of the complex where the apartments were only partially finished and were particularly vulnerable to fire attack. Konefal knew that this was a standard tactic used by ELF as completed structures were much more difficult to burn. In this case the "ELFsters" (or elves, as they call themselves) failed miserably in their goal, as only one of these fires caused any sort of significant damage. Joe sized up the scene and noted that it would have taken several individuals to pull off this event as there were a lot of incendiary materials brought into this scene. This is another hallmark of ELF/ALF attacks: arson by committee.

After initial photography of the scene, Konefal began a detailed examination of each particular area of origin. Even this veteran investigator was surprised at what he found. Joe had been to several ELF/ALF arson scenes in his career and had examined dozens of their incendiary devices. He had never seen devices of this type in the past. He was lucky that a couple almost completely failed, which left him a lot of evidence to examine and photograph.

Each device in the event was basically the same, with some minor deviations. The seven devices consisted of two parts. The main part was a large plastic container (one- to three-gallon size) filled with a liquid that smelled like diesel/gasoline. The mixture was a reddish color, consistent with a particular type of diesel fuel. This was the main fuel load for each fire. Next to the fuel-filled container was a much smaller plastic bottle (pint sized) that had some sort of unknown chemical mixture inside. In each area of ignition, the small plastic bottle was burned and melted to the ground. In some cases, this small bottle got the larger container of fuel to burn as well. In some cases, it failed. In two of the seven scenes, the arsonists had moved large propane cylinders and placed them directly next to the gasoline jugs. Later interviews would reveal that the two propane tanks were owned by the contractors at the site. It was clear the arsonists had moved them next to the incendiary devices in hopes that they would add to the fires. Konefal also found remnants of latex gloves in the scene and remnants of heavily burned sponges.

Joe Konefal was a longtime arson/bomb investigator and had been an instructor in the business for over a decade. He had a strong suspicion about the chemical mixture in the smaller bottle. Joe bent down for a sniff (not the safest method of investigation, still one must do what one must), and his suspicions were confirmed. He smelled the unmistakable odor of chlorine. He knew that an improvised mixture of chlorine (calcium hypochlorite) and glycerin was an old-school incendiary mixture that ELF/ALF groups had used as early as the 1970s. It was rare these days and hadn't been seen in quite some time. This type of mixture, known in our business as a **hypergolic device**, was a time-delayed chemical reaction that reacts over a few seconds or minutes and causes a violent burst of flame. All of this depends on the amount, mixture, and quality of the chemicals involved.

Joe knew that the easiest, most common, and most reliable hypergolic mixture was a combination of swimming pool chlorine and brake fluid. He amazed the FBI evidence techs with this knowledge and advised them to instruct their lab chemists to look for variations of these chemicals when examining the evidence.

Inv. Konefal had correctly concluded that the small containers, the hypergolics, were the ignition source for the larger containers of gasoline/diesel. These devices functioned after a short delay when the chemicals mixed. This fire spread to the sponges between the two bottles and increased the size of the fire. The growing flame then melted the bottle with the gasoline and exposed the gasoline to the flame. The gasoline then was supposed to be enough fuel to ignite the building. This was indeed an educated person who had constructed these time-delay ignition devices.

Konefal also saw that this particular cell of ELF activists was probably a novice or inexperienced group. The devices mostly failed—in several cases the small hypergolic bottle just wasn't large enough to penetrate and ignite the larger fuel containers. The placement of the propane tanks was a pure rookie move since these almost never fail during a fire. In this case they were hardly damaged. Lastly, the arsonists had placed most of the incendiary devices up against finished walls that were already protected with fire-resistant materials. Joe surmised that this group was not all that savvy as to the proper techniques of fire setting. He figured that they would be just as sloppy in covering up other forensics. He ended up being correct.

The fire-scene investigations having concluded, Inv. Konefal and Cal Fire chief Phyllis Banducci began to scour the area for additional evidence. They knew that it probably took several persons to pull off this attack, and they had to have carried the items to the scene. They had also likely driven a vehicle near the scene. All of this would leave lots of trace evidence in the form of debris, footprints, and tire tracks. They soon found parts of several large trash bags that the devices had been carried in. These were collected for forensics. By following footprints, the two investigators found clear footprints in mud and dirt.

They walked further and found tire tracks. Casts of these items were also collected. These footprints were followed to a nearby forest and field, and the two investigators tracked them for a long distance. At some point, the footprints walked through dense forest and through a large patch of poison oak. The investigators collected evidence from this area and came up with the opinion that one or more of the attackers might have a case of poison-oak infection.

Eventually all of this fire-scene evidence was turned over to FBI agents out of Sacramento. The FBI had been keeping loose tabs on a group of ELF activists that had become active in the Gold Country area over the past few months. This attack had failed miserably, but the feds recognized it as a very serious attempt to cause a large fire. They took Joe Konefal's advice and issued a press release about the event and added the facts that red diesel fuel and buckets were used in the attack. They also gave out information that one or more of the suspects likely had a visible case of poison-oak infection. To entice tips, the FBI was able to offer a cash reward for information.

The investigators in the region needed results fast as they believed these recent ELF attacks were escalating in tempo and severity. Three years earlier, in October of 2001, and about 180 miles to the north, on the other side of the Sierras, ALF activists had launched a serious attack on a large ranch property owned by the federal Bureau of Land Management (BLM), near Susanville. The ranch was a supply center for a controversial program where the BLM managed a wild horse and burro facility. ALF had protested this site for years and had finally launched a successful incendiary raid against it. The "ALFsters" had planted four identical incendiary devices in the ranch buildings and hay shed. Only one of the four devices functioned, which caused a large fire that destroyed a massive hay barn. Three other nearby devices failed completely, leaving pristine evidence for investigators to recover and exploit.

Joe Konefal and his partner, supervising arson/bomb investigator Greg Smith, had also been involved in examining these devices at that scene. The devices in that case were constructed of large five-gallon plastic buckets filled with a gasoline/diesel mixture as the main fuel load. The ignition system was highly complex. It consisted of a highway flare taped to the top of the open bucket. Wrapped around the business end of the flare were multiple books of paper matches. Wired into the matches was a model-rocket igniter. The igniter functioned by a digital timer and nine-volt batteries (a time/power unit) sealed in plastic tubs. Each device had two identical time/power units as a redundant ignition system.

This was an incredibly sophisticated device, which often is a reason for the failure. In this case, the device, taken right out of the ELF handbook, had been assembled out of high-quality materials. All four devices should have functioned as designed.

Close analysis by Joe Konefal and Greg Smith showed that the devices in this BLM attack were assembled poorly. The bridge wire from the rocket igniter was supposed to have been weaved through the volatile match heads. The person who assembled these had screwed up and placed the wire just slightly below the match heads on three of the four devices. Consequently, all four devices functioned properly, but only one had the igniter wire close enough to the match heads to actually get a flame. This type of technical failure is common in ELF/ALF attacks.

On December 27, 2004, just two months prior to the Sutter Creek attacks, ELF activists had attacked another construction site in the town of Lincoln, about forty miles from Sutter Creek. In this attack, the target was a tract of new homes that had been built encroaching on a nearby wild land. The first indication that this was an ELF event was that a skip-loader tractor on site had been vandalized with spray paint. Large words saying, "Disarm or Die," a typical ELF sentiment as it refers to the "war against mother earth," had been sprayed on the equipment. Half-finished homes had several slogans painted on them: "You Will Pay," "Leave," "Enjoy the World As Is...As Long As We Can," and "Quit Destroying Their Homes," in reference to the habitat of wild animals. The letters "ELF" were found printed on the street.

FBI and local police investigators had found four failed incendiary devices placed within the partially finished structures on site. A later comparison by Investigators Konefal and Smith would reveal that these were near-clones of the Susanville devices from three years earlier. The devices consisted of large five-gallon pails with a gasoline/red diesel mixture, with a highway flare surrounded by opened books of matches, a rocket igniter, and mechanical kitchen timers with nine-volt batteries. In this case, every device failed, again due to poor assembly of the components. Konefal and Smith were convinced that these items were made by the same cell or group of people who made the Susanville items as the wiring system was an identical match to the previous devices. All of these failed items were forwarded to the FBI laboratories.

The FBI had found that ELF activists had begun targeting urban sprawl and newer construction projects throughout the Sacramento area. Two weeks after the Lincoln attack, a similar attack was located at a commercial-building construction site in the nearby city of Auburn. This attack occurred on January 12, 2005, and entailed the use of five incendiary devices placed at the scene. These incendiary devices were again very similar to the devices found just two weeks prior. They consisted of five-gallon buckets with a gasoline/red diesel mixture, a highway flare, and a manual kitchen timer. Again, all of these devices failed, and there was no fire at all at this scene. Three days later ELF sent letters to the media claiming all of the recent attacks.

With all the activity in recent months, investigators concluded with dread that they had an active ELF/ALF cell working in the semirural areas east of Sacramento. What Joe Konefal and Greg Smith did not know for quite some time was that the FBI had been looking at an increasing tempo of ELF attacks since just prior to 9/11 and had implemented a highly secret task-force known as Operation Backfire. Joe and Greg had become involved in a wide-ranging federal investigation into seventeen major arson attacks across the West.

### ELF and Operation Backfire

ELF had come into being in the mid-1990s as sort of an offshoot of both ALF and a radical environmental group known as Earth First! ELF was mostly just small, local cells or groups of people who wanted to take their protests to a more destructive level. Most of these small cells did not know each other and only communicated through intricate coding systems and via monikers.

There was no national organization, and each cell was a reflection of its local leader. Eventually certain ELF groups were very active in non-arson vandalism attacks while others specialized in incendiary activities.

Some of ELF's early incendiary devices were crude copies of devices found in old military manuals and underground radical literature. Many of these were copies of incendiaries used by the highly skilled Irish Republican Army (IRA) terrorist group, who had pioneered the use of **hypergolic incendiaries**. Indeed, by the late 1990s, a couple of highly organized tacticians joined ELF who specialized in running raids and building sophisticated incendiary devices. Their activities and anti-forensic behavior was so skilled that even after a few dozen major attacks, the FBI had no idea who they were.

While early ELF activists set fires by hand, or with crude devices made of gasoline and pipe bombs, they had very mixed results in their effects. The turning point for ELF occurred in 1997 when an incredibly intelligent man from Prescott, Arizona, named William Rodgers, joined the group. Rodgers was a truly dedicated environmental activist and a student of such successful groups as the IRA. He coauthored a famous manual entitled *Setting Fire with Electrical Timers: An Earth Liberation Front Guide*. Rodgers's book is a must-read for any arson-explosives investigator and gives detailed steps on how to create highly effective incendiary devices designed for maximum destruction of a large target. Rodgers called his devices "cat's cradles," and he instructed readers in detail how to surreptitiously purchase materials, how to create a "clean room" for assembly of these devices in order to defeat forensics, how to scout a location, and how to access a location while bypassing security systems.

Rodgers was highly disciplined and neat in his device making and raid planning. He insisted on highly sophisticated anti-police tactics and strategies. He was later linked to fifteen major

ELF attacks, all with the use of his classic "cat's cradle" devices. By this time he was working frequently with a loose group of men and women from the Pacific Northwest and California known as "the Family." They were extremely active in attacking timber companies and meat-packing companies that dealt with horsemeat. An offshoot of those attacks was the BLM wild horse and burro facilities in Oregon and California, both of which were burned in ELF attacks in 1998 and 2001, respectively. The ELF attacks accelerated in the months prior to 9/11, but still the feds weren't taking these groups seriously and just couldn't seem to get a handle on them. The September 11 attacks changed the entire country's perspective on any sort of extremist or terrorist group, and finally the FBI began to focus on the ELF/ALF groups as homegrown terrorists.

### Ryan Lewis

Operation Backfire was formed just weeks before the cluster of ELF attacks in the Sacramento region. In response to this flurry of arson attacks, the FBI descended on the region. A day after the arson attack in Sutter Creek, a citizen, responding to the appeal of a reward, told the FBI that he was aware that a local man named Ryan Lewis was probably involved in the recent arson attacks. He knew that Lewis had red diesel fuel in the bed of his truck, that Lewis and his truck had been out the night of the fires, and that Lewis had expressed radical environmental rhetoric.

The feds interviewed Lewis's father at his home, and the father admitted that he suspected his own son of being involved. The father had found red diesel, black trash bags, and empty plastic buckets in his son's truck. Agents noted that they saw ELF graffiti written on a skateboard owned by Ryan Lewis. Twenty-one-year-old Ryan Lewis was then interviewed by the feds and quickly admitted that he had transported incendiary materials to the arson scenes. He admitted to stealing the diesel fuel from other construction sites and delivering incendiary-device components to other suspects at the scenes.

Most interestingly, Ryan Lewis had a visible poison-oak infection! Although Lewis admitted his role in being involved in the conspiracy of all of the attacks, he of course diminished his involvement and responsibility. This is a very normal "self-serving" admission given by lots of suspects involved in group crime. It was clear that Lewis was caught red-handed and was trying to save his own skin. Lewis was immediately taken into federal custody for the attacks.

After getting a partial admission from Lewis, the FBI quickly linked him to three other suspects in one of the attacks and arrested those people. Shortly after the arrests of these young people, authorities found two different explosive bombs left in the Auburn area. The local support for the suspects was strong. Eventually the other three suspects gave their own statements to the FBI, not surprisingly naming Ryan Lewis as the leader of this small group or cell. He was the one who brought in the devices and materials. The others admitted to helping him set up the materials in two of the fire scenes. Eventually, all four young people (all from that area) pled guilty and were convicted of multiple counts of arson, attempted arson, and use of incendiary devices. By March of 2006, Lewis had been sentenced to six years in federal prison, while the other three received sentences of two years apiece.

The feds were sure that Lewis was a local cell leader for ELF and exploited his computer for links to other members. They did find some vague connections to other known ELF members, but it was eventually concluded that Ryan Lewis was a fairly new ELFster who had only recently begun dabbling in the arson business. He had not at all been involved in the other major attacks by ELF. Joe Konefal and Greg Smith had correctly concluded that while these recent attacks used devices that closely resembled earlier ELF/ALF devices, the Lewis cell had only copied these items out of ELF handbooks. Lewis and his cell were an isolated group, who were indeed complete novices in the fire-setting business. Nonetheless, all four of these young people now hold the title of "convicted ecoterrorist."

### The Family

This was one of the first arrests for the Operation Backfire agents. Soon the feds were linking suspects from Oregon to Colorado, San Diego and Arizona. By now they had started to identify about fifteen hard-core members of ELF known as "the Family." This ELF cell had originated in Eugene, Oregon, and had set several spectacular fires, with many of them occurring between 1996 and 2001. This eclectic group was a mixture of drug-addicted thrill seekers, latter-day hippies, and sober, intense, and intelligent operatives. The group had computer experts, engineers, and dedicated activists. They worked in small, autonomous cells, where everyone was known only by a moniker, and they seldom interacted with larger groups. They were extremely difficult to identify and track.

When William Rodgers joined the small group in 1997, almost every attack after that was designed to be a major event with multiple, standard-designed incendiary devices employed. They had pulled off major raids in Oregon, California, and the largest ecoterror crime ever—the arson attack of a massive ski resort in Vail, Colorado, in October 1998. Prior to these events, Rodgers forced members to seclude themselves and wear multiple layers of anti-forensic clothing and masks while gathering and assembling device components. They also did extensive pre-raid scouting of their targets. They dressed and worked like skilled commandos, using dark clothing, sterile ready rooms, and night-vision equipment during scouting missions and raids.

By 2001, the Family had changed tactics somewhat and began attacking dealerships that sold large, gas-guzzling SUVs. Their attacks spawned copycat attacks all over the country as many SUVs and dealerships were attacked by ELF sympathizers.

The major break in the Family case came in 1998 when a female member was caught shoplifting incendiary materials shortly before an attack in Washington. A prudent FBI agent named John Ferreira focused on the girl and her drug-addict boyfriend for the next few years, slowly building links in the case and exploiting their dependence on heroin. That same drug-addled female had also left her wallet in a phone booth near a major ELF attack some years before, although it took agents a long time to put those events together.

Drugs were compromising the security and discipline of some members of the Family. Finally, in 2006, when Operation Backfire was in full gear, agent Ferreira approached the heroin-addicted boyfriend, named Jacob Ferguson, and asked him to cooperate or be indicted. The bold tactic worked, and Ferguson became a cooperating federal witness and the key to dismantling the Family. Ferguson agreed to wear a wire and for a year sought out and engaged other ELF members in conversations about past attacks. While some were reluctant and disciplined, Ferguson was convincing enough to pry a large amount of damning information from them. Finally, in the key to the entire case, Ferguson met and debriefed the mastermind of the tactics and incendiary devices, William Rodgers.

On December 7, 2005, the FBI swept across the country and arrested the first seven suspects in a series of highly publicized raids. Eventually the number of arrestees grew to eighteen, with four of the named suspects having fled the country. All were threatened with heavy sentences and most capitulated and agreed to talk, naming other coconspirators and events. As each suspect talked, more coconspirators and sympathizers were exposed. Major ELF cells quickly fell apart due to police raids or their own paranoia that everyone was working for the feds.

The hard-core members of the Family had years earlier sworn to each other to never talk to the feds. They knew from studying other groups and cases that if no one ever talked, then the feds seldom had corroborating evidence. Their early mantra was "no one talks, everyone walks." This was pretty bold talk when you are sitting around a campfire, smoking weed with a bunch of wild-eyed pseudo revolutionaries, but the feds have their own mantra, which has much more impact when you are all alone in a cold, sterile holding cell facing thirty years for terrorism charges. The feds mantra of "he who talks first, walks first" is a tried and true tactic of every federal conspiracy investigation undertaken against mafiosos, gang members, and any other would-be revolutionary or crime group. In the end, cops know that almost everybody always talks.

By early 2006, after many of the suspects had confessed to specific acts and had named their coconspirators, most of the major ELF attacks had been solved. Indictments were handed down on thirteen members of the Family. Some fled the country. Four ELF members were indicted for the incendiary attacks at the BLM ranch in Susanville in 2001. This was for the incident where Investigators Joe Konefal and Greg Smith had found the three intact incendiary devices next to the large burned hay shed. Also solved were almost all of the major attacks in five western states. Each of these events used ELF tactics and devices, and this physical evidence was corroborated by the statements of the suspects. By 2012, all but two of the Family were in prison (or had already served their time). Two minor members of the group had fled to Spain or parts unknown.

Still, the feds were not finished working in the Auburn, California, area. After sifting through Ryan Lewis's computer, they came across the name of an ELF activist named Eric McDavid. An FBI sting netted the arrests of three more ELF activists in 2006 in Auburn. The three were accused of conspiracy to damage facilities. While no damage has actually been done by the three, two of the three pled guilty to conspiracy. The lone holdout, Eric McDavid, refused to admit guilt and was subsequently convicted and is facing twenty years in prison. He and a squadron of lawyers are screaming "foul" due to what they believe are highly questionable tactics used by the FBI.

The main tactician and incendiary genius of the Family, William Rodgers, had slowed or stopped his "direct action" ELF activities and raids after 2001. He had voiced concern over infighting and a lack of security within the group. He had quietly gone back to Prescott, Arizona, where he opened a bookshop while still heavily devoted to the environmental cause. Rodgers was caught surprised when arrested in the first sweep by FBI agents on December 7, 2005. He was jailed in Arizona and believed that he was probably facing thirty years to life in prison for his role in the attacks.

One of the few truly dedicated ecowarriors to the end, Rodgers chose his own exit from the case. On the night of December 21, 2005, he penned a goodbye letter to friends and supporters, which read in part, "Tonight I have made a jailbreak—I am returning home, to the Earth, to the place of my origins." He then committed suicide by suffocating himself in a plastic bag. Rodgers, true to his holy cause, did not talk. He took his secrets to his grave.

It was quite prophetic that Jacob Ferguson was the "snitch" who led to the downfall of the Family cell and that William Rodgers was one of the main players to fall. Ferguson, while he and his girlfriend were early and avid arsonists, were also lifetime heroin addicts. Rodgers had worried about drug use within the group and the threat it posed toward security.

A few years earlier Rodgers wrote an article in an Earth First! publication, where he openly lamented that heavy drug use within the environmental movement was a security threat and was also sapping the will and strength of the group. In a sense he had predicted his own downfall and arrest as it was mainly because of the uncontrollable drug use of a couple of members.

*These cases were worked on by numerous local, state, and federal investigators and agents. Lead investigators for Operation Backfire were FBI Agents John Ferreira and Jane Quimby. The lead criminal investigator in California was FBI Agent Angela Armstrong. In particular, the fire-scene work and analysis of many of the California attacks was done by supervising arson/bomb investigators Joe Konefal and Greg Smith of California State Fire Marshal's Office.*

## ELF ATTACKS SUVS
## WEST COVINA, CA, AUGUST 2003

The year 2003 was a very busy year for ELF operatives. While the actions of the Oregon-based group known as the Family were waning, their major arson attacks spurred on other smaller ELF cells across the United States. This particular wave of attacks by unconnected ELF cells had found new types of targets: gas-guzzling vehicles and their sellers/owners; fast-food restaurants, and construction sites for new homes.

New Year's Day of 2003 opened with an ELF attack at a car dealership in Girard, Pennsylvania. Ecoterrorists set incendiary devices in the car lot and caused $90,000 in damage. Three weeks later in Seattle, ELF attacked another favorite target—the McDonald's fast-food chain. Elves poured a large quantity of gasoline on the roof of the restaurant across from the famous Space Needle. In March, ELF hit several McDonald's in the Chico, California, area with firebombs. In Michigan, on March

21, 2003, ELF used incendiary devices to attack luxury homes in a construction project bordering on wild lands.

### Chico-Santa Cruz ELF/ALF Cell

In April, the ELFs seemed to focus on SUVs. An ELF/ALF cell in Santa Cruz, California, vandalized over ninety SUVs in three different attacks by the use of paint. That same cell was linked to ELF arson attacks in Chico and other fires at a nearby McDonald's and housing tracts. That Chico-Santa Cruz cell was just warming up. By June they had hit car dealerships and several construction sites with vandalism and firebombing attacks. There was clearly a very active cell in the Bay area of California. In all, they damaged or destroyed over 130 SUVs in several raids.

Not to be outdone by the elves, ALF operatives, who had been fairly quiet in California in recent years, attacked a favorite target. They used multiple firebombs to finally torch a slaughterhouse in Petaluma, just north of the Bay area. This same target was hit with firebombs two other times by ALF extremists.

### San Diego Cell

For most of their existence, ALF and ELF activists had not been involved in incendiary attacks in Southern California. The bulk of the incendiary raids had been conducted against targets in the semirural northern and central areas of the state, and further north into Oregon and Washington. That all would change with some very dramatic attacks.

By later summer of 2003, arson investigators found a very active ELF cell in San Diego. On August 1, a massive arson attack occurred at a large condominium construction project in the university area, causing over $50 million in damages, the costliest ecoterrorist attack in US history. Multiple incendiary devices were found, along with two bed sheets proclaiming, "If you build it, we will burn it," and "The ELFs are mad." Within hours of this attack, ELF/ALF activist leader Rod Coronado, a convicted arsonist for a major attack years earlier in Michigan, gave a speech to an environmental group just a few minutes' drive from the massive fire scene. In that speech, Coronado lauded the arson attack and even demonstrated how to construct a "weapon of mass destruction" (his words) incendiary device out of a gallon jug, sponges, and incense sticks as a time delay.

He was not a suspect in the San Diego fire but was in violation of his own federal parole for demonstrating the device. He was arrested and spent a year in jail for this demonstration. That same ELF cell in San Diego, apparently not satisfied with the massive fire they had started, struck again six weeks later on September 19, torching several homes at three other construction sites near La Jolla, just north of San Diego. Again they left taunting banners and remnants of incendiary devices. Despite an intense investigation by local and federal authorities over the past several years, those San Diego ELF incendiary attacks have never been solved. As quickly as the San Diego cell erupted, it went away. There have been no notable ELF events in the San Diego area since the summer of 2003.

### Pasadena Cell

In between the two San Diego attacks, a very small, yet intense ELF cell emerged in Pasadena, California. For a short time period the small three-person group had been content with pulling pranks in the Pasadena area, changing the name of the local Starbucks to "Starfucks," and other such juvenile stunts. The group consisted of a boyfriend/girlfriend combo named Tyler Johnson and Michie Oe, and their odd friend, Billy Cottrell. Tyler and Billy were both students at Pasadena's California Institute of Technology (Caltech), one of the most intense research universities in the country. The two were extremely studious and had met in a class. Both were involved in risky pastimes like bouldering and rock-climbing and had used those skills to complete their high-risk pranks near the campus.

On the afternoon of August 21, 2003, the two were in the midst of a more serious prank. They were both somewhat oriented to environmental issues and both expressed a hatred for sports utility vehicles, as they were gas guzzlers and a menace to the environment. Both claimed that they were not affiliated with ELF, but both were made aware of it and were sympathetic to it from various literature and contacts on campus. Earlier, the two had pooled $200 so that they could order some stickers from Cottrell's mom, who owned a sign business. The stickers proclaimed, "MY SUV SUPPORTS TERRORISM." The pair of thrill seekers planned on spending the hours of darkness slapping those stickers on SUVs in the Pasadena area. The stickers did not arrive in time for their "raid." At some point they devised a more sinister plan.

By one o'clock the next morning, Cottrell and Johnson were out cruising in Cottrell's burgundy Toyota, east of Pasadena, with Michie Oe driving. The trio was wearing old clothes and carrying cans of spray paint. At two in the morning, Cottrell and Johnson were spotted on surveillance cameras at a large car lot in nearby Arcadia. The camera followed them as they strolled down the aisles of cars, occasionally bending down and spraying something on them. Investigators would later photograph typical ELF graffiti: "FUCK SUVS, SUVS=TERRORISM," and "ELF." They stopped in the next town of Monrovia and began spray-painting trucks and SUVs parked on the street. At that time one of them threw an incendiary device into one of the SUVs. The device was a crude Molotov cocktail in a beer bottle. The distraught owner of the SUV would later find the word "POLLUTER" on the hood, red smiley faces, and the word "ELF" on the sides of his burned vehicle.

By three thirty, the small group had moved to another dealership in the next town of Duarte. They painted twenty-one SUVs at a Ford dealership and then crossed the street and painted twenty-six more at a Mitsubishi dealer. This time, Billy Cottrell made a serious and egotistical mistake. He painted an obscure mathematical equation on the side of a Montero SUV.

The trio then drove a few towns east to West Covina, where they attacked a Hummer dealership. Using incendiary devices, the trio started fires that eventually torched twenty Hummer SUVs and partially burned the dealership building. In the midst of this attack, a beer-bottle Molotov was thrown against an SUV, and it splashed on Billy Cottrell, briefly catching his clothes on fire. During the panic of putting himself out, Cottrell dropped a headband at the scene. Their work done, the trio fled the scene back to Pasadena. When firefighters and law enforcement arrived the next day, they found a large amount of ELF graffiti and a pile of burned Hummers. The four-city spree caused vandalism damage to over 130 vehicles and fire damage to twenty-one of them. The total cost exceeded $2.3 million.

The fire scene was worked jointly by a mixed group of investigators from LASD, the San Gabriel Valley arson task force, the ATF, and the FBI. The sheriff's department would soon leave as its assistance was turned down by the local task force. After that, the scene was handled by mostly inexperienced fire investigators and FBI agents, with a couple of ATF guys thrown in. During the extensive scene investigation, an agent recovered the headband, which held three strands of hair. Months later that hair would yield DNA that positively identified Billy Cottrell as the wearer of that headband.

The local cops and FBI/ATF were perplexed by this attack as there had never been an ELF arson attack in the Los Angeles area (although there would later be several ALF-related arson attacks in LA). Nobody had seen this coming, and the FBI's counterterrorism experts, intent on stopping threats from Al Qaeda et al., did not have any information on ecoterrorists in this region at all.

Despite all the investigators, they were unable to locate or recover any evidence of the use of firebombs, with the exception of the SUV fire on the street earlier in the night. This was the first of a few errors made in the case. While errors are common in many investigations, this one had an almost unforgiveable error associated with it. Six weeks into the investigation, the FBI focused on a peace activist who lived twenty miles east in the city of Pomona. The activist, Josh Connole, was decidedly anti-war and had spoken openly against President Bush. At some point the FBI decided he was one of the arson suspects. He was arrested in September. He staunchly proclaimed his innocence. Eventually the FBI released him with no charges, and a year later begrudgingly admitted his innocence. They quickly settled a civil suit with the unhappy peace activist. To this day, no one knows what made the FBI think that Connole was one of the suspects.

Shortly after the arrest of Connole, the *Los Angeles Times* received an email from a fake name claiming that the inept feds had arrested the wrong guy. The emailer convinced the *Los Angeles Times* of his veracity by naming the obscure mathematical formula painted on one of the SUVs. This was important because the investigators had not yet released any of that "case critical" information. The *Los Angeles Times* did its own fact-checking and found that the email came from the Caltech campus in Pasadena.

Eventually the FBI, while clearly not fire-scene experts but are exceptional at investigating computer crimes, figured out which computer the email had come from and that the last user was Billy Cottrell. The FBI began questioning Cottrell and his friends, and eventually the case began to unravel. In February

2004, shortly after being interviewed by federal agents, Tyler Johnson and Michie Oe disappeared. The FBI has immense resources and soon delved deep into the obscure mathematical formula left at the scene of the attacks. They found that it was a highly technical formula invented by an eighteenth-century Swiss mathematician. By leaving this unique calling card, or "signature," Billy Cottrell had practically pointed a finger at himself, as only a math geek would understand something like that.

The feds, and later the world, discovered that Billy Cottrell was indeed a very special math geek. In short, he had been an oddball all his life, with very poor grades and lifelong behavioral issues. However, anyone who knew him realized he was a very gifted genius. He failed high school and was kicked out of other institutions but had scored genius level in math and science at the University of Chicago and had been accepted into Caltech's very prestigious postgraduate program. His parents and defense attorneys would later explain his bizarre actions and confrontational and argumentative attitude by him being autistic and having Asperger's syndrome. Although he had never been diagnosed with either of these conditions before the attacks, it was likely that he did have some sort of issue associated with them.

Cottrell was a study in contrasts. He was a complete and total math and science nerd, yet he loved the outdoors and rock-climbing and pulling stupid little stunts. He was a very difficult person to understand. His mother described him as similar to the subject of the movie "A Beautiful Mind." Indeed, many academics and scientists to include Stephen Hawking wrote to the court on behalf of Billy.

The problem with this case was that Billy eventually told his version of the story, no doubt assisted by a bevy of lawyers and consultants. He admitted to spray-painting the vehicles but stated he was surprised and shocked when the other two began throwing firebombs. His defense team stated that he was conned into this activity by Tyler Johnson, who was much more savvy and domineering. Since Tyler Johnson and Michie Oe had fled the country, they weren't there to tell their side of the story. However, investigators noted that the evidence and statements by Cottrell showed that he had active involvement in the entire incident and was not some sort of dupe.

The US Attorney's Office in Los Angeles, which seldom if ever filed arson charges, wanted blood for this major event (and to probably smooth over the erroneous arrest of Connole), and soon Billy Cottrell was facing a thirty-year sentence for terrorism. Because only one incendiary device had been recovered in all of this mess, and Billy testified that Johnson had thrown that one, the jury gave him a break and tossed out the serious destructive-device charge. Nonetheless, in April of 2005, Billy Cottrell was convicted of conspiracy and arson and sentenced to eight years in federal prison. He later won a partial appeal but eventually served nearly all of his time. He was released in 2011.

Michie Oe has never been seen since this event, and it's probable that the feds aren't looking real hard for her.

Tyler Johnson had not been seen since early 2004. On December 26, 2009, his family announced that Tyler Johnson was found dead after an avalanche in the Corsican Mountains of France. His death was a true mystery and wasn't reported for several weeks. Of course the conspiracy theorists within ELF now believe he was an FBI agent sent in to get Billy Cottrell "dirty."

## LONE WOLF ELFS
## PASADENA, CA, SEPTEMBER 19, 2006

*From the San Gabriel Valley Arson Task Force.*

Analysis has shown that there have been hundreds of ELF or ALF incendiary attacks since the 1980s. They are all similar in ways, and all have a few variances. This case is included as it is typical of a small "lone wolf" ELF cell. It illustrates why it is so difficult to keep tabs on this very loosely affiliated group.

In September of 2006, there was a large construction site operating in Pasadena, California, directly underneath the famed Colorado Street Bridge. Construction crews at the site were building a condominium complex in a deep valley, just blocks from the Rose Bowl football stadium.

When workers arrived to work on September 19, they immediately saw that something was amiss. A large piece of construction equipment at the site had graffiti spray-painted on the side of it proclaiming, "Another Tractor Decommissioned by ELF." The workers investigated and found that the ignition system of the vehicle had been disabled. While there had only been one previous ELF incident in the Los Angeles area prior to this, the workers were aware that ELF historically attacked construction sites and often left incendiary devices in the structures. The construction workers started a detailed search of the site.

A search through the thirty-unit site revealed a sinister-appearing item on the floor of one of the half-finished units. The device was a sixty-four-ounce clear plastic juice container that had been three-fourths filled with gasoline. The cap of the container had been cut open, and a crude ignition system had been built into it. The ignition system consisted of two filtered cigarettes, with more than a dozen paper matches affixed around them. The items were held secured by a rubber band. Even to the untrained eye, this was a crude but effective time-delay incendiary device. The item had been left in the corner of a room, which had only wood framing, wood floors, and pressed-wood half walls. The item had clearly failed to function as designed.

The Pasadena Fire Department arrived and summoned the skills of the local arson-investigation group, the San Gabriel Valley Arson Task Force. The investigators examined the item carefully.

Both cigarettes had been lit but both had self-extinguished before they could ignite the bundles of matches. If this item had ignited, it would have produced enough volume of flame to burn steadily for about ten minutes, which was sufficient time to get the vertical two-by-four studs burning, which eventually would have engulfed and destroyed the entire thirty-unit building, as none of the units had been finished or wrapped in fire-resistant materials. This easily could have been a massive arson fire.

The task-force investigators recognized this incident as an ELF extremist act. They summoned the local FBI, who arrived and took control of the evidence. The item was processed at the FBI lab, and scientists discovered DNA material on the filtered ends of the cigarettes. Three years later the FBI was able to match the DNA to a male named Stephen Murphy. Murphy was tracked down to Texas and was arrested in October 2009. As part of a plea deal, Murphy admitted to building the device with an unnamed friend. He then said he planted and ignited the device in furtherance of ELF causes. Murphy pled guilty to conspiracy and received a five-year prison sentence.

### Investigator's Profile

The three preceding animal liberation/earth liberation attacks are profiled together as all of these attacks under this heading have much the same profile. Since the early 1970s, there have been in excess of 450 documented ELF/ALF incendiary attacks in the world. All but about forty of these attacks used some form of premade incendiary device. The targets of the attacks, along with the type of device used, varied by country and the sophistication level of each cell.

The ELF/ALF attacks were consistent in the following aspects. Almost all took place at nighttime. Most of the attacks involved a physical break-in and entry of the property, along with the vandalism and destruction of high-value equipment and vehicles.

Many of the attackers left distinct graffiti, and most of the attacks were claimed on international websites. The attacks occurred almost always when no humans were at the facilities. The attackers often used clandestine pseudo military tactics including surveillance, pre-scouting, bypassing alarms, penetrating security, and the setting of multiple fires in preplanned areas for maximum damage. Lastly, the overwhelming number of attacks utilized some form of prepared incendiary devices and deployed them in numbers, again for maximum destruction.

These cases are very easy to identify, as a signature or calling card is often found at the scene. With that in mind, it is incredibly frustrating to find out how few of these cases were solved. Despite the best efforts of even the most careful offender, we (the investigations community) should be getting much more forensics off of each device. Most of these suspects really aren't that good. Each piece of forensics needs to be exploited by criminalists, analysts, and dedicated investigators.

Two of the above cases were solved by excellent forensics work. The Auburn cell was broken by footprints and poison oak discovered by investigators. The single device in Pasadena was solved by DNA. Sadly, the biggest event in the group, the West Covina car arsons, was solved mostly by luck and the suspect bragging to a newspaper. It is clear in that case that not enough experienced arson investigators were on scene to locate the several incendiary devices used in that attack.

## ABORTION CLINIC ARSON ATTACKS VARIOUS LOCATIONS, 1979–2015

### The Profile

The profile for this type of extremist arson is fairly straightforward, with some slight deviations based on the large number and variety of attackers. Generally all arson attacks by members of this movement occurred directly against the abortion clinics themselves. Some attackers preferred clandestine nighttime assaults, while others, not at all concerned about being arrested, conducted arson attacks in broad daylight in front of dozens of witnesses. Most of the nighttime attacks occurred from the outside of the building with incendiary materials and devices thrown onto roofs, poured down vents, set against doors, or tossed into windows. The attackers that conducted the bold assaults during daytime often walked into the building and placed or threw flammable materials while shouting some sort of slogan or religious verse.

I conducted an incendiary-device analysis of this movement and found that they did not use prepared devices nearly as much as the animal-rights groups. Almost 100 percent of their attacks used some form of accelerant (usually gasoline or diesel), but less than 30 percent of the attacks used an actual incendiary device. As a general rule, the abortion clinic arsons were very crude and fairly ineffective as far as starting large fires. Members of the movement attacked the same targets over and over again as a large number of attacks simply failed. However the attacks were successful in one aspect. They were excellent methods of intimidation!

The attackers themselves were somewhat predictable as they were all mainly white, and all were closely affiliated with a Christian, Catholic, or Mormon church. Most had been involved in some form of protest against these clinics prior to the attacks. Several of the male attackers had military experience and training and were skilled with weapons and explosives. Many of the female attackers were highly dedicated but were extremely poor fire setters or bombers.

## THE ARMY OF GOD

During roughly the same era that the animal/earth-rights groups were launching their hundreds of arson attacks, a second wave of explosive and incendiary assaults began in the United States. The surprising thing about this wave of attacks was that it came from the exact opposite end of the political spectrum as the animal-rights groups.

In 1973, the US Supreme Court handed down its famous *Roe v. Wade* decision, basically legalizing abortion in the United States. The very first clinic to open and legally provide this service was in New York. In 1979 this same clinic was burned by a twenty-one-year old antiabortion extremist. The attack by this young abortion protester was indicative of a very different type of arsonist than other extremist groups. Many members of this movement simply did not care if they were identified or caught. They firmly believed that they were soldiers of God, and whatever they did was justified.

### Peter Burkin, 1979

On February 15, 1979, twenty-one-year-old Peter Burkin walked through the front doors of an abortion clinic in Hempstead, New York, and lit a flaming torch in the foyer. He picked up a gasoline container over his head and, with the flaming torch in one hand, burst through the doors into the waiting room of the crowded clinic. Burkin yelled, "Everyone out, or this place is going up—I got gas!" Burkin allowed most people in the building to leave and then set the place on fire. He was almost immediately arrested and proclaimed that he was contacted by God, via Morse code, and told to "cleanse the clinic by fire." Burkin was later found not guilty by reason of insanity.

The extremely controversial *Roe v. Wade* legal decision caused an immediate and passionate response by dozens of religious and political groups, who were fundamentally opposed to this issue. The antiabortion movement spread immediately across the United States. This movement started with prayer vigils, peaceful protests, and members attempting to shame or dissuade patients from visiting the clinics. Within a short few years the actions of antiabortionists soon devolved into vandalisms, stench-bomb attacks, assaults, kidnappings, beatings, sniper attacks, assassinations, and eventually arson, firebombing, and explosive-bombing attacks.

Unlike the animal-rights groups' attacks, which seldom if ever targeted people or occupied buildings, the antiabortion wave of attacks started by physical assaults on employees and medical staff. Eventually the arsons, fire bombings, and explosive bombings targeted buildings that were open for business and filled with patients and staff. In many cases, this was truly a violent movement.

However, it was not an easy movement to monitor or exploit by law enforcement. Much like the animal-rights and earth-rights groups, the antiabortion movement was made up of dozens of small, localized protest groups with very little organization and structure. It was extremely difficult to monitor all of the radicalized members of this movement. While the overwhelming number of people with antiabortion sentiments maintained a peaceful and lawful protest, fringe members of the movement radicalized and began conducting "lone wolf" terrorist-style attacks on clinics and medical personnel.

As I mentioned in my first book, *Torchered Minds*, several members of the antiabortion movement became very prolific serial arsonists. Between 1992 and 1995, Richard Andrews, from the Pacific Northwest, conducted no less than eight major arson attacks using prepared incendiary devices on abortion clinics in four states in the Northwest. A female protégé of his, Shelley Shannon, used copies of his devices, and in 1992 conducted six major attacks against clinics in western states before she was arrested trying to assassinate an abortion doctor in Wichita, Kansas. Both of these ardent attackers were members of a very dedicated group known as the Army of God.

The Army of God was a loose affiliation of incredibly zealous members who held extreme religious beliefs against abortion and homosexuality. Members of the Army of God conducted bombings, fire bombings, arsons, kidnappings, sniper attacks, and assassinations of pro-abortion targets, gay/lesbian clubs, abortion providers, and targets that represented the United States' inclusion in the supposed New World Order. The most famous member of the Army of God is serial bomber/murderer Eric Rudolph, who bombed abortion clinics, gay/lesbian clubs, and the 1996 Atlanta Olympic Summer Games.

### San Diego, CA, 1987

Rev. Dorman Owens was a fundamentalist Baptist pastor in the town of Santee, California. Owens was well known for having his congregation actively picket family planning and abortion clinics in the San Diego area. He also led his flock to aggressively picket any pro-gay events and San Diego's annual Gay Pride parade.

The Family Planning Associates Medical Group, a San Diego abortion provider, had received numerous threats from members of the local antiabortion movement. Around three in the morning, on July 27, 1987, police were staking out the location in anticipation of an attack. That night police saw an odd person place an item on the doorsteps of the clinic. They quickly examined the item and found out that it was a timed-delay incendiary/explosive device. The item had been constructed of a two-gallon gas can, with a pipe bomb affixed to it and a "five-minute candle" set as a timer/fuse. This device was lit but failed to function, and the suspect was quickly detained.

The suspect was a thirty-two-year-old white male named Eric Svelmoe, a congregant of Pastor Owens's church. Svelmoe was wearing a disguise consisting of a women's wig and camouflage face paint. He was carrying a loaded .357 revolver. San Diego police and ATF agents interviewed Svelmoe, and he admitted to constructing the device in his home. He was soon indicted on federal charges.

Four months later Pastor Owens and six other members of his flock were arrested by federal agents in connection to this attack and the planned fire bombings of two other abortion clinics in the area. They were charged with conspiracy. Several members of the church were convicted of conspiracy in federal court. Pastor Dorman Owens was convicted in federal court of witness tampering. One member of the church who stood out was Cheryl Sullenger. She was convicted for her role in the conspiracy and sentenced to two years in federal prison along with her husband. After her release she remained an ardent anti-abortionist and joined Operation Rescue, a national movement. She was later accused of gathering personal information on Dr. George Tiller, an abortion doctor. Sullenger was suspected of providing Tiller's personal schedule to an assassin who later murdered Tiller by shooting him in his own church.

### Bakersfield, CA, 1997

At three in the morning, on September 20, 1993, the Family Planning Associates clinic in Bakersfield burned to the ground, with over $1.4 million in damage. The Central Valley of California is a traditional, conservative stronghold, and the clinic had long been a focus of protests and picketing by antiabortion groups. Investigators determined that a single arsonist attacked the building by pouring a flammable liquid along the exterior of the structure. It was a total loss, and no suspects were ever identified. The clinic would eventually be rebuilt, but this arson attack would not be the last extremist event at that building.

On March 17, 1997, antiabortionist Peter Howard, a forty-four-year-old white male filled his pickup truck with over ninety gallons of gasoline in the tank and additional containers in the cab, and placed three propane tanks and a gasoline-soaked hemp rope into the vehicle. He then lit the rope on fire as a fusing system and drove his truck into the front doors of the Family Planning clinic, hoping to end his life and destroy this clinic in a massive fireball. A small fire erupted but not the large fire or explosion that Howard had intended. Howard was immediately arrested and charged in federal court with attempted arson and use of an explosive device. He eventually pled guilty and was sentenced to fifteen years in federal prison.

### Davenport, IA, 2006

In a near-identical, bizarre act, antiabortionist David McMenemy, a forty-year-old white male, drove his personal car through the front doors of a women's clinic in Iowa. By September of 2006, McMenemy had been scouting abortion clinics throughout the Midwest for weeks. On September 11, he found the Edgerton Women's Health Center in Davenport and planned his attack. McMenemy soaked the interior of his car with gasoline and planned to drive it into the clinic, where the impact would cause the car to burst into a firebomb, killing himself in the process. At least that was the plan. In reality, McMenemy drove his car through the front of the clinic, but he survived, and there was no explosion.

He then exited the car, poured a bottle of gasoline onto his crashed car, and set it on fire, which in turn set the building on fire. Realizing that burning to death was probably fairly painful, McMenemy opted to just walk out of the building and surrender himself to the responding firefighters. He fully admitted his intentions and actions. McMenemy pled guilty to arson in 2007 and was sentenced to five years in federal prison.

### The Waning Fervor

The antiabortion extremist attacks started in 1977, reaching a crescendo in the late 1990s before slowly ebbing to single-digit numbers of attacks after 2001. Somehow the movement slowly mellowed out. The National Abortion Federation keeps detailed statistics on all attacks and assaults against abortion facilities and practitioners. They, along with the ATF, which has similar statistics, show that there were about 186 arson attacks against abortion facilities from 1977 to 2015. Additionally, there were forty bombing attacks and one hundred attempts at arsons or bombings to these facilities. It is clear from their statistics that the most violent of attacks greatly decreased after 2001, as did all arsons and bombings in the United States.

In my studies I have formed the opinion that the terrorist attacks on 9/11 caused the acts of bombings and fire bombings to be generally regarded (even in criminal circles) as unfair, underhanded, and wholly un-American. The use of these types of weapons has literally fallen off the charts in this country since then. The antiabortion movement has certainly not died out completely as protests and vandalism attacks against these clinics have continued at a diminished but still healthy pace.

Both the animal-rights attacks and the antiabortion attacks were carried out in almost every state in the country. The attacks were mostly carried out in fairly crude fashion (except for one or two highly skilled cells).

## HOUSE OF WORSHIP FIRES

### The Profile

House of worship fires, or church arsons, are some of the most misunderstood of all arson attacks. In the mid-1990s, President Clinton, citing a wave of arson attacks on black churches by hate groups, launched a multiagency group called the Federal Church Arson Task Force. This group eventually looked at hundreds of church fires and church arsons throughout the United States. After a dozen years of doing so, they (quietly) concluded that the specter of arson attacks on black churches and synagogues by white hate groups was mostly a myth, with only one or two instances ever identified. (It is acknowledged here that racial hatred was responsible for perhaps hundreds of church/synagogue arson attacks throughout the South in the era of Reconstruction and the Civil Rights period. However, these attacks have become extremely rare since the mid-1960s.)

In reality, church fires are fairly common events as a large number of churches, particularly in the rural areas of our country, are poorly constructed facilities with little to no fire-protection systems within. It is fairly common to use candles and open flames in these churches, and the construction and upkeep is usually done by volunteers and parishioners. Consequently, a large number of church fires are, in fact, accidental events.

Church arsons do occur fairly regularly to all types of churches, synagogues, and temples, and each attack must be carefully scrutinized by investigators without leaping to conclusions. Church arson fires tend to get a large amount of media attention, and the investigators must be very diligent not to select the easy answers.

In truth, and after a sober review of hundreds of church fires, the most common arson suspect in a church fire is one of the members of the church. The most common motives for church arsons are the same as other arson attacks: revenge/spite, crime concealment, and profit. Churches that are attacked from the exterior may be related to an extremist group or similar entity. However, if an arsonist enters the church, the investigator should pay attention to the exact target of the attack. An arsonist opposed to the ideals and message of the church, in general, will likely attack the sanctuary of the church. An arsonist who sets fire in the church's office area is sending a different message. That person may be involved in internal theft and embezzlement from the church, which is actually quite common.

Additionally, a person who attempts to burn the entire structure down may, in fact, be involved in insurance fraud.

Churches generate a large amount of money, so theft/embezzlement is common in all churches. A struggle for power within the church or a shift in ideology may create an intense internal dispute and bring about a revenge/spite-based arson attack. All of these motives are much more common than the possibility of a hate crime against the church. Great care should be taken by investigators to determine if the event is staged to appear as a hate crime when in fact the fire was set for a more mundane reason.

If a church fire is, in fact, an arson attack, then special care must be taken to carefully analyze the scene and determine exactly where in the church the fire was started as this is an excellent clue as to the motive for the fire.

## ST. JOHN VIANNEY CHURCH ARSON HACIENDA HEIGHTS, CA, 2011

### St. John Vianney Catholic Church

The St. John Vianney Catholic Church was built in the then-quiet and semirural residential neighborhood of Hacienda Heights, California, in the early 1960s, along Turnbull Canyon Road. Hacienda Heights was a neighborhood of mostly middle-income whites with a few Hispanics sprinkled in. This community is situated along the 60 Freeway, just fifteen miles east of downtown Los Angeles. The church serves a very large Catholic community and at its height had nearly twelve thousand parishioners. Over the next fifty years, the congregation morphed into a more Hispanic flavor, with the large influx of Mexicans into the neighborhood. The church grew in size and consisted of a large main sanctuary and several large outbuildings, including an adjacent rectory for the priests.

Like many churches of the 1960s, St. John Vianney was built with an open sanctuary lined by over twenty glass windows. The windows were clear glass and were easily opened in order to allow a cross breeze on warm days. The large church sanctuary also had a fifty-foot-high ceiling that was open to the roof. The interior of the ceiling was covered with laminated wood, which had a heavy coating of varnish. Huge curved and laminated crossbeams held the large roof in place. These crossbeams were also wood and were laminated for strength. Like the walls, ceiling, and pews, they were heavily coated in varnish and clear coat. The open cathedral was filled with wooden pews. The floor was a mixture of varnished wood and ceramic tile. The massive roof was covered in wood, and then heavy Spanish tiles over that. Like many churches, there were very few modern fire-resistant materials in place.

### Controversy

In the decade of 2002–2012, the Catholic Church worldwide had undergone intense scrutiny for a phenomenon called the Priest Abuse Sex Scandal. This scandal rocked the church to its core and alleged worldwide that there were thousands of Catholic priests involved in the molestations of young parishioners. By 2011, the church had settled dozens of major lawsuits and paid out hundreds of millions of dollars in damages associated with this scandal. A side story to that is that Catholic churches worldwide had been the targets of protests, vandalisms, and other attacks to include arson due to the scandal. In particular, the Los Angeles Archdiocese, the largest in America, was heavily embroiled in the scandal, with much local media attention. All of the Catholic churches in Los Angeles received ongoing threats and protests associated with the scandal.

### The Fire

At just past midnight, on April 16, 2011, a firefighter at the LACoFD Hacienda Heights Station was outside of the station.

The fire station sat on a hill overlooking much of Hacienda Heights. The firefighter's attention was drawn to the neighborhood at the bottom of the hill, just six blocks away. He was surprised to see a jet of flame literally exploding through the roof of St. John Vianney Church. By the time he could alarm the other firefighters and they began pulling the engine out, there was a second jet of flame pushing through the roof. Both of these violent jets of flame were coming from the west end of the sanctuary near the altar. The engine made it to the church in two minutes, and they could now see that the large church was probably beyond help. There was a massive flame front pushing through the roof, with flames reaching up to 180 feet in the air.

The on-scene fire commander, Captain Mike Ponders, summoned a major incident response, and within forty minutes over one hundred firefighters and twenty trucks were on scene battling the blaze. This was mostly a containment operation as the first crews acknowledged that the structure was beyond saving from almost first arrival. However, the first captain, not knowing if any priests or possibly homeless persons slept in the church during the night, attempted to make entry into the very east end of the church. His crew was able to gain access to about forty feet of the front lobby but could see that the entire sanctuary was fully aflame. If anybody had been in there, they would not be alive.

The fire captain was worried the heavy roof might collapse on his men, so he backed out and set up a defensive posture. This defensive posture, known derisively in the business as a "surround and drown" tactic, went on for the next six hours. By four in the morning, large trucks were set up on all four corners of the church, pumping tens of thousands of gallons of water into the structure. The large amount of water flowed out of the church on the north side and created a six-inch-deep river of ash and water several blocks away from the scene.

Arriving arson investigators would see this river and realize with dismay that any evidence in that church was likely spread several blocks away and completely contaminated. After seven straight hours of the surround-and-drown tactic, the flames were out, but hot spots continued to flare up for the next thirty-six hours. An engine company remained on scene for two days following the inception of this fire to deal with all the rekindling hot spots.

### The Fire-Scene Investigation

The first investigators on scene were a trio from LACoFD. They were accompanied by a fire investigator from ATF. Simultaneously, LASD deputies were on scene and holding an evacuation and fire-zone barricade. They requested that the sheriff's department's Arson-Explosives Detail respond immediately to this large structure fire. Eventually this team of investigators from the sheriff's department would take over the entire event. By one in the morning, Sgt. Derek Yoshino of the sheriff's department arrived, along with a fairly new arson investigator.

As the firefighters were battling the blaze, which continued to burn out of control, Sgt. Yoshino and his partner, Sgt. Wendy Zolkowski, began their initial investigation. They started with the basics. Sgt. Yoshino pressed the church staff for information on threats toward the church. Several members said it was fairly normal to have agitated persons come to the church and make harsh comments about the Catholic faith or the recent priest abuse scandal. However, no one could recall a recent specific event or threat.

Sgt. Yoshino questioned one of the priests, Father Roy (a pseudonym), who had observed the initial fire in the sanctuary and had rescued his fellow priest from a sound sleep and led him out of the smoke-filled rectory. Sgt. Yoshino inquired about any security/surveillance systems or alarm systems, as well as who was the last person to secure the buildings for the night. Father Roy advised firmly that there was at one time an alarm system installed, but the alarm service had been discontinued for many years. The priest was young, with dark hair, and was wearing a short-sleeve T-shirt, cargo shorts, and flip-flops. Father Roy, when pressed for details about issues at the church, gave vague, uninterested answers and didn't seem very forthcoming.

Approximately an hour after the first conversation with Father Roy, he approached Sgt. Yoshino and mentioned that he forgot to tell him there was a video camera located inside the main sanctuary and mounted behind the altar. When questioned about this camera, Father Roy stated the church secretary had been on scene at the beginning of the fire and asked whether or not she would be needed to get access to the video feed. Father Roy said he did not think it was that important and told her to go home. Sgt. Yoshino advised Father Roy he needed to call her back and have her respond immediately back to the church. The investigators needed to see the video feed.

Father Roy stated that the reason for the video-surveillance camera above the sanctuary altar was the church had experienced several thefts of artifacts in the recent past and had installed the camera so that it was hidden but focused on a tabernacle box just behind the altar. Yoshino was shocked by this as he had earlier been assured by Father Roy, the head priest, that there were no such systems in the church. The church secretary returned to the scene and took the investigators to an outbuilding where a desktop computer monitored the security camera. Of course by this time the camera had been destroyed, but any footage before the fire would be on the computer.

Sgt. Yoshino and his partner spent a great deal of time with the staff as they finally were able to access the security camera system. What they found was nothing short of fascinating. The hidden camera behind the altar was not a low-light camera, and only showed a dark and grainy image. Nonetheless, it was excellent information. The investigators saw that the camera showed a completely dark church until just a few minutes before midnight. At that time, a spot of light is seen moving in the sanctuary of the church, from the south doors toward the altar. As the light came nearer the camera, investigators could see it was some sort of flame source, like a candle or something similar.

In the glow of the light, investigators could make out a lone male holding it at about face level. The male appeared to be pouring something on the floor, as the floor appeared wet. The light moved around for a few seconds and then investigators got a decent look at the male as he moved the light toward his face. It was a light-skinned male with bushy black hair. He appeared shirtless, wearing shorts, and had a small rectangular mark on his chest just over his heart. The mark appeared to be a possible tattoo. The male had the vague features of an Asian.

The male squatted down on the floor with the light on the south side of the altar (left side if you are looking at it), and the light seemed to grow in intensity and size. It was clear that he had just ignited something on the left side of the altar, near the rear wall. The fire appeared to grow from there, and the male disappeared from view toward the front doors. Upon viewing this footage, Sgt. Yoshino immediately requested additional specialty technicians from the High-Tech Crimes Unit to respond out and secure the footage as crucial evidence.

This fantastic footage gave the investigators two things. It told them almost assuredly that this was a criminal event, and it gave a starting point for the origin and cause investigation. This starting point was also validated as this was the exact area of the building where the first firefighter had noticed the flames jetting through the roof. Yoshino was ecstatic. Because the building was so heavily damaged, and a large amount of it was collapsed or washed down the street, it would have taken several days (if ever) for investigators to be able to piece back enough of the scene to be able to read fire indicators to point toward an area of origin. This video provided a very finite starting point.

What was interesting about the uncovering of the video footage was the fact that everyone was glued to the video screen as the suspect appeared and lit the fire, except for Father Roy. He was seated about twenty feet away at a table by himself and was eating a fast-food meal without a care or interest of what was going on. His continuing suspicious behavior and disinterest in his church burning down was noted by both Sgt. Yoshino and Sgt. Zolkowski.

As sunrise began to approach, none of the investigators were safely able to step into the scene until about seven that morning. At this point, arson was confirmed, but now the questions remained: How many areas of origin? How many suspects? Were accelerants used? What was the motive?

Somewhere around five in the morning, the county fire investigators had left the scene. They were never to return as it was agreed upon decades earlier that any criminal or suspicious fire would be investigated by the sheriff's department's Arson-Explosives Detail. The ATF, though, would be utilized by sheriff's department's investigators several times over the next few days.

By eight in the morning the fire was mostly out. However, fire department safety officers declared the scene too dangerous to enter and recommended bulldozing the building as the massive roof was covered with heavy tiles, and most of the main support beams were charred and at the point of collapse. The interior of the church was filled with debris that was at least six feet deep in places. The fifty-foot-high end walls would also collapse if the roof came down. The hot spots and small fires continued to erupt throughout the building. This was a really dicey scene. It would be another twelve to twenty-four hours before the fire scene would cool down enough to even begin to sift through the debris.

The decision was made after the scene assessment that day that it would not be safe for the scene investigation to begin until first light the following day. Sgt. Yoshino contacted the LASD Crime Lab and asked for the arson criminalists and photographers to respond to the scene on Monday morning. Sgt. Yoshino also asked for an accelerant K-9 from the LAFD to respond as the LASD's accelerant K-9 was unavailable.

During the prior evening of interviews, information was gained on which members of the church staff had access to the church. They confirmed early on that the church was routinely locked at ten o'clock each evening, and all candles were extinguished as a matter of policy. They confirmed that no homeless persons stayed in the church, and they also confirmed the homeless were not allowed to sleep behind the church sanctuary. The only persons with close contact to the church after ten o'clock were the two priests who lived in the rectory, which was just twenty feet away from the fire. These two priests were in their quarters at the time of the fire and were forced to flee from upstairs windows. This easily could have been a fatal or multi-fatal event.

Still, Yoshino, an excellent fire-scene investigator, held all the information originally obtained close to the vest. He brought in the LAFD dog and handler, Frank Oglesby, and asked them to enter the fire scene first and to conduct a search of the area. Sgt. Yoshino did not provide too many details to the handler. Frank and his dog worked for nearly an hour. The dog alerted at several locations on the floor around the altar. In particular, the K-9 alerted at two locations on the left side of the altar, precisely where the video showed the arsonist starting the fire.

Sgt. Yoshino and Zolkowski, after observing Frank Oglesby work his K-9 dog, made a difficult decision. They opted at that time to allow the sheriff's department's arson criminalists to assist them and enter the semi-safe structure to recover some evidence. They spent the next two hours removing debris from the areas around the altar where the K-9 had alerted. The crime lab specialists took fire debris from these areas for later analysis. When the investigators got to the area where they believed the fire had started, they removed the debris and were surprised to find three rolls of toilet paper, side by side, along the wall. The heavily burned remains of toilet paper were soaked with a liquid that was aromatic and smelled similar to a lamp oil. These items appeared to have been the origin of this fire. The crime lab seized these items for analysis.

### The Dig Out

The following day, which was the fourth day on scene, a somewhat exhausted Sgt. Yoshino contacted several other members of the unit including me. He wanted some assistance on this case and needed some immediate advice. A church arson was a very significant event, especially in light of the fact that this fire appeared to have caused over $10 million in damages by early estimates. In this particular church, numerous high-ranking members of the sheriff's department, including the sheriff himself, were personally connected to the church in some way. The sheriff was also a close friend to the local Catholic leader, Cardinal Roger Mahoney. Besides that, the massive fire and complete destruction of the huge church just one week before Easter services caused a megaflood of media attention, even by Los Angeles standards. The fire was getting twenty-four-hour coverage on the local TV stations.

Sgt. Yoshino would remain the lead investigator on this case. However, he knew he could not carry the load on this himself as it was a major case, and he had recently been assigned two large death-penalty cases, which were both arson murders. Yoshino wisely decided to run this operation as a "full unit response." He delegated control of the fire-scene investigation to me and also secured assistance from another detective, Dana Duncan, to help with follow-up and as the tips/leads coordinator. Yoshino also met with the church leaders and their insurance carrier, and they agreed to pay for the heavy equipment, fencing, and full-time security company to secure this property during what would likely be a several-week-long investigation. The insurance carrier also agreed to supply a crane service to insure that the roof was stabilized during the investigation. Part of this service was an asbestos assessment and mitigation team. Finally, Yoshino got the LACoFD to commit one of their large crane trucks to assist in the operation.

Normally the LASD would seldom require assistance from outside agencies as it is one of the four largest law enforcement agencies in the world. We have twenty-two full-time arson and bomb investigators, who each handle up to one hundred fire scenes per year. We seldom work with other fire-investigation agencies for a variety of reasons, but in this case we made the decision to accept some offered help. The FBI, while not in the arson business, does have a nexus to this event through and entity called the Church Arson Task Force. While the Church Arson Task Force is not really in existence anymore, the FBI still has some jurisdiction over house-of-worship fires if they are believed to be hate crimes or acts of terrorism. We work quite well with the FBI in the bomb world, but since they have no arson investigators, we have almost never worked with them on arson events.

In this case we had a massive scene, and our unit had just done some cross-training with the FBI's ERT. We had trained heavily with them in postblast investigation scenes and decided that they might be a great asset at this large church fire. They called Derek Yoshino and offered their assistance, and their offer was accepted. A small caveat of their participation, however, was that for the ERT to be used at a local scene, an FBI investigator also was required to be assigned. We accepted three FBI agents as part of the investigative team, with the explicit rule that LASD was the lead agency, that Sgt. Derek Yoshino was the lead investigator, and that all leads, clues, and decisions would be run through him for his approval. All agreed.

Likewise, I had several contacts with the local ATF in Los Angeles. From the onset they expressed support and a strong desire to be part of the investigation. I was contacted by the local boss from ATF, who offered eight investigators to assist in the case. I accepted his offer. The same restrictions were put on the ATF agents. They all worked for Sgt. Derek Yoshino of the LASD. They agreed and performed their tasks admirably.

On the day of the full dig out, a couple of days after the fire, I was put in charge of the fire scene. I used one investigator as the safety officer to monitor the structure for collapse issues and one civilian as an asbestos monitor. The day prior to the dig out, the fire department and the civilian crane company came in and removed a significant portion of the roof, which was judged to be close to imminent collapse. This caused quite a bit more debris to fall into the fire scene, which would then later have to be moved.

With the building secured for safety, we now established an investigation plan. The ATF and its eight investigators were given a section of the sanctuary to process, with a sheriff's detective overseeing them. The sheriff's team of fourteen investigators handled the areas of all the doors and entryways into the church. Finally, the FBI evidence technicians processed the large area around the altar, with two sheriff's detectives overseeing their efforts. At the height of this dig out, there were over one hundred investigators or technicians moving debris, searching for and documenting fire patterns, and locating and processing evidence. Every bit of this was documented by video and by photographers from two agencies.

The bulk of the work was done that first day. Accelerant evidence was located in several areas around the altar and near the shrines of Mary and Joseph in either wing of the church. All of this evidence was later processed at the LASD crime lab. Over the next few weeks, investigators maintained this massive scene and returned several times. On May 23, we finally were able to clear enough debris on the right side of the altar to gain access to the floor. In a virtual mirror location as the left side of the altar, identical evidence was located on the right side. Four round "ghost marks" indicative of toilet paper rolls were found on this side, along with positive hits for accelerants. This proved that the arsonist had set up at least two identical points of origin for this fire, one on each side of the altar, at the base of the wall and hanging tapestry.

On May 23, 2011, several weeks after the fire, I visited the scene along with three FBI agents and another LASD investigator. We were looking for any type of foot tracks other than firefighters' boot prints. As we did this, we were finally able to closely examine the tall windows on each side of the church. We were able to tell, by burn patterns and protection patterns, that the side windows of the church had been open prior to the fire. In fact, we found that a total of eight of the sixteen windows had been open! This was in direct contradiction to what all the church workers and members had told us about the condition of the building. We just then realized why the church had burned so fast and so furiously. It was a near-perfect fire!

The arsonist had distributed flammable liquids at the base of hanging tapestries, which would certainly accelerate the growth of the flames. Additionally, it appeared that the arsonist had also opened half the windows on either side of the sanctuary, providing a near-perfect ventilated fire, insuring maximum growth and development. Our arsonist was either very experienced and skilled at fire setting or completely lucky. He had taken tremendous steps and spent significant time arranging this scene for total destruction.

### The Investigation

Once the scene was completely done and there was no debate whatsoever that this might have been an accidental fire, the criminal investigation began. This would be one of the more extraordinary investigations in the history of the LASD Arson-Explosive Detail. All of the investigators on the Arson-Explosive Detail have had several years of detective experience even before they are assigned to the unit. It is one of the two senior detective units within the large sheriff's department, and the investigators receive intense, ongoing training while they are with the unit.

In this case, the investigative team, led by Sgt. Yoshino, decided to use some resources that they normally wouldn't use. The ATF was given the task of locating all gas stations within a ten-mile radius (over twenty-five stations) and checking those gas stations to see if anyone purchased gasoline in a container in the four or five hours prior to the fire. The ATF spent the next four days diligently completing this task, with negative results.

The FBI, in the form of three special agents assigned to assist Sgt. Yoshino, volunteered to conduct a computer-based social media investigation. In this manner, the FBI used its very skilled high-tech investigators to comb the Internet for chatter, photos, or any references to the fire. This ended up being a very detailed and successful aspect of the case. Almost immediately, the FBI techs found numerous people "chatting" about the fire online. At least two of these people expressed great joy that the church had burned. One of those expressing great joy also made some extremely interesting comments online, boasting that he was glad to see the church burn and that he and some friends had been involved in lighting other fires in the past.

This subject was a male Asian who lived within just a mile or two of the church. Online photos he had posted of himself depicted a tattoo on his upper chest that was vaguely consistent with the grainy video the detectives had seen of the arsonist. This guy matched in body type, race, and description, and he had expressed anti-Catholic Church sentiments along with admissions to previous fires. He quickly moved to the very top of the "persons of interest" list.

The FBI computer search turned up another Asian male who was making odd comments about the fire. This male also matched the description of the arsonist, and he too had a tattoo on his chest. He also lived within a mile of the St. John Vianney Church. Incredibly, the FBI had come up with two similar Asian males who both lived near the burned church. The FBI really liked the second male as a suspect. His named was Greg Shiga, a Japanese American. The FBI began doing a very detailed investigation into Shiga. Unfortunately, they forgot their deal with the LASD and failed to mention to Sgt. Yoshino that they were pursuing leads on a very good suspect. They kept this information secret from us for months!

### Reward

Meanwhile, our portion of the investigation was continuing. On April 19, 2011, investigators used a rare but sometimes effective tactic. Sgt. Yoshino asked the County Board to create a reward for information about the case. On that date, in a unanimous vote, the board approved a reward of $10,000 for information leading to the arrest and conviction of the person or persons who set the arson fire at St. John Vianney. The reward would eventually reach a much higher total as the case dragged on. An aspect of this reward was that the LASD opened a "We Tip" hotline and began immediately receiving tips in this format.

Several weeks later a tip came in off the "We Tip" line from a local principal. She had contacted the "We Tip" line and also called a local school deputy whom she knew. Sgt. Yoshino listened intently to what the principal was saying and earmarked her tip to the top of the priority list. He then delegated the tip to Det. Dana Duncan, who then shared the tip with the FBI investigators, who immediately went out and contacted the principal.

The principal worked at a private Christian school nearby St. John Vianney but had been a teacher at the campus for many years prior to taking the principal position. When interviewed, the principal related a story about a former student she had in her class many years ago who continued to visit her on and off after he graduated. She said the student had not come by in a long time, but then something odd happened. The principal said two weeks prior to the St. John Vianney fire, the student showed up at her school and wanted to talk to her. The former student began rattling on in a bizarre manner and appeared to be fixated on the Catholic Church and St. John Vianney specifically.

The student did not like the way the church portrayed Jesus and didn't like the church's worship of saints, particularly Mary and Joseph. The principal said the former student made mention that the church would be punished for its beliefs and for the priest scandal. The principal then mentioned that the former student's name was Greg Shiga. She described Shiga as a brilliant student but odd and troubled. She said he had a very high intellect but always acted quite oddly. The FBI found Shiga to be quite interesting. They discreetly kept this name and information to themselves.

Several other leads came in including a lead about some local kids bragging about setting an arson fire at the church. Det. Dana Duncan was dispatched to follow up that lead and found three males who had indeed been bragging about an arson attack. They eventually confessed to setting trash cans on fire at the nearby Los Altos High School but denied knowing anything about the church fire.

### Skateboarders

Another tip came in about a runaway girl and some skateboarders hanging around the church at the time of the fire. It took several days to locate this group of kids, and they confirmed that they had been in the church parking lot the night of the fire. They said that just before midnight they were chased out of the parking lot by an Asian male, who told them to leave because something dangerous was going to happen. The description of the Asian male would later match Greg Shiga, as did the description of the car he was driving.

To the sheriff's department's investigators, Greg Shiga was a good suspect but was no better or worse than the other three that had emerged. We didn't know it for months, but the FBI agents were convinced that Shiga was the suspect and were working him hard. They had gotten his name from two independent sources. They began building a case on Shiga.

Over the next few months the FBI used its massive resources to dig deep into Shiga's life. They found that he was working as a male escort (prostitute) and advertised online several services that he supplied to both male and female customers. They also found numerous photos of Shiga that he had placed online. The FBI guys found that Shiga had a criminal history, which included theft and shoplifting. Anyone who knows arsonists knows that these are two very common crimes committed by serial fire setters.

Eventually FBI agents showed photos of Greg Shiga to other people who had emerged as witnesses to this fire. During this period, they approached church members who had reported seeing an Asian male acting menacingly in the days before the fire. The FBI also approached the three skateboarder kids who had been warned away by an Asian male just minutes before the fire. The FBI agents showed "six pack" photo lineups of Asian males to the witnesses, which included a photo of Greg Shiga. The witnesses all seemed to show interest in Shiga but most refused to commit to him as the suspect. A couple even refused to speak to the agents.

The FBI eventually caused a patrol officer to arrest Shiga on a minor violation. At that time the FBI interviewed Shiga about the church fire. The agents interviewing Shiga believed that he was willing to talk, but he quickly shut them down. Shiga was later released from custody.

Over the next few weeks Shiga pulled a crazy stunt. He was beginning to show his really odd side. He posed as a political polltaker and went to a local college campus to interview female students about a political issue. While the young women were reading the poll questions, Shiga reached down and grabbed their private areas. He did this several times before he was arrested for sexual battery. Shiga was eventually convicted of felony sexual battery and released on probation. These outrageous acts started to show that Greg Shiga was a deviant and a sexual thrill seeker. Once on probation, he continued to remain on the radar of the FBI.

Meanwhile, while all this was occurring, the sheriff's department, through Sgt. Yoshino, was diligently eliminating the other suspects. This long process took several months, but finally Greg Shiga was the only suspect still standing. At that point, Derek Yoshino received a request to accompany the FBI agents to go see the US Attorney's Office in Los Angeles. Yoshino finally learned that the FBI had been building a secret case against Shiga. The assistant US attorney (AUSA) broke the news to Yoshino that the feds were taking over the case and that Shiga was the only suspect. When Yoshino protested that this was a sheriff's department's case, and *he had invited* the FBI to assist him, he was immediately told that as of this moment, the AUSA was in control of the case, and Yoshino and the rest of the LASD were formally ordered to cease working all leads on the case.

We were livid! We had all dealt with federal agencies dozens of times in the past, and each of us had one or two rough experiences with them, particularly the brass at the FBI. What kept us on an even par with them is that the FBI usually had more resources, but the LASD (and LAPD) had much more experienced detectives, who had worked hundreds of major cases. They were kicking us off our own case! The only bone they threw to us was that the AUSA agreed that if she rejected the current case, she would give it back to Yoshino so he could attempt to prosecute at the local level.

About six months later we found out that the AUSA dropped the case because it wasn't "strong enough." We learned through a local prosecutor that two federal agents were attempting to now file the case in state court. The District Attorney's Office would not file it without the sheriff's department being involved. We were back on the case.

This time the FBI agents finally gave us all their info on Shiga They had actually done a very good job amassing evidence. They had gotten his phone records and photos, and they had searched his home and taken his notebooks. These books were filled with ranting and ravings against the Catholic Church and its worship of saints. The written manifestos made references that the church would have to burn or pay in some way. An analysis of his cell phone showed that he had been within a quarter mile of the church on the night of the fire and had been at the church property after the fire, watching us work. His phone also showed him going to a local sex shop shortly after the fire started.

The manager of the sex shop was interviewed, and he pointed out Shiga in photos, saying that he had kicked Shiga out of the shop the night of the fire for acting weird. (You have to be pretty weird to get kicked out of a sleazy sex shop). It seemed that within an hour of the church burning, Shiga had gone to a gym to work out and then had gone to the sex shop, where he entered a small booth to view porno movies. While most of the customers were content with masturbating in the booths, Shiga was kicked out for drilling a hole in the side of the booth to proposition another customer in the next booth.

The FBI had also found some great photos on Shiga's cell phone. Photos taken by his phone confirmed that he had been on the church property at least five days prior to the fire. Despite us being pissed off at the federal agents for stealing our case, we eventually agreed to take them back on the case in exchange for their evidence.

We knew that the feds were not street savvy and had approached the skateboarder kids, who were borderline gang members, in the wrong way. Yoshino and Dana Duncan, two ex-gang detectives, approached the same group in a totally different manner and got them to look at the six-pack photos again. This time the teens agreed to cooperate and quickly identified Greg Shiga as the man who had warned them away from the church just minutes prior to the fire. Subsequent to that, Shiga was identified another four times in photos by other church members. He had come into the church the day prior to the fire and had appeared to have been "scouting" it and looking at all the doors and windows. After these identifications, along with the cell phone evidence and his written manifestos, we believed we had a strong case against Shiga. Now we took the investigation to a new, undercover level. Sgt. Yoshino used the vast resources of the sheriff's department and began setting up an elaborate undercover operation. Meanwhile, we kept loose tabs on Shiga.

### Oddball

By June of 2011, Greg Shiga had legally changed his named to "Nine Shiga." In an increasing sign of his weirdness, he again changed it legally on June 6, 2011, to "Nine Seventynine." His name would remain that way throughout this case. He had also added a great number of tattoos to himself since the fire, many of them being numbers as he had become obsessed with specific numbers.

### The Arrest and Perkins Operation

On Monday, May 14, 2012, led by lead investigator Sgt. Derek Yoshino, detectives from the LASD Arson-Explosives Detail arrested Greg Shiga at his apartment in downtown Los Angeles. The arresting charge would be two counts of attempted murder (the victims were the two priests in the rectory). The attempt murder charge was a seed planted to get the suspect's mind prepped for what was to happen.

Shiga's apartment was a tiny single room on the sixth floor of a very modern and chic high rise. Shiga was wearing an ankle monitoring bracelet due to his being on active probation and having a sex-crimes conviction. An amusing side story to this is that Shiga hesitated in opening the door upon our knock, and when we entered, he was standing next to the open window. We thought for a second he might be attempting to jump. As we searched out of the window, we saw a few feet away on a hidden ledge that he had stashed two new marijuana pipes and a plastic humidor containing "medicinal marijuana." Even after we informed Shiga that he was being arrested for attempted murder and the arson of a church, he was mortified that his probation officer would discover the ounce of pot he had, which was a direct violation of his probation.

Prior to his arrest, an extremely intricate plan had been dreamed up by the investigators. Shiga was booked at a special sheriff's department jail facility that had been prepared for him. Listening devices had been installed, and a particular cellmate had been planted in the booking area near where Shiga was brought. When I brought in Shiga to be booked, I noted with amusement that a former sheriff's academy classmate of mine, from twenty-six years before, was being booked as well. I recognized inmate "Felix," from our Major Crimes Bureau, as one of the most accomplished undercover operators in LASD history. The station "jailer" was actually another Major Crimes detective. The matron at the jail was also another Major Crimes detective.

Greg Shiga had no idea that the rest of his day had been carefully thought out and choreographed by the investigators on this case. Everything that was being done to him was designed to put him at ease and in a talkative frame of mine. Enough information was leaked to him for him to start thinking heavily, but no questions about the case were ever asked. He was given a meal, some time to think alone, and then placed in a cell with Felix. Felix was a master at getting inmates to talk to him.

Undercover detective Felix Osorio, monitored for safety reasons by several hidden detectives, listened intently as Shiga described in intimate details his one-man attack on the sanctuary at St. John Vianney. Shiga told the undercover officer that he entered the Catholic church with a backpack-mounted sprayer that he had shoplifted from Home Depot. The device held a couple gallons of fuel and lamp oil. Shiga ran around the large sanctuary spraying the fuel mixture in specific areas. He had scouted the location at least twice previously and had seen large, forty-foot tall tapestries hanging on either side of the altar. He sprayed fuel from his backpack pump onto the bottom several feet of each tapestry and then placed four rolls of toilet paper at the base of each tapestry. He soaked these items in fuel as well.

Having studied and practiced the art of arson in the past, Shiga new well that a fire would only achieve massive size if it was fed with an adequate flow of oxygen. He expressed in detail the fire triangle theory and knew he had to obtain the right balance between fuel, air, and heat. With this knowledge in his mind, Shiga went along the sides of the sanctuary and opened every other vertical window. These windows were about five feet high and about eighteen inches wide, and were only secured by an old-fashioned latch. Once these were opened and the fire was ignited, the church was doomed. These openings fed a hurricane of air into the rapidly spreading fire and caused the immediate and massive destruction of the wooden structure. By the time the first fire engines arrived, the fate of the church was sealed.

This entire conversation was monitored by multiple hidden microphones and recorded by other investigators. The resulting conversation was also actively monitored by the lead investigators from the sheriff's department and FBI. This type of operation is called a Perkins Operation, after the court decision that allows law enforcement to use this in a very limited capacity. In reality, there are only a few highly skilled investigation units in the country that could pull off this sort of caper. The LASD Arson-Explosives and Major Crimes teams have done it several times.

In a ten-minute period, Greg Shiga confirmed through his intimate knowledge of the arson scene that he had been the arsonist. He later went on to talk about his motive, which was a hatred for the Catholic Church and its practices. He confirmed every piece of physical evidence we had found and even provided us with more evidence we weren't aware of. Immediately after his admissions, Sgt. Yoshino sent investigators out to confirm many of the details. By the end of the day, the case was ironclad!

## The Legal Process

On May 16, 2012, Sgt. Derek Yoshino took his case to a special prosecutor, DDA Renee Rose of the Los Angeles County District Attorney's Office, Arson Unit. Four major arson charges were filed on that day, with Shiga facing nearly fifty years in prison. Shiga's attorney immediately asked for a mental-health assessment of him as he truly was a bizarre guy. The court agreed and sent Shiga out to Department Ninety-Five, which in essence is the mental-health court. Doctors evaluating Shiga believed him to be extremely intelligent and probably faking many of his mental-health maladies. He was certified as "fit for trial" and sent back to the regular criminal courts on December 14, 2012.

Shiga's lawyers immediately saw the writing on the wall and asked for a plea deal. The DA, operating from a position of strength, offered a deal for thirty-one years, about twenty-five of which Shiga would have to serve in prison. Shiga turned this and all other deals down cold. He was determined to go to trial.

The court process went on for months as Shiga kept firing and hiring new attorneys. He would not listen to their advice and believed he could easily beat the case. One of his attorneys, a female, quit after Shiga groped her. A jail inmate came forward and contacted investigators. He later testified that Shiga had admitted the entire arson scheme to him as well.

Shiga didn't limit his bizarre behavior to the courtroom or his attorneys. Shiga was continuing his odd high-risk sexual antics even in the jail system. The Los Angeles County Jail is the largest jail system in the world, with nearly 17,000 inmates on a given day. Many of them are gang members and state-prison convicts. The inmates set the rules in the jails on how other inmates conduct themselves. Shiga routinely violated the inmates' self-ascribed codes of conduct. For instance, while masturbation is probably quite prevalent in the jails, the inmates only tolerate it if it is done in a discreet manner.

Sgt. Yoshino got word from the custody deputies during the case that Shiga had been assaulted in the jails on more than one occasion for openly masturbating in front of other inmates, and, even worse, for exposing himself to family members of other inmates during visiting hours. For those sins, which are quite serious in a custody environment, the rumor was that Shiga had been held down and sexually violated by other inmates.

By the time the case went to trial, Shiga had fired all his own attorneys and was going *pro per*, or acting as his own counsel. The trial was set for late June of 2013. The prosecution put on a two-week-long case with dozens of witnesses. The star was Sgt. Yoshino, who spent three days describing the detailed investigation and evidence. Shiga asked no questions in rebuttal. When it came time for him to call witnesses, he had none, other than some high-school girlfriends he had subpoenaed just so he could see them again. His defense lasted just a couple of minutes and was capped off by him asking the judge if he could have all his property back as soon as the jury acquitted him.

Throughout the trial, Shiga tried to get physically close to any female who came near him. Knowing he had already groped one attorney, the court bailiffs kept him from being within hand's reach of any other females. He even unnerved lead prosecutor Renee Rose as he frequently stared at her intently throughout the case with a leering look on his face.

The jury was treated to several antics by Shiga as he was very animated throughout the trial and acted as if it was one big joke and he would be released the moment testimony was over. He frequently giggled and grinned at nearby reporters.

In the end the jury convicted him within an hour. On July 9, 2013, Greg Shiga was convicted of five counts of arson, burglary, and use of an incendiary device. On July 19, 2013, he was given a sentence of over thirty-two years in state prison.

*This megacase was investigated by Sgt. Derek Yoshino, Sgt. Mike Costleigh, Sgt. Wendy Zolkowski, Det. Dana Duncan, and several other members of the LASD Arson-Explosives Detail and Major Crimes Detail. Federal agents from the ATF and FBI were also heavily involved. The prosecutor was Renee Rose from the District Attorney's Office.*

### Investigator's Profile and Analysis of Extremist-Based Arsons

In comparing the arson attacks by animal-rights groups versus the arson attacks by antiabortion groups, there are some interesting similarities and differences. The groups represented polar opposites in political ideology, and therefore the suspects were polar opposites in lifestyle. The animal-rights groups tended to be mostly white, educated, younger (under thirty), and involved in a very liberal lifestyle involving drinking and some drug use. In contrast, the antiabortion groups were again mostly white, but their ages ranged from younger to more middle aged, and they lived an extremely conservative lifestyle centered on the Christian religion. Both groups had peripheral members, active members, and completely dedicated zealots. It was the zealots in each group who led or conducted the majority of the incendiary attacks.

The animal-rights groups stayed away from physical violence for the most part and attacked structures and equipment at night with no one around. They used incendiary devices at a much more significant rate than the antiabortionists. More of their attacks were carefully planned and executed, and none of the attackers wanted to get caught. Many of their attacks involved them physically entering a structure or compound. They often built consistent devices from manuals and practiced extreme anti-forensics and antidetection behavior. They usually lit multiple fires during a single attack. A couple of the cells in this movement were as highly skilled as any international terrorist group.

In contrast the arson attacks by the antiabortion groups were as varied as were the suspects. Most were fairly crude and involved the use of accelerants but not incendiary devices (other than Molotovs). The nighttime attacks were usually on the exterior of structures and seldom did significant damage. The daytime attacks were really crazy events where the suspect was intending his own death in the process or had very little expectation of escape.

### Federal Failures

Both the animal-rights attacks and the antiabortion attacks were carried out in almost every state in the country by suspects who frequently crossed state lines and belonged to groups or organizations. Most of these attacks interrupted business or commerce or infringed on citizens' rights. By any description these were attacks for the purpose of intimidation and terror and should have been handled by one or more federal agencies. That being said, it is my opinion that for many years these groups were not investigated properly; nor were the crime scenes processed in a serious fashion by government entities. The fault lies primarily with the Justice Department of the federal government, which for years did not regard either of these groups as a serious threat.

Many of the fires set by these groups were investigated by small, understaffed local police and fire agencies. Evidence was missed, overlooked, or not collected properly. Several of these fires have never been solved, and that is a true tragedy.

The two agencies most culpable for not seriously investigating these groups and their crimes are the FBI and ATF. Both, when it suits their needs, insert themselves into arson and explosion investigations, and they go to great lengths to find a "federal nexus" to the crime. I have worked on many cases with both agencies and, for the most part, respect their investigators. However, both agencies are political animals in tune with the political winds that happen to be blowing at that particular time. They both take their cues from Washington.

In 1985, during the height of the abortion-clinic bombings and arson attacks, the director of the FBI himself, William Webster, told the national media that his agency did not see a national conspiracy and, therefore, was not involved in many of these investigations. At the same time the ATF's official policy was that these groups were not involved in any sort of national conspiracy. Bureau spokespeople downplayed the roles of both agencies in the investigation of abortion-clinic attacks. The victims of these attacks, members of the pro-choice movements, were incensed by the lack of concern by the federal government. Many news outlets and writers openly criticized the federal government for failing to act on these increasingly violent attacks.

A decade later, the ELF/ALF groups and cells were conducting relentless vandalism and arson attacks on properties in over twenty states. Again, the FBI and ATF mostly sat back and did very little serious investigating. Only after the 9/11 attacks in New York did the federal government begin to look at these movements as what they truly were—semi organized terrorist campaigns by dedicated zealots—which in that view makes them very close in design and actions to international terrorist groups.

As politics changed, so did the feds' view on these groups. When the Clinton administration entered the White House, the Justice Department eventually formed both the Federal Church Arson Task Force and the Abortion Clinic Arson Task Force. Both of these groups were active for numerous years and had a few successful investigations. However, most of their work produced very modest results. From my dealings with many federal and local arson-explosives investigators, I know through personal conversations that these were never serious task forces and were often (not always, but often) staffed with less-than-stellar investigators. It was not a glorious posting for any FBI or ATF agent.

Exploiting extremist groups is actually quite similar to investigating gangs or organized-crime syndicates. The feds are good at getting intelligence on any targeted group. There are always criminals or extremists who are diehards and are wholly dedicated to the group. These are the main players who plan or execute the attacks by the group. Less dedicated to a degree are the bulk of the group, and even further less dedicated are the fringe "hangers-on" of the group. These are the easiest to exploit for intelligence purposes.

Breaking apart any organized crime or extremist group entails targeting these fringe or general members and using them to point out the actions of the most extreme members. This is a tried and true method used when dealing with street gangs, outlaw biker groups, and Mafia organizations. The same tactics would be easily employable against the animal-rights groups and antiabortion extremists. Because these groups were not traditional crime groups and therefore not as "sexy" a target to the feds, they were left alone to conduct hundreds of attacks and raids.

Now, years after both of these movements have lost steam, the feds treat even the smallest of these types of cases as part of a national conspiracy. However, that still leaves several hundred serious bomb and arson attacks from the 1980s and 1990s unsolved. This is indeed a very poor and embarrassing record for the federal government.

Regarding church arsons by extremist groups, research and history has proven that in the last fifty years, the notion of organized attacks against churches is almost entirely a myth. It undoubtedly occurred in the Civil Rights era from 1945 to 1965, but since that time it has dropped off to almost negligible levels. As stated in the profile, the myth of hate crimes and church arsons by hate groups is just that—mostly a myth.

## EXCITEMENT
## THE MYTH OF PYROMANIA

The salacious use of the term ***pyromania*** has historically drawn everyone's attention to a fire setter without an apparent reason or motive for setting a fire. That was the name that Freudian-based psychologists gave to anyone whose fire-starting behavior did not appear to have a "normal" motive such as revenge or profit. As I mentioned earlier in this book, no educated or experienced arson analyst or investigator uses this term anymore. It was wrong when it came into existence and is even more wrong (if possible) today. If it is used at all anymore, it is by the psychiatric profession whose allegiance is toward the Freudian theories concerning arson.

Freud was dead wrong on his opinions as to what causes persons to set fires. He used a pitifully small test group of just four confessed fire setters and then attempted to explain all fire-setting activities by his observations of this small group. In short, the term *pyromania* would mean an uncontrollable urge to light a fire. I have studied thousands of arson cases in my career and can't think of a single case history of true pyromania. For all of you investigators and prosecutors in courtrooms out there, please do not allow witnesses and "defense experts" to use this outdated and erroneous phrase. It tends to lead jurors and judges to believe that fire setting is an illness that can be treated. Nothing is further from the truth.

### The Profile

The **excitement-based** fire offender does exist, in varying degrees, but usually his motives are mixed with other more common motives such as revenge. There are very few actual excitement-based fire setters. While it is true that a lot of people who commit arson do feel that the event is exciting in some manner, they do not set the fires solely for the purpose of excitement. This is the largest and most pervasive myth in the arson business. The excitement-based arsonist falls under the general heading of an **emotionally based** fire setter and will have no obvious reason for setting fires.

### A Caution

I have heard many arson investigators, after interviewing an arrestee, call me and tell me that they have arrested an excitement-based arsonist. They are sincere in their opinion, but a review of their interview usually finds that they have asked very leading questions of the arrestee. Most of these investigators find a compliant arrestee and at some point ask them, "Did you feel excited after you set the fire?" If the arrestee has already admitted his role and is cooperative, more often than not he will also say that he did feel some excitement.

In the mind of the arson investigators, they believe that they now have a very rare find—a true excitement-based offender! However, an analysis of their interview technique shows that they asked a question in a certain manner with the expectation that they would get a desired answer. In reality, every criminal who confesses to every crime will likely admit a certain amount of excitement during the crime as they know what they are doing is wrong and may lead to imprisonment. This holds true for thieves, robbers, murderers, burglars, et cetera. There is always some excitement when involved in a daring or dangerous act.

The proper question to ask an arsonist is something like, "How did you feel when the fire started?" or "How did you feel an hour after the fire?" Without using the word "excitement," you are asking a more open question. Even if the arsonist uses the word "excitement" in his description, the prudent investigator needs to balance this against the facts of the case. More often than not there will be a much more mundane reason for the fire associated with a motive other than excitement.

Most serial arsonists may appear at first glance to have no motive for their fire setting. However, if you study them and actually sit down and speak to them, and more importantly *listen to them*, you will find that there is some reason why they chose that particular target and set that particular fire. You usually have to dig deep to figure this out with many urban serial arsonists.

Wild-land serial arsonists are a completely different breed, and it would take in-depth interviews, crime-scene work, and analysis to understand their motives for setting such a catastrophic fire. It should come as no surprise that a hefty percentage of wild-land serial arsonists are somehow related to the fire service. Because of this, their motives may include a profit angle if somehow they benefit from the fire. In others it is a need for action, recognition, or relief from boredom. All of these motives are completely different from pyromania. All of the serial arsonists I have met and studied made the mental choice to start the fire, and none of them felt compelled to do it or had an uncontrollable urge to do it.

*"Many (firefighter arsonists) are peer-group leaders and adrenaline junkies...and often consider their job as firefighter more of a religion than a profession"* (Ed Nordskog).

## HERO ARSONISTS

A very close associate of the excitement-based fire setter is the "hero arsonist." This type of offender is most often seen in the form of a firefighter arsonist (almost all of whom are serial arsonists) but can be found in other professions to include persons affiliated with security work, rescue work, photography/film (stringers), law enforcement, and many jobs in the wild-land areas of the world. Hero arsonists tend to set fires where they are actively involved in the suppression of that fire, or the reporting of that event, with the final goal of placing themselves in some sort of heroic position. They may actually physically fight the fire or gain awards, recognition, or attention for "discovering" and reporting the event and, in effect, "save lives."

Classic traits of hero arsonists include the suspect almost always being male, being fairly young or with a history of immature actions, and having issues with alcohol or drugs. The hero arsonist is most often involved in reporting or responding to his own fires. Other traits may include a series of fires all within the same jurisdiction (as a non-hero serial arsonist would have no idea where jurisdictions begin and end), fires set with the aid of accelerants and/or incendiary devices, and fires set to targets of almost no value including sheds, outbuildings, vacant homes or barns, and vegetation.

Many firefighter arsonists share a lot of common traits in that many of them are actually well regarded, gung ho types, who have been named or considered for awards such as "firefighter of the year." Many are peer-group leaders and adrenaline junkies within their departments and often consider their jobs as firefighters more of a religion than a profession. A large number of firefighter arsonists are actually sons and grandsons of firefighters.

Another trait that is shared by this unique group is that many have a history of immature behavior and aggressive-driving issues. Along with juvenile arsonists and extremist (animal-rights) arsonists, firefighter arsonists can operate in groups as well as being lone offenders. There is a significant amount of case history showing firefighter arsonists operating in pairs, groups, or even entire shifts, which is contrary to the bulk of all the other subtypes of arsonists. The following cases show offenders who had an element of excitement within their fire-setting behavior.

## BABBIT FIRE CHIEF
## MINNESOTA, 2010–2012

*This case is from the files of the US Forest Service and the Minnesota State Fire Marshal's Office. The author appears as a consultant/profiler very late in this case.*

**Author's note:** I grew up in Grand Rapids, Minnesota, and lived there through my college years before seeking my fame and fortune in California. This case hits close to home as Babbitt is about ninety miles north and east of my childhood home in the great north woods of Minnesota. In early 2012, just a couple of months after I released my first book on serial arsonists, a college buddy who had been working as a deputy sheriff in northern Minnesota called me to congratulate me on the book. He then mentioned, "We've got one of those guys (serial arsonists) up here. But it's all hush-hush. Nobody's talking." His tone told me that people knew something was up, but it was being kept very secretive by the investigators. Within a year I would be tangentially involved in the Ryan Scharber case.

### Babbitt, Minnesota

Babbitt, Minnesota, is a small city of over sixteen hundred people. It sits on the eastern edge of the famed Iron Range section of northeastern Minnesota. The area is famous for its massive production of iron ore. The ore mined along the Iron Range is shipped by rail to a port along Lake Superior, where it is poured into the cargo holds of giant ore ships bound for the steel mills on the far side of the Great Lakes. The entire Iron Range is dotted with small mining cities and towns, whose collective population is either employed by large iron mines or is supported by them in every other way.

The other main employments in the area are logging and seasonal jobs at the many fishing resorts hidden among hundreds of large and small lakes that fill the pine forests. Just north of Babbitt is a huge body of water called Birch Lake. Its shores are covered by vacation homes, cabins, and well-tended summer resorts. The city of Babbitt, the taconite mine, and all the lakes surrounding the area sit in the middle of the Superior National Forest. The heavily timbered lands creep right to the very edge of the town. Like all small cities in Minnesota, the population of Babbitt is over 98 percent white.

Ryan Scharber worked at the large taconite mine near Babbitt. Ryan was not an ordinary mine worker who drove equipment. He was one of the mine's firefighters, which by law they were required to have on staff. His well-paying job at the mine was to run a very small firefighting team. A young man with a wife and small kids, Scharber wanted to be more than a firefighter at the mine; he wanted to be a full-time firefighter.

In 2005, at the age of twenty-two, Scharber joined the Babbitt Volunteer Fire Department (VFD). Although it was not a full-time job, it was his next step in the process. Scharber was young, clean cut, very smart, and very motivated. He was a family man who didn't drink much and regularly attended a local church with his wife and kids. Scharber had a two-year college degree and soon mastered the skill of writing grants. In any public service, grant writing is the new key to promotion. There are countless millions of dollars sitting in federal vaults waiting for local police and fire agencies to write grants, expressing a need for this money to purchase equipment. Grant writing had become a cottage industry in the wake of the terrorist attacks of 9/11, and hundreds of tiny agencies were using grants to buy enormous piles of modern equipment. Anyone with skill in writing grants was going to be a very favored employee among his peers.

The Babbitt VFD had one full-time employee: the chief. The rest of the thirty-man department were all volunteers, with most of them receiving income as "on call" firefighters. This is a very common method of compensating the three quarters of a million volunteer firefighters in this nation. Basically, a "call" firefighter is a nonpaid position until that person is actually summoned to a real fire or rescue operation. At that point he is "on the clock" and receives compensation for his work.

From 2005 until 2008, Ryan Scharber worked as a "call" firefighter, adding a small amount of income to the decent wages he got paid from the taconite mine. However, despite his youth, he was a rising star with the City of Babbitt, as his grant writing abilities soon enabled the tiny city to purchase all new fire apparatus and equipment for boat rescues and search-and-rescue operations. Scharber was a genius with the grants, and Babbitt soon had the finest outfitted fire department in all of rural Minnesota. As a reward for this skill at grant writing, Ryan Scharber was hired as the full-time chief of the Babbitt VFD in 2008. His paycheck for being the chief was $110,000 at his highest year. He also maintained his employment as fire chief of the mine. Scharber was only twenty-five years old.

### The Fire Surge

Ryan Scharber became fire chief for Babbitt at a time when the Great North Woods was in the beginning stages of a several-year-long drought. Minnesota is the "Land of 10,000 Lakes," but it is also an area that has been the victim of some of the worst fire losses in American history. The Great Hinckley Fire and the Cloquet Fire, both of which occurred in the early logging days of the state, killed hundreds, if not thousands, of people. Even the moist timberlands of upper Minnesota, Wisconsin, and

Michigan can be prone to huge forest fires when every thirty years or so they go through an extended drought. This was the case from about 2007–2012 in northern Minnesota.

The City of Babbitt's fire department had a contract with the federal government. Because the Superior National Forest came right up to the edge of Babbitt, the feds contracted with the local fire agency for firefighting duties in the areas immediately surrounding the city. When a fire occurred in those areas, the Babbitt VFD suppressed the fire and then gave a bill for costs and expenses to the federal government. Each firefighter who responded was paid by Babbitt, but then Babbitt was compensated by the feds. As part of this deal, the chief, Ryan Scharber, double dipped, and received firefighting pay along with his normal chief's pay.

Each response into the federal areas required the chief (Scharber) to submit a stack of paperwork to the US Forest Service (USFS) as supporting documents for his claim. The arrangement also called for Scharber, as the chief, to make an initial determination of the "origin and cause" of all of the fires he attended. Since his agency lacked a formal fire-scene investigator, he assumed the collateral duty as "investigator" for all of the fires attended by the Babbitt VFD. By all accounts, Chief Scharber had no training at all to be a fire investigator.

Any arson fires that occurred in the city of Babbitt or on state lands outside of the city were first investigated by the chief (Scharber) and then forwarded for further investigation to a detective with the St. Louis County Sheriff's Office, the Minnesota State Fire Marshal's Office, and/or the Minnesota Bureau of Criminal Apprehension (BCA). Any arson fires in the contracted Superior National Forest were supposed to be investigated by USFS arson investigators. This confusing arrangement is very similar to how things work in nearly every other part of the United States. The major downside to this is that information and evidence of a fire may end up in one of five possible agencies with overlapping jurisdiction in the area.

In 2008, the Babbitt VFD had three fire calls, two of which were deemed "suspicious." In 2009, there were four "suspicious" vegetation fires—two in the spring and two in the fall. These were not alarming numbers and were consistent with levels going back a few decades. By 2010, something was clearly wrong. The Babbitt VFD responded to sixteen fires. Fifteen of these were vegetation fires, at least five were determined to be "arson," and the remainder were listed as "suspicious" or "under investigation." The vast majority of these fires occurred in two months: April and October.

Things got worse in 2011 when the calls rose up to thirty-three fires, with nineteen of them being considered "arson" or "suspicious," and the rest being labeled "under investigation." State Fire Marshal and USFS experts would later analyze these events for patterns. Some very subtle patterns did emerge. All of these fires occurred in the lands just outside the city of Babbitt. Again, like in the previous year, there were several fires in the spring, with a bit of a drop-off in the summer, and then a tremendous increase in the fall months, when the danger levels were at their worst. The most alarming trend was that up until 2010, there had only been one of these fires that impacted a structure. All of the rest had been wild-land or vegetation fires. The fires in 2011 began to hit structures.

### Timber Bay Lodge

Most resorts in northern Minnesota are seasonal businesses, as very few vacationers dare to brave the brutal winters when the temperatures are around twenty degrees below zero and the ice on the lakes is several feet thick. Because of this, most of these resort properties are closed by Thanksgiving and remain so until late April or May. These vacant properties are routinely patrolled by the few law enforcement officers in the area as they are ripe targets for burglars and squatters who access them by four-wheel-drive truck or snowmobiles.

At five thirty in the morning, on April 14, 2011, a large fire completely destroyed the beautiful Timber Bay Lodge resort on Birch Lake, just outside of Babbitt. The owner was a member of the Babbitt VFD. The Babbitt VFD arrived to fight the fire along with four other agencies, but the main lodge had been destroyed. The resort had just been opened for the summer ten days prior to this. Fire chief Ryan Scharber determined this fire was likely a result of a faulty heater. Scharber was quoted in the local paper: "We don't expect there was any foul play or arson." State Fire Marshals, already concerned about the uptick in fires near the city of Babbitt, were more conservative with their determination. They listed the fire as "undetermined," which left it open to future consideration by arson experts.

Ten days later an arson fire was set to a structure in the rural area around Babbitt. By July 1 there were three more suspicious wild-land fires in the area and a couple of structure fires. In July there were two suspicious structure fires, and in August three more structure fires were confirmed arson attacks. In the midst of that were five suspicious grass fires. In September things shifted into high gear. In that month alone the areas around Babbitt suffered ten wild-land fires, all deemed either suspicious or arson. On September 24, at one thirty in the morning, a grocery store in the city of Babbitt burned. This fire was added to the growing list of suspicious fires in the area. By this time, there were separate investigations taking place by the Minnesota Department of Natural Resources (DNR), the Babbitt VFD, and the State Fire Marshal's Office.

On September 30, 2011, even the local media had figured out that something was going on. They contacted Chief Scharber for an interview, and he admitted that the fire department's calls had doubled this year, and the arson rate had doubled as well. He said he was aware that an arsonist had been burning vegetation in the past year or so, but this year the arsonist had begun to target structures. The chief was worried that his small department couldn't stand the strain of all this activity. Scharber cautioned the public to be vigilant and to see if "someone's showing up at the same fires over and over again." As it turned out much later, the chief's advice was spot-on as, indeed, the arsonist was observed at all of the fire scenes.

After the flurry of fires in September, a meeting was held between the State Fire Marshal's Office and USFS investigators and Chief Scharber. During that meeting he told the investigators that he had suspicions of a local juvenile who may be the arsonist in his area. Scharber let the investigators know that he too was quietly looking into these fires. Chief Scharber gave them the name of the local juvenile who had been identified as a problem fire setter and inquired if the investigators had any hidden cameras staged near his city. The state and federal investigators, as usual, kept things close to the vest.

The reason that the investigators were keeping this investigation somewhat quiet was because they had already begun to suspect that the arsonist may, in fact, be a firefighter from the area. They didn't want to mention their theory to anyone in case they were wrong. They also knew that there were no secrets within the firehouse, and any mention of anything related to something like this would make the rumor mill spin out of control. Eventually the case would be under the control of two senior investigators: Inv. Jim Iammatteo of the State Fire Marshal's Office and Inv. Brian Gierczic of the USFS.

In October there were four more wild-land fires near Babbitt and another fire to a vacant structure near a closed resort. By now the St. Louis County Sheriff's Office and the Minnesota State Fire Marshal's Office had made public their hunt for a possible serial arsonist operating near Babbitt. They set up "tip lines" and posted flyers in the area seeking any information of suspicious activity. They also sent digital flyers to all agencies in the area. They didn't expect much of a response as winter was coming soon and the arsonist hadn't really hit in the winter months.

### Matilla's Resort Incident

By December of 2011, winter had set in hard to the north woods, and all of the wild-land-fire danger was gone, at least for a few months. Almost all of the resorts were closed and shuttered, with the bulk of the resort owners having fled to the city or even south for the winter. One such resort was named Matilla's Resort. The owner of Matilla's was seventy-six-year-old John Matilla. He had closed up his resort at the end of the fall season and had barricaded the road leading toward it. However, he and his wife Erma chose to remain in their home on the resort property. They did this partly because they were concerned about burglars and partly because of the rash of fires that had plagued the area in the past few years. They had grown very concerned when the final fire of the fall season occurred to a vacant garage very near their property. The Matilla home was shielded from the road, and to anyone passing by it would appear that the resort was closed and vacant for the winter.

Around seven in the evening, on December 3, 2011, John Matilla heard a vehicle stop on the road near his property. He went outside into the darkness with a flashlight and saw tracks where the vehicle had driven around the barricades. Matilla followed the vehicle tracks toward his main lodge. He found the empty car parked in front of his garage. He saw that it had firefighter license plates on it. Matilla noted that the footprints in the snow indicated that the driver had exited his car and had retrieved something from his trunk. The footprints then led off behind the garage. Matilla followed them behind the garage and further behind an empty shed.

At that point he encountered a white male emerging from behind the shed. The cantankerous resort owner confronted the man, whom he suspected of being a possible burglar. The man quickly identified himself as Ryan Scharber, the Babbitt fire chief. Scharber told Matilla that as fire chief, he had just been out on patrol and needed to urinate. He said he ducked behind the resort's buildings as a way of just trying to stay out of sight.

The irate resort owner didn't buy this story for a minute. He knew that the area was mostly rural and shrouded by a thick forest, and anyone could urinate on the side of the road without being seen. There was no good reason for the chief to be skulking around his buildings in the dark. He ordered the young fire chief off his property. Matilla then went back to his house and called 911 to report this suspicious activity to the local police. The chief of police for Babbitt called Matilla back within minutes and advised him that fire chief Scharber was sitting in the police station reporting the "misunderstanding" himself.

By now, just a few minutes after the encounter, Scharber's story had changed quite a bit. He told the local police chief that one of his duties as fire chief was to check on the thickness of the lake ice in the area for safety reasons. He said that many people fish and snowmobile on the frozen lakes in the area during winter, and he was going to measure the thickness. This story still bothered Matilla as he advised the cop that the fire chief had been walking toward the buildings and away from the lake when spotted. Matilla also told the cop that Scharber had not been dressed properly for the conditions and for walking out onto the lake. Besides, no one in his or her right mind would be checking on the ice in the darkness.

Scharber's explanation did not sit well with the resort owner. Still irate after getting off the telephone with the police chief,

Matilla grabbed his light and went back out to investigate further. This time he followed Scharber's clear tracks from his car to the shed area. At no time did they ever go toward the lake. He followed the tracks to where they ended behind a shed and was surprised to see a red plastic gasoline can full of gasoline. It was sitting on top of the snow as if just placed there. The can had the words "ice auger" written in ink on the side. This can did not belong to Matilla and was clearly brought to the scene by Scharber. Matilla secured this evidence on his property.

Two days later, John Matilla, who did not trust the City of Babbitt to handle this incident, reported it to the local St. Louis County Sheriff's Office. When he didn't feel they believed him, he took the gas can to another nearby town and gave it to a firefighter. That firefighter then called in a tip to the Minnesota BCA. Eventually the evidence made it to the correct people, and a detective was sent out to interview the resort owner. St. Louis County Sheriff's Office detective Steve Heinrich opened up an investigation of a possible attempted arson, with Babbitt fire chief Ryan Scharber as a suspect.

Two days after this interview with the detective, resort owner Matilla called again to report that someone on a quad runner had entered his property on December 21. That person left clear footprints in the snow behind the resort. The person had walked from his quad to the exact area where the gasoline can had been recovered by Matilla. The quad tracks then drove back out onto the frozen lake. A family member trailed the tracks for a distance until they were lost within the city of Babbitt. Det. Heinrich responded and photographed the tracks and then drove to Ryan Scharber's home where he observed similar quad-runner tracks in his yard. He photographed these as well.

Det. Heinrich then contacted a local search-and-rescue volunteer who was also an expert in foot and vehicle tracks. The track expert assisted the detective and confirmed that the foot tracks leading from the recent quad runner tracks belonged to Ryan Scharber. The same expert also said the vehicle tracks at the resort also matched Ryan Scharber's personal quad runner. It was confirmed that Scharber had returned to the resort to most likely recover evidence he had left there two weeks prior.

Within a short period of time, Det. Heinrich would link up and share information with State Fire Marshal investigator Iammatteo and USFS investigator Gierczic. This was the major break that the small arson task force had been hoping for. However, the incident did not confirm that Scharber was an arsonist. The investigators waited through the long winter.

### Task Force

By the spring of 2012, the fires had begun again. Four suspicious brush fires occurred in March and April, along with a suspicious structure fire. By mid-May a couple of more structures had burned, and now investigators grew worried again. They had done some surveillance work and installed cameras but were unable to come up with any positive evidence. These investigators knew that there had been other cases that may have involved Ryan Scharber. They also knew that the overlapping of several agencies in this area caused a loss of potential information. They were dealing with a small-town environment and just couldn't go around asking anybody about the suspicious actions of the fire chief.

They decided to consolidate efforts into an official, yet secret task force. On May 22, 2012, the task-force members officially met and shared all their information. Present were investigators from the USFS, the Minnesota State Fire Marshal, the Minnesota BCA, the Minnesota DNR, and the St. Louis County Sheriff's Office. Inv. Iammatteo and Inv. Gierczic would continue to lead this task force along with USFS special agent Keith McAuliffe. At a later date they would present their findings to AUSA Andrew Dunne in Minneapolis.

The task force had much to do. The undercover guys and surveillance members began setting up additional secretive cameras in likely places to include near Scharber's home and the fire department. They also installed a tracking device on his vehicle and subpoenaed his phone records. Other investigators began looking at some of the earlier suspects and worked toward eliminating them.

The main investigators met with Scharber and began communicating with him about the arsonist. They sensed that he was possibly aware that he had become a suspect after the incident at Matilla's Resort. He became more proactive with the investigators and at one point even told them that he suspected members of his own department as possible arsonists. He again directed investigators toward a fourteen-year-old male and a volunteer firefighter as probable suspects. Again he made inquiries as to where the agents had placed any hidden cameras. The lead investigators played it cool and didn't let on to Scharber that he was at the top of the suspect list.

The investigators also determined that the two suspects whose names had been given to them by members of the Babbitt police and fire departments were positively eliminated as suspects in any of the arsons. They further found that all of the information that local law enforcement had on those other suspects had, in fact, been given to them by fire chief Ryan Scharber. The task-force investigators knew that early on Scharber had been trying to throw them off his scent.

### ATVs and Quad Runners

The fires slowed down during the summer of 2012; however, for the third year in a row, September became the most active month with additional arson brush fires. This time another pattern started to emerge. The investigators noticed that several of the wild-land fires over the past three years had been started along ATV trails in the woods. The suspect was undoubtedly using an ATV or quad-runner vehicle to access some of his scenes. This reminded investigators that the Matilla's Resort incident also involved a quad runner owned by Ryan Scharber.

Speaking of quad runners, something really bizarre happened on August 19, 2012. Ryan Scharber was out riding his quad runner and was seen driving across a grass field in full view of a crowd watching a local sporting event. Scharber's quad stopped running and within a few seconds burst into flames. Local citizens took cell phone photos and video as they saw the humor in the fact that the local fire chief's personal vehicle was on fire. The arson task-force members later learned of this event and found it to be extremely suspicious. Scharber submitted an insurance claim and received a settlement for this "accidental" fire. This was just another in a long line of suspicious fire events surrounding Ryan Scharber.

At this point in the investigation, the team had dug up a large amount of information. Going back to the start of the known arson series, they had documented thirty-nine fires that were either arson or very suspicious in nature. Besides that, some of the task-force members looked back to 2005 when Ryan Scharber had joined the Babbitt VFD as a firefighter. They found nearly seventy fires that they considered as suspicious events. They realized that they likely could never prove any of those older fires, but they needed to corner Scharber at some point and confront him with his role in any of the more recent fires.

It was crystal clear that from the day he became fire chief in Babbitt, the tiny city led all of the small towns and cities in Minnesota with arson activity. Over the past five years, Babbitt had sixty-five fires, with forty-one of them being deemed suspicious or in fact arson. A nationwide norm of arson fires is that roughly 40 percent of all fires are incendiary in nature. Tiny Babbitt's arson rate was 71 percent or close to double the national average!

The investigators examined a potential financial motive for these crimes. In the years of 2010 through 2012, the Babbitt VFD had suppressed seven suspicious fires in the USFS lands. After these fires, Chief Scharber had billed the USFS for over $24,000 in suppression costs.

After conducting many interviews and doing much investigation, the arson task force had a better understanding of the Babbitt VFD. By almost all accounts, Chief Ryan Scharber was loved by everyone in the city, especially those on his own department. He had brought in a large amount of much-needed equipment and had recruited several young, eager firefighters to join the ranks. The city had appointed him chief after the fire department members had overwhelmingly voted for him to have the job. He had a department that was well trained, well equipped, and actually bringing in money to the city coffers. He was a very popular man.

### The Raid

On December 19, 2012, the task force launched a two-prong raid into the City of Babbitt. Twenty-four investigators from seven different agencies swept into the city to interview thirty-four persons affiliated with the Babbitt VFD. At the same time, two teams served search warrants at the residence of Ryan Scharber and at the headquarters of the Babbitt VFD. This *en masse* operation was designed to throw everyone off balance and to determine if anyone was assisting Scharber with these arson attacks. The quiet, fairly crime-free city was in complete shock over this massive raid.

At eleven in the morning, Scharber was interviewed by investigators at his own headquarters. The interview lasted close to five hours. For more than two hours, Scharber adamantly denied wrongdoing. However, when confronted with the evidence gathered by the task force, he caved in and finally admitted to setting nine wild-land fires and attempting to set Matilla's Resort on fire. Investigators pressed Scharber hard for details and for his knowledge of the other thirty-nine fires. He looked at a list of all the suspicious fires and pointed out the nine smallest fires on the list. Further questioning on the other fires brought only denials. Scharber also admitted to purposely setting his quad runner on fire by cutting through the gas line and igniting the fuel. He said the vehicle wasn't running well, and he wanted an insurance pay out. He purposely set the fire in front of the townspeople as a way of throwing off suspicion.

Scharber admitted to using his vehicle and his quad to access fire scenes and said he used both a cigarette lighter and highway flares to ignite most of his blazes. He self-servingly stated that he only set small fires in areas where he knew that they wouldn't burn very far. He also denied starting any structure fires. At the end of the day, the investigators were convinced that Ryan Scharber was a true serial arsonist and, more importantly, had acted alone. All other department members were soon eliminated as suspects. The investigators left Scharber out of custody in order to complete their investigation. The next day fire chief Ryan Scharber submitted a handwritten resignation letter to the City of Babbitt. He then gave a handwritten letter to the assistant fire chief, admitting to some of the arson fires but not all of them. He then went out and got a good criminal defense lawyer.

After the resignation of Scharber, the new Babbitt fire captain approached investigators and informed them that he believed that Scharber was probably responsible for setting two structure fires at resorts in August of 2011. He said that he was normally the quickest man to the fire department when the calls came out, but when he got there during those fires, Scharber, who lived further away, was already dressed and waiting in the fire truck. He said that Scharber drove to each location without consulting a map. At that point the captain always believed that Scharber had set one or both of those fires.

The USFS eventually filed federal arson charges against Ryan Scharber. Scharber remained out of jail awaiting further developments. He obtained a high-powered defense attorney out of Minneapolis. The case began to wind its way through the federal court system. Running the case through the courts was AUSA Andrew Dunne.

During the early part of 2013, the arson investigators running the case did a unique thing. I happened to be in Minnesota presenting a seminar on serial arsonists in March of 2013. One of the fire investigators hosting the seminar, Chief Steve Flaherty of the Grand Rapids Fire Department, asked me if I would meet privately with a couple investigators regarding a "sensitive" serial arson case. I had not heard of the Ryan Scharber investigation at that point, other than that previous rumor I mentioned at the start of this case.

I sat down with Minnesota State Fire Marshal investigator Jim Iammatteo, and he briefed me on the particulars of the case. He was asking for my expert opinion on the incident. He did not tell me that he had anyone in custody but only mentioned that they were looking to eliminate suspects in an arson series. I asked him many questions about the fires, their locations, time of day, and the specific ignition scenario. When all was said and done, I advised him that with the limited information he had provided me, I couldn't make a detailed analysis or "profile," but that the case had all the appearances of a public official, most likely a firefighter, setting the fires. He confirmed that the number one suspect was indeed a public official—the fire chief.

I also looked at the data they had gathered over the past five years and advised him that it was likely that the fire chief had set many more fires than he admitted to and that in his admissions he was very much minimizing his actions. After that event, I stayed in loose contact with Investigators Iammatteo and McAuliffe.

### Conviction, Sentencing, and the Media

In October of 2013, Ryan Scharber was officially charged in federal court with setting two fires in a federal forest and attempting to set an additional fire at the resort. He was facing a five-year federal mandatory prison sentence. One month later, in November, he pled guilty in front of a federal judge. During his plea he admitted to setting multiple fires over a two-year period. He remained out of custody awaiting sentencing in the spring of 2014.

Scharber was sent to a local psychiatrist as part of a presentencing assessment. The shrink diagnosed Scharber as a "pyromaniac," which Scharber very vocally contested. The defense attorney in the case started a very public campaign to get Scharber sentenced at a much-reduced sentence below the federal mandatory minimum of five years, due to the very small size of his fires. In his plea to the court, the defense attorney argued that Scharber was overwhelmed by some medical difficulties to his third child. He said that Scharber was stressed due to the fact that his child suffered from colic, and he only set fires when he couldn't deal with the stress of the baby.

At the same time, the defense attorney got the word out to Scharber's church to begin a letter-writing campaign to the judge pleading for leniency. The judge was soon drowning in a sea of letters from members of the church, all saying that Scharber deserved a break because the fires were small, and he was not a "true arsonist." He was just stressed.

The defense took it even further and started on a national media campaign to get Scharber's case included in a long list of drug cases being evaluated for the overturning of harsh federal sentencing laws. This caused ABC News to take up Scharber's cause and to feature him on their *20/20* and *Good Morning America* news shows. The original airings did appear to take Scharber's side and gave the impression that his sentence was extremely harsh. The federal judge was feeling the pressure and even publicly commented that Scharber did not appear to him to be a typical arsonist. The judge said that he was hamstrung by federal sentencing laws but didn't believe that Scharber should even go to jail. He granted several delays in Scharber's actual sentencing date and allowed Scharber, a convicted arsonist, to remain out of jail for over a year after his conviction.

Meanwhile ABC News, crusading on Scharber's behalf, wanted to interview the federal and state agencies involved in the Scharber case and confront them about the harsh sentence for just a few small fires. AUSA Andrew Dunne appeared on the television show *20/20* to defend the sentence and to stress that Scharber was a serial arsonist and probably deserved much more time than this. True to form, the USFS brass in Washington got scared by the media attention and didn't want to appear as the "bad guys." The USFS brass refused to let their investigators comment on the case, despite the fact that they were the lead agency. The Minnesota State fire marshal also refused to allow his investigators on camera, and soon ABC News was promoting the perception that all of the agencies were too embarrassed to talk about their role in the case.

The investigators themselves were highly embarrassed by the backpedaling of their agency heads. They felt betrayed as they had worked on this case for over three years and had brought down a serious serial arsonist. They were extremely proud of the investigation, and rightfully so. Eventually they remembered that I had a very minor consulting role in this case, and both the AUSA and two of the lead investigators called me and asked me to appear on ABC News *20/20* as a recognized expert in serial arsonists, to defend their investigation. I agreed and gave an interview to the news agency.

While speaking to one of their producers, I asked them if they were still doing a "sympathy piece" on Scharber and vilifying the investigation. They confided in me that they had finally been able to interview Scharber and found his explanation ludicrous. They felt that he truly was a weirdo, and they quickly abandoned their planned sympathy story. ABC aired the piece in April of 2014 on national news, and it was clear that they had changed their minds about Scharber. He was not at all portrayed in a sympathetic light, and I was allowed to add my opinion that he was most likely setting fires for years, way before his baby developed colic, and that he would be at risk to set fires for the rest of his life.

After seemingly endless delays at the hands of an extremely liberal judge, Ryan Scharber was eventually sent off to prison.

### Investigator's Profile

The firefighter serial arsonist within the subtype of the "hero" is an all-too-familiar scenario in the United States and other countries. Research conducted by several parties has shown that firefighter arsonists have been around since the fire service was formalized. Each year in the United States, nearly one hundred firefighters are arrested for the crime of arson. As I mentioned earlier, they are almost always "serial arsonists" in that they have set multiple fires. Their motives can vary, so they cannot all be painted with the same brush.

Some firefighter serial arsonists are motivated by profit as they may be "call" or seasonal firefighters and will only get paid when there is a fire. This type of arson can be fairly obvious in that it occurs on a certain day and in a specific area. All of this is done to maximize profit and to insure a specific agency or group is called to fight the fire. I have met investigators in Canada and the United States who have dealt with cases where Native American (or First Nation in Canada) tribes have been involved in this sort of activity as firefighting is one of the main methods of income for certain tribes. Many wild-land firefighters have engaged in arson as a means to get paid for seasonal firefighting. Profit-motivated firefighter arsonists would fall under the class of **goal-directed arson**.

A creepier subtype of firefighter arsonist is the excitement- or recognition-based arsonist. These are the "wannabe" heroes. This type of firefighter arsonist would be under the class of **emotionally based** arson. This is the category that I believe best fits Ryan Scharber. The fire service has long had intense training and overly macho instructors who tell young, eager fire cadets that they will be "facing the beast" or "dancing with the devil" or even "slaying the dragon" on a daily basis. These gung ho types get all pumped up in fire training academies and then are let loose in the real world where they seldom see actual structural fires.

Accidental fires occur less frequently each year as fire-safety standards are enacted. Most young firefighters grow incredibly bored with constant cleaning and mundane training, and seldom get to put their adrenaline-pumping skills into action. This type of an issue is always made worse by a lack of mentoring, supervision, and professionalism within the firehouse. This type of atmosphere can help create the recognition-based arsonist.

The main ways to prevent this type of arsonist is to do a full criminal and psychological screening before hiring a firefighter in the same manner that police officers are screened. Look for indications of immaturity, anger, and alcohol or drug use. Looking at someone's driving record is actually a good barometer to reading their maturity and anger level. After hiring and training, the next most important step is a strong mentoring and ongoing education/training program. This sort of progressive activity minimizes the boredom, which can lead to hazing, harassment, drinking, theft, and fighting within the firehouse. Lastly, fire departments of all types need strong leaders and managers who treat the firehouse as a professional workplace and not a clubhouse.

In the above case, Ryan Scharber was an intelligent, highly motivated up-and- comer who had built up his small agency and outfitted it with the best equipment that money could buy. In his small jurisdiction, he had almost no fires to fight and no way for him to get that excitement and hero recognition that he craved. He was also very young and immature and, by his own admission, suffering from some mental-health issues. He clearly lacked a strong moral compass as at least a couple of his fires were set with the side intent of profit on his mind. When he was backed into a corner by investigators, he immediately tried to pin the fires first on a fourteen-year-old boy and then on at least one of the firefighters under his command. Ryan Scharber is truly a bad guy!

Like many arsonists, and particularly the "hero arsonists," Scharber would not admit his crimes until faced with overwhelming evidence. Even as he did so, he attempted to greatly minimize his actions by admitting only to the smallest fires and to add that he set fires in areas where they couldn't grow larger. When faced with jail, Scharber then really showed his true cowardly side and blamed his fire setting on the pressures of raising a colicky baby, which is something that hundreds of thousands of other fathers have successfully accomplished without setting fires. Scharber attempted to hide behind his religion, his baby, and some of the members of his own department. He appears to have no morals and no sense of responsibility.

I stand by the interview I gave to ABC News and believe, based on my knowledge of hundreds of other cases, that Ryan Scharber had been lighting fires for years before these events. He likely had other moral and behavioral issues as well. He is the epitome of the recognition-based arsonist.

Before I leave this case, I must comment that the investigation by this small task force was handled incredibly well. The investigators were able to put together a series of events played out over years in a small-town atmosphere where it is extremely difficult to keep a secret. They weren't able to link Scharber to all of his fires, but they still exposed him for what he was and stopped him before one of his fires killed someone. It was a sensitive investigation that if handled poorly would have blown up in their faces. They did an extraordinary job on this case.

I had hoped that their agencies would recognize the investigators for this once-in-a-lifetime case. However, the USFS has a long reputation of distancing itself from the operations of its own investigators as it wants its image to more reflect the helpful Smokey Bear than as a federal law-enforcement agency. I am deeply disappointed in how the USFS brass responded to the pressure from the media on this case, but I'm not surprised as they have done similar stuff like this for years. As an example, after the five- fatality Esperanza Fire in California in 2006, the USFS downplayed the fact that they had been investigating one of their own fire chiefs as a serial arsonist in that very area. The Forest Service brass was reluctant to bring that up during the case and their arson expert Ron Huxman was left to fend for himself during the trial. As far as the Minnesota case, I am at a loss as to why the other investigative agencies also refused comment on this case. They should have been proud of their work. It was an exceptional investigation by all of the below-listed people.

*The following professionals worked on this lengthy serial arson case: MSFM investigator Jim Iammatteao; USFS investigators Keith McAuliffe and Brian Gierczic; SLCSO detective Steve Heinrich; BCA special agents Chad Museus, Don Newhouse, and Bill Bennett; and AUSA Andrew Dunne.*

## DAVID LIN SERIES
## LOS ANGELES, CA, 2015

At just after ten o'clock, on the night of January 27, 2015, a slightly built, disheveled-looking Chinese man walked into the Guppy House restaurant in Hacienda Heights, California. The business was getting ready to close, and there were not many patrons left inside. The staff watched the man walk directly to the bathroom and go inside. The man emerged within two minutes and then walked directly out the door. He was then witnessed by a customer as he entered a vehicle and began to drive erratically around the parking lot for a few minutes before speeding off.

A minute after the Chinese male left the bathroom, employees saw dark smoke starting to drift out of the room. They ran to investigate and found that the paper towels in the wall dispenser were on fire along with a separate fire in the trash can. The employees quickly extinguished these two small fires.

Nobody got a license plate number for the car, and the suspect's description was fairly generic for that part of town. The suspect was described as being a thirty- to forty-year-old Chinese male of medium height, with medium length hair, and having an extremely thin build. Since that part of Los Angeles was filled with tens of thousands of Asians, it would not be much to go on.

I was in the office when this call came in, and my eyes widened a bit with interest. It is extremely rare to get an arson fire in a business that was open. This was the type of fire that might be considered a prank by a teen or even just a rash act by an upset drunk. It was a very small event with minimal damage. It would normally not get much attention at all, especially if it was a one-time thing. Still, it was also something we had seen a few years before when a doctor had lit over two dozen small fires, some of them in Starbucks restaurants that were open for business. When we got out-of-character fires like this, we tended to take notice. Is this the first in a series? The twenty-first in a series? Or just a simple "one and done" fire by a drunk? We sent an investigator out and waited.

We didn't have to wait long as this was not an isolated event. Two days later, at just past four in the afternoon, a lone Chinese male walked into the L&L Hawaiian BBQ, in the city of Walnut, which is about seven miles from Hacienda Heights. This area also had a large Chinese population. The male walked directly in and entered the women's bathroom. He then exited quickly about two minutes later. A witness said the male appeared to be talking to himself. A short time after this odd incident, restaurant employees noted that there was a small fire burning in the bathroom. They entered and found that a shelf above the toilet, which held a large amount of paper products, was on fire. The sprinkler system activated, and the fire department was summoned. The fire was much larger than the first fire but again didn't do that much damage.

This time Det. Rick Velazquez and Sgt. John Hanson from LASD Arson-Explosives Detail responded. They investigated and found video surveillance of the suspect and noted that he closely matched the suspect description from the previous fire at the Guppy House. We now knew we had a very rare serial or spree arsonist. The same person entered an occupied business during working hours, entered a bathroom, and ignited available combustible items on fire. The suspect was obviously mobile as the locations were a long distance apart. Sgt. Hanson immediately recognized this as a series in the making and started a very small task force to deal with this. He would be the lead investigator of this series of fires.

Sgt. Hanson organized his case quickly and went out to seek video evidence at nearby businesses. He also put out an alert to the other arson groups in the area and described the incidents. Before long Sgt. Hanson was busy again. The very next day, on January 30, at just before noon, a fire broke out in the men's bathroom at an Office Depot store in nearby Rowland Heights. The manager said that the last person to leave that bathroom was a lone Chinese male, thin, and around thirty to forty years old. The male had been a customer of the store in the past and had used their computers. Just before the fire, the male was observed looking nervous and using one of the store's computers.

A worker at the store spoke with the male in Mandarin, and the male spontaneously shouted, "Are you going to call the police? Everyone calls the police on me." This was several minutes before he entered the bathroom. This time the business had a video of the suspect. He indeed matched the description of the suspect in the previous two fires.

Sgt. Hanson and Sgt. Joe Acevedo immediately responded to the store and processed the scene. The scene showed that the suspect had entered the bathroom and started two separate fires. One was in the roll of toilet paper, and the second was to a box containing sanitary toilet barriers that was mounted on the wall behind the toilet.

Later that same night, the same-described suspect entered an Asian restaurant several miles away in the town of San Gabriel. This was not in the sheriff's department's jurisdiction, but the local investigators had been alerted by Sgt. Hanson's request for information. In San Gabriel, the suspect walked into the bathroom and set fire to several rolls of toilet paper. He then fled the scene. San Gabriel investigators found the suspect on video footage and were able to see that he left the scene in an older white Honda with a broken window.

Now Sgt. Hanson was able to look at four identical events. All four were fires in bathrooms in businesses that were open. All had been done by the similarly described suspect. Rowland Heights was the town between Hacienda Heights and Walnut. San Gabriel was just a short five-minute drive away. This suspect had just defined his "target area." We now sat down and studied these events and began to plot out an investigative strategy. The first and third incidents were very close to each other, so we surmised that the suspect lived near that area. He was described as extremely thin, nervous, disheveled, and talking to himself, so we believed that we were looking for someone who had either mental-health issues or was a methamphetamines addict. His fires were small, but extremely high-risk events as he did them in front of witnesses. This guy was a dangerous fellow.

At just past midnight, on Tuesday, February 3, a fire was noticed in the bathroom of a McDonald's restaurant in Rowland Heights. The fire was put out by employees, who neglected to call the police. The fire burned the cardboard sanitary-barrier container that was mounted on the wall above the toilet. Sgt. Hanson found out about this the next day and responded to the scene. He pulled the surveillance video of the event and found the same Chinese male entering the restroom about fifteen minutes before the fire was noticed. This restaurant was just three blocks away from the Office Depot and six blocks away from the Guppy House. We knew it was the same guy, and he wasn't going to quit. We believed that he lived or worked very close to this cluster of fires.

While Sgts. Hanson and Acevedo were still in the vicinity of the McDonald's, checking for witnesses and surveillance video, another fire was observed in the neighboring town of Diamond Bar. At about noon, a thin, disheveled Chinese male walked into a Del Taco restaurant and asked for a cup for water. He went to the dispenser and, instead of water, began to pour himself soda. Workers then watched him dig in a trash can and pull out an old receipt. He then approached the counter and demanded food (in Mandarin), saying that he was never given his meal. Managers tossed the agitated man out of the restaurant. He was visibly upset when he was thrown out. Ten minutes later smoke started pouring out of the women's bathroom.

When Sgts. Hanson and Acevedo arrived, they recognized the suspect in the video as the same man who had set the fire at the McDonald's twelve hours earlier. By now they knew this guy was out of control as his actions were accelerating and growing riskier. They called in a large number of patrol officers to a meeting and began an active search in the area. In this latest fire, he had burned a toilet-roll dispenser in the bathroom.

After the arson sergeants met with uniformed deputies, the deputies spread out to several small businesses in the area of four of the fires. A pair of officers stopped at the closest Starbucks to the area and immediately found a witness. A female said that the man they were describing goes by the name of "David" and comes into the Starbucks on a regular basis. He used to live close by (she gave investigators the address) but said that lately he had been living out of his small white Honda car. This car description matched at least two arson scenes. She said that he has mental-health and drug issues and depends on his mother for money.

The detectives drove to the address described but found out that David had moved out a few weeks ago. However, by searching records from that address, they were able to learn that his full named was David Lin and that his mother lived in another nearby city. The detectives pulled computer records on David Lin and found his photo was a match for four of the videotaped fire scenes. In just four hours of investigating, they had found their suspect. They now distributed this information about his car and photo to the area patrol officers.

Before the detectives had even finished this brief investigation, the suspect struck again. At two in the afternoon that same day, he was seen entering a Chinese tea café in Walnut, very close to the second fire in this series. He went to the bathroom at the café and found that it was occupied. He began pounding on the door, and eventually a customer came out. The suspect entered the bathroom for just a minute and then abruptly left the store. A couple of minutes later a fire was spotted among the toilet-paper rolls. A customer put out the fire, and Sgt. Hanson, along with arson detectives Rick Velazquez and Pat Dorris, responded to the scene. They viewed the video at the café and recognized David Lin again. He had now lit three identical fires in fourteen hours. He was quickly spinning out of control.

By two in the afternoon, on February 3, the detectives had found enough evidence to link David Lin to seven nearly identical arson fires, which occurred over the past six days. His car was confirmed to be a white Honda Accord, which was missing a rear window. The detectives found a small geographic area where he was thought to be hanging around in, very near to four of the arson fires. Almost the entire day shifts from two large LASD stations converged on a two-mile-long strip of businesses within this "target area," looking for David Lin. This extraordinary number of patrol officers included the commander of one of the sheriff's stations.

Additionally, the detectives had uncovered Lin's criminal history, which was predictable in its length and type of crimes. David Lin had a long history of vandalism, trespassing, burglary, theft, physical violence toward women, and narcotics use. He was, as we had earlier suspected, a methamphetamines addict. The detectives then broadcast every bit of information about the suspect that they had out to the patrol officers. The tactic worked out perfectly as within ten minutes of Sgt. Hanson broadcasting the information, David Lin and his white Honda were located within the target area. Deputies initiated a traffic stop, and Lin sped off, leading them on a brief, frenzied car chase that Los Angeles is so famous for.

Several sheriff's department's cars joined the chase, and Lin was seen throwing a brown bag from the car. One deputy stopped and retrieved the bag and found that Lin had discarded a bag of methamphetamines. Lin lost control of his car and came to a jerky stop after a short chase of a few blocks. He refused to obey officers' commands and appeared disoriented, agitated, and hyperexcited. He had to be physically wrestled to the ground.

Sgts. Hanson and Acevedo sped to the scene and eventually interviewed David Lin. They found him to be very talkative but rather cagey. He exhibited all the bizarre physical mannerisms of a longtime addict. He was agitated, jumpy, nervous, and vacillated between violent outbursts and quietness. Although it was clear that he was starting to lose his mind, like all longtime meth users, he was still wise enough to blame his fire setting on "blackouts" or meth use. He eventually admitted to being at all the locations of the fires but said he didn't remember starting them, or he may have blacked out during these events. He said that he had a sickness (addiction) and wasn't responsible for what he did when he was high.

Nice try! That defense, while potentially valid, just doesn't work in California, where arson is a "general intent" crime. It is also considered a serious and violent crime, and David Lin was facing close to life in prison for these seven serious and violent felonies, despite them causing very little damage. Eventually Lin listened to his attorneys and several months later pled guilty to two felony counts of arson, which got him eight years in state prison.

*The following investigators from the LASD Arson-Explosives Detail worked on the David Lin investigation: lead investigator*

*Sgt. John Hanson, Sgt. Joe Acevedo, Det. Rick Velazquez, Det. Rob Harris, Det. Greg Everett, and Det. Pat Dorris. Also working on the case were crime analyst Priscilla Billet and Inv. Gilbert Lee of the San Gabriel Police Department.*

### Investigator's Profile

We are kind of proud of this short but intense case. The LASD Arson-Explosives Detail is a twenty-person unit, which has handled over forty serial arson investigations in the past fifteen years. Most of them were solved, and we have learned how to conduct this sort of investigation in a fairly efficient manner. The lead investigator on this case, Sgt. Hanson, was brand new to the arson field but had been a high-level criminal investigator for two decades. This case was pure police work, nothing more.

When Sgt. Hanson got this case, he immediately sought advice from more experienced people who had dealt with cases like this in the past. We gave him guidance, and he performed brilliantly. I point this out because I have witnessed dozens of police/fire agencies attempt to conduct an investigation of this sort many times in the past, and most struggle and fumble through this process quite badly. Most agencies, the moment they identified a "serial arsonist," would have called a press conference so that the fire chief could warn the public. Next they would almost assuredly begin a series of disorganized stakeouts or surveillance operations of all Asian restaurants. This is exactly how *not* to conduct one of these investigations, which are actually quite common across the United States.

Holding press conferences seldom solves anything and only brings up much unneeded scrutiny. Having the media involved can be very distracting and can be quite detrimental to a case. The use of the media can be a good tactic at a later juncture in the investigation. Lastly, the use of a stakeout or surveillance operation is a last-resort tactic to be used only when a suspect is identified or a very finite area of operation is defined, as was in this case. Too often, agencies will try to flood an area with unqualified surveillance personnel, who only cause more problems than good.

In our case, Sgt. Hanson first gathered in all the reports and then sent detectives and patrol officers to other businesses in the area looking for video. By the end of this case, he had the suspect on video nearly ten times. Eventually the video search found the suspect's car. Sgt. Hanson then used license-plate-reader technology and red-light-camera technology to further identify the vehicle. He then sent people out to canvass for further information, and one of these officers located someone who could identify David Lin.

The rest was mostly academic. Background information and photos of Lin were located, and all of this info was then forwarded to the local patrol cars in the area. It took ten minutes for them to spot Lin. That is exactly how a serial arson case is supposed to end. The suspect is supposed to be picked up by a patrol officer or a surveillance specialist. The investigators are kept busy by building a strong case around the suspect.

Sgt. Hanson also did one other extraordinary thing in this case. He consulted with a profiler. In this case it was me. Every day we spoke on the phone and soon realized that the profile of this guy was somewhat unique. Most serial arson offenders do not drive vehicles, and most do not enter structures to commit arson. This guy went even further and lit fires in occupied structures, which is the rarest of all serial arsonists. This guy was clearly an immediate danger to the community and needed to be caught fast. The funny part was, we recognized his high-risk behavior after his third fire and predicted that we would catch him within a week because his actions were so rash and dangerous. It took only twenty-four hours after we made this prediction that we actually caught him.

The suspect profile is typical of a modern-day, urban serial arsonist. He is a lone male in his forties, has a long history of drug use, and probably is having some mental-health issues associated with that addiction. He also had past criminal behavior consistent with other serial arsonists: vandalism, trespassing, burglary, theft, and drug use. What isn't typical to the nationally known profile of a serial arsonist is that he is Asian. Arson profilers for decades have told us that arsonists are mostly white males. This is a false belief by these experts. This was Sgt. Hanson's second serial arsonist within a month, and both were Chinese Americans.

The last dozen serial arson cases out of our office in Los Angeles showed that of the suspects, ten were male, two female, eight Hispanic, two Asian, one white, and one black. My own profile of the event is that serial arsonists in the urban setting are representative of the ethnic norms of that area. If the area is mostly black, then there is a great chance that the serial arsonist operating in that area will be black, and so forth. This has been proven true to my unit for over twenty years.

David Lin is classified as an **emotionally based arsonist**. There was no known reason whatsoever for him to have lit the fires. He was familiar with several of the locations but had not been involved in any disputes. His real reason for the fires remains locked in his drug-addled brain.

## STAINFACE
## CHARLES KRITZ—SERIAL ARSONIST
## LOMITA, CA, 2006–2011

*This case comes from the author's own case files.*

On Valentine's Day of 2007 I was working the desk at the LASD Arson-Explosives Detail. It was my duty that day to look at all the arson cases that came in the previous night and assign them out to the available investigators. We have a unit of twenty-two full-time arson-explosives investigators, and we get between five and ten arson investigations each day of the year. On that particular day I saw a report indicating that a small arson attack had occurred in a residential neighborhood of one of our coastal cities named Lomita. I read the case quickly and realized that the report talked about two different arson attacks where the suspect had ignited a car cover that was on a car in the driveway of a home and had started another fire a day earlier in the same driveway when he had placed an amount of paper and leaves under a different car and set that on fire. Both of these fires occurred around three in the morning.

The patrol officers had scoured the neighborhood and found a neighbor who lived two houses away with a video camera facing the street (but not the fire scene). A review of the footage on the camera showed a stocky white male between thirty-five and forty years old wearing long shorts, walking toward the area of the fire just before it occurred, and then walking away from the area of the fire immediately after it occurred. The patrol officer's report was very detailed and also mentioned that there had been other small nuisance fires on this same street in previous months.

I assigned the case to one of our investigators who lived near the area. I saw immediately that this case had some workable information and appeared to be either a neighborhood dispute or the potential work of a serial arsonist. The investigator that got the case closed it out quickly with no suspect identified.

In late May, just a couple of months later, I noticed another small arson fire in the same area. The area of the attack was within a block of a large intersection at 261st Street and Western Avenue. All four of the attacks had been within a block of this intersection. The report for that fire was very similar to the previous fire. I did a little research and found that additional fires had occurred on the same street in the two months since the first fire. All of these fires occurred late at night, and all involved someone placing combustible material under cars and igniting it. Most of the damage was quite small. The investigator was advised of this, but because they were small fires, he didn't seem interested. Without much more investigation, he closed out all the cases a couple of weeks later.

Almost four years later I was again working the desk and noticed reports for two trash bin fires behind buildings near the corner of 261st Street and Western Avenue in Lomita. I assigned both of these fires to a different investigator and advised him that we had an arson problem near that same spot four years earlier. This second investigator went to the scene and found that someone had ignited at least three different plastic trash/recycling cans on the street and a large trash Dumpster.

A month later, that same investigator responding to the exact same area and investigated two fires to vehicles. Both fires were started by someone placing trash, wood, and leaves underneath the cars and igniting them. This was very similar to the MO of the arsonist in this same area four years earlier. With these recent fires, we determined that we had at least six different fire scenes within the same block. At that point we knew we had a "firebug" on the street and set up a very small task force. The team included me, Sgt. Joe Guarino, and Det. Cindy Valencia from the Arson-Explosives Detail.

Up to this point, I had conducted about thirty serial arsonist investigations and had a good idea how to go about running this. I would run the overall investigation while Sgt. Guarino wrote all the paperwork and conducted interviews. We had a crime analyst check computer records for every past incident on that street. We also knew from past experience that many small fire events are not reported or are missed by investigators. We began a records research for all fire calls in a mile radius of that intersection. The patrol units were briefed and asked to conduct information stops of all pedestrians, bicyclists, and other suspicious persons in that same area.

Meanwhile the fires started coming in fast and furious. Over the next two weeks we had an additional six fires on the same block. Now the suspect had stepped up his intensity by using accelerant and some crude incendiary devices at the scenes. His targets continued to be trash cans, cars parked on the street, and a power pole. Again, like all the previous events, the fires took place within a two block area near 261st Street and Western Avenue.

The computer records check gave us a lot more information. We found that going back to 2006, there had been a total of eighteen arson attacks in this small area. Many of them were quite similar in nature and targeted cars in the area. Sadly, eight of these incidents had not been reported to the arson unit and were never investigated. Now we knew for sure we had a serial arsonist living in the area. He had gone through three small arson sprees in a five-year period, but his target area and MO remained fairly consistent.

An odd incident came out of the records check. One neighbor had made a complaint that the guy next to him had vandalized his property, stolen some sprinkler heads, and had thrown a bunch of rocks onto his roof several times to annoy him. We had done several other cases where a serial arsonist had been engaged in this odd sort of vandalism and harassment of neighbors, and we felt that this needed to be investigated.

In May of 2011, Det. Valencia and I drove to that area and spoke to the victim who had complained of rocks being thrown. That victim pointed out the guy who lived next to him and called him "Stainface." He said the guy was a mid-forties white male, with a stocky build, and was always wearing long shorts. He said the man is easily identified as he has a large "port wine" pigmentation stain covering most of his face. The victim said the guy has had issues with other neighbors for years and has vandalized several people's cars. He said that Stainface doesn't like people parking in front of his home and has keyed and scratched cars in the past. This victim showed us about twenty small rocks that were thrown on his roof by Stainface. We noted that the rocks were smooth and shiny like aquarium rocks. We collected these as evidence.

We walked outside and saw Stainface on the street. He was short and stocky and wearing long dark shorts similar to what gang members wear. We could see that the port-wine stain was extremely noticeable from a long way away and covered more than half his face and forehead. We saw that his home sat on 261st Street, just thirty yards from the intersection with Western Avenue. He lived exactly in the middle of all of the fire scenes and within fifty feet of at least six of the arsons. That day we did a computer check on Stainface and found that his true name was Charles Kritz. He and his mother had lived at that home for almost forty years. Kritz had a fairly minor criminal record, but the local sheriff's station reported numerous disturbances at his home over the past few years.

We didn't have much to go on, but I recalled that Kritz's description was a close match to that of the arsonist seen on video in the cases from 2007. I went to the original (unmotivated) detective I had assigned some of the earlier fires to and asked him for a copy of the video of the suspect from one of his fires. This fire was less than fifty yards from Kritz's home, and the suspect's actions matched the directions Kritz would have had to walk to start the fire and leave the scene. The earlier detective told me that he had lost or thrown out the surveillance tape of the earlier arsonist. To say that I was irritated would be a gross understatement.

After losing that evidence, we were discouraged but not dead. We knew from several past cases that Kritz's activity fit one profile of a serial arsonist. There is a subset of arsonists who are just angry at everyone around them and constantly harass their neighbors with vandalism, theft, and sometimes arson. Plus, we knew that a large number of serial arsonists had some form of a visible skin or physical deformity. Kritz also matched the profile as he was a grown man living with his mother, and he was not employed.

It wasn't much to go on, and we were only operating on a theory, but the more we looked at Kritz, the better he looked. By now we had looked at a couple of other guys in the neighborhood and eliminated them as potential suspects. Kritz had not yet been eliminated. We went to one of our surveillance teams on our department and asked them to install a surveillance camera near Kritz's home to see if we could catch him (or anyone else) in the act.

The surveillance team set up a "pole camera" across from Kritz's home. The team posed as electrical workers and mounted a tiny but high-tech camera on a power pole. This camera was fed into a computer where a surveillance specialist monitored it at regular intervals. These types of operations are going on in a dozen locations in Los Angeles County on a given day. For the next week the camera captured Kritz as he went through a consistent daily routine. Each day he came outside before the sun came up and walked over to a neighbor's house to steal the newspaper. He varied this routine each day so that the same neighbor wasn't hit twice in a row. We then saw him steal sprinkler heads and even turn a sprinkler to spray on a neighbor's car. He even turned a couple of neighbors' trash cans upside down. This guy was a real asshole! His actions matched those of a few very unique arsonists we had dealt with in the past.

Seven days after we started watching Kritz, a surveillance specialist called us to tell us that Kritz had just set a small fire. In the video, Kritz came out of his home before dawn and stood around. After a few minutes he stepped back into his home and retrieved a small container. He then carried the container out of his yard toward a ten-unit apartment complex directly behind his home. This apartment complex had been the target of at least three of the previous arson attacks.

Kritz was then seen pouring a liquid on top of a row of mailboxes affixed to the apartment complex. He lit the liquid on fire with a small lighter and then sprinted back to his home. He appeared a few times to watch the fire, but the fire quickly fizzled and eventually burned itself out. Nonetheless, our suspicions were confirmed, and we had actually witnessed Kritz start a fire with an accelerant on the outside of an occupied structure. At the time of the fire, there were at least thirty persons sleeping inside of the small apartment complex. When I got to the scene, I found that the damage was extremely minimal. I found an oily substance residue left from the accelerant that Kritz had used.

A few days later Sgt. Guarino obtained a search-and-arrest warrant for Charles Kritz, a.k.a. "Stainface," and his home. We served it at a time when Kritz was just driving away in his car. I stopped him and arrested him for the arson we had witnessed on the video. As soon as Kritz got out of his car, we could see that he was sweating profusely and almost hyperventilating. He said he had numerous medical issues and needed to take some anxiety medicine quickly. We immediately saw an empty gas container in his car and about twenty empty Coca Cola cans. A search of his car showed that he had over twenty pairs of shoes in his car. He had another bag full of shoes in his trunk. He would explain the soda cans and shoes to us in a later interview.

We drove Kritz to his home and executed the search warrant at that place. We found an old aquarium in his backyard that held the exact type of stones that were thrown on the neighbor's roof. This confirmed that Kritz had been the culprit in that event, but it was hardly a serious crime. It did confirm our suspicions that he was a very strange person. In his garage we found an old metal can of lighter fluid that was dented as if used. It was still partially full. We later determined that this was likely the same item used to start the fire at the mailboxes. He also had some empty bottles that were similar to the items used in some of the crude incendiary devices.

When we searched Kritz's room, we found some peculiar items. His room was filled with items of clothing. Each item was obsessively neat in appearance and folded into razor-crisp piles. Kritz later told us that he has obsessive-compulsive disorder (OCD) and has to fold and refold his clothing many times to make it perfect. His compulsions controlled his life. I found a rack in his room that had dozens of used shoelaces hanging from it. The laces were neatly organized by color and length.

Kritz later told us that he had an obsession with shoes and shoelaces. He buys up to twenty pairs of used shoes each week because he can't stand wearing a pair for more than a few hours. He said he will wear his shoes for about four to five hours and then throw them out. He said he buys them at a thrift store, and that the workers are so used to him that they routinely pull out all the shoes in his size and hold them for him. He gets them for about two bucks a pair. Kritz said that it is psychologically impossible for him to wear shoes with laces, so he removes them and hangs them from the rack in his room. He admitted that he has to sort and arrange them by color and length.

Sgt. Guarino and I debriefed Kritz at a local jail. He was very cooperative and immediately took a shine to Sgt. Guarino. The two were roughly the same age and build. After a long time denying he set any fires, we confronted Kritz with the video evidence. He then stated simply, "You've got me; I'm an arsonist." Kritz admitted to the one fire, several vandalisms, the theft of newspapers, and even throwing the rocks. He said he had ongoing problems with all of his neighbors and didn't like them parking near his home and bothering him.

However, Kritz was very cagey when questioned about the previous fires. He never admitted to any other fires, stating simply, "If I admit to them, you will call me a serial arsonist. I don't want to be known as a serial arsonist." We argued this point for nearly an hour with Kritz as he over and over didn't deny the other fires, but he just didn't want to admit to them. The stigma of being known as a serial arsonist seemed to really bother him.

Despite being vague about his fire-setting activities, Kritz was surprisingly very open about his health and personal issues. He told us that he had been born with the port-wine pigmentation and that he considered it a cancer over his body that was slowly killing him. He described numerous other physical and mental afflictions. He said he had migraines and that he walked around all night because he had insomnia. He said he was diagnosed with severe OCD and attention deficit disorder. He also said he suffered from depression, anxiety, and agoraphobia (a fear of open or unknown places).

Kritz said he had hearing and breathing issues, along with heart, kidney, and other internal problems. He said he took a half-dozen different types of emotional and pain medications each day. He said he had traumatic brain injury from past suicide attempts. He described how twice he tried to asphyxiate himself when he was younger. One of those attempts was serious enough to land him in the hospital for a long time. He described at least four different suicide attempts in his life.

Kritz said he was a chain smoker, and when arrested he had six different lighters and two different types of matches in his possession. His car was filled with cheap little toys and other nonsensical items. When we asked about all these things, he said he is drawn to small, colorful items, which is just another obsession. He mentioned that he drank between a dozen and twenty Cokes each day and ate a dozen donuts. He said he was completely addicted to sugar. During our interview he practically begged for a soda. He said he was in the beginning stages of diabetes.

As our interview went longer and longer and we began to really focus on his fire-setting activity, his stress level began to rise. As it did, we visibly watched his large pigmentation stain actually swell on his face and change colors to a dark purple. When we commented on that, he said it happens every time he gets stressed. Kritz told us that the stain was the root of all his problems in life. He said that people had made fun of him since he was a little kid and had always picked on him. He told us that he had been married and had held a good union job but had to leave due to stress. He said he had a twelve-year-old daughter.

The entire time we interviewed Kritz, we noted that he was uncomfortably flirty with us and made several inappropriate sexual innuendos. At some point I asked him if he was gay. He feigned shock and said, "I've been married and have a kid." He didn't answer the question, so I asked him again. He then shocked us and blurted, "Well, I've never sucked a cock, but I'd be willing to try." Since we figured that not many straight men would say something like that, we determined that he was probably latent homosexual.

Kritz surprised us further by telling us with a grin that sometimes he liked to go down to a local bar, where a bunch of straight guys hung out (the local area is known for some fairly tough biker-type bars), and flirt with a guy. He said that several guys have threatened to kick his ass, and a few have actually punched him. He seemed to get a thrill out of that and was smiling and giggling while he told the story.

Sgt. Guarino filed several arson charges against Charles Kritz. The filing DA was Sean Carney, a specialist in arson cases in Los Angeles. Several months later Kritz accepted his fate and pled guilty to arson of an inhabited structure. In a plea deal, the remaining minor arsons were dismissed; however, Kritz had to pay a serious amount of restitution and was sentenced to prison for three years. He ended up doing just a year. We believe that Kritz set between twenty and fifty fires in a several year period. His fires were mostly smaller events. All of his fire setting appears to be related to thrill seeking, excitement, and/or revenge against society for his miserable lot in life.

*The investigators who worked on this case include LASD sergeant Joe Guarino, Det. Ed Nordskog, Det. Cindy Valencia, and surveillance specialist Det. Richie Maier.*

### Investigator's Profile

This case is a textbook example of the most common subtype of serial arsonist in the world—an urban arsonist. The suspect lives in a town or city, accesses his crime scenes by walking or riding a bike, and sets fires close to where he lives. Like most serial arsonists, he is a white male, and for the bulk of his fires he did not use an incendiary device or even an accelerant. By the time we arrested him, he had begun setting more fires and was using accelerants and experimenting with very crude incendiary devices with very poor results. His devices were time delay by virtue of a burning fuse and some fireworks powder, giving him less than ten seconds of a delay.

Like many serial arsonists, he admitted to only the fires we could prove and minimized his other fire-setting activities. He had more traits and physical ailments than any other serial arsonist I have ever met. His attempts at suicide, along with his addictive and obsessive behaviors, are quite common among serial arsonists. The fact that he had a very visible physical deformity may be the key to all his anger and other behaviors. He fully admitted to us that his port-wine stain had stigmatized him throughout his entire life.

We are very confident that Charles Kritz will engage in some sort of arson or other high-risk or self-destructive behavior in the future. He has an element of thrill seeking within his fire setting, and he really enjoyed the attention we gave him. Lastly, he appears to be latent homosexual, or someone who has hidden this most of his life. This again can be a common trait of many serial arsonists and may be a clue to their anger and frustration in life. Charles Kritz is classified as an **emotionally based arsonist**.

## NOHO SERIAL ARSONIST NORTH HOLLYWOOD, CA, 2011

*This case comes from the files of the LAFD, the Los Angeles County District Attorney's Office, and the ATF.*

North Hollywood is a small city within the city of Los Angeles, with about one hundred thousand residents. It is patrolled by the LAPD and has LAFD as its fire service. The city is sort of an "arts district" that has adopted in recent years the fashionable name of "NoHo." It has very little industry but is filled with tightly packed neighborhoods of old homes and many small apartment complexes. The town is filled with several dozen rock and roll clubs, recording studios, and restaurants, and it is bordered by the massive Universal Studios complex. Much like its slightly wilder sister, the city of Hollywood, just five miles away, NoHo is filled with an eclectic mix of artists, wannabe actors, street denizens, and assorted riffraff. It is also a very transient city. For a two-week period in July of 2011, it was besieged by a serial arsonist who went on a bit of a rampage.

In the early morning hours of July 21, 2011, five different vehicle fires were reported along Lankershim Boulevard in a three-hour period. The LAFD normally responds to over twenty arson incidents per day and initially did not think that this was a significant event. Lankershim is the largest, busiest street in

NoHo, and a large number of fire and rescue incidents routinely occur along it. Because of this, the LAFD's arson unit was not notified about the spree of car fires.

Two nights later, on July 23, an additional two vehicle fires were set in the Lankershim corridor in the nighttime hours, and again the arson unit for LAFD was not notified. While these first seven fires were in a very small geographic area, the local fire battalion chiefs did not recognize them as a major issue. The arson unit was not made aware of this problem. That would change drastically the next night.

On July 24, 2011, at two fifty in the morning, an unknown person entered a parking garage on Hatteras Avenue and set two different cars on fire. A blue BMW sedan was set on fire at the driver's-side wheel well. A second vehicle, a Ford Explorer, was set on fire along its driver's side, at a plastic running board. Both fires caused moderate damage to the vehicles. This garage serviced a four-story apartment building that was situated over the garage. The fires endangered several dozen people who were asleep in the above apartments. Investigators noted that the parking garage was in a secured area but that any reasonably fit person could bypass the locked gate by climbing over it.

On the same night and at nearly the same time, a third fire was reported just a couple of buildings away. This fire was in a trash container at the rear of a detached garage of a residence. The fire spread to and consumed the garage and also damaged a nearby parked vehicle.

Almost simultaneous to these fires, a fourth fire was discovered burning at nearby Lemp Avenue. This fourth fire was to another car parked in a carport with occupied apartments overhead. Again, the fire was set in the wheel well of a car.

Just before four that same morning, three additional fires were reported just blocks away from the first four fires. An old RV, which was parked in the 7000 block of Radford Avenue, was set afire at its rear wheel well on the driver's side. This vehicle sustained minor damage.

The second RV to burn was along the same block of Radford. The arsonist set a fire in the exact same place as the previous RV, at the rear wheel well on the driver's side. This too caused minor fire damage and was quickly put out.

The third fire occurred in the same block to a small Dodge camper van/RV. This time the arsonist set the fire in the rear wheel well along the passenger's side. The vehicle suffered moderate to heavy fire damage. Alarmingly, at the time of the fire the owner was sleeping within the vehicle. He escaped unharmed.

Three blocks away, three more fires broke out. Just after four in the morning, two fires occurred within a carport in the 7300 block of Radford Avenue. This time the arsonist entered the open carport and set a fire within the passenger's-side rear wheel well of a Ford Explorer. The arsonist then set a second fire to an adjacent Toyota. This fire was started in the front wheel well area of the passenger's side. These final two fires were quite dangerous in that the carport and cars were directly against an occupied home where residents were sleeping. The fire department, which was already out and dealing with the previous fires, responded quickly and stopped these two fires from causing serious damage to the home.

The final fire of that busy night occurred a block away on Valerio Street where it intersected with Radford. The arsonist lit on fire the contents contained within the bed of a pickup truck, causing minor damage. The busy arsonist had set ten fires within a distance of just a few blocks.

The LAFD arson investigators correctly surmised that their suspect was either on foot or riding a bicycle since the fires were so close together. They had earlier briefed supporting police patrol units to detain any single persons on foot or bicycle in the area. They had used the massive resources of the LAPD and had gotten a helicopter dedicated to scouting out the area for lone pedestrians. The helicopter was equipped with a FLIR (forward-looking infrared) imaging device, which could easily locate persons walking along the dark streets.

### Kurt Billie

Shortly after four thirty in the morning, LAPD North Hollywood Division patrol officers were vectored into a residential neighborhood by the LAPD helicopter. The airship, specially briefed and assigned to this arson investigation, had spotted a lone male running between homes just after the final vehicle fire had been reported. LAPD patrol officers located the male as he walked down a sidewalk on a dark side street. They had been instructed earlier on how to deal with the potential arsonist, so they conducted a very low-key pedestrian stop. Upon seeing the male, they saw that he had a somewhat odd appearance. He was a Native American, which was an extremely rare type of person to be found in Los Angeles, and he sported a rather odd haircut.

The two officers stopped the male and advised him that they were contacting all pedestrians in the area to question them about the spate of arson fires. The male spontaneously mentioned that he "was familiar" with arson. They noted that the male smelled strongly of alcohol. The male told the officers that he was just out taking a walk in the neighborhood. The male advised them that his name was Kurt Billie and allowed the patrolmen to conduct a pat-down search of him. They found a butane cigarette lighter and a clear liquid in a spray bottle in his pockets. The liquid was believed to be some sort of cologne-type substance. Kirk Billie appeared to have soot and burn marks on both of his hands. The patrolmen asked him if he had a criminal record. He surprised the officers by casually stating that he had a prior record for arson.

Recognizing that they had a very real, potential suspect in the arson series, the patrol officers discreetly called an LAFD arson investigator to the scene. LAFD investigator Jose Sanchez arrived and began to question Billie. Billie eventually revealed that he was a former US Marine and that he had been convicted of arson while in Japan with the marines. This explained the odd haircut, as Billie's hair was shaved into the distinct "high and tight" style favored by gung ho marines.

Inv. Sanchez noted that Billie had a driver's license issued from the State of Texas and had only recently moved to North Hollywood. There was no criminal record for Billie in California. Inv. Sanchez found this information to be fascinating, and he took several photos of Billie and tested the substance in the bottle by burning it. He determined that the unknown substance was indeed flammable. Inv. Sanchez was quite sure that Billie was the NoHo arson suspect, but he knew they needed more to link him to the fires. He spent several more minutes casually questioning Billie and then told him that he was not a suspect in the case and could leave. Since they were not sure where Billie resided, he told the patrol officers to escort Billie home so that he would not get stopped by other LAPD units. The officers drove Billie several blocks to his apartment and confirmed that he lived alone in a small apartment dead center in the pattern of arson fires. He was released by the patrolmen.

Inv. Sanchez immediately gave all of this information to the rest of the arson investigators, who in turn requested an immediate surveillance operation be conducted on Kurt Billie. Recognizing the size and scope of this case, LAPD spared no expense and utilized their highly trained surveillance specialists from both their Special Investigation Section (SIS) and their Major Crimes Bureau to begin an ongoing, twenty-four-hour-a-day surveillance of Billie. They would remain glued to Billie for the next seven days. It was really boring work as Kurt Billie didn't leave his apartment the entire time. The stop by patrol officers surely spooked him!

Later that same day the arson investigators were combing the areas around the arson fires, looking for any witnesses or video cameras. Along the area of the final three fires on Radford Avenue, investigators found three cameras on industrial buildings. Later that day they were able to gain access to the footage, and it clearly showed Kurt Billie wandering back and forth on Radford at exactly the time of the final three vehicle fires. He stayed in the area until the first fire engines arrived on scene.

The arson investigators took stock of their growing series of fires. By plotting the fires on a map, they found that all were within easy walking distance of each other. They noted that a tight cluster of ten of the fires was within just a block of Kurt Billie's apartment. He looked like an excellent suspect.

The investigation was being led by Inv. Pat Leonard and his partner Inv. Jose Sanchez. They now were quite sure that they had the right guy. They set about building a case against him. They contacted a local ATF agent, and the two agencies began a detailed background check into Kurt Billie. It eventually came to light that Billie had been born in Arizona and was thirty-four years old. At some point in his life, he moved to Henderson, Nevada, then to North Hollywood, and finally to the San Diego area, where he attended high school and junior college. His grades in his only quarter of attendance in junior college were near failing. He then briefly moved to Florida.

Failing in school, Billie gave up college for the military. Billie enlisted into the US Marine Corps at twenty-two years of age, in 1999. He was and continued to remain unmarried, and he listed his religious preference as Mormon. He supplied the Marine Corps with a certified document confirming that racially he was one-half Navajo by blood. Following his completion of boot camp, Kurt Billie was assigned the military specialty of "refrigerator mechanic." This was a decidedly inglorious field of work for a new marine. A telling footnote lies within his military record. In August of 2000, Lance Corporal Billie received punishment from the marines for an "alcohol-related incident."

## Arson in Japan

Within eighteen months of enlisting, Billie was arrested in Okinawa, Japan, for setting several arson fires. In January of 2001, Japanese authorities arrested and questioned him about setting a fire in an occupied restaurant. He admitted to that fire and seven other fires in clubs and restaurants over a two-week period. He told the Japanese police that he was drunk at the time of the fires. During the same admissions to the Japanese police, Billie told them that he had set two large fires on the American military base, which had destroyed two large buildings. Japanese authorities forwarded that information to Marine Corps officials.

The Naval Criminal Investigative Service investigated and confirmed that there were two recent, large arson attacks on base. Billie was charged with setting a fire on the night of November 2, 2000, which burned down a large military building, causing over a half-million dollars in damage. Billie was also charged with setting a second fire to a military building on December 10, 2000, which caused over $300,000 in damage. He was convicted for those crimes in a military court-martial and sentenced to ten years in a US military prison.

Before he could ship off to the military prison, Billie had also been charged by Japanese authorities for setting the seven fires in restaurants and bars in January of 2001. He was eventually convicted in July of 2001 and sentenced to five years in a Japanese prison for that spate of arson attacks. The Japanese court noted that Billie was under the influence of alcohol during those attacks and lit the fires to "escape reality." Once out of a

Japanese prison, Billie was shipped back to the United States to remain in a US military prison. He ended up serving just over six years in prisons for his several arson counts, with the rest of the time suspended. He was demoted in rank to private and given dishonorable discharge.

Billie was booted out of the marines in late 2006. He was finally released from a US prison in 2008. He moved to Albuquerque, New Mexico, to stay in a halfway house. He got a job working at a food buffet.

### Suspicious Fires in the Southwest

The ATF was aware of Billie as he had come up as a "person of interest" in a small series of fires while living in Albuquerque. An arson fire occurred within the halfway home Billie was living at, and a second fire occurred to a home on the same street. When questioned, Billie told investigators that he had been "out walking" at the time of each fire. The fires stopped when Billie moved out of state.

In 2010, Billie was sent by his employer to El Paso, Texas, to train as a manager. He ended up staying there. Shortly after his arrival, a series of arson fires occurred on construction sites near his home. He again came to the attention of local authorities. As soon as he left the area in March of 2011, the fires in El Paso stopped.

Billie arrived in NoHo in March of 2011. He originally stayed in a canyon in the Hollywood Hills at a homeless encampment. Soon, a Native American assistance organization was supplying him with meals and alcohol counseling. The group eventually moved him to a sober-living facility in NoHo, where he was staying up until his arrest.

### The Surveillance

By August 1, people were getting agitated. The surveillance crews were irritated and grouchy as they had nothing to do but sit in parked cars twenty-four hours a day. Billie had never left his apartment. The brass, as usual, had very little stomach for a drawn-out surveillance and investigation. They were spending lots of money on the surveillance teams and overtime for the arson investigators, and they wanted to wrap this up immediately. Both the LAPD and LAFD brass were going to let the arson unit use the surveillance team for just one more night as they were going to shut it down the next day. What the arson investigators knew was this: Kurt Billie hadn't left his home in a week, but at the same time all of the suspicious fires had stopped. This probably was not a coincidence.

Apparently Kurt Billie was getting agitated as well. On August 2, at just after three in the morning, Kurt Billie finally left his apartment where he had been holed up for eight days. He began walking through the dark side streets of NoHo. Surveillance specialists who were both on foot and in vehicles struggled to keep a close eye on him in the quiet streets without being noticed. At one point they saw Billie stop in front of an older RV vehicle and just stare at it for a couple of minutes. He then moved on. They followed him for several minutes and eventually saw him enter the parking lot of a small strip mall.

Billie walked around back of the building and was seen to crouch behind a semi tractor cab that was parked there. The detectives waited to pounce at the first hint of flames. After a minute Billie emerged from behind the vehicle and wandered back down the street again. He then walked back to his apartment. The detectives had not seen a fire and were perplexed. They eventually sent two investigators in on foot to examine the vehicle. By using flashlights, the cops found that a small fire had been started within the wheel well of the large truck tractor but had self-extinguished. The small fire had caused minor damage to the fiberglass fender of the vehicle. Arson investigators quickly conferred and determined that this was sufficient damage to charge Billie with an arson attack. They ordered the surveillance officers to grab Billie before he could cause a more serious fire. By this time, Billie had again exited his apartment and had wandered a couple of blocks further. He was acting odd and walking in a disjointed manner. A couple of times he was out of sight of the surveillance team.

Eventually the surveillance crew was given the order to arrest Billie. He was grabbed off the street around 4:20 a.m. After they grabbed him, the surveillance officers drove along the areas where Billie had been briefly out of sight. At that time they discovered an old recreational vehicle on fire, which had been stored in a driveway. The fire was burning in the wheel well of the RV and was spreading fast to the occupied home next to it. Suppression crews from LAFD were summoned and assisted the homeowner in extinguishing the blaze.

The arson investigators examined the last fire and saw that Billie had set at least four separate fires on the old RV. He appeared to use a lighter and pieces of tissue that had been piled up in the wheel wells and grille area.

Upon his arrest, Billie was found to have been carrying a book of matches, several sheets of tissue, and a butane cigarette lighter. They also noted that he smelled strongly of alcohol. Investigators Leonard and Sanchez interviewed Billie later that morning. He told them he didn't remember much about his activities that night as he had been very drunk. He then invoked his rights and asked for an attorney.

Inv. Leonard drafted a search warrant of Billie's apartment. They found that he was active on his computer with social networking and even discovered a photo of him in firefighter's clothing, along with several photos of firefighting equipment on the Navajo reservation. There was no record that Billie had ever worked as a firefighter. The investigators also discovered that Billie had a large collection of gay porn. This was their first insight into his social history. They learned that he had recently lived in Albuquerque, New Mexico, and Lubbock and El Paso, Texas.

### The DA

DDA Sean Carney is one of three dedicated arson-explosives DAs in the Los Angeles County District Attorney's Office. He was actively involved in monitoring this LAFD investigation from the very start. As soon as it was discovered that Billie had a prior conviction in another country, DDA Carney knew that he would have to bone up on his international and military law. In order to file charges of aggravated arson, DDA Carney needed to prove a prior conviction for arson. Not only was that conviction in another jurisdiction, it was in another country on the other side of the world. (This would not be Carney's last case of dealing with an arsonist from another country. Six months later, "Hollywood Arsonist" Harry Burkhart, a German national suspected of multiple arsons in Germany, set fifty-two fires in Hollywood. Again, DDA Carney would have significant dealings with the State Department and a foreign government.)

DDA Carney began filling out a myriad of forms, seeking the certification of foreign documents. Luckily, the United States and Japan were close allies, and there was a legal mechanism in effect in the form of a treaty for just this sort of dilemma. This treaty was called the Mutual Legal Assistance in Criminal Matters. With this piece of paper that had been verified by prosecutors in Japan and in the US military, DDA Carney could truthfully assert that Kurt Billie was a multi-convicted arsonist several years prior to the series in NoHo.

DDA Carney continued building his legal case against Billie. Based on the past history of Billie, along with the fact that all of these new charges were "strike felonies" in California, Kurt Billie was facing the possibility of life in prison for these fires.

### The Psycho-Social History of Kurt Billie

Billie's defense team hired psychiatrists to evaluate him and put his life and intentions into perspective. While most defense psychologists tend to give very favorable and sympathetic opinions of the defendant, the sessions gave the prosecution and investigators a good look into Billie's life history and social history. Billie had also undergone psychiatric evaluations in the military. It was clear that Billie had a hard life, but it was also clear that he told a few lies to his evaluators.

Billie claimed he was born the product of an incestuous relationship. He told evaluators that many members of his family engaged in incest. He grew up and lived dirt poor on a Navajo reservation in Arizona without modern amenities. There was no father figure, and his mother was an alcoholic. He was raised primarily until age twelve by his great-grandmother. He did not speak English until the age of twelve. He said he started abusing alcohol to cope while quite young. This all appears to be true.

Billie told evaluators that cleansing by fire was quite normal in Navajo culture, and he practiced it most of his life. He admitted to setting many brush fires starting at six years of age. He stated that at about nine years old, his mother asked him to burn the family home down so that the government would build them a new one. These events actually occurred with the tribal police ruling the event as "accidental." This bit of info appears to be a self-serving statement and may be a bit of an admission to an arson fire he set when younger. Other siblings told the analysts that Kurt Billie was a frequent child fire setter from a very young age, and it was well known in their community.

Billie described having auditory hallucinations most of his life. At twelve years of age, due to his mother's alcoholism, he was placed in a series of foster group homes. He said at that time he was sexually abused by several of the other male wards. He was eventually placed in a foster home in Utah and had Mormonism "forced upon" him. He lived in seven different homes during his teen years. He said that he was sexually molested in at least one of these homes. In adult life, Billie had one older sister who was murdered by a boyfriend, and a second sister who spent time in prison.

Billie reported that he always used alcohol or drugs prior to setting his fires and also felt suicidal during those times. He said he gets so drunk before he sets fires that he has little memory of the events. He stated that he had struggled with the realization that he was homosexual and had severe difficulties with this after he entered the military. Billie claims to have been raped numerous times by men while living in homeless encampments and to have been gang raped by several of his fellow marines while on active duty. During all of these sessions, Billie never gave a reason for setting his fires in NoHo. He was clever enough to avoid direct admissions in these events.

In the end, the court-appointed and defense mental-health analysts determined that Billie suffered from depression and was heavily dependent on alcohol and fire setting as coping methods. They were adamant that he was not a "revenge based" fire setter but more of a "coping" fire setter.

After nearly two years of legal hearings and psychiatric analysis, Kurt Billie's defense team finally came up with an acceptable plea deal. On March 4, 2013, Kurt Billie pled guilty to two counts of arson to an inhabited structure, and he openly admitted in court to setting all seventeen fires in the NoHo arson spree of 2011. He also admitted to the prior arson convictions in Japan. Billie was sentenced on July 11, 2013, to ten years to life in prison for the NoHo fires.

*The professionals who worked on this case include LAFD lead investigator Pat Leonard, Inv. Jose Sanchez, Inv. Frank Oglesby, Inv. David Liske, Inv. Tim Crass, ATF special agent Suriya Khemradhipati, and DDA Sean Carney.*

### Investigator's Profile

Kurt Billie was born and raised a serial arsonist. There was really nothing else that he could have been. Born poor, destitute, and the product of a really sketchy family life, along with the fact that his mother was a hopeless alcoholic, he had very little chance to succeed in life. A study of all criminals will show that almost every single one of them is a direct result of poor parenting. Billie personifies that.

Billie lived a nomadic, transient life and drifted from foster homes to living with relatives in four different states, to living in homeless encampments. He did very poor in school and turned to the military for stabilization. He was not a macho guy and did not fit in well at all in the marines. He was struggling with his sexual identity and found it difficult to engage in a gay lifestyle while in the military. He expressed suicidal thoughts numerous times throughout his life and used alcohol as his main crutch.

All of that makes Billie a very difficult person to identify and arrest. He seldom stayed in one place long enough for authorities to get a bead on him. Only months after his arrest in Los Angeles did it come to light that he was under scrutiny for arsons in New Mexico and Texas. This last bit of information is a bit of a failure on the part of the ATF. Billie was already a twice-convicted serial arsonist when he was released to the halfway house in Albuquerque. There was an arson fire in the same house in which he was living. He was interviewed and identified by police, fire, and federal officers at that time, but they failed to keep close tabs on him. He was the perfect candidate for a detailed investigation and surveillance at that time. He eventually dropped out of sight and his name came up later after some arson attacks in Texas. Again, he should have been a top priority at that time by the federal government. Again, he was allowed to slip away and blend into the very transient lifestyle around Hollywood.

By the time he ended up in Los Angeles and began his final fire-setting spree, he had run into a very professional law enforcement and fire investigation group. This time the arson investigators used time-tested and proven techniques to capture an unknown arsonist. Instead of flooding the streets with firefighters and arson investigators attempting to "go undercover," the LAFD utilized trained and briefed patrol officers to conduct pedestrian stops of all persons out alone at night. They used patrol helicopters to locate potential targets and vectored in officers to conduct the low-key police contacts. This was exactly how a serial arson investigation in an urban setting should have been conducted.

Once Billie was identified as the possible serial arsonist, the LAFD/LAPD then used their brains and began a detailed background check of him while assigning the very best surveillance units in the world to follow him. The result was a perfect investigation and arrest! This case was one of the best I have witnessed and is a blueprint on how to conduct an urban serial arson investigation. It was a great warm-up case for an investigation three times as large just six months later in Hollywood. In that later case, in which I was a colead investigator, we used the exact same tactics to apprehend Harry Burkhart in just four days.

In reviewing his psychiatric reports, I find that much of what Billie told the mental-health experts was self-serving and probably exaggerated. Ritual, controlled use of fire does occur in Native American cultures, but that doesn't include brush fires, home fires, et cetera. There have been hundreds of thousands of Native Americans who practiced some controlled form of the ritual use of fire but did not become serial arsonists. Billie's own siblings told the analysts that Billie was well known as a firebug among his own community. Arson is clearly not accepted within the Navajo culture. Although Billie's life conditions were the major contributors to his behavior, there are hundreds of thousands, if not millions, of Americans with similar, horrible life conditions who do not become serial arsonists.

I also believe that Billie attempted to strike a sympathetic tone with his analysts with lies or exaggerations. He told military officials that he was despondent and set fires due to the death by car accident of his wife and children, when it was clear that he was never married and never fathered any kids. He also asserts that he was raped or sexually molested at nearly every juncture of his life: as a child, in foster care, in homeless encampments, and throughout the military.

I find this to be preposterous. He may have been abused/ molested within one of these settings, but it is clear that as an adult, he purposefully engaged in "high risk" sexual encounters with anonymous men in public settings while drunk. He may have been beaten up or robbed during these encounters and then reported the incident as a rape or a sexual assault. This is a very common outcome of people engaged in this high-risk type of sexual behavior. To the end, Billie used this as a possible reason for his fire setting and refused to accept responsibility for his actions.

In the end, Kurt Billie is a lifetime serial arsonist with serial fire-setting activity going back to his youngest days. He is linked to arson sprees as a child in Arizona, as an adult in Japan, and then back in the United States in Albuquerque, in El Paso, and in North Hollywood. If he ever told the truth, it would be likely that he set over a thousand fires in his life. He has probably set fires everywhere he lived from the time he was ten years old.

This case is also a good wake-up call for the old arson investigators who firmly believe that arsonists always progress to larger and more dangerous fires. There is no proof whatsoever of that assertion, and in fact there are numerous case histories to show just the opposite. In this case, Billie started out by setting brush fires in rural Arizona. He then set huge fires that destroyed warehouses in the military. Shortly after that, he set smaller but more dangerous fires within occupied restaurants and bars. After he got out of the military, he was linked to fires set within occupied homes in New Mexico and then to unoccupied, semi-built homes in Texas.

His final grouping of fires was to vehicles, but some of these were parked along a street, where others were parked up against or under occupied structures. There is no rhyme or reason to a true serial arsonist like Kurt Billie. He just likes starting fires, big or small. There is absolutely no hope that he will ever be rehabilitated from his fire-setting activity.

Kurt Billie is difficult to classify as an arsonist. His targeting and ignition methods were effective but very crude. His targets appear as somewhat random, but he could be a **revenge-based arsonist**, with his revenge aimed at **society in general** for his poor lot in life. However, absent any admissions, I see him as mostly an **emotionally based arsonist**. His fires coincided with depression and very low periods in his life.

## GANG/ORGANIZED CRIME

### The Profile

Gang-related and organized-crime (OC) related arsons come in three main flavors. The first is for the purpose of revenge. In that manner, the target of the attack is a rival gang, biker club, or other OC group. These types of attacks are mostly committed from outside of the target building and frequently employ the use of firebombs or other incendiary arrangements or devices. These attacks are frequently "low performing" events as they are done in great haste and with crude items. These attacks may be preceded by graffiti, vandalism, or shootings at the target building.

The second style of gang/OC-related arson attack is for the purpose of intimidation, usually with the ultimate goal of extortion. In that case, smaller, less damaging fires are set to get the victims' attention and to cause them great fear that they are about to lose their businesses, properties, or lives. Again, incendiary devices in the form of Molotov cocktails are common in these sorts of attacks.

The final gang/OC-related arson attack is the old-school (circa 1970) "**bust out**." This is a well-planned and orchestrated event designed to burn a business for profit. The movie *Goodfellas* has an excellent example of a bust-out arson fire. In that depiction the local Italian mob crew takes over a club/restaurant and begins siphoning profits out of it for months. Eventually this business starts to fail due to diminishing profits, and the owner (a coconspirator with the mob) takes out the maximum amount of insurance possible on the property. On a given evening, when the owner has an airtight alibi, two mob guys enter and begin laying out an exotic incendiary design for the entire structure. In the movie, they wrapped cloths soaked in oil/fuel around all the light bulbs of the club/restaurant. A time delay is set, and in the dead of night the entire building bursts into flames.

These types of events are designed for maximum damage and are usually set from within the structure. This type of event has become fairly rare in the last thirty years but was quite commonplace along the entire east coast during the 1970s.

### The Myth

When I got into the arson business in 1997, I had already been a detective for eight years. In my first five years as an arson investigator, I attended many arson schools at the local, state, and national level. At nearly every one of them, I heard that a common motive for arson involved a "**gang initiation**" ritual. Now, after eighteen years in the arson business and two thousand of my own investigations, I have determined that that concept is a complete myth with almost no documentation to verify it.

Los Angeles (my area) leads the world in all gang activity. My unit has investigated over thirty thousand arson incidents since I have been assigned to it, and we have seen very few gang-related arson attacks. When they occur, they are most commonly failed events involving poorly deployed Molotov cocktails. The typical target is a rival gang member's home or vehicle. We have never, ever seen or heard of a single case where a gang member lit a fire as part of an initiation rite. If anything, we believe that gang members use fire less often than other groups as they have a long history of poor results with fire setting.

Over my career I have sought out the source of this "gang initiation" arson motive, and the consensus among my peers is that the ATF had listed this as a "common motive" in a lot of its training. In the past decade I have noticed that it is not included as a viable motive anymore on paper, yet I still hear the odd investigator invoke it, despite never having a case history to back it up. It remains yet another of the odd myths of the arson world. There may be the occasional case of it out there, but it is clearly not a "common motive."

## THE PUENTE BOYS
## CITY OF INDUSTRY, CA, 2002

*This case comes from the author's own case files.*

The city of Industry is about twenty miles east of downtown Los Angeles. Just like its name says, the city is made up primarily of hundreds of industrial companies that sit between the 60 Freeway and the 10 Freeway. The massive warehouses and factories stretch for miles, and the area is interspersed with several fairly downtrodden Hispanic neighborhoods. Each neighborhood harbors its own street gang. The largest and most active street gang in the area is a collection of young thugs known as the "Puente 13."

At just before midnight, on January 19, 2002, firefighters were summoned to a vehicle on fire in a factory area. The firemen arrived and found a 1997 Nissan Maxima fully engulfed in fire. The vehicle was parked on a darkened, empty roadway between two factories. The firemen made quick work of the burning car and as they were mopping up saw another car drive up to them. Two young men described as Hispanic gang members were in the second car. One of them was burned and in severe pain and claimed to be the owner of the burned car. The fire captain summoned LASD deputies to sort out this strange incident.

Sheriff's deputies quickly recognized both males as being from the local Puente 13 street gang. Both of these two young men were fairly active and were suspected in several recent thefts and assaults. The burned male, who was also the owner of the burned car, was a twenty-two-year-old named Anthony Moreno. He went by the very odd gang moniker of "Laughy." His friend, twenty-one-year-old Mario Rincon, went by the street name of "Stranger."

Laughy told the sheriff's deputies and firemen a really bizarre story. He said that he was at a party with other gang members in another city, where they were drinking and smoking pot. He said he left his car keys on a table, and about an hour later he went to pick them up and found they were missing. He went outside and found that his Nissan Maxima was also missing. He assumed that rival gang members had followed him to the party, entered and stole his car keys, and then stole his car.

Laughy said that he called his buddy Stranger to come pick him up at the party, and then the two began driving around looking for the stolen car. He said that they spotted the car on this deserted roadway as two males were pouring something over it. He said that he and Stranger sped up to them, but they drove off quickly in a "getaway" vehicle. He ran toward his car and saw a small flame inside of it. Just as he got near it, the car exploded in his face, causing burns to his face, his hands, and the side of his body.

His bizarre story sounded like something an eight-year-old would dream up after breaking his mom's lamp. The deputies started laughing at the gangster. He was clearly in some discomfort as he had visible second-degree burns on several places on his body. The deputies took their statements and noted that neither Laughy nor Stranger could recall the location where the party had been, the names or phone numbers of any of the attendees, or even how to get back to that house. They also noted that the gang members were describing a location that was several miles away, but for some reason the "car thieves" had driven the stolen car all the way back to within four blocks of each gang member's home.

Even the newest and most naïve patrolmen figured out that these two gang members had somehow burned this car and were now making up an elaborate cover story. The patrol deputies knew these guys were involved but figured that the detectives would sort it all out in the morning.

The firemen transported the injured Laughy to a local hospital for treatment and left the scene. The patrolmen released Stranger, impounded the burned car, but unfortunately waited several hours before they remembered to call me, the on-duty arson investigator.

### Arson Investigation

Early the next morning I drove to the police impound yard and examined the burned Nissan Maxima. I saw that it had been a fairly nice car before the fire and had all of its components including custom rims and tires. The fire caused complete destruction, both inside and out, but I could still identify some anomalies. I saw that the radio/stereo had been removed from the car, as well as both the front and rear seats. The interior of the car reeked of gasoline, despite the gas tank still being intact. I took a sample of the interior of the car, and the crime lab later identified gasoline as the accelerant used to burn the car.

I saw the vague remnants of a plastic pail with wire handle and several bricks where the driver's seat had been. It was clear to me that whoever burned this car had removed the seats and stereo and then placed a pail and some bricks where the driver's seat had been in order to drive the car a short distance to be burned. We had seen versions of this sort of car stripping/arson on hundreds of past occasions. I noted that the major body parts and engine were still present. It is my experience that persons who steal cars for their parts generally strip all of the major components off the car, leaving little more than the frame. This incident was not at all consistent with a professional auto thief but more consistent with a probable insurance-fraud scheme.

I drove to the fire scene and saw that it was on a vacant street between two large factories. I found a video camera a block away facing the scene, and I eventually retrieved a partial video of the event. The video shows the car being driven with its lights out onto the darkened street. A shaved-headed Hispanic gang member exited the car and then is seen pouring fluid over the top of the car from a gallon-size jug, which is then tossed into the car. The lone male stepped a few feet away from the car and ignited something in his hand. He was immediately engulfed in a ball of fire, and then a second later the car burst into flames.

The event was consistent with a "flash fire," which occurs when gasoline vapors explode. The male was seen putting himself out and then stumbling off camera. He was too far away to be recognized, but his physical description was an exact match for the gang member named Laughy. It should be noted that the direction that the arsonist stumbled off in was exactly the same direction as the nearby home of Laughy.

After I left the scene, I drove to the home of Laughy. He was standing in his front yard along with about ten Puente 13 gang members. As soon as I got out of my car, he recognized me as a detective and asked if he was going to be arrested. I assured him that I just wanted a statement from him. He told me the same story he had given the patrolmen and included the fact that he had already made an insurance claim for the "theft/arson" of his car. I was actually quite surprised to see a gang member who actually had insurance. I noted that he had obvious "flash burn" injuries to his face, his hands, and the side of his body. I was able to photograph the injuries and document them for my report.

At this time I believed I had enough information to arrest Laughy for arson and insurance fraud for burning his own car. However, I needed to confirm that he had actually made an insurance claim (which would complete the crime of insurance fraud) and also verify that the car was co owned by a lending company. I left the scene and Laughy seemed quite amazed that I didn't arrest him. He would think for a couple more weeks that he had gotten away with his crime.

I immediately called his insurance carrier and advised them of my suspicions. They in turn sent him a document to fill out and then took a recorded statement from him and another one from his alibi witness Stranger. In California, giving a false statement in support of a fraudulent claim is a separate felony. Each document or statement that Laughy and Stranger gave to the insurance carrier was one more charge against them.

A few weeks later I had built a strong case against both Laughy and Stranger. They lived close to each other and within just a couple blocks of the arson location. I believed that they had removed the seats and radio from the car before the fire to make it look like car thieves had done this. I wrote a search warrant for both of their homes, seeking evidence that they removed things from the car prior to burning it. In March I went with gang detectives and search teams to do a predawn raid on their homes. Both gang members were caught completely surprised and stunned, which was good for us. Both had stolen and loaded firearms within hand's reach when we burst through their doors. Luckily we overwhelmed them and took them into custody with no problems.

After some initial lies, Laughy became quite docile, especially after we found a stolen handgun and narcotics in his possession. By the end of the day he confessed on tape to having some mechanical issues with his car and wanting to get rid of it. He and his buddy stripped the seats and radio to make it look like car thieves had done this, and then he drove the car to the empty street. He then poured gasoline from a milk jug into and over the car, throwing the empty container into the car. He said that he stepped away from the car as he knew that gas was explosive, but as soon as he lit his lighter, he burst into flames. Laughy wasn't aware that flammable-liquid vapors pool up around your body when you are pouring the liquid. He then enlisted his homeboy Stranger to become an alibi witness for him.

An hour later Stranger confessed to the same story. Both males were jointly charged with arson and insurance fraud, along with several weapons laws. Stranger was storing a half-dozen illegal assault rifles in his home when we raided it and would get another year onto his sentence for that alone. Laughy eventually pled guilty and received a two-year prison sentence. Stranger pled guilty and only received a year in jail.

This case was typical of low-tech arson by young, unskilled arsonists, who lit the fire for the purpose of insurance fraud. Other than the odd twist of insurance fraud, this was a classic street-gang type of arson event. The gangsters learned their lesson about the explosive nature of gasoline vapors. I doubted they would do something that stupid again.

### I Was Right—They Did Learn from This

Almost two years later I was called by an old partner of mine named Pat Tapia, who was now working as a homicide detective.

He asked me to look at a vehicle that had been burned after it had been used in a murder. There were several "catches" with Det. Tapia's request. One was that the car was over sixty miles away in a tow yard in another county. The second was that the car had been burned almost three months ago and had been sitting in the tow yard ever since. The final catch was that the tow yard had been in a foothill area, and after some recent rains, the hillside had collapsed into the tow yard, covering many of the vehicles. I demanded a free lunch from the homicide detective and then drove out to assist him with this old case.

The vehicle in question had been used in a double murder/shooting by some gang members. During his homicide investigation, Det. Tapia learned from some snitches within the gang that the vehicle had been taken out of county and burned somewhere in a rural area to avoid being connected to the murders. This was truly a suspect who wanted to practice "anti-forensics and crime concealment." He had gone to great lengths to hide this vehicle from the LASD Homicide Detail. It had taken Tapia weeks of inquiring in several towns and cities before he located the burned vehicle.

When I got to the tow yard, I could see that the vehicle in question was a small pickup truck. Not only was it burned but it had now become half-full of mud and debris from the landslide. Besides that, the tow yard had the vehicle there for so long that they filled the bed and cab with salvaged parts from other vehicles. This would prove to be a serious evidence-contamination issue.

I spent nearly two hours removing the parts and debris from the pickup. When I finally shoveled out the last few shovels full of sand from the floor of the cab, I could smell a strong odor of gasoline. I cleared the rest of the sand/mud and found a striped beach towel on the floor of the truck that smelled very strongly of gasoline. The towel was intact, but its edges were burned and singed. Incredibly, after sitting in a tow yard for nearly three months, the gasoline evidence was still present. The mud and sand from the landslide, which had occurred a week or so after the vehicle was stored in the yard, had encased the evidence and had not allowed it to evaporate. The towel was sent to the sheriff's department's crime lab, and it was confirmed that it still had gasoline on it.

While Det. Tapia and I were eating the lunch I demanded of him, he told me about his case and that it involved some gang members from Puente 13 in the city of Industry. He said that he had information that several gang members had been involved in the murders and burning of the vehicle. He then told me that the name of the guy who was alleged to have burned the vehicle was known as Stranger, a.k.a. Mario Rincon. When he showed me Stranger's photo, I recognized him as the same guy who had assisted Laughy in the original arson a couple of years back.

In this case, he had obviously remembered how dangerous gasoline was when it was poured onto a vehicle. This time it appeared that he soaked the towel in gasoline and threw that into the vehicle in what he believed was a safer method of arson. This is an excellent example of how a suspect will modify or alter his MO after an accident or a mistake.

Armed with this information about Stranger, Det. Tapia later showed photos of the towel to Stranger and eventually elicited an admission to his involvement in disposing of the murder vehicle through arson. Stranger was stunned that the evidence survived the fire and had led back to him. This time he would get a few years in prison for his role in this fire.

*Investigators who worked these cases include Arson-Explosives detective Ed Nordskog; OSS gang investigator Steve Skahill, Ron Duvall, and Sgt. Louis Duran; and Homicide detective Sgt. Pat Tapia.*

## CLEANERS AND DYERS ASSOCIATION LOS ANGELES, CA, 1931–1938

Los Angeles in the early 1900s was fairly free of criminal gangs and so-called "Mafia" groups. The city had long touted itself, via the very conservative *Los Angeles Times* newspaper, as the last bastion of free, white, Protestant people, and the city and local police took a dim view of Catholics, Italians, Irish, Eastern Europeans, and blacks. Los Angeles in those days was also staunchly antiunion. The city would maintain its mostly white, mostly Protestant antiunion flavor until World War Two caused a massive transformation within just five years' time.

Despite the intolerant views of Los Angeles toward any east-coast influences, specifically organized-crime groups, certain entities began creeping into LA during the Great Depression. The Sunset Strip in present-day West Hollywood was the gambling, whoring, and drinking center of the West Coast. Organized gangsters began to slowly sneak into the city by the 1930s and grew quite powerful before they were stomped out by the LAPD in the late 1940s. These criminal groups inserted themselves into all sorts of businesses and attempted to turn them into moneymaking "rackets."

In 1931 an obscure but sinister "association" was created in the city that mirrored similar groups in Chicago. The association was created by a group of individuals with the goal of bringing all of the cleaning and dyeing companies in the city under their control. A 1939 grand jury investigating the Cleaners and Dyers Plant Owners Association found that the group had basically strong-armed independent mom-and-pop cleaners and dyers into joining their association. The tactics used by the organizers were described by the grand jury as "methods used in Chicago by racketeers."

The basic principle was as follows. The small shop owners were approached to join the association and were then forced to pay steep dues (a.k.a. extortion). The association would then fix prices at an exorbitant rate, and all members had to follow suit. If you didn't join the association or agree to raise your fees to the prescribed rate, you suffered the wrath of the association. The grand jury would find in 1939 that the association's officers did not partake personally in any specific acts of violence or vandalism but contracted these acts out to third-party hoodlums and thugs.

The tactics used by these hired thugs were fairly sophisticated and high tech for the day. One tactic involved the thugs entering the shops and introducing "stench bombs" into the clothing left by customers. These chemical devices were so strong that they ruined all the clothes that were in the shops at the time. A second, less sophisticated tactic was the use of acid on the windows of offending shops. Another tactic was to secrete vials of dye in clothes that were sent to the shops for cleaning. The dye vials would break during the cleaning process and ruin all of the clothing in the washers. Finally, the shop owners were subjected to physical beatings, and their windows were broken over and over again. This ongoing campaign of threats, beatings, and vandalism forced many of the mom-and-pop owners to succumb to the association.

Those shop owners who held out were treated with the ultimate form of vandalism. Hired "torches" were brought in to burn the businesses to the ground. The torches were obviously highly experienced in this sort of attack as they developed an incredibly sophisticated method of attack. The grand jury report noted that the association's thugs had learned how to make an **improvised hypergolic incendiary device** that surreptitiously caused a delayed fire.

One tactic employed by the paid torches was to conceal a substance called "metallic potassium" in clothing sent to the shop. The arsonists knew that the metallic potassium would react to the normal chemicals the shops used in the cleaning process and eventually burst into flames, ruining all the clothes in the vicinity and possibly destroying the shop as well. California investigators learned that this extremely unique tactic had been used by similar "associations" in the Chicago area. This was a learned behavior that was passed on to local hoodlums.

Staying with the theme of fire, the association leaders employed another unique tactic with the aid of a true scoundrel. By the late 1930s, Deputy Fire Marshal Frank D. Scovel, a former fire chief from San Bernardino, joined the conspiracy. While there is no evidence that Fire Marshal Scovel engaged in any of the arson attacks, he approached the independent shop owners from a different racket. He harassed and harangued the independent shop owners with multitudes of fire code violations that cost them large amounts of money. He declared many of the independents shops unsafe or forced them to purchase very expensive fire-protection systems that other shops within the association did not have.

This small, niche racket came to an end in 1937 when a night watchmen at one of the independent shops was murdered on the job. The grand jury investigating his death came upon the hundreds of vandalisms, beatings, and arson attacks that had been perpetrated for an eight-year period by what the District Attorney's Office called "imported Eastern muscle men" and "Chicago hoodlums." In 1939 the grand jury indicted fourteen men for their roles in this ongoing criminal enterprise. The indicted men included Alfred Lushing, who was a commissioner for the Los Angeles Water and Power Department, and Deputy Fire Marshal Frank Scovel.

After the indictments, deals would be made and influence would be exerted on city officials. The end result was that the only persons ever convicted for any of these acts were imported gangsters from Chicago. The actual heads of the association, along with Fire Marshal Scovel, escaped justice.

## MEXICAN MAFIA
## CARSON, CA, 2006

*This case was a combined effort from three major detective groups within the LASD Arson-Explosives Detail, OSS Street Gang Unit, and Narcotics Bureau.*

### Gang Background

This arson investigation is intertwined with ongoing street gang and narcotics investigations. To understand how to properly investigate a gang case of this nature, one needs to know the "lay of the land" in the street gang world of Los Angeles. Los Angeles is easily the street gang capital of the world and has hundreds of active street gangs with over one hundred thousand active members. I have been a detective in Los Angeles for over twenty-five years, and about 30 percent of all my cases involve a gang member or affiliate.

As a bit of background information into this lifestyle, I provide the following. The bulk of all street gang members in Los Angeles are either black or Hispanic. While there is a smattering of Asian and white groups operating as well, over 95 percent of the active street gangs are black or Hispanic. Gangs have their own internal codes and rules, and most gang members are quite racist. It is very rare to see gangsters who are not Hispanic involved in a Hispanic gang. Hispanic gangs are the main threat in Los Angeles, and over 70 percent of all gang members are from a Hispanic gang. There are numerous groups and subgroups within the Hispanic gangs, but all in Los Angeles have a relationship with a group called the Mexican Mafia. Eighty percent of Hispanic street gangs have loyalty to the Mexican Mafia, while about 20 percent are bitter enemies of the Mafia.

The Mexican Mafia is not a street gang but is, in fact, a prison gang. You cannot join it unless you are in prison. It is the most powerful, dangerous, and intimidating prison gang in the nation. Up until about twenty years ago, its influence stayed within the prison walls. However, at some point the Mexican Mafia expanded its influence out of the prison walls and soon began "controlling" the actions of many Hispanic street gangs. They did this by pure intimidation.

Since the Mexican Mafia controls every aspect of prison life, it sent word to the street that if you or your gang did not go along with the orders of the Mexican Mafia on the street, they would punish you the minute you got to jail or prison. Since all street gang members end up in jail or prison eventually, this was and still is a very viable threat. If you or your gang ran afoul of the Mexican Mafia for whatever reason, they put a "green light" on you or your gang. This green light was a mandate to all Hispanic gang members to beat, stab, strangle, anally rape, or kill you or someone from your gang the moment you were seen in a jail or prison. If a Hispanic gang member refused to commit this assault, then he and his gang would be added to the green light list. Since the Mexican Mafia was so dedicated to violence and intimidation, these orders were almost always carried out without hesitation.

Through these tactics, the Mexican Mafia expanded its influence onto the streets. In the past two decades they have proclaimed that they would act more like the Italian Mafia and collect "taxes" or protection money on the streets. If you were involved in an illegal activity like prostitution, drug dealing, or any other act that made money illegally, then the Mexican Mafia would send a "tax collector" around once a month to collect a fee or protection money. Usually the people who collect the taxes are recently released Mafia members who are extremely intimidating in appearance. They collect taxes ruthlessly and punish severely those people who do not or cannot pay. Occasionally, if there are no Mafia members in the area, a local street gang is tasked by the Mafia to collect taxes for them.

The Mexican Mafia is run by a "board," all of whom are locked up for life in some very secure modules in the prison system. Despite this, they are masters at getting orders and information out into the prison system and the streets. The Mexican Mafia is also known by the nicknames "Eme" (Spanish for *M*), or "the Black Hand." All Mafia members have a black handprint tattooed on their chests. Members of the board who make decisions go by the nicknames of "Big Homies." The mere mention of their names instills great fear into even hardened street gang members.

The case you are about to read was caused by a tax collection gone wrong and by some orders being sent down from state prison by the Big Homies. Every investigator in Los Angeles has a familiarity with street gangs, but when you work a case of this nature, you absolutely need an up-to-date street-gang investigator on your team as the gang culture evolves on a monthly basis.

### Tax Time

On November 20, 2006, at just before seven o'clock, shots rang out in a neighborhood in Carson, California. Neighbors summoned the police, and within minutes cars from the LASD's Carson Station arrived at the scene to find two male Hispanics lying in the street. The neighborhood was a clean, quiet middle-class street, which was not known for a lot of gang or narcotics activity. The home where this shooting occurred, at 432 East 229th Street, was clean, orderly, and undergoing an expensive remodel. It did not look like your typical "dope pad."

As both men on the ground were suffering from gunshot wounds, the deputies called fire paramedics. They also noted immediately that one of the victims appeared to be a heavily tattooed gang member. Both gunshot victims were transported to a local hospital, where eventually the heavily tattooed guy died.

LASD homicide sergeant Mike Rodriguez eventually took over the murder investigation. He arrived at the hospital and interviewed the victim with a gunshot wound to his leg. The victim, whose name was Walter Dominguez Llamas, said that two men came to his home and attempted to rob him. He said that they were gang members, and they had told him they were going to kill him if he didn't give them money. Llamas saw that the two gang members were carrying pistols, so he armed himself with a handgun and began shooting at the two gang members. Llamas said he shot both of them, but one of them had run away. Llamas said that one of the gangsters had shot him in the leg.

The homicide detectives noted that Llamas was very vague about the event and appeared to be hiding something. They checked with the local patrol officers and found that Llamas was a suspected midlevel drug dealer. Based on this, they believed that they were looking at a possible drug deal gone bad or even a gang "tax" on the local drug dealer. The homicide detectives spoke to the local gang investigators, who quickly identified the deceased male as a Mexican Mafia enforcer named "Tonito." Through snitches on the street, the gang detectives confirmed that Tonito had been at that home that evening to tax Llamas, who was a Mexican drug dealer. Tonito had been with a local gang member named "Gangster," who at thirty-six was one of the older members of the local gang called "Carson 13."

**Author's note:** It should be explained here that in California, drug dealers from Mexico are generally not affiliated with Hispanic street gangs and pay no heed to the rules and customs of the Hispanic-American gang culture. In this case, the victim (Llamas), engaged in the hyper violent world of Mexican Cartel drug dealing, was not about to be taxed by local hoodlums from a neighborhood street gang. This is why you need gang and narcotics experts to help you sort out who's who in these types of cases.

## The Arsons

Five days after this shooting, on November 25, a neighbor awoke to smell gasoline coming from Llamas's home. The neighbor noted that Llamas's driveway was burned and discolored from a fire and that the garage door was also burned. The fire had apparently put itself out.

LASD arson investigators Joe Guarino and Mike Cofield arrived and processed the scene. They eventually found that a significant amount of gasoline was poured or sprayed over the garage door and then set afire. There were numerous visible suspect footprints at the scene in the dirt portions of the driveway. The detectives noted that the occupants of the home were not home at this time. Cofield, one of the most experienced members of the arson squad, believed that this resembled a gang event in that it was crude, low tech, and had done very little structural damage. The arson investigators believed that this case was related to the earlier shooting, so they forwarded their reports to the Homicide Squad. They learned from the homicide investigator that the Llamas family had fled the area after the shooting in fear of additional gang attacks.

Five days later, the next-door neighbors found a Molotov cocktail device sitting in their driveway. Arson investigators responded and noted that this house was directly next to the Llamases' home. The device was a beer bottle filled with gasoline and had a cloth wick protruding from the neck. It had not been thrown and was just sitting upright as if someone was going to use it and had abandoned it there. It was collected for forensic evidence. Investigators would later learn that this device was indeed part of a second attack at the home, but the attackers had been scared off prior to lighting it.

Later that same day, another neighbor found two brand-new plastic gas cans half-full of gasoline, sitting next to the Llamases' home. It was believed that these two items were also part of the aborted Molotov cocktail attack.

Two weeks later, at three in the morning, on December 18, neighbors reported a fire at the empty Llamases' home. The arson detectives again responded and found that like the first attack, the fire was set from the outside of the home. They determined that someone had poured gasoline through a vent in the rear yard of the home. This fire caused fairly minimal damage to the structure, and again the attackers left good quality footprints and a container.

This time a scorched thirty-two-ounce beer bottle was found at the scene. The arson investigators speculated that someone had thrown the device against the building, and it had failed to break. The suspects then had walked up to the device and poured the contents of it into the open vent at the rear of the home. The bulk of the fire was outside of the home and did very little damage to the stucco and metal frame of the home. However, enough penetrated into the walls of the home that the repairs would cost nearly $30,000. This was a failed Molotov cocktail attack—again a hallmark of gang-related arson activity.

After these four arson events, arson detective Mike Cofield called the homicide guys and told them that whoever was doing this was deadly serious about wanting to burn the home down and would likely try it again. The homicide guys said that they were monitoring the local Carson 13 gang members for information about these attacks. Part of the investigative process of gangs is to keep tabs on gang members who are in jail or prison, as they seldom stop being involved in gang activities. In this case, homicide sergeant Rodriguez had now identified the gang member named Gangster as the second suspect who had attempted to rob and shoot Jose Llamas on November 20. Gangster was in jail as a suspect in that shooting, and the homicide guys were monitoring his phone calls.

Gang members, while quite clever sometimes, have never been known for their brains. When they speak on jail phones, the first thing that happens when they pick up the phone is that a recording comes on advising them that their phone calls are being monitored. This message repeats about every seven minutes during jail phone calls. Despite these admonitions, a large number of inmates, gang members in particular, continue to discuss illegal activities, much to the delight of investigators, who later get a recording of these conversations.

On January 18, 2007, Gangster from Carson 13 was locked up in jail for his role in the shooting that occurred at the Llamases' home on November 20, 2006. Despite all of the recorded admonitions, Gangster, who was talking to his brother and fellow Carson 13 gang member, Jokey, said some really stupid things on the recorded phone line. He told his brother that Eme (Mexican Mafia) had ordered his gang (Carson 13) to burn down the Llamases' home in retaliation for their tax collector (Tonito) being killed by Llamas. The Eme Big Homies were not at all happy that Carson 13 had failed to complete this task in four prior attempts. Eme had sent word through the jail-prison pipeline that every member of Carson 13 would be green lighted if this task was not completed soon.

Even the hard-core, longtime gang-member brothers Gangster and Jokie were terrified of Eme and put out the word to all Carson 13 members to get the job done. If they failed in this task, their gang would be attacked by every Hispanic gang in Los Angeles on the order of Eme. In one detailed phone call, Gangster had defined a major criminal conspiracy and had confessed to his gang's role in an extortion attempt, shooting, and four arson attacks. Because of administrative and technical issues, the homicide detectives would not be able to download and hear this conversation for several days. In the meantime, an additional attack occurred.

The Carson 13 gang took this implied threat seriously, and just two days after that phone conversation, the Llamases' home was attacked again. This time they put a little time and effort into it. At just past midnight, on January 20, neighbors saw a large fire erupt from within the vacant Llamases' home. Two male Hispanic gang members were observed running from the scene. When arson investigators arrived, they found a large crowbar outside of the home and the front and rear doors pried open. They found flammable-liquid pour patterns in several areas of the empty home. A two-gallon red plastic gas can was found lying in the yard. This item was new and unburned. This time the fire damage was fairly heavy and had caused the attic and roof to become involved and eventually collapse.

This fifth arson event had finally given the gang exactly what it wanted—the destruction of the property. Eme should be pleased with the results of this fire.

### Jasmine

Two days after this fire, two LASD deputies saw a suspicious carful of gang members in East Los Angeles (twenty miles from Carson). The car was stopped, and immediately the driver ran off, leaving a male and female passenger to be arrested. The deputies learned that the car was stolen and later determined that the guy who had run off was a Carson 13 gang member known as "Clown." The female in the car was named Jasmine, and she admitted to being the girlfriend of Clown. The car was filled with evidence, and the deputies located a handgun, narcotics, burglary tools, and stolen cell phones. When the deputies searched the trunk, they smelled the overwhelming odor of gasoline. Twenty-six-year-old Jasmine was arrested for being in possession of the gun and stolen items, as well as the stolen car.

The LASD possesses a special unit called Operation Safe Streets (OSS). This investigative unit is the oldest full-time street-gang investigation unit in the United States. All of its detectives are longtime experts on the street gangs in their areas and keep an ongoing intelligence database of what is going on within each active street gang. OSS records are extremely detailed as their specialists personally interview every gang member or gang associate that gets brought into jail. OSS investigators know the families and histories of the gangs even better than many of the gang members themselves.

In this case, Deputy Ernie Valdez spoke at length with Jasmine as he was curious about what Carson 13 gang members were doing way out of their area in East Los Angeles. Dep. Valdez was quite effective as he got Jasmine to talk about a recent arson attack she was involved in.

Jasmine admitted that she had been the "getaway driver" on an arson attempt at a home in Carson on January 19, 2007. She said that she was partying with some Carson 13 gang members when several of them said they were given a "mission" to burn a home. They mentioned that the orders came from the Big Homies in state prison, which she knew to be the Mafia (Eme). Jasmine was given money and sent to a Kmart to purchase two plastic gas cans. She then filled them at a gas station. One of the gang members had stolen a car, and the gas cans were placed in the trunk of the car.

On the night of Thursday, January 18, she drove the car, along with three Carson 13 gang members, Moreno, Droopy, and Lil Man. They drove to the house to be burned but abandoned their plan as they had seen a couple of sheriff's department's cars patrolling the neighborhood. They all went home and agreed to meet again the next night. The same group met at midnight the next day, and this time Jasmine dropped the three gang members off near the house to be burned. They left carrying the two gas cans and a crow bar and returned without them several minutes later. She said that they told her that they had successfully burned the home.

### Moreno

On March 7, OSS gang investigators had located and arrested Carson 13 gang member Moreno on a different charge. He was subsequently interviewed by the gang and arson investigators. During his interview he admitted to being ordered to purchase supplies for one of the arson attacks on the Llamases' home. He said that about a week after the killing of the Eme tax collector, he was called by Gangster, who told him to purchase gasoline, paint thinner, and two Super Soaker squirt guns so that another gang member named "Trooper" could use them to burn the Llamases' home. Moreno, using two young females as his purchasers, went to a local Kmart and purchased the needed items with cash. Later that night he turned them over to fellow gang member Trooper.

### Trooper

All of this information was relayed to the OSS gang investigators in the Carson area, and Det. Luis Trejo began a coordinated investigation into this incident, which would eventually include the Homicide Detail and the Arson-Explosives Detail. Trejo already had some good informants (snitches) within the Carson 13 neighborhood. He knew that some of the older members, like Gangster and his brother Jokey, were helping to do collection of taxes for Eme. He also knew that the pair had ordered that a younger gang member be beaten for failing to shoot someone who refused to pay his taxes.

Det. Trejo, a true expert with the local gang, had cultivated his informants by being a good detective and listening to the people within the neighborhood. One person, the mother of a gang member named Trooper, had called Det. Trejo a few weeks after the first fire and had told him that several of the older gang members had viciously beat her son, Trooper, for failing to carry out a gang mission. She came to the detective for help as her son was on the run from the rest of his gang. Det. Trejo met with Trooper and convinced him to come clean and speak to the arson investigators. By early March, Det. Trejo and arson detectives sat down and interviewed Trooper at a clandestine meeting spot. Trooper admitted that he was an active Carson 13 gang member and had fallen out of favor with the gang after he refused to shoot someone who wasn't paying his taxes.

Shortly after this, the shooting at the Llamases' home occurred, and Carson 13 was ordered to burn the home by orders of some Big Homies from Eme. Gangster ordered Trooper to torch the home as a way to make up for his earlier refusal to shoot someone. On the night of November 25, Trooper went to the Llamases' home with another gang member, Moreno. The two took a plastic gas can, poured the gas on the garage door, and then threw a burning sock into the pool of gasoline. They saw a large fire start and ran from the scene. They were surprised the next day when there was so little damage.

Gangster summoned Trooper, and Trooper told him he had screwed up the job. Gangster then ordered him to burn the home again. The second attack was just a few days later when Trooper and another gang member named "Cartoon" carried a Molotov cocktail to the home. They set it down and then entered the yard to break a window so they could throw it inside. They began making so much noise that they thought they heard neighbors, so the two fled the scene, leaving the intact Molotov next to the location. The investigators noted that this admission by Trooper matched exactly the physical evidence they had found at the scene following the arson attacks of November 25 and November 30. Trooper's shoes were examined and matched the tracks left at the burned home. He was later arrested and charged for both of the arson attacks, along with conspiracy to commit a crime.

Trooper then told investigators that after the failed attacks on the home, Gangster and Jokey beat him severely. They advised him that Eme was going to green light him and the gang and that he was soon going to die. From that day forward, Trooper had been on the run.

Eventually the gang and arson investigators would interview and "break" several additional Carson 13 gang members, who all admitted (at least partially) to some degree of participation in four different arson attacks at the Llamases' home. The one consistency that came from all of the gang members was that these attacks were ordered from state prison by Eme and that the older members of the gang, Gangster and his brother Jokey, were adamant that these attacks be carried out.

The admissions also cleared up why some evidence was left at the various scenes, where the materials used in the attack were purchased, and exactly how many stolen vehicles were used by the various gang members. This investigation would clear up four auto thefts, a couple more shootings, and all four of the arson and firebombing attacks.

In total, seven Carson 13 gang members would be arrested and prosecuted for conspiracy to commit arson, use of an incendiary device, use of an illegal weapon (Molotov cocktail) to further gang activity, and three different counts of burglary and arson. All seven were looking at potential sentences of twelve to twenty years in state prison. Besides that, at least six more gang associates were identified and charged with conspiracy, theft, car theft, and ex-felons carrying firearms.

The list of nicknames of Carson 13 gang members who were eventually arrested and charged for their roles in this ongoing conspiracy is practically comical. The nicknames Trooper, Moreno, Yogi, Droopy, Lil Man, Jokey, Clown, Speedie, Cubbie,

Conejo, Blackie, Cartoon, Spider, Boxer, and Gangster sound more like Looney Tunes characters or the Seven Dwarfs than treacherous, vicious street-gang members.

This case sent a total of thirteen members of the Carson 13 gang back to jail or prison. All eventually ended up pleading guilty to their roles in this far-ranging conspiracy, and the seven members directly involved in the burning of the Llamases' home received plea-bargained sentences ranging from seven years to sixteen years, depending on their criminal history and level of cooperation.

Street gang cases are similar to biker club cases and even other extremist groups like the Animal Liberation Front. There are always a small percentage of hard-core members who are dedicated and ruthless. They will seldom talk or cooperate with police. However, in even the most hard-core gangs or groups, the majority of members or associates do not share that great dedication to the gang as the hard-core members. Law enforcement knows this and frequently finds that many of these less dedicated members are more than happy to talk their way out of lengthy prison sentences by giving up other members of the gang. So is the case with this group of knuckleheads from Carson 13.

Eventually, all but two members of the group cooperated with law enforcement. When one of the gang's senior members, Jokey, found out how many of his gang had snitched or cooperated, he told investigators that he "was embarrassed to be a member" of this gang. This case is an excellent example of a coordinated investigative effort by homicide, arson, and street gang investigators. This is exactly how to expose and dismantle a gang-related conspiracy.

*The following people were involved in this lengthy, complicated investigation: arson detective Mike Cofield, Det. Jim Gonzales, Sgt. Joe Guarino, homicide sergeant Mike Rodriguez,*

*OSS gang detective Luis Trejo, Dep. Ernie Valdez, and Senior Criminalist Steve Phillips.*

### Investigator's Profile

This case was an easily defined case from the very beginning. It was clearly a gang-related set of arson attacks. Gang attacks have many common denominators. The most common is that the target is either another gang member or someone who has run afoul of the local gang. In this case the victim was refusing to pay his "taxes" and in fact embarrassed the local gang by killing a "tax collector." By the code of gang culture, the victim had to pay in a very visible manner. Other commonalities in gang-related arson attacks include the frequent use of firebombs or Molotov cocktails, the poor results of their fire setting, and the use of female acquaintances to purchase materials, act as lookouts, and drive the getaway vehicles. One classic indicator that was missing at this event was the presence of gang graffiti.

All gang-related attacks are usually done by more than one person, and therein lies the means with which to catch them. Gang members tend to be young, impulsive, and very poor planners. They often brag about their exploits, and very soon the local cops know exactly who pulled off a recent caper. In this case, the local gang investigators knew very shortly who was committing the arsons and for what reason. The rest of the investigation involved simply exploiting the gang members' own lifestyles and habits to use against them. Investigators quickly determined who the weak links in the gang were, arrested them, and got them to admit their actions and the actions of their fellow gang members. The investigators then took these admissions, validated them by visiting gas stations and stores where materials were purchased, and compared all of this with the evidence at the arson scenes.

Other unique investigative techniques in this case were the exploitation of jail/prison phone calls, the exploitation of cell phones used by the group, and the forensics collected via DNA and footprints. All of these techniques led investigators to approach specific members of the gang with hard, physical evidence against them.

## VENTURA HELLS ANGELS
## VENTURA, CA, 2011

Ventura, California, is a casual beach town just thirty miles up the coast from Los Angeles. The town is the last affordable beach town in Southern California (other than that cesspool-by-the-sea Oxnard) and enjoys cooler weather, great surfing, and a likable, small-town atmosphere.

In the 1970s, the Hells Angels motorcycle club opened up a Ventura chapter. Its first president was a longtime Angel named George Christie. Christie was a former US Marine and Vietnam-era veteran. He was also smart, well spoken, physically fit, charismatic, and ambitious. By the mid-1990s, the small club had tripled in size to about twenty full-time members. The Hells Angels kept an open presence in Ventura since that time but never became a large problem to the locals and maintained a fairly low profile with law enforcement.

Meanwhile, George Christie expanded his own legitimate businesses and opened a successful martial arts studio and later a tattoo shop called The Ink House, in downtown on Main Street. The Ventura Hells Angels continued to keep a low profile in town until about the mid to late 2000s. By then there were rumors that the Angels were becoming somewhat influential with the flourishing shady business of Asian massage parlors. Asian massage parlors in California are barely disguised fronts for prostitution.

In the late 1990s and early 2000s, law-enforcement intelligence operatives had learned that nationwide, biker clubs were reeling from the enforcement activities of many different layers of law enforcement as it attacked the sellers of hard narcotics such as cocaine and methamphetamines. Every state had narcotics task forces at the local, state, and federal levels, whose main targets were groups distributing cocaine and methamphetamines. Rumors abounded that the Hells Angels at a national level had been trying to get out of the methamphetamines trafficking business to return to making money at more traditional vice-related activities such as strip clubs, bars, tattoo shops, and prostitution. By the mid-2000s, local authorities were investigating rumors that the Hells Angels was taking "soft extortion" money from the owners of the many Asian massage parlors springing up all over Ventura County.

From its start in Ventura in the 1970s until the later 2000s, the Ventura Chapter of the Hells Angels continued to be run by its influential and popular leader, George Christie. In 2007, Christie had a bit of a personal problem that would later unseat him as the chapter president. The increasing popularity of tattoos with average citizens was growing so fast that parlors were springing up everywhere. In particular, two new tattoo shops opened up in the small town of Ventura. These would be in direct competition to George Christie's own shop.

Shortly after they were opened, the owners of each shop received visitors in the form of a couple of burly bikers, who casually mentioned to them that this was a town controlled by Hells Angels, and that as such, they (the tattoo shops) would be well advised to pay some sort of unofficial licensing fee to the Angels in order to do business in town. While the bikers were not wearing official Hells Angels "cuts" (patched vests or jackets), it was very clear to the tattoo shop owners that they were being extorted. They also knew that the Ventura chapter was not that large and that everything done by the chapter had to be sanctioned by its powerful president, George

Christie, who just happened to own a competing tattoo parlor downtown.

Apparently this extortion attempt or implied threat was not heeded by either shop owner. On the night of July 6, 2007, both new tattoo shops in Ventura were firebombed at nearly the same time. Molotov cocktails were hurled through the fronts of the small businesses, causing medium-sized fires that did significant damage to each shop. Several times after these fires, the shop owners were reminded again that they needed to pay a "fee" in order to do business in this town.

It seemed as if there were no leads in these two fire bombings, and local authorities were unable to pin anyone with these crimes, although it was always suspected that George Christie and his Hells Angels had some involvement.

Years went by, and the arson cases seemed to fade away. However, there was more than one way to skin a cat. While no one was talking about the arson cases, other investigations were occurring around the Ventura Hells Angels. Quietly, local narcotics agents from the Ventura Police and Sheriff's Departments, along with some DEA narcs, built a case on some local bikers. They then compromised those bikers and hung some serious narcotics offenses over their heads. By doing this, the bikers had to give up some info that was good enough to get them out of their serious narcotics crimes.

In this case, the feds had long wanted to put some sort of criminal case on George Christie. Christie was something of a local folk hero and had made national headlines more than once by running with the Olympic Torch, suing the Special Olympics, and a decade earlier beating a solicitation-to-commit-murder rap. He was too smart to openly commit crimes himself, but he was suspected to have orchestrated several criminal acts. Christie was a thorn in the side of the federal prosecutors.

The feds were licking their chops to put a case on a high profile biker like Christie, so they used these narcotics informants to expose the long-unsolved arson attacks. Eventually, through the use of informants and "wires," the feds built a conspiracy case against George Christie and three of his Ventura Chapter Hells Angels. On August 11, 2011, FBI agents raided several locations associated with the Ventura Hells Angels and released a detailed press statement about the arrests of George Christie and other Angels. The statement indicated that all four men were facing up to 120 years in federal prison for their roles in the extortions and arsons of the two tattoo parlors four years earlier.

Christie countered with some bold, in-your-face defense tactics and gave many statements to the media. First, he said he had resigned from the Hells Angels months before this and had not been an active member for some time. His contention was that the FBI had yet again entrapped him with illegal tactics. He complained of ongoing harassment of biker clubs across the United States by the federal government and, surprisingly, enlisted the support of mortal enemies, who were the leaders of the Mongols and Bandidos clubs. Both clubs were bitter, deadly rivals of the Hells Angels, but both, through their past presidents, agreed to testify for George Christie in his fight against the US Attorney's Office.

There must have been some serious flaws in the federal case as just a couple of years later it was settled, with George Christie admitting guilt for the crime of arson but receiving just ten months in federal prison instead of the 120 years he was said to be facing. Today George Christie has a television program dedicated to chronicling his life adventures in the Hells Angels. He is more famous, wealthier, and considered more of a hero, rebel, and celebrity than he ever was when he was an active member.

**Author's note:** In 1998 I was attending a high-level detectives' intelligence school when a speaker from the ATF told over three hundred attendees that the Hells Angels had long-used arson/firebombing as one of its favored intimidation tools. The agent advised that one chapter, in an attempt to launder hundreds of thousands of dollars in money made through the sales of meth, purchased a small fleet of catering trucks in the San Francisco area. The lawyers for the Angels kept advising them to launder drug proceeds through these forms of legitimate businesses like the catering trucks and carnivals.

Eventually the catering trucks were making a large amount of money legitimately, and the Angels kept purchasing more and more mom-and-pop catering businesses. When one or two of these small companies refused to sell their business to the Hells Angels, a fire usually broke out in the companies' truck yards, destroying all of their assets. In this way, according to the ATF expert, the Hells Angels was able to gain a monopoly over a niche business. It doesn't appear that there were any arrests or indictments for these attacks.

### Investigator's Profile

This case was included as it was a classic version of an OC arson attack for the purpose of intimidation or extortion. The targets of the attack were vice-related targets and were visited on more than one occasion by the bikers before the actual firebombings. The attacks were carried out in a very open and intimidating fashion with a weapon (Molotov cocktail) that, while crude and not very reliable, is an awesome way for instilling fear. The attackers have little concern if their attack is successful or not as the fear it instills is usually good enough to get their point across.

In this short chapter there are significant differences between traditional Italian Mafia-type organizations and biker clubs as opposed to street gangs. While the Mafia and bikers have a hierarchy and established chain of command, street gangs are without rank, structure, or actual leaders. It is much easier to exploit and arrest street gang members as their actions are usually rash and not well planned out. Street gang members tend to be younger, more impulsive, immature, and less disciplined. Italian Mafia and biker groups tend to have a strong rank structure, in-depth planning, and the use of tried and true tactics. They also are a bit older and more experienced, and many have military training. All of these groups are exploited by law enforcement through good intelligence, the use of informants, and the identification and separation of the members who are less disciplined, less dedicated, and easiest to "flip" or turn into snitches (informants).

# 5

# Female Arsonists

## The Profile

Fire setting and arson activity by women has long been considered an extreme rarity in the arson-investigation field. Many old-time arson investigators pay minimal lip service to the issue of female arsonists. In my early years of training, I was told by a large number of older investigators that they had never seen a female arsonist or that they were extremely rare.

Over the years that myth has been dispelled, as well as many other myths in the arson world. Female arsonists set fires every day in this country for mostly the same reasons that male offenders set fires. Female arsonists are very much in the minority, but they still set roughly 10 percent of all arson fires. The problem with many female-set fires is that because of attitudes in the fire-suppression/investigation field toward women, many of their criminal fires are actually not recognized as criminal events. The overly macho world of firefighting/investigation is mostly filled with men who often do not believe that women would purposely set a fire.

There have been very few true studies of female arsonists, and most of the clinical research has been conducted on very small samples, usually of females who are incarcerated or in a mental-health facility. Other major studies of arsonists make just brief mention of female fire setters. Despite that, I have read enough studies and case histories, along with my own investigations, to notice several traits among female arsonists. In 2004, a team of Japanese researchers conducted an intense and detailed study of eighty-three convicted female Japanese serial arsonists. Despite the large differences between the American and Japanese cultures, the study's results are in keeping with many of my own observations of female American serial arsonists.

Female arson activity, like all other types, can generally be broken down into two main subgroups. The subgroups are classified as **emotionally based fire setting** and **goal-directed fire setting**.

As a review, **emotionally based fire setting** is that type of fire-setting activity that has no apparent motive, such as a serial arsonist. Females that commit emotionally based fire setting often have somewhat similar traits. These traits include the following:

- History of self-harm or suicidal thoughts, threats, or attempts
- History of institutionalization
- History of use/abuse of prescription medication
- History of drug/alcohol abuse
- History of documented mental-health issues
- History as victim of sexual, emotional, or physical abuse

Emotionally based female arson events have several interesting traits and "profiles." While the following are generalities, they seem to hold true a majority of the time. Consistent traits of female-set arsons include the following:

- Fires set within their home or very close to their home (less than one hundred meters).
- Fires set at their work site (if they work).

- Fires set during daylight hours (not all, but more than men).
- Fires set in the presence of their children.
- Fires set that harm them or their children (Munchausen syndrome or Munchausen by proxy).
- Past deaths of their children: sudden infant death syndrome (SIDS), drowning, poisoning, et cetera.
- Past "accidental" fires in their home or family.
- History of frequently moving residences.
- Age tends to be older than other types of arsonists (average age in late thirties).
- Criminal history of fires, thefts, and vandalism.
- Women arsonists/serial arsonists tend to have larger or more masculine features.

**Goal-directed female-set fires** are similar to males. They are set for revenge, crime concealment, extremism, and fraud. Characteristics of this type of female-set fires include the following:

- Fires targeting clothing or beds
- Fires targeting vehicles
- Fires targeting other females
- May have used a "proxy" fire setter (a male acquaintance to set the fire for her)
- History of multiple insurance claims
- History of criminal threats, assaults, and vandalism

Common traits of all types of female fire setters include the following:

- Unsophisticated ignition scenario
- Target their own (or family) property (more often than men)

- Seldom use an incendiary device or accelerants
- Seldom set wild-land fires
- Contentious relations with own family, neighbors, and school officials
- Overly litigious in nature
- Married or had been married at least once

Women involved in serial arson activity are found often in an older age group than males. It is not unusual for a female serial arsonist to be in a late thirties to sixties age groups.

### Analyzing the Female Arsonist

Arson scenes where a female is a possible suspect should be handled no differently than any other investigation. However, the investigator, based on some of the common traits listed above, may discreetly ask more questions of children, neighbors, school officials, and family members to learn a bit about the history of the home, family, and potential suspects. Use caution when considering these general traits as most normal people may have one or two of these. The presence of one or two traits or factors does not automatically mean the suspect is guilty. Arson investigation is a detailed and complex endeavor that takes into account a large number of factors along with evidence and witness statements. Never rely on a single factor to make your case.

## THE GHOST
## ALEXANDRIA, VA, 2013–2014

*This case history comes from the case files of the Alexandria (Virginia) Fire Marshal's Office and from personal interviews with the lead investigators.*

Starting in May of 2013, several small "nuisance" fires began occurring in a large apartment building in the city of Alexandria,

Virginia. The building, known as the Stratford Building, was part of a large residential complex known as Southern Towers. The Stratford Building had sixteen floors and housed over 1,500 tenants, including numerous young children, babies, and the elderly. The structure was built in the 1960s as part of a five-building complex. The occupants at that time were mainly upper-middle-class white families.

Over the years the complex had degraded a bit but was still in fairly good condition. The tenants had become more middle income, and there had been a significant change in the social and ethnic makeup of the occupants. By 2013 there had been an influx of Asian and West African tenants. The building was clean and livable but was a bit dated in amenities. There was no sprinkler system, no security cameras, and only a manual fire alarm. Any sort of significant fire in a building housing so many people could have catastrophic results.

### The Fires

On May 22, 2013, an unknown suspect had placed a newspaper on the carpeted hallway on the third floor of the building. The newspaper was ignited with an open flame and left burning. The damage was minimal, but this occurred around ten o'clock in the evening when many tenants were sleeping. Two nights later, on May 23, an identical fire occurred near midnight, with similar results.

On June 12, 2013, an arsonist set fire to a pile of newspapers in the middle of the hallway on the fifth floor. The time of this attack varied quite a bit as it was set at three thirty in the afternoon. Up until this point, these fires had been viewed as probable vandalism events by teens. Fire investigators arrived and documented the small scene. In the main lobby they found that someone had written a message on a flyer that had been posted to the walls. The flyer was posted by building management advising tenants to bring in items off their balconies during inclement weather. Someone had scrawled across the flyer: "Screw you and your constant harassment!" This note may have struck at the reason for all these nuisance fires.

### The Spree

Just a week later, on June 19, the arsonist dramatically increased the tempo of the attacks. In the evening around seven thirty, the unknown suspect set fire to a pile of newspapers that had been placed onto the concrete floor of the fourth-floor stairwell. This fire caused very little damage. Fire investigators responded to the scene, and by the time they arrived a second fire occurred on the seventh floor in the middle of the hallway. Again, newspapers were set on fire, and again the damage was minimal.

During that same night, the arsonist set fire to a small flyer that was posted to a combustible wall on the fifth floor. This flyer burned but did very little damage to the wall. The fire marshals walked through the building and found similar flyers burned in the hallways of the eleventh and twelfth floors. While investigators were in the building, a fifth fire occurred in the trash room on the seventh floor. Again someone had ignited a newspaper that had been placed on the floor. This floor was made of linoleum tiles, but the fire did not do significant damage.

The arson investigators who responded that night were ATF special agent Chad Campanell and Assistant Fire Marshal (AFM) Andrea Buchanan. AFM Buchanan of the Alexandria Fire Department/Fire Marshal's Office, in Virginia, would assume the role of lead investigator for this emerging case. She was well suited for this role as she had spent thirty-seven years as a law enforcement officer prior to joining the Fire Marshal's Office. The two investigators realized that they were in the middle of an active arson spree, so they set up an ad hoc surveillance operation within the building. Since at least two of the fires had been set on the seventh floor, they stationed SA Campanell in that location.

At just before one in the morning that night, SA Campanell saw an elderly white female exit her apartment on the seventh floor. She walked immediately to the elevator and took it to an upper floor. Within five minutes of the woman being out of view, a fire was noticed on the tenth floor. This was the sixth fire in the building that night, and it was again set on a flyer posted on a wall of the hallway.

Five minutes later, the elderly woman was seen returning to her seventh-floor apartment. She looked visibly shaken and was being assisted by a security officer for the building. The arson investigators would later identify the woman as seventy-four-year-old Shirley Vigneau, a longtime tenant of apartment 717. They learned that another tenant had found Vigneau on the tenth floor just staring at the small fire that was burning on the wall. The other tenant put out the small fire and then escorted the elderly lady down to the security office in the lobby so they could report the fire. The tenant noted that once down in the main lobby, Vigneau refused to approach the security desk.

Noting that there had been two fires this evening on the seventh floor and that Vigneau had been witnessed at a fire scene on the tenth floor, the arson investigators deemed her to be a potential suspect in this spree of six fires. AFM Buchanan and SA Campanell contacted Shirley Vigneau in her apartment and conducted an interview of her.

Vigneau told them that she had been a resident of this building since 1978 and lived alone. She had no relatives nearby. She was a retired secretary and had been married in the distant past, but her husband was deceased. She said she has a lot of trouble sleeping at night and frequently just walks the hallways of the large building in the nighttime hours. Vigneau told investigators that she had seen the flyer on the wall burning during one of her nighttime walks. She said that earlier this same evening, she entered the trash room on the seventh floor and saw a small fire burning but had not reported the incident. Instead she just returned to her apartment because she was having trouble breathing due to the smoke.

Vigneau told the investigators that she did not smoke and did not keep matches or candles around. She did admit that she keeps a cigarette lighter with her. During an interview several months later, she changed her story and admitted to smoking Kent cigarettes. She seemed very reluctant to admit that she was a smoker. Vigneau told them she was aware of the fires in the building but had no idea who may be setting them. The investigators concluded their interview shortly after one in the morning.

Shortly after the interview, SA Campanell remained in the seventh floor hallway to monitor any other suspicious activity. At one forty-five, he saw Vigneau exit her apartment once again and enter the hallway. She took a couple of steps and looked toward the hidden SA Campanell and then abruptly turned around and reentered her own apartment. The investigators found her behavior extremely suspicious. They immediately suspected that this elderly woman might be the serial arsonist.

The night of fire activity produced several very small fires, spread through multiple floors. None of the fires did much damage, and the fires were not regarded as major events by the fire department's brass. AFM Buchanan thought otherwise. Unlike some of her bosses and colleagues, she viewed these "nuisance" fires in a different light. She believed that these may be the beginning fires of a serial arsonist. AFM Buchanan had taken enough classes on serial arsonists to understand that most of them start with small, seemingly inconsequential fires that do little or no damage. She was aware that while many serial arsonists will continue to light small fires most of their lives, a small number of them will actually graduate to increasingly larger and more dangerous fires. AFM Buchanan and SA Campanell started this investigation with that mind-set and began to build a detailed case file around these events.

The two investigators began asking questions about Shirley Vigneau. She was truly an enigma as she appeared to hide in plain sight. She had been a tenant for close to forty years, but no one seemed to know her or be friends with her. Several people commented that she was like a "ghost" as she was slight, gray, and just quietly wandered the halls at all hours of the night. She had a very minor criminal history with a past arrest for shoplifting. Both Buchanan and Campanell found her to be a very suspicious individual and not at all similar to the standard profile of a serial arsonist.

Like so many other fire administrators across the country (and the world), AFM Buchanan's bosses were not impressed by these small fires and were not inclined to devout more than a token amount of resources to the problem. Fire chiefs for eons have erroneously equated small fires as nuisances and large fires with serious offenders, when the size of the fire event has almost no correlation to the danger level and seriousness of the offender. This case brings out the point very dramatically. These fires, while small in scope, were set in the middle of the night (after midnight) in a building filled with hundreds of people. The reckless nature of this act alone makes these fires very dangerous. Most serial arsonists do not set fires in structures, and even fewer set them in occupied structures. The danger level for this offender was very high, yet fire bosses were refusing to acknowledge it.

The very first night that Buchanan and her partners were on scene interviewing witnesses, other fires broke out, including one within fifty feet of where she was speaking to a witness. The arsonist was bold, brazen, and ballsy…or nuts. AFM Buchanan began a serious approach to this offender by contacting the local ATF field office and requesting assistance. Part of that assistance was to get cameras loaned to the case that could be secretly installed in likely areas within the large complex.

While the bosses wouldn't let AFM Buchanan waste time and money on conducting surveillances, she continued to build her case in other ways. AFM Buchanan went so far as to get herself an apartment within the same building. She would conduct her own surveillances while residing within one of the apartments. Over the next few months several more small fires broke out with most of them causing very little damage. AFM Buchanan and SA Campanell approached each fire as a new and separate event and documented each scene and interviewed all witnesses. The investigators began to develop a time line and location map so she could track temporal and spatial patterns. Most of the fires occurred at night and involved trash and other available combustible materials within the hallways of the building. Still, the police and fire department administrators refused to dedicate any more personnel to this growing problem.

With the assistance of the local ATF office, the investigators gathered up enough information for the profilers at the ATF to look at. While the profilers weren't much help in this particular case, it is always a great idea to have a profiler look at an arson series for patterns, along with investigative and interrogation tips. The two investigators used all of these resources.

Finally, one of the fires developed into a larger event, which caught the boss's attention. In December of 2013, the arsonist set fire to an empty refrigerator box filled with packing material that had been left in a hallway on the seventh floor of the building. This finally produced enough heat energy to get other materials burning and caused over $50,000 in damage before it was extinguished. The thick smoke, which filled nearby hallways and permeated apartments, caused a panic with the tenants of the building.

This time the complaints and fears of the tenants caused a typical reaction (or overreaction) from the police and fire brass. Months earlier no one wanted to help AFM Buchanan; now the brass wanted to remove her from the case and assign it to other investigators. This sort of buffoonery occurs all the time the minute the media gets ahold of a case and puts the heat on the brass.

Despite the distractions, AFM Buchanan pressed on. The data that she had painstakingly accumulated over the months was being analyzed at the ATF. The analysts there began detecting subtle patterns within the series. This sort of analysis caused Buchanan to get surveillance cameras and place them in specified "high volume" areas. These cameras remained in place for weeks, with additional fires occurring. Some of these fires were agonizingly just out of view of the surveillance systems. Despite this, AFM Buchanan and SA Campanell were narrowing down the "target area" for the arsonist. Additional cameras were installed and finally hit pay dirt. After nearly twenty-five arson fires, the cameras caught the arsonist at the scene of a fire.

### The Final Fire

By March 18, 2014, security cameras had been installed on the seventh floor, near the trash room. This area had been deemed the "hot zone" for targets as it had more fires than any other part of the building. The cameras were small and hidden but of very high quality. While they were not positioned to view into the room, they clearly showed the face of anyone who entered the trash room. At seven forty-five that night, the hidden camera showed Shirley Vigneau entering the trash room. Vigneau was dressed in gray shorts and a dark top. She was carrying a folded newspaper and a bag of trash. She entered the room and exited in under thirty seconds. She walked directly back toward her apartment.

The next person to enter the trash room was an Asian male, who entered at 9:42 p.m. He was carrying only a very small plastic trash bag. He exited within seconds and walked back toward his apartment. There was no other activity until 10:07 p.m. At that time, Shirley Vigneau reappeared and entered the trash room. This time she was carrying a small plastic drink bottle and a cup. She stayed in the trash room for about twenty seconds and emerged with nothing in her hands. She walked around in front of the doorway for about five seconds and then reentered the trash room. She stayed inside the trash room for an additional twenty seconds before finally exiting. She then walked directly back to her apartment.

This second visit by Vigneau was markedly different from the first. She stayed inside way too long on both entries and loitered in the area for several seconds between entering the room. She was clearly looking for or waiting for something.

The camera stayed operational and nothing from the outside was observed. No other persons entered the room until about twenty minutes later when a security officer walked into view and entered the room. That officer found a smoldering pile of newspapers on the floor of the trash room. Investigators now confirmed that Shirley Vigneau had been the arsonist. She was seen carrying the fuel (newspaper) into the room two hours before the fire. She then entered the room a second and third time for no apparent reason and was the last person in the room before the fire was discovered.

The investigators spoke to the Asian man, and he stated that he lived near Vigneau and that she routinely leaves newspapers on the floor of the trash room. He said he saw one there when he disposed of his trash that night. AFM Buchanan and SA Campanell contacted Vigneau in her room and interviewed her about this latest fire. She made a serious Freudian slip when she told the investigators that she had gone down to the "fire room" twice that night, when she meant to say the "trash room." She denied setting the most recent fire.

The interview was captured on tape, and Vigneau appeared alert, calm, and very interested in the investigation. She had a great recollection of all the fires and even speculated that it was someone from her floor who was setting fires. She said she thought a major problem in the building was that people were leaving trash and other combustible items in the hallways and trash rooms. She believed that a pyromaniac was operating, and these items were easy targets. She believed the arsonist was very bold as he had started several fires when there were people around. She speculated that there had been around fifty fires in this arson series going back one year. She believed the arsonist was male and stated, "I can't imagine a woman doing this."

The investigators were astute enough to inquire about Vigneau's health. She was generally healthy but frail in appearance. She was able to easily walk about the building despite having asthma. She admitted to taking Ambien to help her sleep and to taking two Valium tablets the night of the final fire. She told the investigators that she had no friends and no family. She stated that she was quite lonely in life.

The investigators knew they had their arsonist but were looking for any other corroborating evidence. They left Vigneau in her apartment and then set up a full-time surveillance on her door so that she couldn't light any more fires. AFM Buchanan then drafted a search-and-arrest warrant for Shirley Vigneau and her apartment. By this time AFM Buchanan had done some historical investigating and had found nearly twenty-five arson fires within this building that appeared to be related to Shirley Vigneau. The warrant was issued by a magistrate and was served the next evening by the investigators. During that time they arrested Vigneau and then conducted lengthy interviews of the woman.

*"It was a way of fighting back, maybe, saying I count!"* (Shirley Vigneau, "the Ghost," explaining her fire setting).

Again AFM Buchanan and SA Campanell sat down and interviewed Vigneau. They knew that Vigneau had grown up at the foot of the Appalachian Mountains in Lynchburg, Virginia. As such, they conducted the interview in a very casual and folksy manner, which enabled Vigneau to easily open up to them. At the start of the interview, Vigneau gave a big clue as to her possible motive. She said that although it may sound strange, she wanted people to know that "I count." She went on to say, "It was a way of fighting back, maybe, saying I count." This meant that as a lonely, retired person with no family or friends, she felt isolated and cast aside.

She voiced her sentiments to the investigators and elaborated on them. She said she had been a lonely child and had been married briefly many years before. Vigneau said she worked in a law firm for nearly forty years and had a social structure and support unit within the firm. She retired in 2006 and from that point felt beset by "awful loneliness." She said that the loneliness became more acute during bad weather and during winter months. Physically she was tormented by asthma, insomnia, and an inability to keep warm. She wandered the hallways every night to occupy her mind. She used medications such as sleep aids and anti-anxiety drugs. She was a "neat freak" (like many serial arsonists) and was preoccupied with the trash in the hallways and in the trash room.

The investigators eventually got to specifics, and when she was asked if she had set the most recent fire in the trash room, Vigneau immediately answered, "Yes, I did." She then admitted to all of the fires in the ten-month arson series starting in May of 2013 and could only comment, "I honestly don't know why." Vigneau was asked about certain things she did after her fires. She then dispelled several long-held serial arsonist myths by saying that she never stayed to watch the fires and quickly felt scared after setting them. She did not do it for the excitement or to see firemen. She did not plan her crimes and did not use an accelerant of any sorts other than a lighter. She felt no thrill from the events. She said she lit the bulk of her fires on her own floor out of convenience and for no other reason.

When asked about why she set fire several times to posters/ flyers on the walls of the complex, Vigneau probably tipped off her real reason for setting fires. She stated that she didn't like the "constant harassment" by building managers. This was almost identical to the graffiti phrase written on a flyer several months before. Vigneau admitted that any change in routine stressed her and that the fires were a result of her need to relieve the stress of change.

Shirley Vigneau was charged with several counts of arson to an occupied structure. In a plea deal, she admitted to one count of arson and was given a ten-year suspended sentence and probation. She was released from jail almost immediately.

A year later, lead investigator Andrea Buchanan was formally recognized for her tenacity and determination in solving this series, despite a glaring lack of support and resources by her agency heads. The International Association of Arson Investigators recognized her as its 2015 Investigator of the Year. Well done, Andrea!

*The following professionals worked on this case: Assistant Fire Marshal Andrea Buchanan and Inv. David Garber of the Alexandria (Virginia) Fire Department, and SSA Chad Campanell of the ATF.*

### Investigator's Profile

This case was included in this book of profiles because it embodies two facts. First, it highlights perfectly that there are no hard-and-fast profiles of arsonists or serial arsonists. Arsonists span genders, all races, religions, social classes, and age groups. The second fact that is shown is that there are a large number of these cases in the world, and sadly, due to the lack of support by fire and police administrators, cases like this are frequently dismissed as mere nuisances. This issue has been addressed in arson manuals going back to the 1950s, and yet sixty-plus years later, it still goes unheeded.

It bolsters my ongoing lament that the biggest barrier to solving arson cases has always been, and will continue to be, the fire chief himself. The two lead investigators suffered no small amount of heckling, harassment, and pooh-poohing by colleagues and brass yet still continued working this case to a successful conclusion.

Shirley Vigneau is a major arsonist. She lit twenty-five fires that we know of, and she alluded to around fifty fires. There is no doubt in my mind that she did not begin lighting fires in 2013 and has probably lit dozens more at other stressful phases of her life. There is too much case history evidence out there to not believe that she has been committing arson for a few decades. Most administrators would not consider her case significant at all until one of her fires happened to be lit at the right time in the right circumstances. Had this occurred, there likely would have been casualties and possibly fatalities, and then the fire and police brass would be wondering why something wasn't done earlier.

Vigneau belongs to that rare group of arsonists engaged in **emotionally based fire setting**. She has no clear motive, and that makes her difficult to understand and predict and very difficult, if not impossible, to treat/cure. She tells us in her own words that she is overcome by loneliness and upset with "constant harassment" by the building management. She takes minor annoyances in her life and magnifies them to considerable degrees.

Vigneau has many traits that are consistent with other serial arsonists, particularly women. Although she is slightly built (which is in contrast to many female serial arsonists), she is obsessed with neatness, and has trouble sleeping. She is easily upset by slight changes in her life and has an inability to deal with the stress from those mild changes. The only real power she has is when she lights a fire. Vigneau mirrors other female serial arsonists in that she sets fires in or very close to her home. She walks to fire scenes, uses only available combustible materials, and does not stay around to watch the fires. Like most women arsonists, Vigneau's fire setting is not sophisticated, and she doesn't understand the principle of arranging fuels. Therefore, most of her fires are "low performing" events.

Also like many female serial arsonists, Vigneau set fires at an advanced age. Women serial offenders tend to be much older than male serial arsonists. Her case dispels many myths. Not only was Vigneau not excited about her fire setting, she said that the events actually scared her. I have listened to the audio tapes of her interviews and found Shirley Vigneau to be lucid, candid, and an excellent example to learn from. I also believe that she has lit many more fires in her life than what she has admitted to. She will remain a fire-setting risk for the rest of her life.

This case points out that there are actually quite a few cases of serial arsonists older than sixty-five years old. It also points out how hard work and solid investigative techniques can help you catch even a "ghost."

## MARLENE RAMSDELL
## VENTURA COUNTY, CA, 2006–2009

*This story comes from the case files of the Ventura County Fire and Sheriff's Departments.*

### July 25, 2006

At 4:50 a.m., on July 25, 2006, Ventura County Fire Department (VCFD) firefighters responded to a structure fire in the small city of Simi Valley. The home was a single-family residence, which at the time was being rented out to a family. When the first engines arrived, they found the three occupants of the home standing out in the driveway. One of them was being treated for smoke inhalation while another was screaming hysterically at the firemen. The woman screaming hysterically was identified as forty-five-year-old Marlene Marie Ramsdell. Her sixteen-year-old son, Nelson, was suffering from smoke inhalation. The third person was a subtenant of the property.

Firefighters entered the home and found it filling with smoke from a fire in one of the bedrooms. The front of the house was belching dark smoke while a rear bedroom window had already vented, and a large flame column was boiling out. The firefighters followed the billowing smoke backward and encountered flames in the rear hallway of the home. They fought through these to find that a single rear bedroom was totally involved in fire. The engine crew knocked down the blaze in just a few minutes. According to the protocol at VCFD, the department's arson unit was immediately summoned. The on-duty arson investigator was Inv. Christine Saqui, a sixteen-year veteran firefighter and an eight-year veteran of the arson unit.

Inv. Saqui arrived shortly after the fire was extinguished, and after getting a quick walk-through of the burned home with the battalion chief, she began an interview of Marlene Ramsdell. The best description for Marlene was that she was stout. She stood at five feet six and weighed around 220 pounds. She had short hair and was slightly masculine in appearance.

In this very first interview with Inv. Saqui, Marlene Ramsdell revealed an interesting fact. Almost immediately Marlene stated that she was familiar with fire as she had a fire in a previous home she lived in several years before this fire. This tidbit offered up by Ramsdell prickled the skin of Inv. Saqui as it is extraordinarily rare for anyone to be associated with more than one fire in his or her life.

Regarding this current fire, Marlene gave the following account. She said that she was sleeping in her room at the time of the fire. Her son was in his room, and the other tenant was sleeping on a living-room sofa. Marlene said she was awakened by the smell of smoke and saw flames coming out of her closet and attacking her nightstand. She ran out of the room and woke up her son and the other man. All three occupants safely escaped the growing flames. Marlene was a smoker but never smoked in her home. She also did not use candles in the home. She had no idea how the fire started.

Inv. Saqui was suspicious from the start. Fires in closets are very rare unless there are small children in the home. There were no children in this home, and the fire was in a room controlled by Marlene. There really is nothing in a closet that could fail electrically as most closets do not have electrical outlets in them. A few closets do have lightbulbs, so this was an area of concern.

Inv. Saqui began her scene investigation and quickly determined, based on the fire movement patterns, that the origin of this fire was within a small closet in the master bedroom. The closet was lined with wood walls and had burned completely. The fire had then burned out of the closet into the bedroom and had caused a "flashover" event to occur, which destroyed the bedroom. The fire damage diminished from this room outward. The fire-scene investigation matched Marlene's statement that she saw a fire burning within her closet.

Inv. Saqui conducted a detailed dig out of the closet and found that the floor was unburned, despite the rest of the closet having near-total damage. There was a single bulb outlet mounted on the ceiling of the closet, with the bare bulb broken or missing. Around and directly below this item was a pile of burned clothing. The fire originated within this pile of clothing.

Saqui went through every bit of the pile but was unable to find an ignition source. There was no indication of an accelerant. At the end of her investigation, Inv. Saqui concluded that the only heat source within the closet was the bare lightbulb, but that no clothes would normally be in the area near it.

Inv. Saqui spoke to the owner/landlord of the home. He said that he had recently remodeled the home and rented it out to Section 8 low-income, government-subsidized families. He said that all wiring and safety features had been recently inspected and were in compliance with all codes. He advised that Marlene and her son were the only persons on the lease and that Marlene had been delinquent in paying her rent for several months.

In her final analysis, Inv. Saqui had eliminated any possible accidental source for this fire. She concluded that the fire started among the clothing within the closet and determined that the fire was set by "recent intentional human activity." She concluded that the cause of this fire was "incendiary" or an act of arson. Saqui's investigation and conclusions were forwarded to the Ventura County Sheriff's Department (VCSD) Arson-Bomb Unit for further investigative follow-up.

A week later Saqui and sheriff's detective Larry Bull interviewed Marlene's son, Nelson. He told them that there had been other fires in the family during his life. Nelson said that they had had a fire in a bedroom of a home where they lived in Arizona about twelve years ago. Two years later, there was another fire in a home where they lived in Simi Valley. Nelson also admitted that he and a friend had caused a vegetation fire about two years ago when playing with fireworks. The sixteen-year-old said that he was an alcoholic but had been sober for about a year and a half. He surprised the investigators by telling them that he believed having several fire incidents within his family was fairly normal. He assumed that these sorts of things happen to everyone.

Nelson did confirm on the night of the recent fire that his mom was already alone in her bedroom by midnight, and he did not think she had left the room prior to the fire; nor did he believe that anyone else went into her room. He had no explanation for the fire in the closet.

Shortly after the VCFD finished its scene investigation, the insurance carrier for the owner of the home hired private fire investigator Ron Ablott to conduct an independent investigation. Ablott is a longtime arson investigator in both the public (LASD) and private sector. His independent analysis agreed with Inv. Saqui and found that the fire started high in the closet among the hanging clothing. He left his final analysis of the event as "undetermined" but advised in his report that he found some items suspicious and could not rule out the possibility of a deliberate act of arson.

### October 3, 1996

After the interviews with Marlene and her son, Inv. Saqui dug into the archives and located a fire that had occurred ten years earlier. She found that on October 3, 1996, Marlene, her son, daughter, and then-fiancé had been the victims of a house fire. The fire report listed the incident as a probable "accidental" fire.

Inv. Saqui retrieved the archived report from that case and examined it for any similarities to the 2006 fire. She also located two newspaper accounts of the event, both of which listed the fire as an accident that occurred during a painting/staining operation.

In the 1996 fire, Marlene and family were living in another rented house in Simi Valley. Just prior to the fire, Marlene and her husband, Luke Sisson, were spray-painting the kitchen with a commercial paint sprayer. During the spraying operation, there was a "flash fire," and both Luke and Marlene received flash burns to their bodies. Both were hospitalized for a brief time and then released. Both believed that the fire was ignited by a pilot light from a stove, which ignited the atomized paint particles. The arson investigator at the time, William Hager from the VCFD, agreed with this probability, and the fire was officially deemed an accident.

Inv. Saqui digested this information and noted that there was not much of a similarity between the two events other than the fact that in both cases Marlene Ramsdell was present at the start of the fire. Since the previous event had an additional witness and was conclusively ruled an accident, Saqui did not have much to go on. However, it bothered Inv. Saqui a bit to know that there were other fires associated with this family. Marlene had admitted to a fire in another home in another state, and her son had admitted to starting at least one vegetation fire with fireworks. The veteran arson investigator knew that "normal" people just don't have this much fire activity associated with them. Saqui added the old report and news reports to her case file and then forwarded the entire package to the VCSD. The case file went inactive.

### May 15, 2009

At just before five in the evening, a structure fire was called into the VCFD. As soon as the city firefighters arrived, they began attacking a fire that was burning in the rear bedroom of the property. After it was extinguished, they called their arson investigator to the scene, Inv. Jeff Weins. Weins found that the fire originated within a closet inside the rear bedroom of the home. There was no one present; however, neighbors said that the resident was a female named Marlene Ramsdell. They had seen Ramsdell leave the location not more than ten minutes before the fire was noticed. There were no other persons home for several hours prior to this fire.

Inv. Weins conducted an investigation and determined that the fire started in the closet among clothing, but he was unable to find any source of ignition. There were no electrical services, cords, or outlets within the closet. He found no evidence of a break-in or the use of accelerants, but he maintained a belief that this fire was either due to careless smoking or possibly intentionally set. He eventually classified the fire as "undetermined." Immediately after this fire, Inv. Weins began receiving phone calls from acquaintances of Marlene Ramsdell, who told him that she had been involved in several fires over the years and that she had openly bragged about benefitting from these fires. Despite these tips and the circumstances of the fire, Inv. Weins was unable to conclude that a crime had occurred. He closed his investigation.

The owner of the home had insurance on the rental property. The insurance carrier State Farm sent one of its privately retained fire investigators to the scene. Inv. Rob Rappaport is a longtime fire investigator in both the public (Riverside and Redondo Beach Fire Departments) and private sectors. He conducted his investigation of the latest Ramsdell fire and concluded positively that the event was an arson fire. He was unable to find a source of ignition and determined that the fire was set with an open flame, probably a cigarette lighter.

A couple of weeks after the fire in Ventura City, the VCFD received a telephone call from an anonymous male. The male claimed to be a relative of Marlene Ramsdell. The caller told the VCFD that Ramsdell was purposely setting fires in her rented homes as a means to receive attention and some benefits from the local Red Cross and other charities. The caller said he was aware that Marlene intentionally set at least two prior fires to her residences in Simi Valley. The caller said that Marlene had recently set fire to her residence in the city of Ventura, which was under the jurisdiction of a different fire department.

VCFD investigator Saqui immediately jumped on this anonymous tip as she clearly remembered the very suspicious circumstances of the fire three years prior in Simi Valley. Saqui called VCFD arson investigator Jeff Weins. Weins provided Inv. Saqui with the information he had accumulated during his brief investigation of the house fire on May 15, 2009.

On June 15, 2009, Inv. Saqui and VCSD detective Guy Peach met with and interviewed Marlene Ramsdell regarding this most recent fire in Ventura City. Marlene told them that she was active in a drug/alcohol treatment program and regularly attended meetings. On the afternoon of the fire, she left her home at four fifteen and walked to her Narcotics Anonymous meeting. While on her way to the meeting, she heard the sirens from the responding police and fire engines. She later was informed (by an unknown person) that it was her home that had burned. She confirmed that her son was the only other resident of the house, and he was many miles away at the time.

A later interview with her son confirmed that he was away at the time of the fire. However, he added that before or during the fire, someone took $300 in cash from his room. Witnesses to this event said that Marlene was seen leaving her home about ten minutes before the fire was observed and that she was not acting her normal self.

By this stage of the investigation, Inv. Saqui and Det. Peach now had some very interesting events to consider and compare. From 1996 to 2009, Marlene Ramsdell had been the "victim" of at least three residential fires in Ventura County. She had been present at the start or discovery of each of these fires. She also had freely admitted that there had been a fourth residential fire in her life around 1992 while she was living in another state. She told investigators that she thought her two-year-old son had started that fire while playing with matches.

Neither of these experienced arson investigators had ever heard of any single person having been a "victim" of that many structure fires. They began questioning dozens of other arson investigators in the California region and determined that no one had ever met anyone who had more than two fires in their lives. They found that Marlene Ramsdell was an incredibly unique individual.

*"In my experience as an arson investigator, I have never investigated anyone who has been involved in four residential fires in their lifetime"* (VCSD arson investigator Guy Peach, in an Affidavit for Search Warrant regarding Marlene Ramsdell).

Marlene Ramsdell had a minor but interesting criminal history. She had one conviction for bouncing a check and a second conviction for shoplifting. The arson investigators were quick to note that shoplifting and petty theft were some of the most consistent crimes committed by serial arson offenders.

Marlene also had an interesting social history. She had been married at least three times and had been known by four different last names. It was very difficult to track her past as her name had changed so many times over the years. She was a longtime admitted abuser/addict of both alcohol and illegal narcotics. Marlene was also quite litigious and had been involved as a plaintiff in several lawsuits. Although not exactly hard evidence, the arson investigators knew that women serial arsonists had several peculiar consistencies: their fires were often within their own homes or very close nearby; they were present during fires within their own homes; they tended to be older offenders—setting fires in their thirties, forties, and fifties; they tended to have theft or shoplifting in their backgrounds; and they also tended to be very litigious in nature.

Marlene Ramsdell was hitting on all cylinders as her social history closely matched many other women serial arsonists. It was also learned that Ramsdell had other classic symptoms associated with serial arson activity. She admitted to suffering from panic attacks, depression, anxiety, and posttraumatic stress disorder. She was a longtime user/abuser of prescription medications.

Det. Peach and Inv. Saqui now took their investigation backward into the historical fires. They believed that people in her past would have a better picture of who Marlene Ramsdell was.

Eventually the investigators contacted the owner of the home that had burned in Simi Valley in 2006. The owner provided them with a copy of a very interesting note. He said that he was having problems with Marlene Ramsdell in the weeks and months prior to the fire. She was staying in his rental property on a government-assisted housing program. Despite that, she had illegally sublet a room to another male, which was against her lease and the law. She was behind on her rent, and she and her son had caused some minor damage to the home. He sent her a note on July 24, 2006, detailing these issues and that he expected her to fix the things she had broken and to catch up on her rent money owed. The fire occurred the very next day after Marlene received the note. Now the investigators had a possible motive! They saw that the note may have enraged Marlene and caused her to start the fire out of spite.

It took the investigators several more weeks to locate and interview Marlene's former husband Luke Sisson. They finally were able to talk to him in August of 2009. He told investigators that he was briefly married to Marlene and eventually divorced her after the 1996 fire in their Simi Valley home. Sisson also gave them a unique perspective on the aftermath of the 1996 fire. He said that he and Marlene were featured three times in newspaper articles about the fire, the aftermath, and all of the assistance they had received from charitable organizations. In particular they received a large amount of cash from the Red Cross, two church groups, and citizen's groups. He said that

Marlene seemed to really enjoy the attention they received from charitable groups, the news media, and many citizens who had collected donations for them.

Sisson was amazed that within thirty days of the fire, they had recouped their losses "tenfold" from the various donators. He remarked that Marlene was amazed that total strangers would give so much money to people they didn't even know.

Sisson said that they were collecting so much cash that he grew embarrassed. At the time he was working as a handyman/contractor for cash and brought in nearly $4,000 a week "under the table." His wife, Marlene, was collecting child welfare for her two kids and was also getting assistance money from the county. He said that they were living for nearly free rent through the Section 8 Housing Act. He said they were making more money than they ever had his entire life, almost all of it being nontaxed income. He said that Marlene refused to look for work as she could make more money on welfare.

Sisson pointed out another peculiar fact regarding the 1996 fire. He said that Marlene hosted Narcotics Anonymous meetings regularly at their home and that there had been one the night prior to the fire. At that meeting she had collected over $3,000 cash in dues from the other attendees. The money was sitting in the living room near a ledger book. After the fire, he saw that the ledger book's cover was slightly burned, and the money was missing. He later heard Marlene tell other Narcotics Anonymous members that the money had burned up in the fire. Sisson said he knew for sure that the money survived the fire.

Sisson then dropped a bombshell on investigators. He told them specific details of the 1996 fire that had never been mentioned before. He said he was painting/sealing the kitchen area of the home, and Marlene was very mad at him as she wanted to host a party in the room that night. He said that during his spraying operation she was still mad at him and entered and exited the kitchen several times in an aggressive manner as if she was really pissed off. During one of those times, he heard her aggressively clicking something behind him that sounded like her cigarette lighter. Before he could turn around to tell her to stop, an explosion and fire occurred.

He was immediately covered in melted plastic that he had placed to prevent paint overspray. He said that Marlene made no attempt to help him, and he saw her run from the room. He said that as he was finally able to peel the burning plastic off his body, a second explosion/fireball occurred, blowing him out into the patio area. He picked himself up and made his way to the rear of the home, where Marlene was hiding with her two children. He broke the window to get them out, and he said that Marlene was visibly shocked to see him alive.

Sisson said that at the time, he was sure that Marlene had either purposely set the fire or had been so reckless with her actions of using the lighter in an explosive environment that she had caused this fire. After the outpouring of support for the family, he just decided not to push the issue and let the fire investigator's findings stand unchallenged. Since that day, he had become convinced that Marlene had now started at least four structure fires in her life.

Sisson married Marlene shortly after the fire but soon realized it was a massive mistake. The two slept in separate rooms most of their five-year marriage, and Sisson just continued to live with her because his family didn't believe in divorce. He said that during the entire time he was with her, Marlene Ramsdell was actively committing welfare fraud. Eventually Sisson couldn't stay with her any longer and decided to leave unannounced. Just before he could leave her, Marlene found out about his plans and took her kids and left. That evening the police came to his home and arrested him as she had accused him of spousal battery. Three days later he was released from jail, and no charges were ever filed. The next day he went to the bank and found that Marlene had emptied out their accounts.

Sisson said that Marlene was clever, vindictive, greedy, and mean. He said he and all of their friends in the Narcotics Anonymous network were sure that she was responsible for burning her homes as she loved the attention, the sympathy, and the cash and donations she received after the fires.

On May 11, 2011, Det. Peach and Inv. Saqui believed that they had built a detailed circumstantial arson case against Marlene Ramsdell. They noted that besides the arsons, there was an underlying element of theft and fraud throughout these fires and throughout Marlene's life. They felt that there wasn't enough evidence to present the 1996 fire as an arson attack, and besides that, the statutes on that fire had expired. However, they believed that they could present a decent case on each of the 2006 and 2009 fires. They had exhausted all other avenues of investigation and finally presented their case to the district attorney.

Eventually the case would end up in the lap of DDA Richard Simon of the Ventura County District Attorney's Office. Simon was a seasoned and aggressive prosecutor; just the kind of guy you need on a case like this. The District Attorney's Office poured over the case for two weeks, looking for holes or flaws. They found none, and on May 25 the DA issued an arrest warrant for Marlene for the arsons in 2006 and 2009. She was arrested the next day. Upon her arrest, she was interviewed by Inv. Saqui and Det. Peach. She denied involvement and spoke very little. She was completely devoid of emotion. She quickly asked for an attorney and refused further comment.

The investigators knew that the science of fire would be an issue during the impending court proceedings. They reviewed every detail of the case and looked at possible defense arguments. Two probable arguments (both of which the defense did attempt to use) were that the fire in 2006 was an accident and that the clothing was ignited by either the heat from the bare bulb in the closet or a carelessly discarded cigarette. To test and possibly eliminate these theories, Inv. Saqui and her arson partner Inv. Alan Campbell constructed a realistic mock-up of the closet in Ramsdell's home in 2006. Using old crime-scene photos, they filled it with the appropriate number and types of clothing. They then conducted several "test burns" of the items within the closet using cigarettes, bare bulbs, and eventually a butane cigarette lighter.

The investigators knew that their "field tests" would be seriously challenged in court, so they videotaped them with high-resolution cameras and took dozens of still, digital photos. The results were quite compelling. In every test scenario, both the cigarettes and bare bulb failed to ignite the polyblend clothing hanging in the closet. Each was tested several times, all with similar results. However, the test using a cigarette lighter showed that it was quite easy to ignite these hanging clothes with a cigarette lighter. The investigators noted that Marlene Ramsdell was a longtime smoker and always had a cigarette lighter in her possession. The investigators scientifically ruled out the accidental causes and positively concluded that both closet fires could only have been ignited with an open-flame source like a cigarette lighter. The work by these determined investigators eliminated all defense theories about accidental fires.

Marlene Ramsdell was held to answer after a detailed preliminary hearing on August 15, 2011. She was held over for trial, and her defense attorney promised a major battle. He pointed out that there were no witnesses and that it was well known that most arsonists were, in fact, men and not women. He said that his client was merely "unlucky." He said that all of the fires occurred in rental homes, and Ramsdell had no insurance; therefore, she had no motive to burn the homes, which contained her own property. It was a compelling argument.

The jury trial started in late June of 2012. Prosecutor Richard Simon had done his homework and went aggressively into battle. He presented Marlene Ramsdell as a cold and calculating serial arsonist, who obtained gratification and much-wanted attention by setting these fires. She clearly reveled in being the "victim." The DA described through witnesses her joy at receiving cash, property, and attention after each fire that occurred to her. DDA Simon pointed out through experts the several consistencies that occurred in each of Ramsdell's fires. He also indicated all the traits she had that were consistent with other notorious female serial arsonists.

By June 29 it was all over. Marlene Ramsdell had been convicted by a Ventura County jury for both arsons of her own residences. It was an incredible victory for the investigators and prosecutors who had only circumstantial evidence in the matter. Ramsdell's defense attorney vigorously fought any prison time for this woman who had an otherwise negligible criminal record. The defense demanded that she get mere probation and some psychiatric help. The judge scared the prosecution a bit by stating that he was having issues with why a woman would do these things (start fires in her own home), with no apparent motive like insurance fraud. The judge indicated that maybe she indeed needed some psychiatric assistance. She was sent to a prison hospital for a psychiatric evaluation prior to sentencing. The prison psychiatrist, after monitoring Ramsdell for ninety days, noted that she had expressed no remorse for her actions and that her fires were a danger to the community in which she lived. He opined that "the emotional support and financial rewards she received after the first fire was a strong, reinforcing motivation for setting subsequent fires." He described her as "narcissistic," and "motivated by self-interest and greed."

*"There is nothing in Ramsdell's thinking or behavior that would indicate that she would not repeat this behavior in the future if she thought she could get away with it"* (Prison psychiatrist Dr. Douglas Hoehing on assessing Marlene Ramsdell's potential to reoffend if released from prison).

Armed with the report from the prison doctors, the judge sentenced Marlene Ramsdell to six years in prison. In 2014 Marlene Ramsdell petitioned the California Supreme Court to review her case for a new trial. The court denied her request without comment. Her convictions are final.

This case would be the last in the long and distinguished public careers of sheriff's detective Guy Peach and fire department arson investigator Alan Campbell. Both retired from public service shortly after the Ramsdell case was finally adjudicated. Inv. Christine Saqui continues to be the senior arson investigator for the VCFD.

*The following professionals contributed to the Marlene Ramsdell investigation: Det. Guy Peach, Inv. Christine Saqui, Inv. Alan Campbell, Det. Larry Bull, Inv. William Hager, Inv. Jeff Weins, Inv. Ron Ablott, Inv. Rob Rappaport, and DDA Richard Simon.*

### Investigator's Profile

In my first book, *Torchered Minds: Case Histories of Notorious Serial Arsonists*, I dedicated an entire chapter to an evil group of women who were serial arson offenders. At least three of those women were near clones to the looks, actions, traits, and behaviors of Marlene Ramsdell. By the way, these are some of the most dangerous arsonists ever identified. They pose a great danger to anyone, particularly children who reside with them.

While this subtype of serial arsonist is rare, there are plenty of examples of them out there. They tend to have nearly identical life histories. Most are masculine in appearance, are somewhat physically large or obese, have multiple marriages, move quite frequently, have kids with different fathers, have abuse problems with alcohol/drugs and prescription medications, and seem to derive some sort of financial benefit to their fire setting. Most of these women are quite confrontational to neighbors, landlords, teachers, and other authority figures. Most have petty theft, shoplifting, and fraud in their backgrounds. Many of these women are known to be quite litigious and are frequently involved as plaintiffs in lawsuits.

Many of these women display the same traits and issues as Ramsdell. They suffer from addiction, depression, anxiety, OCD, and other mental issues. Some of these women also display a version of Munchausen's syndrome, where they often portray themselves as victims. In a worse variation, they have Munchausen's by proxy, which is a condition where these women endanger their children, purposely make them ill, or injure them in some other way so that they can receive attention and sympathy.

A good source for information about one of these types of offenders may be to visit the schools where the children attend. Most teachers and principals have a very good idea of parents and students who may fall into these categories. The children of these types of women can also display similar characteristics as their mothers. In this case, the teenage son of Marlene Ramsdell already displayed at least two prior incidents of arson and was already an alcoholic at seventeen years of age. He will be considered at risk for arson his entire life.

Overall, I would have to classify Ramsdell as an **emotionally based** fire setter; however, there are some aspects of profit with her fires. The precise motive for this subtype is a bit confusing. In my case studies, I have noted that the fire setting by this subtype of offender is primarily done out of spite or revenge for some unknown slight. However, following the fire, the female receives a lot of attention, sympathy, and even financial benefit. Future fires are a blend of several motives involving the need for revenge and attention, with the added benefit of financial gain. These traits were shown in my earlier case studies of Belle Gunness, Shirley Baron Winters, and Virginia Rearden, all of whom eventually murdered their own family members with their fire activities.

I don't know the distant past of Marlene Ramsdell, but there quite likely were other fires that we don't know about. She didn't start doing this stuff late in life. Other traits that these women share are that many of them have lost children in their life to nonmedical deaths such as drowning, poisoning, fires, and SIDS. Again, in this case there is no evidence that this occurred to Ramsdell, but we don't know much about her first thirty years of life.

The fires set by this subtype of female serial arsonist are most often within their own homes or within fifty yards of their own homes. They are poorly planned events and seldom involve the use of accelerants or incendiary devices. Their fires tend to injure themselves or their own family members. Quite often they get away with one or two fires as the responding firefighters still have a hard time believing that a woman and mother would set a fire intentionally.

For the investigators out there who may run into these odd "mommy fires," I would encourage you to do what the investigators in Ventura County did and look into the history of these women. The best method is to interview their children, spouses, ex-spouses, and teachers and to do a detailed query of the insurance databases. If you find more than one fire in their lives, then you are onto these most dangerous offenders.

## HORSE WAS AFLAME
## LANCASTER, CA, 2007

On the afternoon of August 20, 2007, Det. Todd Anderson, from the LASD Homicide Detail, was speeding along a remote desert road in the far northern reaches of Los Angeles County. He and his partners Gary Sica and John Corina were putting the final touches on a case that involved two separate murders of people associated with a rural ranching operation. Yesterday they had served search warrants and arrested four persons in connection with the two murders. Today's task, which Anderson would handle alone, was to conduct a quick follow-up interview for evidence from the murders. This took him to the desert ranch, which was fifteen miles west of the city of Lancaster. The high desert, as this section of Los Angeles County was called, was sweltering in heat that exceeded one hundred degrees Fahrenheit.

The ranch that Det. Anderson was heading toward was the root cause of this criminal investigation. The ranch was a gift that the previous owner had given to himself for a life of toil and achievement. The previous owner was a sixty-four-year-old Iranian national named Dr. Esfandiar "Steve" Kadivar. He was a prominent plastic surgeon, who lived in Beverly Hills but had worked at the nearby Lancaster hospital for three decades. Later in life, the doctor wanted to spend time on a ranch and grow the same things that he had helped his father grow in Iran when he was a child. Eight years ago he purchased the two-hundred-acre property in the high desert and began growing olives and pistachios, and raising cattle and goats.

Dr. Kadivar spent many of his free hours on the ranch property. Because of the size of the ranch, Dr. Kadivar hired a foreman, a Mexican man named Nicolas Cordoba, who in turn hired several other Mexican workers as the needs arose. Dr. Kadivar and Nico Cordoba had a long, friendly relationship, and Cordoba resided on the ranch property for several years up until this incident.

Dr. Kadivar had been found murdered on July 5, 2006. His body was found near his livestock pens, and it appeared he was shot to death by a high-powered rifle as he tended his animals. Dr. Kadivar was found by Nico Cordoba, who had been away from the ranch that day. He found the deceased owner when he returned in the evening. Investigators would find that a large safe had been stolen from the property at the time of the murder. The safe was filled with valuables including a trove of gold coins, a large amount of cash, and two expensive hunting rifles.

After Dr. Kadivar's murder, the ranch operations were taken over by his family members. Dr. Kadivar's family knew little about the ranch and how it was run and soon asked the foreman, Nico Cordoba, to find someone they could lease the property to. Cordoba contacted a friend named Efrain Martines, who eventually leased the property from the Kadivar family. This arrangement stayed in place until April 30, 2007, when Efrain Martines was reported to have died from a heart attack. Martines's truck was found about twenty miles away from the ranch on a rural roadside with his body in the rear bed. His body was in a state of decomposition. A coroner's investigator originally believed that Martines had died of a massive heart attack while loading hay into his truck.

Because of the prior murder at the ranch, which was still unsolved at this point, and the fact that Martines had been in control of the ranch since the doctor was killed, LASD homicide investigators thought this second death to be very suspicious. They asked a coroner's doctor to take a second, closer look at the body. A more thorough examination by the medical examiner proved that Martines had been shot six times with a high-powered rifle. He had been shot to death just like Dr. Kadivar. A few weeks later, that murder weapon, an SKS assault rifle, would also be recovered during a search warrant. A few weeks after that, the doctor's stolen safe would be recovered in another search warrant. The recovery of that safe was the day before Det. Anderson's drive into the desert, where this story began.

Det. Anderson was about five miles away from the Kadivar Ranch when he saw a plume of dark black smoke rising up quickly from the desert. He had been to this area several times, and it occurred to him that the smoke was not natural and appeared to be centered near or at the ranch property. Already speeding at about eighty miles per hour, Det. Anderson stomped on the gas pedal, and the detective's sedan soon reached a bumpy ninety-five miles per hour. Within two minutes, he soon could see people running along the road in front of him, so he quickly slowed the car down to a more manageable speed. As Anderson passed the people, he saw that they all appeared to be Mexican ranch workers. About two dozen of them were jogging or running toward the fire at the ranch property.

After passing the group of workers, Anderson could clearly see that some outbuildings on the ranch were fully involved in fire. He approached the property itself and spotted two people walking quickly away from the fire scene. He slowed long enough to see a forty-something Mexican female and a teenaged Mexican male. He would soon learn that their names were Martha Zuno and Adrian Cordoba (her son). The two walked away and soon joined the group of approaching ranch workers.

Det. Anderson slid into the ranch yard and confirmed that the fire was contained to two animal barns. The ramshackle barns were roofed, had three walls, and were held together with a combination of scrap wood, scrap metal, and wire. One of the two barns was fully on fire, and the roof of the second one was beginning to ignite from the radiant heat. The detective could see thirty-foot flames raging from the buildings. In an open corral adjacent to the animal enclosure, Anderson spotted a horse that was running around crazily trying to escape the searing heat of the burning structure. Anderson also saw that the second barn, not yet fully aflame, was filled with several goats and kid goats.

All of the animals were literally screaming as they tried to escape the heat from the fire. Rescue attempts were made by Anderson and several others, but the heat from the fire drove them back before they could unlock the gates to the corrals and pens. To make matters worse, the winds as usual were blowing in excess of thirty miles per hour, and Anderson knew that it would be just a few minutes before the structures and the animals were all destroyed.

Some of the ranch hands had been able to reach fire department dispatchers via cellular telephone but were having a difficult time communicating due to a language barrier. Anderson took a phone from one of the hands and gave detailed information and instructions to the fire department. They assured him that several engines were on their way but advised that the closest engine was at least fifteen minutes from this remote ranch.

Anderson hung up the phone and then joined a group of ranch hands with a pickup truck. By using the vehicle as a ram, they were able to break down a portion of the building and free several of the trapped goats. Anderson and the ranch hands spent several minutes dragging panicked goats from the burning shed and corral. Still, they could all hear the horrible screams of the remaining goats in the enclosure. The half-crazed horse also ran by as the gates were opened. By the time the first fire engines arrived about twenty minutes later, it was far too late as any animals still in the pens were certainly dead.

As the firefighters began knocking down the large fire, they all visibly gasped in horror as they could see that the horse was still on its feet in the ranch yard. The firefighters were stunned to see that all of the hair had been burned off the horse, its eyes and nostrils had been burned closed, and its mane and tail had been burned away. The poor animal had no hair left, and its skin was badly charred.

The firefighters tried to approach the animal, but it was too badly injured to respond. It half-leaned against a fence and began madly smashing its head against a steel pole. The entire body of the horse was shaking in violent spasms as it tried to cope with the overwhelming pain. Several firefighters, in obvious emotional distress at the plight of the suffering animal, ran up to Det. Anderson and begged him to put the horse out of its misery. Anderson, a headquarters detective, had no other weapons with him other than his nine millimeter pistol. A lifetime hunter and outdoorsman, Det. Anderson knew well that this weapon was not at all suitable for terminating an animal of this size. He was very hesitant about attempting it as he was afraid that he just might hurt the horse more, and he didn't want to torture the beast. He knew he needed a rifle or at least a shotgun with slugs for this job; however, there were no other sheriff's deputies within twenty minutes of this scene.

Anderson could not stand any more of the obvious suffering the horse was going through, so he pulled out his pistol and shot the horse twice through the skull. Det. Anderson and the firefighters were very grateful to see the horse immediately drop and then die within seconds. A later assessment by animal-control authorities would conclude that the animal was too far injured to help, and they too would have dispatched the horse with a firearm to end its hideous suffering. They commended Det. Anderson for his actions.

Eventually multiple fire department units arrived including a water-tender and an inmate hand crew. The fire battalion chief put the inmate crew to work with the grisly job of sifting through the downed structures for any livestock. The shocking scene photos show inmate firefighters pulling out the carcasses of several heavily charred goats. Among the group of goats were some newborn kid goats. All in all, it was a pretty ugly scene.

Investigators from the LASD Arson-Explosives Detail were summoned to the scene to conduct an "origin and cause" investigation of the fire. While he waited for those experts, Det. Anderson began his own line of inquiry. He contacted and spoke to the ranch foreman, Jose Soto. He had recently taken over as the foreman of the ranch after LASD homicide detectives (Anderson's partners) had arrested the previous foreman, Nicholas Cordoba, for murder. In an odd twist of fate, Cordoba had been arrested for the murder of Jose Soto's father, Efrain Soto-Martines.

The younger Soto told Det. Anderson the following information. Soto said that the current owner of the ranch (the brother of the murdered Dr. Kadivar) had installed him as foreman shortly after the recent arrest of Cordoba. Today, Cordoba's longtime girlfriend and their joint son (Martha Zuno and Adrian Cordoba) arrived at the ranch property highly agitated. Martha Zuno approached Foreman Soto and told him that she had come to collect the car, horse, and goats owned by her boyfriend, Nicholas Cordoba. Soto, who was well aware that the animals were owned by the ranch and not the previous foreman Cordoba, advised Zuno that he was unable to give the animals to her without permission from the current owner. Jose Soto then said that Martha Zuno became enraged with that decision, and he finally had to escort her off the ranch property. Soto noticed that she appeared to calm down in a few minutes.

Shortly after this brief confrontation, Foreman Soto was organizing several workers to go to a nearby orchard to harvest pistachios. At this time, Martha Zuno approached him again and asked if she and her sixteen-year-old son could assist the other workers in the harvest of the nuts. Soto agreed, and the pair joined the group as they left for the nearby orchard. Soto made sure that the ranch property was locked and secured before he left the scene.

About an hour into their harvest, Martha Zuno excused herself to go to the bathroom. Other workers saw Martha walking toward a trailer, which was about three hundred yards away from the animal enclosure. She was out of everyone's sight for about twenty to thirty minutes. As soon as she returned, other workers near her saw that the animal enclosures were fully on fire. These were in the direction from which Martha had returned.

Anderson questioned the rest of the ranch workers, and all were adamant that no other persons were near the ranch property other than Martha Zuno. Jose Soto said he believed she had lit the fire because there was no means for an accidental fire in that area. There was no electricity to the animal enclosures and no things such as lanterns or candles in use. There had been no machinery in operation in that area for several days. There was no reason at all for the fire to have occurred.

Det. Anderson spoke to Martha Zuno through a translator. She was vague and somewhat belligerent. She told him that she had been picking pistachios the entire time and had not been anywhere close to the animal enclosure.

Sheriff's department's arson investigators would comb the area of the pens later that same day. They too found that there were no accidental sources of ignition in the area as there was no electricity in the structures and no machinery in operation near them. They went so far as to examine the possibility of "spontaneous combustion" of the animal waste and silage, which can be a remote possibility in agricultural operations. In this case, it was positively ruled out as the weather and soil conditions would not support this theory. Later that evening the arson investigators classified this fire as a deliberate act of arson.

Det. Todd Anderson took this case to the Antelope Valley District Attorney's Office for filing. The filing prosecutor, mired in the double murder case at the ranch, was not thrilled about adding a lesser crime like arson to his stack of cases. He told

Anderson that he would file the case but that it was likely that Martha Zuno, possessing a barren criminal record, would probably receive a sentence of probation or very minimal time in jail. Anderson, not used to filing arson cases, took this information without flinching too much. He was well aware that the DA in that area was buried with more substantial cases involving shootings, stabbings, and murders. No matter how horrifying the scene had been to him, when weighing it against the normal mayhem occurring nightly on the streets of Los Angeles County, it seemed to pale a bit.

However, before Anderson could receive the formal filing paperwork, a dramatic change occurred at the District Attorney's Office. A female DA burst into the room, having heard of the case through office gossip. She demanded to see the file and the pictures of the horribly burned horse. She immediately informed all present that she would be filing this case herself and that she would file all charges to a maximum degree and would accept nothing less than several years in jail for the offender. Det. Anderson was surprised and pleased. He would later find out that this new female prosecutor was the most ardent animal lover in the office and would treat this case with the utmost priority.

Martha Zuno was "held to answer" at a preliminary hearing a few weeks later for the charges of arson and animal cruelty. Courtroom observers would note that the judge in that hearing was suitably aghast when he was shown the scene photos. Zuno was facing eleven years in prison. Just before the start of trial, the defense attorneys approached the prosecutor with a plea deal. Martha Zuno then pled guilty to all charges and received a sentence of over five years in prison, which is a fairly stiff sentence in Los Angeles County for the crime of arson. She was whisked away to state prison, having shown no remorse whatsoever for her deed. She would be followed a few years later by her boyfriend, Nico Cordoba.

## Epilogue

The murders of Dr. Kadivar and Efrain Martines would eventually be accounted for.

In August 2007, LASD homicide investigators, led by Det. Gary Sica, arrested four men involved in both the murders of Kadivar and Martines. The principal suspect was Nico Cordoba, the longtime foreman of Kadivar's ranch. The lengthy investigation revealed that Cordoba had long coveted the control of the Kadivar Ranch. He had believed that if Dr. Kadivar was dead, his family in Beverly Hills would have no inclination to run the ranch and would somehow turn it over to Cordoba in some sort of "manage-to-own" arrangement.

A second reason for the murder of Kadivar was pure robbery. Cordoba knew that Dr. Kadivar had a large amount of cash and some gold at the ranch house, along with several weapons of great value. Detectives would prove that Cordoba had two other men murder Dr. Kadivar at his ranch while Cordoba established an alibi. Antonio Martinez and Arturo Verdin shot the doctor with a high-powered rifle as he fed his cattle. That murder remained unsolved for nearly a year.

After the murder of the doctor, Cordoba arranged for Kadivar's family to lease him the ranch for $20,000 per year. Because he didn't have that money himself, Cordoba enlisted a friend (Martines) to help run the property. He lied to Martines and told him that the lease was $40,000 per year and that Martines needed to give him $20,000. Martines fell for this scheme but then took this as an opportunity to own the ranch himself, and soon he and Cordoba began arguing about who was in charge. Animosity grew between the two men. After several months of this, Cordoba promised $5,000 to a man named Marco Garcia to murder Martines so that Cordoba could maintain total control of the ranch operation. Garcia, using an assault rifle, shot Martines on the ranch property. He was then assisted by the original murderers, Martinez and Verdin, as they drove the body away in Martines's pickup truck.

Nico Cordoba reported to the Kadivar family that Martines had died of a heart attack. This complicated set of crimes was committed within the very transient Mexican ranch-hand community in the area, and it was extremely difficult for the homicide investigators to unravel this mystery. The fact that many of the witnesses and suspects in this case were undocumented workers and distrustful of law enforcement greatly complicated the investigation.

Sheriff's detectives painstakingly interviewed reluctant witnesses and pieced together these elaborate crimes. In June of 2007 they threw a series of raids against several possible suspects. In one raid at the home of Antonio Martinez, they located an SKS assault rifle, wrapped in plastic and hidden under a shed. This weapon was tested and found to be the weapon that murdered Efrain Martines. Two suspects admitted that the weapon used to murder the doctor, a 1903 Enfield, had been thrown in the nearby aqueduct. Numerous scuba searches failed to locate this weapon.

In October of 2009, Nico Cordoba, Antonio Martinez, and Arturo Verdin were all "held to answer" on charges of murdering Dr. Kadivar. The three were joined by a fourth man, Marco Garcia, in being held on charges for the murder of Efrain Martines.

On June 4, 2014, Marco Garcia pled guilty to the murder of Efrain Martines and agreed to assist the prosecution in this case. He gave a full admission and named Nico Cordoba as the ringleader.

On August 28, 2014, eight years after the first murder, Antonio Martinez was found guilty of the 2006 murder of Dr. Kadivar. He and ringleader Nico Cordoba were also found guilty of the 2007 murder of Efrain Martines.

In early November 2014, the final defendant, Arturo Verdin, was convicted for the first-degree murder of Dr. Kadivar and the later murder of Efrain Martines. All of the suspects were sentenced on January 23, 2015. Cordoba, Martinez, and Verdin were all sentenced to the maximum of life in prison without the possibility of parole, or LWOP as it is known on the street. The lone cooperating suspect, Marco Garcia, was given a sentence of twenty-eight years to life in prison.

In an ironic twist to this entire story, Det. Anderson would later discover that he had a direct link to the late Dr. Kadivar. Over a decade prior to the murder, Det. Anderson's daughter was injured in a fall. Anderson was set to take the girl to a local hospital near Los Angeles when a family member, who was a doctor, made a special phone call to a plastic surgeon who could help the young girl. An hour later, Det. Anderson handed his two-year-old daughter over to the gentle care of Dr. Steve Kadivar. The connection would not be made by Anderson until all of the suspects in the doctor's murder had been jailed.

### Investigator's Profile

Martha Zuno is the most dangerous of all arsonists: the revenge/spite offender. She, like her longtime boyfriend, Nico Cordoba, was a remorseless, greed-driven individual who would do anything she had to, to get what she wanted. She came to the ranch that day to collect the goats and horse she believed belonged to her. When she was thwarted in her efforts, she decided to destroy the animals in an incredibly horrific manner, thereby depriving anyone else of the animals. Like most revenge/spite arsonists, she showed a callous disregard for the safety of others and was only concerned about her own needs.

Revenge/spite-based arsonists are the deadliest of all as they often set fires in such a fit of rage that they have not considered who else may be in danger or what other property will be destroyed. It is very doubtful that Martha Zuno had one second of remorse for her atrocious act. She was given a very harsh sentence by California standards, for a woman who had no prior criminal record. She deserved every day of it! Zuno is classified as a **goal-directed arsonist** as arson/fire was the weapon she used to get her revenge.

Most big-city homicide detectives see upward of three to five hundred dead bodies in their careers. Many of these bodies are from typical street fights and shootings, and the investigators become somewhat comfortable dealing with this sort of straightforward mayhem. Likewise, not too many investigators have shed so much as a tear over the death of a street gangster or career criminal. However, the cases that really bother even the most hardened of homicide investigators are the kids, the elderly, or other helpless victims who fall prey to a particularly gruesome death. Nothing can erase the image from a homicide detective's mind of something as horrific as a child being cooked alive in a microwave or the decomposing body of a "floater," where the marine creatures have dined on the victim's face, or any number of obscenely vicious deaths against an elderly person or helpless child.

The career-ending rewards for spending several years witnessing these scenes are usually an ulcer, numerous lawsuits against you, stress-induced health issues, and the inability to sleep because you can't unsee horrible things once they have been seen. These are the cases that give detectives nightmares and cause them to turn to alcohol as a coping mechanism. Another coping mechanism used by cops of all types, but particularly homicide detectives, is "gallows humor." The very name suggests extremely inappropriate humor shared by sane people who have witnessed a particularly hideous or gruesome death scene. The true professionals use this as a coping mechanism and attempt to keep it "in house" as your typical citizen just wouldn't understand.

In this case, his partners soon noticed that the suffering of the poor horse greatly bothered Det. Todd Anderson. In true homicide fashion, they worked out a coping method for their partner. By the time Anderson made it back to his office the week after this fire, his well-meaning partners had written a song and crafted a music video of the incident. The song, sung to the tune of the 1970s hit, "Horse with No Name," was entitled, "I Been to the Desert and Shot a Horse That Was Aflame." There is no doubt that the LASD brass would have had a fit had they seen it. Nonetheless, it seemed to help Det. Anderson cope.

You don't work homicide; you wouldn't understand.

*The investigators who worked on this case include homicide detective Todd Anderson, Det. Gary Sica, Sgt. John Corina, Det. Angus Ferguson, and arson investigators Larry Lewis and Tania Owen.*

## WITCHES AND DEMONS
## SANTA CLARITA, CA, 2013

On the morning of April 13, 2013, deputies from the LASD's Santa Clarita Station responded to a modern tract home in a northern neighborhood called Saugus. The call was for a structure on fire and a woman in distress. When they arrived, they found the lone occupant of the home, Esther Su, standing somewhat calmly on the front porch area, with dark black smoke billowing out of the front door of the structure. Her somewhat calm demeanor while her home was obviously on fire was the deputies' first indication that all was not right with this woman. Their second indication that things were amiss was that Esther, a midfifties Asian woman, was stark naked. The confirming fact that she was probably a raving lunatic was the bizarre story she told the patrol officers about the fire. She said she was using the smoke to chase witches and demons from her home!

The deputies detained Esther, found some clothing for her, and watched as the firefighters arrived to check out the home. The source of the fire in the home was in an odd place: the kitchen sink. In that area, firefighters found the molten mass of a coffeepot and the heavy odor of lamp oil. Firefighters found that the pot was filled with gasoline and lamp oil. The fire captain proclaimed that Esther had attempted to burn her home, and this incident was a clear act of arson or at least attempted arson. The smoke damage to the home extended heavily into nearly every room of the house, but the fire was only in the sink area, and the only real damage was to the coffeepot.

In Los Angeles County, all acts of arson are investigated by the sheriff's department's Arson-Explosives Detail. The local deputies placed a call to the unit, and the on-duty team of investigators that night was Sgt. Joe Acevedo and Det. Rob Harris.

Harris and Acevedo, both veteran investigators, realized that this woman was no criminal and that the only fire damage was to her own coffeepot, which was melted flat. The coffeepot had been sitting inside a porcelain sink, which, while heavily stained and covered in soot, was not damaged. They determined that she had not committed a crime per the California arson statutes. However, the two investigators did record through photos and notes that something was truly awry with this woman.

They saw that there was no electricity in the home, despite it being modern, neat and tidy, and filled with expensive personal belongings. They noted that someone (Esther) had set a fire among debris on the concrete walkway just outside of her own front door. They also noticed that the home had a heavy perfume odor consistent with aromatic lamp oil. A search of the home showed that Esther lived alone and had placed lit Tiki torches in several areas of the home. The torches produced heavy soot and black smoke that literally coated many surface areas in the house. The investigators noted where the torches had been moved throughout the home and had caused scorching and heavy soot staining in dozens of areas of the home. The scorching and staining was heaviest around doors and windows, and it appeared that Esther had been holding the several Tiki torches against the walls in these areas.

The investigators were alarmed to find that Esther had brought a propane barbecue inside of the living room of her home and had been operating it. They immediately suspected that this all might have been an attempt at suicide. The investigators were even more alarmed when they spotted large containers of muriatic acid inside of the home.

When Harris and Acevedo went upstairs, they saw the heavy smoke and scorch marks along the ceiling in every room including the bathrooms. Esther had spent considerable time carrying her Tiki torches throughout the home. The master bedroom was the only messy room in the home. Esther had taken every heavy blanket and drape from the home and covered all walls of her bedroom with them. The room smelled strongly of muriatic acid and Tiki torch fuel. This was the room where Esther slept, and the two detectives were having a hard time breathing among the fumes. The investigators also took note of an excessive amount of prescription medications in the home.

Harris and Acevedo went to the attached garage and found a large pile of boxes that had contained large jugs of muriatic acid. This type of material was consistent with persons with swimming pools, but it was an extremely excessive amount. There were at least twenty empty cases of acid stacked up behind the garage. When they entered the garage, they figured out why there were so many empty cases. Esther had an expensive blue Ford F-150 FX4 off-road pickup truck parked inside. The custom truck was completely covered in muriatic acid. A large amount of the acid had been poured onto the concrete floor and driveway and had spilled into the street, creating massive etchings and stains in the concrete.

Harris and Acevedo went to the local sheriff's station to interview Esther. They found the small, slightly built woman to be docile, polite, and very subdued. She spoke to them in a quiet but clear voice. She told the two surprised investigators that she had set the coffeepot in the sink and filled it with fuel for a reason. She explained that she had lit the fuel on fire and then went around her home with torches and acid to drive evil entities out of her home. Esther explained that she had an entity living in her home and in her vehicle, and had learned that the entity did not like smoke or acid. She claimed that the entity came to her in the form of tiny witches, demons, and sprites, and that she had spent weeks ridding her home of them. She admitted to smoking out her truck with torches and covering it in acid in an attempt to rid it of the entities as well.

While the investigators knew that Esther had committed no crime, they were not so sure that she wasn't suicidal. They approved the seventy-two-hour psychiatric hold on the poor woman. Later, we would learn that Esther had been married, raised some good children, and had been employed for several years as a registered nurse. As happens quite a bit in the medical profession, Esther had easy access to powerful prescription drugs and soon became addicted to pain and anxiety medications. The addiction became so powerful that within a few years the drugs began to alter her personality. Eventually her husband left her, and her kids moved away from their crazy mother. There had been several attempts to help the woman over the years, but she continued to act in a bizarre manner.

After the fire incident at her Saugus home, and after being released from the psychiatric hospital following a seventy-two-hour detention and mental-health evaluation, someone in the mental-health field determined that Esther Su was not a danger to herself or to others. Esther went on with her life. She made an insurance claim for the fire and smoke damage to her home. Because she was not charged with the crime of arson, she could legally claim the incident with her insurance carrier. The insurance carrier, as provided in their coverage, arranged for Esther's home to be cleaned, repaired, and put back into original condition. As part of this, they provided a location for Esther to stay while awaiting the repairs on her home. In this case, the insurance carrier housed Esther Su in a very nice, multi-bedroom condominium in a large complex within about three miles of her home.

Sometime in the summer of 2013, Esther Su again came to the attention of the local Santa Clarita Sheriff's Station deputies. One day a traffic officer observed a newer Ford truck speeding on local streets. During the traffic stop he contacted the driver, Esther Su. The officer did not know her and was taken aback at the condition of the vehicle when he walked up to her open window. Outside, the expensive truck was gleaming and in excellent condition. Inside, however, he found that the interior was covered in thick, smoky soot and ash.

Esther appeared to be oblivious to the soot and ash. The traffic officer inquired with Esther if something was wrong with the truck. She explained in a soft, quiet voice that she had been "cleansing" the truck with smoke, and it had left some residue. The officer, not really understanding what she meant, assumed that since she was Asian, there was some sort of language misinterpretation going on. She appeared to be a normal housewife in the area and not up to anything criminal, so he dismissed her statement and finished his business with her.

Later, when he told the odd story at the station, one of the other deputies recognized Esther's name and told the traffic cop about the previous fire event. Esther had apparently performed some sort of fire cleansing ritual on the inside of her nearly new truck, pretty much destroying the interior of the vehicle. At least she had her clothes on for this event.

On September 22, 2013, I met Esther Su. Shortly after moving in to her temporary home in the rented condo, Esther came to the attention of her neighbors and the property manager. Neighbors in the upscale condo complex could hear windows breaking and the sound of someone pounding on walls from within the condo. This was reported to the property manager, who in turn left messages for Esther. At some point the property manager gained access to Esther's apartment and was shocked to find damage to the walls and floor. The manager saw that someone had punched or hammered several holes in the drywall of the master bedroom. There also seemed to be a dark soot coating on one of the closets in the condo.

The manager warned Esther that she would be kicked out and that she needed to repair the damage. Esther later found a friend who came over and attempted to repair the holes in her walls. The repair work and subsequent painting of the walls were both substandard and could be seen several weeks later.

On the evening of September 22, neighbors of Esther Su heard the smoke alarm in her condo sounding and soon saw hazy smoke wafting out of the apartment. They called 911, and soon both the sheriff's and fire departments arrived to investigate. Firefighters forced her door and found the three-bedroom condo empty. They could find no active fire but followed heavy smoke to a master bedroom and walk-in closet. It appeared that a fire had taken place inside the closet. The fire captain noted that there were Tiki torches in the room, and he assumed the woman had used them to start the fire. Besides the heavy smoke and soot, the firefighters soon had trouble breathing and saw there were crystals of acid poured throughout the condo. They called the arson unit, and I was on duty that night.

As soon as I got the call and spoke to the patrol deputy, I recognized the woman from descriptions given by Harris and Acevedo. I called Rob Harris for a little guidance and then drove to the condo. When I entered, I could sense an overpowering odor of acid. I found several empty cases of white crystals that were the dry form of muriatic acid. These crystals had been poured around every door and window of the home, along all counters, and along the walls of every room. This building was practically a hazmat cleanup site.

I went through the home and looked in the closet that appeared to be burned. It in fact was not burned, but the smoke and soot from Tiki torches was so thick that it even fooled the firefighters. I saw that Esther had placed four burned torches inside the closet and had caused nearly a quarter inch of soot on the floor. She did the same thing in a nearby bathroom.

Esther Su had fled the scene prior to the arrival of the cops and firemen, but she returned when I was there. I taped an eerie interview with the petite woman as she walked me through her home. In a completely sober and conversational tone, she patiently explained to me her ongoing war with a demonic entity. She described her actions in her previous home and fully admitted to her recent actions in the condo. She said she was careful not to cause a fire but did admit to "burning the demons out" of the rooms of her home. Once she had cleansed a room with torches, she poured the strong acid crystals on the floor in a circle to prevent them from reentering.

Esther Su described her life among demons, witches, sprites (good witches), and other entities she called "meemies." She described that the sprites and meemies were good and kept the bad demons and witches at bay. While talking to me and the other deputies, she pointed out a half-dozen witches and sprites doing battle around us. She gave me good personal vibes when she told me that I had a large amount of good energy and sprites encircling me to ward of the demons. I thanked her for the insight. In my view of Esther, it was apparent that she truly did "see" these entities and believed in their existence.

At the end of the night, I had the deputies take her again on a seventy-two-hour mental-health evaluation. This time we charged Esther with felony vandalism, as her actions caused tens of thousands of dollars in damage to the rental property. I wrote a report recommending intense mental-health treatment as we were sure that this poor woman was on a path to an accidental fire death or an accidental suffocation/poisoning death. Like every other time she had been detained, she was released almost immediately by the mental-health professionals.

I recently reviewed her file to see if she was staying out of trouble. Esther Su's criminal history reads like every other person who is struggling with failing mental-health and drug addiction. This woman lived a crime-free life for over fifty years, but in the past three years alone she has had six felony arrests. These arrests included assaults, multiple arrests for narcotics (prescription pills), trespassing, and multiple counts of contempt of court. Thank God there have been no more fire incidents, but I do not predict a good ending for Esther Su. She is clearly an extreme danger to herself or any other persons living in the same building as her.

**Author's note:** Esther Su did not actually commit the criminal act of arson, but I told you that story to set up and tell you the next one. These two cases occurred four months apart and ten miles away from each other. Compare the two.

## NINJAS IN MY WALLS!
## CASTAIC, CA, 2014

At just before five o'clock, on New Year's Day 2014, neighbors spotted Kristi Henderson. She was walking up the street, dragging a beat-up suitcase, and talking loudly to herself. In fact, "talking" is not an apt description. It was more like she was ranting to herself and to just about anyone else within earshot. Nobody on the cul-de-sac at the very end of a street named Quail Valley Road was particularly worried about the deranged rants coming from this woman. She was a familiar figure and a longtime resident of the neighborhood of tract homes in Castaic, a small town thirty-five miles north of Los Angeles.

Kristi, her ex-husband, and their kids had lived for over a decade in the home at 31208 Quail Valley Road. The home was a spacious two-story, with a huge yard, which is very rare in California. The family put in a very nice custom pool several years prior. Sometime in the past several years, things had begun to unravel for the family. Kristi was known by her family and neighbors to be a long-term functioning alcoholic. She had severe relationship issues with her mother, who lived in another state, and her husband, and she was dealing with her own minor mental-health issues. Her family knew that Kristi liked to drink in order to cope with these problems. As such, the family began to erode. Eventually the kids became adults and moved away. Her husband left a few years before, and Kristi was alone in the large, modern home.

For a period of several months, she didn't pay the mortgage and was soon in arrears. She finally decided to move out and rent the home to another party so that she could make her mortgage payments. Kristi rented the fully furnished home to a guy for several months, and all seemed well. At some point the renter was told by the mortgage company that Kristi was not applying his rent checks to her mortgage, and she was again several months behind in rent. The renter was actually forced to move from the home by the mortgage company. As such, he lost his security deposit and final month's rent, which was several thousand dollars. He beseeched Kristi to pay him back but soon realized that she was a bit "out of her mind." She refused to acknowledge his issues, and in retaliation the renter took all of her furniture with him when he left.

Shortly after the renter left, the next-door neighbors, Bill and Gayle Farrow, noticed that Kristi had moved back into the home. She acted like nothing was wrong, but soon real-estate signs appeared on the lawn, and it was clear that the bank was attempting to sell the home. Each time a sign would appear, Kristi ripped it down and acted like nothing was wrong. She said the bank was trying to steal her home and that she was all paid up on her mortgage. Several neighbors reported hearing construction work in the home at all hours of the night.

At one point, Kristi approached Bill Farrow and asked him to help her get rid of some people inside of her home. He walked over to her house with her and was shocked by what he saw. He noted that there was almost no furniture in the home, and there were holes cut or broken into several of the interior walls, exposing the wall studs. He believed that there had been several thousand dollars in damage done to the interior of the home. When he asked Kristi what had happened, she gave him a very peculiar reply. She said, "There are people living in my walls." She then asked Farrow if he could help her find them. She indicated that they were in the walls, in the plumbing, and possibly living under the backyard pool. Farrow, shocked by her statements, finally realized that Kristi was losing her mind.

Bill and Gayle Farrow were very sympathetic toward Kristi as they had known her for a long time and realized that her life had been going downhill for the past few years. They had witnessed her devolve from a normal suburban housewife and mom into a raving lunatic, who appeared to be nearly homeless. The Farrows' patience with her would be further tested when one day they noticed that their yard and driveway was flooded under a torrent of water. The source of the flood was Kristi's swimming pool. They saw that she had drained the massive pool of all its water, and some of it had flowed onto their property. This caused several thousands of dollars of damage to the Farrows' home.

Kristi told them that somehow her pool had been sabotaged by either the fire department or the local water agency. The sheriff's department was notified, and puzzled deputies responded to interview the woman. Kristi, who outwardly appeared like a normal suburban mom, told them an outlandish tale. She insisted that somehow the fire department was in league with the local water agency to "steal" her property as there was a lucrative diamond and gold mine directly under her pool. She insisted that she could hear tunneling and miners' voices under her pool. While she never admitted it, she clearly had emptied the pool in search of these voices and miners. The deputies dismissed her as just another housewife who had taken a few too many prescription meds.

Before long, representatives from the bank that owned the home were able to obtain an eviction order for Kristi, who hadn't made a mortgage payment in over two years. Sheriff's deputies served the papers, and Kristi was forced off the property. The bank changed all the locks and put the home up for sale again. A week or two later, as a realty agent was attempting to show the home, he found that Kristi was staying in a tent at the property and that she had changed the locks again. When he spoke to her, she threatened him with some very colorful language. This activity went on several times over the previous summer, with neighbors soon realizing that Kristi was staying in a tent or shed on the property and routinely chasing real-estate agents and bank representatives off of it.

One day, in the fall of 2013, she ran outside and yelled, "Fire, fire." Another neighbor ran to her house to assist her and saw smoke pouring out of it. He called the fire department, and then he entered her home. He could find only a smoldering fire that someone had lit upstairs in some debris. The fire was out, and there was no damage. Three times in the next month, another neighbor was alerted to Kristi screaming that her house was on fire. Each time he responded to find her standing at the door of her home but without any smoke or fire. This neighbor entered her home on each occasion and saw that the home was a disaster, with the carpet having been pulled up and dozens of holes having been cut into the walls and floors. He asked Kristi about it, and she said that when she is out, people come over and do that damage. She also said that people were living in her walls, floors, under her yard, and under her pool.

By Christmas of 2013, the neighbors, sheriff's deputies, and local firefighters had all responded to Kristi's home numerous times. She was clearly losing her mind, and everyone implored her to leave the property and seek mental-health assistance. Her daughter in Las Vegas was notified and made attempts to rescue her mom, all without success. Kristi continued to "squat" in a tent on the property and would only bathe or shower at a friend's house about a mile away. Kristi also continued to drink and was a regular fixture at a seedy bar nearby.

At five o'clock on New Year's Day 2014, Kristi was spotted by two neighbors going in and out of the front door to her home. I later viewed a neighbor's security footage of the event. The footage was equipped with an audio feed, and I could clearly make out what Kristi was saying and singing. I saw that at about 5:08 p.m., Kristi emerged from the home, singing and talking loudly to herself. She was ranting and speaking in a voice consistent with what is often heard in an urban ghetto. She began yelling at the home as if it were a person, saying, "Blaze up, nigga" and "Burn, bitch-ass nigga."

After a few minutes of pacing back and forth and ranting at the home, Kristi eventually sat on the curb line opposite her house and continued to rant loudly. The neighbors, used to this sort of behavior, ignored her and went about their business. At about 5:10 p.m., Kristi yelled more epithets at the home, including "blaze up," and then she started to walk away down the street dragging her suitcase. Almost immediately the glow of a fire was seen reflecting off the neighbors' homes.

At 5:12 p.m., next-door neighbor Bill Farrow walked outside to get something from his truck and saw a large volume of flame erupting from the open front door of Kristi's home. He ran to the house, yelled for Kristi, and was soon joined by his wife and other neighbors. At the same time several of them dialed 911.

When firefighters arrived about ten minutes later, they made entry into the home and found a fully involved fire filling most of the bottom floor. They fought the large fire and realized that the source of the flame was coming from an open gas valve in the kitchen area. This valve was shut off by firefighters, and they recognized that a second gas valve was open in the fireplace in the nearby den. The source of all the fire damage in the home was traced back to these open gas valves.

After hearing the story from the witnesses, sheriff's deputies located and arrested Kristi Henderson several blocks away. She denied knowing that a fire had occurred. Two hours later I drove to the scene with my partner, Det. Kim Ponce. We conducted a fire-scene investigation along with a fire chief and a technician from the local gas company. We documented all the damage to the home that at first looked like normal fire and fire-suppression damage. However, on closer inspection, we confirmed that the majority of the structural damage to the house had occurred prior to the fire. We were a bit surprised to learn that a suburban housewife had committed all of this mayhem.

After confirming that the fire was, indeed, a criminal act of arson and interviewing several neighbors, all of whom had known Kristi for several years, we drove to the nearby sheriff's station to interview this woman. We had heard her very vulgar ranting and yelling on the security video and expected to find a deranged, violent, and out-of-control drug addict in the interview room. We were taken aback by the appearance of a calm, polite, well-dressed and well-mannered suburban mom. Her hair was neat and tidy, her clothes were clean and stylish, and she acted as if she had just been pulled from a school conference or real-estate meeting. We had to check her jail wristband to see if she was actually the same woman who had been ranting and acting crazy on the surveillance video.

Det. Ponce and I spent almost two hours talking to Kristi Henderson. Soon, the calm and collected outward appearance was betrayed by the delusional talk of a woman who had lost her mind. While Kristi never admitted to the fire, she gave obvious lies in the face of plain evidence and witnesses. She denied having even been at her home in the past few days despite video evidence and eyewitnesses. She refused to discuss the fire or anything leading up to it.

However, when the subject of her home came up, the well-dressed, articulate housewife showed her true colors. She began to tell us in a calm, businesslike tone of a massive, secret conspiracy to steal her home and the valuable diamond mine underneath it. She spoke in perfect diction and regaled us with the theory that the sheriff's, fire, and water departments were all acting in concert to steal her home from her so that she couldn't get the diamonds under her pool. She said she had dug inspection holes, had drained her pool, and had even broken the pool concrete and confirmed that there were several massive tunnels under her property where city workers had been stealing diamonds.

When the subject of the holes in the walls and floors came up, Kristi really amazed us. She said that public officials and banks had allowed "ninjas" to enter her home and take residence in the walls and plumbing. Kristi said that sometimes she broke into the walls to chase them out, but sometimes the ninjas broke the walls on their own. She said that the ninjas had destroyed her pool, her plumbing, had eaten her electrical wiring, and had broken through her floors. When we were done with Kristi a couple of hours later, we were convinced that this soft-spoken woman actually believed the stories she had told us.

A couple of days later we filed arson charges against Kristi for the destruction of the home. The home hadn't been owned by her for over a year, and the bank was the true owner. Additionally, we learned that Kristi had confided in a friend that the home was fully insured and that she was going to do something to it after New Year's to get the insurance money. On her arrest, Kristi was in possession of the insurance paperwork for the home. What Kristi didn't know was that she hadn't paid a premium in years, and her insurance had lapsed. This information did give us the idea that possibly Kristi believed she had insurance and thereby had committed an act of insurance fraud.

The case was delayed for months, and the court, worried about Kristi's obvious dangerous behavior, kept her bail at a high level, which she could not reach. Finally, a court officer decided that Kristi had significant mental-health problems. She was sent away to Patton State Hospital for a mental-health evaluation. She was declared mentally incompetent. In early 2015 the hospital changed its evaluation, and Kristi was found mentally fit to be charged with arson. She was sent back to criminal court, and her lawyers realized that we had a very tight case against her and pled her out to a single count of arson of a home.

Kristi Henderson was sentenced to three years in prison. She had to spend one year in jail with the caveat that she also complete a six-month alcohol treatment and mental-health program. She completed those steps, and the rest of her prison sentence was suspended. She is currently on felony probation.

*This case was investigated by the author, Det. Ed Nordskog, and Det. Kim Ponce of the LASD Arson-Explosives Detail.*

## ROSEMARY: SERIAL ARSONIST LOS ANGELES, CA, 2011

In the Los Angeles basin, there are over fifty small cities and a couple of larger ones. The total population exceeds ten million citizens. Crisscrossing this region are several major bus routes and light-rail train lines, all under the authority of the Metropolitan Transit Authority (MTA). From its inception, the MTA had its own police force, but it quickly was overwhelmed by gangs, graffiti, and crime, and was judged to be somewhat ill prepared to deal with all the issues along the rail corridors.

In the 1990s the MTA, realizing its police force lacked the clout of the LAPD or LASD, finally agreed to contract with the nine-thousand-strong sheriff's department for law enforcement services. The LASD, a huge agency with a strong reputation for being very aggressive toward gang members, quickly brought the rail system under control. Twenty years later, through very aggressive enforcement actions and zero tolerance, the MTA system remains fairly free of gang issues and graffiti. The MTA deputies have the most assets of any unit on the sheriff's department. They have undercover details, K-9 units, a counterterrorist squad, fast-reaction teams, and a bevy of detectives. They also have a surveillance-camera system that is state of the art.

On July 7, 2011, MTA officials monitoring video-surveillance cameras saw smoke arising from one of the train station platforms on the route. They couldn't see the source of the smoke but noted that numerous passengers were running around in a bit of a panic. This platform was in an area known as East Hollywood. The platform was extremely modern as it was just a few years old and was mostly underground. The security monitor officers dispatched uniformed sheriff's deputies to the platform to check for the source of the fire. The LAFD also responded. Because of the potential danger level of an underground fire, at least fifty sheriff's deputies, along with a dozen MTA security officials, arrived via car, foot, and train.

When deputies got to the scene, they were relieved to find that the source of the smoke was coming from a metal trash can on the platform. The trash and the plastic interior liner were on fire. Two sheriff's deputies quickly extinguished the blaze with a fire extinguisher. Passersby were questioned, but no one recalled seeing anything. Per the sheriff's department's policy, my unit, the Arson-Explosives Detail, was notified. I was on duty that afternoon, and I responded with my partner Det. Cindy Valencia. Meanwhile, we asked MTA officials to review their video footage backward for up to an hour before the incident.

Due to the typical, heavy Los Angeles traffic, it took us nearly forty-five minutes to get to East Hollywood. Just as we arrived, MTA deputies advised us that they were responding to a second fire at the next train platform to the west, in Hollywood. We sped to that scene and arrived to see deputies extinguishing a second fire in another metal trash container on that platform.

This time the techy geeks were on top of things and had called to say that they had a suspect on video who was seen lighting the trash can on fire with a cigarette lighter. They described the suspect as a black male or possibly female, dressed as a transient in dirty, bedraggled clothing, with a long scarf wrapped around his head, and wearing camouflaged shorts. They gave a detailed description of the suspect, and the MTA deputies began looking for him both in the underground train platforms and on the surface streets above. Meanwhile other citizens approached deputies describing having seen the same person setting multiple fires on at least three train platforms in the area.

By the time we finished examining the two original train station fires, we saw that four trash cans had been set on fire, and it appeared that someone had attempted to ignite one or two more. All of these fires were extinguished by either citizens or deputies, and none spread beyond the cans. While we were examining the small fire scenes, an MTA janitor approached us and told us that she was aware of at least a half-dozen prior small fires on the platforms of the three Hollywood-area stations. The janitor said these fires had been going on for a few months. We later had detectives from the MTA research all records for these events.

Within the hour, an alert patrol deputy found the suspect walking along the surface streets a few blocks from the East Hollywood Station. The suspect was detained and found to be a forty-nine-year-old woman. She was an exact match to the suspect seen lighting four fires on the video screens. Upon her arrest, the suspect was found to be carrying two cigarette lighters, five books of matches, and a pack of cigarettes. The woman, Rosemary Longstreet, was arrested and booked at a nearby jail.

Det. Valencia and I interviewed Rosemary about an hour after her arrest. We attempted to review as much about her background as possible before we spoke to her but could find only a few items in California. We later discovered that she had a significant arrest record in other states, with the bulk of them being in Illinois, where she had spent most of her life. Rosemary had arrest records in four states under seven different names and dates of birth. The arrest records were extremely telling and were quite predictable to us. She had arrests in California for assault, theft, narcotics, and drug violations. She also had numerous arrests in Texas and Chicago going back twenty-five years for theft, shoplifting, assaults, drug use and sales, and prostitution. She had several misdemeanors and one felony conviction.

The moment we met Rosemary we confirmed that her appearance was consistent with her criminal record. She was dirty, smelly, and disheveled and appeared to have been sleeping in an alley for the past six months, which she had. She had her hair shaved close to her head, was quite husky in size, and did have the outward appearance of a man. Her missing and broken teeth and horrifying breath, along with a battered face full of scars and vacant eyes, confirmed that she was an aging prostitute and cocaine addict. She was the living personification of a true crack whore.

Cindy and I had dealt with thousands of these crack zombies that walk the streets and alleys of Los Angeles at night, and we have been able to communicate with most of them as they usually possess at least a little bit of their brains and senses. Rosemary was a true challenge. She grunted and made sounds like a cavewoman. She sat quietly for long minutes, dropped off suddenly into a snoring sleep, and then burst out into animated talking and yelling. We spent nearly ninety minutes trying to talk to Rosemary, and eventually we were able to piece together a disturbing but familiar story.

Rosemary quickly admitted to starting several small fires that night at the train platforms. She said she had approached a police officer for assistance, and when he refused to help her, she had gotten upset and had entered the train stations to light things on fire. She admitted to lighting several fires, but we could only confirm the three or four in the stations. She said she used both matches and a lighter to start the fires.

Rosemary eventually told us that she had grown up in Chicago and had given birth to seven children. She told us that several of them had been killed or died since birth. To her knowledge, only three of her kids were living. She admitted that at least one child died in a fire, and a couple had been killed when they were in gangs. She said that the state authorities (state unknown) took her last two kids from her for neglect reasons.

Rosemary said she had been addicted to crack since the 1980s, and it had caused her to commit thousands of crimes to feed the habit, including theft and prostitution. She said she would do anything in the world to get the crack. Rosemary described how she came to California. She said that the authorities in Chicago were so sick of seeing her that a welfare worker eventually gave her train passes and a credit card to travel to Los Angeles. She said that the welfare workers in Chicago had explained that she could get a lot more benefits in California than anywhere else (this is true).

Rosemary said she has used her free rail passes to travel to several states and back to Chicago numerous times. She has been in Los Angeles for over a year and gets state aid and assistance for numerous psychiatric and physical disabilities. When arrested she had a debit card for a local bank and had several rail tickets indicating that she had traveled by rail across the United States. She also admitted to working as a prostitute to make money or get crack while in Los Angeles.

We focused on the question of fire. Rosemary was very evasive but admitted that she had set fires for years whenever she was upset. She said she seldom burned anything of substance, just usually trash, trees, furniture, or anything she finds on the street. She said she had been caught lighting fires several times by police or security guards but had never been arrested.

Rosemary surprised Cindy and me by lifting up her legs and showing horrible burn scars on both, running from her feet up her legs. She said that once, when she was very upset about the death of a child, she had gone to a gas station in Chicago and pumped gasoline over herself and then ignited it in a suicide attempt. She spent months in a hospital and was released back to the streets. She admitted to other suicide attempts. Rosemary also admitted to starting a fire in one of her homes but that it was almost twenty years before. She said that there had been several fires in her life, but she couldn't remember them all.

We found records of three other fires on the rail platforms. They had occurred two months prior, and both matched

Rosemary's admission. We ended up filing five counts of arson against this habitual fire setter. A few weeks later Rosemary pled guilty and was sentenced to three years in prison. We made several inquiries to Chicago and Texas but could not confirm any of the other fires in Rosemary's life.

*This case was investigated by Det. Ed Nordskog and Det. Cindy Valencia of the LASD Arson-Explosives Detail.*

### Investigator's Profile

Rosemary represents the most common type of serial arsonist: the **urban serial arsonist**. This is the shambling, rambling, wandering, homeless or transient person who sets fire to targets of opportunity that he or she comes across. Urban serial arsonists are often caught or detained numerous times before they are actually brought to jail as their fires normally involved items of little value. They are what fire departments call "nuisance fires" and as such get very little investigative attention. People in this class of serial arsonists can set hundreds of fires in their lives.

Rosemary's profile is a classic urban serial arsonist. She is barely functioning mentally and has numerous physical ailments as well. She has a long history of institutionalization and suicide attempts. She had a nearly thirty-year history of drug addiction, which of course leads back to psychiatric issues. All of the above caused her to have an extensive record of minor crimes. She is unable to drive and is dependent on walking or riding the rails to get around.

She admitted that she lit fires for years whenever she was upset, which is classic as it goes to the motive of **frustration**. Rosemary's attempt at suicide is quite alarming, and it would not surprise me at all if she or her children had been victimized in a house fire she set many years prior. She is classified as an **emotionally based arsonist**.

Rosemary represents several common traits associated with female serial arsonists. Many female serial arsonists have attempted suicide, have lost children to nonmedical deaths, have very masculine qualities, have addiction issues, and have lit fires within their own home or workplace (Rosemary admitted to multiple fires within her homes). While she has no previous arson arrests on her record, it is very likely that Rosemary has been detained by police or firefighters several times for small fire-setting acts. She has likely set hundreds of fires over the past four decades.

## I BURNED YOUR HOUSE! LOS ANGELES, CA, 2014

Patrick Philabaum was a forty-year-old, unemployed ex-felon who lived with his mother in a small apartment building in Rosemead, California. Patrick was a bit down-and-out and had trouble keeping jobs and girlfriends. Besides these issues, Patrick had a girlfriend he didn't *want* to keep; only she wasn't accepting that.

For several months leading up to June of 2014, Patrick had an on-again, off-again relationship with a fifty-year-old woman named Juanita Juarez. Both she and Patrick shared similar life-styles. She was unemployed, had a jail record, and liked to indulge in methamphetamines. In short, she was a tweeker. Like all tweeker relationships, she and Patrick were involved in a constant series of fights, arguments, thefts, assaults, and noisy activity. By early 2014, Patrick's mother could take no more. She had a hard enough time dealing with the fact that her son was an out-of-work ex-con and hanging around the home. She didn't need a half-crazed drug addict, part-time girlfriend hanging out there either. Patrick's mother gave Juanita the boot and got a court order for her not to return to their home in Rosemead.

Like so many "stay away" and "restraining orders," the ink wasn't even dry, and both Patrick and Juanita were in violation of it. If they didn't see each other in person, then they maintained a constant dialogue on the phone and via text. All of these were violations of the court order. Nobody seemed to care.

On June 19, 2014, Patrick and Juanita were having one of their many battles. This time the fight was taking place via text messaging. Luckily for law enforcement purposes, the content of those messages was preserved after this incident. The following is an excerpt from Patrick Philabaum's text messages that day, complete with all of their spelling and grammar errors:

*Patrick: K bitch get the FK out dirty whore*
*Juanita: K see ya*
*(several minutes later)*
*Juanita: Im setting ur housr on fire*

Patrick looked out his bedroom window just seconds after receiving that final text message from Juanita. He could see smoke and flames rising from a fence and bushes directly beneath his window. The fire was threatening the home, and he and his mother (who used a wheelchair) were forced to flee the scene to avoid injury. Juanita was nowhere to be seen. The fire department was able to extinguish the blaze without significant damage or injuries.

Local sheriff's deputies responded to the scene and immediately recognized both Patrick and Juanita from numerous other disturbances at the location. The patrol officers went out into the neighborhood to find the woman. Sgt. John Hanson and Det. Rick Velazquez from the LASD Arson-Explosives Detail arrived a few minutes later. They saw that a medium-sized fire had originated directly below Patrick Philabaum's bedroom window. They found that someone had poured gasoline onto a wooden fence and in some dry shrubbery just below the window. They collected evidence at the scene, including "screen shots" from Patrick Philabaum's cell phone, detailing the text messages sent by Juanita.

This case was a "no brainer," and patrol officers began checking all of Juanita's usual hangouts. They were unable to find her and surmised that she had fled the area immediately after the fire. Sgt. Hanson completed his investigation and found an eyewitness who saw Juanita outside of Patrick's apartment the morning of the fire. Sgt. Hanson placed a BOLO (Be On the Look Out) for Juanita with the local deputies. They were all confident that she would show up sooner or later. Just over two weeks later a pair of alert patrol deputies found and arrested Juanita for possession of narcotics. They immediately notified the arson detail.

Sgt. Hanson rushed to the scene and interviewed Juanita. Juanita might have been half-crazy from years of drug abuse, but she was also very streetwise and clever. She gave an alibi for the event and even named another girl as a probable suspect. However, Sgt. Hanson was persistent and eventually cornered Juanita with the evidence and her ever-changing stories. Eventually she sighed heavily and admitted her actions. Juanita broke down and said she was upset because she was sure that Patrick was having sex with another woman that morning. She went over to confront him and became so upset that she lost her mind and lit the fire to burn Patrick out of his home. Now she apologized and wanted to make amends to the property owner and other tenants. She eventually gave a written confession and a full accounting of how she lit the fire.

For her few moments of vindictiveness in lighting an occupied structure on fire, Juanita Juarez was sentenced to eighteen months in prison.

*This case was investigated by Sgt. John Hanson and Det. Rick Velazquez of the LASD Arson-Explosives Detail.*

### Investigator's Profile

This is definitely a classic female revenge/spite type of fire. Juanita is classified as a **goal-directed arsonist** as revenge was her goal. Sometimes women offenders are so enraged by the actions of their male friends (allegedly cheating—the ultimate betrayal for a woman) that they make no attempt whatsoever to hide their actions. In this case Juanita lit the fire because she was sure that Patrick was cheating (he actually wasn't in this case), and then she sent him a text just to let him know that she had done it. All this was done after another tenant spotted her on the property and asked her to leave. Juanita had virtually no chance of getting away with this sort of act.

The irrational thinking by Juanita could have easily become quite deadly. The location was a multiunit apartment complex, and at least one tenant was in a wheelchair. Luckily, the fire-setting skills of Juanita were quite rudimentary, and the fire stayed outside of the structure long enough for the arrival of the fire department.

# 6

# Juvenile Fire Setting

## The Profile

Profiling juvenile fire setters is perhaps more difficult than dealing with the many subtypes of adult arson offenders. Juvenile arsonists can range in age from six years old to seventeen, with any number of mental-health and social issues that may skew the child's intellectual level. More than adults, extreme caution and detailed investigation must take place with a juvenile-set fire to determine the risk level that the juvenile poses toward society. Investigators and prosecutors should consult *veteran* child psychiatrists, educators, and family and close friends of the family to determine exactly what is occurring in the life of the juvenile before reaching a conclusion of what subtype of arsonist the juvenile is.

Juvenile-set fires run the entire gamut from curiosity, to excitement, to vandalism, to revenge, or worse. It takes detailed analysis to differentiate an act between simple curiosity and a serious "cry for help," or even the onset of a lifetime serial arsonist. Each juvenile fire-setter case is unique and different, as shown in the below case histories.

## PATRICK
## VAL VERDE, CA, 1998

Patrick by all accounts was a good kid. His mother was a hard-working woman, and he lived with an extended family who loved and cared about him. The family was not without its faults. Patrick's aunt lived with them, but she was out of work and struggled with a cocaine habit. She lived upstairs with a boyfriend. Patrick's older brother, Sean, was a good kid too. Despite being only seventeen years old, Sean lived with his girlfriend, who was also seventeen, in another upstairs bedroom. Patrick shared the master bedroom with his mother. Sometimes his mother's boyfriend stayed over, and Patrick would have to sleep in his brother's room.

The extended family lived in a large two-story home in rural Val Verde. They would not have been able to rent such a large home in nearby Valencia, but Val Verde was known as a sort of blue-collar rural area where large properties and homes were affordable. Val Verde was also known for decades by its moniker "smoke town." Most believe that its geographic configuration of a very narrow valley with steep walls caused smoke from campfires and fireplaces to linger in the area.

More recently, Val Verde lived up to the "smoke town" alias due to an unexplained plague of suspicious fires in the area each year. Rumors about the source of these fires ranged from a serial arsonist to a gang initiation. Oddly, despite its very rural location, Val Verde was the home to a very active Hispanic street gang named aptly "Smoketown 13." I tell you this because all of these factors came into play during this investigation.

Patrick and his brother were well liked at home and at their local school. Patrick was very active and very curious. He was a happy boy, who loved his family. On the morning of New Year's Eve 1998, Patrick was seven years old. Because of his curious nature, Patrick would not get any older.

Patrick's mother and her boyfriend loved to prepare their home for a traditional Christmas. As was her long-standing custom, Patrick's mother preferred a live Christmas tree in her home. Her boyfriend, who lived in San Diego during the week, knew just the place to get one. On December 1, he picked up a live ten-footer from a farm in Carlsbad. He put the tree on top of his car and drove it over one hundred miles to Val Verde. On the day he brought it, it was a typical Southern California winter's day. It was dry, windy, and about sixty-five degrees. All this led to a very rapid drying out of the tree.

The tree was put into a stand in Patrick's home. The stand had a large water reservoir, and the family was careful to keep it well watered for the three weeks leading up to Christmas. The home was fully decorated, and the tree sat in a large living room with very high-vaulted ceilings that were open to the upper story. Patrick's mom was careful to use modern, low-wattage Christmas lights on the tree that would not produce heat. Patrick's mother was not aware, however, of how much the fireplace in the room would dry out a tree. The family used the open fireplace about three days a week over the month of December. So, despite the tree receiving a constant supply of water, the dry conditions and close proximity of a fireplace were dehydrating the tree faster than it could take in water.

Every item has something called an **autoignition temperature.** In layman's terms, it means that when an object or substance receives enough outside heat, at a given point, it will simply burst into flames. That point at which it bursts into flame is called its autoignition temperature. Factors that can alter or lower an object's autoignition temperature are prolonged exposure to sun, heat, drying, wind, or any other factor that will literally suck the moisture out of a substance. This exposure can last for as little as hours or as long as years. By December 31, 1998, the Christmas tree in Patrick's home was inching closer to its autoignition temperature.

Some weeks prior to this date, Patrick's aunt and other family members noticed something odd with Patrick. Because the family had begun using the fireplace in the winter months, they saw that Patrick had, like many young boys, been fascinated with the fire. The family routinely used Duraflame logs to start their fires and would then feed in natural wood. A supply of this was kept behind a sofa in an alcove. On top of this pile of wood, the family kept a fireplace/barbecue lighter. At some point they noticed that it was not always in the same spot where they had left it.

About a week before Christmas, they saw Patrick hiding behind the sofa, playing with the lighter. They took it away from him and scolded him about it. Just after Christmas they noticed again that it was missing and found it hidden in Patrick's room. Despite the obvious evidence, Patrick (like all boys his age) lied about even having the item.

This overcurious behavior caused some alarm in the family, and Patrick's mother decided to take steps to prevent an accident. She had her boyfriend install a small screw above the fireplace that was out of reach of Patrick. She then hung the lighter from that hook. This appeared to solve the problem until December 30. Someone lit the fire and forgot to place the lighter back on its hook. Later, Patrick's aunt again found him playing with the lighter in another room. She took it from him and yelled at him again. He just ran away laughing.

On New Year's Eve morning, Patrick's mother awoke early and left for work. Everyone was asleep except for Patrick. As she walked out the front door, she saw Patrick waving at her from the top of the stairs. He was wearing his one piece set of pajamas and was smiling broadly. Patrick's mother closed and locked the heavy front door and then began her half-hour drive to work. It was 7:08 a.m.

At 7:22 a.m., neighbors heard screaming and glass breaking at Patrick's home. Looking outside, they saw a large amount of flames raging from the far-back second-story window. Then, to their horror, they saw a little boy with his head on fire dive out of the upstairs window. The little boy then ran next door to a neighbor's home. At 7:24 a.m., the first 911 call went in to the fire department.

A next-door neighbor described what happened next. She heard pounding on her front door and opened it to see Patrick. He was screaming, and there was smoke and char all over his face and head. He pushed past her and ran upstairs to her bathroom. He then jumped in the tub and began turning on the water. The neighbor ran upstairs to help him and was shocked to see a large amount of his skin hanging from the stair rails and door knob. She began pouring cool water over him. The only thing he would tell her was "my tree was hot."

In the meantime, other neighbors saw that there were more people in the upstairs windows of the home. As the aunt in the front window tried to get out, she slipped and fell off the garage. She later was treated for a broken leg. A female (the girlfriend of Patrick's brother, Sean) had jumped from the rear upstairs window and was on the ground screaming with a broken leg, hip, and severe burns. The worst sight was Sean. Sean was a very heavy boy, who weighed nearly three hundred pounds. He appeared to be stuck in the open upstairs window and was screaming as a torrent of flames ripped out of the same window. He eventually fell to the ground with massive burns to his back area.

By everyone's account, it seemed to take the fire department forever to get there. In reality, the nearest fire station was about twelve miles away, and it took the first engine about twelve minutes to arrive on scene. When they arrived, they saw several groups of neighbors propping ladders against the home and attempting to force open the heavy front and rear doors. They believed there were still two people trapped in the home. The first engine crew finally forced in the heavy front door and began fighting a large fire in the living room just inside the door. A second engine arrived, and this crew was tasked with the rescue/search of the rest of the home. As they began mounting the open stairway adjacent to the living room, they began falling through the heavily burned wood. They were unable to gain access to the upstairs for several minutes after the fire was extinguished. It didn't matter at that point; there were no other persons in the home.

Eventually a paramedic truck arrived and was directed to render aid to Patrick at the neighbor's home. As the neighbor opened the front door, she called up to Patrick, "Don't worry, Patrick; the firemen are here to help you." As they ran up her stairs, they saw a badly burned Patrick leap out of the cooling waters of the bathtub and run away from them into a room, which he locked. When they forced entry into that room, they found him hidden under clothes in a closet. During treatment at the scene, the firefighters would determine that Patrick's and Sean's injuries were "death imminent" and asked for a rescue helicopter to get them to a burn center. As it stood, the only helicopter in the area was performing a rescue in nearby Valencia. Both boys were transported to Grossman Burn Center by ambulance.

I arrived at the scene almost two hours later. By that time the newspapers were out in force, and the firemen were doing a good job of ruining any evidence I had. I asked the fire captain to stop his men from destroying the crime scene, and I began to get an overall assessment of the incident. Immediately a local fire chief with whom I was familiar began making statements that this was an arson fire. This chief, whose judgment was of questionable merit in my mind, based his assessment on the large size of this fire and the fact that multiple people had been injured.

Lastly, this pseudo sleuth opined that the heavily damaged stairway was clear-cut proof that an arsonist had poured a flammable liquid over the scene. He added in several other factors to bolster his opinion, including the rapid buildup of the flames and holes in the upstairs hallway. This fire chief was convinced that a large amount of flammable liquid had been poured into many areas of this home in an attempt to murder the occupants.

Normally, this sort of rushed judgment by an experienced fire official, but an inexperienced fire investigator, is to be expected and doesn't often bother me. I know that a lengthy scene investigation will usually prove what actually started this fire and why it grew and spread so fast. However, in this case, I was irritated because the chief and his public information officer were already talking to the assembled press. Now, I was already being pelted with questions by the print reporters in the area who knew me.

Soon, as usual, the rumors began building, and the neighbors began relating all sorts of conspiracy theories. Within an hour, I was hearing from neighbors who "just knew" that this was a drug-related murder attempt, or it was the work of local gang members or possibly local Nazis as the family was multiracial. Soon, I heard whispers that this was the work of the elusive serial arsonist who seemed to haunt this small valley every few months. The only thing I knew was that I was told two people would probably die, and I needed lots of help to process this scene.

I called my homicide investigators, who merely stalled, saying, "Call us when they die; in the meantime, it's yours." Within about an hour, four investigators from the LACoFD arrived to help. Even though the law stated that this scene belonged to me (LASD), I allowed them to help me process this multi-room home. I then summoned some help from my own office to include an accelerant-trained K-9 named "Billy."

Again, the fire department seemed to be working against me. Since I had to start doing interviews of the survivors, I had assigned the fire department's investigators to process the farthest, least burned rooms in the home. The normal process is to work backward from least burned areas to most burned, which will usually give you the room where the fire originated. My initial walk through had shown that the most damaged room was the downstairs living room, which was just inside the front door. I had wanted to personally process that room with another trusted expert.

The fire department investigators soon tired of their more mundane roles in the farthest rooms and proceeded directly to the living room. While I was outside, I saw them bring in several ordinary firemen to the living room and show them something. This immediately pissed me off as most firefighters are completely untrained as arson investigators and had no business within this crime scene. When I walked in, one of the fire investigators was holding up the severely burned wood of a Christmas tree and stating to the surrounding firemen that this was the cause of the fire. To him, this was just another standard Christmas tree fire.

Well, let's just say this rankled me a bit as I confronted this guy. First, I kicked out all the other firemen, and then I asked this guy if he knew how the fire started since Christmas trees, while a great fuel source, are not a source of ignition. He looked at me blankly like I was stupid and said that it was clearly started by a "short" in the wiring of the tree lights. With that he said that this case was closed, and there didn't need to be anymore done. Within a few minutes, these investigators had "solved" this mystery and packed up their boots and flashlights and left the scene. This was typical in the fire-investigation field to just pick an easy answer and make the call without any supporting documentation.

On their way out, they briefed their chief (the same one who had made the assertion two hours prior that this was an arson attack). A few minutes later, I watched in amazement as the grizzled chief looked squarely into the local TV cameras and warned all the good people of Los Angeles that this is just what happens when you have a dry Christmas tree in the home. He sadly indicated with a gesture of his hand to the burned-out shell of the home.

What irritated me most about this event was that the investigators who had been there had spent less than one hour on the scene. There was no way they could have properly processed this scene in that time. We had two kids who were probably going to die, and the family would want to know what had really happened. I finished my interviews and began my own scene work, such as photographs and diagrams, and waited for investigators from my unit.

During that time I learned something very interesting. The surviving aunt had relayed to me Patrick's recent fire-starting escapades. Also, she told me some critical information. She said that she was absolutely sure that the fireplace lighter was hanging from its hook the previous night. The family had taken steps after Patrick's curiosity to put the lighter on a hook on the wall too high for him to reach. I should be able to find it on the hook or on the floor under it. Lastly, the aunt told me that the family had not plugged in the tree lights since Christmas day, a week prior. This information would help eliminate certain causes for this fire.

Later that day, after being reinforced with six other investigators from my unit and the K-9, I completed a very detailed fire investigation. We all agreed that the fire started in the living room near the Christmas tree. The K-9 alerted in an alcove area for accelerants, but we determined this to be some of the ingredients for the Duraflame logs that were stored there. There was no other gasoline or other accelerants in the home. (So much for the expert opinion of the thirty-five-year veteran fire chief, who had originally told me that accelerants were poured throughout.)

We set up a search grid of the devastated living room and found some interesting things. First, we found the badly burned remnants of the tree lights. They were not plugged in at the time of the fire, so we could quickly eliminate them as a cause. Next, we found the metal frame of a kitchen stool in front of the fireplace. This was in the exact spot where the family had said the barbecue lighter was stored. We were unable to find the barbecue lighter in this area, but we did find its metal components about twelve feet away at the base of the Christmas tree. Lastly, we could find no other forms of ignition in this room. We were beginning to form an interesting theory about what had taken place.

A review of the home showed that its design was a significant contributing factor to the rapid spread of flame. The Christmas tree was near the base of the stairwell. As the tree caught fire, it would naturally burn upward and chimney up the stairway, heavily damaging the stairway. We had learned by this time that Sean, who lived upstairs and at the back of the home, routinely kept his window cracked open a few inches, even in the winter. Because of this, it formed a natural air draw for the flames and literally sucked the flame front laterally across the upper hallway of the home and out Sean's window. This caused catastrophic damage to the living room, stairway, upstairs hall, and Sean's bedroom. It also left the other areas of the home almost untouched by heavy flame damage. The shape of the building and the fact that a window was open on the opposite end of the home caused the major burn patterns in this scene.

I went to bed that night feeling pretty sure that this mystery was solved and that young Patrick had something to do with this fire. First, young males of all races routinely engage in firesetting behavior at that age. Patrick had demonstrated at least three times within the past two weeks his fire curiosity. Patrick was the only person in the home awake just minutes before the fire. Next, the actions of Patrick upon hearing that firemen were here for him spoke about his "consciousness of guilt." He was in the most pain of his young life but still pulled himself out of the soothing water to hide from them.

The fact that the lighter components had been found at the base of the tree instead of hanging from the hook, along with the stool left near the fireplace, told its own story. It's clear that a short person moved that stool to be able to reach the lighter. I surmised at that point that Patrick had somehow ignited the tree and then, in a panic, had dropped the lighter near the base of the tree.

I awoke the next morning to see shocking news in the local rag. A late-arriving reporter had quoted several neighbors about the various rumors. By this time, several family members and now Patrick's mother had been quoted as saying that they believed this event was done by a racist skinhead gang. The local reporter had named anonymous fire department sources as saying that this was a firebomb attack on the home due to either racial animosity or narcotics activity. This claim was bolstered by the fact that local narcotics agents had raided this same home for drug sales about five years prior. I knew this information was outdated because my interviews had shown that Patrick's family had only been renting the home for about two years.

All of these wild theories came from a combination of factors. When we used the accelerant K-9 the previous day, it had in fact alerted just inside the front door. We cleared that area and found the remnants of a Duraflame log right where the family stated they were stored. The log contained kerosene and other accelerants. So, the dog alerted on something, and this alert was witnessed by neighbors and firefighters, who later told reporters that we had found accelerants. While all of this was true, the source of the accelerants was explained and found not to be of a sinister nature. This information was wrongly interpreted by witnesses and firefighters, who reported it to the media, causing a major problem.

A day later things got worse. First of all, young Patrick had died in the night due to his massive burn injuries. Secondly, a cousin of the family, a somewhat militant black preacher from Harlem, New York, had arrived in town and had proclaimed to the media that the sheriff's department was covering up a hate crime and that the fire department did not respond in a timely manner as they had diverted to assist in the attempted rescue of a drowning white girl in nearby, affluent Valencia. After this, the Al Sharpton wannabe got a lot of airtime, and my cell phone started ringing off the hook.

First, Homicide wanted to know why they were never called (actually they were). Secondly, my boss wanted to know why he wasn't informed of this murder (because it wasn't a murder). And lastly, the press wanted to know why we keep hiding the true cause of the fire. All this media attention caused several things. Most importantly, it caused my boss to give me free rein and all the overtime I needed to completely clear this case. It also caused me to interview about sixty-three more witnesses and work for fourteen more days on a case that was resolved within the first eight hours. Either way, the truth eventually came out.

My first stop was the burn ward and later the morgue, where I conducted a detailed examination of Patrick's injuries. It is an extremely sad thing to examine a dead child's body. But the examination was critical because Patrick's wounds told a large part of this story. His palms were burned to the bone. We later opined that he had accidentally ignited the tree and had tried to put out the flames with his hands. The tree, in its dry state, had probably exploded in flame and had caused an immediate massive fire, similar to what several gallons of gasoline might cause. This flame front no doubt chased Patrick up the stairs to his brother's room.

Interviews with his brother, Sean, before he passed out showed that he awoke to find Patrick pounding on his door with his head completely on fire. Patrick ran in and immediately dove out the window. Sean had said that Patrick was followed closely by flames that chased him and his girlfriend out the window behind Patrick. The injuries to both boys verified that story. All of the skin and hair on Patrick's head and face were severely burned, as was his back and the insides of his hands. There were no other injuries on him. Four days later, Sean mercifully succumbed to his injuries. He was only seventeen.

A few days after the funeral, I finally approached Patrick's mother and painfully went through the case with her step by step, leaving out of course the boys' injuries. At the end, I could only feel sorrow for her when she made her own conclusion that her son, Patrick, had accidentally killed himself and his brother by playing with the lighter near the tree.

Eventually, the fire department did an internal investigation and concluded that they had not delayed in responding to this event. Patrick's family eventually dropped the lawsuits it had started against both the sheriff's and the fire departments. After the last witnesses had been interviewed, I closed the case file about two months later. Inside the cover of the case file were two photos I had recovered from the fire debris. The first is a high-school graduation photo of Sean in a suit and tie. The second is a photo of young Patrick in his brightly colored pajamas with a big smile on his face.

**Author's note:** About seven months later, I was asked to attend an awards ceremony in the Val Verde area put on by the local town council. Its purpose was to give valor awards to two local teenaged boys who had helped pull family members to safety that day. According to their citations, they forced open the front door and pulled family members to safety. I contacted the town councilman in charge and told him that no such thing happened. He informed me that his son was one of those persons to be cited, and he was sure that his son would not make up the story. I refused to attend. A few days later I saw in the local paper that the fire department had presented the awards.

*This case was investigated by the author, Det. Ed Nordskog, and his partners Det. Don Powell, Det. Rich McClellan, Det. Sylvia Faris, and Sgt. Don Shively of the LASD Arson-Explosives Detail; and Sr. Criminalist Phil Teramoto of the LASD Crime Lab who handled the lab work.*

### Investigator's Profile

We went into this case with no preconceived notions as to the cause. The actual suspicion that the child had started this fire did not come to us until several hours into this fire and after numerous interviews with neighbors, a relative, and paramedics.

Although I was a fairly new fire investigator at this scene, with under two hundred fire-scene investigations, I knew enough to know that Christmas trees were not an ignition source. Up to that point and in the sixteen years since, I have heard the phrase "Christmas tree fire" used on dozens of occasions, normally associated with major house fires and fatalities. The truth is that trees cannot spontaneously ignite without some sort of external heat source. In reality, most modern Christmas lights are quite safe and produce little to no heat. In our above case, the tree wasn't even plugged in, still, a fire chief and some of his seasoned investigators determined that this was the source of a fire with just an hour's investigation. This sort of "leaping to a convenient conclusion" still occurs frequently in the fire-investigation business as most investigators ignore, or are ignorant to, "**human activity**."

The use of accelerant dogs was also a factor. Dogs can be good tools if utilized properly. In this case, the dog was accurate and found an accelerant. The presence of an accelerant does not necessarily mean that the fire is a criminal act. There may be a very good reason for an accelerant to be where it is found. All homes and businesses have some form of accelerants stored in them. In this case, we positively concluded that there were no sinister accelerants or Molotov cocktails present.

This fire was set by human hands, with no signs of a break-in, and was set by someone inside the home. The physical evidence of the stool and lighter told the rest of the story, as did the burns on Patrick's hands. The rest of the case involved interviews to learn past behavior and to study the "guilty" actions of the child. By the end of our detailed investigation, even his poor mother was convinced that Patrick had set the fire.

Juvenile fires have several consistent factors. They are usually set during daytime, in or around the home, when the adults or caretaker (often a babysitter or grandparent) is napping or otherwise distracted. The fires can be set in any hidden area of the home. Patrick's earlier "fire play" was actually in a hidden alcove behind a sofa. Juvenile fire setters often have multiple incidents, as in this case, and often fight their own fires and/or hide from their own fires. This delayed response in reporting the fire is a "guilty act" and often tragically results in the deaths of siblings or grandparents who are not aware of the fire.

Roughly, juvenile "curiosity" fires are set by boys aged six to ten years old about 80 percent of the time. Young girls can and do set curiosity fires but at less than 20 percent of the time. These curiosity fires should never be confused with teen or truant fires by juveniles, who are a bit older; the cause of their fires is a completely different issue.

In most curiosity fires there is almost no sophistication, and the fire-setting devices are often left at the scene, as in this case. It is usually a lighter or a match, but it can be a rolled-up paper or similar item placed into a gas burner, stove, or furnace. On rare occasions, the use of nontraditional accelerants, such as lighter fluid or hairspray, can be found at the scene.

## *EL DIABLITO*
## PARAMOUNT, CA, 1999

*This case comes from the author's own case files.*

In June of 1999, I responded to a fire at an apartment complex in a gritty neighborhood in Paramount. Paramount is a working-class city in the central area just south of Los Angeles. This area borders on the west with Compton, and while not as crazy and as violent as the gang-stricken neighborhoods to the west, it was just a couple of steps down in intensity. The area at the time was almost entirely Hispanic with a mixture of American-born Mexicans and very recent Mexican immigrants.

At midday on a Tuesday, I began my investigation into a burglary/arson at a duplex apartment. The apartment was occupied by two male roommates who were at work at the time of the break-in and fire. I was fairly new to my arson-investigation career and had investigated only two hundred fires up to this point. However, I had studied enough and spoken to veteran investigators to know that it was a rare thing to have a burglar actually light a fire.

My investigation was fairly quick as the fire did not cause significant damage. I saw that a sliding window had been forced open with a metal pipe and that someone had entered the building via the window. The suspect had stacked a bicycle and some tires under the window to be able to stand on them to climb into the room. This was all done around ten in the morning. The room had been only mildly rifled by the burglar, and only some change and a few loose dollars appeared to be missing. The burglar left valuable items such as televisions and a stereo system. The burglar took the time, however, to remove items from the refrigerator and cupboard and to throw them on the floor, creating a large mess.

I had been a burglary detective for a few years in the past, and this did not look like something a professional burglar would do. They tend to get in, scoop up all the valuable items that they could later sell, and then leave without a lot of noise or fuss. It seemed odd. However, since this area had a large number of halfway homes for ex-felons and plenty of heroin and methamphetamines addicts, I had dozens of potential suspects.

As I was standing in the apartment, I heard a noise, and a child's head appeared at the open window. A red-haired Hispanic kid pulled himself up and looked startled when he saw me. "Who the fuck are you?" he demanded. The little guy looked about eight years old and way too young to be demanding anything, let alone swearing at a cop. I shooed him away and told him I was investigating this fire. I heard him let himself down and speak to another kid. I noted that he was standing on the same pile of items that the burglar had used to let himself into the apartment.

A half hour later I was leaving the scene and walked outside to see the same boy with another young Hispanic kid standing next to him. I spoke to them in Spanish, and the red-haired kid surprised me by getting mad and saying in English, "I ain't a fucking wetback." This kid had a very aggressive and defiant attitude. I smiled inwardly as I realized he was trying to act tough, despite the fact that he looked about eight years old and stood just over four feet tall. The other kid with him was acting more appropriately for a young guy. He looked a mixture of scared and curious about my odd uniform and what I was doing there.

I walked out and went to my car to leave. The two kids followed me out to the street. The red-haired one said, "We know who started the fire. It was a nigger from Compton." I was shocked to hear these graphic phrases from a young kid, and this one talked like he was a hardened twenty-five-year-old gangster. When I asked them how they knew this, the other kid said he didn't know anything and sort of backed away. The red-haired kid, who told me his name was "Donny" (a pseudonym), said that "niggers always come over here from Compton to light fires." I questioned them further, but they then told me that they hadn't actually seen anyone near the fire. I took down the names and addresses of the two kids and left. I later contacted the tenants of the burned apartment, who verified that there had been several small fires in the neighborhood recently but none to structures.

Two days later I was assigned another investigation at the same apartment complex. This time someone had set three trees on fire in the late evening. As I was photographing the scene, sure enough little Donny walked up to me and began engaging me in conversation. Again he pointed out crudely that the suspect must be from Compton. As I was talking to Donny, a maintenance man from the complex saw us and began approaching. As he got near, he began trying to speak to me in broken English and Spanish. He was pointing at Donny and saying, "el Diablito" (Little Devil). Donny swore at him, called him a "wetback," and turned and ran away.

For the next twenty minutes I spoke in broken Spanish with the maintenance man, and he told me a strange story. He said that little Donny was evil and the devil's son. He said that Donny had tried to kill a little girl by setting her on fire and had killed a dog the same way. The man later directed me to a nearby field where he had buried the burned dog. For the next two hours I interviewed about a dozen neighbors from the same complex. All of them were recent immigrants from Mexico, and none had reported any of this to the police in the past. They described that Donny was a firebug and had lit dozens of small fires with gasoline over the past few months. They said he had killed one dog, burned a couple of cats that haven't been seen since, and attempted to burn to death two little girls by pouring gasoline on them. One girl ran from him after she had been doused by gas, but the other girl's hair caught on fire, and she had to go to a hospital. After the injury, the burned girl and her family moved back to rural Mexico.

The maintenance man and the neighbors took me around the complex and the neighborhood and showed me nearly two dozen items that had burn damage on them. Most of these were vegetation and trees, but there was a small shed and another outbuilding as well. All of the witnesses said that Donny has no parents and lives with elderly grandparents who couldn't control him.

I called over another investigator to assist me and began documenting all of the fire scenes. The witnesses told me that the young pyro frequently walks to a nearby gas station to buy gasoline. They have repeatedly asked the owner to stop selling gas to the young kid. I went to the station and spoke to the owner. It was quickly determined that he was aware of the problem but had continued to sell gasoline to the kid. The station owner said that he sold it to the kid because the kid's grandparents weren't able to walk, and they needed it for their lawnmower. I advised him of the problems with the kid, and he promised not to sell any more gas to Donny.

My partner and I then went to interview the little kid who had been with Donny. As soon as he saw us at his door, the little boy began to cry. He immediately said that he had been with Donny when the red-haired boy had broken into the home the day before. He said that Donny talked him into coming into the home and stealing some food and about eight dollars in cash and coins. He said that he got scared when he saw Donny start to pour a cup of gasoline onto the floor. He said that he ran out the door, and then he heard a whoosh, and Donny came running out behind him. He saw that the apartment was on fire. The little boy knew that Donny always carried gas with him and had lit a lot of little fires. He pointed out several fire scenes to us.

We then went to Donny's home. Donny lived with his elderly Hispanic grandparents. They were both in very poor health and not at all ambulatory. They said they were unaware of anything he did wrong but had heard from several neighbors that he was starting small fires. They told us Donny's history. They said that their son, Donny's dad, was a Hispanic gang member who was in prison for a gang-related shooting. He was expected to be in prison for another decade. Donny's mother was a white girl who worked as a prostitute in the area. She was a methamphetamines addict, and Donny had been born addicted to the drug. The mother was currently in prison for fraud. She was due out of prison in a couple of years. The grandparents said the young boy had been aggressive and violent since birth. He was very bitter about being of mixed race in an all-Hispanic neighborhood and hated the fact that people picked on him because of his red hair and freckles.

Donny was ten years old but was very short for his age and was always being picked on. In response to this, he was very aggressive toward others. The grandparents also stated that he had been kicked out of school several times for pulling fire alarms, theft, and fighting. They had caught him drinking alcohol and "huffing" gasoline vapors in the past. They routinely gave him money for lunch, and he was always outside by himself most of the day. He had also stolen additional money from them in the past. In short, they had no control over him whatsoever. At the time of this interview, he was missing.

We went to the nearby grade school and confirmed that Donny had been a student there. The principal knew the family situation quite well and had kicked Donny out for pulling fire alarms and setting two trash bins on fire. There had been other minor fires at the school after hours that they suspected were set by Donny. They said that Donny has attention deficit hyperactivity disorder, fetal alcohol syndrome, and a whole host of other behavioral issues. They determined that he was a risk to other students and were in the process of having him permanently expelled. The school had referred Donny to a Child Protective Services counselor.

On our way back from the school, we saw Donny walking nearby. As soon as he saw us, he began to run. I caught him after a short chase, and we tried to talk to him. He was violent and angry and sat in the car swearing at us and threatening us. He blamed all the fires on either black guys from Compton or other kids in the area. We were stuck in a quandary of what to do with this little hellion.

We drove Donny to juvenile hall and asked to speak directly to the presiding juvenile judge. We knew that juvenile hall did not accept kids under a certain age. In Los Angeles, it is very rare to put anyone in juvenile custody younger than fourteen years of age, as the system is filled with extremely violent, young gang members, who have committed murders, rapes, and assaults. Not only was Donny quite young, but he was very small for his age. He could not be housed with other larger, more violent gang members. We had a special hearing that afternoon and explained the danger level that Donny presented to himself and to others. He had a bizarre fascination with using fire as a weapon of revenge or hate and had nearly killed two young girls.

The judge looked seriously at our investigation and determined that Donny was too much of a danger to the community and himself to be left in the care of his grandparents. He was held in juvenile hall in a special facility by himself until a special court hearing could convene. Ten days later my partner and I had found over twenty-six arson scenes attributed to Donny, or "el Diablito." We confirmed that he had burned the dog and at least two little girls, along with the arson fire during the burglary. We found witnesses who said that he had threatened several other children with fires. We had also found witnesses who stated that they had seen him drink gasoline and other chemicals and brag that he was going to kill himself.

They juvenile courts were perplexed. This kid was the youngest kid ever held in that juvenile facility who had not murdered someone. However, the child psychologists told the judge that Donny was extremely angry, violent, and probably suicidal. They all recommend incarceration and intense therapy. From the day we arrested him, Donny stayed in a secure juvenile facility for nearly two years. We predicted that someday he would end up in prison or dead at a young age. We never heard from him again.

Over a decade later we were inputting known serial arsonists into a database, and I reviewed the case of Donny. I conducted an inquiry of his criminal history since we had last seen him. It was almost predictable. He had been released from juvenile hall and rearrested within a month for a violent assault. This pattern followed over and over again until he was nineteen when it was reported that he committed suicide in a jail facility. There were plenty of assaults, burglaries, and drug arrests on his record but no additional arson attacks. To this day, el Diablito was possibly the angriest kid I have ever run into. The circumstances of his birth doomed him from the start. He never really had a chance in life.

### Investigator's Profile

Donny represents the extreme end of the spectrum for juvenile fire setters. His fire setting is based on a combination of anger and fascination. He was extremely angry at his lot in life and set fires as a way to get **revenge for his overall situation**. Based on what others told us about him, fire was both a weapon and an obsession with him. To tell the truth, we fully expected to see other fire crimes in his criminal history, but there were none. The profile of his fire scenes was typical for juvenile males. They were very overt and not at all sophisticated. He consistently used an easily accessible accelerant and set his fires for maximum damage. His actual fire assaults on dogs, cats, and little girls make him one of the most dangerous persons we have ever come across.

His social history is very reminiscent of the most dangerous arsonist ever identified: Bruce George Peter Lee from England. His mother was a prostitute, and he was stigmatized throughout his life by his size, his mixed-race features, and the lack of parenting. He was born addicted to drugs, which likely caused brain trauma, a very common trait of all serial arsonists. His actions of pulling fire alarms and setting fires at or near schools are also common for most male serial arsonists.

## COCOS FIRE
## SAN MARCOS, CA, 2014

*This case is from the files of the San Diego Sheriff's Office, Arson and Bomb Unit.*

Red-flag days and wildfires have always been the bane of neighborhoods in the urban-wild-land interface areas of the American West. In particular, about once every three to five years, Southern California gets pummeled by massive wildfires. These usually spring up during our Santa Ana wind condition events that occur two to three times a year. The Santa Anas normally occur in October or November and blow hot desert wind down to the coastal plains. These winds pass through the dry, heavily vegetated coastal mountain ranges at speeds of twenty to sixty miles per hour. The temperatures soar twenty degrees above normal, and the humidity drops from its normal 60 percent down to below 10 percent.

These conditions are known as red-flag days and are perfect for the easy ignition of any fire. The conditions also cause fires to act in a very erratic manner. On days like this, fires that would normally be put out in seconds race off into the foothills and become major events. A typical Santa Ana event lasting three days can easily spawn thirty to fifty wildfires.

The overwhelming majority of these wildfires, maybe in excess of 95 percent, are unintentional events. Arson fires do occur in the wild-land areas, but they are fairly rare when compared against all of the accidental and negligently caused fires. It really doesn't matter how a wildfire starts; they all burn the same as soon as they are lit.

On May 14, 2014, a red-flag condition existed all through Southern California. This was the second time in as many years that the Santa Ana winds began blowing in the spring as opposed to their normal time frame in the fall. Fire officials attribute these "out of season" fires to the ongoing drought conditions in the state. By the second day of this event, a dozen fires had sprung up all through Orange, Riverside, and San Diego Counties. A dozen more fires erupted in the following days. Fourteen wildfires were reported to be burning in San Diego County alone.

While two persons were eventually arrested during this fire event, neither was actually a premeditated arsonist. The arrests were for negligently or illegally causing a fire. Basically that's for doing an act that is illegal, such as having an illegal campfire, or so negligent, such as burning trash during a high-wind condition, that the actions are considered "criminally negligent." One person that was eventually arrested had a different reason for setting a fire.

On May 14, at about three in the afternoon, a small fire was reported in a residential neighborhood in the town of San Marcos. Responding firefighters found a large tree on fire in a wooded area behind some homes. The fire pattern around that tree grew to over 4,500 square feet. Embers from that burning tree rose into the air along the buoyant thermal convection plume, and the strong winds carried them out of the scene and to the west. Some embers landed just 14 feet outside the scene and started a small "spot fire" of about 150 square feet in size. Some additional embers carried further downwind about 250 feet away and started a small 100-square-foot blaze.

Both of these two spot fires were quickly brought under control by responding firefighters. However, a third set of embers from the tree fire were raised aloft quite high and blew almost one-half mile downwind on the strong Santa Anas. These embers started a spot fire in a brush-choked canyon that quickly grew and expanded. This small spot fire erupted into a major firestorm and burned for the next seven days, consuming two thousand acres of vegetation. It became known as the Cocos Fire. The fire quickly overran and overwhelmed fire-suppression units and poured a hurricane of embers and firebrands into several neighborhoods. Soon, homes in its path were erupting into flame. Within just a few days, thirty-six homes and four other structures were burned to the ground.

Before the fire had even burned itself out, investigators from the San Diego Sheriff's Department (SDSD) Arson-Bomb Squad learned a very troubling fact. This was not the first fire that had taken place behind those homes on Washingtonia Avenue. Shortly after beginning his investigation, lead detective Arnold Van Lingen learned that a 911 call about a small vegetation fire had gone out the day before the Cocos Fire, at very close to the same time of day. The mother of a thirteen-year-old girl called to say that her daughter had "found" a downed tree branch that was on fire. This fire was put out in relatively quick order without any property damage. The Santa Ana winds were already starting to blow and this could have been a huge problem.

The SDSD arrived and determined that the incident was a deliberate act of arson. Since the fire was so small, the SDSD turned the incident over to the San Marcos Fire Department to investigate. It was later found out that the girl (Jenny) who had "found" the burning log told both her mother and sister that she had started the small fire while playing with a Scripto lighter. She said that she was only curious about what would happen. As soon as the branch caught on fire, she dropped it and ran. She was admonished of the dangerousness of the act by her parents. Police and fire officials were not aware at the time that the young girl had admitted to lighting the fire and never spoke to her. The very next day a second fire (the Cocos Fire) erupted very close to this first fire scene.

Cal Fire and SDSD's origin and cause investigators descended into the area of origin for the Cocos Fire. The area was a steep ravine with thick, heavy brush. They found that there was no homeless activity in the area, no campfires, and no easy way to walk through the brush. They eliminated human activity in that spot as a potential cause for this large fire. They then back-tracked upwind and found that firefighters had extinguished two small "spot fires" on Washingtonia Avenue, in the direct path leading to the Cocos Fire. They found that the sustained wind speeds at the start of the fire were about twenty-four miles per hour but that the topography of the area caused the winds to dramatically increase in between hills and canyons, which were exactly the conditions they found that day.

The fire-scene and fire-behavior experts later conducted some testing, detailed modeling, and research and eventually determined positively that the Cocos Fire did stem from embers blown from the backyard fire on Washingtonia Avenue. They came to the formal conclusion that the embers from the Washingtonia Avenue fire carried downwind a little over four-tenths of a mile to land in the brush-filled canyon.

Det. Van Lingen conducted a very detailed canvass of the local neighborhood and got several witnesses who saw the

Cocos Fire in its very beginning phases. One witness was an avid photographer who took several photos showing the area of origin and the wind direction at the time of the fire. His photos also proved that there was another fire burning upwind at Washingtonia before the Cocos Fire took off. Another witness showed the large tree burning on Washingtonia Avenue. It was in a small, secluded area, which was filled with downed branches, leaves, and other "duff." This was behind the home where the fire had occurred the day before the Cocos Fire.

Det. Van Lingen went to the home where the first fire had occurred the day before the Cocos Fire. He found that it was occupied by a husband and wife, along with their children, which included two teenage daughters and two sons. Van Lingen learned that the young girls had both been adopted by the couple after having traumatic childhoods. Van Lingen interviewed the thirteen-year-old-girl named "Jenny" (a pseudonym) and found her to be shy but polite. She admitted to having some curiosity about fire and that she had used a Scripto lighter the previous day to burn some small leaves and twigs. The fire had gotten out of control, and she ran to tell her sister and mother about it. Jenny denied setting the second fire, which grew into the Cocos Fire.

Van Lingen spoke in depth with the parents of the girl. He noted that both parents were extremely concerned and very cooperative, which can be a rarity in these types of cases. The parents stated that Jenny and her three siblings were adopted when she was younger and had some very traumatic experiences in her prior family. She had been homeschooled since second grade and had no obvious emotional issues. They stated that her grades were fine and that she was an athlete, participating on a highly competitive bike-racing team.

Shortly after this interview, Det. Van Lingen contacted me for some advice on this case. Det. Van Lingen was fairly new to the arson business, and I had assisted him on one prior serial arson case that he had investigated. Among his many concerns was my opinion on the possibility of a thirteen-year-old girl being a firebug or having a fascination with fire. I advised him that it is true that arson is a male-dominated crime, with close to 90 percent of arrested arsonists being male. However, there are still a significant number of female fire setters, to include teenaged fire setters.

I gave him a list of potential traits for a female fire setter and advised him to gather as much information as possible about her background, social history, physical history, and mental-health history. I mentioned that the overwhelming majority of female arsonists have some form of institutionalization in their background (Jenny had been in the foster-care system) and that they set fires at or very close to their homes or work, and they seldom, if ever, used an incendiary device. It was a vague and rough profile, but Van Lingen was already hearing from the doubters in the police and fire departments within his area. Most cops and firemen just don't believe that female arsonists exist, particularly young ones.

The one tactic I suggested to him was to get help from an experienced female investigator with a specialty in crimes against children. These types of investigators have great insight in dealing with juveniles and being able to open a rapport with them. Det. Van Lingen had already decided on that strategy, and he quickly found an expert to assist him.

Within a few short weeks Van Lingen had gathered as much information about the potential suspect as he could legally get from police resources. He knew that she "matched the profile" in several areas but that could be said for thousands of young girls. He had learned that after the fires, the young girl had been giddy and giggling about them when describing them to family members. He knew the only way to solve this case was by admission. The fire-scene experts had done their jobs by proving the fire originated near the girl's home; now they needed some sort of validation.

In June of 2014, Det. Van Lingen and a female juvenile crimes investigator named Claudia Delgado met the thirteen-year-old girl and her mother for a more in-depth interview. This time a rapport was established, and the young girl opened up to them. She admitted that she had lit the second fire (Cocos Fire) in the exact same manner as the one on the previous day. She said that after the first fire she had hid the lighter in a motor home. The next day she went out and retrieved it. She walked a little farther from her home this time and then set some leaves and twigs on fire in a small wooded area, just to "see what would happen." She knew that the wind was blowing quite strong and that there was already a huge brush fire burning nearby but confessed that her curiosity got the best of her. "I don't even know why I did it," she admitted to investigators.

She said as soon as she ignited the vegetation, the wind immediately spread it to a large tree, and it just began to take off from there. This time the girl ran home and hid from the growing fire. Unlike the day before, she did not admit to this fire to her mother or sister.

This entire interview lasted two hours, and the girl later admitted the same information in front of her distraught mother. The girl cried several times and stated that she was sorry and felt very guilty about causing all the damage. After the confession, the girl was released back to her parents, who remained cooperative with investigators. Shortly after leaving the dramatic interview, the mother reported that her daughter, who had been crying and extremely upset in front of the investigators, seemed relaxed and almost happy as they drove away. The teenager was exhibiting some rather odd behavior.

The case was brainstormed within the San Diego District Attorney's Office and eventually assigned to an experienced juvenile prosecutor named Shawnalyse Ochoa. Multiple arson charges were filed, and a trial was set in juvenile court. Prior to submitting the case to the District Attorney's Office, Det. Van Lingen had done a bit of research about wild-land fires, embers, firebrands, and how they travel. As part of his research, he contacted a man named Doug Allen. Doug Allen was a fire-investigation instructor at a college in the San Bernardino area and had been a long-retired Cal Fire arson investigator. Van Lingen sent him an email inquiring about firebrand and ember travel during a Santa Ana event. Mr. Allen replied via email that firebrands and embers can travel up to a mile in Santa Ana conditions, creating spot fires way ahead of the source of the firebrands.

A two-week-long trial in juvenile court ensued in March of 2015. The crux of the trial was not whether the young girl started small fires on two different days during a Santa Ana wind condition; she had already admitted those facts to the police and members of her own family. The fact in dispute during this trial was whether the embers from the second fire could have traveled far enough downwind (nearly one-half mile) to land in the rugged canyon and ignite the Cocos Fire. This trial was focused on fire behavior, wind behavior, fire science, and the opinions of two opposing wild-land fire-behavior experts.

Cal Fire, through the testimony of fire-behavior expert Tim Chavez, brought in the scientifically based results of an exhaustive analysis of the fire, the terrain, the wind direction and speed, the gusting capabilities of the wind, and the phenomenon of thermal lift during a wildfire. It was the contention of the experts at Cal Fire, citing lengthy research and testing, that burning embers and firebrands can be carried significant distances downwind during Santa Ana conditions. They brought in detailed documentation and computer modeling, backed by modern studies of hundreds of wild-land and vegetation fires to support their conclusions. They linked the Cocos Fire point of origin to be in the same exact axis as the two other spot fires that had grown from the fire set by the girl.

In contrast to that, the defense brought in a forty-plus-year fire/arson expert who was also a longtime retired Cal Fire chief and investigator himself. Doug Allen had surprisingly joined the defense team after already having given information to the prosecution. It would come back to haunt him.

Mr. Allen testified that in the conditions present on the day of the Cocos Fire, it would be very unlikely that a firebrand or ember could travel that far (nearly one-half mile) downwind. However, the prosecution countered that Allen had been long retired from active investigations and had not refreshed himself in years when it came to wildfire behavior. The prosecution contended that Allen was unfamiliar with modern computer models and systems used to calculate wildfire behavior. The prosecution then produced the very email that Doug Allen himself had sent to Det. Van Lingen on this very case! This was the email where Allen had previously stated that embers could easily be blown over a mile in Santa Ana wind conditions. In effect the defense expert testified against himself.

The judge was clearly not impressed by this contradictory defense testimony. Mr. Allen's experience and expertise were clearly outdated and not consistent with the very modern technology used by current Cal Fire investigators. Doug Allen's testimony would not be given much weight in the judge's decision.

On March 24, 2015, the final arguments were given by the attorneys to the presiding judge. After some deliberation the judge found that the prosecution had proved their assertion that the tree fire deliberately started by the young girl had spread into the massive Cocos Fire. They showed that the girl had been warned previous to this about the dangers of wildfire and was aware of the extreme wind and heat conditions of the event. The judge found that there was willful criminal conduct by the young girl. The judge commented that while Jenny did not deliberately intend to burn down the property of others, her actions were criminal in nature. She was convicted on three counts of setting a criminal arson fire.

The sentencing for young Jenny went as expected. Prior to the hearing, the court had asked for a psychiatric evaluation of Jenny. All juvenile records in cases like this are normally sealed, but the judge indicated at sentencing that issues came up during the psychiatric evaluation. The juvenile court judge noted for the record that the girl had gone through a traumatic early childhood, without getting into the specifics. As such, the court was looking at rehabilitation instead of incarceration. The troubled young girl received no time in jail and was allowed to continue competing in her bicycle races. She was ordered to write letters of apology to the victims and to complete four hundred hours of community service. She was also ordered to enroll in a rehabilitation program. While the total cost of this fire exceeded $10 million, the girl's family was forced to pay just a small fraction of that amount.

*The lead investigator on this case was Det. Arnold Van Lingen of the San Diego Sheriff's Department Arson-Bomb Squad. Juvenile crimes Det. Claudia Delgado assisted in interviewing the suspect. Cal Fire investigators David LaClair, Chris Palmer, and Tim Chavez assisted as wildfire-behavior specialists. The prosecutor was DDA Shawnalyse Ochoa. I was asked to consult with the lead investigator and prosecutor prior to the trial.*

### Investigator's Profile

In this particular case, the lead investigator actually consulted with an arson profiler after he had identified a thirteen-year-old girl as a probable suspect. While the circumstances of the fire were consistent with both male and female juvenile arsonists, the investigator knew that the public (and court's) perception was that a young female was incapable of such a crime. Consulting a profiler didn't solve the crime, but it gave the investigator a starting point of what to look for, how to approach the suspect, and how to prepare this case for a courtroom presentation.

The investigator conducted detailed interviews of the suspect's family members, as well as examining other social and psychological factors. The investigator wisely brought in an experienced female investigator who was instrumental in getting the young girl to open up about the events. Lastly, in this case, the investigator and prosecutor consulted with me, a profiler, on what to expect from the defense and how to counter any defense tactics. In this case, the prior preparation by the prosecution rendered the defense expert's opinion moot.

This case was included in this book as it highlights several important profiling aspects. It shows a typical wild-land fire setter, who was curious about fires in a time frame when there were dozens of fires all around her home. There could be some aspect of excitement with this event. It also shows both a typical juvenile fire and a typical female fire, in that it was set in a crude manner in or near the home during daylight hours. It should be noted by investigators that both fires occurred at nearly the same time of day, which is another strong indication that the fire setter for both was the same person. Another aspect of female fire setting is that the female often "self-reports" the fire, which occurred in this case. Jenny also hit the female fire-setter profile on several other important points.

The scary part of this case is that no one knows why Jenny lit fires, not even her. She will be classified as an **emotionally based** fire setter, which is the type we understand the least. It is also the type that tends to continue in his or her fire-setting behavior throughout his or her life. While I would agree with the court that rehabilitation is preferred in this case over incarceration, Jenny will be at risk for similar type activity for much of her life.

# 7

# Wild-Land Arson

*In writing this chapter, I relied on my own experience in about two hundred wild-land arson investigations, along with my personal and professional relationships with several of the more accomplished experts in the field of wild-land arsonists and arson investigation. These experts include SSA Paul Steensland, USFS (retired); Inv. Ron Huxman, USFS (retired); Chief Alan Carlson, Cal Fire (retired); Cap. Tom Oldag, Cal Fire (retired); Supv. Inv. Joe Konefal, Cal SFM/CDF (retired); Inv. Chris Vallerga, Cal Fire (retired); Inv. Brice Trask, Lake County, CA (retired); Senior Inv. Ken Ness, Saskatchewan, Canada Ministry of Environment; Supt. Richard Woods, Australian Rural Fire Service; and Chief Jim Engel, Cal Fire. Please refer to my first two books,* Torchered Minds *and* Fireraisers, Freaks, and Fiends, *for excellent case histories of significant wild-land arsonists.*

## The Profile

The above group of experts has investigated thousands of wild-land fires and has arrested and interviewed several dozen wild-land arsonists and serial arsonists. While we as a group of experienced investigators don't always agree on every aspect of an issue, we are in general agreement with the following offered profiles of wild-land arsonists.

The wild-land arsonist shares only a few of the traits and profiles of the urban arsonist. There are very significant differences between these two subgroups of arsonists. Where the majority of urban serial offenders tend to have serious mental-health and addiction issues, many of the wild-land arsonists are more stable mentally and are actually employed or have held jobs throughout their life. Most urban serial arsonists do not drive vehicles and generally access their fire scenes via foot, bicycle, or public transport. The vast majority of wild-land serial offenders drive vehicles to access their scenes, and history shows that most of them, in fact, drive a certain type of vehicle: an SUV or light truck. Most urban arsonists/serial arsonists set their fires in the nighttime hours, while the vast majority of wild-land arsonists will set fires in daylight hours. These are the major differences between the two subtypes.

There are some similarities between the subtypes as well. Like their urban counterparts, the wild-land serial arsonists are overwhelmingly male, with estimates near 90 percent. The urban serial arsonist is mostly male (about 80 percent), with a slightly higher percentage of female offenders.

The use of incendiary devices by urban arsonists is extremely rare and almost unheard of for urban serial arsonists (with the exception of extremist groups). However, among wild-land serial arsonists, the use of incendiary devices is quite a bit more common.

Race is not a factor in either urban or rural arsons. Most experienced investigators will agree that the race of the arsonist most often reflects the racial makeup of the area where the fires are occurring. Indeed, a large percentage of wild-land serial arsonists are Caucasian, which coincides with the large percentage of Caucasians living in rural or wild-land areas.

Age can be a factor in wild-land arson investigation. The fact that the ability to drive a vehicle is important for the wild-land arsonist would exclude most juvenile offenders. However, beyond that, age is not much of a factor.

**In general, the following traits are common to wild-land arsonists/serial arsonists:**

- Majority are male, up to 90 percent.
- Race of suspect is reflective of the population of the target area.
- Age ranges from sixteen to eighty, with the majority in the mid-twenties to mid-thirties range.
- Women offenders likely a bit older in age range.
- Majority of fires are "hot sets" to available combustibles.
- Use of an incendiary device is rare but more common than urban arsonist.
- Incendiary devices may evolve until they reach reliability status and then stay the same.
- Devices are usually very simple unless suspect has unique training or skills.
- Device design shows a commonality in certain geographic areas.
- Most offenders access scenes via a vehicle, usually a truck or SUV.
- Alcohol/drug use is a factor.
- Majority of offenders are employed.
- Many work/live in area or pass through target area to work.
- A significant number have a connection to the fire service (up to 30 percent).
- If in fire service, offender often reports/fights his own fires.
- Fires tend to increase in frequency but not necessarily in size.
- Offenders tend to leave scene of fire but often watch it from a distance.
- Serial offenders can light fires for years or even decades.

- Fires are mostly set in daylight hours.
- Long-term serial offenders tend to subconsciously form patterns.
- Pattern analysis can show import clusters of activity—anchor points.
- Wild-land arsonists can set dozens to hundreds of fires.

Using the above list of common traits, wild-land arson investigators can immediately start an investigation by plotting time and location maps of the fires. This temporal/spatial analysis is the basis for pattern recognition, which can eliminate whole groups of offenders from the suspect list. The next most important step is to determine the sophistication of the ignition event. If a device is used, that is a direct indicator toward the type of offender who set the fire. The use of a device is learned behavior and points directly at the sophistication level of the arsonist. This again may eliminate entire groups from the suspect list.

Common investigative strategies for wild-land cases include temporal/spatial plotting and analysis, incendiary device analysis by a crime lab, analysis by a profiler, forensics in the form of footprints, tire tracks, cell phones, license plate readers, and the use of cameras and live surveillance assets.

## MA SPARKER
## MT. SHASTA, CA, 1994–1995

*This case comes from the files of the US Forest Service*

In August of 1995, a fairly small serial arson case in Northern California made national headlines. The media attention was not due to the size, scope, or number of fires in the arson series but was directly related to who the investigators eventually arrested. It was a case that opened a lot of eyes and dispelled quite a few myths within the arson-investigation business.

Mt. Shasta, California, is a small town situated at the base of the iconic peak whose name it bears. The town of over 3,500 residents sits in the middle of the Shasta-Trinity National Forest. Any fires in that area are suppressed and investigated by the US Forest Service (USFS). Up until the summer of 1994, the USFS investigators noted an average of one wild-land arson per year in the forestlands surrounding Mt. Shasta. There were so few fires in the area that the USFS was considering the deactivation of a fire engine and the laying off of a few wild-land firefighters.

In the fall months of that year, USFS special agent Frank Packwood detected a small arson problem along Everitt Memorial Highway, west of Mt. Shasta. Everitt Memorial Highway is a two-lane asphalt road that winds from the northern edge of the town of Mt. Shasta for about twelve miles toward the northeast and up the slopes of the mountain of Mt. Shasta, where it terminates at a trailhead for the higher alpine slopes.

In a fairly short time period, USFS suppression crews had responded to eight suspicious wild-land fires along that rural roadway. All of the fires were knocked down without serious consequence, but all of them caused the investigator to worry. The fires were set in dry vegetation that immediately led into a heavily forested mountainside. The fires were set in daylight hours a short distance off the highway. The fires had to be arsons as they were too far from the road to be related to vehicles and were nowhere near any other accidental sources. The fires left no evidence and were deemed to be "hot set" blazes. This type of fire is where the arsonist uses a lighter or matches to quickly set the combustible vegetation on fire and then walks away.

Other than the odd footprint or tire track, these "hot set" fires leave almost no evidence for an investigator to work with. To further hinder investigators, many wild-land suppression crews responding to a roadside fire have the unfortunate tendency to park their vehicles on or near the area of origin, and they often obliterate any tire or foot tracks left by a suspect.

SA Packwood realized that based on the similar circumstances of all eight fires, he likely had a serial arsonist active in his area. He noted that all of the fires were in a fairly small area and coincided with the same engine companies responding to most of them. In wild-land arson investigation that is a huge red flag that may indicate that someone on that suppression crew was involved in fire setting. A common reason for fire setting in wild-land firefighter ranks is that many of the crews are part time or "paid/call" employees. This means that they only get paid when there is a fire. These sorts of thoughts ran through Packwood's head that fall as he called fellow USFS investigators and told them of his suspicions. By the time an investigation could be formed up, the winter weather had descended upon the Shasta-Trinity National Forest, and the fire season was over.

SA Packwood knew from his training and experience that wild-land arsonists tend to be seasonal creatures, who can light fires on an off for years and even decades. Some go dormant for months at a time and then begin their fire-setting behavior the moment their lives start to slide into the toilet. Packwood fully expected the Shasta-Trinity arsonist to resume his arson activity the following spring and summer when the fire season began again. In the meantime he quietly explored his theory that these fires might be attributed to a firefighter. He assembled lists and schedules of fire crews and began a sort of time-and-space analysis of the fires.

By the spring and summer of 1995, SA Packwood had been reassigned, and the arson investigation had been assigned to a veteran USFS arson expert named Paul Steensland. SA Steensland was well educated and highly experienced in the phenomenon of wild-land arson, and he and SA Rix Calloway picked up Packwood's case and began a confidential investigation.

The USFS investigators had several things going for them. The most important thing they had was a fairly finite target area along a rural roadway, with only a small number of people who normally drive on it. Since the fires had been strung out for a time period, the investigators believed that they could rule out a tourist or camper, who would only be in the area for a few days or more. This series showed that it was someone who was routinely in the area.

The Everitt Memorial Highway was the only major roadway in the area, with just a few smaller roads intersecting it. It was not a busy highway, and that limited the number of people who drove on it, which of course limited the number of potential suspects. The flip side of it being a rural roadway was that there were no witnesses and no video-surveillance systems in place to capture suspicious activity. The USFS investigators would change that dynamic in the spring of 1995.

The two major wild-land fire-investigation agencies in the United States are the USFS and its local cousin out West, Cal Fire (or CDF, the California Department of Forestry and Fire Protection, as it was known in those days). Between the two large agencies, they investigate more wildfires and arrest more wild-land arson suspects than any other group in the country. They have a handful of very experienced and highly skilled investigators in the niche business of wild-land arson investigation. These experts had learned many facts through several decades of wild-land investigations and employed investigative tactics based on these facts.

The first thing investigators did was to maintain a degree of secrecy about this case. There is an old saying in the fire world that "there are no secrets in the firehouse." These wild-land investigators rarely discussed their investigations with local firefighters and agencies as they knew well that a shockingly significant number of wild-land arsons are set by persons related to the fire service. In this case, SAs Steensland and Calloway brought in surveillance members from outside the area. They included USFS special agents and Cal Fire arson investigators. These investigators then installed static cameras hidden in the vegetation at critical points along the target area.

The problem with the cameras in those days was that they did not have a live feed. After a fire occurred, investigators would retrieve the cameras and examine the videotape, looking for vehicles that had passed through the area shortly before or after the fire. They would have to investigate these vehicles and drivers after a fire had occurred. Later on in the investigation, some of these investigators would actually don camouflage clothing and lay along the roadways with cameras.

*"Give me the repeat offender any day. Every fire they light adds to the evidentiary pile, and the net draws ever tighter over time"* (Senior Special Agent Paul Steensland, USFS retired, after thirty-seven years investigating wild-land arson).

A cruel twist of any serial crime investigation is that investigators on a difficult case actually hope for additional events to occur. The longer a series of crimes continues, the more data and patterns emerge. In a bizarre irony, the arson investigators had no good leads after the fall of 1994, so they needed more fires to occur so that they could gather more information. By June investigators were not disappointed. The arsonist was back, and a small spate of roadside fires began again along Everitt Memorial Highway.

Early on in the investigation that summer, after a couple of fires, investigators noted that a particular Oldsmobile Cutlass vehicle had passed through the view of the cameras around the time of the fires. They would later see that same vehicle on two other occasions around the time of a fire. For a while, they were unable to identify the vehicle or its driver.

### Firefighter Arsonist?

Meanwhile, the investigators had been working on their theory that the fires were related to a local firefighter. They knew from many past cases that the most likely suspect in a case like this might be a recently hired, fairly young male, working as a volunteer, seasonal, or part-time firefighter. This sort of person would likely have maturity issues manifested by speeding tickets, anger issues, or other work-related incidents. They further knew from past cases that if the fires had been lit by a firefighter, then he likely would have reported some of them and fought some or all of them.

By their careful analysis of this growing string of fires, the investigators found that the same fire crew had been present at all of the fire scenes. They also became aware that this crew had been slated the previous year to be eliminated due to a lack of fires in the area. A few of the firefighters were scheduled to be "let go" by the brass.

Eventually, in the summer of 1995 as the fires continued to occur along the highway, the investigators found a potential suspect with several red flags associated with him. Seasonal firefighter Jason Robertson was a nineteen-year-old local boy with a few problems in his life. He was a recent hire to the USFS and had some documented maturity issues. In the fall of 1994, his engine was scheduled to be deactivated. Jason Robertson had his own problems. Jason was on probation with his USFS fire crew as twice he had been late for work. As a new hire, he was very close to getting fired. Shortly after these problems emerged, the string of fires began along the slopes of Mt. Shasta.

By midsummer of 1995, the investigators had still not identified a suspect. At one point, Jason Robertson and his engine were deployed to assist in a large forest fire in another area of the West. The crew was out of the area for twenty-one days and incredibly the string of fires around Mt. Shasta stopped! Shortly after the crew returned to the Mt. Shasta area in July, the roadside fires resumed again. Investigators were very sure that their arsonist was probably among the ranks of the engine crew in question, and Jason Robertson was at the top of the list of potential suspects.

In late July investigators had narrowed the fires down to specific areas. They had gotten a break, and twice more had seen the same Oldsmobile Cutlass in their "camera traps" near the time of the fires. By reviewing the footage, they saw that the car was being driven by a white woman who appeared to be in her fifties or sixties. She hardly fit the profile of a wild-land serial arsonist. Eventually the investigators in the field (literally, they were hiding in the fields) saw the older woman very near two fire scenes immediately around the time of two fires. Since they had not seen her start a fire, they assumed at first that it was a coincidence.

Eventually, the lead investigators on the case realized that it was no coincidence that the same car and driver appeared at three different arson scenes. They ran the plate of the Oldsmobile and saw that it was registered to an eighty-year-old local woman, who was much older than the woman they had observed driving the car. They began a discreet investigation into that eighty-year-old woman.

### Charmian Glassman

Eventually, like in all good cases, the hard-working investigative team got a nice break. One of the Cal Fire investigators was in town at a convenience store and saw the Oldsmobile Cutlass leaving the same business. It was driven by a short-haired older woman—the same woman spotted driving near the fire scenes. The Cal Fire investigator took a big gamble and asked the store employees if they knew the name of the woman in the Oldsmobile. Employees identified her as a local citizen named Charmian Glassman, who was sixty years old. She lived locally at 309 East Lake Street, in Mount Shasta. The investigators noted that her home was just three blocks away from the street that led into Everitt Memorial Highway.

Eventually the investigation would reveal that Glassman was a local artist who routinely drove the car that was registered to the eighty-year-old woman. She was also the mother of firefighter Jason Robertson! When this information was learned, the arson investigators didn't know what to think.

The fire total had now grown to over twenty fires. By this time the investigators had been able to scour the fire scenes and were able to gather full and partial footprints along with tire tracks from the suspect vehicle. SA Paul Steensland took a full-size photo of one of the tire tracks to a local Oldsmobile dealership to see how it compared to the tires on the new cars. The suspicious track was a close match. While this comparison was not done by a forensic specialist (that would come later), this was some positive news that the investigation team was focused on the correct vehicle.

The team now had the problem of wondering if they had two arsonists or if the arsons were being done by the son or the mother. Their best guess was that it was both, since no one had ever heard of a sixty-year-old grandmother being a wild-land serial arsonist.

By the end of July the investigative team set up and focused their surveillance activities on Charmian Glassman and her Oldsmobile. They were able to follow her one day out to the target area, and an undercover investigator was hidden nearby when he observed Glassman park her car by the side of the road, pick up a pine cone, and walk several feet into the dry vegetation. She then ignited the pine cone with a plastic cigarette lighter and tossed the burning item into the brush. They had their arsonist!

Glassman was quickly arrested, and a search warrant was served at her home. She was brought into a carefully prepared interview room where she met SA Steensland and SA Patricia Anjola. Steensland had carefully placed a few props in the room including aerial photos of the target area, a large photograph of a tire track, and photos of the arsonist's footprints. The two USFS investigators soon engaged Glassman in a very one-sided interview. When SA Steensland told Glassman that the very shoes she was now wearing were linked to several of the fire scenes, she quickly pulled her feet under her chair and tried to hide them from view.

Glassman at first denied involvement in the fires but changed her tune when SA Steensland told her that they believed that her son was involved with her. He laid down in front of her a police photo of her son, Jason. This shocked Charmian, and she immediately confessed and stated, "He didn't have anything to do with it."

Shortly Charmian Glassman admitted to setting five of the recent fires. She surprised the investigators when they asked her about her reasons for setting fires. Glassman had adopted her son, Jason, at a very young age and had rescued him from an abusive family. She was an aging single parent, and her son was the focus of her life. She doted on the young man and was happy that he was trying to become a firefighter.

She had grown dismayed in recent months when a series of events began to negatively affect both her and her son. Jason had started dating a young girl and had impregnated the seventeen-year-old. Soon a baby came to the young couple, who barely had any income. The baby had been born somewhat unhealthy and had lingering medical issues. Jason was in trouble at work and had been told that he was possibly going to be let go. The fire engine he was assigned to was set to be deactivated due to a lack of business. Charmian knew her son was about to lose his job as a firefighter. Charmian eventually told investigators the shocking news that she had decided to set the fires so that her son would have a chance to make some money and could possibly be seen as a hero. She was hoping that his heroic deeds would help him find full-time employment as a firefighter. Charmian Glassman was a firefighter arsonist by proxy!

The investigators were forced to take Glassman's confession on its face value. She had a spotless record and had no history of alcoholism, drug addiction, mental-health issues, or any of the other problems often associated with serial arsonists. She had many longtime friends in the local community. In the end, they took the case to the local district attorney, Christine Stark, who filed charges related to five arson fires in the series.

The investigative team showed its diligence by continuing to examine Glassman's son, firefighter Jason Robertson. He was positively cleared and did not have any involvement in the fires. Sometime after his mother's arrest, Jason Robertson resigned from his firefighting duties.

In an arranged deal, Charmian Glassman pled guilty to setting five arson fires during July of 1995. In January of 1996, a state judge accepted Glassman's plea deal and sentenced her to 120 days in jail and five years of felony probation. She was also ordered to pay restitution in the form of investigative costs to both Cal Fire and the USFS. Glassman maintained a low profile, normal life after this series of fires. Charmian Glassman passed away quietly in her hometown of Mt. Shasta, in May of 2010. She was never linked to any other fires in her life.

*The professionals who worked on this case include USFS senior special agent Paul Steensland, SA Frank Packwood, SA Rix Calloway, and SA Patricia Anjola, with DDA Christine Stark.*

### Investigator's Profile

This case made the national news that year and comes up all the time in the discussion of "famous" arson cases. Most of that hype was generated by the media, who gave Glassman the moniker "Ma Sparker," in witty reference to the notorious female leader of the Barker bank-robbing family of the 1930s, Ma Barker.

While her nickname gives her immortality in the arson world, seasoned investigators now know that she is not the only female serial arsonist; nor is she even close to being the oldest. This book has a serial arsonist older than Glassman (Shirley "the Ghost" Vigneau) who set more fires than Glassman. There are many other examples of female serial arsonists in the same age group.

This case is important because it gives the history of a woman who was quite unique in her motive for fire setting. She did not set fires due to excitement, depression, anger, rage, mental illness, or revenge. She set them to benefit her son, the firefighter. SA Paul Steensland called Glassman a "**firefighter arsonist by proxy.**" This is a very small niche group of arsonists who set fires in an attempt to somehow benefit a family member involved in firefighting. This is most often seen among groups involved in seasonal wildfire suppression and can include Native American families and tribes along with Canadian First Nations tribes. This classification would put Glassman in the category of a **goal-directed arsonist.**

While Charmian Glassman certainly defies the norm when it comes to a wild-land serial arsonist, she is a good reminder for all in this business that everyone can be a potential suspect, and an investigator cannot simply eliminate suspects based on race, gender, and age.

The fires in this series were consistent with other female fire setters in that they were low-performing events lacking any sort of sophistication, and the suspect operated in a very small and predictable target area. Glassman was not sophisticated enough to obscure her foot and tire tracks and did not use a delay incendiary device that may have given her some time to escape the area. She is very typical of a female serial arsonist.

## FELONY STUPID
## CORRAL CANYON FIRE, CA, 2007

On November 20, 2007, Cal Fire, the fire management, suppression, and investigation agency for California, issued an urgent press release. The press release stated that Cal Fire was "mobilizing for Santa Ana winds." The press release predicted a strong Santa Ana wind condition over the next several days, with widespread gusty winds over a large region of Southern California. The temperature was expected to remain fairly warm for November, and the winds were expected to blow from over thirty miles per hour in the flatlands and up to seventy miles per hour in the canyons, mountain passes, and foothills. The chief of Cal Fire stated that the conditions would be so dire that they "just increase the chance of a single spark becoming a major fire due to the dry vegetation in Southern California."

In preparation for what surely would be a busy week of fires, the chief ordered the prepositioning of hundreds of firefighters, engines, wild-land and inmate hand crews, and firefighting aircraft throughout the region. This prepositioning of massive forces was a normal agency response to something the chief called a "red-flag warning." To make matters even worse, according to the US Drought Monitor, the Southern California coastal foothills were classified as being in "extreme drought" condition. In other words, the upcoming week had all the ingredients for a potential catastrophe.

The worried Cal Fire chief had every right to be concerned. The fall of 2007 had already been one of the most disastrous fire seasons in Southern California history. In the month of October alone, during a searing hot Santa Ana windstorm, thirty wildfires erupted across seven southern counties. Seventeen of these grew to become major events stretching the resources of firefighting and police agencies to their limits. Fifteen hundred homes had already been destroyed and fourteen people had been killed during these fires.

At least two of these fires were intentionally set by arsonists. One of the arsonists was killed by police as they attempted to apprehend him, and the second, Ricky Jimenez, was arrested by LASD arson investigators after he lit eight fires in the wild lands north of Los Angeles. Jimenez, a convicted serial arsonist, already had three prior arson arrests on his record. He would later be sentenced to fourteen years in prison for his fires in 2007.

On October 21, due to eleven of these large fires still burning, the dangerously low relative humidity in the region, and the threat of more Santa Ana winds, California governor Arnold Schwarzenegger formally proclaimed a state of emergency for the seven Southern California counties. This formal proclamation was still in effect when Cal Fire issued its press release on November 20.

At just past three in the morning on November 24, the Remote Automated Weather Station in Malibu reported a temperature of fifty-nine degrees, with steady winds from the north at twenty-four miles per hour, and with gusts to forty-three miles per hour. The relative humidity was an arid 7 percent. The Santa Ana winds, this time without their normal heat, were in full effect.

## The Fire

At 3:23 a.m., on November 24, 2007, a brush fire erupted over a ridgeline just to the east of Corral Canyon Road, along Mesa Peak, in the mountains above Malibu. Residents in the canyon reported hearing a car horn sounding frantically at just past three in the morning. This car horn was later believed to be a warning given by one of the persons involved in the start of the fire. The first flames were spotted just three miles north of the coastline and above the sprawling campus of Pepperdine University.

Sgt. Rob Knudson, of the Los Angeles Sheriff's Malibu Station, was among the first responders. Upon arrival at the area near the start of the fire, Sgt. Knudson was informed that the first flames were spotted coming from the vicinity of "the cave." Knudson knew, like all the cops and residents in the area, that the cave was a notorious party spot high atop a ridgeline in a remote area overlooking the coast. The cave was a natural cavern in the mountain rocks that was big enough to hold eight to twelve people, and it had a view extending down slope to the coast three miles away. The cave was a comfortable and easily accessible location and had been a covert party spot for teens for decades.

Sgt. Knudson could see a small fire burning near the cave, but he could also see that the winds were howling along the ridgeline, already pushing the head of the fire down slope, southward toward the heavily populated beach area of Malibu. He began orchestrating a massive evacuation of the dozens of expensive ranches that filled Corral Canyon between the caves and the coast.

Captain Alvin Cunningham, with the LACoFD, was in charge of Engine No. 271 based in Malibu that night. He was dispatched to the Mesa Peak area at 3:23 a.m. on November 24. The area was on state parklands, and had a gated roadway. The area had been closed and gated for months due to the dry conditions and threat of fire. Cunningham had to cut the locks off one of the gates in order for his engine to access the area. When he arrived with his crew, they could see a three to five acre brush fire burning in the area of the cave. He said the winds were extremely heavy and were pushing the blaze in a southeast direction toward the coast.

He called for immediate backup from several more engines and began to fight the fire. The local chief knew that there were no power lines in the area of the cave and immediately deemed the blaze suspicious. He placed a call to the fire department's arson investigators, asking them to respond to this event, which he now christened the "Corral Fire."

While the sheriff's deputies frantically tried to evacuate the dozens of ranch properties in Corral Canyon, the fire agencies attempted to set up hasty firebreaks and structure protection. They knew they had to get a handle on this fast as the winds would surely double in strength by dawn, just two hours away. Despite the actions of two of the largest public agencies in the world, there was just no stopping this fire. The gusting winds drove the fire so fast that it made it to Pacific Coast Highway within two hours, even before the winds started reaching speeds in excess of sixty miles per hour.

The fire agencies then conducted a superhuman blocking operation, by literally lining fire engines up bumper to bumper along the coast highway. If the fire crossed this wide road, it would surely decimate the heavily clustered beach homes at the water's edge. In desperation, the fire bosses used the aligned engines with their water cannons, backfiring operations, and even used predawn helicopter water drops, a very risky maneuver to blunt the force of this blaze. Amazingly, they were able to knock down the flame front and protect everything south of Pacific Coast Highway. The raging front of this fire collapsed at the coast highway.

The strong winds had two unique effects on this fire. Due to the wind speed, the fire was focused in a narrow front and did not endanger many properties on either side of the canyon. Additionally, the fire was moving so fast that the flames were burning laterally over the ground. In this fashion, they moved too quickly to burn everything in their path and literally skipped dozens of homes and ranches.

The effect of this was apparent when the sun arose and helicopters took to the air. They could no longer see a major flame front but could see pockets of fire and burning buildings all up and down the canyon, with other pockets of unburned vegetation and buildings in the middle of it all. The people who were spared the blaze rushed to their homes to account for their pets and ranch animals, no doubt thanking their lucky stars. Meanwhile, their stunned next-door neighbors stood staring at their own devastated properties, wondering what they had done wrong to be cursed by the fire gods.

For the next several days, the firefighters, while not hampered on trying to control a moving flame front, nonetheless were kept quite busy extinguishing over ninety structure fires in the coastal region.

The City of Malibu, in conducting a final tabulation of the event, concluded that ninety structures were destroyed in the fire, with fifty-five of them being occupied family homes. Several of these belonged to celebrities and the elite of Hollywood. An additional fifty-three structures were damaged, with forty-three of them being homes, along with thirty-seven vehicles being destroyed. A total of 4,900 acres of wild land was burned. By dawn, fourteen thousand residents of Malibu had been evacuated. The total amount of damage for this fast-moving fire was later estimated at $100 million. This clearly was a major disaster.

In addition to the loss of property, five firefighters suffered minor to moderate injuries during the fire-suppression efforts, with injuries including burns, broken bones, and breathing issues. Miraculously, not a single person was seriously injured or killed.

Almost immediately rumors began to swirl that the fire was an intentional act. The normally liberally bent, kicked-back, live-and-let-live-minded landowners in Malibu were incensed. There was a piercing cry for blood and justice from the rich, mostly former hippies, who were usually a pretty forgiving lot.

### The Arson Investigation

By eight in the morning, Ranger Brian Lincoln was aware of the fast-moving fire. Lincoln was employed by the California Department of State Parks. He immediately suspected that the fire may have originated in the area of the cave. Ranger Lincoln had encountered numerous persons in the past drinking alcohol, smoking pot, and having built illegal campfires within the cave area. He had issued many citations to area teens for all of these above activities. At 10:50 a.m., Ranger Lincoln arrived at the cave and immediately saw evidence of a recent campfire. Ranger Lincoln also saw alcohol containers, food wrappers, marshmallows, and graham crackers. All of the items appeared to have been left there within the past day. The brush at the mouth of the cave was five to fifteen feet high and was comprised of very dry chaparral and manzanita. Ranger Lincoln contained the scene and called LACoFD investigators.

Arson investigations in Los Angeles County have confused people since the 1930s, when, due to cost-cutting measures, the county fire department begged out of "arson" investigations in the unincorporated areas. They argued that arson was a police crime and that the investigation should fall to the sheriff's department. Since that era, the LASD has maintained a full-time arson unit, merging it with the Bomb Squad in the 1970s. This Arson-Explosives Detail is one of the few full-time arson-investigation units run by a police agency in the United States, where the bulk of arson investigation is conducted by fire agencies.

The sheriff's department's arson investigators are among the highest trained in the world and have a long-standing reputation for aggressiveness and case solving. This particular fire would be even more confusing as the State of California, through the investigators working for Cal Fire, would have a say as well in the outcome.

The fire originated on state parklands, and Cal Fire dispatched battalion chief (investigator) Andy Anderson to handle its end of it. LACoFD sent Inv. Chuck Doremus to monitor its part, and the LASD sent Det. Irma Gonzales as the lead investigator. Irma brought along experienced sheriff's investigators Det. Greg Everett and Sgt. Mike Costleigh. This small group would form into the ad hoc Corral Fire Task Force. Irma would eventually be the lead investigator for the entire case, with Sgt. Costleigh and Det. Everett conducting the bulk of the follow-up investigation.

By noon, all of these investigators met at Pacific Coast Highway and Corral Canyon Road. They traveled to the cave area and met Ranger Lincoln. The group as a whole conducted an "origin and cause" investigation for this fire. It was clear almost immediately that the fire started near the open mouth of the cave. Brush fires that occur during high winds are the easiest ones to investigate. The primary factor in fire direction is the wind, and by just proceeding upwind to the very edge of the burn pattern, investigators can easily locate the origin area for the fire since fires generally cannot burn against high winds.

In this case, the area of origin was just a few feet wide, in some brush at the base of the cave's opening. It should be pointed out here that the open mouth of the cave was raised about fifteen feet above the ground and brush below it. A piece of burned firewood was found directly at the point of origin. This wood partially remained intact and displayed indications that it had been a chunk of wood split and sold commercially as firewood, as opposed to just a piece of downed tree wood or a branch on the ground.

Adding to this theory, the investigators quickly spotted a piece of orange plastic twine in the area of origin. This piece of twine had come off a larger piece and appeared consistent with that found to encircle a bundle of commercial firewood. Within inches of this twine, the team located a single wooden match that had been lit at one point.

The investigative team entered the cave itself. The cave was about twelve feet deep and twenty feet wide. It had a rock floor and was tall enough to stand in. The team quickly discovered a large amount of old debris, bottles, and cigarette butts littering the floor. It was clearly a long-used party location. Vulgar graffiti covered the walls. Most of it was not gang related. It was more the type used by older teens. Much of it referred to smoking marijuana.

In the center of the cave, directly next to the open mouth, were the remnants of a recent campfire. Alongside that were six pieces of wood from a bundle of commercial firewood. The bundle had been secured by an orange plastic twine, identical to what was found in the area of origin. It became apparent to the investigators that the chunk of burned firewood found in the origin of this fire was from this nearby bundle.

Other items of interest in the cave were the burned remnants of small tea candles and some recently discarded food items. Investigators found and collected a burned bag of Kraft Jet-Puffed marshmallows and an uneaten graham cracker. Stuck in a tree just outside the mouth of the cave were two plastic grocery bags from the Ralph's chain. Pages from a *Malibu Times* newspaper were strewn about the cave. The paper was dated November 22, 2007.

The investigators noted that the floor of the cave was directly above the area of origin for this brush fire. The burned piece of wood and match were the only items in the area of origin that could have started this fire. The only question was whether they were deliberately thrown from the cave into the brush, which would make this event an arson attack, or were they accidentally allowed to travel from the cave to the brush, making this a negligently caused fire. Either way, the investigators ruled this fire as "human caused" and not due to an accident. The ensuing investigation would hopefully provide the answers to who started this fire and why.

Cal Fire investigator Anderson took some weather data at the area of origin. The actual mouth of the cave and area origin was in the lee of the rock outcropping and mostly out of the wind. The wind speeds in that spot were about five to seven miles per hour. He then walked fifteen yards east along the path of the fire and soon was exposed to a southeast wind blowing at over twenty-five miles per hour. The investigators came to the mutual conclusion that the fire was likely an unintentional act and that it was started in an area with mild winds. However, within seconds of igniting, it likely reached into a windy area and soon was too far out of control for anyone to stop it.

### Posted Signs

Sheriff's investigators had to prove that the persons who had set this fire, while having no criminal intent, had acted in a grossly negligent manner. To show this, they had to prove that the individuals should have known that starting a fire in the conditions or location was negligent or unlawful. There were two main routes of access to the cave area. On both routes, there were clear signs indicating that the area was off limits to camping, open flames, and ground fires of any sort.

One sign had bold red letters proclaiming "Danger—Extreme Fire Hazard Area—No Open Fire—No Smoking." A second sign along the hiking trail stated, "No Ground Fires" and had graphics depicting no camping and no open flames. Rangers would testify that these signs had been freshly erected just weeks prior to this fire.

## The Investigation

Realizing that there was a Ralph's grocery store in nearby Malibu, sheriff's investigators Mike Costleigh and Greg Everett drove to that store to follow up on the food items found within the cave. They immediately hit pay dirt. The store manager found a receipt for some of the items found in the cave. She found a receipt purchased with a debit card. She printed that receipt and gave it to the investigators. The receipt showed that at 9:53 p.m., on November 23, just four hours before the fire, someone had purchased twenty-eight dollars' worth of marshmallows, graham crackers, and Hershey bars, all the makings of the campfire treat known as S'mores.

There was associated store security video showing several young adults purchasing the items. At the same time, a male member of their group stood around the store entrance, looking about in a suspicious manner. He appeared to be acting as some sort of lookout. The detectives noted that he was standing right next to the outdoor rack that held firewood. Next to this was a newspaper rack for the *Malibu Times*. While the video failed to show the exact area of the racks, the investigators went outside and saw that the wood in the rack was bundled with orange plastic twine, identical to the items found in the cave. Further, the current newspapers still in the rack were dated November 22, 2007. The detectives surmised that one of the group must have stolen the wood and newspaper at this time.

Detectives wrote a search warrant to learn the bank associated with the debit card used at Ralph's. They then wrote a separate warrant for that bank account and learned that the debit card was owned by a twenty-three-year-old man named Patrick

Earley, living in Redding, California. A subsequent search of social media showed that Earley had a Myspace account. Detectives accessed that and were shocked to see that Earley had posted photos of himself and several others sitting around a campfire in the cave, just a few feet from the area of origin. Although the photo was not dated, it clearly linked Earley to the cave.

On November 29, lead investigator Irma Gonzalez received a phone message from a mother who lived in the Malibu area. The mother said that her teenage daughter had been with a group of young people in the cave the night of the fire. The mother wanted her daughter to give a statement about the actions of this group. This group would come to be known as "the first group" to arrive at the cave.

Later that same day, Det. Gonzalez interviewed the young woman. The young woman (witness) stated that she, along with a couple of other teenage girls, went to the cave with two young men named Eric Ullman and Dean Lavorante. They arrived at the cave about nine thirty on the night of the twenty-third, and there were no other persons around. The two young men (Ullman and Lavorante) brought a case of beer and scraps of wood. The two males started a small campfire with the wood scraps. The witness said the group was worried about causing a fire in the high winds, so they kept their campfire very low and monitored it carefully.

After eleven o'clock, a second larger group showed up with two girls and six young men. The witness said the second group had several bundles of firewood and a couple of Ralph's bags with the ingredients for s'mores. The first group watched as the second group made s'mores and listened to music on a laptop computer. At midnight, the first group left the cave. They did not see anyone playing with the fire or throwing embers around. When her group left, the witness said the second group still had a campfire burning in the cave. She identified a white male in the second group by his nickname "AJ." She said another male named Brian appeared to be the leader of that group. The witness was shown a photo lineup of persons who may have been in the second group. She immediately identified the photo of Patrick Earley as a member of the second group in the cave.

The witness told Det. Gonzalez that after the large fire occurred and made the news, her friends had been called by AJ, who threatened to "kill them for telling people" about what happened in the cave.

### Patrick Earley

The same day as this interview with the young woman, detectives contacted Patrick Earley by phone, and he agreed to meet with them in person. He admitted to being in the cave that night and also told the cops that another person from Redding named Andrew Ramos was with him. He identified Ramos as having the nickname "AJ." The sheriff's detectives, along with polygraph examiners and their equipment, flew to Redding, California, to meet with Patrick Earley and Andrew Ramos on November 30, 2007.

Both young men told investigators that they had visited friends in the Los Angeles area over Thanksgiving. On the evening of the twenty-third, they drove with several friends in two cars to the Malibu area. Earley admitted purchasing the food items from the grocery store. The two told investigators that a couple of their friends, Will Coppock and Brian Anderson, had stolen wood from the front of the grocery store.

The group drove up to the locked gate near the cave and had to walk the rest of the way. In the cave, they saw another group of young adults partying around a small campfire. At some point, they started adding the stolen wood to the small campfire, and it soon got too hot and smoky inside the cave. Three of the males, Brian Anderson, Will Coppock, and Brian

Franks, began goofing around and kicking the flaming logs and embers around. Some of these items fell outside of the cave mouth into the brush below and started small fires. Brian Franks went outside to stomp out the small fires, and Brian Anderson threw a burning pillow at him as a joke. Eventually Franks put out all the small fires, and the group left the scene.

Earley and Ramos claimed to be very concerned about the fire and the guys fooling around as they described the conditions as "super windy," with wind speeds of around forty miles per hour. They said that most of their group was drinking vodka and beer. They claimed to have left prior to about one thirty in the morning. Earley also stated that as they left, one of the kids started honking his car horn as he drove down canyon as a joke. This group of young males became known by investigators as "the second group" to arrive at the cave.

The investigators noted that Earley had given them some self-serving statements. He had implicated others in drinking and playing with fire while denying that he had done either. He took a video-recorded polygraph exam and was found to be "deceptive" in certain parts.

### William Coppock

William Coppock was located and interviewed on December 3 by sheriff's investigators and polygraph examiners. Coppock reiterated much of the same information as Earley had. However, he added that the embers came out of the cave when the group decided to leave the cave and go home. They began kicking at some of the smoldering logs in an attempt to put them out. During that time they accidentally kicked some embers into the brush below. Coppock denied doing this himself and indicated that Brian Anderson had thrown or kicked a burning pillow into the brush. He said that Anderson was drunk at the time.

He claimed that all of the small fires were out when they left the scene. However, he admitted that the logs in the cave were still glowing red when they left. The polygraph examiner determined that parts of Coppock's statement were "deceptive."

### Brian Anderson

Brian Anderson was interviewed on December 3 by sheriff's investigators and polygraph examiners. Anderson stated that he had partied at the cave over fifteen times in the past few years. He went with the second group of people. He brought a twelve pack of beer and then purchased a bottle of vodka at the Ralph's store with his debit card at the same time Earley was purchasing s'mores. He said that Wil Coppock had stolen bundles of wood from in front of the store.

Anderson gave roughly the same story as the others, with some editing on his own behalf. He said that the first group's fire was a bit small, so he added an entire bundle of wood to it at once, causing it to get very hot and smoky. He said that the fire got a bit too large, and they decided to put it out by kicking the logs. He did not recall any embers getting away but did see some small fires start in the brush below the cave mouth. He sent Franks to put out the fires in the brush. When Franks was doing that, Anderson kicked a piece of burning pillow at Franks as a joke. He was sure that Franks had put that out as well. He believed all fires were out when they left the cave. The polygraph examiner took Anderson's statement and believed him to be untruthful about who kicked the wood out of the cave.

### Brian Franks

Brian Franks was interviewed on December 3 by sheriff's investigators and polygraph examiners. Franks again gave roughly the same story as the others. He added that it was he and Wil Coppock who had stolen four bundles of wood from in front of the Ralph's store, at the direction of Brian Anderson. Franks also took a newspaper from the nearby rack in order to use it for kindling the fire. Franks said that around two in the morning they decided to leave the cave. They kicked out the burning logs, causing some embers to fly out of the cave into the brush below. Franks said he went into the brush and put out the small fires that had occurred. At that time Brian Anderson threw a burning pillow at him. This caused a small fire, which he quickly extinguished. Franks said they soon left, and it appeared that all fires were out when they left the cave.

### Eric Ullman

Eric Ullman was interviewed by sheriff's detectives on December 5. Eric stated that he and Dean Lavorante were part of the first group that went to the cave. They picked up some young girls, some firewood, and an eighteen pack of beer. They arrived after eight in the evening and started a small campfire. Ullman admitted that he and Lavorante used lighter fluid and a lighter to ignite the campfire. They hung out until the second group arrived, and then they left around midnight.

### Dean Lavorante

Dean Lavorante was interviewed by sheriff's detectives on December 5. Lavorante gave an identical story as Ullman. He added that on November 27, after detectives had spoken to Patrick Earley in Redding by phone, he had received a cell phone call from AJ, who he knew to be Andrew Ramos from Redding. Ramos put Earley on the phone with Lavorante. At that time Earley told Lavorante, "I know you man...I'm gonna come fucking kill you." Lavorante explained that the two men in Redding did not know how the cops found them or got their names, so they assumed that Lavorante snitched on them.

## Other Interviews

Four other persons gave interviews of the events of that night. All remained somewhat consistent with the original story. The main consistent themes were that the original group of young girls and the two males, Ullman and Lavorante, had started the original fire, which was continually described as fairly small. When the second group arrived with Franks, Anderson, Coppock, Ramos, and Earley, the size of the fire soon changed. Almost all witnesses described Anderson as being the ring-leader or instigator. He was by all accounts drunk, loud, and a bit out of control. He seemed to have a degree of influence over Brian Franks as he frequently ordered him about and made him do things for him.

All witnesses stated that Anderson made the fire much larger by applying a large amount of wood at once. The witnesses also indicate that while several men began kicking at the burning logs to put them out, it was Anderson who purposefully kicked or threw the burning pillow into the brush below. By everyone's account, he was out of control.

Most of the group admitted that they were drinking beer and vodka, plus several were smoking marijuana. No one recalled having seen any signs stating the area was closed due to a fire hazard, but all recalled bypassing the locked gate. Another mystery that was cleared up through interviews was the honking of the car horns. This signal was originally believed to be a warning given by someone to alert the citizens of the fire. The interviews showed that at least two of the drivers, in a fit of revelry and alcohol, were just speeding down the canyon sounding their horns as a bit of a prank. Most importantly, almost everyone in both groups was aware of the cold and windy conditions, and all expressed concern that the campfire was a risky thing to have in such bad conditions.

### The Prosecution

The original task force members, who included Cal Fire and LACoFD investigators, met with LASD detectives. They all reviewed the detailed investigation that the sheriff's department had completed up until this point. All reached the same conclusion that the Corral Fire was not an act of arson. After reviewing the scene evidence, weather conditions, and statements made by numerous participants and witnesses, they all realized that this case was more likely an act of gross criminal negligence.

In California, the arson statutes have a series of codes for something called "negligent fires." The layman's version is that these are fires that are human caused but without criminal intent. They are further described as fires set in a manner, which is defined by the conditions or location, as being grossly negligent. The Corral Fire was clearly in this category.

On December 12, 2007, LASD detectives, led by Det. Irma Gonzales, presented the facts of this case to the District Attorney's Office for filing consideration. They also supplied a list of all those present in the cave, their respective roles, and the detectives' opinions as to who were actually involved in causing the fire. As a result of this investigation, the DA filed multiple felony counts of illegally and negligently causing a fire, which led to serious injuries and massive property damage. Felony charges were filed against Brian Anderson, who was deemed to be most culpable after it was established he threw the burning pillow and kicked burning wood into the brush. Three felonies were also filed against William Coppock for his role in stealing the firewood, creating a large fire, and kicking embers into the brush. Similar charges were filed against Brian Franks.

Eric Ullman and Dean Lavorante were viewed to have similar but lesser roles. However, they were the persons who set the original fire and were filed on in the same manner as the previous three suspects. All other participants were given a pass. In truth, the DA anticipated using the non-charged persons as witnesses against the charged persons.

LASD detectives swooped down and immediately arrested Anderson, Franks, and Coppock the next day. That afternoon, Ullman and Lavorante turned themselves in to a local sheriff's station. They immediately posted bail. Over the next two years a series of court hearings and legal machinations took place. Codefendants began attempting to separate themselves from each other.

At their first joint hearing, the lawyers for one part of the group began blaming the fire on the other part of the group. A couple of the lawyers issued passionate arguments that what occurred wasn't even a crime and should be in civil court instead of criminal court. Defense counsel also cited tremendous community, media, and government pressure to make arrests and prosecute suspects in this case, when in their minds it was an accidental event. The defense even went so far as to point out that the presiding judge in the case was a resident of Malibu and had been personally affected by the fire, insinuating that he may have a bias against the defendants. All of these arguments were in vain as the judge placed high bails on the defendants and ordered them held over for preliminary hearings.

In 2008, Brian Franks in a plea agreement pled "no contest" to the charges against him. He then provided testimony in a preliminary hearing against Brian Anderson and William Coppock. Franks received a felony conviction, a five-year probationary sentence, and was ordered to pay restitution.

On September 8, 2010, a superior court judge took "no contest" pleas from Brian Anderson and William Coppock. The judge sentenced them to one year in jail and ordered them to write letters to all fifty-three homeowners who lost their houses in the fire. They were also ordered to pay $7.7 million in firefighting costs, and an undetermined amount of money in restitution.

Six weeks later, on October 20, 2010, the final two defendants of the Corral Canyon fire pled "no contest" in superior court. The received felony convictions and got five years of probation each, along with $1,000 in restitution fees.

Although the total cost for this fire was in excess of $100 million, there is little expectation that the defendants will ever make any sort of restitution. All of them were adults around twenty years of age, with menial-type jobs and very little income at the time of this event.

Shortly after the final court proceedings in this case, lead detective Irma Gonzales retired after an exemplary thirty-year career with the LASD.

*The following detectives or investigators played major roles in this investigation: Lead investigator Det. Irma Gonzales, LASD; Det. Greg Everett, LASD; Sgt. Mike Costleigh, LASD; battalion chief investigator Andy Anderson, Cal Fire; Inv. Chuck Doremus, LACoFD; and Ranger Brian Lincoln of the California Department of Parks.*

### Investigator's Profile

Readers will note that this case is not classified as a deliberate criminal fire or arson (per California statutes). There was no malice aforethought, no premeditation, and no criminal intent by the offenders. As such, the criminal motive for this fire is nonexistent. In its place, we insert the words "dumbass" or "moron." In cop lingo, that's "felony stupid." Normally, a case like this would never make it into a book on criminal profiling.

However, in the world of criminal fire setting, negligent or reckless fires that lead to serious damage or death are commonplace, and therefore this subject needs to be discussed because virtually every arson investigator deals with negligent fires fairly often. The real crux of the question and goal of the investigator is to determine if there was ordinary, everyday negligence (such as a housewife leaving the bacon cooking too long) that caused the fire, or if the act was so grossly negligent in manner or scope that it rises to the level of *criminal negligence*.

Sadly, in the fire-investigation world, these investigations become heavily skewed by administrators and managers of fire agencies wanting to classify all fires as criminally negligent so that they can pursue cost-recovery efforts. This mind-set and quest for money has clearly contaminated several agencies and has cast a shadow on legitimate arson investigations. This issue is a major hot-button issue in the western United States, where there are annually thousands of devastating wild-land fires. Most of those can be classified under two major headings. They are either an "act of God or nature," which is usually a lightning strike, or they are caused by "human activity." Human activity can be classified as accidental, intentional arson, negligence, or gross criminal negligence.

This above case clearly points to gross criminal negligence. These kids ignored numerous warning indicators and set a fire in conditions in which an open fire should not have been set. They were trespassing, drinking, and engaged in petty criminal conduct. The only saving grace for this group was that no one was injured or killed in this rapid-moving firestorm.

# 8

# Vehicle Arson Profiles

## The Profile

A surprisingly large number of arson-investigation agencies do not investigate automobile fires. Each time I ask an investigator why his agency does not investigate these fires, the answer is mostly the same. The chief doesn't want to waste resources on fires that are mainly an insurance problem. This is just another reason why arson investigation should be taken away from fire chiefs. They simply do not understand the crime of arson at all.

In the Los Angeles basin of over twelve million people, vehicle arsons are the most common arson events we deal with. I am quite sure that nationwide that holds true, especially in any urban environment. In an analysis of our own files covering tens of thousands of arson investigations, we have discovered that around 90 percent of vehicle arsons are "**owner involved**," **for the purpose of insurance fraud**. In these cases, the owner has torched his own car or more commonly has solicited a relative, friend, or coworker to do it for him. These cases are painfully obvious to figure out, and the majority of the arrests my unit makes involve "owner involved" car fires.

The other 10 percent or so of vehicle arson attacks involve the **revenge/spite motive**, as someone is really, really mad at you and has attacked your car with fire. The differences between the two arsons are very dramatic and obvious. A small percentage of other vehicle arsons may involve the crime concealment motive. In this scenario, the vehicle was used in some sort of serious crime and was then torched as an anti-forensics measure. This remains a fairly rare motive for vehicle arsons.

The key to figuring out which motive you have in a vehicle arson is to examine all aspects of the crime scene and event. In a typical revenge/spite arson attack on a vehicle, the vehicle is set on fire from the exterior. Sometimes a window is broken and an accelerant is poured inside. Sometimes an accelerant is poured over the vehicle. In almost all of these attacks, the vehicle is targeted when it is parked at the victim's home or workplace. The vehicle is normally not stolen, and there are seldom parts missing from the vehicle. Quite often the attack is part of a very overt dispute and may be preceded by vandalism in the form of window breaking, "keying" the car, or flattening tires. The victim almost always knows the suspect as they are usually involved in a dispute.

In direct contrast to the revenge/spite attack is the financial gain attack. In most cases, the owner is actively involved and wants his vehicle burned for a specific reason. The incident is planned out and often a coconspirator is involved so that the owner can have an alibi. The fire event is often preceded by a "staged theft," where the vehicle is "stolen" from a public place. Typical staged thefts have occurred at shopping malls, movie theaters, or when the victim is away from home for several days.

The vehicle is then found burning in a remote or hidden area. Occasionally there are some parts missing to give it the appearance of a theft by an organized auto-theft group. More often than not the vehicle is set on fire from the interior. There are several common factors that are often present during these staged "theft/arson" events:

- Vehicle is less than five years old.
- Vehicle has insurance.
- Vehicle registration has expired or is near expiration.
- Vehicle may have excessive miles or wear.
- Vehicle lease is due to expire.
- Vehicle may have major mechanical problem.
- Victim has an obvious alibi.
- Victim recently tried to sell or trade in vehicle.
- Victim purchased new vehicle.
- Victim experiencing financial hardship.
- Victim has history of suspicious insurance claims.
- Victim may have reported the loss of his keys in the days or weeks prior to the event.

In general, burglars and car thieves are profit-oriented criminals, and there is little incentive for them to burn a vehicle. The value of the vehicle is in its parts, and true auto thieves want to renumber the stolen car or "part it out" for a maximum profit. Auto thieves very rarely are involved in the burning of vehicles.

The most common suspect to burn a vehicle is a male. If a female is the owner of the vehicle, quite often a male relative or friend is the suspect. The most effective investigative technique for this sort of case is by exploiting cell phone forensics to determine who is talking to the victim around the time of the event.

## RAZO THE BAD COP
## LOS ANGELES, CA, JANUARY 2009

### The Arson

At 12:55 p.m. on January 4, 2009, patrol deputies from the LASD's East Los Angeles Station saw a dark and angry column of thick black smoke rising into the air. They sped to the scene, which was a cul-de-sac in a quiet industrial neighborhood, and found a very nice-looking 2005 BMW LI car on fire. The fire had fully engulfed the trunk area of the vehicle. The deputies called the local fire department, which quickly arrived and extinguished the car fire. There were no persons in the car or around who could identify the car.

Because the car was very high dollar in appearance and because no one was around, the deputies suspected that the car may have been involved in some sort of crime. They ran the license plate of the car and found that it was registered to a man named Anthony Razo.

## The Theft

At 1:55 p.m. on the same day, Anthony Razo stepped out of a drugstore in the city of Monterey Park, which is right next door to East Los Angeles. At that time he made a cell phone call to the Monterey Park Police Department and advised them that he was an off-duty LAPD detective and that his car had "just been stolen." A young patrol officer was sent to the scene to take a report from Detective Razo. The patrol officer was a rookie who was just barely off training. He arrived at the drugstore within minutes to find a fifty-something-year-old veteran detective of the LAPD, which was the largest police agency in the western United States.

The patrol officer was a bit intimidated taking a report from a man who had been a cop for over twenty-five years. The patrolman noticed that although Razo had told him that this incident had "just occurred," he already had a replacement vehicle at the scene. The older cop explained that a relative had been nearby and had responded quickly to the scene with Razo's other car.

As soon as he made contact, Razo told the young officer about the "theft." He said that he had been at the drugstore since about noon and had been shopping for about two hours. When he exited the store just before two in the afternoon, he found that his 2005 BMW had been stolen. The young patrolman took detailed notes and carefully examined the scene where Razo stated the BMW had been parked. There was no broken glass and no other indications of a car theft.

While the patrolman was filling out his report, Razo began volunteering extra information. He told the patrolman that he had been at the store for so long because he was awaiting a prescription to be filled. He mentioned that as he waited, he had eaten lunch at a nearby restaurant. At this point the young officer showed an incredible amount of intuition. He knew from being at this small strip mall recently that the restaurant Razo had referred to had been closed for several months. The circumstances of this case were a bit strange, and the veteran police detective seemed exceptionally nervous.

The young patrolman then casually reached down and secretly turned on his digital recorder on his belt. He wanted to get this information right. He then repeated his line of questioning with Razo and noted that the details were somewhat different this time around. He then told Razo that the restaurant was closed. Immediately Razo got very nervous and started to stammer out a different answer. Despite the strange behavior of Razo, and the obvious lie he had told about where he ate, the young patrolman continued taking the information for the report.

He asked Razo for his car's license information and was shocked that Razo just happened to have the registration for the stolen car in his pocket. The patrolman then tried to enter this as "stolen" on his car's computer terminal. The patrolman found that Razo's car was already listed as "impounded" by the sheriff's station in East Los Angeles (ELA). He had his desk call the ELA sheriff's station, and they confirmed that they had found the vehicle burning at one o'clock, or nearly one hour before Razo claimed it was stolen. Something was very wrong, but the young officer figured the detectives would sort it all out.

## The Arson Investigation

Mike Cofield, the senior detective at the LASD Arson-Explosives Detail, was on duty that afternoon when the call came in about the burned car. The ELA patrol officers had spoken to the Monterey Park police desk and learned that the car they had found burning belonged to an undercover LAPD detective. Somehow, by the time the ELA deputies notified the Arson-Explosives Detail, they had confused some of this information and told Det. Cofield that the burned vehicle was a stolen LAPD undercover car. As a matter of professional courtesy, Cofield determined he was going to supply our brother agency LAPD with the highest quality of service possible.

Cofield began a detailed investigation into this incident. He saw that the car was indeed a high-dollar car and marveled that LAPD could afford such a nice, custom car for its undercover detectives. The car was a customized 740 Series BMW. It had custom rims and tires and all of the luxury upgrades. Cofield estimated that the car was worth something just under $100,000.

Det. Cofield determined that the car had been torched with a flammable liquid that had been poured into the trunk and rear area. This was very odd since most torch jobs were in the passenger compartment of vehicles or sometimes poured over the roof and hood. So far the scene had two oddities or anomalies. The time of the fire was odd since most arson fires occurred at night, and the area of the car set on fire was also odd since the trunk area is rarely targeted. Cofield took note that nothing on the car had been stolen or stripped, which is something true car thieves would have done. He also found a set of heavily damaged golf clubs in the trunk of the car.

Later Det. Cofield would learn that the car was not an LAPD undercover vehicle but was in fact a private car owned by an off-duty LAPD detective. From the start Cofield was deeply troubled as he realized that this arson fire had all the characteristics of an "owner involved" arson-for-profit scheme.

Shortly after this fire-scene investigation, Det. Cofield spoke to the car's owner, Anthony Razo. Razo confirmed that he was a longtime LAPD Major Crimes detective, who worked out of the nearby Hollenbeck Division. He reiterated roughly the same story to Cofield that he had told the young patrol officer, but this time he greatly changed his time line. He told Cofield that he had been golfing all morning and had arrived at the drugstore shortly after one in the afternoon. He said that he had shopped in the store for about thirty-five minutes. He also told Cofield that he was a very active golfer and that he had a bag of golf clubs in the trunk of the car. He described them as Ping brand worth over $1,000. He told Cofield that he had already reported the loss of the car to his insurance carrier, Farmers.

A few days later Det. Cofield made contact with investigators from Farmers, and each agreed that this case was highly consistent with possible insurance fraud. Each investigator agreed to pursue independent investigations of Anthony Razo. At this time Det. Cofield learned that Razo had made an official insurance claim for the burned car, and he had added a secondary claim for three bags of Ping golf clubs and other personal items totaling over $15,000. Cofield had conducted the fire-scene investigation and knew that there was only one set of clubs in the trunk of the car and that they were a very cheap brand, and certainly not the Ping brand. Anthony Razo had just committed at least one act of insurance fraud.

This little trick of alleging that high-priced items were lost in the fire is known as "padding the claim" in the insurance world. It is a felony in the criminal justice world.

The investigation continued for a few weeks while Cofield gathered evidence. He wrote a search warrant for Razo's cell phone and confirmed that the cell records did not match Razo's story. Three minutes before the ELA deputies happened upon the burning car, Razo's cell phone was not at the drugstore where he told the patrolman but was in fact within one block of the fire scene. Further, the cell records showed that he had not called any relative in his family to assist him after he reported his car stolen to the Monterey Park Police.

Clearly, his cell phone told the story. Razo had driven the BMW to the cul-de-sac by himself. The burn site was less than a half mile from his home. He had then walked home, picked up his second car and had driven to the drugstore to form an alibi. He had most likely chosen the drugstore as an alibi because he was witnessed on security cameras. This backfired on Razo as the security footage showed him entering the store just twelve minutes prior to him calling 911 to report the theft and not the thirty-five minutes he had told investigators.

Curious about how a cop could afford such an expensive car, Det. Cofield delved into Razo's finances. He found that Razo also had a real-estate license and was known as a golfer who was very close to professional in his skill level. He was also known as a heavy gambler who bet a lot of money on sports and his own golf games. Cofield discovered that Razo had paid over $75,000 for the BMW and had recently paid it off in two large payments. Cofield found that Razo had been apparently committing real-estate fraud for several years and had pulled several mortgages out of a property by illegally inflating its value on paper.

At the time of this fire, Razo was several hundred thousand dollars in debt and had a vicious gambling habit. Research was done on his visits to Las Vegas, and it was learned he had lost several thousand dollars at several casinos in that city. Razo's cell phone records showed that he had over 130 calls from debt collectors over the previous few weeks. By all indications, Anthony Razo was in the middle of a financial crisis!

Det. Cofield contacted BMW, who sent experts to examine the car. The experts confirmed that the car's ignition had not been bypassed and that it was "virtually impossible" for someone to steal this car without the key and remote due to some very intricate "antitheft" devices installed. The BMW experts advised Cofield that whoever drove that car to the burn site had the key and the key remote in his possession. Razo had those items in his possession when he contacted the Monterey Park officer.

Within three weeks Det. Mike Cofield had come to the conclusion that Anthony Razo had staged this event for the purpose of insurance fraud. Since he didn't work internal affairs, Cofield was deeply troubled about implicating a fellow officer. He knew by this time that Razo, although he was close to retirement and not considered a real hard worker at this stage of his career, had a traumatic history with the LAPD. Twenty years before this incident, Razo and a partner had been involved in a dramatic shootout with felons. During that shootout, Razo's partner had been murdered. Razo spent the next two decades working high-level detective assignments within LAPD. Mike Cofield really didn't want to arrest a decorated LAPD officer.

Cofield approached me to conduct a peer review on his case. Cofield was our best investigator, and I confirmed that he had done a meticulous and exhausting investigation and that his case was solid. He could easily prove that Razo had committed insurance fraud and arson. Cofield opted to report the case to both the LAPD and LASD internal affairs bureaus. Both units monitored it closely, but told Cofield to conduct his investigation as he would any other suspect. They would jump in after charges were filed.

Still, Cofield was not thrilled about this case and decided to give Razo a chance to come clean. He called Razo in the last week of January and asked him to come in for an informal interview. Razo knew something was up and asked Cofield if he was going to arrest him. Cofield assured him he was not but did tell him that we needed a clear statement from him. Razo assured Cofield he would be in on Friday, January 29. That morning Razo failed to show up for the interview with Det. Cofield. Later that day Cofield spoke to him again, and again Razo asked him if he was about to be arrested. When Cofield told him no, Razo promised to come in Monday morning, which was February 1.

Again Det. Cofield confided in me about the case and his concerns about how to file it. Neither one of us was thrilled with being involved in this case. That night I went home and met with a buddy who was a homicide detective. He had worked in the ELA area for years, and I asked him if he knew LAPD detective Anthony Razo. He did not, and I gave him a brief rundown of the insurance-fraud scheme Razo had concocted. We both felt a little bad for him.

### The Shooting

At seven in the morning, on Sunday, January 31, my homicide buddy, Det. Todd Anderson, called me at my home. "What was the name of that LAPD detective you told me about the other night?" I told him the name was Tony Razo. "Well," he wryly replied, "Tony Razo was just shot outside of his home in East Los Angeles." Det. Anderson said that Razo was alive and conscious but told patrolmen that he had been shot during an attempted robbery by two Hispanic gang members.

Det. Anderson went on to explain that the initial story that Razo told patrol officers was that he was leaving his home at just before five in the morning to go golfing. He had just pulled out his car and had placed his golfing gear inside when two thugs walked up behind him with a revolver. Razo said that one thug stuck the gun in his back and demanded the keys to Razo's car.

At that time, Razo claims to have quickly reacted and disarmed the man holding the revolver. During this struggle, Razo said his own weapon, which had been in his waist, fell out onto the ground and was picked up by the second suspect. Razo said the second suspect pointed the gun at Razo, and Razo was forced to grab the gun.

A violent struggle took place, and Razo was able to first eject the magazine out of the gun and then place his hands into the trigger mechanism to stop it from firing. Somehow, Razo said his weapon fired during the struggle, and the bullet struck him in the upper chest. As Razo fell to the ground, both suspects fled the scene on foot, taking the revolver with them.

Homicide detective Anderson said that the story Razo gave was fantastic and incredible, but it just didn't seem to match the evidence at the crime scene. He said that something seemed "staged" and not right. I reminded him that Razo was suspected of staging a very elaborate arson scene and had also been involved in several real-estate fraud schemes. He was very knowledgeable and clever and an experienced cop. He very well could have staged this entire incident to avoid answering to arson charges he knew were coming just a day later. This case had gone from a simple arson caper to an extremely elaborate "attempted murder of a police officer."

### Let Loose the Dogs

Anybody would tell you that you can't shoot a cop and get away with it. Most agencies would not rest for a second if they thought a cop killer was out there. LAPD and LASD are not most agencies. They are considered to be two of the largest, most modern, and most aggressive policing agencies in the world. They each have over 8,500 sworn officers within their ranks, and each has a massive division of detectives. Neither agency has ever had an unsolved murder against one of its officers. In this case both agencies were involved as the "attempted murder" occurred against an LAPD officer who resided in an LASD area. Although Razo had not been killed, the brass from each agency was not going to waste a second in rounding up the suspects. There was some intense recent history regarding this sort of thing.

On March 26, 2006, LASD deputy Maria Rosa was outside of an apartment in Long Beach in the predawn hours on her way to work in the Central Jail. As she was loading her gear into her car, she was shot twice in the head by two Hispanic street gang members. It took an intense undercover investigation over a year to track down the suspects. No motive was ever given, but robbery seemed to be the reason.

On August 2, 2008, almost exactly five months to the day prior to the Razo shooting, LASD deputy Juan Escalante was leaving his home in the predawn hours for his job at the downtown Central Jail. Escalante lived in the Boyle Heights area, less than five miles away from Razo's home in East Los Angeles. As Deputy Escalante was loading his gear into his car, several Hispanic street gang members approached him from behind and shot him to death with a handgun.

At the time of Razo's shooting, the Escalante case was still unsolved, but investigators had zeroed in on a local street gang that was targeting any cop in retaliation for one of its own being killed by an LAPD officer. The attack on Razo was a virtual clone of the Escalante murder five months earlier. It was also in roughly the same section of the city. The two previous, unprovoked attacks on police officers had occurred in the dawn hours, outside of their own homes, as they were loading items into their cars. The Razo shooting was eerily similar. Maybe too similar.

From the beginning of this incident with Razo, there were two different investigations going on. The first was by the shooting team, which eventually included a select group of LASD and LAPD homicide investigators, the District Attorney's Office's shooting experts, and arson detective Mike Cofield. That investigation was closely and quietly examining the possibility that this entire shooting was a staged event. The investigation by this small cadre was kept extremely quiet, and many members of both large agencies had no idea it was taking place. Only the highest brass of each agency realized that Razo was a potential target in this case.

Meanwhile, the agency heads for LASD and LAPD opened up a second investigation into the possibility that this attack on Razo was part of a wave of attacks on law enforcement that included the earlier Deputy Escalante murder. The task force for this part of the investigation numbered in the hundreds of detectives. The outraged heads of both agencies dedicated over a dozen homicide investigators each, along with several dozen street gang and major crimes investigators. Federal agents, state agents, parole officers, and probation officers all pounded the pavement looking for even the slightest lead in this case.

For the next several weeks, every Hispanic gang member on the east side of Los Angeles (and there are thousands of them) was grabbed off the streets and interrogated in an interview room. Snitches and informants were questioned, and dozens of search warrants and raids were conducted in nearly every gang neighborhood east of downtown. Jail and prison investigators used every trick in their books to pull information out of inmates and prisoners. The agency heads had indeed let loose the dogs, and the investigators started getting leads.

In the vernacular of the cop movies of the 1980s, "the heat was on." No ex-con or gangbanger could draw a free breath without a probation officer, parole officer, or police detective dragging him into a jail cell for a very vigorous interview. When law enforcement gets together on a coordinated task, it is really an awesome thing! Crimes will get solved, and in this case, it led indirectly to the solving of a major crime. It just wasn't Razo's shooting.

Several weeks after the shooting, the massive investigation had turned up not a single suspect or clue regarding Razo. In fact, local gang members came forward and told investigators that Razo had never been a problem to them, and they were familiar with him from living in the neighborhood all his life.

Another big problem was the shooting scene. The LASD had reconstructed Razo's life-and-death struggle with two armed assailants and had presented it to at least three top police-shooting experts. All of the experts came up with the conclusion that the scene and the evidence did not at all match up to Razo's story. An injury that Razo suffered on his hand was conclusively found by several experts to have been caused by Razo holding his own gun backward and shooting himself. All of the experts examined the scene and the story and found it nearly comical.

Razo was a short, physically unfit middle-aged man, with a belly and very few muscles. His story of deftly disarming two young, muscular, and healthy gang members conjured up an image of action stars Steven Seagal or Chuck Norris on their finest day. It was ludicrous to think that Razo could have pulled off even half of this derring-do.

Razo told his story several times to investigators, friends, and family members, and each time the story varied. Pretty soon there were a half-dozen versions of the event, and none of them matching the actual forensics.

Razo had been seriously wounded during the shooting as the bullet had struck his collarbone and gone downward into his body cavity, nearly killing him. During his emergency medical treatment, doctors had taken blood samples and found that Razo had a significant amount of narcotic painkillers in his system at the time of the shooting. It was theorized that he had planned to shoot himself in an effort to wound himself, and he took the painkillers in anticipation of the trauma.

The investigation was extremely detailed. Razo had told investigators that he was going to golf with his usual buddies the day he was shot. Investigators followed up and found that he was not scheduled to golf until seven that morning, over two hours after the shooting. The golf course was just a couple of miles away. Razo's story made no sense whatsoever.

Meanwhile gangbangers were still going to jail, and no leads at all were developing about this shooting. In a side note, the community members and officers from Razo's duty station, LAPD Hollenbeck Division, conducted fund raisers for the injured officer and eventually presented him a check for $35,000.

By March the major task force had run out of leads on the Razo case. There simply was no evidence or clues to examine. The shooting task force had more of a problem. They had officially but quietly concluded that the entire event was a hoax. Through the detailed reconstruction, it was clear from his various injuries that Razo had shot himself with his own gun in an attempt to somehow make it seem like he was yet another cop targeted by Hispanic street gang members. The theory was that he staged this because he knew he was about to be arrested for the arson case. Investigators believed that Razo could now "sell" the arson case as all part of an elaborate plot by street gang members.

The homicide investigators met with Razo for a formal interview on March 19, 2009. He told them the same story he had given earlier and denied staging this shooting event. He also refused to take a polygraph exam about the shooting. At that moment, arson detective Mike Cofield was brought into the room to face Razo. As soon as Razo saw Cofield, he realized that they all suspected him of staging both events. He then admitted that he had lied about the events that happened at the drugstore and the theft of his BMW. He then admitted to removing items from the car and burning it with a combination of lighter fluid and a highway flare.

Razo was immediately relieved of duty by the LAPD after this interview. Three days later the team served a search warrant on Razo's home and found several items that he had removed from this car prior to torching it. He had reported those items as stolen and burned to the insurance company.

The case was taken to a special branch within the District Attorney's Office. It went to a merciless prosecutor (now superior court judge) named Christian Gullon. Gullon filed five felony counts against Razo for arson and insurance fraud. No charges were mentioned about the staged shooting.

Five days later an extraordinary meeting with Razo and his attorney took place. Present were police brass from LAPD and the LASD, the District Attorney's Office, and all of the principal investigators on the case. The topic was this. Since the LAPD and LASD never, ever clear a police officer shooting case without a criminal filing, they were compelled to keep Razo's shooting case open for perpetuity. They knew he staged the event, but there wasn't enough evidence to charge him with any sort of crime, and nobody wanted to keep the shooting case open forever.

The DA made a brass-balls decision. In no uncertain terms, he castigated Razo and his deeds. He told Razo that he had only one small shot at a plea deal on the arson case, or he would spend several years in prison. The DA told Razo the only way he would allow him to make a plea deal on the arson case was for him to come clean on the shooting and make things right. Razo and his attorney adjourned for a short "come to Jesus" talk.

On April 7, 2009, Anthony Razo pled guilty to insurance fraud and filing a false police report. During this hearing he admitted in open court that he purposely staged the theft and arson to his own car for the purpose of insurance fraud. He also admitted in open court that his gunshot wound on January 31 was "self-inflicted," thereby closing the massive police investigation that had been ongoing for three months. He was sentenced to one year in jail and returned $5,400 of the money that had been raised for him by fellow officers. The money went back into a police charity fund.

The fallout was short but intense. Local liberal papers were livid that a bunch of gang members had been harassed for weeks after this faked shooting. A newspaper did a detailed look into Razo's past and discovered his gambling and other sordid activities. It seems that he had a lengthy history within his own community of less than stellar activities. They wrote a headline entitled "Razo, Bad Cop." They weren't exaggerating.

The only good thing that came out of the Razo case was that the massive ass-kicking task force that hit the streets looking for any information actually came up with a bunch of clues that eventually led to the solving of the Deputy Juan Escalante murder. Eventually five local Hispanic gang members were identified and successfully prosecuted for Escalante's murder. The two gang members who murdered Deputy Maria Rosa in 2006 were also identified, apprehended, and prosecuted. As I write this in 2016, there are no unsolved police-shooting cases in Los Angeles County.

*The following professionals were the lead investigators on this case: arson detective Mike Cofield, homicide detectives Todd Anderson and Mike Valento, DDA Phil Stirling, and DDA (now superior court judge) Christian Gullon.*

## CHRIS NANCE
## LOS ANGELES, CA, MARCH 2009

*This case comes from the author's own case files.*

At just past noon on Saturday, March 21, 2009, Sgt. Derek Yoshino and I were working the weekend shift at the Arson-Explosives Detail. My cell phone began to ring, notifying me of an "immediate response" arson case. At the moment I took the call, Derek and I were at the home of an LAPD officer who had been convicted of torching his own car. We were just finishing up dealing with some of his property. Arson by a cop must have been contagious because the moment I took the call and heard the details, I knew that it was very likely that an LASD deputy had just done the same thing!

I was called by a young patrol officer, who was working the day shift in the desert town of Palmdale. He had received a call of a vehicle on fire. The patrol officer responded to the scene and found a 2003 Nissan 350Z with its entire rear area on fire. The vehicle was parked with no one around on a vacant street behind a housing development. The fire department extinguished the flames and found that someone had poured a flammable-liquid accelerant on the back deck of the hatchback car and set it on fire. At the time of the fire, the doors were all locked, and the vehicle's alarm was sounding.

This would normally be a non-emergent investigation as my unit received about six of these types of smaller arson cases a day. This scene would have been investigated on Monday, along with about a dozen other noncritical arson cases. In this case, the patrol deputy informed me that this was an "immediate response" request as the burning car was registered to a sheriff's deputy named Chris Nance. The car had not been reported stolen, and there was no body in the car. The deputy who found the burning car had not been able to reach Chris Nance through his work assignment, which was at a courthouse.

Almost immediately Derek Yoshino and I groaned at the news. We got a lot of car fires in our unit, and we instinctively knew that the majority of them were "owner involved" insurance schemes. We had a general rule of thumb that was almost always accurate. If the car was torched in the owner/victim's driveway, at his work, or near his home, then it was likely a revenge/spite-related attack. In that case the owner/victim had a clear enemy, and he most likely was aware of who had done this. If, as in this case, the car was found burning in any sort of remote or hidden area, then there was a very high likelihood that the owner was involved in this "staged theft" for the purpose of insurance fraud.

Of course, that was not our final conclusion as we had not even looked at the scene, but it was usually the correct assumption. In this case, there was a wrinkle or anomaly. The overwhelming number of arson cases occurred at night, with the notable exception of wild-land arson. In this case, the fire had occurred near high noon, a very untypical time of day for arson. Our interest was piqued.

I told the patrol deputy to use all available resources to try to locate the deputy sheriff who owned the car. As law enforcement officers, we were always concerned when something happened to another officer. There was the (remote) possibility that he may have been targeted because of his job. I told the patrol officer that if Deputy Nance was located alive and well, then I wanted him to call me on my cell phone so that I could speak to him as the investigating officer on his car fire.

In truth, I had already developed my suspicions about this incident and was already employing investigative tactics and strategies. If Nance was located and called me, then my cell phone would have a digital log to his phone. I knew that I could use that in a future phone analysis to find out where Nance was at the time his car was found burning. Secondly, I always spoke to the victim of an incident, so I needed to talk to him to get his initial statement on what happened to his car. It would lock him into a story without going through a formal interrogation process.

Right now, Deputy Nance was a victim and would be treated as such, despite my and Derek's immediate profile of the event. If and when we factually cleared him as a suspect, he would have no idea that we ever suspected him. However, if he was eventually determined to be the suspect in this case, then he would have no idea that we had already started to draw a snare around him before we had even spoken to him.

Palmdale was in the desert eighty miles north of my office in Los Angeles. By two in the afternoon, Derek and I were driving up the 14 Freeway and had almost made it to the scene of the fire. It was at that time that I got a call on my cell phone from Chris Nance. He told me that he was sleeping at his father's home in Pacoima (the San Fernando Valley area of Los Angeles) and had been awakened by his sergeant calling him to tell him his car was on fire. Nance told me that he was still at the Pacoima address and had been sleeping there all day since about seven in the morning when he got off work. He confirmed that he was calling from his own cell phone. I had now locked Nance to a phone and a location. From that information I could get cell records and determine if he was being truthful.

I asked Nance about his car. He told me that as far as he knew, his car was still parked at his home where he had left it the previous evening when he had gone to work. Nance's home was about thirty miles from Palmdale. Nance said he lived alone, and nobody had permission to drive or move the car. Besides, there was only one set of keys, and Nance had them in his possession at the moment. Nance explained that he was just this week assigned to a patrol station after having spent three years working as a bailiff in the courts. He said he routinely drove his Nissan 350Z to work until he started working in patrol. He said he found out that he didn't have enough room in his 350Z to carry all his patrol gear and that last night was the first night he had driven his other vehicle, a small truck, to the patrol station.

This was what I was looking for...**an anomaly**! I had investigated hundreds of insurance-fraud fires and found that in many of them, the owner/suspect does something different on the day of the event than he normally does. This sort of behavior is indicative of the suspect staging a scene or manipulating the event. We call it an **event or crime-scene anomaly**.

Nance told me a few other anomalies. He said that he normally parked his spare vehicle in a garage, except for last night. Last night he left his 350Z on the street in front of his home for the first time ever. He gave the lame excuse that he was trying to hold a parking spot. Nance said that he last saw the car at about ten o'clock that evening when he left for work. He drove his truck to work and worked the night shift as a patrol deputy until six in the morning.

He then drove his truck home from work (about thirty miles) but was too tired to drive all the way to his own home. He said he stopped at his father's home in Pacoima to sleep instead of driving all the way home. I knew while he was telling me this story that it was complete bullshit. His father's home in Pacoima was only about ten miles away from his own house. He easily could have driven home. Nance said he went immediately to bed and was only awakened around two in the afternoon by his sergeant calling him. He said his keys for both vehicles were on the nightstand next to him as I spoke to him.

After getting Nance's full story, we knew that this was a staged event. Nance's story was filled with anomalies that made no sense whatsoever. He deviated from his normal schedule for no good reason and expected us to believe that the very first day ever that he parked his car on the street it got stolen. This was ridiculous. Still, I told Nance we were going to the scene and that I would be in contact at a later date.

Derek Yoshino and I drove to the scene of the burned vehicle. The scene was a vacant street behind a housing tract, hidden by low desert hills. The street was a dead end and had been blocked off by a series of barrier signs on the open end. My SUV could not get down the street. We noted that Nance's car had been burned at the very end of the street and that only a very small vehicle, such as the 350Z, a VW, or a Porsche, could squeeze through the barriers. This was a very important factor in this case.

We knew that it was very difficult to steal a modern car without its key. It is extremely difficult to bypass the ignition lock and hot-wire any decent modern car. The art of auto theft has greatly diminished as security systems in cars have gotten more sophisticated. While there were some very highly skilled thieves out there, most of them only stole very high-end cars and then would strip them to the frame instead of burning them. The entire purpose of auto theft was to make a profit. The car's parts are always worth much more than the car itself.

So, while Chris Nance had a very nice car, it was more of a street racer that did not rise to the level of a "high end" luxury or sports car. There is no way that a professional auto thief would waste his time on a car of this type. Lower quality thieves stole cars by tow truck, which is always a factor to consider. In this case, it was physically impossible for a tow truck to have driven between the barrier signs on this vacant street. The location of the dump/burn site excluded the use of a tow truck in this case. The rough desert and hills in the area made it impossible for the car to have been driven off road to get to this spot.

We knew, based on the location, that the 350Z had been driven to the scene, and therefore the suspect would need a key or fake key to do so. Nance had already confirmed that he had only one key to the car, and it was currently in his possession. He would later turn that key in to the insurance carrier.

Sgt. Yoshino and I could find no evidence at the scene, except for tire tracks and footprints. The patrol deputy had already towed the car to an impound yard. We did find, however, that two of the barrier signs at the open end of the street had been bent inward and had a bright blue paint transfer on them. We measured the height and distance of the signs and recovered a small paint-transfer sample from them.

Yoshino and I then drove to the police impound yard and examined the 350Z. We saw that it was relatively unburned and still drivable. The only fire damage had occurred on the back deck of the hatchback. The remainder of the car was intact and hardly damaged. We were able to examine the door locks and found them undamaged. We looked at the ignition lock and found that it had been damaged on the outside as if it had been hit by a screwdriver-type instrument. This coincided with a large screwdriver found on the floorboards beneath the steering wheel. We processed the car and found that an ignitable liquid had been poured over the back deck of the car and set on fire.

In examining the small car, we saw that it had two long scratches along each side of the car. We noted that these scratches were deep and were exactly the same height of the bent barrier signs at the burn site. Based on these scratches, we confirmed that this car had been physically driven through the signs at the burn site, bending them and causing the paint to transfer between the signs and the car.

On the seat we found a piece of notebook paper with writing on it. On the notebook paper were three entries that described vehicles for sale at a local Dodge dealership. The vehicles were all used but were high-end muscle cars. The paper gave a vehicle description, mileage, price, and phone number to the dealer. It also gave the name of a salesman. From this paper we concluded that someone was trying to buy a used car.

We took stock of the entire car at the tow yard. We saw that the car had newer, high-quality custom rims and tires, a front "bra," and very high-quality aftermarket upgrades to its exterior and engine. None of these items had been damaged or stripped, which is not something a car thief would leave. A car thief would have stripped all of these expensive items off the car prior to burning it. This case did not look at all like something a car thief would do.

We also learned that the patrol deputy who found the car burning had found a claw hammer on the ground outside the car. This, along with the large screwdriver on the floor, looked to us like items that had been planted at the scene by the arsonist in an act of "**staging**." These items had been used to make the impact mark on the ignition lock, but it did not appear that they had actually been successful. These are not items that a car thief would leave at a scene.

Chris Nance called me after I left the impound yard. He asked me if his car was completely destroyed. If so, he was going to make an insurance claim on the car. I told him that it was burned, and there were signs of a burglary, but I was careful not to advise him to make the claim. He could later say that I (as a more senior cop) ordered him to make the insurance claim. I told him to email me via the department's computer system if and when he did make a claim. Later that day Chris Nance made an official claim to his insurance carrier, which at that point completed the crime of insurance fraud.

At this point, Sgt. Yoshino and I had a bit of a problem. We were very sure that Chris Nance had been involved in this staged car theft and arson. We greatly outranked him in our department, and neither one of us worked in Internal Affairs. There were some very peculiar legal details that were required when interviewing someone of less rank than you who is suspected of a crime. I contacted the department's Internal Affairs experts, and they told me to continue our investigation, and they would monitor Nance. They advised me that it would be best for me not to interview him personally as I greatly outranked him, but that I could ask him questions by email. From that point on we never spoke to Nance in person. We conducted all business over email.

The next day I drove to the Dodge dealership from the notebook page and inquired about the vehicles listed on the paper. The used-car manager confirmed that his company had all three of those vehicles for sale about two weeks ago. He checked his records and found that a male named "Chris" had called inquiring about the vehicles. The dealer's notes said that "Chris" was seeking a cop discount and wanted to trade in a 350Z. The dealer said that Chris owed way too much money on the 350Z for them to be able to strike a deal. The dealer maintained Chris's phone number in the computer, and it was a match to the cell number of Chris Nance.

Now it was clear to me that Chris Nance had attempted to trade in the 350Z just a couple of weeks prior to the fire but was turned down because he was "upside down" on his loan for the 350Z. The motive for this case was starting to come together.

That same afternoon I wrote a warrant for Nance's cell phone records. Two weeks later we got the information back from the cell phone carrier. The carrier confirmed that Chris Nance's cell phone was not at his father's home in Pacoima at the time of the fire but was, in fact, over forty miles away and within a half mile of the fire scene. In fact, I found my own number on the cell phone bill and realized that when Chris Nance called me around two in the afternoon that day, his phone (and presumably he himself) was very near to the site of the vehicle fire. His story was falling apart rapidly.

I immediately contacted the insurance carrier on this case, Mercury Insurance, and spoke to the company's special investigator, Shannon Hubbard. I had worked with Inv. Hubbard on at least one previous case and found her to be an extremely dedicated and tenacious investigator. She began a detailed investigation into Chris Nance. Part of that was to get a forensic vehicle examiner to conduct detailed testing on the ignition lock of Nance's car. Mercury Insurance hired a forensic ignition analyst to conduct testing on Nance's car key and ignition. In the end, the forensic examiner scientifically proved that only the key provided by Chris Nance had driven the 350Z to the scene of the fire. The forensic specialist also confirmed that the damage to the ignition lock was caused by the screwdriver from the car, but it had been minor cosmetic damage only and had not caused the ignition lock to fail.

In the end, through cell phone forensics and vehicle forensics, we had proven that the cell phone and car key owned and controlled by Chris Nance were at the scene of the fire in Palmdale at the time of the event and not forty miles away as Nance had stated.

By this time Inv. Hubbard, through interviews and recorded statements, had locked Chris Nance into his story. He had given sworn affidavits to the insurance carrier of his phony story, thereby implicating him in this insurance-fraud scheme.

As usual in any case, there were certain aspects we did not know. We knew that Nance had to have an accomplice for this event, but we were never able to identify that person. It would not have been possible to pull off alone.

Meanwhile, we continued building our case. I later found two other dealerships where Chris Nance had attempted to trade in his 350Z. Both turned him down but kept records of his name and phone number. His last attempt to turn in the car was on the night prior to the fire.

I learned through searching pay records that Nance was a very poor sheriff's deputy. He had been suspended twice in the previous year for misconduct while off duty. He had also transferred from bailiff duties, where there is a lot of overtime pay, to patrol duties, where there is very little overtime. He had recently purchased a second car and a townhome. At the same time his personal expenses had gone through the roof, and due to his suspension from work, Chris Nance had lost a total of $30,000 in income. He was living way beyond his means.

His 350Z car was a financial nightmare. He had installed many custom items and had taken out a second loan on the car. The car, which was valued at around ten thousand dollars, had loans against it totaling over $18,000. Besides being a poor sheriff's deputy, Chris Nance was a very poor financial manager of his own resources.

Five months after the staged fire and theft, we descended upon Chris Nance at his townhome. He had no idea we were ever looking at him! We had just asked him a few questions over email and had then handled the rest of the investigation discreetly through his insurance carrier. When we showed up to serve a warrant at his home and interview him, he was completely in shock.

In the fall of 2009 we took our case to special prosecutor DDA Susan Schwartz, and she brought it before the county grand jury. The grand jury immediately handed down an indictment against Chris Nance for arson and insurance fraud. A day later he was suspended without pay and arrested. Within a month Nance pled guilty to the charges and was convicted. He was forced to sell his townhome and other cars in order to pay restitution on this case. He was sentenced to a year in jail. To show you how naïve Chris Nance was, he actually asked us if he could have his job as a deputy sheriff back after he got out of jail. Luckily that will never happen. He is now a convicted felon for life.

We later learned that Chris Nance had several cousins who were involved in criminal activity and that one of them had assisted him with this staged theft and arson. We were never able to prove which cousin was the coconspirator. Once he had served his time, Chris Nance met me again when we returned some property to him. At that point, he personally apologized to me for making us go through the heartache of investigating a fellow sheriff's deputy.

*This case was investigated by Det. Ed Nordskog and Sgt. Derek Yoshino of the LASD Arson-Explosives Detail, Inv. Shannon Hubbard of Mercury Insurance, and DDA Susan Schwartz of the Los Angeles County District Attorney's Office.*

# Bibliography

Acuna, A. "Minister, Six Others Seized in Bomb Case." *Los Angeles Times*, November 6, 1987.

*American Arsonists.* Memphis: Books, LLC, 2010.

Anderson, T. *LASD Case File Number 407-21407-1188-272.* Los Angeles: Los Angeles County Sheriff's Department, 2007.

Armstrong, A. "FBI, United States Department of Justice Criminal Complaint—*United States of America v. Ryan Daniel Lewis.*" *Auburn Journal*, February 18, 2005.

Blanchard, D. and T. Prewitt. *Religious Violence and Abortion: The Gideon Project.* Gainesville: University Press of Florida, 1993.

Brussel, J. *Casebook of a Crime Psychiatrist.* New York: Bernard Geis Associates, 1968.

Buchanan, A. *AFD Case File Number 14-004055.* Alexandria: Alexandria Fire Department. Alexandria, 2014.

Bureau of Alcohol, Tobacco, and Firearms. "Bakersfield Abortion Clinic Arsonist Sentenced to 15 Years." Fresno: ATF Press Release, February 10, 1998.

California Court of Appeal Decisions. *People v. Cowan; Crim. No. 394. Fourth Appellate District.* California. March 29, 1940.

California Court of Appeal Decisions. *People v. Marlene M. Ramsdell, 2d Crim. No. B246053; Super. Ct. No. 2010012821;*

*Ventura County*. Ventura: California Court of Appeal, Second Appellate District, Division Six, 2014.

Celona, L., Stuart Marques, Marcia Kramer, Eddie Borges, and Mike Santangelo. "Investigators Say They Have an 'Airtight Case' Against Happy Land Social Club Arsonist in 1990." New York: *New York Daily News*, March 27, 1990.

Cofield, M. *LASD Master Case File Number 407-00025-3310-999*. Los Angeles: Los Angeles County Sheriff's Department, 2007.

Curry, W. "Against Abortion: Clinic Fires a Holy War, Bomber Says." Los Angeles: *Los Angeles Times*, January 11, 1985.

DeHaan, J. and D. Icove. *Kirk's Fire Investigation*, 7th ed. Upper Saddle River: Pearson Education Inc., 2012.

Department of the Army. *TM 31-201-1 Unconventional Warfare Devices and Techniques: Incendiaries*. Washington: Headquarters, Department of the Army, 1966.

Edwards, R. *LASD Case File Number 498-00379-3399-339*. Los Angeles: Los Angeles County Sheriff's Department, 1998.

Elwell, G. *BHPD Case File Number 11-674*. Beverly Hills: Beverly Hills Police Department, 2011.

Federal Bureau of Investigation. "Former President of Ventura Hells Angels Chapter Arrested on Federal Extortion and Firebombing Charges." Los Angeles: FBI Press Release—Los Angeles Field Division, August 12, 2011.

Flacco, A. *A Checklist for Murder: The True Story of Robert John Peernock*. New York: Dell Publishing, 1995.

Fulkerson, C. *LASD Case File Number 011-03550-6413-275*. Los Angeles: Los Angeles County Sheriff's Department, 2011.

Gabbert, W. "Battle of Investigators During Cocos Fire Trial." Posted in *Wildfire Today* on March, 22, 2015, from http://wildfiretoday.com/2015/03/22/battle-of-investigators-during-cocos-fire-trial/.

Gonzales, I. *LASD Case File Number 407-07744-1012-279*. Los Angeles: Los Angeles County Sheriff's Department, 2007.

Gonzales, R. "Environmental Extremist Gets 5 Years for Attempted Arson of Pasadena Condos." Pasadena: *Pasadena Star News*, April 5, 2010.

Gordon, T. "Mill City Reacts to Finance Clerk's Arson Arrest." Retrieved on August 23, 2001, from http://www.msnbc.msn.com/id/44212052.

Hager, W. *VCFD Investigative Case Number 96-91214*. Camarillo: Ventura County Fire Department, 1996.

Hanson, J. *LASD Case File Number 014-07364-0532-271*. Los Angeles: Los Angeles County Sheriff's Department, 2014.

Hanson, J. *LASD Master Case File Number 915-00045-3310-999*. Los Angeles: Los Angeles County Sheriff's Department, 2015.

Harrison, P. and D. Wilson, D. *Hunting Evil: Inside the Ipswich Serial Murders*. London: Sphere Books, 2008.

Harris, R. *LASD Case File Number 013-05011-0641-461*. Los Angeles: Los Angeles County Sheriff's Department, 2013.

Hoeffel, J. "2 West Hollywood Medical Marijuana Dispensaries Raided by Federal Agents." Los Angeles: *Los Angeles Times*, March 15, 2011.

Kandel, J. "Takeover at Studio City Pot Clinic." Retrieved from *Mean Streets* blog, February 1, 2008.

Kaplan, T. "Daughter, 18, Says Father Threatened to Murder Her." Los Angeles: *Los Angeles Times*, December 22, 1987.

Katz, A. et al. *Case File Number 12HF2145—The People of the State of California v. Rainer Klaus Reinscheid*. Santa Ana: Orange County Superior Court, 2013.

Kelm, K. "Behavioral Investigation of the Arsonist. Parts I, II, and III." International Association of Arson Investigators, *Fire & Arson Journal*, vol. 62, issue 4; vol. 63, issue 1; vol. 63, issue 2 (2012).

Keppel, R. *Signature Killers*. New York: Pocket Books, 1997.

Konefal, J. *CSFM Case File Number 05-JWK-007*. Sacramento: Office of the California State Fire Marshal, 2005.

Leibowitz, E. "The Accidental Ecoterrorist." Los Angeles: *Los Angeles Magazine*, May 1, 2005.

Leslie, E. *The Devil Knows How to Ride*. New York: Random House Inc., 1996.

Leung, W. "Ex-Hells Angels Leader to Serve Prison Term." Ventura: *Ventura County Star*, September 3, 2013.

*Los Angeles Times* staff. "BAR BOMBED; 6 DIE! Victims Turned into Human Torches." Los Angeles: *Los Angeles Times Extra*, April 5, 1957.

McAuliffe, K. *USFS Report of Investigation Number 12-09-9285528*. Minneapolis: US Forest Service Region 9, 2013.

Miller, A. *LASD Case File Number 014-00034-0976-272*. Los Angeles: Los Angeles County Sheriff's Department, 2014.

Mozingo, J. "Some Southern California Pot Shops Make Big Money." Retrieved on June 17, 2012, from www.latimes.com.

National Abortion Federation. "National Abortion Federation—Violence Statistics & History." Retrieved on August 18, 2015, from http://prochoice.org/education-and-advocacy/violence-statistics-and-history/.

Nordskog, E. *LASD Case File Number 602-01168-1415-091*. Los Angeles: Los Angeles County Sheriff's Department, 2002.

Nordskog, E. *LASD Case File Number 609-05106-2610-277*. Los Angeles: Los Angeles County Sheriff's Department, 2009.

Nordskog, E. *LASD Case File Number 011-01770-1713-277*. Los Angeles: Los Angeles County Sheriff's Department, 2011.

Nordskog, E. *Torchered Minds: Case Histories of Notorious Serial Arsonists*. Indianapolis: Xlibris, 2011.

Nordskog, E. *Fireraisers, Freaks, and Fiends: Obsessive Arsonists in the California Foothills*. North Charleston: CreateSpace Independent Publishing Platform, 2013.

Nordskog, E. *LASD Case File Number 013-13054-0642-461*. Los Angeles: Los Angeles County Sheriff's Department, 2013.

Nordskog, E. *LASD Master Case File Number 913-00035-3310-999*. Los Angeles: Los Angeles County Sheriff's Department, 2013.

Peach, G. *VCSO Case File Number 06-0020471*. Ventura: Ventura County Sheriff's Department, 2006.

Peach, G. *VCSO Case File Number 09-0020039*. Ventura: Ventura County Sheriff's Department, 2009.

Peernock, R. *Window 18, Robert J. Peernock: Serving Life Sentence without Parole*. Retrieved on July 17, 2012, from http://freerobertpeernock.com.

Perry, L. and R. Perry. *A History of the Los Angeles Labor Movement, 1911–1941*. Berkley: University of California Press, 1963.

Plummer, W. "In the Heat of the Night." New York: *People Magazine*, vol. 41, no. 24 (1994).

Quinn, J. "Man Goes on Trial in Wife's Fatal Beating." Los Angeles: *Los Angeles Times*, July 9, 1991.

Romero, D. "Weed Shop Owner Set Rival's Beverly Hills Home on Fire." Los Angeles: *LA Weekly*, March 31, 2014.

Sanchez, J. *LAFD Case File Number 2011-07-0247*. Los Angeles: Los Angeles Fire Department, 2011.

Sapp, A., T. Huff, G. Gary, D. Icove, and P. Horbert. *Essential Findings from a Study of Serial Arsonists.* Quantico: US Department of Justice, Federal Bureau of Investigation, National Center for the Analysis of Violent Crime, 1996.

Saqui, C. *VCFD Investigation Case File Number 06-13086.* Camarillo: Ventura County Fire Department, 2006.

Spencer, G. *LASD Master Case File Number 409-00039-3300-999.* Los Angeles: Los Angeles County Sheriff's Department, 2009.

The Canyon Weekly. "Trial of Joy Cronin—Mill City Arson Case Update." Gates: *The Canyon Weekly*, March 13, 2013.

Turvey, B. *Criminal Profiling: An Introduction to Behavioral Evidence Analysis*, 4th ed. Waltham: Academic Press, 2011.

Usborne, S. "Denmark Place Arson: Why People Are Still Searching for Answers 35 Years on from One of the Biggest Mass Murders in our History." Retrieved on August 30, 2015, from http://www.independent.co.uk/news/uk/home-news/denmark-place-arson-why-people-are-still-searching-for-answers-35-years-on-from-one-of-the-biggest-mass-murders-in-our-history-10467987.html.

Van Lingen, A. *SDSD Case File Number 14-124431*. Sam Diego: San Diego Sheriff's Department, 2014.

Wachi, T., K. Watanabe, K. Yokata, et al. "Offender and Crime Characteristics of Female Serial Arsonists in Japan." *Journal of Investigative Psychology and Offender Profiling*, no. 4: 29–52 (2007).

WeHo News Staff. "Sunset Strip Pot Club Red Tagged and Closed by WeHo." Los Angeles: *WEHO News*, February 7, 2011.

WeHo News Staff. "Illegal Sunset Super Shop Pot Store Shuts Down." Los Angeles: *WEHO News*, December 20, 2012.

Weins, J. *VFD Investigative Case File Number 2009-0027955-000*. Ventura: Ventura City Fire Department, 2009.

Yelles, W. "Pot Shop Has 'Nothing to Hide' in Wake of Homicide Probe," Los Angeles: *West Hollywood Patch*, September 6, 2010.

Made in the USA
Middletown, DE
09 September 2021